D1242196

AN IMPOSSIBLE MISSION WITH EVERYTHING TO LOSE!

D-Day, June 6, 1944. The Allied invasion of Europe hinges on a critical opening gambit:

- Land several companies seven kilometers west of the right flank of Omaha Beach, on a narrow strip of beach at the base of Pointe-du-Hoc.

- Scale the 120-foot sheer cliffs under heavy enemy fire.

- Cross the heavily mined, obstacle-filled top, and destroy six 155-mm cannons located in open, reinforced concrete artillery emplacements.

U.S. ARMY RANGERS ARE CALLED TO DUTY BECAUSE
ONLY RANGERS ARE TRAINED TO FIGHT
ANYTIME, ANYWHERE, AGAINST ANY ENEMY
AND WIN!

TO FIGHT WITH INTREPIDITY...

The Complete History of the U.S. Army Rangers
1622 to Present

Second Edition

JD Lock
Lieutenant Colonel, U.S. Army

With a foreword by

Lieutenant General Harold G. Moore, U.S. Army (Ret)
The New York Times best-selling co-author of
We Were Soldiers Once ... and Young

First edition (June 1998) by POCKET BOOKS, a division of Simon & Schuster Inc. 1230 Avenue of the Americas, New York, NY 10020. ISBN: 0-671-01528-1

This edition (2001) Published by FENESTRA BOOKS™
610 East Delano Street, Suite 104, Tucson, Arizona 85705, U.S.A.
www.fenestrabooks.com

International Standard Book Number: 1-58736-064-0 (hardcover)
Library of Congress Control Number: 2001094968

Publisher's Cataloging-in-Publication
(Provided by Quality Books, Inc.)

  Lock, John D.
    To fight with intrepidity-- : the complete history of
  the U.S. Army Rangers, 1622 to present / J. D. Lock ;
  with a foreword by Lieutenant General Harold G. Moore.
  -- 2nd ed.
    p. cm.
    Includes bibliographical references and index.
    LCCN 2001094968
    ISBN 1-587-36064-0

    1. United States. Army. Commando troops--History.
  2. United States--History, Military. 3. Rogers, Robert,
  1731-1795. I. Moore, Harold G., 1922- II. Title.
  III. Title: Complete history of the U.S. Army Rangers

  UA34.R36L63 2001   356'.167'0973
           QB101-1181

Cover photograph of Sergeant Jerod Boggess, 1st Battalion, 75th Ranger Regiment, provided courtesy of Russ Bryant

Copy of Medal of Honor Certificate provided courtesy of Mrs. Carmen Gordon.

Book design by Atilla L. Vékony

Printed in the United States of America

To fight the enemy bravely with a prospect of victory is nothing; but to fight with intrepidity under the constant impression of defeat, and inspire irregular troops to do it, is a talent peculiar to yourself.

American Revolutionary War General Nathanael Greene
to Brigadier Francis Marion, the "Swamp Fox"

[Intrepidity (in-tré pid é tē): "resolute courage"]

The views expressed in this book are those of the author and do not reflect the official policy nor position of the Department of Army, Department of Defense, or the United States Government.

DEDICATION

To those Rangers who have gone before. The standards you set, the self sacrifice you made, your devotion to a cause, and your love of the profession have laid the firm foundation that we who follow attempt to emulate. May neither you nor your sacrifice for the nation ever be forgotten.

Table of Contents

Foreword

Only a proud American Army Ranger could have authored such a superb book. Only a proud American Army Ranger could clearly capture in writing the brotherly love, pride, discipline, respect for and loyalty to one another, and belief in the vital importance of mission accomplishment that pervades all U.S. Army Ranger units.

This book, meticulously researched and brilliantly written, is a gold mine of information on American Rangers. Want to know the fascinating details of Rogers' Rangers and their 43 Battle Honors, and the shrewd tactics of Francis the "Swamp Fox" Marion? It's all here. The astonishing exploits of Rangers in World War II, and their controversial usage in Korea? All here. Operations of the American Ranger companies in Vietnam are highlighted with descriptions of gallant deeds. Want to know the details on the tragedy of April 1980 at Desert One in Iran; the bravery and foul-ups in the October 1983 Grenada operation, and the actions of Rangers in Panama and Iraq? Read this book.

For me the most enlightening—although depressing—part of Lieutenant Colonel Lock's book is his recounting of the results of the ill-fated altruistic commitment in 1992 of U.S. military forces, into harm's way, in the loser's game of Somalia—a Fourth World tribal country shot through with deadly internecine politics and motives of different tribes, clans and their leaders. In Somalia, humanitarian and nation-building actions by foreigners, backed up by combat troops, were viewed as threats to their power by clan leaders and outside interference in the internal affairs of their country. Anti-U.N. and anti-American propaganda increased and by late summer of 1993 had escalated to ambushes, mortar attacks, mine explosions, and firefights. "Mission Creep" had taken over. The shocking result was that terrible 1993 October day in Mogadishu when eighteen Americans were killed, seventy-three wounded on a mission which had nothing whatsoever to do with any U.S. national interest. Lieutenant Colonel Lock's vivid, heartbreaking descriptions by name of the actions of men who were killed, wounded, or survived the most vicious battle

1

since Vietnam are absolutely riveting. His thoughtful, candid analysis of the entire Somalia commitment and the 3 October 1993 tragedy is extremely perceptive. In these years of shrinking American Armed Forces being sent into costly and sometimes dangerous "Operations Other Than War" across the world, Senior U.S. Political, Military, and Cabinet leaders would be well advised to study carefully Lieutenant Colonel Lock's writing on the Somalia disaster.

This book will be a valuable addition to any Military bibliophile's library and is a must for those who want to know more about U.S. Army Rangers.

Harold G. Moore
Lt. General, USA (Ret)
Crested Butte, Colorado January 1998

Praise for JD Lock's
To Fight with Intrepidity...

Lieutenant Colonel Lock has provided an exceptional history of our nation's Army Rangers. It is a work and tribute long overdue. I recommend it for anyone interested in our nation's military history.

Senator Bob Kerrey,
Medal of Honor recipient

Lieutenant Colonel John Lock's *To Fight with Intrepidity...* is a great achievement. For the first time, the history of the world's premier light infantry force has been written. His scholarly researched description of Rangers in combat through the centuries establishes the rationale for the vigorous training that aspirants for the coveted Ranger Tab and Ranger Scroll endure. This tough, realistic training and the great demands that Rangers place on themselves are the reasons 'Rangers Lead the Way!'

Colonel Ralph Puckett, U.S. Army (Ret),
Honorary Colonel of the 75th Ranger Regiment

The history of American Rangers is the history of America. When Americans go to war, Rangers lead the way. Now one of their own has taken time to tell their stirring story. And what a story it is! Ranger School graduate John D. Lock writes with an authority and attention to detail certain to make this the definitive history of America's oldest military elite.

Dan Bolger,
Author of *Savage Peace*

This book is by far the best all-inclusive history of any facet of combat arms that I have ever read. Lock has meticulously researched and presented the entire history of the US Army Rangers in this long awaited book. In short, *To Fight with Intrepidity...* is a smartly compartmentalized, thoroughly exhaustive, and intellectually stimulating volume on the history of the US Army Rangers.

Dominic J. Caraccilo,
Author of *The Ready Brigade of the 82nd Airborne Division in Desert Storm*

Introduction

After the train had been captured by 150 Boers, the last four men, though completely surrounded, and with no cover, continued to fire until three were killed, the fourth wounded. On the Boers asking the survivor the reason why they had not surrendered, he replied, "Why, man, we are the Gordon Highlanders."

Lord Kitchener,
telegram from Pretoria to Edward VII (10 August 1901)

U.S. Army Rangers are among the most elite, if not *the* most elite, combat soldiers in the world. Being a Ranger is a function of attitude and state of mind, as well as a matter of skill and training. It is the fraternity of a highly select group within the profession of arms that few will attempt to join and into which even fewer will be initiated. To be a Ranger is a mark of excellence indicating a degree of success that few will achieve. The challenge of being a Ranger is to prove your ability to lead and command while undergoing significant mental, emotional, and physical stress. For those who have mastered this challenge, the coveted title of "Army Ranger" is their reward.

The foundation of principles upon which being a Ranger is built, its very roots, can be readily comprehended from the history of the United States Army Ranger. It is that history, that lineage, that tradition constructed by those generations past and present, whose dedication, honor, courage, perseverance, blood, and ultimate personal sacrifice to which we owe so much. For those desiring to understand what a Ranger is, read on; for those who are Rangers, read the heritage of which you are part.

The early lineage of the United States Army Ranger is over two hundred years old and can be said to have "unofficially" begun with the implementation of Rogers' Rangers of the French and Indian War. When one reviews the history of the Rangers, it can be noted that the lineage falls into two distinct periods of time. The early years encompass the pre-American Revolution period with Robert Rogers, the American Revolu-

5

tion with Francis Marion, and the American Civil War with John S. Mosby. Though not "formally" trained in accordance with the standards prescribed by today's prestigious U.S. Army Ranger School, the early deeds of Rogers, Marion, and Mosby easily meet the standards and intent of today's modern Ranger. In actuality, they do more than meet the standard. They are the standard. Consequently, no history of the United States Army Ranger can be complete without them.

The second historical period can be referred to as that of the "Modern" Ranger, which began with the formation of Darby's Rangers during the Second World War. This more conventional view of the Rangers, if one can refer to them as being "conventional" at all, encompasses not only World War II but also the Korean Conflict, the Vietnam Conflict, Desert One (Iran), Grenada, Panama, and Somalia.

RLTW
JD Lock

AUTHOR'S NOTE: To fully appreciate the scope of their accomplishments and to hopefully understand the environment in which they operated, I have placed the Ranger's history within the context of the historical events that surrounded them for perspective. History is not black and white and events do not occur in a vacuum. They occur for a reason and this work attempts to provide that foundation of understanding. While every attempt has been made to verify and ensure the accuracy of what has been written, this work was never intended to be a documented and footnoted doctoral dissertation. It is a novel about history and not a history book, per se. Where primary sources were not available, the author took care to refer to other works that had been written based on primary source references. What initially started as a simple overview of Ranger history developed into the life form of its own that you see before you because there is no one centralized work that deals specifically with Ranger history.

CONTACT THE AUTHOR: Comments can be forwarded to:

JDLock82@aol.com

The Ranger Creed

U.S. Army Rangers are highly trained and motivated professionals who live by a code called "The Ranger Creed." It is sacrosanct. It is a way of life, a guide for how Rangers conduct themselves. It is the source that binds through loyalty the individual to his Ranger buddies and to his unit.

Recognizing that I volunteered as a Ranger, fully knowing the hazards of my chosen profession, I will always endeavor to uphold the prestige, honor, and high esprit de corps of the Rangers.

Acknowledging the fact that a Ranger is a more elite soldier who arrives at the cutting edge of battle by land, sea, or air, I accept the fact that as a Ranger my country expects me to move farther, faster, and fight harder than any other soldier.

Never shall I fail my comrades. I will always keep myself mentally alert, physically strong, and morally straight, and I will shoulder more than my share of the task, whatever it may be. One hundred percent and then some.

Gallantly will I show the world that I am a specially selected and well-trained soldier. My courtesy to superior officers, my neatness of dress, and care of equipment shall set the example for others to follow.

Energetically will I meet the enemies of my country. I shall defeat them on the field of battle for I am better trained and will fight with all my might. Surrender is not a Ranger word. I will never leave a fallen comrade to fall into the hands of the enemy, and under no circumstances will I ever embarrass my country.

Readily will I display the intestinal fortitude required to fight on to the Ranger objective and complete the mission, though I be the lone survivor.

Rangers Lead the Way!

Command Sergeant Major Neil R. Gentry, 1974

CHAPTER 1

Pre-American Revolution

The only good Indians I ever saw were dead.

P.H. Sheridan

The Ranger lineage predates the very birth of this great nation. The term "Ranger" evolved as far back as thirteenth century England, when it was used to describe a far-ranging forester or borderer. By the seventeenth century, the term emerged to serve as a title for irregular and unique military organizations, such as the "Border Rangers" who defended the troubled border frontier between England and Scotland. The term crossed the Atlantic to the North American continent with England's early settlers.

The first "Ranger" references in the New World began shortly after the start of a war between the native American Indians and the colonists of the Commonwealth of Virginia on 22 March 1622. Outside of the larger towns and villages, the Commonwealth was populated with a series of isolated plantations and farms owned by titled landowners, each responsible for the defense of his family and his workers. To successfully defend against a surprise Indian attack, advanced warning of a war party's approach was necessary. Consequently, armed men were selected to roam, or "range," the countryside to provide this warning or to search for targets of opportunity.

In a 1622 report to Virginia Governor Sir George, Captain John Smith — of Pocahontas fame — reported the following: "Yearly ranging the shore of Weanock, could see nothing but their [Indians] old houses which he burnt." The General Assembly of Maryland drew up a list of conditions by which "raingers or scouts" were to be regulated in 1648.

The designation of "rainger" had taken root and continued to be used during the intermittent Indian wars from 1675 to 1715. The first of these wars, referred to as "King Philip's War," raged throughout much of New England for several years. Meacomet, otherwise known as King Philip, was chief of the Wampanoags Indians. For years, Philip had gained growing influence among his neighboring tribes and was attempting to lace together a far-reaching intertribal conspiracy against the British when the war started. Full-scale war soon evolved as the three Puritan colonies of Plymouth, Massachusetts Bay, and Connecticut joined as allies. The isolation of many of the frontier villages and family farmsteads made them exceptionally vulnerable to surprise Indian attacks and presented a perplexing problem for local defenses.

The challenges facing the colonists were significantly different than those military challenges faced by the regular armies of the Old World. The New World was much more rugged and the enemy significantly different. Toughened by the environment, accustomed to moving great distances by foot, and loath to fight pitched battles, the American Indian employed stealth and reconnaissance to select targets, execute a surprise and devastating attack, and quickly withdraw. Extremely competent in their movements, the Indians also showed themselves to be very adept at displaying their skill in the art of ambush. Cruel and ruthless in their application of force, the American Indian instilled a great deal of fear throughout the colonies.

Employing new methods and tactics, and expanding on the original concept of the individual "rainger," the colonists raised small, organized groups of men who began to move out from the defensive walls of the settlements and into the forests and mountains. These mounted troops traversed or patrolled the frontier, screening between frontier forts and blockhouses. Looking for signs of enemy movement and serving as early warning scouts, these groups would cover the countryside and submit reports that, among other things, would state, "This day, ranged 12 miles." Hence, the name "Ranger" was also attached to them.

Captain Benjamin Church, considered by many to be the first American Ranger, commanded one such local company. Raised in 1675 and organized to defend the colonists and to take the war to the Indians, Church's Rangers was manned by colonial volunteers who were daring, aggressive men, attracted to the dangers and hardships of this type of service, and in search of adventure and spoils of war. Additionally, and unlike most other militia organizations, Church incorporated friendly Indian auxiliaries into his independent company, employed for scouting and tracking, and treated as fellow soldiers.

A veteran of previous Indian battles, Church was an innovator who learned quickly from his adversary. The Indians were quick to note that the colonists always moved together as a group and never scattered. Hence, the Indians were able to engage a target-rich environment with little concern of being attacked by any unseen elements. Realizing this, Church developed a mode of operation very similar to that of his enemy. Leading with his own Indian scouts, Church's Rangers would advance through the woods in a loose formation, providing no massed target and allowing for a maneuver element to deploy quickly when engaged, thus demonstrating with great precision the field tactic of encirclement.

Philip's war entered its final stage in the spring of 1676. Pursued by Captain Church and a mixed party of colonists and Indians, King Philip was finally hunted down in a Rhode Island swamp and killed on 12 August 1676. With his death, the war in southern New England came to a close.

The New England colonies were not the only providences needing the services of Ranger-style military organizations. In 1732, a group of twenty prominent men were named in a charter from the British Parliament to found a thirteenth and final colony. In this group, was a thirty-six-year-old Member of Parliament, James Oglethorpe, who named the colony Georgia, in honor of King George II. To defend the frontier regions of the colony between its border garrisons, Oglethorpe formed in 1734, partly at his own expense, a small, mobile Ranger organization.

Although their numbers never grew to more than fifteen officers and one hundred twenty-two men, when they peaked in 1746, the Rangers proved to be an invaluable resource throughout the early years of the Georgia colony and especially against Spanish forces entrenched in Florida. Unfortunately, despite their distinguished service, unique skills, and Oglethorpe's attempts to the contrary, the Rangers, as a cost-cutting measure for the British Crown, were disbanded as the war with Spain, which had commenced in October 1739, drew to a close.

One of the first Ranger companies enlisted primarily to support the British Army was Gorham's Ranger Company. Raised and organized in 1747, Gorham's company was composed of frontiersmen, hunters, mixed-bloods, and Indians. Identified by the British Army as "Independent Companies of Rangers," this unit scouted and raided along the frontier borders on behalf of the British Army. Ultimately, Captain John Gorham went on to raise six companies that served on the periphery of the new colonies and in Quebec, Canada. Following his death in 1751,

Gorham's brother, Joseph, would continue to command the organization until 1759.

The Georgia Rangers were revised a second time in 1757, when Henry Ellis was appointed governor of Georgia. Soliciting the Crown for monies to support Ranger forces, he was provided enough funds to organize and maintain a unit of twenty men. On the orders of the British Prime Minister, the First Troop of Rangers was officially assigned as part of the British Army in North America on 18 May 1759. On 1 January 1760, the Second Troop of Rangers followed.

Ellis' successor as governor was Governor James Wright. Because of Ellis' efforts, Wright had two troops of Rangers with a total of fourteen officers and cadets and one hundred forty enlisted men under his control. The most significant distinction between his Rangers and the local militia was that the Rangers were full-time soldiers and could consequently always be counted on in times of emergency.

The Rangers' primary concern was external defense against Indians. Averaging approximately thirty Rangers per site, they defended four forts, or garrisons—Savannah, Fort Augusta, Fort Argyle, and Fort Barrington—located around the outer perimeter of the colony. The Rangers continued to receive a diversity of responsibilities reflective of their growing renown. Increasingly, the Rangers represented the military in official ceremonies to include the honor of firing the volleys on the King's birthday in 1764 and 1765. Relative peace and calm reigned over the territory until 1765.

The French and Indian War had proven to be a very expensive affair for the British, doubling the government's debt and significantly increasing the territory to protect in America. In 1765, the Stamp Act was passed to obtain partial support of these troops. The act required that British government stamps be purchased and used on all important documents, periodicals, almanacs, pamphlets, and playing cards. Decrying "Taxation without representation," many of the colonists resisted. Soon societies such as the Sons of Liberty sprang up in the various American colonies in opposition to the Stamp Act.

British merchants pushed for a repeal of the act, which finally occurred in March 1766. During the crisis, the colonial governors found that they could not depend on the local militias to maintain or restore public order during the Stamp Act crisis. Other than troops of the British Army, the Rangers proved for the governor of Georgia to be the only soldiers upon whom he could depend.

With the Stamp Act crisis a memory, the Rangers went about their routine peacetime duties. Ironically, though they had proven to be the most loyal of soldiers in support of the governor, they were the first military organization to be disbanded soon thereafter. General Thomas Gage, who would be the British military commander-in-chief in North America at the outbreak of the American Revolution, did not think very highly of the Ranger organizations, believing them to be "an expensive sort of Troops" and had obtained the assistance of the Secretary of War to discharge Governor Wright's Rangers on 31 March.

Without the Rangers, Governor Wright's concerns only grew over time. In the early 1770s, the Georgian population was 18,000 whites and 15,000 blacks. The Creek Indian population was estimated to be 12,000 with over 4,000 warriors. Against this perceived border threat, a small body of twelve scouts was raised to protect settlers on the fringes of the border. From this small group would be reborn, for the third time, the Georgia Rangers.

By September 1773, Wright had organized a troop of Rangers, seventy-five officers and enlisted strong, to be supported from land sales of over two million acres of land from the Creek and Cherokee tribes, referred to as the Ceded Lands. Their mission was to keep good order among and to protect the settlers of this region.

The Rangers garrisoned Fort James, a one-acre area they constructed at the fork of the Broad and Savannah rivers near Dartmouth. From this garrison, the Rangers, divided into three divisions, patrolled the frontier. On Christmas Day 1773, the Creek Indians destroyed the peace between themselves and the white settlers with a series of swift and brutally destructive attacks against frontier settlers.

The Rangers, supported by local militia, responded quickly but, on 24 January, two seemingly frightened Indians easily lured a group of ten Rangers and twenty-five militiamen into an ambush. Moving across the crest of a hill, the Rangers and militiamen were fired upon by a large force of Indians who had been hiding in the long grass near the top of the hill. Having been surprised by a force of up to sixty Indians, the colonial group quickly withdrew on horse to their camp after firing a few shots, leaving behind what they presumed to be three dead.

One of the "dead" left behind at the ambush site was Ranger Lieutenant Daniel Grant. Two published newspaper accounts from the time indicate that the lieutenant had only been wounded during the engagement. Seized by the Indians, he was bound to a tree and shot full of arrows, a total of twelve to thirty, depending upon which account one is to believe. Keeping with what seemed to be Indian tradition, Grant's genitals were either cut off or a "red hot" gun barrel shoved up his rectum, or both. A hatchet to the head and groin combined with his scalp and ears being cut off only added to the grisly picture. Whichever account may have proven true, the lieutenant's death certainly, as a minimum, could be described as torture.

The colonial situation continued to deteriorate as the militia deserted in large numbers upon hearing of the skirmish and the knowledge of Grant's torture and mutilation spread. The Rangers were not immune, either, for it was reported that five or six of them might have deserted, also. Time, though, eventually began to show that these Indian attacks were isolated and not part of an overall uprising against the colonists. Gradually, a sense of normalcy began to return to the colonies as the likelihood of a major Indian War diminished. The Georgia Rangers remained in service patrolling and securing the Ceded Lands until 6 March 1776, when they were disbanded for the final time.

CHAPTER 2

Rogers' Rangers:
The Beginning—1755

As the proposition advanced ... that hereafter war will be made altogether with artillery, I consider that this observation is wholly erroneous.... For whoever wishes to train a good army must ... train his troops to attack the enemy sword in hand, and to seize hold of him boldly.

Niccolò Machiavelli

Commencing in 1754 and lasting until 1763, the French and Indian War on the North American continent served as part of a larger conflict called the Seven Years' War in Europe. The British, having seen how successful Ranger units were against this new and unorthodox style of warfare, began recruiting American frontiersmen to form similar units to serve as auxiliaries of their Regular army. The impact of the war upon British infantry techniques and tactics was tremendous. Impressed by the successful combination of loose-knit Indian fighting and disciplined light-fighting skills, the British Army sought to incorporate these style units within their organizational structure.

The Ranger unit that eventually would leave its indelible mark on American military history and the lineage of the United States Army Ranger was originally formed as the Ranger Company of the New Hampshire Provincial Regiment under the command of Robert Rogers. Rogers would not only win lasting renown as a Ranger leader but he would also be immortalized in American literature as the main character of Kenneth Roberts' classic novel, *Northwest Passage.*

In February 1755, Governor Wentworth of New Hampshire awarded Rogers the captaincy of the 1st Company of Colonel Blanchard's New

15

Hampshire Regiment for having raised twenty-four recruits within one month. Rogers' company was composed of approximately fifty men. The men were skilled and accomplished in defending themselves and their homes against Indian raids. They were well trained in the ways of the woods, having gained considerable experience from trapping beaver to hunting and pursuing Indians. Over time, as a function of these skills, they came to be known as Rogers' Rangers, the Ranging Company of the Regiment. Gifted as a leader, Rogers set out to make a name for himself and his soldiers.

In that the unit had not been permanently established as a distinct corps, the Rangers, like other Provincial troops, were supplied with only food and blankets. The majority of Rangers wore their hunting frocks of deerskin and used their own muskets. Choosing his own officers, Rogers selected his close friend, John Stark—whose words "Live Free or Die" would serve centuries later as a state motto—to serve as a lieutenant. Later, on 4 October 1755, Rogers' younger brother, Richard, signed into the company and was commissioned a lieutenant on 28 November. Rogers began to build his reputation with his first reconnaissance into French-held territory during the early morning hours of 14 September 1755 in support of British General William Johnson's Crown Point Army.

Embarking on a bateau with two of his Rangers and two Connecticut Provincials, Rogers landed at dawn on the west side of Lake George, in the vicinity of Bald Mountain, approximately twenty-five miles from Fort William Henry. Leaving the two Provincials behind to guard their boat, the three Rangers moved through the woods for three days to arrive at Crown Point. Moving under the cover of darkness, the group quietly infiltrated the enemy picket line, moved through a small village, and concealed itself in a freshly dug entrenchment on a small hill only 150 meters from the main fort. There the Rangers remained throughout the evening, eating a cold meal while Rogers made notes on the fortification.

Seeking a different perspective of their objective, Rogers moved the group to a large hill located a mile away on the other side of the fort. Somewhat fatigued, the Rangers were able to leisurely rest all day while observing the enemy's movements. Despite troop movements all about their position, Rogers' group remained undiscovered and departed the area later that evening.

On their return trip, the group passed within two miles of Fort Carillon, a new fortress under construction at the northern outlet of Lake George to Lake Champlain. Eighty-five miles northeast of Albany, this fort would eventually fall to the British in 1759 during the French and Indian War and be renamed, after the nearby village, to its universally known name of Fort Ticonderoga. This fort would later change hands again when captured 10 May 1775 by a small force of colonial American Green Mountain Boys led by Ethan Allen.

Unfortunately, with provisions nearly exhausted, the Rangers were unable to stop at the fortress site to determine the percentage complete. Taking less than two days to get back their landing site, the group was "mortified" to find the two Connecticut men, their boat, and all provisions gone. Left with no other alternative, Rogers and his two companions moved cross-country to Fort William Henry. Fatigued, hungry, and cold, the Rangers arrived late at night on 23 September. In that harmony needed to be maintained between the various colonists that comprised the provisional unit, there is no indication that the two Connecticut men who had so readily neglected their duties were punished. Shortly thereafter, a scout party composed of Rogers and five Rangers departed on the evening of 27 September to check on Fort Ticonderoga's progress. Moving up Lake George in a canoe and passing a number of Indian patrol campfires along the shore, the Rangers landed at Friend's Point, near Isle au Mouton. Leaving three Rangers behind to secure the site, Rogers and his other two men moved forward on foot to encounter a large advance guard defending the perimeter. Crawling through the enemy's perimeter, the Rangers counted nearly one thousand men. Moving on, Rogers spent the night of 28 September within the fortification.

Returning late the next morning, the group of three Rangers noted a bark canoe manned by nine Indians and a Frenchman moving south on Lake George. Arriving at their hiding site, Rogers was informed by the security element that the bark canoe had landed on an island five miles farther south in the middle of the lake. The enemy element remained on the island only briefly, for shortly thereafter, they departed the island heading north once more. Unknown to those in the canoe, they were heading straight for Rogers' location. With plenty of time to prepare, the Rangers opened fire from their hidden position when the canoe closed to approximately one hundred yards. Within minutes, the enemy suffered four dead and two wounded. The Rangers gave chase in their own canoe as the enemy withdrew in the direction of Fort Ticonderoga. Roles were soon changed, though, as three additional enemy canoes sallied forth to assist the four remaining survivors. Rogers' Rangers' first skirmish concluded with his small group being pursued most of the way back to the other end of Lake George.

The Rangers' exploits became the talk of Johnson's army. Having had no contact with the enemy in over two weeks, the army regaled in Rogers' "bold adventure," which placed Rogers firmly in Johnson's favor. With the terms of the Rangers' enlistments complete, Rogers' Rangers returned to New Hampshire. Prevailed upon by Johnson to remain in service "to continue scouting and insure the safety of his army," Rogers was able to cajole and convince with his persuasive personality twenty-eight of his men to continue their service to the Crown, even though they might not be paid for their services. These volunteers would compose the nucleus of Rogers' Rangers.

The fame of Rogers' Rangers grew but there were those jealous of his success. Despite insidious innuendoes against his character, Rogers continued to be accredited by General Johnson as "the most active man in [his] army." To the New York governor, Sir Charles Hardy, Johnson wrote, in no uncertain terms, "I believe [Rogers] to be as brave & honest a Man as any I have equal knowledge of, & both myself & all the Army are convinced that he has distinguished himself since he has been among us, superior to most, inferior to none of his Rank in these Troops."

Rogers returned to Fort William Henry with his reduced company and immediately began conducting operations. A scout party of forty Rangers and Provincials led by Rogers from 7 to 12 October failed to decoy any French or Indians into an ambush. Two days later, Rogers landed three hundred yards from the fort at Crown Point with four other Rangers in an attempt to capture a prisoner.

One of the Rangers with Rogers on this mission was Israel Putnam. Soon to become quite famous for his exploits with Rogers' Rangers, Putnam would later be appointed a major general in the Continental Army at the start of the American Revolution and was one of the leaders at the battle of Bunker (Breeds) Hill. It is he who is most often credited with having given the famous order, "Don't fire until you can see the whites of their eyes" as the British troops advanced against the entrenched colonists on 17 June 1775. Leaving the other three behind, Rogers and Putnam crept nearer to the fort just prior to dawn, concealing themselves behind a large pine log and handheld bushes. Large numbers of French soldiers left the fortress, too many in number to obviously capture one and too many in number to allow them to safely withdraw from their position. In great peril, the Rangers were forced to lie quietly. Finally, the French reentered the fortress.

Unwilling to depart the area without a prisoner, Rogers waited. His patience—and courage—was soon rewarded when a single French soldier exited the fortress. Rogers sprang from hiding and jabbed his fusee—a fuse for detonating explosives—in the Frenchman's chest and demanded his surrender. Unfortunately for Rogers, the "prisoner" was a huge fellow who had no intention of surrendering. Preferring to fight, the Frenchman called out to a nearby guard, pulled a dirk, and proceeded to attack Rogers. A fierce hand-to-hand struggle ensued. Though Rogers was the undisputed champion wrestler of northern New Hampshire, he was more than meeting his match with the large, dirk-wielding Frenchman.

Putnam soon had to intervene when the nearby guard began to approach. With the two combatants locked in a death grip, he ended the duel with a fatal blow from the butt of his musket to the back of the Frenchman's head. With the garrison now fully roused and preparing to pursue, Rogers and his group of Rangers beat a hasty retreat, but not before Rogers scalped the Frenchman.

Eight days later, on 29 October, Rogers was ordered by Johnson to intercept enemy canoe patrols that were reported by a French deserter to be routinely observing the American camp. Eagerly looking forward to engaging these patrols, Rogers devised a plan that provided considerable firepower with little sacrifice of mobility. Assembling four bateaus, he spent the 30th outfitting each with a miniature cannon called a "wallpiece"—a rare small-arm artillery piece with a four-and-a-half-foot barrel. Weighing thirty-five pounds, these field pieces were usually used over parapets or low protective walls or on earth and stone embankments.

Embarking later that evening, Rogers and thirty-two of his men quietly began their movement up Lake George on a clear, cold night. Shortly before dawn, the Ranger amphibious force landed within a half mile of the enemy's advance guard camp on the west side of the lake. Having concealed the boats and posted sentries, Rogers sent three of his Rangers, including Putnam, on a reconnaissance of the advance guard camp.

The following evening, one of the Rangers returned to report that the enemy had no fortifications about their camp and that the entire guard camp lay open to assault. Rogers immediately sent a group of thirteen Rangers, six of whom were ill, back to the American camp with a request of General Johnson to send a force of sufficient strength to attack the guards' camp.

Left with only a detachment of twenty Rangers, Rogers spent the remainder of the day conducting his own personal reconnaissance of the enemy camp. Around 1000 the next morning, Putnam and his scouting partner finally returned. Unfortunately, their reconnaissance of the camp had been compromised when they inadvertently found themselves inside it. English custom is to place fires around the perimeter of a camp with sentinels posted inside. The French, on the other hand, had grouped their campfires in the center of the camp and placed their sentinels in the surrounding darkness. Discovered before they could withdraw, the two

Rangers took flight for their lives with Putnam's partner taking a musket ball through the thigh.

Soon after their return to the Ranger camp, two French scouts appeared on a crest overlooking the Ranger position. Soon thereafter, a force of thirty men in two war canoes appeared and held their position in the middle of the lake. Realizing that the canoes were waiting for a dismounted element to arrive and catch him in a crossfire, Rogers felt there were only three options available to him: he could retreat and have his courage questioned; he could stand his ground and plan a suicidal defense; or he could take the initiative and take the fight to the enemy with a daring and aggressive maneuver.

Leaving Putnam, six Rangers, and a bateau on shore, Rogers manned the two remaining boats with seven Rangers each and proceeded to attack the waiting enemy canoes. Needing to decoy the enemy to close within range of his wall-pieces, Rogers made it appear as if he were trying to slip by the blocking force. Completely duped, the French closed in on Rogers' bateaus to cut them off.

At one hundred yards, the wall-pieces opened up. With the dead and wounded piling up, the French canoes tried to escape the cannon fire but, in the process, maneuvered too close to the shore and were engaged by Putnam's shore detachment. Seriously holed by the fires, the French had to bail with half their surviving crews while the remainder paddled for all their lives trying to move the canoes out of the line of fire.

Noting the arrival of the French dismounted party, Rogers shouted a warning to Putnam to withdraw. Carrying Putnam's wounded scout partner, the small force was able to launch the remaining bateau under the covering fires of the other two Ranger boats, which were able to hold the superior land-based enemy force at bay until Putnam's boat was safely out of range.

Rogers was not finished. Closing on the enemy canoes once again, Rogers' three boats delivered another broadside to drive any thoughts of further engagement from their minds. The tiny Ranger squadron continued in hot pursuit of the enemy, following them up the lake to their landing, four hundred meters from their advance fort, Coutre Coeur. A force of one hundred Frenchmen gathered on the shore to cover the war canoes but Rogers closed to within two hundred meters and discharged another broadside that drove many of the enemy into the bushes.

Recognizing that he was pushing his luck against a superior force and within the shadow of Fort Ticonderoga, Rogers opted not to linger in the neighborhood. Rogers triumphantly began to withdraw to the British encampment on the southern end of Lake George. He had successfully engaged and driven from the lake in a two-hour engagement an advance guard of over 150 French with a force of only twenty Rangers and at a cost of only one wounded.

Halfway up the lake, Johnson's reinforcements that had been requested the previous day were encountered only to return with Rogers. The fame of Rogers and his Rangers was now firmly established and the name of Rogers' Rangers echoed from the army camp to the firesides of New England. Needless to say, Johnson was most pleased with his protégé. At the age of twenty-three, Rogers had just executed his most successful, most complete, and boldest victory.

Late November found Rogers forming a unique company of Rangers for winter service. While the British and French armies withdrew into their garrisons and cantonments each winter, Rogers recognized a need to conduct continued scouting operations during periods of adverse weather, such as those encountered during the winter in northern New York. By 14 December, Rogers had enlisted a total of forty-three officers and men to serve in his command.

On 19 December 1755, despite the forbidding weather, Rogers departed on the final scout of the year to Fort Ticonderoga. Paddling fifteen miles up the lake, Rogers and three other Rangers landed by Great Mountain, where they rested until the following morning. The next day they traveled twenty miles overland. By noon of the 21st, they came within sight of the fort. The area was still very active as construction continued. Overall, the Rangers counted approximately five hundred Frenchmen.

Hoping to capture a prisoner or "take a scalp," the Rangers set an ambush later that evening along a road. Approximately thirty minutes later, a group of ten Frenchmen walked by but the Rangers "were so weak [they] durst not fire on them, and so let them pass." Just around sunset, a smaller party of five moved into the area to gather some wood. Leaving their ambush site, the Rangers attempted to close on the Frenchmen before they returned to the fort, but to no avail. The Frenchmen escaped not knowing how close they'd been to capture or death.

By then, it had grown so cold the Rangers could not sit still in an ambush. If they were to do so, they would freeze to death. Needing shelter from the elements, they located and occupied a hut for the remainder of the night. Daybreak found snow falling so hard, the Rangers were obliged to depart. A hard march to their boat and the movement down the lake found the Ranger patrol arriving at Fort William Henry around two in the morning, Christmas Day, thus bringing to a close the first campaign of Rogers' Rangers.

CHAPTER 3

Rogers' Rangers:
Campaign of 1756

Every mile is two in winter.

George Herbert

The winter of 1755–56 was fierce. Despite the conditions, Rogers' Rangers executed three audacious expeditions against the enemy to secure prisoners. Rogers felt the capture of prisoners extremely important, for from them he could obtain not only information about reinforcements to Ticonderoga and Crown Point but he could also learn what improvements had been made to the fortifications.

Rogers' first winter foray began on 14 January, when he and seventeen of his Rangers departed Fort William Henry, put on skates at the lake's edge, and began to glide briskly up the frozen lake. By the end of the second day, they arrived at the waterfall located to the north. As night fell, the Rangers moved over the snowy terrain that separated Lake George and Lake Champlain. On the shore of Lake Champlain, the Rangers once again put on their skates and quietly skated past the lights of Fort Ticonderoga.

Moving across the lake, Rogers selected a strategic point of land from which he could ambush small parties passing on the lake between Crown Point and Ticonderoga. Waiting in ambush, their patience was rewarded shortly after sunrise by the arrival of "two Frenchmen with a horse and [sleigh] loaded with fresh beer" for Ticonderoga. The two Frenchmen were quickly captured. Unfortunately, Rogers was unable to make off with the beef. Hearing gunfire and viewing a group of men skating their way from Crown Point, Rogers was forced to sink both the sleigh — with the beef—and the horse under the ice. With the two prisoners in tow, the Rangers arrived safely back at Fort William Henry on the 17th.

Ordered to "take a view" of Crown Point "or to distress them," Rogers set out once again nine days later. Arriving within sight of the fort with his entire company of Rangers and six additional volunteers, Rogers and his force scaled a steep mountain from where he could make a sketch of the fortifications. Later that evening, he descended to a road that led from the fort to a nearby village to establish an ambush. One prisoner was quietly captured but two others were able to outrun the pursuing Rangers and raise the alarm with the fort's garrison.

Knowing that a strong party would soon sally forth from the stronghold, Rogers ordered his force back through the village, setting fire to houses and barns that stored abundant amounts of grain. Withdrawing safely, the Rangers left behind a village in flames and fifty dead cattle. The following morning, Rogers split his party when one of his Rangers fell ill. Sending the main party forward with the ailing Ranger, he formed a rear guard with seven other Rangers to face any enemy pursuit. The next day, 6 February, with no contact having occurred, Rogers and his rear guard closed on Fort William Henry.

Rogers' final excursion for the winter began 29 February. Planning on a scout of fifteen days, Rogers departed William Henry with a force of sixty-five men that included the majority of his Rangers. The force marched north along the western shore of Lake George for five days covering distances of 12, 14, 10, 13, and 11 miles, respectively, through fresh, slippery snow. On day six, the 5th, the sixty-one-man force—five having fallen ill and returned to the fort on the first day—crossed over to Lake Champlain.

Halting within site of the Crown Point fort that evening, Rogers made the decision to try and cross the lake to the east side in the dark and establish an ambush along the St. John's Road. Setting out at 0200 the next morning, Rogers led the patrol to the lake only to slip and plunge twenty-six feet down the embankment and through the thin ice along the rugged shoreline. It was only with a great deal of effort that Rogers was extracted from the icy waters.

Having determined through Rogers' personal "reconnaissance" that the ice along the lake's edge was too weak to bear their weight, the force remained out of sight for the remainder of the day. At 0300 the following morning, Rogers and three other Rangers tested the ice but once again found it too thin. Abandoning his plan to cross the lake, Rogers decided to march south for twelve miles to set up an ambush along the road that ran from Crown Point to Ticonderoga.

The site was in the vicinity of the village he had burned on his previous scout. Setting up in the woods on the outskirts of the village, Rogers
waited. By nightfall, with no enemy encountered, Rogers moved his force
into the village, posting twenty-four men in a house while Rogers and
thirty-six men hid in a barn nearly four hundred meters away. Again,
throughout the next day, there was no contact. A quick reconnoiter by
Rogers and one other Ranger found no French outside the walls of the
fort.

Deciding not to wait much longer, Rogers had his force torch two
houses and nine barns storing eight hundred bushels of wheat, oats, and
peas that evening around 2100. Unfortunately, one of the Rangers' Indians was asleep in a barn and was mortally burned before he could be rescued. Carrying the dying Indian with them, Rogers marched four miles
and "lodged in wet land." The following morning, they marched an additional eighteen miles, wading across Putnam's Creek, and settling down
once again without a fire to warm them.

The next day, Rogers, along with Putnam and seven other men, separated from the main body "in order to find a good wagon road to or by
the Ticonderoga rapids" that could be used by the Americans or British
for an assault later that summer. The remainder of the force continued
their march towards Fort William Henry. Twenty-one miles farther
south, they encountered a day-old set of tracks left by a French and
Indian scouting party of 160 men. Seeing the raging fires on the Crown
Point horizon, this enemy force had suspected that Rogers was on the
prowl again and had moved south in an attempt to intercept the Rangers.
Angered and frustrated by the fact that Rogers had, with two raids,
destroyed an entire village and a significant portion of the French garrison's food resources, the enemy scouts even went so far as to post written
warnings on trees stating that if Rogers or any of his Rangers were caught
"they would burn them directly." Able to avoid the enemy force, the
Ranger main body marched the final eighteen miles to arrive at 0200 on
the 12th, exhausted and weak from "having had nothing to eat for some
time."

Rogers and his small group, meanwhile, had marched to Fort Ticonderoga, where he crept into the trench directly beneath the fortress wall.
From this vantage point, he could look directly up and observe the sentries. Having obtained all the information he desired about the defenses.
Rogers left clearly visible confirmation of his presence in the trench and
returned to Fort William Henry around 0100 on 14 March, having spent a
total of fifteen — mostly unsheltered — days in the freezing northern New
York winter. It was this type of sharp and successful winter excursion,

conducted at a time when all other military campaigning had ceased, which made Rogers' Rangers most famous.

On 17 March, Massachusetts Governor Shirley, the acting commander-in-chief of British forces in the Americas, offered Rogers the command of an Independent Company of Rangers. To command such a unit had been one of Rogers' eventual objectives, for it would rank him above a Provincial officer and move him closer to his ultimate goal of a commission as a Regular officer in the British Army. The title of Rogers' new command made it exceptionally unique, for it was neither a Provincial nor Regular company. As commander of His Majesty's Independent Company of American Rangers, Rogers was independent of each. Though subject to orders from British officers through Rogers, the company was "free of the line," hence enjoying more autonomy and less oversight than a Regular organization.

Rogers was commissioned captain of an Independent Company of Rangers on 24 March 1756 and authorized to raise a company of sixty privates, three sergeants, one ensign, and two lieutenants. Enlistment requirements were strict. Only men accomplished in hunting, tracking, long marches, and having displayed courage and loyalty would be accepted. For those who passed the muster, each was provided ten Spanish dollars toward clothing, blankets, and arms. And for each Indian or French prisoner or scalp brought in, a reward of five pounds sterling silver was paid.

Rogers organized his new command into two subunits, one of which — under the command of his brother, Lieutenant Richard Rogers — he directed to Fort William Henry to link up with his original company, which was encamped there. The remainder of the company, including his other lieutenant, John Stark, marched to the most advanced frontier town and fort — referred to as Number Four — in the Connecticut Valley to await an expected St. Francis Indian attack. When the attack failed to materialize, Rogers was ordered on 28 April to return to Fort William Henry by way of a reconnoiter of Crown Point and Ticonderoga.

Rogers cautiously advanced along the Connecticut River and established a hide along with nine other men opposite Crown Point in the hopes of capturing any small parties crossing the lake. Encountering no one, Rogers' group had just completed slaughtering twenty-three head of cattle when he noticed a war party of eleven canoes heading straight across the lake for them. Realizing the Rangers had a better chance of eluding the approaching French and Indians individually rather than as a group, Rogers ordered each man to exfiltrate on his own, each moving along a different route, to a rendezvous point at Lake Champlain. This technique of eluding pursuers would become a standard Ranger tactic. Rallying at Lake Champlain, Rogers and his Rangers built a raft, crossed the lake, and conducted a reconnaissance of four advance guard outposts that lay in the valley between the foot of Lake George and Ticonderoga as they marched back to Fort William Henry, where they arrived on 11 May.

Rogers' arrival at Fort William Henry in May ended a two-month absence from the fort. Unfortunately, during this absence, his encamped Rangers had suffered their first defeat at the hands of the enemy. On 11 April, Sergeant James Archibald and a squad of five Rangers departed up Lake George on a scout. Having covered only two miles, the group encamped on an island in the first narrows. At exactly 0410 the next morning, Fort William Henry sentries heard three or four musket shots followed quickly by a volley of thirty to forty shots from up the lake. Having observed the small Ranger force encamp, a party of French-allied Indians numbering close to two hundred had staged a predawn attack on the sleeping Rangers.

Though it seemed a few of the Rangers awoke in time to discharge their weapons, the small force was quickly overwhelmed. Three of the Rangers were shot, stripped of their clothing, and scalped. The other three, including Archibald, who would later escape, were captured and carried off to Montreal as prisoners. A group of ten Provincials departed by two bateaux at 0600 to the campsite. Proceeding cautiously, they came upon the remnants of the three scalped Rangers. One of them "the barbarous Indians had cut quite across his breast and turn'd it under his chin, and left his inwards exposed to the wild beasts."

The French and Indian War was gaining a full head of steam in 1756 and the British were relying heavily on units that could track, scout, procure intelligence, and act as advance guards for the frontier garrisons and Regular army units. In May 1756, Shirley was able to strike a deal with the Stockbridge Indians from Massachusetts to raise a company of fifty men. Enlisted for the duration of the war, the company would be raised during the spring of each year and disbanded in late fall so the Indians could return to their village and assist their people through the winter. This Indian company was initially garrisoned at Fort Edward but was soon attached to Rogers' Rangers, where Rogers commanded them for the remainder of the war. Intermingling his own Rangers with the Indian force, Rogers found the unit to be of valuable service as an advance guard for his own Rangers.

Nine days following his arrival, Rogers was provided the opportunity to gain some revenge for the massacre and mutilation of Archibald's detachment. Ordered by General Shirley to reconnoiter the French advance guards, Rogers and his eleven Ranger scouts quickly complied and deployed his men. Selecting a path between Fort Ticonderoga and the nearest fortified advance camp, the Rangers lay in wait. After allowing a large group of 118 French soldiers to pass, the Rangers were soon rewarded with the appearance of a smaller twenty-two-man party. The Rangers killed six and captured the party's leader. By the time the survivors were able to raise the alarm at Ticonderoga, the Rangers, like apparitions, had disappeared and were on their way back to Fort William Henry with their prisoner.

From 24 March to 6 June 1756, Rogers' command consisted of both his original company at Fort William Henry and the new company he had raised. The original company's term of enlistment was completed 6 June and the unit was disbanded. Fourteen of the original Rangers reenlisted, bringing the strength of the new Ranger company to sixty-seven officers and men.

Rogers embarked in bateaux with a force of thirty-seven Rangers on 13 June to revisit the Ticonderoga advance guards. During the scout, a Ranger named Samuel Eastman was lost. Departing the Ranger camp early one morning without informing Rogers, Eastman returned to the hill from where they had observed the French camps to secure a knapsack he had left there. Informed at daybreak that there was a Ranger missing, Rogers sent out a patrol in an attempt to find the missing Ranger but to no avail. Waiting all day for Eastman to return, Rogers left some provisions behind in case the lost Ranger should return to that site, and made his way back to Fort William Henry. Fearing the worst had happened, the Rangers were pleasantly surprised when Eastman sheepishly staggered into the fort five days later on 23 June "almost famished for want of subsistence."

Upon his return from the scout, Rogers found an unexpected "present" from Albany built specifically for him: six light whaleboats. Aching to put them to the test, Rogers embarked with fifty Rangers in five of the light, but strong, boats on 28 June. Landing ten miles up Lake George on the east shore, the Rangers carried the boats for three and a half days in sweltering summer heat over a gorge and through the mountains for a distance of six miles to a tributary of South Bay.

Having rested the afternoon of 3 July, the Rangers set out that night rowing with muffled oars down the narrow body of South Bay and Wood Creek, passing so close to Fort Ticonderoga that they could hear the watchwords being called by the sentinels. By morning, the Rangers were six miles beyond the fortress and hidden in the woods. Five miles short of Crown Point, Rogers' group had a respite the next night, unable to continue in their boats for fear of being exposed by a luminous full moon. The next day, the Rangers quietly observed from their hideout nearly one hundred boats of Brigadier General Louis-Joseph Montcalm, commander of the French Regulars in New France, pass on their way to Ticonderoga.

The following night was dark and the Rangers rowed forth, passing Crown Point and landing ten miles beyond. During the day, thirty boats and a schooner passed by their position on their way to Canada. Later that evening, Rogers rowed eight miles to the mouth of Otter Creek. From that point, he sent scouts to reconnoiter along the shore to the southern point of Buttonmould Bay, from where they returned with word of a schooner anchored a mile offshore.

Rogers planned to board and capture the schooner but, just as his boats were preparing to launch, two armed bateaus crewed by twelve men and laden with rice, flour, wheat, wine, and brandy appeared intent to land at Otter Creek. The Rangers fired a volley into the bateaus and called for their surrender. Unwilling to do so, the Frenchmen in the boats pulled for the far shore. The Rangers loaded their whaleboats and rowed in pursuit, quickly seizing the heavier and slower boats. The Rangers' lakeshore ambush had killed three and wounded two, one mortally.

Informed by the prisoners that they were part of a five-hundred-man force located only six miles away, Rogers had his men secure the wine and brandy they'd captured, sink the two enemy boats, and securely hide their whaleboats on the west shore. Rogers also felt compelled to have the mortally wounded man executed, for he could not march and he did not want to leave him behind to be discovered. Taking an overland route, Rogers and his force returned safely to Fort William Henry on 15 July with eight prisoners and four scalps.

Rogers' foray caused a great deal of consternation with the French. How could English whaleboats be operating north of Crown Point and Ticonderoga? Convinced there was a new water route from Lake George to Lake Champlain, the French launched numerous scouting expeditions to locate it. Unable to find this "water" route, they grew more confused with time.

Following his return, Rogers had an audience in Albany with Major General Abercrombie, the new and temporary commander-in-chief who had succeeded Shirley. Arriving with his newest prisoners, Rogers requested and was granted the authority to raise another company of Rangers on 24 July 1756. Abercrombie breveted Rogers a major and placed Richard Rogers in command of the newly formed company.

Prior to Rogers' request, Shirley had authorized the formation in May of two additional Ranger companies under the command of Captains Hobbs and Speakman. The two Ranger companies commanded by Hobbs and Speakman each had an authorized strength of three officers, two sergeants, two corporals, and fifty-eight privates, for a total of sixty-five men. Though short on enlisted men, they did have their full complement of officers, one of whom was Robert Rogers' older brother, James, who was serving as Hobbs' ensign. Of the six officers in these two companies, only James and one other would survive the war. Of the remainder, Hobbs would die of smallpox at Fort William Henry on 22 February 1757, Speakman would be scalped alive and mutilated after being mortally wounded, and the other two would die on the field of battle.

Rogers set out to reconnoiter the French fortresses and their advance guards on 2 August with a force of twenty-five Rangers and fifty Provincials. Following a probe of Ticonderoga, the Provincials returned to William Henry while Rogers and his Rangers skirted the hordes of Indians in the valley of Ticonderoga and continued on to Crown Point. While lying in ambush, a French deserter whom Rogers had brought along as a guide attempted to betray their position. Subdued and searched, the deserter was found to be carrying in his waistcoat meticulously sketched plans of both Forts Edward and William Henry. Failing to ambush any French soldiers there, the Rangers killed forty horses prior to being discovered. With a swarm of French, Canadians, and Indians in hot pursuit, Rogers' force hastily retired to Fort William Henry with their turncoat guide in tow. The deserter was subsequently sent to Albany where he was executed.

Rogers had been determined since his first scout of the year to raid the French Quebec Province settlements along the Richelieu River, an outlet of Lake Champlain that connected with the St. Lawrence River at Lake St. Peter. Petitioning Lord Loudoun—who had replaced Abercrombie as commander-in-chief—for permission to conduct the raid and receiving no answer in return, Rogers wrote him again on the 16th stating that the eagerness of his company to go on the scout had forced him "to comply with their wishes." Rogers departed the same day, wanting to be long gone should Loudoun opt to cancel the raid.

Having launched Stark earlier in the morning with a section of men in whaleboats, Rogers followed later that evening with the second section. Linking up the next morning and hiding their boats, the Rangers moved cross-country to their hidden whaleboats on Lake Champlain, recuperating after their long march with the wine and brandy they had obtained from the two armed bateaus they had captured and sunk during their raid to the region in early July.

Moving only at night on the water, the Rangers approached Isle la Motte—a two mile by six mile island located in the northern section of Lake Champlain within the state of Vermont—around midnight of the second night only to discover a schooner sailing toward them. A brisk wind propelled the schooner by the Rangers at too quick a pace to board.

Having been thwarted a second time from capturing a schooner, Rogers continued northward with his men for another two nights. Landing at Wind-Mill-Point on the east side of Lake Champlain at the Richelieu River, the Rangers established an ambush along the narrow waterway, waited, and waited some more. Finally, with their provisions running out, Rogers had to abandon the position. Hiding their whaleboats in a small cove on the east side of the lake and eight miles from Crown Point, the group took a French family of three prisoner as they passed by the fort on their return to Fort William Henry.

In September, Rogers received orders assigning both of his Ranger companies that had been based at Fort William Henry, and the attached Stockbridge Indian Company, to an island opposite Fort Edward, now under the command of Abercrombie, in the Hudson River. They did not have to move far, though, for they were already located at Edward, having served a short assignment from 31 August to mid September in support of General Webb's troops on the Mohawk River in central New York. More fearful of an assault on Fort Edward than Fort William Henry, Loudoun concentrated the "elite" of his army to provide support for the garrison stationed there.

This new post was soon called "Rogers' Island," and it would serve as the base and headquarters for Rogers' Rangers for the remainder of the campaign and as winter quarters. Though a large blockhouse was built, the Rangers chose to live in groups of four in bark huts. The blockhouse eventually became a hospital where smallpox victims could be kept in isolation.

The Rangers "ebbed and flowed" from their Island. Un-uniformed and augmented with Indians at times, their patrols appeared wild and barbaric as they paddled by the sentries of Fort Edward, usually in the dead of night or early morning hours. Occasionally, panicked guards would fire shots and sound the alarm believing they were an enemy force. Eventually, a system was established to prevent this type of fratricide from occurring. Though Rogers' Island was now their base of operations, Fort William Henry still served as the Ranger point of departure for operations against Ticonderoga and Crown Point.

On 22 October, Rogers and twenty of his Rangers departed from Henry in two whaleboats to recon Ticonderoga. Landing the boats, the group moved up the Ticonderoga Valley. As they approached the fort, a sentry was spotted on the forest road within shouting distance of the fortress. Followed by five of his men, Rogers boldly walked up the road directly toward the sentry. Challenged in French, Rogers answered in French. Confused, the sentry failed to halt Rogers' approach. Realizing his error, the sentry asked Rogers in amazement, "*Qui êtes vous?*" to which the Ranger responded, "Rogers." The sentry was quickly seized and spirited away to Fort William Henry. Interrogated, the prisoner provided a great deal of important intelligence, including the news that Rogers' four whaleboats concealed in the cove on Lake Champlain had been discovered, thus solving that perplexing French mystery of the "new water route" from Lake George to Lake Champlain.

Though Rogers and his men were a considerable expense, Loudoun was unable to rely on Indian allies and, therefore, judged his Rangers indispensable, depending on them to safeguard his camps, his marches, and to report on enemy activity. He fully realized that his army could not exist in the forests of America without the eyes and ears of the American Ranger. Loudoun developed his winter plan of defense entirely around five companies of Rangers: the four companies that would eventually constitute the corps of Rogers' Rangers and a fifth detached Ranger company of the New York Provincial Regiment commanded by Captain Jonathan Ogden and garrisoned at Saratoga.

Loudoun's plan of defense called for the garrisoning of Fort William Henry with four hundred Regulars under the command of Major Eyre, as well as Hobbs' and Speakman's Ranger companies of forty-three and fifty-five officers and men apiece. Fort Edward was defended by five hundred Regulars under Major Sparks with Rogers' two companies of approximately fifty men each settled nearby on their island. The defenses were rounded out with Ogden's Rangers at Saratoga.

The year closed out with Rogers' Rangers patrolling around their two English forts and conducting one final scout of little consequence to Crown Point. The main body of Loudoun's army was withdrawn from Fort Edward and quartered from Saratoga to New York. Rogers was left with orders to remain at Rogers' Island with his corps of two Ranger companies — the Stockbridge Company of Indians having disbanded on 11 November for the winter — to secure the region.

CHAPTER 4

Rogers' Rangers:
Campaign of 1757

Everything which the enemy least expects will succeed the best.

Frederick the Great

The winter campaign commenced for Rogers and his men on 15 January 1757, with an operation that would eventually transform their reputation from that of a scouting corps to that of a fighting organization. Ordered by Major Sparks to conduct a reconnaissance of Forts Ticonderoga and Crown Point and to "harass the enemy in any way that he saw fit," Rogers departed Fort Edward for Fort William Henry that day with fifty-two Rangers from both his companies. Arriving at Henry that night, Eyre was informed of the Ranger mission and the requirement to obtain an additional thirty-three Rangers for the patrol. From a multitude of volunteers, Speakman and sixteen of his men were accepted while James Rogers and fourteen others joined from Hobbs' company—Hobbs himself being unavailable and in the hospital with smallpox from which he would eventually die. Though unofficial at the time, Hobbs' and Speakman's companies came under Rogers' command on that date, thus constituting a part of Rogers' Rangers.

The next two days were spent preparing for the operation. The uniform and weapons for Rogers' original two companies were greenish buckskin battledress, individual muskets flintlocks or firelocks, scalping knives, and hatchets or tomahawks. Rogers' company officers also carried compasses in the large end of their powder horns, a practice that would soon be emulated by all of the Rogers' Rangers officers. Hobbs' and Speakman's Rangers wore gray duffel coat with vest, buckskin breeches, leggings, and water resistant moccasins and socks. On them, they carried regulation muskets, cartridge boxes, King's regulation shoes, and contractor-supplied hatchets.

Ammunition and provisions were gathered and issued. Each man was supplied enough powder and balls for sixty rounds. Food rations were carried in a knapsack strapped over a shoulder and consisted of two weeks' supply of dried beef, sugar, rice, cornmeal, and peas. Rum was carried in their wooden canteens. Though Rogers' two companies had come prepared for the winter campaign, the new companies were untrained in the art of winter warfare. Consequently, Rogers' experienced men had to teach them how to make snowshoes for the march. Forming his patrol of eighty-five men on the fort's parade ground on the evening of the 17th, Rogers personally inspected each and every man to ensure that he was properly equipped and provisioned.

Wrapped in blankets—the Ranger winter campaign coat—the patrol moved out in single file, marching the few miles to the first narrows on Lake George. The patrol encamped in an exceptionally defensible position with a steep mountain slope to their rear and the frozen surface of the lake to their front. Sentry posts consisting of six men each were positioned around the perimeter. Two of them were to remain alert at all times. Relief would be done noiselessly and, in the event of needing to sound an alarm, one of them was to silently retreat to notify Rogers in the hope that he could redeploy his Rangers quietly to turn the tables on their attackers. Small fires could be built at night but they had to be placed in the heavy part of the woods and in pits three feet deep.

In the morning, at the break of dawn, the men were roused—the precursor to what would be called "stand-to"—as that was a favorite time for the French and Indians to attack. The still warm coals from the nighttime fires were rekindled and a hot breakfast of cornmeal gruel was cooked to be washed down with a swig of rum. Rogers made his way around the camp as his men ate, asking about their condition, having noted that several of them had fallen during the evening march. None would admit to any disability and it was not until the march was started once again that Rogers, standing to one side, was able to identify eleven lame men as the patrol filed past. In spite of their protests, Rogers ordered them to return to Fort William Henry under the charge of one of their number. The Rangers departed, mumbling their protestations as they hobbled away.

Having already ascertained with small reconnaissance parties that the local area was secure, Rogers and his now seventy-four-man Ranger detachment marched within sight of the lake's shoreline in single file, extended order, with each man maintaining a large enough interval to keep any two of them from being hit by the same musket ball. An advance guard preceded the main body and flanking parties moved on both sides, at approximately twenty yards' distance. They encamped that second night at a point three miles from Sabbath Day Point.

The following morning, donning their snowshoes, the Rangers moved northwest cross-country through the hills for eight miles to their next camp. By the evening of the 20th, Rogers' force found itself three miles west of Lake Champlain. A few more miles of marching the next morning found the Rangers on Lake Champlain at Five Mile Point midway between Ticonderoga and Crown Point, which were five miles in both directions-hence the name.

The weather was bad. Rain and mist reduced visibility. Almost immediately upon their arrival, Rogers' scouts reported two sleighs from Ticonderoga coming toward their position. Ironically, it was from this same location that Rogers had captured two sleighs the winter prior. Rogers quickly organized the ambush. Sending Lieutenant Stark and twenty of Rogers' men farther up, past the point of the shoreline toward Crown Point, Rogers took thirty men with him and moved toward Ticonderoga to cut off the enemy's escape route. Captain Speakman, in the center with his men and positioned where Putnam's Creek-La Barbue Creek joined with the lake at a point that jutted out, waited. When the sleighs were opposite his position, Stark was to move out onto the frozen lake to block their movement, thus allowing Speakman to easily capture them.

Unknown to Rogers at that point in time, he had a rather significant problem on his hands. Earlier that morning, the Ticonderoga commandant had ordered a resupply mission to proceed to Crown Point to load some brandy and forage. A total of ten sleighs, eighty horses, and thirty men set out with two sleighs and ten men in advance. The two advance sleighs were almost abreast of Speakman's position when Rogers saw the other eight sleighs slowly emerging from the cover afforded by the mist and falling rain.

Rogers quickly dispatched his two fastest men on snowshoes in an attempt to inform the other two sections to execute the ambush when the main body of eight sleighs passed by. Cutting through the woods and gasping out Rogers' orders to Speakman, the two Ranger messengers couldn't reach Stark in time. Unable to see the other eight sleighs because of the bend in the point, Stark and his Rangers sprang from the north side of the lake and, with bloodcurdling war cries, spread out on the ice and headed toward the two advance sleighs.

With the ambush sprung, both Speakman and Rogers closed in on the two sleighs. Of the ten accompanying soldiers, seven were captured. The other three, upon seeing and hearing Stark and his men, had jumped on the backs of three horses, cut their traces, and galloped away toward Ticonderoga. Spotting the second group of sleighs, the Rangers removed their snowshoes and gave chase across the ice after the fleeing men and the other eight sleighs. Observing the pack of Rangers bearing down on them, the unloaded sleighs were able to quickly outdistance Rogers' men and make their way back to the safety of Ticonderoga. Rogers wisely halted the pursuit.

The prisoners were kept isolated from one another and brought before Rogers one at a time. His interrogation revealed that two hundred Canadians and forty-five Indians had just arrived at Fort Ticonderoga with an additional fifty Indians to join them from Crown Point that evening or first thing the following morning. Combined with the three hundred fifty Regulars at Ticonderoga and six hundred Regulars at Crown Point, Rogers realized there was a formidable force that could soon make him the pursued.

Rogers was caught in a dilemma. He could not wait in his current position, for it would provide the French an opportunity to gather their forces and catch him between both fortresses. He could not cross the lake and return by way of Wood Creek out of concern of being observed from Ticonderoga and having an ambush set to catch him. Despite the opposition of some of officers, Rogers believed there was only one true recourse left: return by the same route they had traveled in hopes of slipping by Ticonderoga unobserved.

Marching as quickly as possible through the snow, the Rangers moved back to their previous night's encampment, rekindled the fires, and dried their powder and weapons. Rogers gave orders to Sergeant Walker, commander of the security detachment, to kill their prisoners should the Rangers be attacked in force. Forcing down a hasty meal, the force moved off in single file with their weapons held under their blanket-coats to keep them dry in the soaking rain. Rogers led the way with Speakman in the center and Stark bringing up the rear of the main formation. Sergeant Walker followed with the prisoners and a rear guard.

As the Rangers were withdrawing, the French were moving to engage. The supply sleigh commander, Major De Rouilly, dispatched a soldier on horse to ride ahead and inform the Ticonderoga commandant, Major De Lusignan, that Rogers had just attacked the supply train from the west. Surmising correctly that Rogers would return west of Ticonderoga through the mountains, Lusignan dispatched a total of 104 Indians, Regulars, and Canadian volunteers under the dual command of Captains De Basserode and La Granville to intercept them.

Eager to finally have an opportunity to engage Rogers, the French force departed Ticonderoga with only a few rounds of ammunition per man and very little in the way of supplies. A half hour later, Lusignan dispatched an additional ten men loaded with ammunition and supplies to follow. Basserode's scouts located Rogers' column at around 1400, three miles northwest of Ticonderoga. Realizing that the Rangers' route would require them to cross a seventy-five-foot-wide ravine through which Putnam's Creek ran, Basserode moved to the location and established a crescent-shaped ambush among the trees and bushes that ran along the crest of the far side gully where it took a turn.

Though a dangerous tactic, Rogers chose to pass through the ravine in an attempt to remain concealed rather than continue along the high ground. This decision resulted in one of the Rangers' bloodiest battles of the war. Having traveled a mile and a half from where they had briefly halted to dry their weapons, the Rangers descended into the ravine. Holding his fire long enough to allow Rogers and the following twelve men to almost reach the summit of the ravine, Basserode's force of 114 men opened fire. The sprung ambush found Rogers caught in the upper kill zone of the ravine, Speakman with the center section on the floor of the ravine, and Stark's and Walker's rear elements on the opposite hill for they had yet to enter the ravine.

The vast majority of muskets were probably aimed at Rogers. While half of them misfired because of the rain, the other half amazingly failed to do no more than place one glancing shot across his forehead. Wiping the blood from his eyes, Rogers shouted orders to withdraw back across the ravine. Unfortunately, there were those who could not obey: the initial barrage had killed two and wounded several more.

As the Rangers in the ambush attempted to retire back across the ravine, their attackers, not taking the time to reload after their initial volley, burst forth and charged down into the ravine with fixed bayonets. Again, it was another miracle that the sections under Rogers and Speakman did not find themselves cut off from the rear. This miracle did not save them from a serious beating, though. Rogers' advance column had just linked up with Speaker's center section when the enemy fell upon them, slashing, stabbing, and shouting. Veteran French Regulars, French Canadians in buckskin, and Indians in war paint joined in the fierce melee within the creek's little ravine.

Rogers' loaded muskets, which had yet to be fired, greeted the cold steel of French and Indian bayonet and tomahawk, but that did not stem the enemy tide. Outnumbered in the ravine nearly two to one, the Rangers heard the welcome volleys of Stark's rear formation from the opposite hill. Having discharged their muskets, Rogers again ordered the advance and center sections to withdraw. The men moved back across the creek and up the gully's side as quickly as they could in their snowshoes. But the going was not easy, for they not only had to fight the enemy that was on their tail, but they were also fighting their way through four feet of snow. Moving only a few feet at a time up the ravine, a Ranger would have to turn and fight before he could move farther up. The frenzy of the pursuers and the raging survival instincts of the Rangers made for many fierce duels. Captain Speakman fell wounded but was able to conceal himself under a bush as the shouting enemy horde passed him by.

The screams of bayoneted and tomahawked Rangers rose from the ravine floor. With the Rangers below finally spreading out, Stark's men were better able to place supporting fires from above without fear of hitting some of their own men. Rogers and the survivors made it to Stark's position just as Basserode attempted to envelop the Ranger position with a flanking movement. Upon being informed by Stark of the threat, Rogers dispatched a detachment of marksmen to deal with it. Led by Sergeant Bill Phillips, a noted half-breed Indian, the marksmen placed such devastating fire into the flankers that their attempt ceased immediately and they promptly withdrew back to the main body.

Despite their failure to flank the Ranger position, the French and Indians were still flushed enough with their initial success to attempt an attack along Rogers' entire front. The enemy slowly worked their way up the ravine, firing from behind trees and bushes until they were within a few yards. Rising en masse, they charged. The high ground and dense cover provided Rogers with the advantage now. The charge failed to advance against what seemed like constant firepower. One of the secrets to Rogers' success was a unique tactic he used to control his fires. Rather than allow all of his men to fire in a single volley, half would discharge their weapons. Then, while they were reloading, the other half would fire, after which the first section would be completed with their reloading. This simple tactic, practiced at this time period exclusively by Rogers' Rangers, allowed for what seemed to be continuous volley fires. The attack dissolved as the French and Indians broke and ran back down the ravine where they established positions from which they could take potshots at the Rangers.

Following a lull in the fighting, the firing soon increased on Rogers' left as another flanking attempt was attempted. Ensign James Rogers and twelve Rangers were dispatched to end this threat. Their effective fires soon drove off Basserode's third attack. Having gained the time, Rogers reorganized his defenses, placing Stark in the center, Ensign Brewer on the left, Ensign Rogers and fourteen men on the summit to the rear of the hill, while he took the traditional place of honor on the right side of the formation.

Out of his original force of seventy-four Rangers at the start of the battle, fifty-seven remained. Ten had been killed and seven captured in the ravine. Of the fifty-seven who survived, two were too seriously wounded to fire a weapon. The remaining wounded occupied a place on the line. Security of the seven prisoners was no longer a concern, for they had been executed, per orders, at the outset of the battle.

Neither Basserode nor his men had the stomach to try a fourth attack. They had suffered heavy losses in their three previous attempts and could no longer muster an overwhelming force at any point along Rogers' perimeter. Sending off to Ticonderoga for reinforcements, Basserode attempted another stratagem, that of attempting to talk Rogers and his men into surrendering. Calling Rogers by name and flattering him and his Rangers' bravery, Basserode and his officers attempted to convince them that they would be humanely treated if they gave themselves up. If they did not do so, the only alternative was to die when the requested reinforcements arrived. In response, Rogers assured the French that he had plenty of men and supplies left and he himself would "do some scalping and cutting to pieces" if another charge were attempted.

Basserode's request for reinforcements incredibly only brought an additional twenty-six soldiers to his position, bringing the French total to 115 by their account and 250 by Rogers' Rangers' estimate. Bush-fighting warfare continued throughout the afternoon as the French and Indians crawled as close as they dared and traded shots with the Rangers. This sniping was not without its consequences, for Basserode was mortally wounded.

At sundown, Rogers was wounded with a shot along the hand that went through his wrist. Though no longer able to load a musket, Rogers hid the true nature of his wound to ensure the men would not become discouraged. Two other Rangers were seriously wounded with one, Private Joshua Martin, taking what was believed to be a wound to the stomach that shattered his hip.

Calling a council of war of his officers after sundown, as he was prone to do, Rogers and his officers agreed that the most prudent action to take was to "carry off the wounded of [their] party and take the advantage of the night to return homeward, lest the enemy should send out a fresh party upon them in the morning, [besides, their] ammunition being almost expended [they] were obliged to pursue this resolution."

Gathering in the dark their seven wounded men, the Rangers were relieved to find that with three arm wounds, two head wounds, and one each in the mouth and side, none had sustained any wounds to his legs. Under the cover of darkness, Rogers and his men moved off, making fairly good progress. Seeing a fire in the middle of the woods and concerned that it might represent a hostile party, Rogers decided to take a long route around it to place some distance between a potential trouble spot and his exhausted Rangers. The next morning found them on the shore of Lake George, six miles south of the French advance guard positions in the vicinity of the second narrows. Physically drained and unable to advance much farther on foot, the wounded needed to rest.

Despite their fatigued condition, Stark and two others volunteered to march on to Fort William Henry to bring back assistance. Discarding their snowshoes, the three Rangers took to the frozen lake, and despite the effects of the previous long marches, the battle, and their long march during the night, they covered the forty mile distance to the fort by evening. Exhausted, they stumbled into the fort to inform Major Eyre of the engagement and Rogers' situation.

Sixteen Rangers immediately sallied forth with sleighs to carry the wounded. Their journey was not long, for the following morning, 23 January, they linked up with Rogers and his fifty-four survivors as they came staggering through the first narrows of Lake George, wounded in tow.

Soon after Stark's departure, Rogers had reconsidered his position. With the French and Indians so close and Fort William Henry so far, he decided he dared not wait for the sleighs to arrive. Gathering the wounded, the Rangers trudged tiredly after Stark down the lake. Happening to glance behind him, Rogers noticed a dark form following the group. Believing it was a straggler from their column, Rogers sent some men back to get him.

Rather than a straggler from their column, it turned out to be Martin, the private who'd had his hip shattered by a bullet through the stomach. Left for dead on the field of battle, he had recovered himself enough to make off to the woods. There he built a fire to keep from freezing to death. It was his fire that Rogers had skirted and it was this skirting that slowed Rogers down thus allowing Martin, as wounded as he was, to drag himself after his comrades and to overtake them. The moment the Rangers reached him, he collapsed from exhaustion. Much to everyone's surprise, Private Martin not only survived what appeared to be mortal wounds, but he was later promoted to Sergeant and earned an ensigncy in the Ranger Corps.

Despite the Ranger's efforts to ensure none of their men were left behind alive after this engagement, there were others who would not be as fortunate as Martin. Having concealed himself under a bush during the enemy assault up the ravine, Captain Speakman managed to crawl down the gully, following the creek out of the battle area. This distance proved to be farther than Rogers' men could look for survivors. Later that day, he was joined by Robert Baker, a British volunteer who had tagged along to see how American Rangers operated, and Private Thomas Brown of Speakman's own company, both men seriously wounded.

Speakman's and Baker's wounds were so serious, they could no longer move. Brown, being the only one still capable of movement, built a fire. Speakman called to Rogers and the Rangers but to no avail. Their only answer was from the enemy. Realizing they could not travel or escape, they decided they would surrender to the French, hoping this could be accomplished prior to being found by the Indians. Just as this decision was reached, Brown observed an Indian moving toward them from over Putnam's Creek. Crawling away from the fire, Brown observed the Indian come up to Captain Speakman. Unable to offer any form of resistance because of the wounds, Speakman was stripped and scalped alive. Baker, nearly just as helpless, attempted to pull out a knife and stab himself but he was stopped by the Indian and carried away.

Speakman was still alive and called out to Brown, begging him "for God's sake!" to give him [Speakman] a tomahawk with which he could end his life. Brown could not bring himself to do so and could, in the end, only "[exhort] him as well as I could to pray for mercy, as he could not live many minutes in that deplorable condition, being on the frozen ground, covered with snow." Speakman's final request was to "let his wife know if [Brown] lived to get home the dreadful death he died." Following Speakman's demise, Brown attempted to flee the area but was captured. He later managed to escape but was once again recaptured. His freedom was finally achieved at a later date with an exchange.

As it so happened, Speakman was not the only Ranger to be tortured in such a manner. Lieutenant Samuel Kennedy had been mortally wounded and, also, left on the field of battle. Incapacitated and unable to defend himself, he had died under a hail of tomahawks.

Both sides claimed victory. Rogers' Rangers had sustained fourteen killed, nine wounded, and seven captured of seventy-four engaged. The French force of Regulars, Canadians, and Indians numbered anywhere from 145 to 250 men, depending on whose numbers one is to believe. Either way, Rogers was outnumbered a minimum of two to one. French losses based on their reports—which were always a bit suspect—were put at eighteen killed (to include the seven prisoners) and twenty-seven wounded. When one considers the significant advantage the French had as a function of surprise and numbers, it would seem that the Rangers' claim to victory, based upon turning a desperate situation into a well-for-mulated plan of stubborn defense, had greater validity. In the overall scheme of the war, though, the battle that would be known as the Battle of La Barbue Creek would prove to be, strategically, of no consequence.

Word of the battle traveled throughout the colonies. It raised colonial spirits. Abercrombie sent Rogers and his Rangers "thanks for their behavior, and recommended both him and them strongly to Lord Loudoun." Rogers' wrist wound had become worse and he had to go to Albany to obtain better medical treatment. Unfortunately, he also came down with smallpox, which he may have contracted previously at Forts Edward or William Henry. The illness, though, did not prevent Rogers from conducting a letter campaign in an attempt to expand his Ranger force. On 25 January, Rogers received authorization to raise an additional one hundred Rangers, to bring the original two companies to a complement of one hundred each.

Though breveted a major and addressed as such by his Rangers and the Provincials, Rogers' title was not a true commission and the British Regulars still addressed him as "Captain." Though he now commanded a battalion-sized element, Rogers would not receive his majority until over a year later, in April 1758. The deaths of the two Ranger commanders, Hobbs and Speakman, created openings that needed to be filled. Lieutenant John Stark, the Rangers' most senior lieutenant, was strongly recommended for and given the command of Speakman's old company. Hobbs' vacancy was filled by Lieutenant Charles Bulkeley, who was subsequently promoted to captain.

The war did not stop while the Rangers recuperated from the La Barbue Creek battle and reorganization. With Rogers still incapacitated in Albany, the Rangers at Fort William Henry, a total of eighty-two officers and men from both Speakman's and Hobbs' old companies, fell under the command of Captain Stark, who proceeded to increase the Ranger fame with some insightful thinking.

On the evening of 16 March, Stark overheard that his Rangers, many of whom were Irish or Scot-Irish, were planning a celebration the following day in honor of St. Patrick's Day. Knowing that the majority of the Regulars stationed at Henry were also Irish, Stark grew concerned with the knowledge that the fort would be vulnerable to French attack if both his Rangers and the garrison soldiers celebrated by indulging themselves in excessive quantities of rum and spruce beer. Fully realizing the negative consequences of his actions on the morale of his Rangers and his reputation as a new commander should he be wrong, Stark gave explicit orders that no "spirituous liquors" would be issued to his Rangers without written orders from him. As the requests came pouring in that day, he pleaded a "lameness of his wrist" that prevented him from signing them.

The garrison soldiers partied after the evening mess on the 17th as the Rangers watched and fumed about the injustice. Hung over, the majority of the Regulars were in a mellow stupor and Stark's Rangers literally hated their new commander by the time a French force of 1,600 men under the command of French Canada governor-general Vaudreuil's brother, Rigaud, arrived to capture Fort William Henry late at night on the 18th.

An alert Ranger sentry raised the alarm. Stationed on the east side of their hut-fort compound—the Rangers lived outside of the actual fort—the Ranger had observed a light moving on the lake. Immediately informed of the occurrence by Stark, the garrison commander, Major Eyre, ordered the Rangers into William Henry. Roused from their stupor and quietly moved into position on the ramparts, the Regulars took their place alongside the Rangers, who had reluctantly abandoned their own village.

The fort's garrison consisted of 346 Regulars and Rogers' Rangers, who could field only sixty-three combat effectives, for a total defending force of 409 soldiers, including those still drunk. Outnumbered four to one, the defenders opened fire against a surprised French force as they approached the fort. Having so unexpectedly met heavy resistance, the French withdrew and were not seen throughout the rest of the day.

Attacking once again under the cover of darkness that night, the enemy attempted to scale the walls of the fort with their assault ladders. But, as the night prior, the fires were too heavy and accurate and the French withdrew for a second time.

Campfire smoke gave the French camp away the next morning and Stark sent forth a reconnaissance party of Rangers to gather some intelligence. Returning before noon, the scouts reported that the enemy was numerous and preparing to attack again.

At 1200 and within sight of the fort, the entire French force marched out on the frozen lake, two men deep and extending for more than a mile and a half. A French representative under a flag of truce was received by Eyre, who rejected any terms of surrender. With a general assault now expected, every man who could walk or crawl to the ramparts to defend the fort "to the last man" did so, including eleven Rangers who were seriously ill with scurvy.

A general assault did not ensue until later that evening when the French concentrated their attention—and their forces—on the Ranger compound and flotilla of lake boats in dry dock outside of William Henry's fortified walls. Watching their personal belongings go up in flames, the Rangers begged to be allowed to make a sortie. Finally, with the flames threatening the fort itself, Eyre authorized the charge.

Leading a group of volunteers, of which he had no problem gathering, Stark and the men swarmed out of the fort and attacked with a vengeance. Met with such determination, the French abandoned their interest in the Ranger stockade and began to focus it on the attacking Rangers. Overwhelmed by the sheer numbers of enemy, Stark, one of three wounded Rangers, and his group of volunteers were forced to return to the fort or be cut off.

Leaving behind seventeen burned Ranger huts, the French next went after the dry-docked British flotilla. Another sortie of Rangers and Regulars sallied forth from the fort but, as with the huts, they failed to save the "fleet." What they did manage to save, though, was a considerable amount of provisions—particularly rum—from the fired storehouses. With part of the force providing covering fires, the remainder were able to evacuate all the kegs of rum to the fort.

Having failed to take the fort, Rigaud's force withdrew up Lake George on the morning of 23 March. The defender's losses were placed at four Regulars killed and three Rangers wounded. French losses were reported to be fourteen men killed and three wounded. Too wounded to travel the distance back to Canada, the three Frenchmen were left behind as prisoners.

From these three prisoners, it was learned that two of Rogers' Rangers who had been taken prisoner by the French at La Barbue Creek had turned and offered their services to their captors. Privates Benjamin Woodall and David Kimble of Richard Rogers' company had been offered 7,000 livres each—a considerable amount, for a livre was a silver coin equal in worth to an English pound—if they would show Rigaud the best route to Fort William Henry and the fort's most accessible and vulnerable places to attack. Private Thomas Brown, another Ranger captured at La Barbue Creek, had been the one initially approached. Questioned by Rigaud while held at Ticonderoga, Brown responded to Rigaud's request to assist his army by stating "I [am] sorry that a Gentlemen should desire such a thing of a youth, or endeavor to draw him away from his duty.... I [am] not to be bought with money, to be a traitor to my country and assist in destroying my friends." Encountering the other two privates in the guardhouse later, Brown was disappointed to hear that they had become willing traitors.

With Rigaud's failure, the two Ranger traitors' fortunes changed significantly. Not only did they not receive their money, they were put in irons and returned to the guardhouse. It is believed they were eventually turned over to the Indians in order to help pacify them following the failure to take William Henry. Brown, while in captivity, heard reports that two Rangers had suffered grisly deaths at the hands of some Indians. Perhaps both Woodall and Kimble had received their just reward, after all.

At Fort William Henry, a battalion from Fort Edward relieved Eyre's scurvy-ridden garrison. Rogers' Rangers were not so fortunate, as they had to remain at the fort and lick their wounds as best they could. Fortunately, the newly enlisted recruits were on their way. By the end of April, the companies were at established strength, all chain of command positions were filled, and Ensign James Rogers had even been promoted to first lieutenant in Hobbs' old company, two days following Bulkeley's promotion to captain and commander of that unit. The Fort William Henry Ranger companies had been successfully infused with members of Rogers' original companies, thus making for a truly homogeneous corps of Rogers' Rangers.

Loudoun's plan for the year was to attack Louisbourg—a heavily defended town and harbor along the Canadian coast—from where he could launch an assault on Quebec afterward. In order to accomplish this feat, he unwisely drained the bulk of his army from the interior forts and moved them to New York. In that he felt it was "impossible for an Army to act in [Canada] without Rangers," he included the majority of Rogers' corps in the task organization.

On 22 April, just seven days after dragging his cured but fever-weakened body from the room where he had battled smallpox for forty days, Rogers received orders to prepare his Rangers for "Foreign Service." Considered one of the most experienced of the companies, Richard Rogers' Rangers were moved to Fort William Henry to serve as the eyes and ears of Webb's army left behind to guard Lake George. Stark and Bulkeley redeployed to Fort Edward, linked up with Robert Rogers' Rangers, and marched to Albany. From there, they embarked down the Hudson River on sloops to New York to await passage to Louisbourg via Halifax, located on the southeastern coast of the Canadian province of Nova Scotia. At New York, Rogers' corps was augmented with a new company of New Hampshire Rangers under the command of Captain John Shephard, which had been formed on 25 February 1757, under Loudoun's authority.

While waiting to sail aboard their transports, Rogers was assigned a sixth company of Rangers. These one hundred men belonged to a Provincial company raised in New Hampshire and commanded by Captain John Titcomb.

Though Rangers in name, they were not Rangers of the status of Rogers' Rangers, for they were paid and equipped by the New Hampshire government and not out of the King's contingent funds. By the time the expedition came to a close, this Ranger company was no longer under Rogers' command.

The ships finally departed New York Harbor on 18 June and dropped anchor at Halifax on 1 July. There, Loudoun had to wait for the British fleet from England before he could advance on Louisbourg. The local Ranger captain, Captain Joseph Gorham of Gorham's Rangers—who had taken over command following his brother John's death—was not pleased with the implication that Rogers' brevet rank of major and title of Ranger corps commander made him the de facto commander of all Rangers involved with the campaign. Unable to resolve it between them—for there was nothing but "hollering" between Rogers' and Gorham's Rangers—the two commanders took the matter to Loudoun to settle the issue of who the senior captain of Rangers would be. No record was kept of how it was settled but it is noted that the two rugged individuals and their units were sent in different directions, never to work together.

The fleet finally arrived and the army embarked on the 1st and 2nd of August. Unfortunately for the English, the wait proved costly. Twenty-two French ships-of-the-line and a heavily reinforced Louisbourg fortress awaited them. With the odds no longer for certain in their favor, the expedition was abandoned for that year.

Meanwhile, disaster had struck the northern frontier of New York. Concerned about the area's security, Loudoun rushed from Halifax on 7 to 10 August, with Rogers' Rangers in advance of his Regulars. Returning to New York Harbor, the Rangers had to wait until 7 September for sloops to transport them up the Hudson to Albany, where they arrived on the night of the 14th. Following a two day layover, Rogers and his Rangers marched to Fort Edward.

For Richard Rogers and the Rangers left behind at Fort William Henry, events had not gone well during the absence of Loudoun's main body. Prior to his departure, Loudoun had been persuaded to sign on a company of New Jersey Dutch Bateaumen commanded by Captain Philip Burgin as Rangers to be instructed by and to augment Rogers' Rangers at William Henry. Richard Rogers soon found that they were not the caliber of soldier required to be Rangers and thus stationed them at Fort Edward in place of Ogden's company of New York Provisionals, who replaced them at William Henry.

For the English and American Rangers, the stockade at the far end of Lake George, Coutre Coeur, had been a thorn in the side to all scouts marching to Ticonderoga. Richard Rogers formulated a plan to destroy it.

Arriving in the vicinity of the objective during the early morning hours of 6 June, a detachment of Rangers composed of both Rogers' and Ogden's commands surprised the French, shooting three of them on the ramparts. The defenders, though, were able to rally faster than the Rangers could rush the gate. Forced to retire, the Rangers shot and killed a French officer as they withdrew into the bushes on the edge of the clearing.

Having been alerted by the fire, a force deployed from Ticonderoga to engage the Rangers. With the arrival of these reinforcements, the Rangers fired one final volley at the stockade and at the relief party and withdrew in their boats to Fort William Henry. Rogers had inflicted four dead and a number of wounded at the cost of four men wounded. Though a relatively insignificant battle, it earned considerable fame for Richard Rogers and Ogden, as it was given lengthy notice in the colonial daily.

Robert Rogers was able to proudly hear of his brother's exploit prior to sailing to Halifax. Unfortunately, the raid proved to be Richard's last. Contracting the smallpox almost immediately upon his return, Richard Rogers died on 22 June. Lieutenant Noah Johnson assumed command.

Johnson continued to send forth numerous scouts toward Ticonderoga and Crown Point. On one such mission on 1 July, the Rangers were ambushed and seven Rangers killed before they could extract themselves from the trap. Later, on 16 July, the Rangers were able to return the favor when they ambushed an eleven-man boat patrol from Coutre Coeur. Positioned on La Barque Island, an island opposite Sabbath Day Point that provided a commanding view of the lake, the Rangers spotted the French boat approaching the island. Landing in the Ranger ambush, the French – with two dead and four wounded – were able to embark under fire and escape the Rangers pursuing in their boats. The Rangers soon gave up the chase out of concern they were rowing into an ambush themselves.

For some time, the French general, Montcalm, had been determined to destroy Fort William Henry. Having entered the army at the age of fourteen and attained the rank of colonel by the time he was twenty-four, Montcalm was not one to hesitate when an opportunity presented itself, as it did with the departure of Loudoun's main body. Two weeks following the skirmish at La Barque Island, he advanced on Fort William Henry with an army of 7,600 men. With Montcalm's advance guard attacking, some of Rogers' Rangers desperately held the French and Indian tide of demonic humanity back while their picketed camp was evacuated and anyone outside of the fortress was brought safely inside the walls of the fort or within the confines of the entrenched camp outside.

Major Monroe, who had relieved Major Eyre following the previous attack on Fort William Henry, had a total force of 2,200 Regulars, Provincials, and Rogers' and Ogden's Rangers under his command. Realizing that the French vastly outnumbered him, Monroe sent three Rangers to General Webb at Fort Edward, begging for reinforcements. Though later condemned for his lack of action, Webb, concerned by the fact that Loudoun's expedition to Louisbourg had left the entire frontier open to attack, opted not to march to Monroe's relief. Fort William Henry and its valiant defenders were on their own.

With the completion of his first set of siege trenches, Montcalm opened with an artillery barrage. Battery and counterbattery fires continued for days as the French dug closer. With a French battery just 250 yards distance from the fort, the situation became virtually untenable for the men in the fort. Smallpox was rampant throughout and over three hundred of the defenders were dead or wounded. All major pieces of artillery or mortar had been destroyed. Two sorties by Rogers' Rangers — one from the fort and another from the entrenched camp — were fearlessly fought and repulsed with heavy losses on both sides.

The fortress surrendered on 9 August after it was resolved that the defenders would be escorted to Fort Edward by French troops where they would be released, agreeing not to serve again for a period of eighteen months. Unfortunately for the British and Rangers, someone forgot to tell the Indians. Having killed and scalped all the wounded left behind in the fort, the Indians poured forth and turned their attention on the survivors who were lined up outside of the fortress, preparing to march to Fort Edward. Bloodthirsty and scalp-hungry, the Indians began dragging victims from the ranks, usually tomahawking them as they did so. Order was established only after Montcalm and his French Regular officers entered into the fray.

At the rear of the column, Rogers' Rangers suffered only one killed and two missing during the Indian's reign of carnage. Others were not so fortunate, as the Indians butchered fifty to one hundred of the unarmed prisoners and carried off another two hundred. Those carried off would have undoubtedly wished to have been killed in the initial slaughter. Some of the prisoners were roasted and eaten by the Indians, who compelled other prisoners to partake of the feast. Ranger Private John McKeen, captured after a desperate struggle, was stripped and tied later that night to a tree referred to as the torture pole. In this position, the victim served as a target for the knives and tomahawks of liquored, excited, and dancing warriors. By the time the dance was complete, McKeen had been hit and gashed at virtually every point of his body. Not finished, the

Indians stuck each wound with pitchwood splints and, in one final barbaric climax, set the splints on fire, creating a human funeral pyre.

In the end, however, the Rangers gained some measure of revenge — biological in nature. Still thirsty for scalps, the Indians proceeded to dig up and skin the corpses buried in the graveyard of Fort William Henry. Many of these fallen soldiers, including Captain Richard Rogers, had died of smallpox. Having unknowingly contracted that disease from the infected scalps, the Indians returned to their villages where the virus wreaked great havoc among them. One entire nation of the bravest and staunchest allies of the French, the Pouteotame Indians, almost entirely perished from the resulting epidemic. The final closure to this massacre took place on 25 June 1758 when the British posted notice at Fort Edward that the capitulation agreement had been broken as a result of the massacre and, consequently, those who had surrendered could once again take up arms.

Robert Rogers returned to the frontier to find his brother Richard dead, his company paid up and discharged from the corps on 24 August, and Fort William Henry razed and burned to the ground. The spring, summer, and early fall of 1757 had not been a good one for Rogers' Rangers.

One item of favorable note for the Rangers did occur during that period and that was the establishment of Rogers' famous Ranging School. The culmination of the British Prime Minister's and Loudoun's plan and desire to impart Rogers' ranging skills and tactics to British volunteers, the school was formed during Rogers' two-day layover in Albany. Its official existence began on 14 September with the issuance by General Abercrombie of certificates to British Cadet volunteers who desired to serve with Rogers. Each certificate listed the Cadet's name, the Regular regiment he had been attached to, and informed the volunteer that "being desirous to go out with a Party of Rangers is hereby permitted to serve in that quality." Starting on the 15th, they formed a Cadet Company and were to place themselves under "the command of Captain Rogers and to be ready to march at a minute's notice."

Training the new recruits in the techniques of ranging, discipline, and methods of fighting, Rogers' school was, in essence, the first light infantry school in history. For the benefit of his students, Rogers codified his Ranging Rules; rules that, based upon past experience, were the foundation upon which Rangers were trained and disciplined. Other than the change in weaponry, these nineteen rules, which have come to be known as Rogers' Rangers Standing Orders, still serve as the cornerstone of today's standing orders for all tactical units, not just light infantry or Ranger organizations.

AUTHOR'S NOTE: Read Appendices A, B, and C

Rogers offered one caveat to his Standing Orders or, to be more historically correct, his Rules of Discipline. While these orders were to serve as a foundation upon which to operate, they were not inviolate or to be adhered to blindly. There were a "thousand and one" circumstances that could make it necessary to deviate from them. These rules and one's common sense and judgment were to employ the tactics that best fit the given situation. Above all, Rogers directed all to "preserve a firmness and presence of mind on every occasion."

Despite the loss of Fort William Henry, the scouts and patrols to Ticonderoga continued. Several Cadets always ventured on these excursions. On 3 October, a Ranger hunting party was nearly encircled by a force of French Allied Indians, attracted by the Rangers' shots as they tracked fresh meat. The Rangers effectively eluded their entrappers by every man dispersing and moving along a separate route to an appointed rendezvous.

Within the week, Rogers increased the number of scouts and patrols. On one of these patrols, Rogers was accompanied by Lord William Howe, who would later be the commander-in-chief of British land forces in North America from 1775 to 1778. Intent upon learning the Ranger method of marching, ambushing, retreating, and other Ranger tactics, Howe returned from the journey full of praise for the Rangers' methods, tactics, and abilities. Howe was so impressed that he would later institute many reforms in the British Army based upon what he had learned with the Rangers.

With winter bearing down, the Provincials were disbanded and the Regulars began to withdraw to their winter quarters during the early days of November. On 8 November, the Cadet Company was officially disbanded, with some of the Cadets withdrawing with the Regulars to their winter quarters while others remained as permanent Cadets of Rogers' Rangers.

Around mid-November, Captain James Abercrombie, General Abercrombie's nephew and aide-de-camp, ordered a "grand scouting party" formed to create some "mischief to their enemy." With Rogers ill with scurvy, Captain Stark formed a party of three hundred Rangers. The raid was Stark's first opportunity since he'd contracted smallpox to command his company in battle but, much to his chagrin and frustration, Abercrombie superseded him in command on the patrol.

Throughout the patrol, Stark did very little to assist Abercrombie, especially in regard to controlling the Rangers. On the march to Ticonderoga, Rangers fired at game despite Abercrombie's orders to the contrary. By dusk of the sixth day, Abercrombie, two British officers who had accompanied him, and ten Rangers had approached to within nine hundred yards of the fortress when they spotted twenty to thirty boats along the water side of Ticonderoga. Abercrombie was in favor of burning the boats but the Rangers rejected that proposal and decided to establish an ambush along the road instead. Setting up the ambush site, Abercrombie ordered a fifty-fifty watch, half the men on security while the other half slept. Much to his amazement and contrary to his orders, Abercrombie noted that all Ranger officers and men were soon fast asleep under their blankets.

At dawn, the ambush party was woken. Two hours later, six armed men moved into the area. Waiting an additional thirty minutes to see if they would approach closer, Abercrombie finally ordered an officer and ten men to stealthily sneak up on the Frenchmen and capture them. Those left behind in the ambush site were given the strictest orders to remain quiet and not to stir. Despite their stealthy attempt, the advancing party of Rangers was spotted by one of the six potential prisoners, who let out a holler and took off running. Without orders, Captain Stark, who was located right next to Abercrombie, let out with an Indian war cry and, with his men rising after him, set off after the six men, all firing and yelling like a mob.

Some rounds from the Fort Ticonderoga cannon soon put a stop to the chase as the group ran toward the fortress. Giving up the pursuit, the Rangers halted, began calling out "God save King George," and proceeded to damn the French for not coming out to fight. The French response was to fire eleven rapid cannon rounds. Sounding retreat, the Ranger party quickly dispersed and fell back out of artillery range. It took Abercrombie a number of miles while on the return march to persuade the Rangers to form a rear guard.

Upon their return to Fort Edward, Abercrombie forwarded a report to Loudoun that recommended, based upon his perception of a lack of discipline, that officers of the Regular army be assigned to the Ranger units. As the senior Ranger representative of what would become known as the Misbehavior Scout, Stark's performance was inexcusable. Though there may have been reason to dislike young Abercrombie, Stark went out of his way to gall the captain and to deliberately oppose him. Not only did this attitude not enhance the good name of Rogers' Rangers, it also endangered the entire Ranger party by disregarding a number of Rogers' Ranging Rules, rules that some members of the corps would rather die to uphold rather than disobey.

On 17 December, Rogers, having recovered sufficiently enough, marched from Fort Edward with a force of 150 Rangers. Moving through three inches of snow, an additional twelve inches were dumped on them that night. By the next morning, eight Rangers had succumbed to frost-bite and had to return to Fort Edward. Passing by the charred remains of Fort William Henry and Richard Rogers' grave, Rogers' party discovered a large cache of cannon balls and shells that had been hidden by the French after the fall of the fort.

Leaving a mark so the ammunition could be recovered later, the Rangers continued on through the ever-increasing snowfall. Slowed by the snow's depth, cross-country progress averaged only eight miles a day. By the fifth day, nineteen more Rangers had to be returned to Fort Edward because of illness, leaving a force of 123 officers and men to continue on.

On Christmas Eve day, 24 December, the Rangers established an ambush six hundred yards from Ticonderoga. The Rangers quickly and quietly captured a French sergeant of marines who had strolled out of the fort and into their hands. The sergeant's interrogation brought to light the fact that the fortress's garrison was only 350 strong. Given this information, Rogers quickly conceived of a plan to capture the fortress.

The plan called for luring the garrison to venture forth from the fort with a body of men. If this could be accomplished, Rogers and his Rangers would cut back in behind them, Indian-fashion, to storm the gate. Seeing a hunter returning toward Ticonderoga, Rogers ordered a group of his men to pursue him to the edge of the clearing in front of the fort. There, they were to capture him, firing their weapons to get the garrison's attention, thus hopefully inducing the French to sortie from within their walls while the bulk of the Rangers waited in the woods, prepared to strike. Unfortunately for the Rangers, their reputation had preceded them. Noting the buckskin uniforms of Rogers' Rangers as they attempted the deception, the French failed to budge, rightfully wary of a trap.

Disappointed that the garrison refused to accept the ruse, Rogers set about to harass them. Locating seventeen oxen just outside the range of the fort's cannon, the Rangers butchered them within view of the garrison. Rogers then torched five large stacks of firewood that had been laboriously cut and stacked. Finally angered, the garrison fired cannon in their direction but to no avail. The Rangers continued to harass the defenders with their marksmen until 2000, when Rogers finally withdrew, leaving a "receipt" for the oxen on the horns of one of the slain animals, addressed to the commandant of Ticonderoga: "I am obliged to you sir, for the rest you have allowed me to take and the fresh meat you have sent me. I shall take good care of my prisoners. My compliments to the Marquis of Montcalm."

Leaving the audacious note behind—but modestly leaving it out of his official written account—Rogers and his Rangers returned to Fort Edward. The scout was considered a great success and, despite the fact that he was unable to secure the fortress, the fact that Rogers had even attempted to take Ticonderoga with a garrison three times the size of his force did much to restore the character of the Rangers.

CHAPTER 5

Rogers' Rangers:
Campaign of 1758

Imperturbable calm in the commander is essential above all things.

Sir Ian Hamilton

On 9 January, Loudoun discussed with Rogers the formation of additional Ranger companies based on Rogers' recommendation of a 1,000-man Ranger corps. After much deliberation with the Ranger, Loudoun authorized the formation of five additional companies for a total of nine. While waiting for Loudoun to finalize the commissions of his newly appointed Ranger officers, Rogers developed a plan to take the fortresses of Crown Point and Ticonderoga.

In that Ticonderoga was the most exposed French fort in the region, it remained garrisoned with 350 soldiers during the winter months. Crown Point, farther north, however, was only garrisoned with 150 men. Rogers' proposal was to take four hundred Rangers and march along the backside of the mountains west of Lake George to Lake Champlain. At the lake, they would intercept a group of sleighs traveling along the frozen surface between St. John's and Crown Point. Outfitting some of his men in the clothes of his prisoners, the "Trojan Horse" sleighs would continue on with some French-speaking Rangers to get the Crown Point garrison commander to open his gate. With the gates open, the remainder of the Rangers concealed nearby would rush the gate and storm the fort before the commandant could learn of the deceit. With Crown Point captured, the umbilical cord of supplies to Ticonderoga would be cut, leaving the fort vulnerable to a siege.

Rogers presented his plan to Loudoun on 13 January. It was an excellent plan with great potential for success. There was only one problem: Loudoun had his own plans for a winter siege of Ticonderoga. Knowing Rogers as he did, Loudoun knew that Rogers could succeed and, if he were to do so, it would diminish his own hopeful success at Ticonderoga. Considering how unsuccessful his unaggressive campaigns had been to date, Loudoun was not about to concede any success to another. He put Rogers off by telling him to address the campaign with Abercrombie, who would inform him at a later date when to make the attempt.

On 14 January, Rogers departed New York. In Albany, he ordered new uniforms for his Rangers, sent notice to his new officers of their commissions, and directed the recruiting of the necessary privates. On 21 January, he conferred with General Abercrombie about his Crown Point campaign. Abercrombie and his nephew listened to the Rangers' daring plan attentively. Rogers trusted the apparent sincerity of the two Abercrombies but it would prove to be a misplaced trust. That same evening, the two British officers wrote and submitted to Loudoun their own proposal to take Crown Point that did not involve Rogers' Rangers. Faced with the dilemma of offending either party, General Abercrombie or Captain Rogers, Loudoun opted to authorize neither of their efforts.

Rogers returned from Albany on 25 January. The next day, a scout of Rogers' men composed of Sergeant "Shanks" Shankland, Private Joshua Goodenough, and two Mohegan Indians, set forth on one of the most harrowing odysseys ever experienced by such a small Ranger detachment. Near Ticonderoga, this four-man group ambushed and defeated a French patrol. Then, as they made their way to Fort Edward, they encountered and maintained a running fight against a strong French scout.

Deserted by the two Indians, Shankland ended up with two fights on his hands. Not only did he have to engage and keep the pursuing enemy at bay but he also ended up having to periodically kick Goodenough into consciousness, as he continually fell asleep from sheer exhaustion, in order for them to outdistance their pursuers to the safety of the fort.

Loudoun's winter expedition to Ticonderoga came to light on 28 January when a large convoy of sleighs loaded with artillery shells and provisions arrived from Albany. Due to government demands, Loudoun had to turn over command of the expedition to Lord Howe on 2 February with orders to destroy both Forts Ticonderoga and Crown Point. On the same day, Rogers sent Stark on a scout to the first narrows to determine if the lake was adequately frozen.

During Stark's absence, Langy De Montegron, the most notable of the French Canadian partisan leaders on the Lake George front and an accomplished rival to Rogers for daring, struck at Fort Edward. Arriving in the late afternoon of 7 February with a force of one hundred Regulars, French Canadians, and Indians, Montegron noted a wood-cutting party clearing the forest around the fort. Realizing this was probably a routine detail, he prepared an ambush for the following morning.

A security force of twenty-five Regulars of the 27th Regiment cleared the fort at 0900 the next day followed by a large party of unarmed Regulars and Provincials. None of them wore snowshoes so they walked within a previously beaten trail. Foreseeing this, Montegron deployed his men in the three to four-foot-deep snow on either side of the trail. Then, while engaging the armed covering party in front, a portion of his detachment on snowshoes swung to the rear and began to herd the unarmed woodcutters as they would sheep. While the covering party gave a good account for themselves, they were soon overwhelmed. Of the twenty-five men, thirteen were killed, five captured, and four wounded. The snowshoeless woodcutters were at the mercy of the Indians and they were slaughtered at will, hip-deep in snow.

Upon hearing the fire, Rogers, on his island, attempted to ascertain the strength of the attackers and to organize a force of appropriate size to cover Stark, who was due back from his scout. Unfortunately, it took nearly an hour and a half to gather the available snowshoes and set out in pursuit with 140 Rangers. Spotting Montegron's tracks and realizing that he was taking the Wood Creek route back to Ticonderoga, Rogers attempted to intercept him by taking a shortcut along Lake George. Meeting Stark's scout at Half-Way Brook, the combined detachment continued on the forced march. Crossing over to South Bay, Rogers found that the French party had already passed. Rogers would soon regret not having been a bit quicker in his pursuit of Montegron.

Thirty light sledges — a sled with low runners used to transport heavy loads — departed Fort Edward on the 11th with Regular drivers and an escort of forty-three Rangers under the command of Captain Stark to test and survey the road and lake in preparation for the winter expedition to Ticonderoga. Marching in advance on snowshoes they themselves had manufactured, Stark and his Rangers attempted with little success to level a road for those who followed with no snowshoes. The weather was exceptionally adverse and the next day found many of the Regulars and even ten of the hardened Rangers suffering from frostbite.

With the injured returned to Fort Edward, Stark, the Regular commander, and ten Rangers departed for the lake, leaving the sledges to follow. Arriving at the lake around 1100, the group found four to five feet of snow on either bank. When the sledges arrived at 1630, it was observed that the lake was frozen enough to sustain their weight. The Regular commander returned to Albany on the 14th to make his report to Howe.

The most significant problem in regard to the Ticonderoga plan was that Loudoun, while an able administrator and organizer, was repeatedly making grand preparations to attack the wrong place at the wrong time. In the dead of a violent winter, the depth of the snow prevented, no matter how many snowshoes were to be employed, the transportation of artillery and logistics the size and amount necessary to lay siege to a fortress like Ticonderoga. Only a bold and audacious attack by a Flying Party—the term used then to describe a fast-moving partisan force—could hope to succeed under those conditions. Such was the attack that Rogers had planned.

The French, feeling that something was in the wind based on their interrogation of prisoners taken in the vicinity of Fort Edward on 8 February, sent Captain Wolff with an escort of sixteen men under a white flag of truce to reconnoiter the British on the pretext of discussing an exchange of prisoners. Arriving at Fort Edward, Wolff was able to note little change in the normal garrison activities, for Howe's invasion troops had yet to arrive and the newly arrived artillery and logistics were out of sight. Not allowed to linger, Wolff was asked by Rogers "about the fresh meat they let him [Rogers] eat." Wolff's ominous and prophetic retort to Rogers was "to be careful of himself when he came again."

Three thousand of the finest British Regulars moved into the area and supplies continued to arrive. The recently recruited members of the Ranger corps made their way to Rogers' Island. The new Ranger uniforms even began to arrive. The weather cleared on the 26th and all was set. The following day, the word arrived that the expedition had been canceled.

No sooner did Colonel Haviland, the new garrison commander of Fort Edward, receive word of the cancellation, than that same evening he ordered Captain Putnam to command a large scout to Ticonderoga to capture a prisoner. Concurrently, he publicly gave notice that Rogers would be leading a four-hundred-man Ranger expedition upon Putnam's return. At 1300 the next afternoon, 28 February, Putnam and 114 Rangers departed. On 6 March, Putnam returned one man short. It was reported that John Robens had apparently gotten lost and been captured by the French while others believed he intentionally deserted. Though aware of Rogers' plans, courtesy of Haviland's public proclamation, Robens is never mentioned in French records nor is there any indication that the

French were aware of Rogers' movements until 13 March, the fated day of Rogers' next battle.

On 10 March, Rogers received from Haviland a change to his previous orders. Rather than lead an expedition of four hundred men, Rogers was authorized to lead an element "of 180 men only, officers included." Even if he had opted to attack Crown Point per his originally proposed Trojan Horse ploy without Haviland's authorization, Rogers no longer had enough men to do so even with the element of surprise on his side. Rogers, according to his journals, believed that Haviland was setting him up and leading him into a trap. While it will never be know if that was true, it must be remembered that Haviland included eight officers and men from his own 27th Regiment of Regulars in Rogers' expedition. Despite his clear dislike for the Rangers, it is hard to believe that he would intentionally sacrifice three of his own officers, three volunteers, a sergeant, and a private when he did not need to.

All members of this expedition were volunteers, though Rogers selected only from among veterans of his four original companies. His only exception was to allow three of the five new companies to be represented by an officer. Each of these three officers, Ensign Andrew Ross, Lieutenant Archibald Campbell, and Ensign Gregory McDonald, were former members of Rogers' Cadet Company. Unfortunately for each of these three men, their first battle as commissioned officers of Rogers' Rangers would also be their last.

The task organization included twelve Ranger officers—of whom only four would survive—eleven sergeants, 150 privates of Rogers' Rangers, eight British Regulars, and a corporal of Putnam's Connecticut Company. In all, 182 officers and men.

Departing from Fort Edward at midafternoon on 10 March with Rogers at point, the detachment marched only as far as the Half-Way Brook before settling in for the evening. By the end of the next day, they had reached the first narrows and had encamped on the east side of Lake George. Rogers was extremely cautious and seemed to almost have had a premonition about the scout. He sent a party three miles farther up the lake on a reconnaissance. Their report was negative. He posted sentries on the lake and on land that night.

Up at dawn the next morning, they had traveled three miles on the lake when they noticed a dog running across it. Since dogs sometimes traveled with Indians—as they did with Rangers—Rogers established a security perimeter and had a party reconnoiter some islands on the lake. Again the scouts returned with a negative report. Rogers, still taking no chances, had his force put on their snowshoes and kept to the woods until

1000 when they were opposite Sabbath Day Point. They remained there the rest of the day, keeping a sharp lookout, and proceeded on the lake later that night. The advance guard was on skates ranging out front while Rogers kept the main body tight to prevent a break in contact. A detachment flanked them to the west, close to shore.

Approximately eight miles from the French advance guard at Coutre Coeur, a campfire was reported on the east shore. Advancing to attack, the Rangers could find no evidence of a fire, the advance scouts quite possibly deceived by a patch of bleach snow or rotted wood that sometimes turned phosphorescent and fooled the best of scouts. Returning to the west bank where they had dropped their packs, they remained there for the remainder of the night.

On the morning of the 13th, Rogers held a council of war with his officers. The decision was made to go with snowshoes and travel the back of Bald Mountain to maintain a distance from the French advance guard posts. From 0700 to 1100 they marched, until they were opposite Coutre Coeur. Halting on the back side of the ridge, they ate a cold meal and waited for the enemy Trout Brook patrol that passed by daily on its return to Ticonderoga, intent on ambushing them.

Believing the moment had arrived, Rogers had his men resume their march down the valley of Trout Brook at 1500 with the frozen brook close on their left and Bald Mountain—soon to be renamed Rogers' Rock—to their right. The snow was deep, approximately four feet, and even with snowshoes the travel was tough. A mile and a half later the report from the advance guard came back: enemy in view, approximately ninety-five, mostly Indians.

The opposing force was making its way up the valley, along the frozen creek, and they would pass on the left within seventy-five meters of their current position. Assuming this to be the main body of the enemy, Rogers moved forward and formed an ambush within a few yards of the bank and waited. With the enemy patrol's leading element opposite their flank, the Rangers sprang the ambush. About forty Indians were killed in the initial volley, with the remainder falling back in disarray. Rogers ordered his Rangers to pursue, sending Captain Bulkeley and his section after the fleeing enemy down the draw. Those remaining behind worked on scalping the fallen Indians. Within fifteen minutes, unforeseen events would begin to unfold that would change the Rangers' feelings from the thrill of victory to the agony of defeat.

Unknown to Rogers, on the previous evening of the 12th, a force of two hundred Indians and thirty-plus French Canadians commanded by Ensign Sieur La Durantaye had arrived at Ticonderoga. The next morning, while Rogers and his men were marching toward Trout Brook, the

Indians applied to the fort commandant and received provisions and brandy.

Returning to their camp, they broke open the liquor. One of their number, claiming to be a witch doctor, consulted the "spirits," who revealed to him that there was an English war party about and not too far distant. Soon thereafter, a scout of six Indians who had been scouting the foot of the lake arrived to confirm the witch doctor's prognostication with news of seeing fresh tracks of two hundred men where Rogers' detachment had left the lake.

Unfortunately for Rogers and his force, Langy De Montegron was resting at Fort Ticonderoga between raids on Fort Edward. Unable to resist the call to action, Montegron gathered a force of fifty French Canadian and Regular volunteers. In total, a force of 290 Regulars, French Canadians, and Indians were prepared to move against Rogers. La Durantaye preceded the main body with an advance guard of ninety-five; the same ninety-five men Rogers ambushed. Just minutes behind, another 195 Indian warriors and soldiers followed.

Having heard the firing just ahead, Montegron deployed his force on the march into a bush-fighting formation and quickly moved forward. Soon, La Durantaye and his fifty-four survivors rejoined Montegron. Moments later, Bulkeley and his pursuing Rangers ran right into the opening volley of the French and Indian muskets. Unaware that there was any other force in the area, especially one as large as they had just been engaged by, the Rangers were taken totally and completely by surprise. The French and Indians poured on withering fire and a furious attack. Bulkeley and three of his officers were killed almost instantly, along with nearly fifty of his men. Lieutenant Increase Moore and Ensign McDonald, though both mortally wounded, managed to rally the survivors and withdraw them to Rogers' location before they died.

Rogers' force was scattered. The remnants of his pursuit party were falling back. Others were still scalping Indians killed by the Rangers in their ambush. Unable to form a front against Montegron's and La Durantaye's attacking force, Rogers soon found his detachment threatened with envelopment. Ordering his men to fall back to their original position on the slope of Bald Mountain the Rangers did so at the cost of another ten men lost.

Rogers' men returned fire and fought with a ferocity that forced the enemy to withdraw. The French and Indians rallied again to attack along the front and to the sides. Only the mountain to their back prevented the Rangers from being encircled. Still inebriated and seeking revenge for their recently scalped comrades — as well as the loss of one of their prominent war chiefs in the ambush—the Indians ferociously pressed their attack.

Rogers was down to fewer than 120 men and he was outnumbered by about two to one. Montegron and La Durantaye capitalized on the Indian intoxication and rage by having the Indians throw themselves at the Rangers in hopes of wearing them down by attrition. Rogers' men held, however, as the Indians attacked and the Canadian marksmen took their toll.

Repulsed for a third time, the enemy rallied and attacked again forty-five minutes later. With skirmishes to the front, Montegron and La Durantaye attempted to envelop the flanks by sending the Indians on the left and the Canadians on the right. Attacking first, the Indians pressed hard on the Ranger flank. Rogers continued to send small parties of Rangers to reinforce the sector. Fighting was furious and from a distance of only twenty yards. Friend and foe, at times, found themselves inter-mixed but the Ranger line continued to hold.

Evening was fast approaching and Montegron and La Durantaye knew that if they were to finish Rogers off, it had to be before darkness set in. A final, simultaneous, and unrelenting assault from all three sides was launched. Having lost eight officers and one hundred men, Rogers only had Ensign Joseph Waite and thirty-one Rangers left to hold his cen-ter, his newly promoted Indian Ensign Bill Phillips and eighteen men to hold his right, and Lieutenant Edward Crofton, Captain-Lieutenant Prin-gle, and Lieutenant Roche—the last two being British officers Haviland had sent—with twenty-two men to secure the Ranger left flank.

The right flank was the first to be enveloped. Surrounded by the bulk of the Indians, Phillips and his men were quickly losing ground. Rogers and Waite managed to hold the center until they were down to twenty-one defenders. Finally, separated from Phillips, nearly fighting hand to hand and in perilous danger of being totally cut off, Rogers ordered the center group to break contact and make their way to Crofton and Prin-gle's position, which was still relatively intact on the left flank.

As Rogers was withdrawing, Phillips was surrendering to La Duran-taye. Encircled by an overwhelming number of Indians and promised humane treatment, Phillips and his small band of survivors capitulated. Despite the strong assurances, the entire party were tied to trees and slowly tortured and hacked to pieces when several fresh Indian scalps were found in the coats of slain Rangers. Phillips proved to be the lone survivor of this group. While the Indians were busy mutilating and tor-turing other captives, he was able to free a hand, secure a knife from his pocket, open it with his teeth, cut his deerskin cord bond, and escape, only to be captured again. Incredibly, rather than butcher him, he was taken to the Indian village of Sault St. Louis, near Montreal, where he was once again able to work his magic and escape for good.

Linked with the remnants of his left flank and realizing that his right flank had surrendered, Rogers knew the fight was near its completion and that the only thing left to do was to save as many of his men as he possibly could. Implementing one of his Ranging Rules, Rogers ordered his men to disperse and for each to take a different route to the rendez-vous point, which for this scout was where they had concealed their hand sleds on Lake George, the southern end of Rogers' Rock.

The approaching darkness helped facilitate their escape, but until it descended completely, several of the retreating Rangers were intercepted and captured. Some could not exfiltrate individually, such as the two surviving British Regulars. Unfamiliar with the terrain, Rogers offered Pringle and Roche a sergeant to guide them through the mountains to the rendezvous point, but they declined. Having damaged their snowshoes during the fight, both realized they would be easy prey for any pursuers and a burden to any Ranger. Making their way from the field of battle under the cover of darkness, the two officers met Rogers' orderly, who guided them astray. On the 19th the orderly died from the cold. The next day, the British officers gave themselves up as they came within sight of Fort Ticonderoga. Their very survival proved to be dependent on a foot-race between the French officers they were surrendering to and Indians who had also seen them.

Rogers' escape was to become the stuff of legend. Discarding his green jacket that also contained his 24 March 1756 commission—which for a while led the Indians and French to believe he was among the dead for surely he would not leave so precious and treasured a document behind—Rogers began to climb the west slope of Bald Mountain. At the summit, he looked down the sheer smooth wall of rock that formed the eastern slope that ran to the frozen surface of Lake George more than one thousand feet below. Behind and below him, he could hear his pursuers shouting excitedly as they located his trail in the moonlight. Conceiving an idea to make those following believe he had gone over the summit to slide down the slope, Rogers loosened the thongs of his snowshoes and turned about-face without moving them. Then, having laced them back up, he proceeded to backtrack along his trail for some distance until he was able to swing himself by a branch off the trail and into a defile, thus leaving no telltale indications that he'd departed the pathway.

The Indians reached the summit just as Rogers was making his way down to the lake, having followed the defile down the mountain. Convinced that he had slid down the slope and that he was being watched over, the Indians did not continue the pursuit. Rogers, the *Wobi Mada-ondo*, "White Devil," led a charmed existence.

It was approximately 2000 when Rogers began to move across the lake's frozen surface. Within a short time, he encountered other survivors and several wounded men whom they carried to the rendezvous point. From there, Rogers dispatched three Rangers on skates to move with all haste to Fort Edward and bring back reinforcements, for Rogers still expected a pursuit. These skaters were soon followed by four injured Rangers, each strapped in a hand sleigh with two Rangers pulling each sleigh. Remaining behind with the handful of survivors, Rogers waited for others to arrive. With no blankets and unwilling to chance lighting a fire, the small group nearly froze to death as they waited through the night. Their lingering was not in vain, though, for the next morning a few more Rangers wearily staggered in, some wounded. Under Rogers' care, the group started up the lake to Fort Edward.

The three ice-skating messengers arrived at Fort Edward about noon on the 14th. All the Rangers that could be spared were dispatched with Captain Stark to assist the survivors. Encountering Rogers at Sloop Island, about six miles from the head of Lake George, Stark remained there with Rogers for the night, sending back for three horse sleighs to carry the wounded. With the sleighs arriving the next morning, small groups of Rangers began to enter Fort Edward around 1500. Rogers was the last to arrive at 1700, bringing up the rear.

The numbers were not pretty. Rogers had brought back fifty-two survivors, eight of whom were seriously wounded. A total of 122 officers and men had been lost on the field of battle. Of those 122, only one was a prisoner, Ensign Phillips. The remaining 121 were dead. The French accounts are difficult to accept at face value for La Durantaye claimed to have suffered only eight Indians killed. How does one reconcile that with the forty men Rogers stated to have killed in the ambush? All told, it is probably safe to claim that the Rangers killed at least eighty and wounded a similar number.

Despite the totality of the defeat, General Howe, the new commander of the New York front—General Abercrombie having succeeded Lord Loudoun—was extremely impressed by the fact that Rogers' detachment, surprised and wounded as it was, still had the ability to repulse two assaults by a significantly superior force. Provincial papers applauded their valiant stand and the incredible battle only served to enhance Rogers' fame more.

Following an audience with Howe, in which he was well received, Rogers reported to Abercrombie in New York. Despite the press and the enhancement to his fame, Rogers was in a rather foul mood. He had been denied the opportunity to try his Trojan Horse ruse that ultimately led to his first defeat and, he had just learned from Howe that four of the five new companies he had worked so hard to raise, half his corps, had been rerouted to the Louisbourg front. Frustrated, Rogers mentioned to Abercrombie that he wanted a majority over his independent companies. If he did not get one, he would resign from the service.

While surprised that Rogers was rather brazen and not more docile after having suffered such a crushing defeat, Abercrombie was also alarmed to think that he might lose the invaluable services of his Ranger chief. The British Prime Minister, William Pitt, had been very explicit when Abercrombie assumed his new duties about maintaining the Ranger force. Though he had a much lower opinion of the Rangers as an organization, Abercrombie, despite his attempt to double-cross Rogers on his Crown Point expedition, still realized that Rogers was the force behind the organization. "Without him, the Rangers would be good for nothing," he had once penned to Loudoun.

Before giving Rogers a reply, Abercrombie learned from Loudoun that Rogers had been promised a majority at some time. Realizing that he would have to fulfill Loudoun's promise in order to keep Rogers, Abercrombie commissioned Rogers "Major of the Rangers in His Majesty's Service" on 6 April 1758. Rogers was now the commander of a battalion of Rangers. His dream had come to fruition.

Returning to Rogers' Island, Rogers set about rebuilding his corps and retaliating for his defeat at Rogers' Rock. Five scouts were sent out within a short period of time primarily to secure prisoners who might reveal the strength and movements at Ticonderoga or Crown Point. The most successful of these five scouts was the one led by Captain Jacob Naunauphtaunk who commanded the Stockbridge Indian Company that was reconstituted again for that year's campaign. Leading a patrol of eighteen Stockbridges and one Rogers' Ranger, Naunauphtaunk and his men ambushed a party of forty-five woodcutters crossing the lake in three bateaus opposite Ticonderoga. Allowing the first boat to land, the Rangers immediately surrounded the occupants, taking ten prisoners while killing and scalping seven who resisted. Wanting no part of the action, the other two French bateaus fled.

Rogers' Rangers soon lost another fight. Returning from a scout, Ensign Etowaukaum of Naunauphtaunk's company, leading a scout of twenty-one Stockbridges and four Rogers' Rangers, was ambushed by thirty-one French Indians who were able to envelop the Rangers approximately six miles from Ticonderoga. Etowaukaum and twelve others were able to fight their way clear and return to Edward. Of the remainder, two Rogers' Rangers and two Stockbridges were killed with two Rangers and seven Stockbridges taken prisoner.

On 28 May, orders were received giving notice of Abercrombie's campaign in the Lake George region. Lord Howe arrived at Fort Edward on 8 June and ordered Rogers to recon and map roads, fortifications, and terrain of Ticonderoga as well as the landing site for Abercrombie's army at the north end of Lake George. Departing on 12 June from Fort Edward with a force of fifty men composed of Rogers' Rangers, Brewer's Mohegan-Rangers, Stockbridge Rangers, and Ensign Downing of the 55th British Regiment, Rogers linked up with a wagon train of whaleboats at the Fort William Henry ruins the following day and embarked up Lake George to the vicinity of the abandoned French advance post of Coutre Coeur. Landing on the east side of the Ticonderoga River, Rogers split his group into three sections. Naunauphtaunk and thirty-five of his men remained to secure the landing site while Lieutenant Porter and ten Rangers scouted Ticonderoga and Rogers and three of his men marched to Rattlesnake Mountain from whence they could map the valley.

Mission completed, Rogers had returned to within three hundred yards of Naunauphtaunk's position when Lieutenant Wolfe and thirty to fifty French and Indians attacked Naunauphtaunk on three sides. Surprised and overestimating the size of the force he faced—and no doubt overly "sensitive" to Ensign Etowaukaum's earlier experience—Naunauphtaunk elected to withdraw to the boats in the rear of his position, which his Mohegan-Rangers were only too glad to do. Those Rangers in the group that were Rogers' refused to run. Veterans and well versed in the Ranging Rules of extricating themselves while under fire, these Rangers fanned out along a front and maintained a steady fire as they retired in good order to the boats.

Rogers, meanwhile, skirted Wolfe's flank to rally his troops at the boat site. Loading and casting off in boats while under fire is a somewhat difficult task. Fortunately for the Rangers, many of the French Indians were not sober, thus seriously hindering the accuracy of their fires. Rogers' losses were five killed—including Ensign Downing—and three captured. Among the wounded was Rogers, who sustained a flesh wound to the leg while covering the embarkation of his Rangers. Wolfe's losses were placed at three killed.

Lieutenant Porter and his Ticonderoga scout also returned during the skirmish. Hearing the intensity of the battle and unable to get his Mohegan-Rangers to throw their weight into what they perceived to be an unequal fight, Porter believed it more prudent to bypass the battle and march to Fort Edward. On their return, both Naunauphtaunk and Porter encountered Howe and 3,000 of his men at Half-Way Brook. Believing that "Rogers must be either killed or taken," all were amazed when he returned to Fort Edward on the 17th.

With the campaign picking up steam, Howe ordered Rogers to consolidate his Ranger Corps and join the army in the vicinity of the Fort William Henry ruins. Encamping 400 yards in advance of the army on the west side of the lake on 22 June, Rogers would use the location as his base of operations for the remainder of the campaign. Seven Ranger companies were under his command. Captains Stark, Shephard, and Jonathan Burbank—who had assumed command of Bulkeley's company after his death at Rogers' Rock—and Rogers, commanded the four main Rogers' Rangers companies. Naunauphtaunk commanded two companies of Stockbridge Indians, fifty men each, while Moses Brewer commanded the third Indian company, the Mohegan Indians, from the Connecticut, Rhode Island, and Massachusetts regions.

Unfortunately for Rogers and his commanders, only Rogers' original company was at strength with 106 privates. Learning of Rogers' understrength commands when he arrived at Lake George on 28 June, Abercrombie ordered Rogers to "draft" volunteers from the Provincial Regiments. Five officers, five sergeants, and 164 privates signed on, bringing the Ranger companies to their authorized strength of one hundred men each.

Four small scout parties were launched on 23 June to recon the lake and area around Ticonderoga. Unfortunately for the one party to travel by boat, they were spotted and surrounded on the 25th by a superior force at the Second Narrows. Lieutenants Simon Stephens, Nathan Stone, and their seventeen Rangers were all taken prisoner. The commander of the French force was none other than Langy De Montegron—Rogers' nemesis at Rogers' Rock, now an ensign in the French army.

Under the command of Lord Howe, Abercrombie's army of 15,400 men embarked on Lake George 5 July and arrived at Sabbath Day Point at dusk where they rested that night. Rogers' Rangers moved in fifty whaleboats and served as an advance guard for the force. They had not proceeded far in the early dawn hours when they identified a force of 150 French and Indians in boats waiting to spring an ambush near Sloop Island. Commanded by Montegron, the enemy elected to quickly withdraw and lose themselves among the islands of the First Narrows rather than engage the six hundred Rangers bearing down on them.

Detailed scouting reports during the night indicated that there was an enemy force at the landing site located on the northern end of Lake George. Once again in the vanguard, Rogers and his Rangers set down at the site around noon on the 6th. Unwilling to commit to an engagement so far from his entrenchments around Ticonderoga, Montcalm's defending forces withdrew. Driving the French landing guard before them, the Rangers marched an hour to high ground within a quarter of a mile of Montcalm's 1,500-man encampment.

Rogers launched some small scouting parties to determine Montcalm's exact location. One of these parties, manned by Sergeant Paige, Corporal Wright, Private Maxwell, and Private O'Brian, was attacked and pursued by French Indians. Wright was killed and the wounded O'Brian captured. Maxwell, fleet of foot, managed to outrun all but two of his hunters. Shooting one dead, Maxwell escaped the other when he cleared a fallen hemlock tree hurdle while his pursuer fell upon it with a grunt.

Rejoining Sergeant Paige at their rally point on the Ticonderoga River, Maxwell encountered one last obstacle. Safety lay across the river and Maxwell could not swim. Leading by example, the determined sergeant swam across the river with Maxwell and their two weapons strung across his back.

The French advance party, now composed of Captain Trepezac and Montegron and totaling 350 men, had been observing the movement of the British Army down the lake from atop Rogers' Rock. Slow to react, the group soon found itself cut off from Ticonderoga. Attempting to carefully work their way back by way of the first rapids from Lake George, Montegron was attacked by Howe's advance guard. Hearing the fire, Rogers, leaving only Burbank and 150 Rangers to keep observing Montcalm, rushed forward and hurled his 450 Rangers against the trapped French. Placing himself between Trepezac's and Montegron's units, Rogers forced the fight. The only exit out for the French were the cascades and waterfall of the Ticonderoga River on their right flank. Approximately fifty French, including Montegron, managed to escape. Of the remaining French force, 151 were captured with the remaining 150 either being killed or drowned in their attempt to escape.

Though Rogers' Rangers had avenged the battle of Rogers' Rock, Abercrombie would not see another victory this campaign, having lost his most trusted advisor when Lord Howe was killed while driving his men on during the battle. Refusing to seek any advice other than that of his ignorant aide-de-camp and nephew, Captain James Abercrombie, Abercrombie would soon lead his army to their defeat.

The morning after Montegron's rout, Rogers ordered Stark with two hundred Rangers to guide Captain Abercrombie and the chief engineer,

Matthew Clarke, to the top of Rattlesnake Mountain (Mount Defiance) to inspect the French fortifications. Apparently forgotten or not considered by Rogers was the fact that there was a very strained relationship between the aide-de-camp—and the chief engineer, who'd also been on the patrol—and Stark as a result of the "misbehavior patrol." Consequently, as the officers considered what strategy to employ for the siege, Stark's sage advice to cut behind Ticonderoga to sever the French retreat and to drag cannon to where they stood to shell Ticonderoga fell on deaf ears.

Abercrombie and Clarke returned with their own misguided advice and proposal. Overwhelmed by the magnitude of events and relying solely on their recommendations, General Abercrombie ordered a general assault against the French fortifications without first softening them up with the heavy artillery that was on its way. At 0700 on 8 July, Rogers received orders to lead the attack.

Lieutenant James Clark of Stark's company led the Ranger corps with an advance guard of fifty Rangers. Fired on from a two-hundred-man French ambush three hundred yards from Montcalm's entrenchments, Clark held his ground while Rogers deployed his corps on line and advanced. Acting as skirmishers, the Rangers advanced in the center with Gage's light infantry on the right flank and Bradstreet's Bateaumen to the left. At 1000, Rogers received orders to force the enemy's advance parties to disperse or to fall back into the entrenchments in anticipation of the British main attack. Mission accomplished, Rogers' men, per orders, dropped in intervals to a prone position behind fallen trees that had been abandoned by the French to allow the British Grenadiers to push forward.

The French breastwork consisted of large trees, felled and piled together to form a height of eight feet. Easily vulnerable to cannon fire, they were not to fall to unsupported dismounted infantry. With the Rangers providing volumous covering fires from their positions, the British infantry threw itself against the French defense, but to no avail. Six attempts were made with some of the Rangers even attempting to storm the works "but were stopped by the bristling mass of sharpened branches."

Total British losses were 1,944 officers and men. The Rangers, more skilled at brush warfare, suffered only three killed, eighteen wounded, and two missing. Despite the fact Abercrombie still outnumbered the French two to one even with such heavy losses, he chose to retreat from the field of battle and return to the south end of Lake George. Serving as the army's rear guard, Rogers' men provided covering fire from 1800 to 1900 as the British gathered up their wounded and embarked on their boats. The Rangers were the last of the British Army to melt into the night and make their way south with the taunts and jeers of Montcalm's Frenchmen ringing in their ears.

Within the week, Rogers was once again on the prowl for prisoners and information. On the 28th, La Corne, a Canadian partisan, massacred a wagon train convoy of 116 men and women between Fort Edward and Half-Way Brook. Captain Burbank, with forty-five of his Rangers, was located in the vicinity of Half-Way Brook when the alarm gun was fired at Fort Edward. Moving toward the fort, Burbank encountered Colonel Hart and four hundred Provincials sallying forth. Joining up, the two bodies of men picked up La Corne's trail. Observing the three hundred French and Indians of La Corne's patrol staggering half drunk through a swamp, Hart decided to withdraw to the wagon train massacre site a half mile away, somehow fearing an ambush. Once there, his men proceeded to get drunk on the same wine that had inebriated La Corne's men.

Outnumbered seven to one, Burbank and his small force of men held their ground, attempting to persuade Hart through messengers to move forward to attack. Hart eventually relented by sending a detachment of one hundred men who no sooner had marched a fourth of a mile before all but eight came running back. Disgusted, Burbank could do little but take shots from a distance as the enemy withdrew toward Ticonderoga.

Having been alerted by one of Burbank's officers at 2100 that evening, Abercrombie detached Rogers with seven hundred Rangers to intercept La Corne. Departing the fort at 0200 the next morning, the 29th, Rogers quickly moved by bateau to Sabbath Day Point, where he force marched across the mountains to Two Rocks on the narrows of lower Lake Champlain where he intended to establish an ambush. Unfortunately, he and his men were too late. The French and Indians had passed just a half hour prior to their arrival.

Rogers' seven hundred men moved to Sloop Island to encamp and recover. On 31 July, a scout of eleven Rangers led by Sergeant Hackett was tracking a force of fifty Indians, when the Indians surprised and surrounded the Rangers. The Rangers put up a fierce fight, killing seventeen Indians, but they were eventually overwhelmed. With eight Rangers dead and two captured, Hackett, the lone survivor, was able to escape. Hackett reported to Abercrombie upon his arrival at Fort Edward that he had observed fresh enemy tracks moving in the direction of the fort. The general sent word to Rogers to intercept the enemy, if he could.

Having to leave some of his men behind who were still fatigued from the earlier forced marches, Rogers was able to augment his force with volunteers from Haviland's troops. Putnam was with Rogers and he, too, was now a major. Though Rogers was the senior officer, there was a degree of jealousy between the two men that was not helped by Haviland's obvious favoritism towards Putnam. The Ranger force conducted another march, this time breaking into two ambush elements with Putnam moving to South Bay and Rogers to the junction of Wood Creek and East Bay. On 6 August, a boat of Indians escaped their trap with an ill-timed challenge from one of the augmenting Provincials. Two other boats escaped from Putnam the same way.

Rejoining forces, the Rangers moved on 7 August to the ruins of Fort Anne, where 530 of them encamped, the other 170 having been sent on to Fort Edward. Rogers and his reduced force departed at 0700 the next morning to return to Fort Edward. Tight discipline was not maintained during the march with some, maybe even Rogers himself, taking potshots at marks or pigeons on a wager. Within earshot was the French Canadian colonial officer Marin with his partisan band of five hundred Canadians and Indians.

Quickly and quietly moving his men forward, Marin established a crescent-shaped ambush along Rogers' route of march at the edge of a clearing. Putnam and his three hundred Connecticuts led the Ranger party, having to march three quarters of a mile across a brush-filled clearing before they would encounter the woodline in which Marin hid.

Physically grabbed and restrained, Putnam and four of his Rangers at the head of the column were dragged off into the undergrowth. Overwhelmed, the Connecticuts quickly fell back behind detachments of the 80th and 44th Regiments, Regulars under the command of Captain Dalyell who were following just behind. The battle centered on a huge fallen tree. Withstanding volley after volley, the Regulars and Connecticut Rangers wavered but held their ground.

Rogers quickly arrived with his Ranger and Provincial rear guard. Establishing the Regulars as the center of his position, Rogers hastily formed a line of battle with Captain Giddings' Massachusetts Provincials on the left of the Regulars in support of the Connecticut Rangers and his own Rangers and a detachment of Partridge's Provincial Light Infantry to the right. Evenly matched, the two forces waged a fierce struggle for over an hour, as the battle became one of individual actions in the dense brush.

In one close encounter, an enormous, howling Indian chief bounded upon a fallen tree, killed two Regulars, and was immediately butt-stroked to the head by a British officer. Showing little effects from the blow, the enraged Indian was about to dispatch the officer with his tomahawk when Rogers shot and killed the behemoth. The Indian measured over six feet four inches—exceptionally tall for the time—and was the largest Indian Rogers had ever seen.

Marin attempted to force the issue with four attacks against Rogers' right flank but the unyielding Rangers successively repelled the assaults. Rogers extended the flanks of his position. With some Canadians giving ground, Rogers' force took to the offensive. Advancing, they implemented their technique of continual fire by having one half of the men fire while the other half reloaded. Unable to face the continuous fire, the French and Indians broke and ran.

Victory in sight, the Rangers, Regulars, and Provincials pursued. The use of Rogers' own dispersal technique against him was the only thing that saved the remainder of Marin's unit from being totally annihilated. Dividing his force into small groups, each group exfiltrated the area to reunite later that evening at a location surrounded by impervious swamps.

The field of battle was Rogers'. Returning to bury their forty dead, the victors constructed litters made of branches to carry forty wounded to Fort Edward. As they departed, they left behind fifty-two scalped enemy and twenty-five additional dead that would not be discovered until 15 August, for a total of seventy-seven enemy killed. French reports placed their wounded at twelve but, based upon the number of dead and the traditional three to one ratio of wounded to dead, that number is rather suspect.

Though Rogers was also able to report the taking of two prisoners, he had lost five, including Major Putnam. Dalyell reported to Abercrombie that Rogers "acted the whole time with great calmness and officer-like." In his correspondence with Prime Minister Pitt, Abercrombie noted that "Rogers deserved much to be commended." As a result, not only did the fame of Rogers' Rangers continue to expand in America, but it also took root in Europe.

For the remainder of the summer and fall, the British maintained three bases of operation: Fort Edward, Abercrombie's camp in the vicinity of the Fort William Henry ruins, and Half-Way Brook. From 16 August to 6 October, the Rangers ran continuous scouting and small ambush operations from these bases. Rogers kept his Rangers actively employed in an attempt to prevent idle time that would allow them to get in trouble. If they were not out on scout, they were on detail cutting wood, training to march or bush fight, or standing inspection.

One of Rogers' final missions for the year was to position whaleboats along the lake so they'd be close at hand for scouts come the spring. His men hid over thirty boats in the brush of Northwest Bay after carrying them over the peninsula and hid others in the vicinity of Long Island.

Well hidden and sunk, none of these boats were found by the French who looked for them to no avail throughout the winter.

One of Rogers' companies that was not stationed with him was that of Captain Wendell. Stationed at Fort Stanwix—also known as Fort Schuyler—near Rome, New York, in the Mohawk Valley, these Rangers figured prominently in the capture of Fort Frontenac located on the north shore of Lake Ontario. Under the command of Colonel John Bradstreet, Lieutenant William Hair and sixty Rangers of Wendell's 105 officers and men accompanied a Provincial force of 2,600 men. With Chief Red Head and forty Onondagos, the Rangers and Indians formed a scout detachment under the command of Captain Tom Butler. The scouts performed their duties so well that the fort fell after only one day's investment. Hair and his men returned heroes and even Rogers praised their work in his dispatches.

Rogers' Rangers were also performing exceptionally well on the Louisbourg front where his four newly raised Ranger companies had been spirited away. The overall commander of the invasion was Baron Jeffrey Amherst. Prime Minister Pitt had ordered that 600 Rangers be on the expedition. The four companies selected were those commanded by Captains James Rogers, John McCurdy, Jonathan Brewer, and Captain William Stark. Authorized one hundred officers and men, Abercrombie ordered them expanded to 125 men each to meet the Prime Minister's directive when combined with Gorham's one hundred Rangers already in Halifax. These four companies sailed on 2 April and disembarked at Halifax on the 7th from whence they departed with the Army on 28 May to begin the attack.

While feinting a landing at three other locations, the main amphibious force moved to its real site at Freshwater Cove. Unfortunately, the feints did not deceive the French and the landing force came under heavy, continuous fire from artillery and muskets while still in their boats. Despite the ground commander's order to abort the invasion, four boats of fifty men loaded with Rangers and light infantry mistook or intentionally disregarded the signal and headed straight for a rocky area of the beach out of reach of the French's covering artillery. Two of the boats were stoved-in when the pounding surf threw them against the rough shoreline. With some soldiers drowning, the remainder of these boats' occupants, some only armed with tomahawks and scalping knives, scrambled over the slippery boulders and linked up with those of their comrades who were fortunate enough to make a dry landing. A surgeon onboard the H.M.S. *Kingston* who observed the daring landing noted in his diary that "the Rangers landed first" and "behaved to admiration."

Initially, the French, believing this flank section of the beach impenetrable, had posted very little in the way of security. Unfortunately, despite this lack of defense, those on shore had observed the landing party. Consequently, by the time the small landing force made it to the summit of the rocky flank, they found a welcoming committee of approximately one hundred French and Indians with more on their way. Despite the odds, the fifty Rangers and light infantry held their ground. The Ranger leader, Ensign Francis Carruthers, was cut down in the fierce fight. The Rangers retaliated by killing and scalping a prominent Indian war chief.

Having changed his mind based upon the daring of this small group, the ground commander, Brigadier General Wolfe, soon had his brigade-sized element established on the beach and pushing inward. With one of their main leaders dead and significant pressure being placed on them, the Indians retreated, forcing the French to withdraw and relinquish the nearest artillery guns. With additional landings on the other flank, the French defenders found themselves in grave danger of being cut off from Louisbourg.

Abandoning their artillery batteries, the French and Indians retreated through the mountains to the port city with a loss of fifty men killed and seventy men captured, in addition to the loss of their cannon. Ranger losses were modestly light with only three killed, one wounded, and one missing in addition to British casualties of one hundred killed or wounded. The fact that Carruthers died in the assault did not allow for a very accurate description of the attack and has resulted in historians giving much, if not most, of the credit erroneously to the British light infantry.

Two days later, the Rangers encountered a French and Canadian party on a reconnaissance mission and forced it to withdraw with a loss of three men. Later, on 10 and 11 June, the Rangers flushed out and captured seven horses and twenty soldiers.

Several Rangers, officers mostly, had dogs that accompanied them on scouts and to attack the enemy in battle. These canine Rangers received credit for killing more Indians "than any individual of the Corps." Captain Stark had a wolf dog named Sergeant Beaubier who accompanied him and became quite famous. Not only was the dog honored but in addition "Sergeant" was placed on the rolls and drew pay and rations, which, of course, went to Stark. During the tracking missions, in particular, the dog earned its pay.

The Rangers continued to perform an assortment of missions that ranged from helping artillerists prepare cannon positions to maintaining security around critical positions. On the 13th, they had an hour and a half skirmish with three hundred French who had sallied forth beyond Gallows Hill only to be pushed back to Louisbourg. Six days later, the Rangers were ordered to encamp on the west side of the Mire Road, in the vicinity of Barachois Lagoon, to provide continued observation of Louisbourg. French ships of the line routinely fired on British entrenchments under construction and on the 21st, short rounds were falling in the Ranger camp. Their request to withdraw out of range was denied but, as time would tell, their positions were spread enough that their losses to this fire were minor. These advance positions proved to be of exceptional value, for enemy sorties were observed and usually repelled from this vantage point.

The Rangers were involved in two French assaults. At 0100 on 9 July, a force of 724 French attacked Ranger pickets and trenches located at the Cap Noir side siege works. Quickly overrunning the pickets and taking the trenches, the Rangers counterattacked with the support of Grenadiers to recover the work and force the French to withdraw. Later, on 15 July, the partisan, Boishebert, launched a predawn attack against the Rangers posted at Northeast Harbor. A sharp firefight ensued but by the time support elements could move forward, Boishebert had already withdrawn so quickly, he could not be overtaken. Louisbourg surrendered on 26 July.

On 30 August, Rogers' three companies commanded by Stark, Brewer, and McCurdy, and Gorham's Rangers embarked with a force of Regulars to capture Fort St. John, Boishebert's headquarters, at the mouth of the St. John River. Upon their arrival, though, they found the fort abandoned. Moving upriver, the expedition burned two abandoned villages and returned to Fort St. John—renamed Fort Frederick—from where they advanced along the Peticodiac River to destroy two schooners that, because of the lateness of the season, had been trapped in ice within the vicinity of a large settlement. Locating the ships, the Rangers were determined to bring them in as a prize, which they did, literally cutting them out "with much difficulty."

Departing with their prizes, the Rangers torched the settlement of one hundred houses and barns. Unfortunately for a few of the Rangers, some of the Acadian residents—the term identifying the original French settlers of 1605 and their subsequent ancestors—were lurking in the woods. Straggling too far to the rear of the main body, Lieutenant Caesar McCormick of Stark's company and three Rangers of his detachment, along with two light infantry privates, were snared and captured. A party of Rangers was dispatched the following morning but to no avail. They could not "find anything" of McCormick's group.

The Rangers arrived at Fort Frederick with their two prizes and thirty prisoners on 18 November. With the season finally upon them, they went into winter quarters. Stark's and Brewer's companies wintered in Halifax; Gorham's Rangers wintered at Lunenburgh, a coastal town forty miles southwest of Halifax. James Rogers' company remained at Louisbourg.

The strength of Rogers' corps had begun to erode as the summer gave way to fall. On 24 August, the Provincials who had volunteered to augment and to serve with Rogers for the summer were released to their respective regiments. Then, on 11 October, Abercrombie discharged Naunauphtaunk's two Stockbridge Indian companies. Overall, these discharges reduced the Ranger force by nearly a third. By the 29th of that month, with six of the seven authorized Ranger companies in winter quarters at Rogers' Island and Fort Edward and, with the desertion of most of Brewer's Connecticut Mohegans, the total corps strength was fewer than two hundred men.

CHAPTER 6

Rogers' Rangers:
Campaign of 1759

Man is a creature fit for any climate, and necessity and determination soon reconcile him to anything.

Ferdinand Wrangell

The start of 1759 found Rogers' Ranger Corps severely depleted. In January, Brigadier General Gage, commander of the New York forts for the winter, ordered the Fort Edward commandant, Colonel Haldimand, to augment the understrength Rangers with two hundred of his Regulars. This was an experiment that had been suggested by British officers in the past but would prove a failure as future events unfolded.

Wanting to ensure Amherst, who by now had succeeded Abercrombie, had all the intelligence necessary for an advance on Ticonderoga following the winter, Gage had Rogers conduct a large-scale expedition against the fort accompanied by Lieutenant Brehme, a draughtsman from the Royal Americans who would sketch a detailed map. The force was composed of ninety Rangers, 217 Regulars, and fifty Mohawks commanded by Captain Lottridge, who had just arrived from the Mohawk Valley. Captain Williams, the Regulars' commander, made an issue of who the expedition commander should be—in that he commanded the largest component—but the issue was decided in Rogers' favor.

The force departed Fort Edward on 3 March and encamped at Half-Way Brook that evening. Wanting to avoid being observed, Rogers marched the men that night. Weather conditions were exceptionally adverse. The temperatures were subzero and by the second day of the mission, twenty-three men had been frostbitten and were returned to Fort

Edward. Reaching Sabbath Day Point at 2300 of the third day, the group, "almost overcome with the cold," rested for three hours and continued on to reach the end of Lake George by 0800 the next morning.

Having confirmed with a small advance party that the Ticonderoga Valley was free of enemy parties—though woodcutting details were noted on the west side of Lake Champlain—Rogers and a security force of ninety-four Rangers and Mohawks accompanied Brehme to the top of Rattlesnake Mountain from where he could observe the fort during the day. Later that evening, Brehme and ten men went forward to walk the fortress entrenchments from end to end, much to the amazement of the French who discovered their tracks the next day.

By midnight that night, the Regulars, not equipped with snowshoes or other proper winter gear, were suffering terribly. Rogers, having decided to launch an attack the following day and not wanting to be hampered by the ill men, ordered them back under the escort of thirty Rangers to Sabbath Day Point where they could build fires and secure Rogers' return march.

Rogers' remaining force was composed of ninety-two officers and men including Rogers: three Ranger lieutenants, forty Rangers, one Regular, and Captain Lottridge with forty-six Mohawks. At 0300 on 7 March, the force moved out. Making their way through the snow-covered mountains that separated them from the lower Lake Champlain, Rogers and his men crossed the arm of the lake around 0600, where they discovered the tracks of fifty Indians who had passed the day before on their way to Fort Edward.

Continuing on for eight miles, the Rangers arrived at Little Mary River where they came upon a French cutting party of forty soldiers. Stripping off the blankets that served as an outer cloak, Rogers fanned his men out and prepared to attack. It so happened that the Ticonderoga commandant, Hebecourt, warned by some of his reconnaissance scouts in the area of Rogers' presence, fired his signal gun to warn and recall his woodcutting party at the same moment Rogers attacked. Charging with a combined Ranger-Mohawk battle cry, the Rangers and Indians overran the woodcutting site. Rogers' men killed four and captured seven. The remainder, to include four wounded, managed to escape to Ticonderoga with Rogers' party pursuing them to within pistol-shot distance of the fort.

Now the pursuers became the pursued as Rogers' force withdrew across the lake. Hebecourt quickly launched a force of eighty Canadians and Indians after him, soon to be followed by an additional 150 Regulars. At a hill approximately one mile south of where they attacked the woodcutting party, Rogers hastily formed an assault line that easily repelled the first enemy attack. In a delaying action, Rogers continued to withdraw and entice the enemy to continue skirmishing for another half mile.

Reaching a long ridge, Rogers' men made a second stand. Defeating the Canadians and Indians' second major attack, Rogers turned the tables and launched a counterattack that routed them before the French Regulars could move up to assist. Disinclined to pursue any farther, the French let Rogers and his men withdraw to Sabbath Day Point, which they reached around midnight that night after an extraordinary day's march of fifty miles in four feet of snow and frigid temperatures.

The weather had taken its toll, however. Though the fires of Captain Williams' Regulars were indeed beneficial, over two thirds of the entire force was frostbitten, including Rogers. Ranger Lieutenant James Tute was dispatched to Fort Edward to gather sleds that linked up with the injured at the ruins of Fort William Henry. Following their arrival at Fort Edward, Rogers was so fatigued, he could not compile his log until a few days later. Later, even though he felt that Williams and his Regulars could have been better employed, Amherst, as he read Rogers' report, could not help but feel a sense of accomplishment in knowing that Rogers would be assisting him in his advance on Ticonderoga.

During the spring, the Rangers suffered some moderate setbacks. On 1 May, a four Ranger scout was attacked. One Ranger was killed and two captured. Only one managed to escape. On 11 May, Captain Burbank and thirty Rangers were attacked at dawn while encamped at the site of Fort William Henry by a superior force of Indians. Surprised and overwhelmed, three of the Rangers were killed, including Burbank, who was savagely and inhumanely butchered by the Indians in the mistaken belief that he was Rogers. The Indians appeared sorry for having killed the captain when informed of their mistake, for they were St. Francis Indians and Burbank had "shown them kindness" as a captive during his youth. The remaining twenty-eight Rangers were taken captive. Surprisingly, twenty-five of them were later sold to the French who repatriated them in a prisoner exchange on 15 November 1759.

In preparation for the advance on Ticonderoga and Crown Point, there were ten companies of Rogers' Rangers on the Lake George front by the end of May. In addition to the seven Regular companies, there was a new company raised and under the command of Jonathan Brewer's brother, Lieutenant David Brewer—who had not yet received his captaincy for he had yet to raise enough men, and the two revived Stockbridge Indian companies under the command of two Naunauphtaunks, father and son.

Prior to the army's embarkation, the Rangers were involved in two brief but significant engagements. On 5 July, the elder Naunauphtaunk's company was badly mauled in an ambush. Carelessly proceeding during daylight in three boats on the lake, the party was observed and pounded at the Second Narrows by an enemy force twice its size. Using his boat to cover the landing of the other two, Naunauphtaunk and the nine men with him were attacked by Iroquois Indians before the Rangers could scale a steep embankment at their landing site. Five Stockbridge Indians were killed and, Naunauphtaunk and four others were captured. Infuriated by their own losses, the Iroquois tortured and killed four of the prisoners, electing to keep Naunauphtaunk alive for the high price he'd bring with the French. In all, over half of the elder Naunauphtaunk's Stockbridge company of thirty Indians were killed or captured.

The second engagement was a ruse on Rogers' part to entice a force of partisans prowling in the First Narrows to expose themselves. A force of Rangers, Grenadiers, and Gage's light infantry led by Majors Rogers and Campbell departed before dawn and rowed along the east shore until they reached the Narrows' islands. Rogers moved on with his one hundred Rangers while Campbell lay in wait with the Regulars and an eighteen-pound cannon on a boat.

Rogers' lead boat was fired on and one Ranger was killed with a second wounded. Returning fire, the Rangers drove the enemy down the lake with eight volleys of fire. Campbell moved to support Rogers but fired the cannon too soon. Keeping their distance, the two hundred enemy Indians withdrew up the lake. Though certainly not as successful as it could have been, the ruse did clear the Narrows for the large-scale expedition to follow.

On the 17th, Rogers was allocated a total of forty-three whaleboats and bateaus for the Ticonderoga expedition. The final Ranger scout returned on 20 July to report that the French advance guard had withdrawn to the Ticonderoga Valley. The next day, Amherst's invasion army set out. As usual, Rogers' Rangers led as the advance guard. Following their landing at Ticonderoga Valley the following day, the Rangers advanced and surprised a force of four hundred French and Indians led by Captain Bournie that was securing the bridge crossing the Ticonderoga River. Following a brief fight, the bridge was taken and Bournie was pushed back with the French losing four dead and three prisoners.

With the path clear, Amherst's army seized the heights in the vicinity of Saw Mills and began to bring forward cannon to invest Ticonderoga. Seeing this, the French began to withdraw from those entrenchments that were within range of the large guns. Rogers was assigned the task of securing the entrenchments north of the fortress and out of the range of the investing artillery. Captain Moses Brewer and two hundred Rangers easily accomplished this task. Brewer remained in the entrenchments with his company while Amherst posted the remainder of Rogers' Rangers to secure his rear from Partisan attacks. A party of Indians attempted to drive Brewer from his newly acquired position the next day but were themselves driven back. As the British settled into the siege, Rogers' men found themselves involved in specialty missions on nearly a daily basis. On the evening of the 25th, sixty Ranger sharpshooters were posted in the trenches, firing at watchtowers and gun turrets, to serve as a distraction for skilled artificers to go about their business.

The following evening, Rogers was entrusted with the secret assignment of destroying the boom that was extended across the lake to prevent British boats from passing. Rogers embarked in three boats that had been hauled overland with sixty Rangers and cutting saws. They were halfway to the boom's end at 2100 when an explosion resonated from the fortress.

Amazed, Rogers and his men watched as the French abandoned Fort Ticonderoga in their boats, having intentionally destroyed their ammunition magazine. Though seriously outnumbered, Rogers found himself in an excellent position to harass their retreat. Making his force seem larger than it actually was by spreading it out, Rogers was able to capture ten boats, a quantity of French coats, fifty barrels of powder, sixteen prisoners, and Hebecourt's portmanteau, a large leather suitcase that opens into two separate compartments that contained many important letters.

With Ticonderoga secured, Amherst turned his attention to Crown Point. Rogers' Rangers were posted beyond Saw Mills to intercept partisan bands as the British portaged their boats to Lake Champlain. Small scouts were launched that provided nearly hourly updates on the French. Some of these scouts were exceptionally daring. During one such scout, a Ranger entered a French camp and returned with a British deserter.

On 1 August, at noon, a detachment from Lieutenant Fletcher's scout returned to announce that Fletcher was in possession of Crown Point, the French having abandoned the fortress and destroyed it, as they withdrew to the northern end of Lake Champlain on the Isle aux Noix. Captain Moses Brewer and two hundred Rangers posted themselves on the strategic location until the remainder of Amherst's army could move forward to secure it on the evening of the 4th.

While Crown Point was being abandoned by the French and scouted by his Rangers, Rogers was on a reconnaissance with Captain Abercrombie, revealing his legendary Secret Water Passage east of Sabbath Day

Point that allowed him to so easily traverse the mountains separating Lake George and Lake Champlain. This route proved to be critical, for a communications and logistics trail needed to be constructed securing Fort George—a new fort being constructed in the vicinity of Fort William Henry—and Fort Ticonderoga.

Rogers returned in time to advance with the army to Crown Point, where Amherst's next task was to build a fleet of vessels to protect his waterborne forces as they advanced on Isle aux Noix from the four French sloops that commanded Lake Champlain. For a while, Rogers' Rangers became pioneers cutting roads for cattle to be herded and cutting timber to construct a new fort at Crown Point. John Stark with two hundred Rangers cut an eighty-mile road through a pathless wilderness from Crown Point to Fort Number Four on the Connecticut River within one month.

One amusing anecdote of the time involved Amherst and Ranger Private Stilson Eastman. Amherst had a strong preference for fresh milk and retained a cow in camp that had the liberty to roam in search of greener pastures. One day it roamed too far and could not be found. Despite the Regulars' best efforts, they could not locate the bovine. Eastman was given the task and, to Amherst's great relief and joy, found her. As a reward, Amherst ordered Eastman's canteen filled with rum. Realizing he had a great deal, Eastman would periodically drive the cow to its favorite pasture, a pasture unknown to anyone else, and would bring the dairy cow in for his reward when no one else could find it.

On 5 August, Amherst asked for a Ranger to volunteer to get a message through French occupied Canada to Wolfe at Quebec. Two days later Ensign Benjamin Hutchings stepped forth to undertake the perilous mission. Departing Boston by sloop for Fort Halifax on the Kennebec River, Hutchings, accompanied by a guide and two men, proceeded cross-country to Point Levi, where he hoped to meet Wolfe. Without food for the last four days of a seventeen-day march, Hutchings' group were about to give themselves up when they were able to capture three natives who informed the Ranger he was not far from Quebec. Sticking it out, they delivered Amherst's message to Wolfe on 3 September.

Hutchings' travails were not yet over. Departing four days later, he began his return trip aboard a sloop commanded by Captain Haynes. While off the coast of Cape Sable on 29 September, the sloop was hailed by an English voice. Their deception was not exposed until the enemy vessel opened fire at close range with four swivel guns. With fifty French privateers swarming aboard, Hutchings and his fellow Englishmen discharged three hundred rounds from their small arms before they were compelled to strike their colors. Fortunately, Hutchings was able to throw overboard his dispatches from Wolfe to Amherst prior to his being forced to strip.

The pirate captain took the captives to Beaver Harbor on the Cape Sable shore. Two days later, he crammed Hutchings and fifty other English prisoners aboard a small fishing schooner and with only one day's provisions, allowed them to set sail. Good weather allowed them to make Halifax three days later. Hutchings embarked the following morning for Boston and, hence, Crown Point.

Wanting to double his chances for success, Amherst had attempted to get another group—composed of two Regular officers, Captain Naunauphtaunk, and four of his Stockbridge Rangers—through to Wolfe by another, more deceptive means. The group was to make contact with the St. Francis Indians under the pretext of offering them a peace plan, their answer to be taken by Naunauphtaunk and the others to Wolfe. The St. Francis Indians were not that naive, for they quickly captured the party and presented the prisoners to the French General Montcalm.

Rangers were sent throughout the area to scout unexplored territory. Some were sent along the La Barbue, Upper Hudson, and Otter rivers. Others explored Isle aux Noix. One scout pitted a Ranger whaleboat and three wind-assisted French warships in a race that was won by the Rangers when one of the Rangers, a former New England fisherman, recommended they rig sails with their blankets. Thus jury-rigged, the Rangers held their own until the French gave up the race as they approached Crown Point.

On 22 August, Amherst ordered two scouting missions to St. Johns River. Lieutenant Fletcher led one detachment of ten Rangers. Sergeant Joseph Hopkins, a future Ranger sergeant major, commanded the second party of eight. After agreeing to rendezvous at a specific location and time, the two groups separated approximately one mile from the river with Fletcher moving toward La Prairie—across the river from Montreal—while Hopkins continued on to St. Johns. A superior force soon discovered Hopkins' group. Employing their time-tested escape and evasion maneuver, the detail dispersed in different directions.

Hours later, Hopkins linked up with four of his Rangers near Isle aux Noix. Deciding to set an ambush to capture a prisoner, the five Rangers observed three enemy soldiers swimming in the vicinity of four armed vessels. Hopkins immediately stripped and entered the water. Fluent in

French, the sergeant engaged the three soldiers in conversation as he approached. Enticing the soldiers with the tale of a fishing spot "prodigious" with fish, Hopkins led them back to his four hidden Rangers, who quickly swarmed out into chest-deep water to make off with all three. Though alerted by the captives' yells, the armed vessels and sentries on nearby ramparts could not fire for fear of hitting their own men. It proved to be fortunate for Hopkins to have captured these men, for they informed him that Fletcher and his men had not only been captured but they had also divulged their rallying point with Hopkins.

Later, it would be learned that seventy Indians had come upon Fletcher's beached boat and its two guards. Securing the boat and one of the guards, they tracked Fletcher and his eight other men near La Prairie. Though surrounded by overwhelming numbers, Fletcher and his men put up a good fight. With three dead and three having been able to break out of the trap—one of whom was captured shortly thereafter—Fletcher and his two remaining men had little choice but to surrender. Fletcher would subsequently be exchanged for a French Captain Marin Dinsantrie—a Ranger lieutenant for a French captain. This spoke well for the value of a Ranger.

Fortunately for Hopkins and his men, they had not placed their whaleboat at the exact rendezvous point. Thus, Hopkins, his four men, and their three prisoners were able to move off in their boat just as the French appeared and began firing on them. The group arrived at Crown Point to find that the other four men of the party had preceded them the previous day.

Having gained full faith and trust in Hopkins' abilities, Amherst entrusted the sergeant with a hazardous assignment three days back from Isle aux Noix. Upon his return from the scout, Hopkins had reported the launching of a new French sloop that was now in the process of being fitted for sea duty. Amherst's order to Hopkins was to burn it. His commando party consisted of four Rangers, two Provincial officers who volunteered to serve under the Sergeant, two Regulars, and two Provincial privates.

Traveling only at night, the raid party reached the coast on 11 September. At 2000 that night, Hopkins and four of his best swimmers swam out to the sloop with one of the men carrying a darkened lantern with lit match on his head. The remaining four men carried fire darts and hand carcasses in a similar manner. Stealthily swimming to the stem, the swimmers were surprised to discover a Frenchman fishing from a boat. Unseen, they swam to the bow where one man was nearly completed screwing in his fire dart and another just starting when the Frenchman who had been fishing spotted them as he looked over the bow.

The alarm was immediately sounded. While the French began throwing their magazine powder overboard out of fear the ship was on fire, the raiders scattered for their lives. The guards on Isle aux Noix and from the sloop, itself, began firing on them. All, with the exception of one man with a thigh wound, reached the shore without a scratch to safely rejoin their covering party. Escaping into the darkness, Hopkins brought all his men back to Crown Point. Unfortunately, increased French patrols around their ships prevented any further attempts to fire at them.

Amherst had another hazardous mission for Rogers' Rangers. Needing to ascertain the status of Brigadier General Gage's lethargic advance on the St. Lawrence River to La Gallete and the feasibility of moving his own army, Amherst had Lieutenant Tute and eleven Rangers and Regulars take a whaleboat up the Sable River as far as possible. From there, they began to move overland to the St. Lawrence. Having taken only twenty-five days' provisions, Tute realized by the seventeenth day that he would soon be running short and sent a sergeant and four men to obtain some more.

Coordinating to link up with these five men later, Tute continued to march, reaching the St. Lawrence on 20 September — twenty-seven days out — a few miles below La Gallete. Starving, Tute was resolved to complete the mission. Sneaking forward to reconnoiter La Gallete and take a prisoner, the Rangers were forced to abandon their attempt when Corporal Cauley of Gage's 80th Infantry Regiment was sent forward to scout and deserted to the enemy — no doubt because of hunger.

Tute wrote a quick note describing the results of their scout and dispatched it with a messenger to Gage. The scout party then withdrew as fast as their weakened condition would allow to their boat and the five men he'd left behind to secure provisions on the Sable River. Unknown to Tute, the messenger was captured and his party's route of march compromised. Trailed, the remainder of the group were captured the same day, 22 September, taken to La Corne at La Gallete, then later moved to Montreal.

During Tute's absence, Rogers' request to attack the Canadian St. Francis Indians — also known as the Abanakis — was finally approved. Having learned of Naunauphtaunk's capture by those Indians while under a flag of truce, Amherst ordered Rogers on 10 September "to chastise those savages with some severity." For the next two days, Rogers personally hand-selected the two hundred Rangers, Regulars, and Provincials who would accompany him on the mission. With only the word out that Rogers was leading an expedition, destination unknown, Rogers was able to select from the multitude of volunteers only the best.

Rogers and his expedition departed in seventeen whaleboats on the night of the 13th with a total of 190 men. Reaching Buttonmould Bay, they remained concealed throughout the day and continued to the Otter River the following evening. While waiting for a dark evening so they could pass the three French warships guarding the mouth of the river, Rogers' force began to diminish in size as a result of injuries and personal illness. Overall, Rogers had to send back to Crown Point forty-eight of his detachment—twenty-five Rangers and Stockbridges, sixteen Provincials, and seven Regulars. Despite the loss of 25 percent of his force, Rogers was comforted by the fact that the remaining 142 officers and men were of "phenomenal endurance."

Finally, one evening, the warships sailed farther up the river toward Crown Point, allowing Rogers and his men to slip behind and proceed on their journey. Knowing that the Rangers traveled at night, the French had left some booby-trapped boats anchored at various points in hopes of ensnaring those inquisitive enough to look, but the Rangers were not tempted enough to fall for the trick.

Arriving at Missisquoi Bay on 23 September, Rogers disembarked, hiding their boats in the tiny southern arm of the bay. The attempt at concealment was of little help, for two days after they began their northward march, the two Stockbridges who had been left with the boats as messengers caught up to the group to inform Rogers that the boats had been discovered by an enemy scout and burned.

Knowing full well that an enemy party would soon be in pursuit, Rogers implemented part of his original 1756 plan. Deciding to return by way of Lake Memphremagog—a one to four-mile-wide and thirty-mile-long lake located in south Quebec Province and northern Vermont—and the Connecticut River, Rogers dispatched Lieutenant McMullen, who was lame, and six other men to return to Crown Point on foot. They were to cover the 120 miles in nine days to request that Amherst send Lieutenant Samuel Stevens to the Connecticut and Wells Rivers with provisions for Rogers and his men.

The French commandant at Isle aux Noix, Bourlamaque, posted 360 men at the burned whaleboat site in ambush and launched an additional three hundred men in pursuit of Rogers. Following the departure of McMullen, Rogers and the remainder of his men also marched for nine days, but their march was through the foot-deep Missisquoi swamps. Forced to sleep in hammocks strung between spruce trees above the bog, Rogers was able to throw off the enemy, who were unable to track them through the swamps. In an attempt to anticipate Rogers' moves, the

French assumed he was moving against the closest Indian settlement, the Wigwam Martinique on the Yamaska River. Consequently, the French positioned 215 men to reinforce the Wigwam Martinique and another three hundred French and Indians at the mouth of the St. Francis River.

Rogers and his raiders reached the St. Francis River, fifteen miles north of the St. Francis village, twenty-two days after departing Crown Point. Finding himself on the opposite side of the river and with no time to build rafts, Rogers led a group of his tallest Rangers across the river to form a human chain by which the remainder could ford the river. By the end of the day, the force was in position only three miles from its objective.

A reconnoiter that evening by Rogers and three other men found the Indians drunk in celebration of a wedding. One of the men, Lieutenant Turner, was captured when he moved forward for a closer look. Another of the group, a Stockbridge private named Samadagwas, deserted to inform the town of the impending attack. A large number of the Abanakis Indians heeded his warning and abandoned the village to conceal themselves in the surrounding woods.

Rogers returned to the main body not knowing that Turner had been captured and that Samadagwas' warning had allowed for some of his enemy to escape. Moving into position at 0300, Rogers attacked the village from three sides a half hour before dawn. Despite the prisoner and deserter, and the departure of a large number of the villagers, the surprise, incredibly, was complete. The Abanakis were unable to organize any form of resistance and were annihilated.

Many of the Indians refused to surrender, choosing to remain hidden in the cellars and attics of their well-built homes. Most of them would perish when the town was torched. All told, the Indian losses were placed at sixty-five to 140 Indians dead, one town destroyed. Of the twenty women and children captured, all were released with the exception of Chief Gill's wife, Marie-Jeanne, and her five children, who returned with Rogers. Rogers' losses were one badly wounded—Captain Ogden—and six lightly wounded. Turner's release as a prisoner was secured. To a degree, justice was served when the Abanakis killed Samadagwas.

With the raid over by 0700, Rogers had to make a hasty retreat south. Grabbing enough corn from three of the village warehouses to sustain them for the first eight days of their march, the force began their return with a land movement via Lake Memphremagog and the Connecticut River. Later, with provisions running out and pressure from his officers to do so, Rogers divided his force into nine groups, each with knowledgeable guides, to increase the force's ability to scavenge and to hunt scarce game. At the appointed rendezvous, they would hopefully meet with Lieutenant Stevens and his provisions.

Sergeant Benjamin Bradley led one of the groups. Unknown to Rogers, he and a few of his men had pilfered the village and its church of many valuable possessions: a rare ruby, a golden calf or lamb, a great number of necklaces, silver broaches, sacred chalices, a solid silver image of the Madonna that weighed ten pounds, and even scalps. Weighed down with their ill-gotten gains, Bradley and three others struck out for his home in Concord, New Hampshire. Mistaking the Upper Cohase for the Lower Cohase, Bradley led his greedy followers erroneously into the White Mountains. For days, they wandered the mountains, trying to find their way out, only to have each succumb to the elements and die, some to be found the following year, others to remain missing forever—along with the silver Madonna.

Not far behind the Rangers were the Indians in hot and frenzied pursuit. Ensign Avery's party was attacked and seven were taken as prisoners. Another party of twenty men under the leadership of Ranger Lieutenant Turner and Regular Lieutenant Dunbar—Rogers' student three years removed—were attacked. Overwhelmed, the two officers and ten others were killed while the remainder were able to escape to later be rescued from starvation by Rogers. Fortunately, these were the only two detachments to be attacked.

For the remainder of the groups, the situation required exceptionally desperate measures—Darwinism of the purest kind. Survival called for the par-boiling of leather accoutrements for food. Others turned to boiling birch bark. A party led by Sergeant Evans was so reduced by hunger that, when they came across the massacred remains of Dunbar's and Turner's men, they resorted to cannibalism and "most of them sliced off choice portions for food." For two days, Evans refused to eat human flesh. Finally giving in, he cut a piece from one of three human heads he found in a Ranger's large knapsack. Broiled in coals, he ate the piece, declaring it the "sweetest morsel he ever tasted," but that he would die of hunger before he would do it again. Hunger made beasts of them all.

Evans' group was not the only to resort to cannibalism. Lieutenant George Campell's party also stumbled upon the mutilated and butchered Rangers after Evans. They gorged themselves on the remains, with some of the Rangers eating the flesh raw. Lieutenant Phillips' group of sixteen men marched directly for Crown Point via the mouth of the Otter River. Nearly incapacitated by hunger, they were about ready to kill and eat one of their three Indian prisoners when a Ranger was lucky enough to kill a muskrat. Divided among all the members of the party, it proved to be just enough to keep them from turning cannibal and to get them to the mouth of Otter River where they were met on 8 November by fifteen Rangers in three whaleboats loaded with 150 pounds of biscuits and a gallon of rum "to refresh the starving Rangers." Another group was able to barely feed itself with the carcass of an owl.

Rogers' own small party sustained themselves by sheer willpower. Unfortunately, Lieutenant Stevens had failed at his mission, for he was not at the rendezvous point with the provisions when Rogers arrived. Reaching the point on the Connecticut River, Rogers was stunned to find the still warm embers of Stevens' fire, for he had just departed hours before to establish a new unauthorized base of operations five miles farther south. Rogers' men were able to hear Stevens' signal guns farther down the river but the lieutenant became alarmed when he heard the discharge of Rogers' weapons in return. Believing Rogers and his men to be Indians, Stevens repacked the provisions in his canoes and returned to Crown Point on 30 October.

It would be ten more days before Rogers' arrival at Fort Number Four. Canoes loaded with provisions for his starving men were immediately dispatched to provide sustenance to the starving Rangers scattered about. Some were sent to Fort Wentworth while other similarly loaded canoes embarked up the Merrimac River. For thirteen days, seventeen men paddled the rivers. Of the 138 officers and men, including Rogers, who crossed the river to attack St. Francis, eighty-seven returned; a loss of 37 percent of the raiding force. Of the forty-nine men to die following the raid on St. Francis, only seventeen were combat-related deaths. The remainder were from starvation. When one considers that sixty-five percent of the casualties could be attributed to the culpability of just one man, Stevens, and combine that with the fact that the raid covered four hundred miles and nearly sixty days, the feat was an extraordinary military achievement. With this raid, Rogers was at the pinnacle of his career.

Rogers and those who volunteered to remain after discharge returned to Crown Point early in December where they linked up with the only two Rangers companies remaining at the fort for the winter encampment. Still bothered that Stevens' negligence and cowardice resulted in so many unnecessary deaths, Rogers took the time and considerable effort to gather the evidence that would ultimately see Stevens court-martialed, found guilty, and dismissed from the Rangers.

Amherst discharged the forty-two surviving Rangers of the two Naunauphtaunk Stockbridge Indian companies—though eight Stockbridge Indians were still with Rogers on his St. Francis raid—on 27 October. On 15 November, an exchange of prisoners took place between the

British and French forces that included fifty-two of Rogers' officers and men, to include the five men just captured on the Isle aux Noix scout. Some of those exchanged had served on some of the Ranger corps' most notable and famous operations: one from Rogers' Rock, one of Fletcher's fight near La Prairie, two who'd been on the Naunauphtaunk mission to the St. Francis Indians and captured under the flag of truce, two of Tute's men captured near La Gallete, fourteen from a collection of other scouts throughout the years, and twenty-five from the Captain Burbank "massacre" of May 1759. The three officers exchanged were Lieutenants Tute, Stone, and Fletcher. Not among those exchanged were the five Rangers captured during the withdrawal from St. Francis, for the Indians had refused to turn them over to the French, opting to butcher them in retribution instead.

All told, a total of four Rogers' Rangers companies remained in service throughout the winter period, forming a scouting perimeter that served the advance fortresses of the British Army. Rogers' company, under the command of newly promoted Captain Tute—John Stark and Moses Brewer having retired from active duty—and Captain Noah Johnson with a second company were garrisoned at Crown Point. A twenty-six Ranger detachment from these two companies was posted at Fort Number Four. A reduced company under the command of Captain Waite was stationed on the west end of Lake Oneida at Fort Brewerton while the fourth company, under the command of Lieutenant Moses Hazen, was in support of Brigadier General James Murray's force at Quebec. Amherst retained all of the officers of the disbanded companies on full pay until he decided how many companies he would reconstitute come the spring. On 24 November, 275 Rangers were mustered out.

The year closed on an unfortunate and ironic note for Rogers' Rangers while their commander was in Albany. On 25 December, Haviland ordered a British captain and one hundred Regulars and Rangers to Ticonderoga from Crown Point to transport new clothing. Not very pleased with the assignment, the force departed with many wearing regulation shoes on the march rather than the more durable and winter-resistant moccasins and socks. The stupidity of this action cost every Ranger and Regular who wore the regulation shoes frostbitten feet. Upon their return to Crown Point, the surgeon had to cut off more than one hundred frozen toes. The result of this ill-planned resupply effort— referred to as the "100 Toes Expedition"—left nearly 25 percent of the men assigned to the two Ranger companies either incapacitated or crippled for life. Eventually, twenty of the Rangers were reluctantly discharged.

Rogers' companies in Louisbourg and Nova Scotia executed several daring expeditions from their winter quarters in early 1759 prior to their attachment to Wolfe in support of his Quebec campaign. Captain John McCurdy's company was tasked with making an expedition up the St. John River valley on a scout for refugee Arcadians reported to have settled there. Ironically and unfortunately for him, he was killed in a freak accident the day prior to the mission during a firewood detail when a tree cut down by his men fell on him.

Lieutenant Moses Hazen succeeded McCurdy and marched out of Fort Frederick with twenty-two Rangers on an exhausting trek of 180 miles along the banks of the St. John River to Saint Anne, now Fredericton, the capital of New Brunswick, and back. Having arrived at Saint Anne, the Rangers found that the habitants of the substantial village had evacuated their homes prior to the arrival of their small force. Taking full advantage of the situation, Hazen had his men torch 147 houses, stables, and granaries.

Prior to their withdrawal back down the river, the Rangers noted smoke coming from a house's chimney in the woods. Moving forward, the Rangers were ambushed by a force of ten Arcadians. Reacting quickly, the Rangers were able to overwhelm the smaller force, killing six of the enemy and capturing the remaining four in a brief engagement. Pleased with the results of the raid and with the endorsements of other noted British Regular officers, Amherst soon thereafter approved Hazen's captaincy.

A similar expedition had been conducted at about the same time by Captain James Rogers' company of Rangers garrisoned in Louisbourg. Marching to the Lake Labrador region, Rogers' Rangers were able to locate and capture a large force of Arcadians. Without a struggle, the eighteen armed men and one hundred other men, women, and children were secured and brought back as prisoners.

In May, the four "overseas Companies" were consolidated with the army at Louisbourg. The Rangers fought their last skirmish on this newly acquired province soil on 1 June. On 6 June, the last British ship in support of the Quebec expedition departed Louisbourg Harbor.

On this very final day of departure, a schooner carrying Lieutenant Simon Stephens arrived. Stephens had been one of John Stark's officers sent by boat to scout around Ticonderoga. Stephens, Nathan Stone, and seventeen other Rangers were all taken prisoner when spotted and surrounded by a superior force at the Second Narrows of Lake George on 25 June 1758. Following their capture, he and Stone had been taken to Quebec where they planned with Major Putnam — captured on 8 August 1758 at the start of the ambush that was initiated but eventually lost by the French Canadian colonial officer Marin — to escape by way of the Kennebec River that flows from Moosehead Lake 190 miles to the Atlantic and on to Fort Halifax on the Maine coast. Major Putnam was exchanged, though, before the attempt was made.

With the passing of winter, Stephens was planning another escape attempt come spring. Stone elected not to make the attempt when Stephens decided he would follow the St. Lawrence to Louisbourg. A party of nine, including a family of five with three children, set out in a birch canoe on the night of 1 May. By morning, they reached Isle Madame. The second day found them unable to reach shore as a strong wind and current required two of the crewmen to continuously bail water while the remainder paddled to stabilize themselves in the middle of the river. By the 3rd, they were able to reach shore, where they laid up to dry themselves out.

The next day found them encountering a canoe of Indians, which they were able to elude by hiding in a fog bank. Unfortunately, the same fog bank forced them once again to remain on the river, unable to reach shore safely. On shore the next afternoon, they discovered and captured an Indian and his squaw — who were killed and scalped when they attempted to escape — and their two muskets and supplies. The 6th found them fighting for their lives as they battled for over an hour a whirlpool that attempted to suck them, literally, into an underground section of the river. Free of the vortex and totally exhausted, the canoe and occupants found themselves on Green Island. Adverse weather kept them at the location for the following two days.

While mending their canoe on the morning of the 9th, a small two-masted cutter moved in their direction. Lying in wait, the escapees captured the four-man crew as they landed. Setting sail in their prize and having the prisoners row whenever becalmed, Stephens and his compatriots made good time. Later that night, their hearts quickened while rowing against the tide as they slipped quietly by the strong French advance guard on the Isle of Bic. Having slipped by the Isle, they encountered an armed sloop that fired on them on the far side. Only a fortunate shift in the wind allowed their escape.

The following morning at sunrise they were passing the Isle Barnaby when a French frigate "saluted" them with a broadside that missed. Ten leagues — thirty miles — later, they beached at the River Metis. Resting and releasing their prisoners, Stephens and group set out once again, rounding the Gaspe Peninsula, which projects into the Gulf of St. Lawrence, and sailing into the Baie des Chaleurs, a favorite haunt of French pirates.

Discovering an uncrewed sloop near the shore, they made an attempt to board her but the tide and approaching nightfall hindered their effort. Taking shelter in a cove, the group attempted to board the sloop during the next two days, but each attempt was disrupted by winds blowing from the wrong direction that nearly drove them into the shore. Giving up on the sloop, the group set out en route to Port Daniel with only two days' worth of provisions left. Potential starvation was staved off when they were able to catch twenty-four codfish the next day. The second day out, a hard rain and severe winds drove them to the security of the shore, where they sheltered under a canvas mainsail employed as a tent. By the time the storm abated, the boat had been driven ashore, caving in a plank. For two days, they attempted to repair the boat but to no avail. It was no longer seaworthy.

With the situation becoming desperate, they earnestly contemplated striking out cross-country for the nearest British garrison, Fort Cumberland. Stephens and one other conducted a short scout in its direction only to still find snow, four feet deep in some areas. Their prospects appeared dim.

Luck intervened the very next day with the appearance of a sloop and the schooner they had seen just a few days previously. The decision was made to board them. Capturing the four men who crewed a canoe to the shore, the group was able to learn that eight men remained aboard the two boats. Launching their own damaged boat, Stephens and the rest quietly rowed to the schooner at 2200 that night. With the mother of the family guarding three of the prisoners on shore, the fourth prisoner was taken to serve as a pilot. Rowing and bailing water, the crew pulled alongside the schooner by 0100. Stephens grappled and boarded the schooner to find everyone aboard asleep. A brief skirmish ensued in which some crewmembers were killed while the remainder were taken prisoner.

With the schooner theirs, they set sail toward the sloop. Refusing to come aboard as ordered, the sloop's crew was engaged by a heavy concentration of small-arms fire that finally convinced them to immediately call for quarters—meaning mercy or clemency. The crew received mercy and joined the other prisoners in the schooner's hold. Stephens, two group members, and the sloop's master boarded the sloop and removed those items of use prior to setting the boat afire.

Having returned to their embarkation site to collect the woman and three prisoners, the schooner set sail. Five leagues later, six of their prisoners with three days provisions, one musket, and some ammunition were set ashore. Retaining the two ships' masters and three additional prisoners to crew the vessel, Stephens and his group set sail for St. John Island, where they arrived safely on 27 May. From St. John, they then proceeded to Louisbourg. Pursuant to General Whimore's order and Stephens' request, the lieutenant joined Wolfe's army attached to one of Rogers' Rangers companies.

Wolfe arrived before Quebec with a force of 9,000 soldiers and 140 ships. The French force, under the command of Montcalm and Francois-Gaston Levis, was 6,000 men strong and occupied the Beauport shore and the area of terrain, the plains, just above the city. The campaign was to endure for twelve weeks as Wolfe conducted a series of probing attacks that gained little ground. Finally, in early September, the climactic finale was played out.

The four Ranger companies attached to Wolfe served with great distinction during the expedition to Quebec and served in twenty-two recorded scouts and actions. Though both James Rogers and Moses Hazen were very popular leaders, Hazen garnered the greater share of recognition and was routinely mentioned in Wolfe's daily Journal. The Rangers first action in the campaign was on 30 June with two small actions at St. Joseph and Beaumont, the shore opposite of Quebec. This was followed the next afternoon with an ambush of a guerrilla force of Indians at 1500 as they moved into position to fire on British Regulars entrenching on Point Levi — Wolfe's base of operations for the siege of Quebec. Surprised and completely routed, the Indians left nine of their dead behind to be scalped.

Wolfe's next move after securing Point Levi was to secure the east bank of the Montmorenci River, opposite Point Levi on the Quebec side of the St. Lawrence. The landings took place at L'Ange Gardien on 8 July. The two participating Ranger companies, Hazen's and that of a new commander, Danks, were instrumental in taking the heights. With the high ground and plateau secured, the two Ranger companies advanced into the neighboring woods to expand the local perimeter.

Danks was also given the task of reconning fording sites across the Montmorenci River. Danks and his men located one that also proved to be an ambush site. Four hundred Indians under the command of the partisan Langlande attacked them. Danks' losses were heavy as he and his Rangers were forced back into the positions held by Hazen and a detachment of Regulars. Hazen's Rangers held their ground against the onslaught and were able to repel Langlande's attack. Langlande's retreat cost him twelve prisoners taken by Hazen but, in the end, his Indians were able to recross the ford with the scalps of thirty-six of Danks' Rangers. While the French fortified the fording site, the British entrenched themselves on the eastern shore of the Montmorenci.

Hazen's performance established his reputation with Wolfe and missions continued to flow his way. On 9 July, Hazen and a picked detail of Rangers canoed up the St. Lawrence to locate and determine the size of the French fleet. On the 24th, while on a scout for prisoners, he brought in eight of them after a successful skirmish. The next day found Hazen and his Rangers engaged in a major firefight as nearly 1,500 French and Indians launched a foray at a fording site just above the Montmorenci Falls against an equal sized body of British Regulars and Light Infantry. The contest could have gone either way. Hazen's company, which had been reconnoitering ahead, redeployed to turn the left flank of the Indians, thus forcing the entire enemy force to break and retire in disorder. In his journal, Wolfe credits Hazen's company as the deciding factor in the battle.

Raids against suspected guerrilla homesteads and bases of support in parishes above and below Quebec were conducted throughout much of August as Wolfe grew irritated by their hit-and-run attacks against his outposts. Hoping to draw these forces back to defend their home territory and families, Amherst directed that these raids torch all of the buildings in the suspected villages with the exception of the churches.

Hazen was even able to entice the guerrillas to engage his Rangers during one of his operations that allowed him to affect a crushing defeat on them. Later, on 1 September, Wolfe ordered a 1,600-man force, one that included all of his Rangers, to conduct a full-scale raid along the southern shore of the St. Lawrence. As a result of this mission, the Rangers would not participate in the Battle of the Plains or the capture of Quebec.

Rogers' Rangers volunteer, Ensign Hutchings, arrived after his extraordinary travels with a letter from Amherst to Wolfe on 3 September informing Wolfe that he could expect no assistance from him. With the knowledge that he had all the resources available that he could have, Wolfe moved to seize the initiative. The final battle for Quebec began with the landing of Wolfe's troops on the night of 12 September two miles above the city. By morning, they were arrayed for battle on the Plains of Abraham.

Montcalm's force moved from Beauport to confront them. Within a few hours, the French defenses would lie broken, with both opposing commanders, Wolfe and Montcalm, mortally wounded. Wolfe would die the very same day he had attained his greatest victory. Montcalm, who replied, when informed that he would not live, "Thank God! I shall not live to see the surrender of Quebec," died the following day.

Following the fall of Quebec, Rogers' Rangers returned to patrol the main logistics routes from the city and to serve as an early warning should the defeated French Army attempt to return. On 26 September, three hundred and fifty Rangers deployed to Isle Madame to cut wood for the winter garrison of Quebec. Realizing this task was a bit above and beyond for such soldiers, the British offered the incentive of one gill of rum per day — the equivalent of a quarter pint — and five shillings above their regular pay for each cord the Rangers cut and placed on board ship. Employed in such a manner until the second week of October, all but Hazen's command — augmented by twenty-five volunteers from Stark's and Brewer's companies — soon set sail for Boston where Amherst had James Rogers', William Stark's, and Jonathan Brewer's companies disbanded on 30 November 1759. Swelled to 134 officers and men, Hazen's Ranger company remained in Canada.

CHAPTER 7

Rogers' Rangers:
Campaign of 1760

Ruses are of great usefulness. They are detours which often lead more surely to the object than the wide road which goes straight ahead.

Frederick the Great

The New Year started off with an ignominious defeat for Rogers' Rangers and his near death or capture. Returning to Crown Point from Albany via Ticonderoga with fourteen sleighs full of new Ranger arms, gear, and sixteen Ranger recruits — who for some unknown reason were unarmed — Rogers was ambushed by his old foe, De Montegron, and a force of seventy Canadian and Indian partisans in the vicinity of Five Mile Point on 12 February. Five Mile Point had been Rogers' old ambush grounds and now the tables were turned on him as he fell into a familiar trap.

Riding in the lead sleigh ahead of the rest, Rogers was identified and targeted by De Montegron, who abandoned seizing the remaining sleighs for the chance to get Rogers. With the opening shot, the caravan quickly turned and made its way back to Ticonderoga. Rogers' sleigh horses were all shot, rendering his sleigh immobile and him and his sixteen new recruits vulnerable. Though there were thirty-two new muskets in wooden crates on the sleigh, there was no time to break them out before the ambush party was upon them.

In the bloody hand-to-hand fight that followed, the new Rangers showed their mettle by fighting with anything they had at hand. While five of them were killed and four others taken prisoner, Rogers and the remaining seven recruits were able to battle their way free and make their escape to Crown Point, leaving behind in addition to the muskets, fifty-five pairs of moccasins, one hundred hatchets, and £11,961 of New York currency — £3,961 of which was Rogers', the remainder pay for his soldiers at Crown Point.

Rogers was ready to pursue De Montegron immediately, but Haviland would not authorize it based upon the scurvy and frostbitten conditions of the garrisoned Rangers and Regulars. When Rogers was finally able to return with a scout, he found that De Montegron's Indians had left behind a derisive remembrance of his defeat: one of his recruits, an Indian, had been scalped alive and left to hang from a tree with a small mirror placed before him so that he could watch himself die. Close by lay the butchered corpse of his squaw.

Six weeks after the Ranger Recruit Massacre, the Rangers suffered another loss. At 0100 on 1 April, Captain Tute, Lieutenant Fortescue, Ensign Stuart, three Rangers, and three Regular privates, were authorized to cross the lake to fish and hunt near White Rock. Crossing over in a bateau through an unfrozen part of the lake, the party was attacked by French and Indians — once again led by De Montegron — the following morning. Leaping into their boat, the Rangers and Regulars quickly paddled their way back across the lake with the enemy deftly running on the thin ice after them.

Having paddled three hundred yards and with only two hundred more to go to hit the vast open waters of the lake, the group discovered too late that their passage through the ice had refrozen overnight. Overtaken, they surrendered without a shot being fired. Tute became a prisoner for a second time within a year but he would be exchanged later, in time to advance on Montreal with his Ranger company. As for De Montegron, Rogers never would get his revenge. It was learned later by a Ranger who escaped from Montreal that the French partisan drowned in the St. Lawrence River just days following his return to Canada with Tute and the others.

Four Ranger companies had remained in service throughout the winter: Rogers' own and Captain Johnson's at Crown Point, Captain Waite's at Fort Brewerton, and Captain Hazen's at Quebec. In preparation for the continued conquest of Canada and advance on Montreal, Amherst ordered the raising of four more Ranger companies. All of the Ranger officers who had been wintering in New England on full pay were called back to duty and required to recruit the new Rangers.

On the night of 4 May, Sergeant Thomas Beverly and Ranger Private Francis Howgill stumbled on the advance Northwest Blockhouse manned by four of Rogers' Rangers. Both men had been prisoners in

Montreal and had escaped on 27 April. Beverly was one of the captives taken on 12 February during the Ranger Recruit Massacre. Having won the favor and interest of the French governor-general of Canada, Pierre-Francois de-Rigaud, marquis de Vaudreuil-Cavagnal, Beverly had been a guest in his home and thus had a great deal of useful intelligence to divulge to Amherst.

Departing Crown Point in a whaleboat at 0300 on 9 May, Beverly and seven other men began to row for Ticonderoga. Finding the wind and water too rough, the boat landed at the southernmost Crown Point block-house, where the party left the boat and proceeded on foot. Four miles south of the blockhouse, they were ambushed and surrounded by French Indians. Beverly, who happened to be at the rear of the march column, was able to slip away into the night and make his way alone to Ticonderoga. Of the remaining seven, all but two were also able to escape and make their way back to Crown Point.

Rogers' Rangers entered a new phase of operations late April and early May with the recommissioning of two sloops and the brig *Cumberland* moored at Ticonderoga. Rangers with shipboard experience began to make the necessary repairs and brought the brig and one of the sloops to Crown Point where they were placed under the command of Ranger Lieutenant Alexander Grant with orders from Amherst to "give all assistance to Ranging scouting parties...." Furtive travel by night in whaleboats now became a thing of the past as the Rangers patrolled the river and Lake Champlain in broad daylight.

On 9 May, following the attack on Beverly's party, the *Cumberland* and one of the sloops were patrolling toward Isle aux Noix on their first cruise of the year. A whaleboat was dispatched from Crown Point to relay the information about the attack to Rogers, who was aboard the ships with sixty Rangers and thirty light infantrymen. While the message arrived too late for Rogers to locate the Indian party's canoes and thus ambush them, he was able to surprise the returning Indians by placing the *Cumberland* between them and their base of operations eight miles away, Isle aux Noix.

Rogers was on the shore, scouting towards the isle with two other Rangers. The sloop was posted six miles closer to Isle aux Noix to prevent the brig from being surprised. The four Indian canoes closed on each other in the lake, confused, as the *Cumberland* hoisted French colors to deceive them. The brig's two boats were lowered and manned by Rangers armed with hand grenades. In that all of the Ranger officers were otherwise engaged, a naval officer was placed in command of the two boats.

One of the Indian canoes advanced to challenge the boats and was fired on by the Rangers. Damp gunpowder forced the *Cumberland*'s guns to misfire as the Rangers gave chase to the fleeing canoes. Landing on the western shore and leaving behind five dead, their canoes, and supplies, the Indians took flight cross-country to the safe refuge of the isle.

The second sloop completed its fitting at Ticonderoga and sailed to join the other two ships only to find that a smallpox outbreak had struck the *Cumberland*, forcing the entire expedition to return to Crown Point on 19 May. In the new sloop's dispatches were orders for Rogers to report to Amherst at Albany.

Rogers met with his commander on the 23rd. The true purpose of the meeting was brought to light when Amherst, unable to support the British Army in Canada any other way, ordered Rogers and three hundred of his men to destroy the villages of St. John's and Chambly in the Richelieu River Valley, and Wigwam Martinique—a notorious Indian settlement on the Yamaska River—in an effort to draw French troops away from Levis' siege of Murray at Quebec.

With orders in hand on the 25th, Rogers gathered the necessary equipment and returned to Crown Point five days later. Having been apprised of the urgency and necessity of the mission by Amherst, Haviland, for once, proved to be supportive of Rogers' efforts. Rogers' force of 225 Rangers, two Regulars, and twelve light infantrymen embarked the night of 1 June with the remainder of his force, fifty Rangers of Solomon's Stockbridge Indians, to rendezvous with him at the end of the lake as soon as they arrived at Crown Point from Albany.

Rogers sailed directly for Missisquoi Bay. On 3 June, Sergeant Beverly and three volunteer Ranger privates were landed on a mission to deliver a message to Murray from Amherst that explained the objective of Rogers' expedition. Lieutenant Holmes, Ensigns Samuel Stark and Bill Phillips, who had escaped as a lieutenant from captivity in 1758 only to find upon his return that there were no longer any lieutenant slots left to obtain, and forty-eight other Rangers were also dispatched to shore to conduct their raid on the Wigwam Martinique.

Returning to Lake Champlain, the two sloops distracted the French on Isle aux Noix while Rogers and his remaining men landed at King's Bay on the night of 4 June. A heavy rain the next morning delayed his departure and, later that afternoon, he grew concerned as he observed a number of small enemy craft maneuver about his two sloops as they cruised off Windmill Point. Concerned about French attempts to board the vessels, Rogers rowed out to the sloops after dark to order them to return to Isle La Motte where the *Cumberland* was holding station.

Unknown to Rogers, he was spotted by enemy scouts on the lake as he returned to shore from the *Cumberland*. A subsequent reconnaissance on land determined Rogers' numbers and location, a report of which was delivered to the French commander, Bourlamaque, at Isle aux Noix. A force of over three hundred French Regulars, Canadians, and Indians under the command of the famed partisans La Force and Longville were dispatched to do battle.

Having anticipated possible trouble from the isle, Rogers had posted a reconnaissance element opposite the fort. Forewarned by his men, Rogers was able to prepare a welcome for his uninvited guests by deploying his force along the Pointe aux Fer peninsula—on the shore of present-day King's Bay—in anticipation of the enemy's probable point of attack. The bay with his whaleboats drawn up on the shore was to his left. To his right was a bog—by the edge of present Griffith Bay—through which he had dispatched seventy of his Rangers under the command of Ensign Farrington with orders to fall upon the enemy rear.

The green uniforms of Rogers' men blended exceptionally well into the natural hues of the surrounding forest as they waited for the enemy to approach. Finally, around 1130, the French advance party walked into Rogers' trap and the battle commenced. With Farrington making his way through the swamp, Rogers and the remaining 144 Rangers and light infantry had their jobs cut out for them. Fortunately, Farrington and his men were not long in arriving. Surprised from the rear and pressured by Rogers from the front, the French Regulars soon broke, to be followed by the remainder.

In pursuit, the Rangers followed the retreating enemy west for approximately a mile before they allowed them to slip away into a thick cedar swamp by 1430, three hours after the engagement had begun. The intensity of the action can best be understood from the fact that Rogers' men had expended nearly all of the sixty rounds each man carried.

With it raining heavily once again, Rogers gathered up his dead and wounded and embarked in his whaleboats to Isle La Motte where he encamped, buried his dead, and dispatched his wounded to Crown Point on one of the sloops. Though the wounded were attended aboard ship by an English surgeon, James Jameson, Jameson had been dispatched from Albany by his superior, Surgeon-General Napier, without any bandages, medicine, or instruments. Thus, despite Jameson's best efforts, many of the wounded died on the trip back to Crown Point. Included in those deaths was Captain Noah Johnson, who had been badly wounded in three places. Overall, Rogers' losses during the Battle of Pointe aux Fer were seventeen Ranger dead, including his invaluable company commander, and eight wounded. The attached light infantry losses were one dead, two wounded. French losses were placed at thirty-two dead and nineteen wounded. Both of the French commanders were wounded, La Force mortally.

The Stockbridge Company of Indians joined Rogers three days later. Having arrived at Crown Point with only thirty Indians, five of whom had to be left behind for illness and support, Solomon joined up with Rogers, bringing a total of twenty-four Stockbridge and thirty-two Light Infantrymen with him. Despite the fact that the element of surprise had been lost and Levis had withdrawn from Quebec, Amherst confirmed in a letter written 10 June that Rogers was to proceed with his operation to disrupt the enemy as best he could.

Departing prior to the receipt of Amherst's confirmation on the 11th, Rogers landed that evening on the western shore of the lake with 220 men. Force marching through swamps and streams, they arrived at St. John's on the night of 15 June. Finding the fort too well defended to attack directly, Rogers elected to attempt a Trojan Horse tactic similar to the one he had proposed to Lord Loudoun in 1758 to take Crown Point by surprise. Turning their white-lined coats inside out, his Light Infantry component would march up to the fort under the command of Lieutenant McCormick, who spoke French fluently. McCormick would then inform the gate guard that he had a dispatch for the fort's commandant from Montreal. Once the gate was opened, the British detachment would secure the gate long enough for the Rangers to rush it and capture the fort. The plan was innovative and insightful. Unfortunately, as they neared the fort, they noted that the sentries were exceptionally diligent while others were sweeping their field of vision with watch glasses. Given the heightened security, Rogers called off their plan.

Abandoning their effort to take the St. John's fort, Rogers and his men marched nine miles down the Richelieu to the fort at Ste. Therese, a vital communications link to Isle aux Noix. Arriving at 1000, the raiders watched as a convoy of hay wagons were about to pass through the fort's gates. Breaking his group down into three separate detachments under Captain Brewer, Lieutenant McCormick, and himself, Rogers had each detachment rush the gate simultaneously from three different directions before the wagons could clear it.

Having captured the fort without a single casualty to either side, Rogers fired the fort and its neighboring village and crossed the Richelieu with twenty-seven French prisoners — after having released fifty-two old men, women, and children — in boats and canoes he found under the fort. From the far shore, Rogers looked back and saw a large body of men on the Ste. Therese shore. Unknown to him at the time, they were British prisoners under guard and being sent to Crown Point to be exchanged. The boats Rogers' men had captured and burned from the fort were to have conveyed the prisoners to Crown Point. Captain James Tute was one of these prisoners who was able to personally admire Rogers' handiwork.

Rogers continued along the eastern shore of the Richelieu, making a detour around Isle aux Noix. His advance party engaged and defeated a similar-sized French force that was a mile ahead of a six-hundred-man pursuit force from Isle aux Noix. With his French prisoners still in tow, Rogers quickened his pace to the Windmill Point rendezvous. Constricting breeches hindered the prisoners' ability to maintain the rapid march. The situation was quickly remedied by the Rangers' knives, which were used to cut the leggings off the Frenchmen's pants. A small force of Rangers had been sent forward to signal by smoke their support ship. Arriving at Windmill Point, Rogers' force immediately boarded the waiting boats just minutes prior to the six hundred pursuing enemy frustratingly erupting from the tree line on the shore.

The Ste. Therese Raid is considered by many to be Rogers' most successful operation of the war. Well timed and executed, the mission cost Rogers not one single man while it obtained the desired effect of creating a great deal of turmoil for the French. Believing that the entire British Army was advancing from Crown Point, French soldiers were shifted from the vital St. Lawrence region to St. John's in the Richelieu River Valley.

On the following day, the 21st, Rogers sent fifty of his men and his twenty-six prisoners to Crown Point while he and the remainder of his detachment waited on a sloop for the return of Lieutenant Holmes and his force. Holmes returned that evening, having failed to accomplish his mission. Having mistakenly followed a waterway other than the Wigwam Martinique. Yamaska River, he and his men found themselves in the vicinity of the Richelieu amid a number of roaming bands of Indians. Having been instructed by Rogers to avoid unnecessary risks, Holmes returned, having accomplished nothing more than a reconnaissance of the countryside. Returning to Crown Point, Haviland directed the Rangers to encamp at Chimney Point, also referred to as Rogers' Point throughout the War, opposite Crown Point on the east shore of the lake.

Meanwhile, the third element of Rogers' force, the squad led by Sergeant Beverly, had successfully completed their five-hundred-mile journey across St. Francis Indian Territory and had delivered Amherst's message to Murray at Quebec as he prepared to advance upon Montreal along the St. Lawrence. Mission completed, Beverly and his men linked up with Hazen's company of Rogers' Rangers as they supported the British advance up the St. Lawrence.

The conquest of Canada was to be accomplished with a three-prong attack on Montreal from the south, east, and west. Amherst planned for Haviland to move by way of Lake Champlain while Murray moved from Quebec along the St. Lawrence with Amherst advancing along the St. Lawrence from Oswego. While detachments of Rogers' Rangers were assigned to each of the expeditions, the bulk of the Ranger corps—six companies under the command of James Tute, brothers Jonathan and David Brewer, Rogers' brother James, Lieutenant Simon Stevens, and Solomon with his Stockbridge Indians—were attached to Haviland with Rogers.

As the army at Crown Point set about to prepare for its movement north, enemy activity was spotted in the area by a vigilant scout of Rangers on 17 June. The following evening, small fires were observed on the west shore of the lake approximately eight miles from the army's encampment. Haviland dispatched captains Jonathan Brewer and James Rogers along with some Provincials on a reconnaissance. Three boats with thirty men pulled for the fires but were unable to arrive prior to their being extinguished. Remaining on the lake in the vicinity, the force waited until daylight when it fired a shot that was answered from the shore. Much to their amazement, Rangers Christopher Proudfoot, wounded and captured in Rogers' "Three Battles" of 7 March 1759, and Ebil Chamberlain, captured February 1760 during the Ranger Recruit Massacre emerged from hiding, having escaped on 7 June from Montreal. Captain Tute, captured 22 September of the previous year while engaged in a reconnaissance mission for Amherst and having been informed by the boastful Rangers of their plans to escape, had sent his compliments with these two Rangers. Tute was soon to follow these two Rangers himself, for he was exchanged shortly thereafter and quickly rejoined Rogers.

The early morning hours of 8 July found a Ranger element engaged in a skirmish despite the maintenance of constant patrols. At approximately 0600, a party of forty French and Indians surprised a small detachment of Rangers under Captain Jonathan Brewer who were making a raft near the Ranger compound. The Ranger force lost one killed and six wounded, including Brewer, before they could force the raiding party to withdraw. Rogers immediately dispatched a force to pursue the enemy but they were forced to give up the chase after traveling eight miles without gaining ground.

Of the six wounded Rangers, two would die within days. Captain Jonathan Brewer recovered in time to rejoin his command for the advance on Isle aux Noix. A third Ranger not involved with this engagement was to die also, on 10 July. Private Jacob Hallowell, considered by many of his peers to be one of the most courageous Rangers, died on a hot, sweltering day in the hospital of wounds received at the Battle of Pointe aux Fer.

A flurry of activity continued during the remainder of the month of July and into the first two weeks of August as Haviland's army prepared its advance. Short of men, Rogers' corps was augmented on 4 August by 284 New Hampshire Provincials. After bringing his line companies to full strength of one hundred men each, Rogers had the remaining one hundred Provincials form a sapper company of "Hatchetmen" under the command of Captain Samuel Hodge, Jr. On 16 August, Rogers' corps, serving as the advance guard of Haviland's army, consisted of five Ranger companies, one Stockbridge Indian company, and one company of pioneers formed.

Moving by water, the army encountered strong winds and heavy rains three days into its movement. Eight of the Rangers were drowned when choppy waters split their canoe, spilling them and three others into the water. Riding out the weather, the Rangers, Light Infantry, and Grenadiers landed unopposed on the east shore the next day. Followed by the rest of the army, Rogers encamped on the northern end of Haviland's line, opposite the rear of Isle aux Noix.

Gun batteries were quickly erected. Later that night a whaleboat of Rangers moved into the channel near the French fort to take soundings. Discovered, the reconnaissance party was challenged by a volley of grapeshot that killed one Ranger and wounded three, one of whom drowned.

The siege commenced the following day with the initiation of a bombardment from the newly emplaced gun batteries. As the week progressed, Rogers was ordered to provide a diversion by cutting and stacking chords of wood sixty yards in front of his position to be burned each night. Disturbed with the fact that this would invite long-range enemy fire into his camp, Rogers complied and entrusted the mission to his new company of Hatchetmen.

Ranger scouts were also employed. On the 22nd, the efforts of a nine-man volunteer Ranger scout were rewarded with the capture of four prisoners on the Isle aux Noix early that morning, in addition to thirty-seven pounds, sixteen shillings from Haviland for their bravery and success.

The climax of the siege occurred early on 25 August when a force composed of Rogers and five of his companies, including the Stockbridge Indians and two companies of Light Infantry all under the command of Haviland's Colonel Darby moved into position to capture the small

French fleet supporting the isle. The French naval force consisted of a schooner, a sloop, a brig, and a rideau. Emplacing three artillery field pieces that had been silently hauled through the wood opposite the vessels located behind the isle in the Richelieu River, Darby opened fire on the unsuspecting enemy ships.

A lucky first shot cut the anchoring cable of the largest of the four ships, the rideau, which was driven ashore by a strong west wind and swiftly secured by the Light Infantry. Immediately weighing anchor, the remaining three vessels made sail for St. John's only to find themselves stranded in a bend of the river. Along the shore and in hot pursuit were Rogers and his Rangers.

Closing on the stranded ships, part of Rogers' force remained along the shoreline placing suppressive covering fires on the ships while the remainder of the force swam out with tomahawks between their teeth to the vessels. Boarding one of the ships, the Rangers were able to quickly drive the astonished crew below decks or into the water. Demoralized, the remaining two crews surrendered to Darby when he closed on them in the British-manned rideau he had captured earlier.

Devastated by the intrepid and triumphal exploits of Darby and Rogers, the French commander, Bougainville, and his garrison abandoned the isle on the night of 27 August and withdrew twelve miles through the forest and swamps to St. John's. Rogers, in quick pursuit with Haviland's army following, arrived at St. John's only to find it in flames.

Leaving two hundred Rangers behind to secure the lakeside, his boats, and baggage, Rogers continued to march with his remaining 370 Rangers and Stockbridge Indians. Encountering and engaging the French rear guard of nearly two hundred men, Rogers' men broke the guard, with the loss of two Ranger dead and two wounded, and forced them back on the main body of 1,500 soldiers. Attempting to force Bougainville to make a stand and fight, Rogers and his men pursued, flanked, and harassed the retreating enemy force. Not willing to take a stand, the French withdrew across a river to a fortified camp on the far shore. With the raising of the bridge leading into the camp, Rogers' pursuit came to a close.

Accompanied by seventeen French prisoners, Rogers rejoined Haviland and continued with the army to encamp at Ste. D'Etrese. Rogers and his men soon had the task of administering the oath of allegiance to his Britannic Majesty to the French-Canadian populace down the Richelieu River. Completing this, Rogers, upon his return, joined with Colonel Darby to invest the relatively small fort at Chambly. Not too thrilled with the thought of repelling an assault, the fort capitulated after the firing of one cannon shot.

Chambly's capture completed Haviland's part of the three-pronged attack on Canada. A Ranger officer was dispatched to establish communications with Murray. The officer returned with orders for Haviland to immediately have Rogers' Rangers, his Grenadiers, and his Light Infantry to close on Murray's position, to be followed soon thereafter by the remainder of Haviland's force. By the time this message arrived, though, Haviland had already redeployed to La Prairie under orders from Amherst.

While Haviland's main body remained under orders from Amherst, Haviland did send Rogers and his Rangers to join Murray. Finally, upon Rogers' arrival at Murray's encampment at Longueuil and following a long two and a half year separation, Hazen's company of Rogers' Rangers rejoined the corps.

CHAPTER 8

Rogers' Rangers: Campaign of 1761

The fact cannot be concealed. The best thing for an army on the defensive is to know how to take the offensive at a proper time and to take it.

Lieutenant General Antoine-Henri Baron de Jomini

The onset of winter proved to be exceptionally harsh. Driven from their tent encampment on the plains, Murray's army moved to the shelter of Quebec. Cut off from the British fleet, and thus reinforcements, until the following May, Murray and his men were isolated. In an effort to establish communications with Amherst, Lieutenant John Butler and four other Rangers attempted to make it cross-country to New York with dispatches. Foul weather and Indians forced them to return after ten days.

Butler made a second attempt on 26 January along a shorter route. The detachment was increased in size to two sergeants and ten Rangers. Though the Rangers were under the command of Butler, Lieutenant John Montressor, an engineer of distinction, who had also been assigned the task of mapping their route along the Chaudiere River, commanded the entire patrol. The adversity and hardships endured by these men proved to be as severe as any "previously encountered by the Rangers," to include those experienced by the St. Francis Raiders.

Their route took them along the Chaudiere to its source at Lake Megantic. From there, they moved directly south, passing between the Rangeley and Mooselucmeguntic lakes, and through the Blue Mountains of Maine. Finally, out of food, the detachment was forced to survive and subsist by eating their leather shoes and bullet pouches. Compounding their arduous journey was the freezing weather they encountered along the trek; weather so cold that one of the Rangers froze to death.

On 15 February in an attempt to save his command, Montressor dispatched Butler and a second Ranger to move ahead of the main body to the settlement of Topsham located at the mouth of the Androscoggin River to procure urgent provisions which they were able to do five days later. Resupplied by two of the settlement's inhabitants, the remainder of the detachment arrived twelve days after they had first run short of provisions.

Following a period of recovery, two of the Rangers retraced their steps to Quebec while Montressor and Butler rode horseback to Newport from where they sailed on a sloop to New York. The two lieutenants arrived in New York on 3 March to deliver their verbal message to Amherst. The other two Rangers arrived in Quebec on 13 March to report to Murray of the detachment's success.

On 19 April, Butler sailed for Boston to obtain Ranger recruits Amherst had enlisted for Hazen's company. Rounding up the recruits, Butler embarked on a cattle boat for Quebec, arriving in time to assist with the relief of the city that had found itself besieged from Levis, who had moved his army from Montreal in April.

In anticipation of Levis' movements, Murray had fortified two outposts at Ste. Foy and Old Lorette. Hazen's company of Rangers was stationed in a house not far from the outpost at Old Lorette and figured in some fierce actions that winter.

The first of his actions occurred in February when he and twenty-five of his Rangers stopped a much superior force of French Grenadiers who were attempting to drive off a herd of cattle at Old Lorette.

A few weeks later, a force of over 1,000 French, Canadians, and Indians secured a strong position in the vicinity of a church at Point Levi. Murray organized a force composed of Hazen's company of Rangers and a detachment of Light Infantry under the overall command of Major Dalling to oppose this incursion. With Hazen's Rangers leading the advance, the British force crossed the frozen St. Lawrence River. Having secured a footing on the heights overlooking the river, the Rangers placed suppressive fires on the enemy as the Light Infantry followed. Trained by the Rangers on snowshoe warfare, the Light Infantry and Hazen's men routed the French and their allies following a sharp engagement, killing and capturing a significant number. After establishing a third outpost at the church, the victorious Rangers and Light Infantry compatriots returned to Quebec.

Hazen and his Rangers found themselves heavily involved in a third engagement the following month. Having been informed by a Ranger scout that a large enemy force was moving to attack them, Hazen detached a small security element of fifteen men to secure their house near Lorette and moved with his remaining men toward the outpost at Lorette to obtain reinforcements.

Shortly thereafter, Hazen encountered the French force, which attempted to envelop them. Ordering his men to withdraw to their house, Hazen found his men disinclined to do so for they "felt spry" and wanted to demonstrate to their Regular counterparts that Rangers could fight as well as any Redcoat. Accepting their request, Hazen ordered his men to charge the enemy and deliver a close volley of buckshot.

Having put those they charged to flight, the Rangers found themselves engaged from the rear by another French detachment that was attempting to cut them off from their retreat to the house. Facing about, the Rangers attacked and drove off this second group as they had done the first. With the enemy seemingly vanquished from the area, Hazen continued his movement to Lorette.

Unknown to him, though, the two enemy elements had joined forces and moved to attack the house guarded by the fifteen Rangers. A brisk fire from the defending Rangers met the French. Hearing the engagement behind him, Hazen quickly abandoned his attempt to seek reinforcements and returned to the house, falling on the rear of the attacking enemy. Soon the French found themselves caught between two closing forces as the house defenders sallied forth and attacked them in front. Routed for a third time that day and pursued for two miles, the French were repelled with a loss of six killed and seven captured.

The remainder of Hazen's Rangers were quartered in Quebec and, in at least one instance, were deceptively used by Murray to help bolster British morale. To counter false rumors spread by the French among the populace of Quebec that packets had arrived from France with news of a favorable peace in Europe and that large numbers of French reinforcements were on the way, Murray had a Ranger sergeant and four of his men carry out a psychological ploy. Departing Quebec unobserved, the five Rangers crossed the frozen St. Lawrence and entered Quebec as if they were messengers from Amherst with favorable dispatches for Murray from his commander and from England. This stratagem did much to counter the French rumors and lift British spirits.

Murray was forewarned of Levis' advance in April when a deserter from Montreal delivered him a letter. The letter was written by one of

Rogers' officers who was a prisoner at that location. In the letter, the Ranger warned Murray that a force of 11,000 men were preparing to attack Quebec. Upon Levis' arrival before Lorette in late April, the British advanced guard and Hazen's Rangers withdrew to Ste. Foy. Levis maintained the pressure and followed.

On the morning of 27 April, Murray advanced from Quebec with half of his garrison and ten pieces of artillery to support the withdrawal of his remaining outposts. From heights in the woods overlooking Ste. Foy, Murray's force was able to engage Levis' entire force as the outposts, to include Hazen's Rangers, withdrew to the safety of Quebec, soon to be followed by Murray.

Rather than wait out a siege, Murray opted to attack even though his forces were seriously inferior in number. Deploying from garrison the very next morning, Murray's army of 3,000 men sallied forth to meet Levis' advancing army. Hazen's company covered the left flank and included a hundred Highlander volunteers. Dalling's Light Infantry covered the right. The line consisted of eight battalions with two in reserve.

The initial stages of the battle went well for the British as their cannon opened with telling effect. Ordered to withdraw to the cover of some woods, Levis' left flank fell back. Mistaking this movement for a retreat, Murray left his advantageous position and advanced through deep snow against the French line. Unable to move their artillery through the snow, the British cannon had to cease fire as their infantry advanced.

With the threat of the indirect fire removed, the French left flank charged from the wood line and overwhelmed the Light Infantry of the British right Bank. Despite the Light Infantry being thrown back upon the main body, the battle continued to ebb and flow for an hour. Hazen's Rangers and attached volunteers, though engaged by deadly fires, managed to take two blockhouses but could not hold them. With Hazen wounded and the volunteer commander killed, the British flank began to buckle under the overwhelming pressure of numbers. With both of his flanks enveloped and giving ground, Murray soon realized that he stood a great chance of being totally surrounded, cut off from Quebec, and destroyed. A retreat was ordered.

The French continued to press, hoping to sever the line of communications the British were moving along. Supported by his servant while making his way toward the city gates, Hazen observed at a great distance a French officer leading a detachment of soldiers across the rising ground. Briefly halting, Hazen obtained a rifle from his servant, seated himself on the ground, took aim, brought down the officer with a single shot, and then proceeded to move back to the city.

Losses were heavy for both sides, but especially for the British, whose casualties were greater than a third of their number with over a thousand killed, wounded, or missing. Ranger losses, besides the wounding of Hazen, were relatively light, considering the fierceness and length of the engagement, at two dead, nine wounded. French losses were placed at 833 men. With their withdrawal into the city, the British Army now found itself under siege.

Murray's forces settled in for the siege as Levis entrenched himself along the bank of Buttes-a-Neveu. Nighttime patrols became routine for Hazen's Rangers as they covered the area between the entrenchments and town limits. During these patrols, the Rangers made every effort to harass the French. On the night of 4 May, in particular, Hazen's Rangers sallied forth unobserved, stealthily made their way up to a section of the enemy's siege line, poured in a volley of fire, and returned without a single shot fired at them in return.

With the stalemate on land, the eventual victor would be determined on sea. Apprehensive eyes remained focused on the St. Lawrence, waiting to see if the first ships to sail the unfrozen channel were from England or from France. Soon, that question was answered as the first fleet to approach Quebec flew the cross of St. George and not the fleur-de-lis. Levis withdrew to Montreal on 17 May.

The siege lifted and his army supplied and reinforced, Murray set about fulfilling Amherst's directive as the third leg of the attack on Montreal. Embarking on 15 July with a force of 2,450 men, Murray slowly made his way toward Montreal. Included in this force and under the command of Lieutenant Patton were fifty of Hazen's 139 Rangers. Unfortunately for Hazen, himself, he was forced to remain behind in a Quebec hospital as a result of his earlier wounds.

Landing periodically, the British force skirmished with detachments of enemy soldiers who followed along the shore. During one such landing on 18 July, Hazen's Rangers observed an approaching party of forty soldiers under the command of a noted partisan, Lieutenant Hertel. Coordinating with the accompanying two hundred Regulars who had landed with him, Patton prepared an ambush for Hertel. With Regulars posted on both sides of the road that Hertel was traversing, Patton's Rangers initiated the ambush with a rush that forced the enemy between the two Regular forces. Finding themselves surrounded, the Canadians continued their desperate struggle, which resulted in nearly all of them being killed, wounded, or taken prisoner. Hertel was one who would die from his wounds.

Pacification of the local populace was another of Murray's objectives during this movement. To accomplish this aspect of his mission, Hazen's Rangers were often landed to follow abreast of the fleet, disarming the inhabitants and administering the oath of neutrality along the way.

The fleet arrived alongside the Ste. Therese Island on 27 August, just south of Montreal. Having landed and captured some prisoners, the Rangers obtained information that a force of two hundred Canadians and a detachment of French Regulars was located on the eastern part of the shore just opposite the British location in the village of Varennes. Requiring the village to serve as his initial base of operations against Montreal, Murray moved to secure it.

Murray attacked at dawn on 31 August after posting strong detachments north and south of the objective. The assault element consisted of Hazen's Rangers and the Light Infantry. Their landing was followed by a spirited engagement that secured Varennes after killing or wounding eight and capturing twenty.

Reembarking the security elements he had posted both north and south of the village, Murray ordered Hazen and two of the Light Infantry companies to remain behind as a security detachment until needed later for the army's advance. Later that afternoon around 1300, while fortifying a church within the town, a force of eighty Canadians from Boucherville attacked Hazen's Rangers.

Moving forth to do battle, the Rangers were able to defeat the enemy attempt, first by burning a barn they had tried to occupy then by occupying the church just moments prior to a Canadian attempt to seize it. Finally, with assistance of a small Light Infantry detachment's assault on the enemy flank, the Rangers were able to break the enemy formation with a strong frontal assault. Pursuing the defeated enemy for nearly a mile, the Rangers returned with seven wounded prisoners to add to the three enemy they had killed during their attack on the church. Ranger losses were only three wounded.

Ironically, this engagement would prove to be the last significant engagement of the French and Indian War. It was only fitting that it was conducted by an element of the Ranger corps. Shortly thereafter, Murray landed on the Ste. Therese Island. This landing was followed on 5 September with Murray's deployment to reinforce Haviland at Longueuil, located directly across from Montreal, with Hazen's Rangers, the Light Infantry, and Grenadiers. It was the following day, 6 September, that Hazen's Rangers joined Major Rogers and his corps after an exceptionally long two and-a-half -year separation.

Hazen's command was not the only company to be separated from Rogers' command for a considerable length of time. Back in November 1759, a reduced company of Rogers' Rangers under the command of Captain Joseph Waite, a veteran of the battle of Rogers' Rock, was stationed on the west end of Lake Oneida at Fort Brewerton. Braving the harsh winter, Waite's small command of thirty Rangers had been spared from any attacks that winter. A strong recruiting effort by Waite in the spring raised his strength to ninety-one officers and men, including his brother, who was serving as his ensign.

Concurrently, Captain Amos Ogden, a St. Francis Raider and former New Jersey Provincial—not to be confused with the fifth detached Ranger company of the New York Provincial Regiment commanded by Captain Jonathan Ogden and garrisoned at Saratoga that was cited earlier in the formation of Rogers' Ranger corps—was granted the authority to raise a company of Rangers in New Jersey. Provided £500 in advance funds in March, Ogden was able to raise a company of one hundred officers and men. When informed of this new Ranger company, Rogers replied that he was "heartily glad" that Ogden had received his own company.

Assigned to Amherst's command, Waite's and Ogden's Ranger companies were to participate in Amherst's advance on Montreal. As part of his 10,000-man army encamped at Fort Ontario, the two Ranger companies ran daily patrols from advance posts on the perimeter. Amherst thought very highly of his Rangers and mentioned them very frequently in General Orders and correspondence.

On 15 July, each company provided one officer and fifteen men to serve as decoys on three whaleboats in an attempt to capture a French brig and schooner. After playing cat and mouse for more than a week in the eastern portion of Lake Ontario, the two French ships withdrew back into the St. Lawrence on the 23rd.

On 7 August, Colonel Haldimand's advance force embarked in advance of Amherst's main body with the majority of the two Ranger companies, a total of seven officers and 184 enlisted. Three days later, Amherst deployed with his main body and soon joined Haldimand at Man Island, after which he continued his movement down the St. Lawrence to Fort Levis on Isle Royale.

On the 17th, Amherst attacked the French fleet and laid siege to Fort Levis the following day. The bombardment intensified on 23 August as Amherst's three heavy ships concentrated on the mainland and the neighboring islands. To isolate the invested fort, the Rangers were posted opposite it on Isle a La Cuisse. Outfitted with fourteen whaleboats, their mission was to attack any boats coming or going from Fort Levis with reinforcements or escaping garrison. Unable to hold out any longer, the garrison finally surrendered on the afternoon of the 25th.

Four days later on the evening of 29 August, Captain Jacob Naunau-phtaunk, a former commander of the Stockbridge Indians who was captured along with Captain Kennedy prior to the St. Francis Raid, arrived at Fort Levis escorted by French Indians. Father Robaud, who was very influential with the French Indians, had secured his release from the French at Montreal. As a measure of good faith, the Father had returned Naunauphtaunk along with a letter offering peace between the British and the Indians who desired peace. Accepting the offer, Amherst employed the Ranger captain as a peace envoy with the remnants of the St. Francis Indians.

Departing Fort Levis—renamed Fort William Augustus—the army progressed down the rapids with the two Ranger companies and Gage's Light Infantry in advance. Disembarked, the Rangers scoured the wooded embankments of the rapids to defend against any ambushes as Amherst's army made its way through the watercourse, which took a week for the force to traverse.

The army finally found itself on 6 September before the walls of Montreal. Realizing the futility of resisting, French Canadian Governor-General Vaudreuil entered into capitulation negotiations on 1 September. By the next day, the capitulation document transferring all of Canada and its dependencies to the British was signed. Four days later, Waite's command was ordered to rejoin their corps commander, Major Rogers.

With the long war finally over, the difficult task of consolidation began. The surrender of the far-flung western French forts and outposts Forts Detroit, Miamis, St. Joseph, Quatanon, La Baye, Michilimackinac, and Sault Ste. Marie would prove to be very difficult, for the troops assigned this task would be required to travel through country infested with unfriendly Indians, most of whom were not aware of the change of masters. Realizing that the administration of the oath of allegiance to the Canadians and Indians would require the utmost discretion and delicate handling, Amherst selected Rogers and his Rangers as the emissaries to accomplish this important mission.

Few of Rogers' men would accompany him on the corps' final mission. Those who did not were returned to Crown Point. On 30 September, all of the Provincials who had been drafted into the Rangers were returned to their respective units while the remaining Rangers ferried Regulars from St. John's to Crown Point by bateau.

With Major Rogers departed on his expedition, it fell to the next senior Ranger, his brother Captain James Rogers, to handle the final details. Paying off the Number Four detachment on 25 October, he paraded and embarked the remaining Rangers, with the exception of Ogden's company, for Albany where they were paid off on 11 November, as were the bulk of Ogden's company who had been left behind.

A small nucleus of Rogers' Rangers remained, though. Needing to ensure communications between Crown Point and Montreal, especially during the harsh winters, the British retained a small detachment of Rangers from Ogden's company, thirty-one in all. The communications plan called for the group to be broken into three details to be garrisoned evenly at St. John's Island, Isle aux Noix, and Crown Point. Ranger Lieutenant van Tyne was one of the thirty-one and in command. Following an exceptionally harsh winter, Van Tyne and his remaining Rangers were discharged on 20 May by Haviland and paid off at Ticonderoga the next day.

Rogers embarked at noon on 13 September from Montreal up the St. Lawrence to Lake Ontario. Traveling in the fifteen whaleboats with Rogers were Captain Jonathan Brewer, Captain Waite, seven lieutenants, two ensigns, fifteen sergeants, and 111 Rangers for a total force of 198. In addition, an engineer and artillery lieutenant were attached to the force to map and determine defensive requirements at the far-flung forts. On 29 November, Fort Detroit was surrendered with its garrison of two officers and thirty-five Regulars.

Setting out on 10 December to execute the final tasks of Amherst's assigned mission, Rogers moved to bring the final outlying posts of the former French territory under British control. Detachments were dispatched to the garrisons at Forts Miamis and Quatanon, an outpost at the lower Shawnee Indian town on the Ohio River, and to the upper Shawnee villages.

While the two Shawnee missions were accomplished with little note, the same could not be said for the third mission. Rogers had tasked Lieutenant John Butler and his twenty Rangers with the mission of taking possession of Forts Miamis and Quatanon. These two isolated forts were located in the wilderness near Vincennes in the Mississippi Valley. This isolation, exacerbated by adverse conditions and relief force difficulties, did not provide Butler and his men an opportunity to muster and be paid off for the final time until 2 January 1762.

Nearly a year prior to Butler's mustering out, Rogers had arrived at Fort Pitt on 23 January 1761, where he instructed Lieutenant McCormick and the balance of Rangers yet to be paid off, thirty-six in all, to march the Rangers to Albany where they were to be disbanded. Rogers departed

Fort Pitt a few days later and arrived at his destination, New York, on 14 February, where he received not only Amherst's congratulations but also a captain's commission dated 25 October 1760 in the Regulars of His King's Service as a reward for his exceptional services during the French and Indian War.

CHAPTER 9

Rogers' Rangers:
Beyond the French and Indian War

It is always more difficult to defend a coast than to invade it.

Sir Walter Raleigh

Though no longer required for duties in the colonies, the British did have a further need for Rangers during their conquest of the French West Indies. When Waite's command was mustered out in the spring of 1761, Waite and forty-four of his men remained in service. In addition to Waite, Captain Amos Ogden, part of whose command had been retained for courier service between Crown Point and Montreal for the winter, was authorized to recruit during March and April for new volunteers. Over all, Ogden was able to sign four sergeants and sixty-two privates, including a number of men from Hazen's old command. By the summer of 1761, these two companies, though not led by Major Rogers, represented Rogers' Rangers' participation in the French West Indies.

Amherst had been ordered by Prime Minister Pitt to deploy a force of 2,000 soldiers to Guadeloupe to assist the governor of that area with the conquest of Dominica, St. Lucia, and Martinique. These forces, to include Waite's and Ogden's companies, set sail on 3 May from New York. Arriving at noon on 6 June before the Dominican port of Rosseau, Lord Rollo, the expedition commander, demanded their surrender. The French opted to resist. Landing with the main force on the beach, Rogers' Rangers immediately assaulted the enemy entrenchments before they could be reinforced. With the entrenchments lost and their commander and his

119

deputy prisoners, the French offered no further resistance and swore their allegiance to the Crown the following day.

Having waited for additional reinforcements, the invasion force arrived in Barbados on Christmas Eve. The Rangers did not have to linger long for the new expedition commander, General Monckton, to advance, which he did on 5 January 1762. The army made land at St. Anne's Bay on the southern point of Martinique on the 7th. Following the landing, Monckton needed to march three miles overland to Fort Royal. The route wound its way through deep gullies and treacherous ravines defended by redoubts erected and defended by the French. Defending these redoubts from the rear were artillery batteries situated on a hill named Morne Tortenson.

Needing to clear the route prior to moving his own cannon forward to invest Tortenson, Monckton assigned the mission to the two Ranger companies. Employing their bush-fighting tactics and supported by the Highlanders, the Rangers quickly drove back the enemy's advance posts and cleared the route for the main advance of the 24th.

Driven back to Fort Royal and Morne Grenier, a higher hill north of Tortenson, the French did not have to wait long for the next engagement. Two British brigades, one of which was Haviland's with the two Ranger companies attached, attacked the batteries on Tortenson and, after a great fight up the steep mountain, drove the enemy back to Grenier. Rogers' Rangers, in the thick of the battle, suffered the death of two Rangers, one of whom was Lieutenant van Tyne, thirteen wounded, and two missing.

Now in range, the British brought up their artillery to engage Fort Royal. On the 27th, the French on Morne Grenier attempted to change the inevitable outcome by storming down the mountain to hit the left side of the army—Haviland's brigade, the Highlanders, and the Light Infantry. In their haste, the French exposed their flank to Rogers' Rangers, who quickly assaulted and routed the French attack with some assistance from the Highlanders. The French formations disintegrated and the rout was on as the British Army pursued them to Morne Grenier.

Leading this pursuit were the Rangers, Highlanders, and Light Infantry. Following the retreating French down the hill from their positions, through a ravine at the foot of the mountain, and then up Grenier, the Rangers led the swarm through the French positions. The operation continued throughout the night as the French were cleared from the mountain, position by position. Possession of the mountain and its batteries cost the British one hundred killed and wounded. Ranger casualties were one dead, one wounded, and one missing.

With Tortenson and Grenier in British hands and new batteries being constructed within four hundred yards of Fort Royal, the French realized there was little to do but capitulate, which they did on 3 February. With Fort Royal lost, the remainder of the island fell by the 12th. Recognizing that resistance was futile, the islands of St. Lucia, St. Vincent, and Grenada fell without a fight. The foreign service of Rogers' Rangers came to a close on 16 June 1762 when the two Ranger companies returned to New York and were disbanded.

Even though there was finally peace on the continent between the British and French, a war did erupt in late 1760 between the British and Cherokee Indians, whose home territories were in Georgia, Tennessee, and the Carolinas. South Carolina governor, William Bull, requested the assistance of the King's troops. The 77th Royal Scott Highlanders, under the command of Colonel Archibald Montgomerie, were dispatched. Moving through the Cherokee territory from Fort Prince George, burning villages along the way, the overconfident Highlanders fell prey to a bloody ambush at Etchoe Pass, approximately six miles from the Cherokees' principle village of Etchoe. Rallying his soldiers, Montgomerie was able to drive the Indians from their position with heavy losses.

Greatly concerned that the severely mauled Highlanders and his South Carolina militia would not be able to protect the colony from the inflamed Cherokees, Bull requested additional troops from Lord Amherst. Lieutenant Colonel Francis Grant and 1,200 Regulars of the 42nd Highlanders were dispatched to replace Montgomerie for a campaign against the Cherokees. Included with this force were representatives of Rogers' Rangers, the Stockbridge Indians. Having paid off the bulk of Rogers' Rangers in Albany in late 1760, Amherst prudently realized there may be a requirement for the Stockbridges' services and retained thirty to forty of them in service under the command of Captain Quinton Kennedy.

On 7 January 1761, the Stockbridge Indians had arrived in Charleston, South Carolina. Three months later, another detachment of Rogers' Rangers was to follow. This detachment of fourteen Ranger recruits and one lieutenant, Jacob Farrington, was in actuality a group from Rogers' — now Captain Rogers of the Regulars since his commission in October 1760 — new command of the South Carolina Independent Company. Kennedy's command was now a smorgasbord of detachments composed of not only his Stockbridges, but also of Mohawk, Chickasaws, and Catawba Indians in addition to the newly arrived component of Rogers' Rangers.

Grant's expedition began its movement in mid-March up the Santee and Congaree Rivers, following Montgomerie's previous route. Within two days, the army was at Etchoe Pass, the scene of Montgomerie's earlier ambush.

Grant became very wary when greeted at the pass by an ominous silence. Expecting to be met by peace envoys, Grant and his men instead were fired on from the rear by a force of Cherokees early the following morning. This attempt at misdirection by the Indians would have proven successful if it hadn't been for the sharp eyes of Rogers' Rangers, who around 0830 spotted the Indians' true positions on a high hill to the right that overlooked the pass.

Of special note was a regiment of South Carolina militia attached to Grant's command. One of the Regiment's lieutenants was named *Francis Marion* – who would gain considerable fame fighting the British during the American Revolution as the "Swamp Fox." Selected by Grant, Marion and a South Carolina detachment of thirty men joined Kennedy's lead elements for the attack.

Leading the advance of Kennedy's command, the Rangers moved down into the defile, moving from tree to tree. Though outnumbered, Kennedy's attack was so forceful that the Cherokees fell back before the onslaught. British losses were heavy with Marion's detachment alone suffering twenty-one dead or wounded. A half-mile later having pushed the enemy back, Kennedy and his men crossed the Cullasaja River at a fording site to secure the high ground on the far side. Posted along the banks, they provided cover for the passage of Grant's main body.

The movement of Grant's army through the ford took all morning, during which Kennedy, his Indians, Light Infantry, and Rogers' Rangers continued to place fires that kept the Cherokees a safe distance away. The employment of Indian-style tactics by Kennedy and the Rangers proved to be exceptionally disheartening to Great Warrior. So much so that during the heat of the battle, the Cherokees called out to Kennedy in desperation to come forward within reach of their fires, obviously a request he and his men were inclined to disregard.

With their ammunition running low, the Cherokee fires began to slacken around noon as the last of Grant's forces were crossing the river. Having haphazardly maintained fires throughout the early afternoon, Great Warrior and his men finally withdrew around 1,500. Grant and his officers recognized Kennedy's forces for having performed an invaluable service. Total losses for the British were eleven killed and fifty-one wounded. Kennedy's corps only suffered one Indian killed.

Continuing on with their mission, Grant's army reached the Cherokee village of Etchoe that evening, which they reduced to ashes around 2100. Grant continued to move unopposed through the Cherokee territory, sweeping the Little Tennessee and Tuckaseegee Valleys. Grant continued on for another thirty days, destroying every Cherokee village encountered along the way. The Rangers figured prominently in the destruction of the Neowee, Canouga, and Ayoree villages.

On 11 June, the Rangers and Stockbridges were deployed to destroy Burning Town when the Cowhitchi River proved too difficult for the main body to cross. By that evening, the village had been laid to ashes. Despite the total destruction, only two Cherokee braves had been encountered throughout the campaign. One was killed; the second, while wounded, was able to escape. Grant realized that he had accomplished all he could. His men were so seriously fatigued they could barely travel without assistance. Returning to Fort Prince George, the expedition made it back with only two days rations remaining. By the time they reached Fort Prince George, nearly 1,000 of Grant's men were without shoes of any type.

Exhausted, Grant and his men waited to see what the results of their efforts would be. They did not have long to wait, as several Cherokee chiefs arrived at the fort to sue for peace. Grant sent the chiefs to meet with Governor Bull and a successful treaty was soon signed thus bringing to an end the Cherokee-English War.

Rogers, having been tied up in administrative work, finally arrived at Fort Prince George on 26 August with an additional eighteen ex-Rangers. Joined by Farrington and his detachment, Rogers received orders from Grant to redeploy his men to Charleston. The final active component of Rogers' Rangers was finally deactivated as the men assigned to Rogers' command donned the bright red cloth of the British Regular Army and became members of the South Carolina Independent Company.

CHAPTER 10

The Temporary Revival of
Rogers' Rangers

Eternal peace lasts only until the next war.

Russian proverb

In 1763, Rogers' Rangers found itself activated for duty one last time against one of Rogers' old friends. Despite having made peace with Rogers during his expedition to consolidate the isolated French posts and the British Empire in November 1760, the great Indian chief, Pontiac, was encouraged by the French to wage war once again against the British by the fact that a peace plan had yet to be signed to officially end the conflict. Pontiac's influence was still so great that he was able to secure alliances with all of the tribes formerly allied with France. Then, in May 1763, he attacked. In a lightning fifteen-day campaign, Pontiac and his warriors surprised and either massacred or scattered the garrisons of eight British forts.

In August 1762, Rogers' command, the New York Independent Company, was inactivated and Rogers found himself without a company and on half pay. At this time, Pontiac had placed Detroit under siege. For relief, Amherst dispatched his aide-de-camp, Captain Dalyell, whom Rogers had first met during his battle with Marin on 8 August 1758. Extremely discouraged by the loss of his command and the opportunity to command the relief expedition which he felt was his, Rogers nonetheless felt the urge to battle and allowed himself to be nominated for a junior rank and to be placed under the command of Dalyell.

While on the march, the expedition stopped at Fort Ontario, where Rogers elected to revive his Rangers. Encountering his brother James at the fort, Rogers recruited a platoon that signed up on 30 June for a three-month period. Consisting of Rogers, his brother, and six other men, this platoon added an additional lieutenant, named Bean, a sergeant, and twenty-eight Privates from the New York Provincials prior to their departure from Ontario.

On the evening of 28 July, the expedition reached the straits at the mouth of the Detroit River. In the dark, Rogers and his men guided the expedition up the river. Paddling their canoes, they made a final sprint on the water for the besieged fortification. Midway between the fort and the village of the Pottawattamie and Wyandottes Indians, the British were met with a hot fusillade of shot from Pontiac's braves surrounding the fort. The force returned its fire in kind and the accuracy of fire from the Rangers proved to be the deciding factor in holding the enemy off long enough for boats to gain the security of the fort. Casualties were high with fifteen dead and wounded.

The reinforcements, provisions, and ammunition were of tremendous relief to the garrison. Coincidentally, upon his arrival, Rogers was met by one of his old lieutenants, Caesar McCormick. McCormick and some of the traders and their servants attached themselves to Rogers' command, thus bringing the number of officers and men under him to more than forty.

Swelled with confidence gained from their success to date, Dalyell boldly, but rashly, petitioned the garrison commander, Major Gladwyn, to lead a sortie from the fort upon Pontiac's encampment. Reluctantly, Gladwyn approved the captain's request. Departing at 0200 on 31 July, Dalyell and Rogers led a force of 250 men quietly through the fort's gate. The men marched along the road in two files while two large bateaus, each with a swivel cannon on the bow, rowed up the river abreast the land movement.

Unknown to the British, their approach was being observed and the Indians were lying in wait. Parent's Creek settled through a wild and rugged hollow and flowed into the Detroit River amid a growth of rank grass approximately a mile and a half from the fort. Crossing this creek by a wooden bridge just a few rods from its mouth, the column apprehensively—for they were aware of the potential dangers of this dangerous pass—continued their march uphill where a large body of warriors waited silently along the summit in ambush.

The advance guard were halfway across the bridge with the main body just beginning to cross when a frightful fusillade of war whoops and bullets erupted to their front with the initiation of Pontiac's ambush.

Half of the advance party was dropped where they stood while the survivors attempted to push their way back across the bridge. Confusion reigned supreme as the remnants of the lead element intermingled with the main body. Dalyell and Rogers rallied their men despite a second volley of fire and led the attack across the bridge and up the far embankment to the ambush heights beyond.

Encountering no Indians at the top of the hill, the British pushed on into the darkness. Resistance was stiff though, as the Indians continued to employ their guerrilla tactics with harassing fires from the front and flanks. While the Regulars found this style of warfare extremely disturbing, Rogers and his men quite naturally emulated their foes and returned fire from behind rocks and trees.

Further British advancement was out of the question and the decision was made to withdraw and await daylight. Pontiac had something else in mind, though, and deployed a large force to the British rear in an attempt to cut off their line of retreat to the fort. Learning from some Canadians of the Indian attempt to cut them off by occupying some houses that commanded the road below, Dalyell ordered an immediate withdrawal to the fort.

Passing a group of buildings, the retreating force was engaged with a heavy volley of fire that felled a large number of British soldiers, including Dalyell himself. In possession of a house nearby, Indians were firing from the upstairs windows down onto the British soldiers. Rogers and his men rushed the house, broke the door down with their hatchets, and drove the warriors out. Then, moving to a second house that provided better command of the road, the Rangers posted themselves at the building's windows and provided covering fires for the Regulars who were quickly falling back.

The scene in the house was one of pandemonium. In the cellar were the women of the town, terrified and screaming over the turmoil playing out above their heads. On the trapdoor stood the house's master, Old Campau, who had to fight off frightened British Regulars who were trying to find safety and shelter down below. Incredibly, other Regulars had located a keg of whiskey in one of the rooms, which they quickly drained. Rogers and his Rangers proved to be the only levelheaded troops present and above the din of battle, it took Rogers some time to restore order within the building.

Assuming command after Dalyell had fallen, Captain Grant rallied the remnants of the advance guard and moved forward about a half mile to positions behind some trees and fences. As soldiers straggled in, Grant had them move to the rear under cover of Rogers' fire until he had secured his line of retreat to Fort Detroit. For the next hour, Grant withdrew his men to the fort until the only soldiers left to withdraw were Rogers and his men from the house.

Rogers and his men now had a slight problem. Besieged by a force of two hundred Indians or more, they could not get out of the building they had secured for an overwatch of the withdrawal. Through Lieutenant Bean, Rogers relayed to Grant the need to move the two armed bateaus up the river to support his retreat. Arriving at a point opposite Rogers' position, the two boats opened fire with their swivel mounts. The swivel's canister rounds quickly cleared the area above and below the house of Indians. Rogers' men had barely departed through the back door escorting the women from the cellar when the Indians rushed the front of the house.

Supported by Grant on land and the two bateaus on the river, Rogers and his men were able to move back house by house. Despite being seriously pressed by Pontiac's warriors, Rogers and Grant were able to steadily disrupt the enemy and prevent any overwhelming concentrated attacks. After six hours of movement and combat, the final detachment composed of Rogers' Rangers closed on Fort Detroit at 0800. From that night on, Parent's Creek would be referred to as Bloody Run.

Other than a few small skirmishes beyond the security of Detroit, the garrison remained safely within the confines of the fort for the remainder of Pontiac's siege. Without artillery, all the Indians could do was maintain a noose around the fort, which they did until November. Finally, Pontiac realized his cause was lost with the receipt of two bad pieces of news. The first piece of bad news was word that a strong British force was closing on Detroit from Niagara. The second, and more damaging, piece of information received on 21 October was the crushing news that the French had signed the Peace of Paris, which officially ended the Seven Years' War. Knowing that he could no longer expect any assistance from the French, Pontiac withdrew his warriors from around Detroit and retreated to Maumee.

With the siege over, Gladwyn, no longer having a need for so many soldiers, reduced the size of his garrison and redeployed two hundred men under the command of Major Rogers, including his Rangers, to Niagara. Rogers and his Rangers remained at Niagara throughout the winter and were disbanded again that following spring.

CHAPTER 11

The American Revolution:
The Queen's & King's Rangers

I only regret that I have but one life to lose for my country.

Nathan Hale

At the onset of the American Revolution, it was not known for whom Rogers would fight. As it would turn out, Rogers' loyalties lay with the Crown and against his fellow countrymen. In the end, the venerated *icon* of the United States Army Rangers was a Tory who fought against the establishment of the United States as an independent nation!

At the start of the Revolution, Rogers petitioned King George III for the rank of lieutenant colonel and command of a Provincial corps. The Crown rejected Rogers as the King bestowed the rank and command on Joseph Gorham, instead. Attempts by Rogers to obtain a commission in the new American Continental Army were equally rebuffed by a suspicious General George Washington, who was not convinced of the Ranger's loyalty.

In July 1776, Rogers made his way to General Howe, encamped with his newly arrived army on Staten Island. Joyously received by Howe and having had the King's faith restored in him, Rogers was commissioned the rank of lieutenant-colonel-commandant and empowered to raise a battalion of Rangers. After eleven years of lying dormant, Rogers' Rangers lived again.

The nucleus of this new Ranger corps was recruited in August when the remnants of the Queen's Royal Rangers, a corps from Virginia, were renamed Rogers' Queen's Rangers. It would just so happen that Rogers newly formed Rangers would play a significant part in the capture and execution of one of this nation's greatest American heroes. As the Rangers formed and trained near Huntington, detachments of Rogers' Queen's Rangers would conduct reconnaissances with the H.M.S. *Halifax* along the western shore of Long Island. During one such scout, a detachment landed near Flushing Bay on 21 September and encountered Nathan Hale in civilian attire preparing to return to the mainland with notes and maps on Howe's army. Taken to the British headquarters at Beekman's Mansion by Rogers himself, Hale identified who he was and confessed to his mission. Without a trial, American patriot was led to the gallows at 1100 the next day, 22 September 1776, where he met his destiny.

Shortly following this infamous encounter, Rogers and his force of four hundred Rangers were deployed with Howe's army to pursue Washington and the Continental Army, which had been forced from the Brooklyn Heights of New York to White Plains. Landing approximately ten miles up the East River on 12 October, Rogers and his men were assigned the task of shielding the eastern wing of Howe's army during its advance a week later.

Ordered the evening of 20 October to move three miles ahead of the British lines and secure the stores located in the town of Mamaroneck, the Queen's Rangers attacked at sunrise, driving off the defending militia companies and capturing a large stockpile of Continental provisions. Later that day, Rogers positioned his battalion on the smooth Portion of Heathcote's Hill and posted his sentinels at dusk along the passes and roads in the direction of Washington's army, the lines of which were only ten miles away. Considering the avenues of approach into his camp from the direction of the British Army of negligible concern, Rogers left them lightly guarded.

As his men settled in for the night, Rogers was not aware that local patriots had reported the exact, location of his battalion and sentries to the nearest American general, Lord Sterling. Seizing upon the opportunity, Sterling dispatched his crack Delaware Regiment led by Colonel Haslet and a detachment of 150 men from the First and Third Virginians under the command of Major Greene to surprise Rogers. Overall command was Haslet's and he had 750 men to accomplish the task.

Led by guides, Haslet and his men marched in silence from White Plains to Mamaroneck. Moving cross-country with guides removing obstacles along the way that would create noise, the Americans searched for the first of Rogers' sentries, a young Indian, around 0400. With some difficulty in the darkness, they finally located the lone sentry and a group of men pounced on him. Unfortunately for the young sentry, he put up such a good fight, the Americans felt compelled to kill him to keep him quiet.

Having approached from Rogers' least defended side, the way was now open as the American force silently moved in for the eagerly anticipated kill. As usual, though, lady luck was smiling on Rogers as she had so often done in the past during the French and Indian War. Having made a meticulous inspection of his sentries some time after 2100 the evening prior, Rogers had grown concerned about the lack of sentries on his exposed southwestern side. With his sixth sense telling him that a daring force could create problems if it knew of this weakness, Rogers had ordered one of his company commanders, Captain Eagles, to take up a position with sixty Rangers as an advance guard between the rest of the battalion and the lone Indian sentry. Satisfied with the increased security, Rogers retired for some sleep.

Advancing quietly toward Rogers' bivouac site, the Americans' advance column led by Major Greene stumbled on the Ranger company, all of whom, amazingly, were asleep! With both units equally surprised by the unexpected encounter, the American command was first to seize the initiative and demanded an instant surrender. While some of the British Rangers moved to do so, the remainder resisted, putting up a stiff fight.

Hearing the commotion from behind Greene, Haslet moved forward with the remainder of the American force, completing the encirclement of Eagles' small command. Facing total annihilation, the resourcefulness of the Ranger commander came to the forefront. With Rangers and Greene's Virginians intermixed and mostly un-uniformed, Eagles began to act and sound like an American, shouting, "Surrender you Tory dogs!" Quickly picking up on their commander's cue, the Rangers began to heap abusive and disparaging remarks on themselves also. To further confuse the Americans, Rangers began grappling with fellow Rangers. In the darkness and resulting confusion, nearly a third of Eagles' Rangers were able to escape the trap with this ruse.

By now, the din of battle had roused Rogers and his battalion. Quietly in the darkness, the Queen's Rangers formed their line of battle. Having gathered what prisoners and arms they could, Haslet re-formed his men and continued to advance up Heathcote's Hill. Ordering his men to hold their fire until the American force was within range, Rogers finally ordered "Fire!" and a well-directed volley checked Haslet's advance. Believing they were facing a much superior force than they actually were, Haslet elected to immediately withdraw back to Sterling's position with his twenty-eight Ranger prisoners, leaving Rogers in control of the field of battle. Additional Ranger losses apart from those captured were twenty killed and nine wounded. Haslet stated his losses at four killed and fifteen wounded, including Major Greene. The next morning, Howe advanced General Agnew's Sixth Brigade up to support Rogers' exposed position.

As was customary, Rogers did not take his previous evening's defeat lightly and sought retribution with the execution of a raid the following day. In a bold and audacious move, he and a detachment of his Rangers penetrated colonial positions to Bedford, Connecticut, and were able to return with eight Royal Navy officers and men who had been held prisoner by the Americans.

The remainder of 1776 closed out quickly for the Queen's Rangers. Rogers was attached to General Knyphausen's command to participate in the capture of Fort Washington. Three days later, one hundred Rangers were detached from Knyphausen and marched with Brigadier General Charles Marquis Cornwallis' detachment in pursuit of Washington and his Continental Army. Detained for a short time at Hackensack Bridge by an American rear guard action, Cornwallis and the Rangers were finally ordered by Howe to give up the pursuit in the vicinity of Trenton.

After the chase, Rogers and his men settled into winter quarters at Fort Independence, New York, as part of Knyphausen's division. For the garrison, all was quiet until the morning of 18 January 1777, when an American force of 2,500 men under the command of General Wooster appeared before the gates of the fort, demanding its surrender. Offering lenient terms to the Hessians but not guaranteeing the same for Rogers' Queen's Rangers and the New York Loyalist companies, Wooster's efforts were met with a brisk cannonade, which was promptly returned. The battery fires continued for some time until Wooster retired to Courtland's House where he established his headquarters.

Rogers advanced from the fort with two of the companies and secured a large house that stood before the fort. On the evening of the 23rd, a strong detachment of American soldiers deployed to attack this advance post. Aware of the effort, Rogers turned the tables on the attackers. Waiting until their approach was close, he and his men sallied forth and completely routed the American attackers, who had believed the enemy number was significantly less than that which it turned out to be. Killing several of the Americans, Rogers returned to the house with seven prisoners.

Despite the success of Rogers and his unit, this action would prove to be the last for Rogers' Queen's Rangers. Later that month, Colonel Alexander Innes, the newly appointed Inspector-General of the Provincial forces, conducted an inspection of the Queen's Rangers and was disturbed with what he found. His report to General Howe noted that Rogers had abused his authority and the confidence given him by the Crown by issuing warrants to "improper persons as inferior officers" and by recruiting Indians, mulattos, Negroes, sailors, and rebel prisoners "to the disgrace and ruin of the Provincial service."

In defense of Rogers, the composition of his Rangers was no different from that of his corps during the French and Indian War. He was, in essence, an equal opportunity employer who quite simply recruited, for the most part, the best soldier he could find, regardless of social status. Unfortunately for Rogers, a clique of resentful British officers, many of whom greatly desired command of the Queen's Rangers because of its far-reaching fame, were able to use this 'mixed' composition to their advantage.

Empowered by Howe to discharge those who had been improperly commissioned or enlisted, Innes proceeded to do just that. This action proved to be too much for Rogers. Already frustrated with the conspiracy against him by his fellow officers and the loathing of his rank as a captain in the Regular Army, Rogers relinquished command of the Queen's Rangers and proceeded to seek advancement from Governor-General Haldimand in Canada.

Rogers' efforts to raise a corps of Rangers in Canada under the auspices of the governor-general were not well received. Haldimand denied Rogers' petition to raise a corps of Rangers under the pretext that other similar corps had precedence in Canada. On 1 May, Howe's successor, Sir Henry Clinton, authorized Rogers' raising of two battalions, one of which was to be designated the King's Rangers. Later, informing the Crown that he had recruited a total of six hundred men, Rogers was awarded his commission as a lieutenant colonel, commandant of both battalions. Rogers then appointed his brother as major of the first battalion, designated as the King's Rangers.

Rogers had a truly major problem, though, for, while he had informed Haldimand that he had seven hundred Rangers in the vicinity by this time, he only had, in reality, a total of forty men raised. Pressed by Haldimand to enjoin with his command, Rogers realized that a significant uproar would result when his deception was exposed.

Rogers' world was beginning to crash down about him as he departed in March for Penobscot. Despite his overwhelming professional success, Rogers' personal life had seen a number of low moments. Repeated indiscretions had left him without family, friends, and fortune. Creditors were petitioning Haldimand for the collection of Rogers' debts and outstanding accounts. Additionally, having been somewhat suspicious of Rogers' activities and hesitancy to join with his unit, Haldimand had queried the Penobscot commander, Brigadier Maclean, about the newly recruited Ranger status. Haldimand's anger erupted upon hearing the truth that there were only forty Rangers recruited.

Realizing that his deceit was soon to be disclosed, Rogers had immediately set sail upon his arrival at Penobscot for Halifax. Remaining in Halifax until the end of the War for Independence, and thus safely out of Haldimand's providence, he sailed the Atlantic to London, where he remained for the rest of his life. Subsisting off the half pay provided by his retired captain of the British Army status, Robert Rogers, the quintessential and consummate Ranger warrior, died at the age of sixty-three on 18 May 1795 and was buried at St. Mary, Newington, in the southern part of London.

Despite Robert Rogers' absence, the corps that Rogers had been warranted to raise, slowly took form as Rogers' brother, Major James Rogers, took up the task. Having been assured by Haldimand that his brother's "extraordinary conduct" would not prejudice his career, James Rogers established his headquarters on the Richelieu River at St. John's to recruit his battalion. Though authorized six hundred men organized into ten companies of sixty men each, the battalion was never able to muster more than 183 men assigned to four companies.

Throughout the remainder of the war, the King's Rangers served principally as a garrison battalion within Haldiman's area of operation. The only major exception to their garrison activities occurred in October 1780, when a company of King's Rangers serving as part of a two-hundred-man expedition were dispatched by Haldimand to destroy threatening American forts that had been established at the head of Lake George and along the route from the Hudson River to Lake Champlain.

Conducting some raids along the Hudson as they marched, the force moved against Fort Anne and Fort George. On 8 October, the King's Rangers company advanced boldly against the rebuilt Fort Anne on Wood Creek. Arriving at the fort on the 10th, the Rangers surrounded it, received the surrender of its seventy-five-man garrison, and then burned it to the ground.

Rejoining a smaller detachment that had split to conduct a raid on the mills and barracks at Saratoga, the Rangers and the expedition's force advanced against Fort George. Having moved to within a mile and a half of the fort, the expedition was stumbled upon by two men passing on a road who were able to escape and notify the fort's garrison. Believing the enemy force was a small Indian scouting party, Fort George dispatched a fifty-man detachment to deal with it.

The advance guard Indians initiated the fight against the detachment that was over within half an hour when the King's Rangers and the Regulars arrived in support. Of the fifty-man force, twenty-three were killed and seven taken prisoner. British losses were one Ranger and one Regular killed. Continuing their advance on the fort, it did not take much to convince the remaining forty-six men in the garrison to surrender. With the destruction of the fort, the expedition returned to St. John's.

In the spring of 1781, the King's Rangers were involved in one final expedition. As part of an expedition to serve as a decoy for the more important British expedition of Major Ross from Oswego, the Rangers advanced up Lake Champlain to the Hudson under the command of St. Leger, the commandant of St. John's. One party of Rangers under the command of Captain John Myers was detached for a quick foray in the Mohawk Valley to Ballstown. Myers and his men returned to St. John's on 8 July, the last major excursion for the once vaunted Rogers' Rangers. For the remainder of the war, the Rangers found themselves relatively inactive — with only a few, select individuals detailed to serve as spies.

On 24 December 1783, the King's Rangers battalions were disbanded. Though the war was over, the adventurer's spirit was still carried by many of the Rangers. With Major James Rogers, his wife, and his children, over two hundred of Rangers joined to march into the Canadian wilderness in quest of a new home. The majority of men who accompanied James Rogers settled on the shores of the Bay of Quinte, in the township of Fredericksburg. They were a courageous and adventurous group of men to the end.

CHAPTER 12

The American Revolution:
Francis Marion — the "Swamp Fox"

History will record his worth, and rising generations embalm his memory, as one
of the most distinguished Patriots and Heroes of the American Revolution.

Eulogy written on Francis Marion's tombstone

The American revolutionaries were not without their Rangers, either. On the brink of war, the Continental Congress passed a resolution on 14 June 1775, on what is known as Flag Day, that "six companies of expert riflemen be immediately raised in Pennsylvania, two in Maryland, and two in Virginia." From these beginnings of the Continental Army, a group of expert riflemen composed of hardy frontiersmen were formed in 1777 into an organization George Washington referred to as The Corps of Rangers. Commanded by Dan Morgan, this Ranger force was singled out by British General John Burgoyne, the commander of British forces intent on isolating the New England colonies, as "the most famous corps of the Continental Army, all of them crack shots."

Given command of a company of Virginia riflemen in 1775, Morgan and his company joined Colonel Benedict Arnold as part of an 1,100-man force on a secret expedition to Quebec. Departing Cambridge on 12 September 1775, the expedition made an amazing march through the frozen Maine wilderness. Losing their bateaus and narrowly escaping destruction in river rapids, the expedition arrived 8 November on the St. Lawrence opposite Quebec, hungry, cold, and fatigued. Only six hundred men remained of the original force, the remainder having died or been forced to return because of illness or injury.

137

Augmented with an additional three hundred soldiers deployed from Montreal and commanded by General Montgomery, the expedition attacked the city and its 1,800-man garrison on 31 December under the cover of a heavy snowstorm. The attack was an American disaster with Montgomery killed in the initial assault. Though wounded, himself, command passed to Arnold, who bravely carried the first defensive barrier but was eventually stopped in a bloody struggle at the second. With nearly one hundred dead or wounded and another three hundred more captured, to include Morgan, the Americans withdrew. Arnold and the expedition maintained a siege for the next five months before withdrawing upon the arrival of a British fleet and an accompanying twelve thousand soldiers.

Morgan, in the meantime, was the prisoner of the military governor general, Guy Carleton. Following an attempted escape, Morgan was offered a colonelcy in the British service, which he indignantly rejected. Finally, nearly a half year later with the siege lifted, Morgan's petition for parole was accepted.

Upon his return and based upon his actions during the expedition, Morgan was appointed a colonel of the rifle regiment. Morgan's Corps of Rangers was coming to fruition. For the remainder of the war, the fame of Morgan and of his Rangers continued to grow as they deployed throughout the colonies engaging British forces.

One such engagement occurred on 7 October 1777 as the Continental Army closed in on Burgoyne and his 6,300-man army around Saratoga, New York. In the Battle of Bemis Heights, Morgan's corps routed the British light infantry as the Americans counterattacked against a desperate British assault. Morgan's riflemen we're credited with playing a significant role in the loss of over six hundred redcoats. Finding himself outnumbered over three to one, Burgoyne would finally surrender his army on 17 October.

Morgan would continue to fight in support of the American Revolution in a number of significant battles, including the battle at Cowpens, South Carolina, on 17 January 1781. An attack against Morgan and his "crack shots" by a British force of 1,100 men would result in a brilliant double envelopment that has been called by historians the "American Cannae." The British defeat was total with over 110 soldiers killed and 830 captured. Morgan's losses were placed at twelve killed and sixty-one wounded.

Though titled Rangers by Washington and a grateful American people, Morgan's Rangers were not, in essence, Rangers in the sense of the uniquely trained, motivated, and challenged soldier. When one considers those parameters, there truly was only one group of American revolutionaries who could be considered an excellent example of early American Ranger prowess. This highly successful group of Partisans was known as "Marion's Brigade."

Formed in 1780 as a result of the brutality of British General Cornwallis' severe measures, this unit was commanded by Brigadier General Francis Marion, considered by many to be one of the boldest and most dashing figures of the American Revolution. Taking refuge in forests and swamps, for which he earned the appellation the "Swamp Fox" from his enemies, Marion's brigade kept the British off-balance with quick movements that captured British troops, destroyed supplies, and disrupted lines of communications.

Most crucial was the fact that between 15 August 1780 and 8 September 1781, Marion and his men *alone* held eastern South Carolina from the British. Hiding in his lair on Peyre's Plantation or Snow's Island by day and stealthily emerging at night to strike around midnight, Marion and his men would wreak havoc on British units from White Marsh to Black Mingo before fading once again into the morasses of the Santee or Peedee Rivers. Immortalized in song and story, Francis Marion became a hero of the Revolution second only to the commander-in-chief and first President of the United States, George Washington.

Having fought with the Continental Army regiments of South Carolina since the start of the Revolution, Colonel Francis Marion found himself the most senior and respected officer in that state by the summer of 1780. Unfortunately, much of the Continental Army in that southern state had been severely mauled in the interim and Marion was basically a commander in name only. Aware that there was a group of Scotch-Irish militia in Williamsburg already armed and under the command of Major William James, Marion proposed that he assume command of this unit and conduct a boat-burning raid up the Santee, south of Camden. Approval was obtained from the Continental Army commander in the south, General Gates and, on 15 August, Marion and a small group of South Carolina officers and men rode out of the American army encampment and into American history.

Marion and his men arrived at the Williamsburg militia camp at Witherspoon's Ferry late afternoon of 17 August. Though short in stature, limping on a bad leg, and forty-eight years of age, Marion was met by an exhilarated Major James and his militiamen. Without hesitation, the militia readily accepted him as their commander, though he had no legal authority to command as an officer of the Continental Line without rank in the militia. Quickly acquainting himself with his men, Marion set about to carry out his orders from Gates by moving along the Santee in the proximity of Lenud, burning flatboats and destroying canoes as they moved north toward Camden.

The South Carolinian situation for the Continentals had reached its nadir. All major military units within the state had been routed or captured following a disastrous battle in the vicinity of Camden on 16 August between General Gates and Lord Cornwallis. The British occupied the state capital. There was no civil government in the state. In essence, South Carolina lay defenseless before the Crown. Despite the debacles, Marion would prove to be at his best when the odds seemed to be most desperate. Concealing the Camden disaster from his troops, he continued his mission of marching and burning, operating as an independent element.

The evening of 24 August found Marion and his men in bivouac at Nelson's Ferry when their scouts returned with a report that a group of 150 American prisoners under British escort were camped for the night in Thomas "Gamecock" Sumter's house at the Great Savannah. Rousing his men and moving during the early morning hours, Marion closed on the house as he prepared to initiate his first partisan action. Despite the fact that surprise was lost when one of his patrols stumbled upon a British sentinel who was able to fire a warning shot, Marion and his men were able to storm the building and capture twenty-two prisoners.

Though the 150 released prisoners were Continentals of the Maryland Line, only sixty-five were willing to obey Marion's commands or to join his efforts. The remaining eighty-five insisted, much to Marion's distaste, that they were still prisoners and should be allowed to continue on to Charleston. Gathering his prisoners and the Continentals who would follow, Marion departed and withdrew across the Lynches River at Witherspoon's Ferry. Sadly, of those Continentals who returned with Marion, all but three deserted. Overall, of the original 150 Maryland prisoners, only sixty of them would rejoin their corps.

The Marylanders were not the only troops to depart. Having crossed the Lynches, Marion found that most of his Williamsburg militia were also deserting back to their homes. This action would become a relative norm for Marion's command. Rallying to his call, his men would follow his commands to sally forth and engage the enemy. But, once that mission was accomplished, most would return to work and wait for Marion's next call to arms.

Still accompanied by some stalwart companions, to include Major James, Marion crossed the Peedee to Port Ferry where he waited for Colonel Peter Horry and his patrol, which Marion had deployed on an earlier mission. As he waited, Marion wrote his official report and had it delivered to General Gates at Hillsboro, North Carolina, where he was encamped with what remained of his shattered army.

On 9 September, Gates reported to the Continental Congress of Marion's successful actions. Considered by many to have been a brilliant exploit, the news of Marion's efforts did much to cheer the flagging spirits of a war-weary nation. An extract of Gates' letter about Marion's exploits was published in the leading Whig newspapers in the country and for the first time the name of Francis Marion was known to all. Unfortunately, some things never change no matter what the time period. His name had been misspelled "Marien."

The region in which Marion had stopped was relatively secure, for it contained a high population of fervent Whigs. But close by, on Catfish Creek along the Little Peedee, were communities still loyal to the King of England. They had formed a regiment of Loyalists under the command of Major Micajah Ganey with Captain Jesse Barefield as his executive officer. The word of Marion's encampment at Port Ferry spread quickly and Ganey called out his loyalist militia to attack. Mustering 250 men, he moved on 4 September with an advance guard of forty-five horsemen while Barefield marched with the remaining infantry.

Marion was not one to be caught by surprise, though. With scouts out, he quickly learned of the Tory's muster and set about to meet their advance. Marion's main problem, however, was the fact he only had fifty-two men with him. Formulating a plan, Marion roused his men early in the morning on 4 September. Mounted, he and his men rode from their bivouac trailing a group of handpicked men who were serving as an advance guard under the command of Major James.

Two hours later, one of James' scouts returned with word that a troop of armed horsemen had blocked the road they were traveling. James, without hesitation or further orders, spurred his horse and led a charge straight toward the blocking horsemen. Recognizing Ganey, James dashed toward him, sword flashing high. Caught off guard by the totally unexpected assault, Ganey's men turned to flee, scattering in every direction. Noting that he now stood alone, Ganey elected to follow the actions of his men and flee also.

A half-mile chase ensued, major chasing major. Pulling up to a group of his men, Ganey turned to face James as he came bearing down. Realizing he had outraced his men, James never hesitated. Deceptively shouting as though his men were right behind him, James wheeled into the group of Tories. Never looking back, the Loyalists once again turned and fled into the marshes of Little Peedee Swamp.

Amazingly, none of the loyalists considered warning Barefield and his advancing infantry of Marion's presence in the area. Informed by his prisoners that Barefield was only three miles away, Marion raced off to engage them ten minutes later. Barefield was no amateur, though, for he had learned many of his tactics from Marion, himself. Quickly forming a line of battle, the Loyalists held their ground against the advancing cavalry. Faced with two hundred muskets at the ready, Marion signaled a halt to his frontal assault and withdrew.

Out of sight, the Colonial left the road and began to circle back. Concealing his men in a screen of dense scrub pines and undergrowth, he waited. He did not have to wait for long. Encouraged by their apparent success, Barefield and his men had thrown caution to the wind and were excitedly and quickly moving down the road. Marion led the charge from the brush as he and his fifty men burst forth.

Maintaining some poise, Barefield's men delivered one volley that wounded three of Marion's men and killed two of his horses. Unable to reload and hard-pressed by the saber-wielding and pistol-firing mounted rebels, the dismounted infantry Loyalists broke ranks, making for the woods and the Little Peedee Swamp beyond with Marion's men in pursuit. With the enemy broken, Marion reassembled his men and gathered the wounded, both his and Barefield's. He proceeded to march with them and his prisoners back to Port Ferry, much satisfied with the victory attained.

Throughout the next day, sixty more volunteers rode into camp to join Marion as he prepared for what he anticipated would be the inevitable British attack. Constructing a small redoubt built of logs and clay across the enemy's main supply route on the eastern bank of the Peedee, Marion emplaced two small cannon for supporting fires. On 28 August, Lord Cornwallis ordered Major Wemyss and his 63rd Regiment to march to Kingstree to sweep the countryside clear of rebels from there to Peedee. Major James Moncrief and his Royal Fusilier Regiment, the 7th, were ordered to fortify Georgetown. Loyalist militias in the area were ordered to support their operations.

Wemyss' unit was weak from malaria and having to move 150 miles would not be an easy feat for the ground infantry. To solve his transportation problem, Wemyss deceived the local Whigs of High Hills into attending a meeting while his men scoured the neighborhood, rounding up in their absence the Whigs' horses. Enraged by such actions, many of the Whigs would actively join with Marion against the British in the days to follow.

With his men now mounted, Wemyss deployed on 5 September. Marion had anticipated this deployment, though. On 7 September, he had Major James reconnoiter Kingstree with a picked squad of men. Leaving fifty men behind to guard his rear and the camp, Marion rode with the remaining one hundred men across the Peedee to Indiantown.

Later that evening, James and his men hid along the high road into Kingstree in a deep thicket. It was not long before Wemyss and his tired men filed past. Allowing the main body to pass, James and his men sprang their ambush on the very last horseman of the rear guard. Weary and taken totally by surprise, the rider was captured, bound, and dragged off without a shot being fired. A half hour before daybreak, the prisoner was brought before Marion.

Questioning the prisoner, Marion quickly learned that two hundred infantry already occupied Kingstree with Wemyss' command to add another two hundred to the total. With Moncrief in Georgetown and the militia mustered, Marion now found that the eight hundred Regulars and Loyalist militia in the area would seriously outnumber his command of one hundred men. Deeming it foolhardy to engage such a force, Marion detached' a ten man force to remain behind and gather intelligence while he withdrew during the early morning hours with the remainder back across the Peedee to his redoubt.

During the afternoon, his scouts informed Marion that Wemyss had crossed the Peedee at Yauhannah and was moving to position himself behind Marion's little fort. Moncrief had also dispatched a small force across the Peedee to approach from the south. Additional militia were being mustered. The total force now facing Marion was between 1,000 and 1,500 men. Even worse was the fact that Marion was now down to sixty men. Dismantling his fort, he chose to fight another day. Leaving their two spiked field pieces behind in a swamp, Marion and his men rode virtually nonstop for approximately eighteen hours across gray sand hills, warn causeways, and desolate swamps.

Forty miles later, Marion encamped in the sympathetic Whig settlement of Amis' Mill on Drowning Creek. Concerned for the security of the civilian population left behind, Marion dispatched Major James and a few volunteers to return to observe how the redcoats were treating their wives and families. With James gone, Marion continued his retreat in the direction of Cape Fear to link up with General William Harrington's corps of North Carolinians in the vicinity of Cross Creek.

Ten days later, James rejoined Marion, who was concealed with his small force in the Great White Marsh. The news James brought was not good, for the British had pillaged and torched Williamsburg, killing and destroying in a swath of destruction from Cheraw to Georgetown. To prevent Marion's return, Moncrief had constructed and manned a redoubt in Georgetown with Colonel Cassel's militia. To secure Williamsburg, Moncrief posted the fifty militia men of Colonel Wigfall's command near Black River Church while Colonel Ball and his even smaller command of forty-six men were garrisoned at Shepherd's Ferry on Black Mingo River.

Lord Cornwallis was greatly concerned with this deployment, believing they were too exposed. His concern would prove to be a valid one. The afternoon of 24 September, Marion led his men out of the Great White Marsh to arrive in Kingston later that evening to bivouac. Striking camp before dawn the next morning, the group made their way into the Little Peedee Swamp. Three miles later, they arrived at the Little Peedee River. With no alternative other than swimming across it on their horses, Marion led the way by plunging into the river, despite his inability to swim and his great fear of water.

Reaching the far shore, the rebel militia continued on their way, reaching Port Ferry late on the afternoon of 28 September. Passing through their old redoubt, Marion crossed the Peedee River on flatboats and continued to Witherspoon's Ferry, crossing the Lynches River in the evening twilight. Linking up with some forward scouts, Marion was informed that a force of Loyalist militia under the command of Colonel Ball was garrisoned at Shepherd's Ferry under very light security.

Despite the fact that he and his men had crossed three rivers and ridden thirty miles since dawn, Marion did not hesitate. Colonel Ball's camp was west of Black Mingo Creek, approximately twelve miles distant. Arriving around midnight, Marion's movement was compromised as he crossed an old, poorly maintained causeway. As the planks rumbled and the noise echoed along the Mingo, a sentinel in Ball's camp fired his musket in alarm.

Without hesitation, Marion spurred his horse forward. Just short of the Red House Tavern, which was serving as Ball's encampment, Marion dismounted a large percentage of his force in an infantry frontal assault with a supporting element on the right flank. To the left, he deployed his small cavalry element, while he followed the attack with a small reserve.

Warned by his sentry's shot, Ball quickly roused his men and deployed them into a field west of the tavern. In the distance, he could hear Marion's horses and their deployment. The supporting attack advanced first. Ball waited until they were thirty yards away before giving the command to fire. The British volley lit up the night and wreaked havoc upon Marion's advancing men, striking a number of them. Disheartened, the supporting attack began to withdraw in disorder.

Major James' son, Captain James, rallied and steadied the men, forestalling their retreat. Slowly, they began to advance, firing at every shadow they saw. As they did so, the frontal assault advanced against Ball's right flank. Caught between the two, Ball's men began to waver. As the screams and cries of their dying and wounded comrades increased around them, Ball's men began to discard their empty weapons and scatter for the safety of the Black Mingo Swamp.

The total time of battle was fifteen minutes. Of forty-six engaged, Ball's casualties were three dead and thirteen wounded or prisoners. Several of those wounded would die. Marion suffered two dead and eight wounded. Having abandoned their encampment, Ball and his men left behind their guns, ammunition, baggage, and horses. Marion claimed Ball's spirited horse, as well as bridle and saddle. Renamed Ball, the captured sorrel would serve as Marion's steed throughout his South Carolina campaign. Of his prisoners, Marion proved to be so compelling that he was able to convince five of them to renounce the King, swear allegiance to the United States, and to join his men.

Tired, Marion's men began to press for some time with their families. Praising their fortitude, gallantry, and bravery, he bade them, "Go to your families." Having accomplished his primary mission of delivering retribution, Marion, five of his officers, and twelve other men made their way back twenty-six miles to Amis' Mill on Drowning Creek.

On 11 October, Gates forwarded a letter to Marion congratulating him on his successes and providing encouragement to continue waging his partisan warfare. Upon receipt of this letter in Port Ferry, Marion issued a call for his militia to muster. Much to his consternation, the troops did not assemble as rapidly as he expected. The war had passed Williamsburg by and it was no longer the major focus of the area. Despondent and discouraged, Marion gathered his officers to inform them that he would abandon the state's low country and rejoin General Gates. Marion's closest friend in the council, Major Hugh Horry, begged and cajoled him to remain in South Carolina.

Over the next few days, the militia began to stagger into camp and, as they did, Marion's discouragement began to fade. As his unit began to form, he dispatched five- to ten-man patrols in every direction to depart at sunrise and return by sunset. On 24 October, a patrol returned from upper Williamsburg with a report that Marion found most interesting. To augment the British line, Loyalist militia from High Hills had been mustered. Unprepared and untrained, this militia was encamped on a field bordering the Tearcoat Swamp under the command of Colonel Tynes.

Recognizing the opportunity, Marion was able to quickly muster 150 men. Setting off for Kingstree, he deceptively planted rumors that he was riding toward McCallum's Ferry to attack the militia there. Arriving at Kingston on the morning of 25 October, he moved toward Salem and forded the Black River. Coming upon the Tearcoat Stream, Marion's scouts soon located Tynes' men camped in an overgrown field, with many of the command fast asleep and the remainder relaxing around campfires.

Marion divided his 150-man force into three elements that would hit the British camp from the left and right flanks as he led the frontal assault. At midnight, they attacked. Total surprise was achieved and the rout of the two hundred Loyalists was complete. Tynes disappeared as three of his men were killed, fourteen wounded, and twenty-three taken prisoner, many of whom would join Marion's ranks. Eighty horses, their equipment, and an equal number of muskets were captured. Marion's losses were two horses killed. Tynes would be captured a few days later in the hills of Santee by a detachment of men sent out by Marion.

Lieutenant Colonel Banastre Tarleton and his Green Dragoon were directed by Cornwallis to reestablish order in the region. Tarleton, whose motto was "Swift, Vigilant, and Bold," was one of the England's best and was always willing to inflict pain and suffering on the King's enemies. The Colonel and his horsemen departed Brierley's Ferry on the Broad River on 3 November and made Camden that afternoon to be informed that Marion and his men were assembled at Singleton's on the Wateree River. Spurred on by Cornwallis' letter urging him to "get at Mr. Marion," Tarleton began to move along the Santee Road on the 5th.

Marion and four hundred of his horsemen were also moving along the Santee Road, planning to disrupt and delay the flow of supplies. Late on the evening of 5 November, Marion bivouacked ten miles north of Nelson's Ferry on Jack's Creek. A Whig informed Tarleton of Marion's campsite and he immediately set out for battle. As he advanced, Tarleton spread false rumors that he was returning to Camden while he dispatched patrols in an attempt to entice Marion into an ambush.

By the evening of 7 November, the British dragoons had reached the plantation of the late Brigadier General Richard Richardson where they encamped with two cannons and men at the ready. Marion was aware of the enemy's encampment but not aware of who the enemy was or their size. Quietly moving into the area in anticipation of launching a surprise attack on the bivouac site, Marion was warned by Richardson's son of the ambush. Realizing that to continue with his plans against such a large, well-trained, and waiting force would prove to be rather disastrous, Marion turned his corps around with little additional thought and led his men by Woodyard Swamp and across Richbourg's Mill Dam on Jack's Creek, where they finally halted for a rest.

During their flight, Marion's men accidentally allowed a Tory prisoner to escape. The prisoner was brought to Tarleton just prior to dawn the next morning. Learning of Marion's movements, Tarleton immediately called his men to arms and galloped off to Richbourg's Mill Dam. Marion was not to be so easily caught, though, for he had also remounted his men and departed before dawn that day.

Those men most familiar with the terrain were placed in the van to lead the formation. Major James and a select group of men trailed the force as a rear guard. At a gallop, Marion's steed Ball set the pace as they raced to the head of Jack's Creek and then down to the Pocotaligo River. For hours, the group galloped through swamps, pine woods, and harvested fields. Finally reaching familiar territory along Black River, Marion slowed the pace and came to rest his men and their mounts at Benbow's Ferry.

Tarleton pursued Marion for over seven hours and twenty-six miles of tough terrain. Realizing the futility of continuing, Tarleton called a halt to the pursuit before the roadless bog of Ox Swamp, approximately twenty-three miles above Kingstree. Turning to head back and deciding to seek battle elsewhere, Tarleton called out to his men "Come, my boys! Let us go back, and we will find the Gamecock [Sumter]. But as for this damned old fox, the devil himself could not catch him!" Little did Tarleton realize at the time that this moniker would be seized upon as the title of a soon to be legend, the "Swamp Fox."

Following Tarleton's departure, Marion moved to Murry's and Nelson's Ferry, hoping to intercept some of the British boats making their way to and from Camden. Unable to seize any of the shipping, Marion advanced against Georgetown intending to rout its fifty-soldier garrison and to take control of the town. The odds turned out to be just a bit greater than Marion had anticipated, though, for Captain Barefield and two hundred of his Tories had arrived the evening prior.

Instead of finding a town ripe for the taking, Marion found a British force moving against him and his men as they arrived at the outskirts of town. The engagement was brief, however, with the British sustaining three dead and twelve men captured. The remainder of the Tory force retreated back to the safety of the town. Marion's losses were one officer and private killed, three wounded. Unfortunately for Marion, the dead officer was his nephew, Lieutenant Gabriel Marion.

Cornwallis was greatly concerned with Marion's growing strength. Under the command of Major Robert McLeroth, a force of 275 men and two three-pound cannons were assembled to seize the Whig stronghold of Kingstree. Arriving at the village green on the evening of 20 November, McLeroth waited in anticipation of the arrival of Marion and his men. A Tory village messenger was dispatched to the Black Mingo with word of the British force's arrival.

Electing to wait rather than to attack, Marion mustered his militia and reestablished his base camp twenty-six miles away on a bluff overlooking the Peedee. From there, Marion corresponded with Brigadier General Harrington, the senior militia officer in South Carolina — though he was North Carolinian by birth — headquartered in Cheraw. Marion's letter requested additional cavalry support to drive out the invaders, knowing full well that the request would not be approved.

To General Gates he wrote another letter, detailing the events that had recently occurred and the resources he would need if he were to continue his partisan-style campaign. More importantly, though, Marion closed his correspondence with the question that haunted him the most. Where was the American Army? He was losing men and local support because many believed there was no army to assist them. Marion and the people of his region needed some assurance, some hope.

While Marion wrote, his reputation was at work in Kingstree, where McLeroth grew increasingly paranoid about the Swamp Fox's disappearance. Throughout the day and long into the night of the 21st, the Major anxiously awaited the shot that would signal the start of a furious charge against his position. Unable to stand the pressure any longer, McLeroth retreated before dawn of the next morning, fleeing toward the Santee.

Unfortunately for Marion, this "victory" would prove to be exceptionally damaging to his unit. The situation was dire. His men had not been paid in months. They had no uniforms, no ammunition or food. They had little if any recognition from the government of South Carolina, the American Army, or the Continental Congress. Their homes and crops had been destroyed. And now the British had withdrawn from Kingstree. With the British gone from that town, they felt their thankless task had been accomplished. Sad and despondent, Marion watched his militia disband as individuals and small groups departed. With nothing left other than a tiny band of loyal followers, Marion crossed the Peedee for the swamps of Britton's Neck.

Marion and his small group moved to a high, dry, and inaccessible hiding place across the Peedee called Snow's Island. On this island was the plantation of William Goddard, an ardent Whig who was more than willing to support the cause of the revolution by turning over to Marion his cabin, barn, and crops. Marion found Snow's Island to be a perfect base for his operations—should he be able to raise his regiment again, that was.

The island was a low ridge five miles long and two miles wide encircled by rivers, creeks, lakes, and swamps. Pitching camp near Goddard's cabin, Marion and his men quickly constructed crude lean-to huts. Bins were erected to store supplies and the barn was reinforced to serve as a prison for captives. For security, all boats were drawn onto the island's shores with those not being needed, destroyed. Trees were felled into fords to serve as obstacles and planks were removed from causeways and bridges. A small redoubt was constructed on the lower side of Dunham's Bluff on the neck side of the Peedee and garrisoned with a guard from the Britton's Neck militia.

With a new burst of confidence, Marion once again sent out the call for the re-formation of his regiment. As volunteers arrived and his unit strength swelled, Marion dispatched patrols far and wide. From these scouts, he learned that Colonel Tynes had constructed a militia strongpoint on Upton Hill near the Wateree River in the High Hills. Garrisoned with fifty men and two cannons, the redoubt was named Fort Upton.

Spurred into action, Marion saddled his troops and advanced to reconnoiter Tynes' position at Fort Upton. A detachment of men was dispatched to reconnoiter the area. Stopping at the tavern of a well-known Loyalist, the commander, Lieutenant Colonel Peter Horry, questioned the owner while the owner's wife, unknown to Horry, was busy showing his troops a barrel of apple brandy. Before he knew it, Horry found that all his men were drunk. Realizing that his men were too intoxicated to continue on, Horry led them whooping and hollering, as a band of drunkards would, back to Witherspoon's Ferry where Marion was waiting. Embarrassed, Horry had to explain the farcical tale. Amused, Marion informed the crestfallen officer that he had done the right thing to retreat but to ensure to "keep a careful eye on the apple water next time."

Interestingly enough, the ruckus created by Horry's men ultimately resulted in a great deal of mission accomplishment. Having heard the drunk soldiers on their return to the ferry, the Loyalists along Black Mingo River had grown exceedingly frightened. This incident combined with the belief that Harrington was approaching their position with the American army resulted in all but twenty men deserting the fort's garrison. Tynes, believing the twenty men remaining too small a garrison, proceeded to desert them. His subsequent request to resign his commission was readily accepted.

In early December, recruits of the Royal Fusiliers were to be marched from Charleston to Winnsboro. Learning from his spies of this march, Marion sounded the muster and with seven hundred mounted men passed Nelson's Ferry by 12 December. Approximately twenty miles beyond the ferry, just above Halfway Swamp, Marion's force overtook the unprepared recruits as they straggled along under the command of Major McLeroth and members of the 64th Regiment.

The battle was immediately commenced as Marion's men drove in the British pickets. Engaging the rear guard with musketmen of his own, Marion wheeled the bulk of his force around the enemy flank and commenced a direct attack. Dragging as many recruits as they could with them, the veterans of the 64th retreated to a field enclosed by rail fences. From behind the fence, the British force was able to hold off the charging horsemen.

Withdrawing out of range, Marion waited. Under a white flag of truce, a British officer approached to commence arguing with Marion about the uncivilized nature of shooting pickets. Marion countered by maintaining that burning the houses of patriots was indefensible. Marion finally offered the British officer a solution to their standoff. "If Major McLeroth wishes to see mortal combat between teams of twenty men picked by each side, I will gratify him." McLeroth accepted the challenge.

The battleground selected by both parties was near an old oak tree that stood in the field. Marion slowly and deliberately handpicked each marksman. None refused his selection. The decision was made by Marion's men to fire at fifty feet. As they advanced toward the British twenty, who were formed on line, a British officer passed quickly along the enemy line. Before Marion's men could fire, the British had shouldered their arms and retreated.

The British major had only been stalling, waiting for help in the form of 140 mounted infantry to arrive. Tasked to escort the recruits, these mounted men had been contacted by one of McLeroth's couriers and apprised of the situation. Much to McLeroth's consternation, however, rather than advance forward and assist their beleaguered comrades, the mounted unit's commander, Captain Coffin, withdrew and took up a defensive position behind the Swift Creek. He would not join McLeroth until later the next day following the skirmish at Singleton's Mill.

Later that evening, McLeroth's troops lit large campfires as they burned the fence rails, danced, and sang. But it was all part of a deception. As midnight approached, they quieted down, pretending to get some rest. Noiselessly leaving their baggage and supplies behind, McLeroth and his men slipped out of the field and down the road to Single-ton's Mill.

Discovering the trick early that morning, Marion dispatched one hundred men under the command of Major Hugh Horry to get ahead of McLeroth and arrive at Singleton first. Early in the "race," Horry realized that he would not be able to overtake the British force in time. Consequently, he dispatched a squadron of men with the fastest horses under the command of Major James to secure the buildings.

James and his men swept up Singleton's Hill just as McLeroth's men were arriving at the bottom. Dismounting, the squadron secured the buildings and delivered a volley of fire into the approaching British. Then, amazingly, the partisans raced out of the buildings, jumped on their horses, and fled in all haste. In the midst of the fight, they had learned that the Singleton family was ill with smallpox!

While this amusing event was occurring, Marion had stopped at a local tavern to check on some of his wounded men. It was there, he found that McLeroth had a streak of humanity in him that most other British officers did not possess. Marion learned from the tavern owner that, during the skirmish around Halfway Swamp and Singleton's Mill, McLeroth had gathered the wounded from both sides and placed them comfortably in the tavern under the care of one of the Crown's own physicians. Polite and courteous, McLeroth had even paid for a fortnight's lodging for the wounded. Following his talk with the tavern owner, Marion remarked to Horry, "Well, I suppose I feel now very much as I should feel were I in pursuit of a brother to kill him."

Upon the return of his men from Singleton's Mill, many, upon learning of McLeroth's generosity toward their comrades, voiced the fact that they no longer had the desire to fight him. Realizing that it would be a lost cause to continue pursuit, Marion opted not to force the engagement any longer. As for McLeroth, he soon found himself relieved of command, in essence for being too humane and compassionate with the rebels.

On 22 December, Marion received a piece of correspondence from General Nathanael Greene, who had relieved Gates as the commander of the Continental Army of the South, that would do much to raise his spirits and lead him to believe that the struggle for liberty was still alive and victory in the South was still attainable. Greene acknowledged Marion's contribution to the revolution by stating his "services in the lower part of South Carolina, in awing the Tories and preventing the enemy from extending their limits, have been very important." Furthermore, Greene directed Marion to continue where he was and serve as his eyes and ears in the Charleston area.

Marion took his time returning to his lair on Snow's Island following his encounter around Singleton's Mill, stopping all traffic on Santee Road and River along the way. Major John Campbell and his 64th Regiment moved to engage, but he reported to his superiors that Marion was too secure at Nelson's Ferry and too large a force for him to successfully attack. On 24 December, Marion and his men rode back to the Santee and patrolled all Christmas Day down the long and winding road between Nelson's and Murry's Ferry. Later that day, Marion called in his patrols and returned to his hideaway at Snow's Island.

On 26 December, Lieutenant Colonel John Watson and His Majesty's 3rd Regiment of Guards marched to an area ten miles north of Nelson's Ferry where they constructed a formidable redoubt on Wright's Bluff overlooking Scott's Lake. This fort was complete with abatis, parapets, fosse, and gun ports for his two cannons. An eighty-foot Indian burial mound was in the center of the fortification on which he placed a firing position for his sharpshooters. Upon completion, the regimental commander vainly named it after himself, Fort Watson. Unknown to Lieutenant Colonel Watson, Fort Watson was in Francis Marion's future.

The month of December also found General Greene redeploying some of his forces throughout the Carolinas to interdict Cornwallis' lines of communications or to compel him to reposition. Realizing that it was critical to drive Marion and his regiment of militia from his left flank prior to dealing with Greene's deployments, Cornwallis ordered a campaign be initiated to do so. The King's American Regiment under the command of Lieutenant Colonel George Campbell was deployed to Georgetown while reinforcements were drawn from the north, to include Captain John Sanders and his Queen's Rangers, the unit originally formed at the start of the war by Robert Rogers, to assist.

With the deployments complete, the offensive commenced on the 28th. Campbell was ordered to move up the Peedee to secure Kingstree. Watson was directed to deploy a force from his fort to move against Marion, intending to push him into Campbell's force in the process. Unknown to them, Marion had already figured out what was about to transpire and, in anticipation, had begun his operation a day earlier.

On the evening of the 27th, Lieutenant Colonel Peter Horry had mustered a troop of horsemen to determine the enemy's strength in Georgetown. Riding through the night, they crossed the Black River at Potato Ferry and hid in ambush at The Camp. Later that morning, a carriage containing two ladies passed through the ambush site undisturbed. Unknown to Horry, it had initially been escorted by two officers of the Queen's Rangers who had turned back a short distance before to obtain a larger escort.

A while later, Horry and his men decided to obtain a late breakfast at the home of a well-known Whig. Entering, Horry was surprised to meet the two ladies who had passed through his ambush earlier that morning. Acting out a charade with the home's Whig owners in the presence of the two Tory ladies, Horry and his men repaired to the barn, where they obtained provisions for the men and their mounts. Just as his men were finishing their meal, shots were fired by Horry's posted sentries who hurriedly dashed into the barn with the two Ranger officers and a squad of mounted Queen's Rangers they had returned with for escort hard-pressed on their heels.

With his men mounted, Horry shouted "Charge!" and his cavalry surged with sabers flashing and pistols firing into the Rangers. Overwhelmed by the turn of events, the outnumbered British Rangers turned and fled down the lane, back to Georgetown, with Horry and his men in pursuit. At the outskirts of Georgetown, Major Ganey and his Tory militia, who had been mustered and deployed to the town earlier, rode forth to do battle.

As the two forces engaged, Ganey's men once again deserted him. During an attempt to get away, Ganey was ridden down and bayoneted by one of Horry's sergeants. Incredibly, Ganey would recover from these wounds and once again command his militia later in the war.

A bit of timely intelligence led to the final military operation of the year when Marion was informed by a Whig friend of an unguarded treasure located at Waccamaw Neck. The "treasure" was 150 bushels of salt, a very precious commodity worth over ten dollars in silver for every bushel. The British had intended to use the salt to cure sixty head of cattle they had collected but Marion had other plans for it. A detachment of men and wagons secured the salt and, with a bit of dramatic Robin Hood-type flair, he distributed it all to the families of Whig supporters.

At the start of the New Year, a detachment of forty men under Peter Horry was dispatched to collect boats and to drive off cattle on Waccamaw Neck. The patrol captured a slave from a nearby plantation and secured him per Horry's directive. Later that night, Captain Clarke, who knew the slave, released the prisoner. Unknown to Horry or his men, a detachment of sixty-five of the Queen's Rangers under the command of Colonel Campbell had been dispatched to Waccamaw Neck as a result of the salt heist in late December. At sunrise, the Rangers picked up the slave. Terrified, the slave betrayed the presence of Horry's command.

As the Rangers galloped to the camp's location, Horry and his men were moving forward with an advance guard of five men lead by Captain Clarke. Clarke and Campbell saw each other at the same time. Campbell blew a horn and ordered Clarke to stop. Clarke, on the other hand, believing he had stumbled on to a hunting party, told his men to hold their positions. Campbell and twenty of his men quickly secured Clarke as a prisoner before he even knew it. Not so foolish, Clarke's four companions had turned and run. Campbell treated the captain with courtesy and respect and took his parole, only to soon see Clarke escape into the wilds of Waccamaw Swamp.

Having been alerted by the sound of a scuffle ahead, Horry and the remainder of the detachment dashed forward, scattering the small group of Rangers. Having retained the ground, secured his prisoners, and believing himself the victor, Horry was surprised to see Campbell return with his entire command. Horry and his men quickly scattered before the superior-sized force. The engagement cost the Rangers three dead, two prisoners, and four horses lost. Horry and his men continued to live a charmed life, having suffered only one wounded and two dead horses.

In answer to one of Marion's prayers, General Greene was able to dispatch a force of colonial Regulars to assist him. Though numbering only 260 men, Lieutenant Colonel Henry Lee—the father of the future Confederate commander, Robert E. Lee—and his legion were considered by many, including the British army, the finest combat force in the American army.

Unfortunately for Lee, he encountered some difficulty in finding the Swamp Fox, who had been appointed by South Carolina Governor Rutledge on 30 December 1780 a brigadier in command of all the regiments eastward of Catawba, Wateree, and Santee. Lee's difficulty was coincidental for it just so happened that the green uniforms Lee and his men wore were nearly identical to those worn by Tarleton's Green Dragoon and the Queen's Rangers. Apprehensive, the local Whigs refused to divulge the location of Marion's base camp, thus causing Lee some serious delay.

Frustration had set in on the British in regard to Marion, and the decision was made by Cornwallis' replacement as field commander in South Carolina, Lord Francis Rawdon, to try and eradicate the pest once and for all. A double-pronged attack was planned with Lieutenant Colonel Watson marching down the Santee to attack Marion while Colonel Welbore

Ellis Doyle crossed the Lynches River to cut off the rebel's escape. On 5 March, Watson began his movement, marching from Fort Watson. Late that afternoon, he bivouacked south of Nelson's Ferry. Later that evening, one of Marion's scouts reconnoitered the camp and rode off to warn his brigadier.

Marion was located past Murry's Ferry. When brought word of Watson's deployment, he correctly realized that this was a strategic attempt by the British to drive him from the southern region of the state. Watson's Buffs were considered to be one of the finest regiments in the British army. Marion knew that an engagement with them would not be easy and he could expect no support from the American army. The only unit capable, Lee's Legion, had been recalled to the north to support Greene. As with all his previous battles, he was on his own with this fight.

Undaunted, the Swamp Fox ordered an immediate advance and moved to position himself at Wiboo Swamp. There, Marion waited, knowing that Watson would eventually appear. Soon, the British regiment marched into view. Both Watson and Marion rode out to face each other across a quarter-mile causeway spanning the mire and marsh of the swamp.

Watson did not take long to initiate the fight. Sending forth his Loyalist cavalry to cross the causeway, Marion met the charge with one of his own led by Peter Horry and his mounted men. Following a brief skirmish on the narrow land bridge, both sides withdrew. Advancing his main force as support, Marion again ordered Horry to charge. Undaunted, the British Regulars held their ground, unlimbered their field cannon, and repelled the attack.

As Horry withdrew, Watson's mounted Tory dragoons advanced right behind, successfully crossing the causeway. A countercharge of the remainder of Marion's cavalry pushed the dragoons back across the land bridge. With his cavalry defeated, Watson advanced his guards. Imposing and silent, highly disciplined and trained, impressive in their bright red uniforms, the guards led with bayonets that gleamed and sparkled on the ends of upraised muskets. Realizing that he had done enough and that his men would not be able to stand in the open ground against such a disciplined and highly trained force, Marion had his men remount and follow him, leaving the field of battle to Watson.

The morning following their initial engagement, Watson resumed his march down the Santee Road with Marion slowly backing away before him, remaining out of the range of the British artillery. That evening both sides encamped, though Marion did order his night patrols to take shots at Watson's sentinels.

Morning arrived and Watson again resumed his march with Marion leading. At Mount Hope Swamp, Marion had his men disassemble the bridge. A covering force of riflemen were swept aside by Watson's artillery, allowing Watson's guard to ford the stream unopposed. The cat and mouse advance continued on the far bank.

Crossing the road that led from Murry's Ferry to Kingstree, Watson continued to follow Marion toward Georgetown. Soon, though, just as Marion had expected, the guardsmen wheeled around and made their way back to the Kingstree intersection. Lower Bridge was only twelve miles away. To cross it would put Watson deep within the heartland of the Whig resistance. This was the decisive point of the campaign that required Marion to attack.

Seventy men, thirty of whom were sharpshooters, were dispatched to ride ahead to secure and hold the Lower Bridge under Major James. With knowledge of the land, James and his men were able to secure the bridge before the arrival of Watson's dragoons. Within minutes, the planks had been removed from the center of the bridge and the stringers burned on the east end. The sharpshooters were placed at the abutment where they had the clearest shot at the far end of the bridge while the remaining musketeers secured their flanks. Marion and his brigade soon arrived and forded the river. Pleased with James' deployment, Marion reinforced him with an additional company and moved to a reserve position to the rear and out of sight.

The east bank of the river was low, open, and swampy. The west bank was a high bluff with the roadway passing down through a ravine to the bridge. The distance from bank to bank was the perfect sharpshooter distance, fifty yards.

Realizing that he needed to clear the far bank first before his soldiers could safely enter the defile to cross the bridge, Watson emplaced his cannon. But the bluff was too high and the artillery canister just passed overhead of the defenders on the east bank when fired. An attempt to move the cannon and depress the muzzles led to the crews being run off by the highly accurate fire of the sharpshooters.

Curtailing his attempt to clear the far side first, Watson formed his men in column and ordered the first column forward with its captain out front. Upon reaching the ford site, the captain was killed with one shot from the Marion's sharpshooter commander. Four men running forward to recover his body were also killed in sequence.

Baffled about what to do next, Watson waited on the bluff until evening, when he withdrew to a plantation a mile north of the bridge. To the plantation's Whig owner, Watson acknowledged he had "never seen such shooting before in his life." While Watson established his headquarters in the plantation house, Marion and his men bivouacked in the woods of the ridge south of the ford. Marion and his men had won the day's skirmish. But they were engaged with one of the finest regiments in the British army and, thus, in the world. Marion knew that if he did not continue to press, they'd be back—with a vengeance.

Before daybreak, Marion roused his men and deployed his troops. To get things off to a spirited start, he dispatched a detachment of sharp-shooters across the river to the plantation where Watson and his troops were housed with orders to shoot his sentries and to wreak havoc. These sharpshooters were proving to be so successful that Watson felt com-pelled by noon to redeploy his regiment to a large open field about a half-mile away.

Unfortunately for Watson, the lack of trees and concealment did not diminish the fires, nor their accuracy. With his men in a panic and the number of wounded and suffering growing, Watson shelved his pride and addressed a letter to Marion not only requesting permission to send seven of his most seriously wounded through the lines but once again alluding to the fact that Watson believed Marion was conducting himself in a manner contrary to civilized war. Marion's response was to once again reiterate his position that he was only responding in kind to British transgressions. In addition, he sent a pass for the safe passage of the wounded and their attendants.

Watson and his men remained where they were, subsisting off the plantation, gathering from those homes around them anything else they needed. Scouts abounded about the British regiment. Watson was cut off from outside information, for his messengers could not break through Marion's cordon. As his situation grew more desperate with each passing day, Watson finally decided to retreat.

Leaving his dead in an abandoned rock quarry and loading his wounded on wagons, Watson and his crack regiment began their with-drawal at the double-time on 28 March toward Georgetown. Seven miles later at Ox Swamp, he encountered destroyed bridges and an abatis across the causeway. The situation was not good. Swamp to his left and right, passage blocked to the front and Marion closing in from the rear, Watson had to quickly choose whether to flee or fight.

Choosing escape, Watson abruptly wheeled his Regiment to the right and proceeded to move at a quick pace across fifteen miles of marsh and pine lands to the Santee Road. In pursuit was Peter Horry, firing on the retreating forms from every bush and thicket. The infantry moved at a trot the entire way, stopping only to fire a volley to their rear. Within the formation were the wagons, periodically stopping to gather more wounded—or dead.

Nine miles from Georgetown, the harried regiment approached the Sampit River. Having dashed ahead to destroy the bridge, Horry and his men were positioned fifty yards across the river. Undaunted by the destroyed bridge or the rebels' fire, the lead guardsmen closed column and plunged across the river. As the advance guard made its way across the river, Marion fell upon the rear guard.

A quick fight ensued with heavy firing. Watson rode back to rally his men only to have his horse shot from under him. Mounting a second animal, he ordered his artillery to open fire with grapeshot. As Marion's men turned back from the fires, Watson loaded two wagons with wounded. Leaving twenty dead from the engagement, he, the wagons, and the remainder of his regiment forced the ford.

Safely camped in the vicinity of Georgetown later that evening, Watson was extremely bitter, complaining that Marion and his men would "not sleep and fight like gentlemen." Instead, "like savages," they were "eternally firing and whooping around us by night, and by day waylaying and popping at us from behind every tree!" Marion and his partisan group of "uncivilized" American militia had soundly defeated the Buffs Regiment, one of the finest fighting combat units in the world.

Unfortunately for Marion, he was unable to bask in his incredible victory for long. His base of operations at Snow's Island had been located and destroyed during his absence. Marion's focus on Watson had led him to neglect putting out scouts or placing guards at various ferries. Consequently, he was surprised to learn from a messenger the day after his victory that Colonel Doyle and his New York Volunteers had successfully made their way through the swamps and bogs towards Snow's Island, following the trampled paths and trails cut out by Marion's riders.

Though his deputy, Colonel Hugh Ervin, and the small stay-behind contingent attempted to put up a spirited defense, they were quickly overwhelmed by the superior force at the boat landing on Clark's Creek. Withdrawing to the island's cottage after having suffered seven dead at the boat landing, Ervin was forced to release the twenty-six prisoners located on the island in addition to leaving behind an additional fifteen American militia who were too ill to escape.

Unable to bring any of their stores or equipment with them, Ervin and his survivors abandoned Snow's Island. Doyle, having captured the island without losing a single man, torched the structures and supplies and hastily recrossed Clark's Creek, concerned that he would be caught in a trap should Marion and his men suddenly return.

Marion and his exhausted men pushed hard to reach the Island prior to Doyle's departure. The nature of the militia began to show again as the men began to slip off without leave or authority as the force made its way through the countryside. By the time Marion arrived at Indiantown, the proud brigade that had just defeated one of the world's finest regiments had been reduced to seventy men without a single shot being fired at it.

Refusing to become despondent, Marion launched his scouts at daybreak to locate Doyle. They returned with reports that placed Doyle's foragers at Whig plantations south of the Lynches River. Hugh Horry and his mounted infantry were dispatched to drive them off. Finding Doyle's men ransacking a plantation, Horry and his men killed nine and took sixteen prisoners. The fleeing raiders were pursued back to Doyle's camp across the Lynches River.

Arriving just as Doyle's panicked rearguard were scuttling the ferry, Horry had his sharpshooters take up position and begin to place effective fire on Doyle's camp. Doyle responded aggressively by forming his infantry in ranks along the river and returning volley fire. But his fires proved to be ineffective at that range, especially against the well-covered and concealed Americans. Realizing he was in a no-win situation, Doyle struck camp and marched off toward the Peedee.

Despite their great victory against Watson, Marion and his men were starting to become somewhat discouraged. Marion had now been in command for seven months. Their recent deployment against Watson had them in the field for three continuous weeks. Some of the militia had been killed, with many others wounded. The vengeful British had burned over one hundred of their homes to the ground. What little supplies they'd accumulated had been destroyed on Snow's Island. And no matter how many victories they achieved, it seemed as though the British always returned stronger the next time.

A heavy cloud began to hang over those who remained. Finally, after giving it much thought, Marion had his small force mustered. Standing before them in a dirty, faded, and worn Continental uniform, looking gaunt, shaggy, and unshaven, Marion addressed the remnants of his brigade, reminding them of their duty, their service, and the sacrifices they'd already made. He reminded them of the taxes demanded by a government that truly did not represent them. He reminded them of the outrages perpetrated in the name of the King by his soldiers and allies alike. In closing, he left them with this one final thought.

> Now my brave brethren in arms, is there a man among you who can bear the thought of living to see his dear country and friends in so degraded and wretched a state as this? If there be, then let that man leave me and retire to his home—I ask not his aid. But, thanks to God, I have now no

fears about you: Judging by your looks, I feel that there is no such man
among us. For my own part, I look upon such a state of things as a thousand times worse than death. And God is my judge this day, that if I
could die a thousand deaths, most gladly would I die them all rather
than live to see my dear country in such a state of degradation and
wretchedness.

To cheers and rousing enthusiasm, the Swamp Fox had revived the
lagging spirit of his men. In response to their shouts that they would fight
beside him to their death, Marion declared, "Well, now, Colonel Doyle,
look sharp, for you shall presently feel the edge of our swords!"

Calling in all his riders, Marion struck camp and led his men
upstream of the swollen and flooded Lynches River to a swamp behind
the James Plantation. With no illumination, Marion spurred his mount,
Ball, into the dark waters. For many, such as Peter Horry, no other experience had ever placed them "so near the other world." Horses, men, and
equipment were swept away. Amazingly, no one was killed but many
did have to wait until daylight to continue their movement across the
river, having found themselves caught in trees or sandbars in the raging
water.

Fires were built on the far shore to thaw bodies and to dry clothes.
Then, weapons primed with dry powder, Marion and his men rode on. In
the evening, they arrived at the plantation of a noted Whig named Burch
to find that Doyle and his men had encamped there just the day before.
Burch informed Marion that a message from Lord Rawdon was delivered
that evening, after which Doyle destroyed his heavy baggage and hastily
set out toward Camden, sixty miles away. Marion would soon learn that
Greene had elected to return with his army to South Carolina in late
March.

Though disappointed that his efforts had not led to Doyle's destruction, Marion was exhilarated by the fact that the Continental Army's
focus was once again South Carolina. Intuitively, Marion visualized
another strategic plan as a result of these changing sets of circumstances.
Directing Lee and his legion — which had set out to rendezvous with Marion on 4 April — to meet him, Marion and his brigade deployed to intercept Watson, whom he knew would be marching from Georgetown
toward the British concentration in Camden. Moving through Williamsburg, though, Marion was once again faced with the continuing problem
of homesick men who would depart the formation as they passed

through their residential area. The brigade's strength was down to eight men by the time it reached the bridge over the Black River.

Lee and his men effectively linked up with Marion and his depleted and nearly nonexistent brigade on 14 April. The affection and respect of each commander for the other was genuine and, after much discussion of what had transpired since their last meeting, they both began to coordinate their joint campaign. Lee's knowledge of the strategy Greene had for the Carolinas figured immensely in their strategy. At daybreak on 16 April, they began to implement their plan.

With Lee detaching a patrol of dragoons toward Georgetown to report on Watson's movements, the remainder of the force moved through Nelson's Ferry to Wright's Bluff to begin their siege of Fort Watson. The fort's commandant, Lieutenant James McKay, assessed his situation. Morale was high and quantities of ammunition and food plentiful. And, though Marion's sharpshooters cut him off from his water sources, he was able to have a well dug within the confines of his stockade, striking water on 18 April. Despite the fact that Watson had taken the only cannon with him on his deployment, McKay felt confident that he had enough resources to hold the redoubt.

Realizing that the siege could become somewhat lengthy, Lee developed an alternative and requested in writing that Greene loan the brigade a field piece. "Five minutes will finish the business, and it can be immediately returned." Unfortunately, disaster in the form of smallpox struck Marion's men as they awaited the cannon. Many of the militia had never been inoculated against the illness and it spread rapidly throughout the camp. Deserting in large numbers, the healthy fled to avoid coming down with the affliction; the ill departed to seek medical care and nursing.

Having been chastised earlier on the 16th by his oldest and most respected friend in the army, General Moultrie, for supposed transgressions against the local populace by his militia, Marion was already feeling a bit dejected. The desertion of his soldiers and the inactivity of the siege just compounded the problem further. Lee grew concerned over Marion's decreasing disposition, for he was thoroughly sympathetic to the Carolinian's situation, knowing full well that it was only through the Swamp Fox's efforts that the British had not totally overrun South Carolina after the colonial army's retreat.

Attempting to seek some form of acknowledgment for Marion's services, Lee wrote Greene, requesting that he write a long letter to his militia brigadier. Though Greene held Marion in high regard, he did not feel the same about the militia. While there were "brave and good officers" in command, "the people with them just come and go as they please." While words of appreciation or thanks in regard to the militia would not be coming from Greene at the moment, he soon would have cause to do so. Though Greene would not send the letter per Lee's request, he did send a cannon with gun crew, and a detachment of infantry to escort it.

Unaware that their request for the cannon had been approved and that it was on its way, Marion, given his depressed state of mind, began to seriously consider lifting the siege and withdrawing. To date, his force had suffered two killed and six wounded with nothing to show for their efforts.

Fortunately for the militia, there was an alternative to the cannon and a newly assigned officer in the Brigade, Major Hezekiah Maham, proposed it. Considering and then accepting Maham's recommendation, Marion set his men to work constructing an old-style siege tower built of logs that had a floor in the tower that was higher than the fort walls before them. To protect the marksmen who would be inside, the front of the tower was reinforced with a dense shield of timber.

The morning of 23 April dawned to display a tower filled with sharpshooters looming over McKay and his men. The piercing noise of the sharpshooters' bullets echoed throughout the fort while the return fire of the British muskets failed to penetrate the tower's thick shield. Unable to raise their heads above the palisade unless they wanted to lose them, McKay could only watch in frustration as militia pioneers breached the abatis that encircled the fort and began to attack the logs of the stockade's wall itself. Behind these men stood Lee's infantry with fixed bayonets. A white flag was soon raised from inside the fort. The eight-day siege was about to come to an end.

The American commanders offered generous terms to McKay and his men as recognition of their displayed bravery. Officers were allowed to sign paroles, keep their swords and baggage, moving to Charleston to await an exchange. Both the Regular and Loyalist troops were treated alike as prisoners of war.

The fall of Fort Watson established an operation that others would emulate along the Santee. American troops for the first time had toppled a British fortress in South Carolina. Even better, it had been accomplished by a joint militia and Regular army initiative. In Marion's official report, he gave great credit to Maham and Lee.

Departing Fort Watson to encamp on Bloom Hill in the High Hills, Marion arrived to find the long letter Lee had suggested Greene write.

> When I consider how much you have done and suffered, and under what disadvantage you have maintained your ground, I am at a loss which to admire most, your courage and fortitude, or your address and

management. Certain it is no man has a better claim to the public thanks, or is more generally admired than you. History affords no instance wherein an officer has kept possession of a country under so many disadvantages as you have; surrounded on every side with a superior force; hunted from every quarter with veteran troops, you have found means to elude all their attempts, and to keep alive the expiring hopes of an oppressed Militia, when all succor seemed to be cut off. To fight the enemy bravely with a prospect of victory is nothing; but *to fight with intrepidity* under the constant impression of defeat, and inspire irregular troops to do it, is a talent peculiar to yourself. Nothing will give me greater pleasure, than to do justice to your merit, and I shall miss no opportunity of declaring to Congress, the Commander-in-chief of the American Army, and to the world in general, the great sense I have of your merit and services.

It would seem that General Nathanael Greene's opinion of Brigadier Francis Marion's contribution and the abilities of his militia had risen greatly with the fall of Fort Watson.

Buoyed by his success against Fort Watson and by his commander's letter, Marion continued to carry the war against the British. A detachment of eighty men was dispatched to conduct a raid through the High Hills, along Rafting Creek, to the source of the Black River. Instilling fear within the Tories and disrupting the flow of supplies throughout the region, the raid resulted in significant pressure being placed on the local British garrisons.

The general success of the American Army and their proximity to his location, soon forced Rawdon to abandon Camden. Shortly thereafter, Greene met with Marion for the first time. Each grew to admire the other as their talk on strategy progressed. Following this meeting, Marion moved down the Santee as Henry Lee marched on Fort Grandy. Laying siege to the fort on 14 May, Lee was able to negotiate a surrender on 15 May of the garrison and its 340-man garrison, including two cannons.

Meanwhile, Rawdon had crossed the Santee on 13 May and was on his way to assist the garrison at Fort Grandy. The morning of the fort's surrender found the British Army at the road junction that led to the fort and McCord's Ferry. Unfortunately for Rawdon, the local Loyalists were so terrified, he could obtain little in the way of useful information from them. All he could learn was that there were American forces in the area. Mistaking the force as Greene's Army, Rawdon withdrew to Moncks Corner.

Marion, meanwhile, had located another lair to serve as his base of operations. On the Peyre Plantation was an island surrounded by streams and marshes. Shelters and storage facilities were constructed and patrols were sent forth. Seeking intelligence on Rawdon's disposition, Marion assigned his innovative Major Maham the specific task of observing Lord Rawdon.

Maham located Rawdon at Moncks Corner. Realizing that Georgetown had little more than a garrison of eighty Regulars and militia to defend it, Marion begged Greene on 19 May for the opportunity to seize it, knowing that its loss would unhinge the entire British line. Despite renewed pleas for action, there was no response to his messages. Unknown to Marion, Greene and his army were in the process of investing the large fortress of Ninety-Six—which he would fail to take when Rawdon arrived with reinforcements—and partisan activities were not on his agenda at the moment.

Finally, with no response and having operated independently for far too long, Marion moved to seize the initiative. Crossing the Santee, he bivouacked at Cantey's Plantation, from where he issued a call to muster to his militia. On May 27 with his brigade at full strength, the Swamp Fox departed Cantey for Winyah Bay and Georgetown. Arriving before Georgetown on the 28th, Marion immediately began to entrench and lay siege.

For the British, their hearts were not in it. Later that evening at 2100, the small garrison boarded a galley, two gun boats, and an armed schooner in the bay and withdrew. Marion immediately seized the town and reduced its defenses. Following a dispatch to Greene of his success, Marion was prepared to proceed across the Santee and encamp near Moncks Corner where he would await further orders from his commander.

Toward the end of June, Rawdon departed Fort Ninety-Six and moved to link up with Watson's former regiment, which was now under the command of Lieutenant Colonel Alexander Stewart following Watson's retirement. Hoping to prevent the joining of these two British units, Greene moved in advance of his army accompanied only by an escort of cavalry. Marion was directed to move from Nelson's Ferry to Moncks Corner. Assembling four hundred horsemen, the Swamp Fox maneuvered around Rawdon's fatigued, ill, and insubordinate soldiers on 6 July to take up his assigned position.

Breaking camp at 0100 on 8 July, Marion and his men began to slowly and quietly make their way down the broad road that ran from Moncks Corner to Orangeburg in anticipation of encountering Stewart. But Stewart had anticipated such a move and was traveling a much less traveled route. Consequently, the two forces passed each other in the night. Realizing his mistake, Marion sent Peter Horry in pursuit of Stewart's guards. Though they were able to engage the rear guard and capture several supply wagons, Horry was unable to prevent the Stewart and Rawdon linkup in Orangeburg.

Now facing a sizable force, Greene ordered the concentration of his army, both Continental and militia, at Ancrum's Plantation on the Congaree River. For the first time in the war, Greene, Sumter, Marion, and Lee had joined under one immediate command. On 10 July, Greene deployed his force to the north side of Turkey Hill, four miles north of Orangeburg. For two days, Greene offered battle that was declined by Rawdon. Finally, on the 12th, after having determined that the British held too strong a position, Greene withdrew his army across the Santee and took up camp around Bloom Hill.

While Greene planned, Sumter received authorization to reduce the British post at Moncks Corner. Deploying Marion and Lee on the evening of 12 July, Sumter attempted to surround and cut off Lieutenant Colonel John Coates and his 19th Regiment. Aware of the Americans' approach, Coates would not fall prey to such a tactic. Evacuating Moncks Corner and establishing a sound defensive position around Biggin Church and its three-foot-thick brick walls, Coates lay in wait for the American attack.

As the night progressed, though, Coates grew more alarmed by Sumter's movements. Finally, at 0300 on 17 July, he withdrew from his position, setting fire to the church and retreating down the Cooper River.

The American force set out in pursuit, finally catching and engaging Coates' regiment later that day after a forced march of eighteen miles. Attacked at a bridge site spanning the Quinby Creek, Coates and his men were able to hold off Lee and take up a strong position on the Shubrick Plantation. Lee waited for Marion to move up.

With Marion's arrival, the combined force forded the creek and conducted a reconnaissance. The reconnaissance indicated a formidable defensive position with the infantry formed in its traditional square before the plantation house, a howitzer to its front, and plantation equipment serving as obstacles along its flanks. Both Marion and Lee determined that the position was too strong to attack and awaited Sumter's arrival.

The Gamecock and his infantry joined the two officers and their commands around 1700. Unfortunately, he had failed to bring along his artillery piece. Despite Marion's protest against assaulting such a well defended position, Sumter ordered an attack. To the far right he placed Horry's cavalry. To their left were Sumter's troops. To Sumter's immediate left, Colonel Thomas Taylor's regiment was posted. Marion held the far left flank.

Charging forward, Sumter's men sought the safety of some cabins from which they could fire. Taylor's men advanced against the square, only to be repelled by the redcoats' bayonets. Marion's men took position behind a fence, delivering a steady fire into the square to cover Taylor's retreat.

Marion's men held their ground against a heavy fire. Early in the battle, Lieutenant Colonel John Baxter, a large man in full uniform, was struck by a shot.

Shouting to Peter Horry, "I am wounded, colonel," Horry responded, "Think no more of it, Baxter, but hold your place."

"But I can't stand, colonel. I am wounded a second time," came the response.

Still unfazed by the colonel's wounds, Horry stated, "Then lie down, Baxter, but quit not your post."

But Baxter was not yet finished. "Colonel, they've shot me again. If I remain here any longer, I shall be shot to pieces."

"Be it so, Baxter, but stir not," replied Horry. Despite his wounds, Baxter valiantly maintained his position, surrounded by fifty other members of his regiment who lay dead or wounded.

Having exhausted their ammunition, Marion ordered their withdrawal, stunned and grief-stricken by the senseless waste. Marion had never held Sumter in high esteem and this action vindicated his reluctance to cooperate with the general. Marion silently left the field, resolved to never fight under Sumter's command again.

Taylor was more direct. Approaching Sumter, he informed the general, "I don't know why you sent me forward on a forlorn hope, promising to sustain me, and failed to do so, unless you designed to sacrifice me. I will never more serve under you!" Sumter's rashness had far exceeded his common sense.

Marion and Lee gathered their dead and wounded. They rode for fifteen miles before halting and establishing a bivouac. Incensed and resentful of the fact that Sumter's men had remained covered and concealed in the cabins while they were sacrificed in the open, Marion's men deserted throughout the night. Dawn found only one hundred of Marion's men remaining. Without a word to Sumter, who still was in command of the corps, Marion and Lee each headed their separate ways; Lee to Greene's location in the High Hills and Marion to Cordes' Plantation across the Santee.

Sumter elected to heap insult upon injury, refusing to even acknowledge Marion's participation in the Battle of Quinby in his first report to

Greene. His second report noted, "When we overtook the enemy he [Marion] had scarcely 100 [men] left." In his fifth and final letter about the engagement, Sumter reported that "General Marion was upon the left and suffered considerably by supposing the enemy would not fire upon his men ... when moving up in a certain direction ... he soon found his mistake ... but had his men brought off ... and behaved well upon every occasion."

Despite this attempt at slander, the actions of Marion and his men had been flatteringly relayed to Greene, courtesy of Harry Lee. In Greene's letter to Marion, he so noted. "The gallantry and good conduct of your men reflects the highest honor upon your brigade. I only lament that men who spilt their blood in such noble exertions to serve their country could not have met with more deserved success."

Sumter's days were soon numbered. Under pressure from Governor Rutledge, exhausted, pained by an old wound, distrusted by his fellow officers, and disliked by his own men, Sumter relinquished command of his partisan brigade and retired, leaving Marion the senior brigadier general of militia in South Carolina.

With all of South Carolina—except a small district around Charleston—recovered from the British, Marion found himself expending a great deal of effort helping to restore order and government throughout the region. Large bands composed of four hundred to five hundred Tories were ravaging the countryside south of Charleston. To help instigate this disorder, Major Thomas Fraser and his regiment of dragoons had been dispatched by the British to raid the region south of Edisto. Fraser, it just so happened, had been an active participant in the hanging of Colonel Isaac Hayne, a friend of Marion.

Seizing the opportunity, Marion handpicked two hundred men from his brigade and set out in pursuit of Fraser. Unobserved by the British, Marion rode a hundred miles, crossing the Edisto, and joining with a militia unit under the command of Colonel William Harden on 13 August. Informed that Fraser was in the process of returning to Edisto, Marion planned an ambush on the causeway leading to Parker's Ferry. Concealing his main element in the swamp, he dispatched a detachment of his fastest horses to lure the British into his trap.

Marion's decoy worked and Fraser set off in pursuit. Across the causeway, the dragoons thundered. As Fraser and his men drew abreast of Marion's hidden position, the ambush was initiated. From a distance of fifty yards, the militia fired their first volley. The line of dragoons reeled, horses reared, and men fell. Fraser valiantly attempted to rally his men and lead them on a charge across the swamp against Marion's position.

The delay as Fraser rallied his men allowed Marion and his men time to reload and fire a second volley. Soon thereafter, a third volley by the militia sent the dragoons fleeing. Low on ammunition and aware that a large body of dismounted infantry was moving in his direction, Marion and his men slipped away through the swamp. A reconnaissance the next morning by Marion's scouts counted twenty-seven dead horses along the causeway. Knowing that his sharpshooters had targeted the riders and not the mounts, Marion was comforted by the fact that a high price had been extracted for Isaac Hayne's murder.

On 22 August in support of General George Washington's combined American-French campaign against Lord Cornwallis in Yorktown, Virginia, Greene commenced the resumption of offensive operations. Having concentrated all of his forces with the exception of Marion and Harden, Greene broke camp and advanced on Stewart and his regiment, who were bivouacked on the Congaree. Crossing Howell's Ferry in anticipation of a fight on the 28th, Greene found that Stewart had hurriedly departed and moved thirty miles down the Santee and secured a strong position around Eutaw Springs.

In that one of Greene's primary missions was to keep the British occupied in South Carolina while Washington struck up north, Greene and his army set a leisurely pace for their continued advance, having sent Lee and his legion forward to keep an eye on Stewart. On 4 September, Greene notified Marion to advance from his camp at Peyre's up the Santee. With surprising dispatch, Marion bypassed Stewart and was waiting for Greene seventeen miles north of Eutaw Springs at the Henry Laurens' Plantation by the very next day.

Greene paused his men at the plantation for a day, allowing them to prepare for the upcoming fight as he formulated the plan of attack. In accordance with contemporary American tactics, Greene divided his army into four basic elements: an advance guard to include Lee's legion, a rear guard, a column of Regulars under the command of General Jethro Sumner, and a column of militia under the command of General Francis Marion.

Moving into position, the army advanced to attack at 0400 on 8 September. Greene's attack took Stewart by surprise. The British commander had believed until that point that Greene and Marion were much farther away and not yet combined. Though warned of the impending attack by two American deserters while Greene was still four miles north, Stewart did not take the warning seriously, believing it was just a small American detachment the two deserters were talking about. The quick defeat of one of his detachments of horse and infantry over one hundred soldiers strong, soon convinced Stewart otherwise.

Greene's army continued to advance and stopped to form their line of battle. Marion had three brigades under his command and, dismounted, they formed the lead elements of Greene's attack. With a South Carolina brigade formed on the left, the North Carolina militia formed in the center, and Marion's own brigade holding the right wing, the colonial militia attacked across Congaree Road against Stewart's formation, which had moved out to meet the attack.

Moving through the woods, the militia drove the British skirmishers back before setting upon the main British line. To the astonishment of both British and colonial regulars, the militia steadily and unfailingly continued their advance into the very hottest fires the British could create. Greene was later to write to General Von Steuben "such conduct would have graced the veterans of the Great King of Prussia."

The militia under Marion's command held their ground, firing seventeen volleys into the British lines. Then, with their ammunition expended and their mission accomplished, they conducted an organized withdrawal as the colonial Regulars advanced. The spirited American advance forced Stewart's left flank to give ground and fall back in disorder. Seeing an opportunity, Lee threw his cavalry into the struggle against the British left flank to add to their confusion and turmoil.

The British center held as the colonial and British Regulars engaged each other with fists, bayonets, rifle butts, and swords. But the British inability to hold on the left eventually led to the entire line giving way with one terrific volley of fire from the Marylanders. Stewart rallied his troops and reformed his line, slowly giving ground before the colonial advance. His line of retreat took Stewart through his camp in Roche Field and this would prove to be his saving grace, for within those tents lay abundant food and drink. Tired, hungry, and thirsty, the colonial soldiers could not resist the temptation to stop and pilfer what they saw. Quickly, the entire front line lost all semblance of order. Soon, the tables were turned and, with all control lost, Greene ordered his regulars to retreat.

As British snipers rained down heavy fires from a nearby brick building and British cavalry clashed with American, Greene rallied his men along the edge of Roche Field. Having collected his wounded, Greene had his army retrace their earlier morning steps. Though Stewart retained the field of battle and claimed a victory, it was a Pyrrhic victory at best, for his army had been shattered.

Fearing a second attack, he dispatched messengers for reinforcements, destroyed his supplies, and retreated to Moncks Corner leaving his dead unburied and seventy wounded under flag. Despite a valiant effort by Marion and Lee, they were not able to intercept Stewart prior to reinforcements arriving to assist him. Having accomplished what he'd originally set out to do, keep the British forces in South Carolina occupied, Greene withdrew north along the Santee and encamped near Nelson's Ferry. Marion and his men arrived at Cantey Plantation where he dismissed his men, who had conducted themselves so valorously.

In July, Greene requested that Marion take a post at Wadboo. Agreeing to do so, the Swamp Fox established a base of operations and constantly patrolled against roving bands of the King's cavalry or Tories. On the morning of 29 August, Marion received word that Major Fraser had set out to attack the guards at Biggin Bridge and Strawberry Ferry with a force of one hundred dragoons.

Posting his marksmen in the vicinity of the objective, Marion dispatched a reconnaissance detachment. These men soon encountered Fraser in the woods. The detachment led the dragoons right into Marion's ambush. The militia's opening volley dropped twenty men and five horses. Unfortunately, it also spooked the militia's horses pulling the ammunition wagon, causing them to bolt. Unable to recover the wagon and running low on powder, Marion ordered the retreat of his men to the Santee, having fired his last ball at another human being.

The British evacuated Charleston on 14 December 1782. Early that morning, General Anthony Wayne secured the city. At last, the soil of South Carolina was free of the King's men. With there no longer a need for a standing militia, the units began to disband. With no fanfare, General Francis Marion conducted his final muster under the cedars of Fair Lawn. Expressing his thanks and the nation's debt for their gallantry, patriotism, and valor, Marion wished them much happiness and prosperity. Then, mounting his trusted steed, Ball, he rode off toward Pond Bluff.

Francis Marion returned to his home to find it plundered and burned by friend and foe alike. His horses and cattle had been driven off or confiscated and his slaves kidnapped. Unconquered by the British, he would prove to be unconquerable to these circumstances also. Though unpaid for his services in the militia and unreimbursed for his losses despite the use of his land and property by the American army, Marion was able to recover from his loss.

The aging General lived revered and honored by all. Periodically, he would heed the calls from campaigns past. During those times, both he and his wife, Mary, would pack and go camping in the High Hills of Santee. As they'd walk, he'd stop at a swamp or clearing to "visit" with old comrades.

Marion's health began to fail quickly in 1794 at the age of sixty-two. Francis Marion was buried in the family cemetery on Gabriel's Plantation on Belle Isle, having died at Pond Bluff on 27 February 1795.

CHAPTER 13

Post-Revolutionary War Years

The safety of the people must be the supreme law.

Roman proverb

At the war's end, most of the Continental Army was disbanded, including all of the Ranger-style forces. But the early years of this nation's existence still saw continued unrest along its frontier. In due course, the states and eventually the federal government began to raise Ranger units again, in the style and tradition of those raised during the early colonial years.

In January 1812, six companies of Rangers were raised to protect frontier settlers. General Andrew Jackson, himself, raised a Ranger company in 1818. In 1832, a mounted Ranger battalion was formed as a show of force against the Indians. Also during the 1830s, the Texas Rangers were established and employed along the Texas frontier.

Eventually more than twenty Ranger companies would be serving in Texas during the 1850s. And, though General Zachary Taylor held a poor opinion of Ranger units, he found them to be vital as scouts during the Mexican War.

CHAPTER 14

The American Civil War:
John S. Mosby — Mosby's Rangers

*There were probably but few men in the South who could have commanded suc-
cessfully a separate detachment in the rear of an opposing army, and so near the
border of hostilities, as long as he did without losing his entire command.*

Lieutenant General Ulysses S. Grant,
of Mosby in Memoirs

The Civil War — or "War of Rebellion" — found a total of 428 units officially and unofficially designated as Rangers during the conflict with the
majority being Ranger-style units in name only. With few exceptions,
nearly all of these organizations were Confederate. Given the nature of
the war in the South and the type of operations it was forced to conduct,
it can be readily seen why they were forced to attempt such an unconventional and partisan style of warfare. Unfortunately for them, most of the
Ranger units proved to be ineffective and their contributions to the war
effort relatively obscure.

The only long-term major exception to this fact was Mosby's Rangers
of the Confederate army. Officially designated the 43rd Battalion of Virginia Cavalry, Mosby's partisan Rangers were lead by John Singleton
Mosby, who believed that by resorting to aggressive action, he could
compel his enemies to guard a hundred points and thus expend valuable
troops and resources needed elsewhere. These Rangers were particularly
active in Virginia and Maryland for a twenty-eight month period from
1863 to 1865 and maintained an excellent reputation within the Confederate army. This type of reputation was the exception rather than the norm

when it came to Confederate Ranger units, for their own officers usually described them as being no better than robbers and plunderers.

Within the South, a real debate about the legitimacy and effectiveness of partisan- or guerrilla-style forces had arisen. Early attempts to establish such units met with official disapproval from many including Jefferson Davis and General Robert E. Lee. It was believed that guerrilla warfare not only drained the strength of Regular forces, but the units organized would prove to be undisciplined mobs that roamed the countryside terrorizing and victimizing civilians and inviting reprisals from Federal forces. Brigadier General Henry Heth characterized such organizations as composed of nothing more than "notorious thiefs [sic] and murderers, more ready to plunder friends than foes."

Military necessity and the overwhelming onslaught of Union armies, resulted in such units being assembled throughout the South as a form of self-defense. To many Southerners looking for inspiration and someone to emulate, they did not have to look very far to cite as a renowned historical example Francis Marion, the Swamp Fox of South Carolina.

As the war progressed and the number of partisan commands grew with it, the Confederate government, in the end, sanctioned the formation of such commands as an attempt to provide them legitimacy. In April 1862, the regulation was codified by the Confederate Congress and signed into law on the 21st by Davis, to authorize the creation of partisan Ranger commands. This law authorized Davis to "commission such officers as he may deem proper with authority to form bands of partisan rangers, in companies, battalions, or regiments, either as infantry or cavalry." As a further inducement to enroll, and to assuage, somewhat, the hardships of joining such a unit, the Confederate Congress, in essence, authorized such units to plunder and to pilfer and to receive payment for the "full value" of any arms and munitions seized as a result of their operations.

Six regiments, nine battalions, and a number of independent companies of partisan Rangers had been formed in eight states by September 1862. Unfortunately, much of what had been argued against their formation began to take place as numerous protests about the partisan units inundated the Confederate government. Reluctant to disband the units, the War Department, in June 1863, ordered commanders to combine partisan Ranger units into battalions or regiments. In addition, they were to be placed "under the same regulations as other soldiers in reference to their discipline, position, and movements."

Despite the success of some of the partisan units, such as Mosby's Rangers, complaints from military authorities and civilians still continued to flood the Confederate Congress in regard to the "irregulars" thievery and undisciplined ways. Lacking the support of most of his senior commanders, to include Lee and cavalry commander Brigadier General Jeb Stuart, in regard to this issue, the Secretary of War ultimately conceded that the experiment had been a failure and drafted a bill to repeal the authority for the formation of the partisan units and to consolidate them into the organizations of regular battalions and regiments.

On 17 February 1864, the bill was enacted into law. Only two partisan commands were exempted from the reorganization and allowed to retain their identity as an independent command. These two exceptions were the commands of John McNeill and John Singleton Mosby. On 1 April, Lee informed the adjutant and inspector general of the Confederacy, Samuel Cooper:

> I am making an effort to have Col Mosby's battalion mustered into the regular service. If this cannot be done, I recommend that this battalion be retained as partisans for the present. Lt Col Mosby had done excellent service, & from the reports of citizens & others I am inclined to believe that he is strict in discipline & adds protection to the county in which he operates.

Mosby first voiced the concept of a Ranger-style cavalry unit in December 1862. Following a raid against Burnside's Army of the Potomac, Brigadier General Jeb Stuart and his cavalry withdrew to Loudoun County in northern Virginia for a few days of rest and rehabilitation — R&R. As they rested, Mosby — an enlisted member of his command — approached Stuart to discuss with him an idea that he'd been considering for quite some time.

During the winter months, armies usually limited their maneuvers and bivouacked in winter quarters. Mosby, on the other hand, wanted to continue operations and conduct guerrilla forays in Loudoun County during those months of "hibernation," until the cavalry returned in the spring from the vicinity of Fredericksburg. With nothing but "unlimited confidence" in his junior enlisted subordinate, Stuart approved his request.

Later that day, Stuart and his command departed, leaving Mosby behind with a nine-man detachment. Years later, Mosby was to state that Stuart "made me all that I was in the war, but for his friendship I would never have been heard of." He was "the best friend I ever had."

Mosby's original intent had never been to organize as an independent partisan command but, unknown to him, Stuart's withdrawal to Fredericksburg would be the start of twenty-eight months of attacks, ambushes, and raids against the Northern forces within the region. The area in which Mosby would operate was a 100-mile stretch of territory that ran between the Federal capital of Washington, D.C., and the Confederate capital of Richmond, Virginia. The region in which Mosby and his Rangers would ultimately operate would encompass the counties south and west of Washington, south of the Potomac River, and those in the northern portion of the Shenandoah Valley at the base of the Blue Ridge Mountains. Much of this area was hills and wooded mountains interspersed with fertile farmlands, which would prove to be very conducive to guerrilla warfare.

Based in southern Loudoun County and in the northern and western portion of Fauquier County, Mosby and his men would eventually strike eastward into Culpeper, Fairfax, or Prince William Counties. Operations would also take him westward into Warren, Clarke, Jefferson, and Frederick Counties. Much of this region would become known as "Mosby's Confederacy," for many of his men would be quartered with their parents while others would reside with family or friends. By Mosby's definition, his Confederacy encompassed the roughly 125 square miles that was bordered by a line that ran south along the Blue Ridge Mountains from Snickersville to Linden at the Manassas Gap, east through Upper Fauquier to The Plains, north along the Bull Run Mountains to Aldie, and west back to Snickersville.

Mosby's philosophy was simple. "If you are going to fight, then be the attacker." He was never one who could stand still to receive a charge. Most of his men also adhered to this philosophy of warfare. On one occasion, Mosby had ordered one of his newly promoted lieutenants, Harry Hatcher, to make a demonstration with some men against a force of Federal soldiers. Hatcher proceeded to ride forth with his men in an attack that dislodged the Union force from behind a fence. When questioned by Mosby as to why he had disobeyed his orders, Hatcher reminded Mosby that "[y]ou told me to make a demonstration to get them from behind the fence, and if that didn't mean charge 'em, I don't know what it did mean." For most his Rangers, the commander's intent was clear. Even Mosby, apparently, needed to be reminded of that once in a while.

Union operations between the two capitals, or down the Shenandoah Valley, exposed their communications and supply lines to the type of guerrilla operations Mosby had planned. He believed that the Federals' rear would be the most vulnerable section of their lines. Mosby was certain that "[a] small force moving with celerity and threatening many points on a line can neutralize a hundred times its own number." As for the benefit of such insurgent groups, Mosby would later write, "The military value of a partisan's work is not measured by the amount of property destroyed, or the number of men killed or captured, but by the number he keeps watching."

Within days of Mosby and his small detachment being left behind, Union forces in the area began to report a series of perplexing raids against their camps at night. Stealthily the apparitions would appear, attack, and then suddenly vanish, usually with prisoners in tow. By 17 January, Mosby had captured seventeen Federals.

Throughout February, as the word was passed that a small detachment of Jeb Stuart's Confederate cavalry had remained behind to conduct partisan activities, Mosby's command nearly doubled in size as recruits, enamored by the booty and adventure, began to enlist. The original ten members of the detachment would call these new men "conglomerates."

Mosby's first large raid with his new recruits was launched 25 February. Having been informed of the raid nearly a week earlier, the twenty-seven men who rendezvoused departed late in the day for a Union cavalry outpost located two miles from Germantown. Reaching the outpost at 0400 on the 26th, Mosby placed his men on line and charged against the fifty Federal soldiers occupying a log house. Though they occupied a strong defensive position from which they could fire their carbines from behind thick wood walls, the Yankees woke and ran from the house and into the surrounding woods. The unit's commander, a lieutenant, and three of his men were killed. Five other soldiers and nearly all the horses were captured. This raid would prove to be the first of many successful operations conducted by Mosby and his men.

The Federals responded to this attack on 2 March when 200 soldiers of the 18th Pennsylvania Cavalry entered Middleburg in search of the partisans. Under the command of Major Gilmer, the troopers arrested a few citizens and threatened to burn the village but their efforts brought them no additional information about Mosby. The command departed Middleburg and rode east for Aldie.

Apparently drunk, Gilmer became spooked when he observed a fifty-man detachment of mounted men as he was clearing Aldie. Ordering an immediate retreat, the panicked Gilmer was eventually ridden down by members of the 1st Vermont Cavalry, the unit he had mistaken for Mosby. Calmed, Gilmer informed the Vermont commander, Captain F. T. Huntoon, that his Pennsylvanians had cleared Aldie and Mosby was not in the town. As Gilmer and his men proceeded to ride west, Huntoon returned to Aldie to rest and feed his men and horses on the eastern side of town.

Unknown to either Federal commander, Mosby had entered the town from the west with twenty-eight of his men. Fortuitously coming upon the dismounted and resting Union cavalry, he quickly ordered an attack. Galloping into the midst of the surprised Federal soldiers, Mosby's men made short work of the enemy, capturing Huntoon and fifteen of his officers and men. Mosby's casualties were only one man wounded.

Mosby's success seemed to result in the Union cavalry remaining in camp for a week or so. This additional time allowed Mosby to plan and conduct what would prove to be possibly his most notable and audacious raid. The order had been issued to assemble on 8 March 1863 at Dover Mill, just west of Aldie in Loudoun County. In groups of two and three, twenty-nine of Mosby's riders arrived amid the drizzle of a miserable day.

With the men assembled by dusk, Mosby mounted his horse and announced, "I shall mount the stars tonight or sink lower than plummet ever sounded." The men followed, not knowing that their objective was to penetrate Union lines to capture Colonel Percy Wyndham, the commander of a cavalry brigade, who was reported to be camped in his headquarters at Fairfax Court House. The mission was a vendetta for Mosby. Frustrated by Mosby's recent successes and his own command's failure to stop the Confederate Rangers' forays around his capital, Wyndham had resorted to calling Mosby "a common horse thief" and had threatened to burn the homes of those he believed supported the partisans. Taking Wyndham's comments rather personally, Mosby had decided to "put a stop to his talk by gobbling him up in bed and sending him off to Richmond."

Proceeding eastward on the Little River Turnpike, the Rangers moved in a cold rain through the pitch black of night and fields of mud. Leading the column between the flickering Union campfires to the Warrenton Turnpike, Lieutenant James F. "Big Yankee" Ames—a Union deserter from the 5th New York Cavalry—was able to avoid the challenge of any pickets and turn northward toward Fairfax. A mile and a half from the courthouse, they veered again, this time eastward to avoid the campfires of Vermont infantry troops. Unfortunately, in the process of their maneuvering, the column had split and nearly half of the Rangers had become disoriented in a pine forest between Centreville and Chantilly. It was 0200 before the column had reunited and entered Fairfax.

Quietly moving through the town and capturing sentinels, the raiding party quickly cut the telegraph wires and secured the horse stables and various other buildings. Arriving at the building he thought housed the Union cavalry commander, Mosby was informed that his information was incorrect and that Colonel Wyndham was housed in a building on the other side of town. A squad was quickly dispatched to the second site only to learn that their quarry had been unexpectedly summoned and had spent the night in Washington, D.C, rather than with his troops in the field.

Disappointed, Mosby opted to make the best of it. An interrogation of some prisoners soon revealed an even greater prize, for it was learned that the commander of the Vermont infantry brigade, Brigadier General Edwin H. Stoughton, was headquartered in town. The son of a wealthy family, Stoughton had been the youngest general in the army a year before at the age of twenty-four. On this particular night, he had hosted a champagne party and had retired to bed to sleep off the effects of his revelries.

Mosby and some of his men walked to the brick home of Dr. William Presley Gunnell, where Stoughton was staying for the evening. A knock on the front door brought the head of one of the general's staff, Lieutenant Prentiss, out of a second-story window. Upon being informed that there was a "dispatch for General Stoughton," the lieutenant came down and opened the door.

Grabbing the startled Union officer, Mosby and his men forced their way into the house. Convincing with a bit of coercion that Prentiss lead them to his commander's bedroom, the Confederates found the young twenty-five-year-old general sound asleep. Accounts differ as to what happened next. Witnesses state that Mosby simply shook the general awake while Mosby's memoirs have him removing the covers, lifting the nightshirt, and unceremoniously spanking the Federal general's backside.

In either case, the general found himself rudely awoken with a group of strangers gathered around his bed. Confused and demanding to know who was present, the general was asked by the twenty-nine-year-old Confederate lieutenant who was wearing a captain's uniform during this raid, "General, did you ever hear of Mosby?"

"Yes, have you caught him?" queried the Union officer.

"No, but he has caught you," came the response. "Stuart's cavalry has possession of the Court House; be quick and dress."

Allowing the general to dress, though he was a bit slow about it, the group moved back to the town square with their captives by around 0330. With scores of dazed and confused Union soldiers scattering about the town trying to gain some semblance of order and trying to determine what was happening, Mosby and his men began to ride out of town with their thirty Union soldier captives and a large number of Union horses.

The column had only traveled a few hundred feet when the command, "Halt! The horses need rest!" was bellowed from a second-story window. Answered by silence, the voice continued, "I am commander of the cavalry here and this must be stopped." Realizing that he was addressing rebels below him, Colonel Robert Johnstone, commander of the 5th New York Cavalry, quickly ducked back in the window of the house as two of Mosby's men broke through the front door. Encountering Mrs. Johnstone in the hallway, the men were delayed just enough to allow the naked colonel to escape through the back door and unceremoniously conceal himself under an outhouse on the grounds.

The Confederates continued their withdrawal along the same route they had entered for approximately a half-mile when Mosby left the highway and began to move cross-country to throw off his pursuers, whom he knew would soon be following. The terrain was harsh and, with no moonlight, it was difficult to see. The column began to get strung out and prisoners began to escape, disappearing into the darkness. Encountering Warrenton Pike, Mosby turned over command of his column to William Hunter, who moved out at a fast trot with the group while Mosby and a second Ranger formed a rear guard.

Fleeing through the night, the raiders skirted the Federal camps located in Centreville and continued on, the clatter of their hooves, if heard, probably mistaken as that of Union cavalry. Encountering the swollen Cub Run, the Rangers, with some degree of difficulty, were able to swim their horses across. Taking the lead on the far shore, Mosby and a second Ranger led the raider force across the Bull Run creek and through the field of battle that had been bloodied in July 1861 and in August 1862 as the new day's sun was commencing to rise. Mosby's raid had netted one Union general, two captains, thirty enlisted men, and fifty-eight horses. Not a shot had been fired nor a man killed or wounded.

The "Stoughton Raid" was proclaimed by Jeb Stuart as "a feat unparalleled in the war." As a result, Federal camps and headquarters began to feel a sense of insecurity and vulnerability to the partisans' roving patrols. This accreditation of Mosby's prowess even made its way to the very highest levels of Washington where a belief surfaced that the president and his cabinet might be the Confederate Ranger's next target. Acting on those fears, the Union army ensured that the link across the Potomac between Washington and Virginia, the Chain Bridge, was obstructed each night for a week with the removal of its flooring planks.

Lincoln, though, rather than fearful for his safety, was amused by the incident stating "he didn't mind the loss of the Brigadier as much as the horses. For I can make a much better General in five minutes, but the horses cost one hundred and twenty-five dollars apiece."

Mosby was appointed a captain on 19 March, with a date of rank of 15 March. The special orders from Lee read, in part, "The General Commanding is confident that this manifestation of the approbation of his superiors, will but serve to incite Captain Mosby to still greater efforts to advance the good of the cause in which we are engaged."

Stuart offered some unsolicited but what would turn out to be sage advice for his subordinate. "You will proceed to organize a band of permanent followers for the war but by all means ignore the term 'Partisan Ranger.' It is in bad repute." In closing, Stuart provided Mosby with what was perhaps the most sound piece of counsel anyone had ever given him and that was "not to have any established headquarters anywhere but 'in the saddle.'" This was advice that Mosby would follow to the very final day of the war.

Mosby resumed his raiding on 16 March with a strike against two cavalry outposts, unaware that he was one day into his time in grade as a captain. Two hundred Federal horsemen immediately set out in chase of Mosby and his fifty-man raider force. With the Union cavalry slowly gaining ground, Mosby allowed them to close to within one hundred yards. Then, wheeling his column around, he led a charge against his pursuers. Stunned by the turn of events, the Yankees scattered and fled. The Rebels pursued the blue uniformed rabble for four or five miles, killing five, capturing thirty-six, and wounding a significant number of others. The following day, Mosby and his men were able to add a twenty-five-man picket post to their collection of prisoners.

Later, on 23 March, the same day Special Order #28 was read, Mosby and his men returned to Fairfax County and attacked a picket post of Ames' former cavalry regiment, the 5th New York. Quickly scattering, the New Yorkers beat a hasty retreat to a reserve picket post. A Union counterattack soon came thundering down the Little River Turnpike, driving the Confederates before it for three miles. Dismounting, Mosby drew his men up in a line behind some fallen trees and loosened a volley into the approaching Federal cavalry. With the bluecoats momentarily halted, the men in butternut gray remounted and completed their escape unscathed and with thirty-six prisoners and fifty horses.

On 10 June 1863, Mosby, who had been promoted again to the rank of major, rode into the village of Rector's Cross Roads — now Atoka — accompanied by four of his men: James William Foster, William L. Hunter, William Thomas Turner, and George H. Whitescarver. Inside a stone house and acting under the authority granted him in the letters of

23 and 25 March by Robert E. Lee and Jeb Stuart, Mosby sat down and signed the paperwork that officially created Company A—the first mustered company of what would become the 43rd Battalion of Virginia Cavalry.

Mosby's first action following execution of the paperwork authorizing the formation of his new command was to select the company's officers. Heeding Stuart's advice, Mosby selected Foster as the company commander, Turner as first lieutenant, Hunter as second lieutenant, and Whitescarver as third lieutenant. Departing the village, Mosby and his four officers rode to a wood line where seventy of his men awaited. Encircled by these men, Mosby informed them they were no longer guerrillas but an officially sanctioned and authorized company of partisan Rangers, Mosby's Rangers to be exact. Thirty men of Captain William G. Brawner's company of partisan Rangers were also formed with Mosby's men but this unit would not be enrolled in the 43rd Battalion.

On 23 September, Mosby and four men rode into Fairfax County. Rumored to have been killed in an earlier engagement, Mosby intended to dispel that talk with another daring capture similar to that of his Fairfax Court House escapade with General Stoughton. Mosby's target this time was the governor of West Virginia, Francis H. Pierpont, who was temporarily headquartered in Alexandria.

Under the cover of darkness, the five Rangers passed through the Federal pickets and dismounted before the governor's mansion. Fate again intervened when it was discovered that the governor was staying in Washington that evening, just as Wyndham had previously done earlier in March. Riding to the home of the governor's military aide, Colonel D. H. Dulany, Mosby and his men were let in by the unsuspecting colonel, who had assumed the small party were Federal scouts disguised in Southern uniforms. Only upon noting that his son, French, a known member of Mosby's Rangers, was part of the group did the Colonel come to realize that he had been taken prisoner. While Mosby's daring raid into Alexandria served little in the way of military purpose, it did leave little doubt in the minds of the Union that Mosby was still very much alive.

In the final days of September, Mosby organized a second company, Company B, to help expedite the achievement of his objectives, which was to renew operations against the lines of communications of the Army of the Potomac currently deployed along the Rapidan River. The number of Rangers riding with him now numbered one hundred and fifty or more, such a number of men couldn't be effectively commanded by one officer.

A rendezvous of all his men was ordered on 1 October at the small village of Scuffleburg. With all the men mustered, Mosby selected sixty men to step forward. Designated the new members of Company B, they voted for the slate of officers Mosby presented: Captain William R. "Billy" Smith, commander; First Lieutenant Franklin Williams; Second Lieutenant Albert "Ab" Wrenn; and Third Lieutenant Robert Gray.

As what would prove to be Mosby's tradition for newly formed companies, he ordered Company B to conduct a raid the following day. Rallying in Salem, Smith and forty of his men proceeded to Warrenton, reaching it by dusk. In the face of a howling rainstorm, the captain turned his column around and led them to his home, where they were fed and dried out. At daybreak, Smith ordered his men to scatter and reassemble later that afternoon at a home six miles from Warrenton.

The company mustered at 1600 and continued with its mission. Three miles past the town and around midnight, a Federal campsite was located on the crest of a hill. Smith and two of his Rangers approached the camp to scout its defenses. All was quiet and security was so lax they were able to dismount and walk through the camp unchallenged. A count indicated approximately 250 Union soldiers.

Returning to his men, Smith had them remount and move to the rear of the enemy camp where they closed to within ten yards of the tents. At that point, Smith shouted the charge and the Confederates streaked through the sleeping camp. Though total surprise had been achieved, the company was only able to capture six Yankees and twenty-seven horses before the remainder made off into the woods. With no casualties on their side, they had achieved a modest degree of success for their baptism of fire.

Less than a week later, Mosby assembled both companies again. Selecting forty men from the overall group present, he proceeded to direct those selected to the vicinity of Frying Pan in Fairfax County while he rode before them with a small scout. Mosby linked up with his men later that evening around 2300 on the 9th and slept for a few hours with his Rangers. Before daybreak, he was back in the saddle again with four of his Rangers to ride forth on another scout through Federal lines to Falls Church, just eight miles northwest of Alexandria.

Mosby relayed instructions through one of his scouts for the main body of Rangers to ride to Guilford Station, approximately four miles northwest of Frying Pan. The movement took the Rangers three hours and they arrived at the station around 0100 on the 10th, where they halted to feed their mounts and grab a few more hours of rest. On the move before daylight, they moved to a point five miles from Alexandria where Mosby, once again, linked up with them.

Mosby and his men waited throughout the morning hours and into the early afternoon. Finally, late in the day, a large wagon train with an escort of 150 Union soldiers made its way down the pike before them. With so many soldiers intermingled with the train, Mosby believed himself to be at a disadvantage.

With the caravan's passing, it was noted that two wagons had been left behind, unguarded and stuck in a large hole in the roadbed. Carefully approaching the buckboards, Mosby and his men soon discovered that they contained between 150 to 200 pairs of cavalry boots and some food inside. Dividing the plunder, the Rangers returned to their quarters with little — other than boots — to show for their efforts over five days.

The New Year of 1864 started off with a Union cavalry sweep by eighty soldiers under the command of Captain A. N. Hunter. Passing through Upperville and riding on to Rectortown, the Federals arrived just as a rendezvous called by the Company B commander, Billy Smith, was taking place.

With only a small number of Rangers on hand, the Confederates quickly scattered upon the appearance of the men in blue. As the Union cavalry continued on toward Middleburg, Smith gathered thirty-two of his men and rode after the Yankees in pursuit. At a road junction called Five Points, the Confederates caught up. Though the Union soldiers had halted and deployed prior to Smith's charge, Hunter's men broke ranks and fled in the direction of Middleburg after his horse was shot from under him. A total of fifty-seven men were killed, wounded, or captured by Smith and his men along with the seizure of sixty horses.

A week later, Mosby learned that a Yankee cavalry unit encamped on Loudoun Heights was vulnerable to an assault. Another of Jeb Stuart's favorite scouts, Benjamin Franklin Stringfellow, had provided this information. Mosby ordered a rendezvous for 1200 on 9 January at Upperville. In addition to the one hundred Rangers who rallied, Stringfellow, having received authorization to temporarily ride with Mosby's Rangers, also joined the group.

The Rangers rode northward through the snow and intensely cold temperature. Around 2000, they halted at a Ranger's home in Loudoun County to feed their mounts and to warm themselves. By 2200, they were back in their saddles and moving almost due north to Hillsborough.

As the temperature continued to plunge, the Rangers rode with their hands in their pockets and reigns in their teeth. Periodically, as their feet began to freeze, they'd dismount to walk beside their steeds. In the small valley between Short Hill and the Blue Ridge, Mosby and his men linked up with Stringfellow who had been scouting ahead.

Estimating the Federal strength in the camp at three hundred, String-fellow outlined the camp's layout. Mosby proceeded to lead his command off the road and down to the southern bank of the Potomac to skirt the Union pickets. Turning west, the Rangers moved to the foot of Loudoun Heights. Halting at the entrance to a ravine, Mosby dismounted his men and began the ascent of the heights on foot.

The Rangers came to a halt approximately two hundred yards from the rear of the Union camp. There, Mosby assigned Stringfellow a detachment of ten men and the mission to capture the unit's commander, who was headquartered in a house at the northern end of the camp. Stringfellow was not to initiate his attack until he heard the firing of the main group's assault. Mosby then made off with the main body to the eastern side of Hillsborough road.

By 0430 on the morning of 10 January, Mosby had his men on line and prepared to charge. But before he could initiate the attack, gunfire erupted from the direction of where Stringfellow and his men had been posted. Immediately following the burst of gunfire, cavalry galloped into the north perimeter of the camp. Not realizing the men thundering toward him were those who'd been left with Stringfellow, Mosby mistook the approaching cavalrymen as Federals and signaled a charge straight into the ranks of the approaching unit. Confusion reigned supreme for the next few minutes as the Confederates fought among themselves.

Granted this brief respite of chaos by the Confederates, the Union men quickly awoke and, grabbing their weapons, which they now slept with by their sides, quickly sought the nearest rock or tree for cover. While the dark prevented positive identification of friend or foe, a number of Northerners smartly—and correctly—called out "shoot every soldier on horseback."

The initial volley fire caught Mosby's men in the open, along the road. As the only men on horseback, they were easy targets. Veterans of the group were cut down. First Lieutenant Turner of Company A, an original "charter" member, slowly died in the arms of fellow Ranger Walter Frankland as he was led away. John Robinson, a Scotsman and former officer in the British army lay dead on the soil of a foreign land. Five other Rangers would lay dead or dying. A sixth, Captain Billy Smith, commander of Company B, was mortally wounded while attempting to rescue one of his injured men.

Despite the casualties and sudden turn of events, the Rangers withdrew in good order when Mosby issued the command. Moving off with six prisoners and fifty to sixty horses, Mosby briefly halted at a home to drop off one of his mortally wounded men. Then, prior to remounting, he directed two Rangers to return to the Federal camp under a flag of truce in an attempt to exchange their six Union prisoners for the dead and mortally wounded Rangers who had been left behind. The Rangers' request was rejected.

The ride back to their territory was a miserable one for the Rangers. Mosby had lost eight dead, five wounded, and one captured. Three of the dead were killed—so it was believed—by Southern bullets. On an even more personal level, one of the wounded was the commander's eighteen-year-old brother, William Mosby. Fortunately for William, his wounds were light. The Union's losses were six killed and fourteen wounded in addition to the six captives.

The loss of the two Confederate officers, Turner and Smith, in particular was especially disturbing for they were both "universal favorites" among the Rangers. One of the remaining six who were either killed outright or mortally wounded was Charlie Paxson. Back in the Federal camp, as he lay dying on the ground, Paxson asked if Samuel McNair was still assigned to the battalion Mosby had just attacked. It just so happened that nearly a year prior, McNair had been the one lying wounded on another battlefield near Leesburg. Located and cared for by his brother, H.S. McNair, the wounded McNair had been transported by a kind-hearted civilian who just happened to be Charlie Paxson's father.

The father had secured from H. S. McNair his word that should his son, Charlie, a member of Mosby's Rangers, need help in the future, the McNairs would reciprocate in kind. Samuel McNair soon arrived. With Paxson's identification, McNair promised the dying Ranger that he would send word to his father. Dying shortly thereafter, Paxson was the only one of the eight killed who was not buried in a common grave. A few days following the engagement, Paxson's father arrived to return his son's remains home to their final resting place. A debt of honor had been repaid.

One of the greatest threats against Mosby and his men was not from Union cavalry but from some of his own men, deserters who felt wronged and attempted to get even by informing the Federals of the Rangers' whereabouts. In mid-February, one such man, John Cornwall, enraged by the fact that Mosby had disallowed some expenses claimed when he brought in a wagonload of ammunition from Charlottesville to Fauquier, swore retribution against Mosby and his command. Turning himself over to the Yankees for interrogation, Cornwall promised to lead them to the Ranger safe houses.

A 350-man force from the 1st and 3rd Pennsylvania, the 1st New Jersey, and the 1st Massachusetts departed from Warrenton midmorning on

17 February. Under the command of Lieutenant Colonel John W. Kester, 1st New Jersey, the group found the day to be exceptionally cold with a wind-chill that penetrated even their heavy winter overcoats. The frigid temperatures of the previous night had forced the Ranger guards into cover from their exposed positions. Consequently, no warning was relayed of the Yankees' approach as they spread out to cover the country-side from Paris to Markham. Every house was searched, with the turn-coat Cornwall pointing out those that served as safe houses.

The secret hiding places within many of the safe homes were put to the test by some Rangers while other Rangers were scrambled out a back or side window to make off into woods or up mountains either on foot or horseback. Unfortunately, all those surprised were not so lucky. Five Rangers trapped in one home were compelled to surrender when the Federals threatened to torch the house. Others were located under beds or couches. One Ranger was even discovered under a pile of "Southern Belle"-type hoopskirts. Overall, the Union raid netted twenty-eight Rangers, approximately two hundred horses, a cache of medical supplies, and some barrels of whiskey.

Not all of the Rangers were caught unawares. A small detachment of Mosby's men under the command of William Chapman skirmished with the detachment of 1st Pennsylvania Cavalry at Belle Grove but the small group of thirty Rangers was unable to accomplish much against the larger force. By the evening of the 18th, the Union cavalry had returned to their camp, having inflicted the greatest single loss of men on Mosby's Rangers.

Union cavalry once again rode through Mosby's Confederacy on 20 February on the hunt for more partisans. On this particular morning, a two-hundred-man force under the command of Major Cole entered the town of Upperville and rooted out nine Rangers who'd gone into hiding. As the cavalry was riding out of town with its prisoners around 0800, two more Rangers were detained as they unknowingly rode into town. A twelfth Ranger was encountered a short distance out of town at a safe house. The Ranger, named McCobb, was able to run to his horse, mount, and spur his animal into a gallop. Unfortunately, though he was able to outdistance his pursuers, he was unable to safely jump a fence. Thrown from his saddle, McCobb's fall resulted in his death from a broken neck.

Mosby, who had been promoted to Lieutenant Colonel with a date of rank of 21 January 1864, and three of his fellow Rangers were leisurely enjoying breakfast when the younger brother of one of the men burst into the house warning of the Federal cavalry's advance toward Piedmont. Quickly mounting their horses, the four Rangers rode to a point that allowed them to observe Cole's men as they watered their mounts. Dismounting, Mosby and a second Ranger engaged the Union force with long-range fire from their carbines, killing one trooper and a horse. After trading fire with Mosby and his small band of men, Cole finally had his men remount and ride back toward Upperville.

Alerted by the exchange of gunfire, Rangers began to move to the sound of the guns. Rallying a group of fifty to sixty Rangers on the outskirts of Piedmont, Mosby set out in pursuit of the withdrawing Federals. The horsemen, both North and South, thundered at a gallop through Upperville with the Confederates slowly gaining ground in the race. Finally, realizing that he would need to take a stand or be run down, Cole halted and dismounted his men behind a stone wall at Blakeley's Grove School three miles northeast of Upperville. Mosby deployed his men on line in preparation for battle.

An exchange of fire between the two stationary forces was soon followed by a Federal officer, Captain W. L. Morgan of the 1st New York Cavalry, riding forward into the open area between the two opposing forces. Accepting the challenge for the Confederates was Ranger Richard Montjoy, who rode forth to do battle. A well-aimed shot from the Ranger's revolver left the Union officer lying dead on the field of battle. In response to this loss, the Yankee cavalry charged Mosby's position, only to be repelled. A subsequent second and third assault by the Federals also met with the same results.

The battle swirled around the schoolhouse with each side looking for an opportunity to rout the other. Finally, Mosby divided his force and outflanked Cole's position behind the stonewall. Despite being outmaneuvered, Cole's men disengaged in good order, withdrawing with a rear guard of men providing covering fire from a succession of stonewalls. Cole's reported losses were two killed, three wounded, and one missing. Other than those eleven who'd been captured earlier during the Union sweep and unfortunately retained during the fight, Mosby's losses were only three wounded.

The next morning, during the funeral services for McCobb, a scout reported the presence of another Union cavalry force in Middleburg. Abruptly concluding the service, Mosby and the approximately 160 Rangers gathered with him were on the road riding again into battle. Arriving at Middleburg, Mosby dispatched the majority of his men under the command of William Chapman to a location six miles south of Leesburg at Ball's Mill, while he and a small detachment trailed the Union cavalry who were apparently now riding toward Leesburg.

The Federal cavalry were 127 officers and men under the command of Captain J. Sewell Reed. Composed of three companies of the 2nd Massachusetts and one company of the 16th New York, the force was on what was termed a "roving commission." Serving as a guide was a deserter from Mosby's command, Charley Binns, who had escaped Mosby's grasp prior to his ordered arrest around 3 November.

Reed established a campsite around 0200 on the morning of the 22nd, approximately six miles beyond Leesburg, where Mosby and his scouts caught up to him. Leaving his small detachment behind to continue monitoring the Yankees' movements, Mosby rode cross-country to link up with his main body, which he'd kept informed throughout the day and evening. Mosby met up with Chapman at the Guilford Station depot on the Loudoun & Hampshire Railroad where the Ranger commander woke his sleeping men and led them on a march toward the Leesburg Alexandria Pike, despite the fact he'd been in the saddle for nearly twenty-four hours.

Along the Pike, Mosby located a thicket and stand of trees just two miles west of Dranesville that would serve as a suitable ambush location. Dividing his force into three detachments, Mosby placed fifteen dismounted men with carbines in the center under Richard Montjoy on the south side of the Pike, deployed Lieutenant Frank Williams to his right with a mounted group in a column of fours, and a similarly organized group to his left under Captain William Chapman. Three men serving as bait to lure the unsuspecting Federals were stationed on the road with orders to engage the leading enemy elements, turn, and ride past their compatriots' ambush position.

Reed and his men advanced slowly and came into view around 1100 that morning. His formation indicated that he anticipated trouble. A van of fifteen men rode about three hundred paces ahead. In turn, a point man consisting of four horsemen rode one hundred paces ahead of the van. Upon observing Mosby's decoy men on the road, the Union vanguard gave chase after the Confederates. Not realizing that the men before them were only the lead element of Cole's force, Montjoy's dismounted men fired, blowing several of the mounted troopers off their horses.

With the ambush initiated, Mosby blew a whistle to lead the mounted charge across the Pike. Given that only a small percentage of his men were actually engaged, Cole's counterattack was both swift and unexpected. Confused, Mosby and his men turned to face this unexpected attack from over one hundred men. The battle flowed and raged across the Pike and into the nearby fields as it became personal and close-quarters. In the midst of the turmoil rode Mosby, "fighting hand-to-hand with every man who would stand before him." Fortune proved to be on his side as his horse carried him through the engagement on three legs, the fourth leg having taken a bullet early in the fight.

As the battle progressed, Ranger Baron Robert von Massow, a former Prussian officer, captured Captain Reed. Keeping with tradition, Reed was allowed to retain his firearm as von Massow turned his attention to other Yankees. It was then, contrary to the rules of engagement, capture, and parole of the times, Reed proceeded to shoot von Massow in the back. Captain Chapman shot and killed the Union captain seconds later. Von Massow would recover from his wounds but not enough to ever ride with Mosby again.

Von Massow was the second Ranger to be shot under similar circumstances. Earlier in the battle, John Munson had also been shot in the back by his prisoner, with the bullet entering just an inch from his spinal cord. Munson would also survive his serious and near crippling wound.

Mosby's superior numbers finally began to overwhelm the embattled Federals, who broke and began to scatter across the countryside. A few of them were pursued and driven into the Potomac where some of them drowned. The Confederate deserter and Federal guide, Binns, disappeared during the fight and escaped.

Referred to as the Second Dranesville, the Union cavalry suffered at least twelve men dead, twenty-five wounded, and seventy captured. Nearly one hundred horses were seized. Mosby's losses were one killed and five wounded. Unfortunately for the one killed in action, J. Pendleton Chappalear, the battle was the first — and last — he participated in.

On the morning of the 28th, the Union cavalry brigade's commander, Brigadier General Charles Russell Lowell, complying with a directive of the commander of the Department of War Union Cavalry Major General Christopher C. Augur, conducted a raid against some specific homes that had been identified as harboring some of Mosby's Rangers. Deploying the 16th New York and the 2nd Massachusetts, Lowell advanced on Leesburg that afternoon. Unknown to Lowell, a number of Rangers were in Leesburg. Unfortunately for the Rangers, they, likewise, were unaware of Lowell's approach as they enjoyed themselves in Pickett's Hotel. By the time they learned of the Yankees' approach, the Federals were within two hundred yards of the town square.

Scrambling, the Rangers attempted to unhitch and mount their horses only to be spotted by the vanguard of the approaching Union cavalry. The skirmish was brief as one Ranger was shot dead, a second wounded, and six captured. Only two of the Confederates escaped, making their way out the rear of the hotel. Lowell's men continued into Upper Fauquier, where they captured twelve and killed one as they swept through the territory. Finally, on the 30th, they returned to their camp late in the day, having suffered three killed, two wounded, and four missing.

Mosby lost his mentor and best friend on 12 May. During an engagement the day prior with Union cavalry at Yellow Tavern, north of Richmond, Jeb Stuart received a wound in his right side, just below the ribs. Taken to Richmond, he would die in the early evening nearly twenty-four hours later. With Stuart's death, Mosby soon found himself reporting directly to Lee, the only commander below corps level to do so.

The war allowed little time for mourning, though, and within days, Mosby was in action again. Leading a group of fifty Rangers who had rendezvoused with five days of feed for their horses, Mosby made for Belle Plain. The following day found them hidden in the woodline along the Potomac, three miles from their objective. From this point, they observed Union infantry units pass by and a large Federal flotilla at anchor on the river. Moving forward with two other Rangers, Mosby reconnoitered. The next morning, they located a park of wagons but the decision was made to wait until evening before attacking.

Leaving his men under the command of Lieutenant Alfred Glascock, Mosby extended his reconnaissance into Fairfax County. Later that same day, Glascock was warned that their position had been compromised by their tracks and a regiment of infantry and cavalry were on their way to deal with the rebels. In no time, the men were in their saddle and moving out.

Approaching a railroad spur, they found that they were too late, for the infantry barred their escape route. Glascock was equal to the challenge though. Quick thinking and innovative, he spurred his horse into a gallop, racing towards the bluecoats, shouting, "Mosby is after us! Get out of the way!" Believing the oncoming cavalry to be Union, the infantry quickly scattered, allowing the lieutenant and his men a clear escape.

On 20 May, Mosby departed Paris with a force of ninety-nine men. Moving west across the Blue Mountains, they reached the Shenandoah River around dusk only to find it too swollen to cross on horse. While the Rangers bedded down for the evening, Mosby secured a skiff and crossed the river to scout ahead. The next morning the detachment arrived at the river to find six boats waiting for them at the bank, courtesy of their commander. With their mounts swimming alongside the craft, the Rangers crossed. On the far shore, a messenger sent by Mosby directed them to take the back roads toward Guard Hill, a forested knoll four miles from

Front Royal and on the road to Winchester. The group arrived in the vicinity of Guard Hill later that evening where Mosby met them.

Later that evening, Mosby and a small detachment of men reconnoitered Guard Hill, which was garrisoned by the 15th New York Cavalry. Coincidentally, the Federals were holding a party that evening that eventually turned into a brawl among themselves. During the disturbance, Mosby and his men captured one of the 15th's picket posts. From the guards, Mosby learned that the garrison of two hundred cavalry was twice the number he had originally expected but that fact did not deter him.

Mosby's attack commenced at sunrise on the 22nd with Sam Chapman—William Chapman's brother—and six additional Rangers opening fire with their carbines. The initial volley signaled Mosby's charge. Thundering into the camp, the mounted Rangers began to gather the sleeping Federals. But the Union troopers were quick. Despite their surprise, many were able to scramble from their sleeping locations and safely make it to the nearby woods and brush. The raid netted Mosby seventeen prisoners, including a captain who rode into camp after the attack demanding to know what "all this fuss" was about, and seventy-five horses.

On 16 July 1864, Major General Jubal Early's army slowly made its way through Snicker's Gap and into the Shenandoah Valley after it had defeated a Union force under the command of Major General Lewis Wallace in the Battle of Monocacy on 9 July and tested the defenses of the Union capital, Washington, D.C. Having entered the northwest quadrant of Mosby's Confederacy, Early was approached by Mosby, who offered his services in support of the bloodied and tired army. Early, though heavily outnumbered, seemed to ignore the offer. During the next four months, Mosby would operate without guidance or direction from Early as the Confederate general attempted to defend the Shenandoah Valley against Brigadier General Philip Sheridan and his Army of the Potomac cavalry who had been assigned the mission by Lieutenant General Ulysses S. Grant to destroy all organized resistance in the valley.

To Mosby's credit, he attempted to assist the embattled Confederate army the best he could. The very next day, the 17th, as Early's men rested, Mosby's Rangers observed the approach of the 22nd Pennsylvania Cavalry as they rode toward Snicker's Gap. Later that evening, the Rangers attacked the 22nd's bivouac site, inflicting approximately fifteen casualties without a single loss of their own.

The Pennsylvanians were just a precursor of what was to come, however, for 18 July found the roads to Snicker's and Ashby's Gaps clogged with the blue uniforms of Federal troops. Mosby rallied four of his companies at Upperville and moved to Middleburg to encamp for the night. Splitting his forces the next morning to harass the Union army, Mosby dispatched Dolly Richards and Company B to Fairfax County on a scout that netted little.

Companies A and D, under the command of Richard Montjoy and joined by Mosby, himself, scouted between Snicker's Gap and Leesburg. Trailing a Union column, the Rangers were able to capture 102 gaggling infantrymen on the 18th.

The third group of Rangers, Company C under the command of William Chapman, were tasked with the mission of harassing the Federal cavalry in Ashby's Gap. At the gap, Chapman encountered a rear guard under the command of Brigadier General Alfred Napoleon Alexander Duffié. Chapman's charge against this group resulted in the capture of thirty Yankees and forty horses. Confederate losses were placed at two dead and two captured.

For a week, relative inactivity reigned. During that time, Mosby organized two additional companies. Company E was officially formed in Upperville on 28 July with ninety-six men officially mustered. Mosby's proposed, and endorsed, slate of officers were First Lieutenant Samuel Chapman to captain and command, Fount Beattie as first lieutenant, William "Willie" Martin as second lieutenant, and Sergeant William Ben Palmer to third lieutenant.

The second company organized was an artillery company. Having requested and received from the Secretary of War three more artillery pieces, Mosby now had a four-gun battery. Though manned by the smallest number of men, the company received its full complement of officers. The unit's commander was Captain Peter Franklin. His three officers by rank were John J. Fray, John P. Page, and Frank H. Rahm. William H. Mosby, John S. Mosby's brother, was appointed the battalion adjutant to replace Sam Chapman.

As was the custom, a muster was ordered for the battalion and a raid launched the same day Company E was formed. Crossing the Potomac River and entering Adamstown, Maryland, the following day, Mosby encountered no Union forces. Returning to Virginia with the main body, Mosby had Chapman and his new company remain behind to scout deeper into the territory.

South of Frederick along the Monocacy River, Company E encountered a detachment of the 8th Illinois Cavalry on the 30th. The initial engagement went well for the Confederates, who captured twelve prisoners. But a Union counterattack broke through the rear guard led by Beattie that resulted in the entire Confederate company scattering and fleeing.

Though Chapman did not lose a man, it was not the most impressive of starts.

Events were about to come to a head in the Valley and Mosby's Confederacy. Farther north in Chambersburg, Pennsylvania, Early's cavalry under the command of Brigadier General John McCausland had looted and incinerated eleven square blocks of the town, destroying over two hundred buildings, in retaliation for the Union's torching of the Shenandoah Valley. An editorial in the *New York Times* noted that the foray into the north was "the old story over again. The back door, by way of the Shenandoah Valley, has been left invitingly open." Lincoln now felt compelled to shut and bolt the back door forever.

On 31 July, following a meeting between Lincoln and Grant, George Meade's cavalry commander, Philip H. "Little Phil" Sheridan, was given the command of what would become the Army of the Shenandoah, Middle Military Division. Grant's orders were short and specific. He was to "put himself south of the enemy and follow him to the death. Wherever the enemy goes let our troops go also."

Sheridan's army moved from Harper's Ferry on 10 August and into the Shenandoah Valley. Fully understanding that Early was outnumbered almost three to one, Mosby took the initiative to assist the Confederate army as well as he could. Mosby planned two continuing operations in support of the Confederate army. His first plan was to guard Early's flank along the Blue Ridge Mountains while attacking the Federals' outposts and disrupting their supply lines on an almost daily basis.

Mosby's second plan of support had him dispatching detachments into Fairfax County where they would attack the outer ring of Washington's outposts. It was Mosby's belief that pressure on the Federal capital would make the local commanders less liable to reassign defending units to reinforce Sheridan's Valley campaign.

To support these efforts, Mosby relied more heavily on Dolly Richards, Richard Montjoy, and the two Chapman brothers. The Valley was divided into three sectors. Each of these Ranger leaders were assigned one of these sectors — to include a sector in Fairfax County — and authorized to plan and conduct their own raids as they saw fit. Operations requiring multiple companies would be planned and led by Mosby.

In the lower, northern, valley, Berryville served as the hub for Ranger operations in the region. Safe houses were scattered about, providing the soldiers with food, shelter, guides, and information. Mosby's most valuable scout was a Berryville native, John S. Russell. Russell's family had lived in the Valley for over half a century and his knowledge of the terrain and its occupants was matchless. Amazingly, on any given night,

Russell and a small number of Rangers could be found prowling within the lines of Sheridan's headquarters' security.

Mosby's initial operation against Sheridan was literally against the general. Based on Russell's reliable information and his proposal, Mosby agreed to attempt to capture the Union commander who had just arrived in the valley on the 6th. The kidnap attempt was launched the night of 8 August.

Mosby, a small contingent of Rangers, and Russell entered the valley and began to make their way toward the home of Haight Willis in the Charlestown area. Throughout the next day, Mosby and his men tested the perimeter of the Union army, taking several prisoners in the process. That night, they stealthily moved to within three hundred yards of the Willis residence.

Ranger John W. Hearn was ordered to move forward to scout the number of troops around the headquarters site. Unfortunately for Mosby and his men, and quite fortunately for Sheridan whose successful career may have been terminated that very night, Hearn accidentally landed among some sleeping Yankees after he vaulted a fence. When challenged, Hearn grabbed for the sentry's musket and quickly disappeared as the guard shouted the alarm. Compromised, Mosby terminated the extraordinary mission.

The strange events outside of his headquarters of the evening before did nothing to prevent Sheridan's movements the following morning as he mobilized his army to press southward toward Early. As the Army of the Shenandoah advanced, the Army of the Valley retreated before it, hesitant to engage. Warned by Russell on the 11th of the movement and made aware of the vulnerability of Sheridan's supply trains, Mosby ordered a rendezvous on the 12th for noon at Rectortown. Between two hundred and fifty to three hundred Rangers of Companies A, B, C, and D reported, as did the artillery crews with two guns. That afternoon they passed through Snicker's Gap and crossed the Shenandoah River at Castleman's Ferry to bed down for a few hours' rest three miles from Berryville.

Russell scouted ahead while Mosby and his men caught some sleep. Approximately two hours later, Russell returned with the news that the Charlestown-Berryville Pike was crowded with dozens of parked wagons at Berryville. Russell led Mosby and three other Rangers back to select a site from where to attack. With a site selected, Mosby ordered the main body to report to him.

Once arrived, they were formed into their line of battle before the assembled wagons, which were only one hundred yards distant. Dolly Richards was placed on the left flank and Chapman on the right. Mosby remained with Company D on Barnett's Hill to act as the reserve and to secure the cannon, there being only one on hand for the second had been left behind where it broke a wheel as it crossed the rugged terrain.

The howitzer was unlimbered. Two rounds fired from it would signal the start of the attack. Unfortunately for the gun crew, nature elected to actively involve itself. As the cannon was moved into position, it rolled over a nest of yellow jackets. Incensed by the disturbance, the bees quickly took flight and scattered the gun crew. Mosby's own horse nearly threw its rider. A brave band of cannoneers rushed the weapon and manhandled it to a more hospitable location. Finally in position, the crew was prepared to fire the first round.

Sheridan's supply trains consisted of nearly six hundred canvastopped wagons each drawn by a four-horse team. Cavalry escorts rode vanguard before the train with infantrymen intermingled throughout the wagons all along the column. The section that had stopped at Berryville was the support train of Sheridan's cavalry corps. The detail assigned to secure the wagons were companies of the 144th and 149th Ohio National Guard. Coffee was being brewed and horses being hitched when Mosby's gun crew lit the fuse.

The first shot fired from the Confederate cannon exploded, beheading a mule. A few seconds later, the second shot followed with Richards' mounted Rangers right behind, heading for the center and trail of the halted train. Pandemonium ensued at once as those in the Rangers' immediate path broke and scattered. Some of the Ohio infantrymen were able to drop their breakfasts, grab their rifles, and get to cover behind a stonewall at Buck Marsh Church. The remainder, many of whom had no combat experience and less than a month left in service, joined the wagon drivers in their flight. Those who remained behind the wall fired a volley that killed one Ranger, mortally wounded a second, and wounded two others. The single volley was the only resistance offered as the remaining men scrambled upon an Ohio captain's shouted command to save themselves.

Chapman and his men of Company C, meanwhile, charged the wagons where they entered the town. Resistance was light, with only one Ranger sustaining a wound. A brief skirmish resulted in the scattering of all the Federals. For his efforts, Chapman secured over two hundred head of cattle. Overall, Mosby and his men captured about one hundred wagons, up to six hundred horses and mules, and approximately two hundred prisoners.

Scouring the wagons, the Confederates secured food and grain for themselves and their mounts and secured what bounty they could carry on their saddles. In their haste, they overlooked a paymaster's chest loaded down with $112,000 in cash. With their task completed, the Rangers set fire to the wagons and withdrew eastward around 0630. Within thirty minutes of their departure, the 1st Rhode Island Cavalry arrived at the scene of the raid. They were able to extinguish eighteen of the fires and save the overlooked cash box.

Returning to the location where they had left their second cannon, the artillery crews lifted the disabled cannon on top of the other and moved out. Arriving at Rectortown, Mosby immediately promoted his trustworthy scout, John Russell, to lieutenant for his contribution to the "Berryville Wagon Train Raid." The captured horses were divided between the Rangers and Mosby designated a detail to drive the cattle and mules to Richmond.

Despite the constant harassment by the Rangers, Sheridan did not feel compelled to vigorously pursue Mosby and his men. Grant had assigned him his primary mission and that was the destruction of Early and the valley's ability to feed Lee and his army in Petersburg. Though he did not feel that he could commit the requisite number of cavalry necessary to eradicate Mosby, Sheridan did authorize, based on a suggestion from Major General George Crook, the formation of a small independent command whose sole mission was to operate against the Confederate Rangers.

In early 1864, Crook had organized a hundred-man force to scout and suppress guerrilla activity. The organization was designated the "Legion of Honor." Now, with his Army of West Virginia assigned to Sheridan, Crook proposed in mid-August that this legion be assigned the task of dealing with Mosby and his Rangers. Sheridan agreed to the proposal. Even more, he requested some of the latest weaponry for their use—the seven-shot Spencer repeater rifle. Sheridan elected to retain the unit's commander, Captain Richard Blazer. Officially designated Company G of the 23rd Ohio, the unit would eventually come to be very well known throughout Mosby's Confederacy as "Blazer's Scouts."

Blazer had his men operate in a manner similar to that of Mosby. Moving swiftly, they would swing into their saddles before sunrise and ride until well past sunset. Raids would, on average, run three days with scouts circling along the main body's perimeter to defend against surprise attacks. Unlike his compatriots, Blazer also believed that kindness by him and his men toward the local civilian populace would ultimately result in their not being so compelled to report to Mosby on their movements.

Blazer and his men commenced their newly assigned mission late in August. Their search for Mosby began as a reconnaissance along the Shenandoah River and Blue Ridge Mountains, watching fording sites and passes into Loudoun County. Blazer's reports during this time stated that he had killed six and captured four Rangers by the end of the month but indications were that none of these Confederates were part of Mosby's command.

On 3 September; as Sheridan's army marched to Berryville, Blazer and his command moved east toward the Blue Ridge Mountains. Heavy rains impeded their ride and by evening, they bivouacked short of the ridge. Later that evening, Blazer received word from an informant that Mosby and a large force of Rangers were at Snickersville on the eastern side of Snicker's Gap.

The information was reasonably accurate. Mosby and ninety of his men were in the area, encamped in the gap at the top of the Blue Ridge and not in Snickersville. Earlier that day, Mosby had assembled his A and B Companies at Rectortown and moved through Snickersville to his present location. Preceding him was a second detachment of Rangers composed of Companies C and E under the overall command of Sam Chapman. They had entered the valley the day prior with the orders to move to the Millwood-Berryville area to harass Sheridan. Approaching Berryville from the southwest, they were a half-mile from the town when they encountered the 6th New York Cavalry Regiment in a farm field.

The regiment was commanded by Major William E. Beardsley and was serving as the advance guard for Sheridan's army. Having received word from his scouts that Confederates were reported to the west, Beardsley had positioned the main body of his regiment in a field enclosed by a fence and dismounted skirmishers to cover his front and flanks. A volley from the skirmishers placed out front met Chapman's movement down the road. Splitting his forces in two, Chapman ordered Company E under the command of Lieutenant W. Ben Palmer to attack through a gate in the fence around the field while he led his company in a charge down the road.

Palmer and his men advanced, only to be met with successive volleys of fire from the New Yorkers' repeating rifles. Compounding their troubles was the fact that the Rangers had to halt in order to unlatch the gate. Rangers Robert Jarman and Benjamin Iden attempted, but were killed in the process. Palmer was the third to try and his effort proved to be successful.

With the gate open, the company thundered into the field. As the Union skirmishers scattered to the rear before the oncoming rebels, Beardsley shouted the charge to initiate the counterattack with his mounted cavalry. Reeling under the weight of the attack, Palmer's men gave ground momentarily until Chapman and his men, pouring in through a gap in the fence, arrived to help change the tide. Finding himself almost surrounded, Beardsley ordered his men to fall back toward the woods and reform.

The Confederates continued to pursue relentlessly. Driven into a corner of the fenced-in field, the Federals escaped total annihilation only as a result of a gate that was opened, allowing their escape. Regimental records reflect that Beardsley's regiment suffered forty-two dead, wounded, or captured. The losses for Chapman's detachment were two dead, three mortally wounded, and one wounded. The Rangers withdrew from the area, arriving back in Mosby's Confederacy on the 4th.

Meanwhile, Mosby and his detachment had moved to Myers' Ford on the Shenandoah River, approximately six miles to the southeast of their objective, Charlestown. Mosby crossed with fifteen men and scouted north while Dolly Richards forded the site and moved west with a small detachment to search for Federal soldiers. Lieutenant Joseph Nelson was left in command of the main body. Richards returned shortly thereafter, having been informed that the Union cavalry were in the vicinity of Nelson. Scouting with Company B north along the river shore, Richards decided that the report was incorrect. Nelson and his seventy or so Rangers resumed their leisurely wait as Richards recrossed the river on a scout.

The day that had started so warm, sunny, and restive for the Confederates changed dramatically around 1400 with the sudden arrival of Blazer's Scouts, who had spent the day tracking the Ranger main body from the Blue Ridge Mountains to its current location at Myers' Ford. With little warning, the scouts attacked Nelson and his men.

Finding themselves at a serious disadvantage, the Rangers scrambled after their weapons and mounts. Nelson rallied a few men to serve as a rear guard while the majority of his men fled demoralized in all directions. Dismounting a number of his soldiers, Blazer was able to place a heavy volume of fire with their new Spencer rifles, forcing the remaining Rangers out of the woods and into the open.

The battle between the Rangers' pistols and the scouts' rifles continued for thirty minutes, with the Rangers getting the worst end of the deal as their losses continued to accumulate. Blazer himself was to note later that the Confederates "fought with a will, but the seven-shooters proved too much for them." A final charge from the woodline by the scouts routed what remained of Nelson's command, which scattered again, every man for himself. Behind they left two dead and four prisoners. Four others, including Nelson, were wounded. Blazer reported the loss of one killed and four wounded in action. His use of Mosby's own tactics earned Blazer and his men the respect of Mosby and his command.

A two-week interlude between the two main Valley protagonists, Sheridan and Early, found both sides conducting little in the way of offensive operations. The Rangers undertook no major forays into the valley as the Union cavalry sealed the Rangers' main entry points through the mountains and observed the Shenandoah's fording sites.

Two minor Ranger operations conducted by small detachments did occur during this time. One such operation by Lieutenant Alfred Glascock and ten men proved to be an overwhelming success when the Ranger lieutenant and his men were able to ride through an encampment's pickets without being stopped or questioned to capture fifteen Yankees in the camp with no losses to themselves.

A second raid had mixed results when Chapman and his Company C skirmished with a contingent of the 8th Illinois Cavalry. While the Rangers were able to capture eighteen Federals and forty of their horses, Chapman lost one killed and five prisoners.

The decreased operational tempo allowed Mosby the opportunity to activate a seventh company in Piedmont on 13 September. Company F enlisted sixty to seventy men that day. Mosby's slate of approved officers were Captain Walter Frankland, First Lieutenant James F. "Big Yankee" Ames—the Union deserter—Second Lieutenant Walter Bowie, and Third Lieutenant James Frank Turner, whose previously highest rank had been private until this promotion.

Unlike previous activations, Mosby did not initiate the unit's formation with a raid. Instead, on the following day, Mosby went on a scout with two other Rangers into Fairfax County. Unfortunately for Mosby, he should have stuck with his tradition. Clearing Centerville, the three Rangers were attacked by five cavalrymen from the 13th New York. There was a brief exchange of pistol fire leading to a chase with the Yankees in pursuit. A mile later, Mosby stopped and turned to engage the Federals. Firing with both his pistols, Mosby killed the mounts of two of the riders and halted the other three men.

Pinned under his horse, Corporal Henry Smith fired his last round at Mosby. The round struck one of Mosby's pistols and ricocheted into his groin. Reeling in his saddle, Mosby was able to remain upright and disengage from the fight. Leaving the small Union detachment behind, Mosby and his two escorts arrived at The Plains, where his wound was dressed. The decision was made to not attempt to remove the bullet, which Mosby would carry for the rest of his life. Mosby ultimately transferred himself to Amherst County to recover with his father near Lynchburg.

The battle for the valley reached its peak on 19 September. Sheridan's overwhelming numbers prevailed and Early's army scattered in a complete rout from Winchester. A second assault by Sheridan against Early on the 22nd resulted in an even greater rout as the Confederate left flank was crushed and their entire line rolled up.

The following morning found Chapman and a small detachment of Rangers scouting toward Milford ahead of their main body of Rangers. A few miles north of the town, they observed an ambulance train with what appeared to be a small escort slowly moving along the Luray-Front Royal Pike. Hurrying ahead, Chapman linked up with his main force outside of Front Royal where he divided his force. Forty-five Rangers under Captain Walter E. Frankland would strike the front of the train as it apparently made its way toward Winchester while Chapman and seventy-five other Rangers flanked the column to the east and struck them from the rear.

As Chapman as his men closed on the column, he halted on the crest of a bluff to look down upon the Union column. Spread below were the ambulance wagons creaking along. Unfortunately, unseen until now and following immediately behind for as far as the eye could see was also an unbroken column of Union cavalry. Incredibly, the ambulances were in reality the van of two divisions of cavalry under the command of Brevet Major General Alfred T. A. Torbert. While he could halt the attack of the seventy-five Rangers riding with him, Chapman was not sure he could halt in time Frankland's attack to the front with his forty-five men.

Ordering Lieutenant Harry Hatcher to withdraw with his detail to Chester Gap, Chapman spurred his horse on towards Prospect Hill in an attempt to stop what could prove to be a suicidal attack by Frankland and his men. Having located Frankland, Chapman galloped up yelling, "Call off your men! You are attacking a brigade!"

Frankland, not clearly hearing what Chapman was shouting replied, "Sam, we can't stop now. We've got them whipped!"

Whipped was putting it mildly and the term was not to be used on the Union, for as the two commanders were speaking, Frankland's Rangers, who were already among the ambulances and shooting the wagon drivers and escorts, were quickly overwhelmed by the cavalry who rode from the rear of the column. Though the forty-five men attempted to make a valiant stand, common sense quickly prevailed and they began to scatter to save their lives.

Riding into the foray, Chapman and Frankland began to rally the men and lead them across the fields toward Chester Gap. In the finest of Ranger tradition, Hatcher disobeyed Chapman's previous orders to wait at the gap and, instead, stopped short of the gap to await link-up with the remainder of their force, unwilling to abandon his comrades to an unknown fate. The two elements met in the bottomlands of the Oak Hill farm, near the Chester Gap Road.

Unknown to the Rangers, the regiment that had responded to their attack on the ambulances, the 2nd U.S. Cavalry Regiment of Lowell's reserve brigade, had divided its forces. While one detachment rode to the head of the column to assist the drivers and their escort, a larger force had scaled the embankment along the pike and galloped toward Chester Gap to cut off the Southerners' escape route. In the vicinity of Oak Hill, the two forces collided.

Encountering the Yankees, the rebels charged forward, attempting to punch a hole through the Federal cordon. Each individual Ranger was on his own, attempting to make his escape any way possible. Small, narrow openings were created as pistols fired and Union horses were either knocked off their feet or wandered from the line, riderless. Amazingly, most of the Rangers were able to make it through the line with only six captured and none killed.

During this battle, an incident occurred that would linger and affect both sides for months to come. One of the Union casualties was Lieutenant Charles McMaster, who was mortally wounded on the road in the gap. At the start of the engagement, a bullet severed the bridle of McMaster's horse. Unable to control his mount as it panicked, McMaster found himself in the midst of Chapman's Rangers.

What happened next is unclear. Mosby's men were to later claim that McMaster was shot in the head as they made past him unable, under the circumstances, to stop and take prisoners. Two local women reported differently. One of them, Tee Edmonds, reported in her diary that she had learned from some Ranger boarders "[o]ur men had captured a Colonel [an obvious mistake for McMaster was a lieutenant and the only officer captured] and were overtaken, surrounded by the enemy. Our men shot the Colonel, giving him several shots after his begging and pleading with them not to kill him."

The second woman, Catherine Cochran, also had noted in her journal that the Rangers had shot several Yankee prisoners. In his memoirs of the incident, Ranger John Scott admitted that the Union lieutenant had dismounted his horse, "it is supposed, intending to surrender."

Whether intentionally shot as a combatant or as a prisoner, McMaster survived until 15 October, long enough to tell his men that he had been gunned down after he'd surrendered. True or not, though there seems to be a great deal of validity to the claim, the allegation unleashed a fury of retribution in the streets of Front Royal. As the story spread, the Yankees clamored for revenge as the six Rangers captured during the engagement with Chapman were brought into the town.

The first two Ranger prisoners to be executed were Lucien Love, who was only seventeen, and David L. Jones. Marched to a town lot, they were quickly executed within the shadow of the Methodist Church. A third prisoner Thomas E. Anderson, husband and father of two, was shot under an elm tree on Perry Criser's farm.

The fourth Confederate to die was not a member of Mosby's Rangers. Henry Rhodes was a seventeen-year-old boy from Front Royal who had dreamed of riding with Mosby. When Chapman and his men moved through Front Royal on their way to attack the ambulances, Rhodes borrowed a neighbor's horse and rode after them. Unfortunately for the young Ranger wannabe, his mount collapsed during the race to Chester Gap. Rhodes was led to a farm field on Rose Hill where, despite pleas for mercy from his mother, a single shot from a revolver ended his life.

The final two to be executed were William Thomas Overby and a Ranger named Carter, about whom little is known. The two men were mounted on horses under the limb of a walnut tree with nooses placed around their necks. The crack of two whips sealed their fates. For the people of Front Royal, 23 September would forever be known as "The 'dark day' of 1864."

With Mosby's return to command six days after the execution of his men, he authorized another of his dramatic capture missions and assigned Lieutenant "Wat" Bowie of Company F the task of carrying it out. Mosby's target this time was Governor Bradford of Maryland. Bowie was a logical choice for the mission. He was a native of Maryland in addition to having operated within the state as part of a courier service for the Confederate secret service earlier in the war.

Bowie and his team of twenty-five Rangers arrived in the vicinity of Charles County, Maryland, on 2 October. Unable to ferry his men and horses across the Potomac River from Virginia to Maryland, Bowie crossed in a small boat for a quick reconnoiter, instead. Informed by a Southern sympathizer of a small party of the 8th Illinois Cavalry encamped at the courthouse in Port Tobacco, Bowie returned to his men and released eighteen of them to return to Mosby with all their horses. He and the remaining seven Rangers crossed the river, surprised the Illinois detachment, tied them up, and rode off with their horses.

The evening of the 3rd found Bowie and his men making their way to the Bowie family home, approximately fifteen or so miles west of their target in Annapolis. Brune, Bowie's younger brother who was home recovering from wounds received while serving with the 1st Virginia Cavalry, joined the band or Rangers. On the 5th, the group moved to the village of Collington. Entering Annapolis to scout alone, Wat Bowie determined that the governor was too well protected to attempt a seizure. Rejoining his men, he led them to Sandy Spring that night, a village north of the District of Columbia, where they ransacked a village store before continuing their journey south.

The following morning, a seventeen-member posse from Sandy Spring followed in pursuit of Bowie and his men. Three miles from Rockville, the posse located the Rangers encamped in a thicket of pine trees. The battle-hardened Confederates easily repelled the townsfolk's attack. Mounting their horses, the Rangers charged in pursuit of the fleeing posse. One of the civilians, a blacksmith and carriage-maker named William H. Ent, held his ground. Shotgun leveled, he fired both barrels at a charging rebel, riddling Wat Bowie's head and face with buckshot. Cared for by his brother in a nearby farmhouse, the Ranger lieutenant would die from his wounds a few short hours later.

With Mosby's return in late September, a series of minor raids were conducted in the Shenandoah Valley. Sheridan's supply lines ran for nearly one hundred miles between his army's current location at Harrisonburg and his supply base at Martinsburg. Between these two points, Union wagons shuttled back and forth. Escort duty was not lightly thought of. It was described as "hard and very dangerous work for experienced men who were so near used up from hard service during the war."

Detachments of Rangers roamed the roadways, searching for poorly defended convoys. On 11 October, Dolly Richards encountered a single ambulance wagon with a fifty-man escort from the 17th Pennsylvania Cavalry just south of Winchester near the town of Newtown. Resistance by the cavalry was light as the Union escort scattered, leaving behind twelve captives and the ambulance. Unfortunately, the two occupants of the ambulance, Colonel Cornelius Tolles, quartermaster of Sheridan's Sixth Corps, and Doctor Emil Ohlenschlager, Sheridan's medical director, were both mortally wounded during the brief skirmish. The war between Mosby and Sheridan's army was soon to grow even more personal.

On the same day as Richards' attack, one of Mosby's scouts, Jim Wiltshire, returned to report that he had located a chink in the Union security of the Baltimore & Ohio Railroad between Martinsburg and Harper's Ferry. Anticipating Mosby's wishes, Wiltshire had even obtained a timetable for the trains using the rail.

At noon the next day, eighty Rangers rendezvoused at Bloomfield in southern Loudoun County. Once again, as they had done many times before, Mosby led them through Snicker's Gap and across the Shenandoah River. Riding on through the night and early morning hours, they finally came to a halt before daybreak. The Rangers relaxed, as they remained hidden throughout the day.

As dusk fell on the evening of the 13th, Mosby and his men followed Wiltshire to a "long, deep cut on the railroad." Deciding to derail a westbound train, Mosby consulted the schedule that his scout had provided. Allowing an eastbound train to pass, the Ranger commander directed fifteen men under the guidance of Lieutenant Hatcher to remove a rail. That task completed, the men situated themselves up on the bank of the cut where many of them fell asleep.

The train was on time and derailed shortly after 0200. Veering off the track approximately a quarter of a mile beyond Duffield's Station, the locomotive crashed into the embankment causing the boiler in the engine to explode. The Rangers swept through the cars. Soon, all of the passengers were off the train that was set afire, but not before a U.S. Army quartermaster moneybox was secured. Gathering his lieutenants, Dear, Aldridge, Brisk, Wiltshire, and Groan, Mosby had them divide the money, place it in their saddlebags, and ride ahead of the main body to Bloomfield. Within an hour of the derailment, Mosby and his men were on their way.

The raid members rallied at Ebenezer Church in Bloomfield on the morning of 15 October to apportion out the money. A count of the greenbacks showed that there was a total of $173,000, which provided each of the eighty-two members of the operation, who would call themselves the "stockholders," an equal share of $2,109. The only one to not accept a share was Mosby. Weeks later, the stockholders would present Mosby with a thoroughbred named Coquette that would become Mosby's favorite horse and serve as a reminder of the great "Greenback Raid."

All was not cheerful, though, upon their return. During Mosby's absence the battalion's artillery was captured. Again, the Rangers had fallen victim to another turncoat. John Lunceford of Company B surrendered to the Yankees on 13 October, stating that he no longer desired to serve with Mosby.

Under a cooperative agreement, Lunceford led Colonel Henry Gansevoort and his command of the 13th New York Cavalry and two infantry companies to the location of the four Ranger cannon on Big Cobbler Mountain. The eight-man Ranger security detail was easily overwhelmed without a shot being fired.

Sheridan's success had changed the strategic situation within the valley region and for three days his cavalry roamed the full breadth of the valley, systematically destroying livestock, crops, mills, and barns. The swath of destruction would be referred to for a long time to come as "The Burning."

Incredibly, Early and his men still had some fight left in them. Following an all-night forced march, Early's troops attacked at dawn on the 19th, striking the Federal camps at Cedar Creek, routing nearly all of Sheridan's three infantry corps in his absence. Sheridan soon rejoined his command around 1030 and launched a massive counterattack around 1600 that completely overwhelmed Early. The Battle of Cedar Creek destroyed what little had remained of Early's army in the valley.

Years later, Mosby was to ask one of Early's staff officers why they had never informed the Ranger of their plans to attack or sought his assistance to pressure Sheridan's rear. Apparently, a member of Early's staff had asked the same thing of the general. Early's response was "By God, I was not going to do the fighting and Colonel Mosby do the plundering." Though Mosby had gained Lee's complete trust and confidence, he had not gained Early's. Needless to say, it would be Early who lost out in the end.

Despite Cedar Creek, Mosby still continued to conduct offensive operations within the region even though his was the only major organized Confederate unit left within the Valley's area of operation. At sunrise on 24 October, nearly four hundred Rangers rendezvoused at Bloomfield. Through Snicker's Gap and Castleman's Ferry they moved, bivouacking near Summit Point that evening.

The next morning found them positioned along the Valley Pike, six miles north of Winchester. Shortly after their arrival, a small wagon and an escort of twenty-five cavalrymen rode into view. The escort was quickly scattered and the wagon captured. Inside the wagon, they found Brigadier General Alfred N. A. Duffié, a cavalry commander who had previously threatened to hang every Mosby Ranger his men captured. Upon learning of the general's capture, Sheridan immediately requested his dismissal from the army. To Sheridan, Duffié was "a trifling man and a poor soldier. He was captured by his own stupidity."

The day was still young and Mosby and his men waited to see if they would encounter any additional Union units. Within an hour, a two-hundred-wagon train with an infantry and cavalry escort of up to 3,000 men and two cannon marched into view. Unhesitatingly wasting no time, Mosby formed his men into a line of battle.

At his signal, they charged. The Union cavalry did not even exchange a shot before they turned and ran. The infantry and artillery were more stoic, though, and stood their ground. The rifle and artillery fire proved to be more than Mosby and his men could handle, requiring the Ranger to disengage his forces. Mosby's efforts were not in total vain, though. Turning southward, the Rangers were able to seize seven wagons just outside of Winchester prior to recrossing the Blue Ridge Mountains.

The events of the dark day of 23 September in Front Royal were never far from Mosby's mind and a seventh Ranger, Absalom C. Willis, had been captured and hung on 13 October. Lee had approved a request by Mosby on 4 November to conduct similar prisoner executions. Two days later, the time had come. Twenty-seven Yankee prisoners were escorted from a brick store building in Rectortown and marched a half mile to the banks of Goose Creek. Twenty-seven slips of paper were placed in a hat with each man drawing one slip. Those who drew one of seven marked slips — one for each known Confederate Ranger execution — were to be executed.

The condemned were soon led to their place of execution in the Shenandoah Valley, their left wrists tied together with bed cord, escorted by the detail commander, Edward Thompson, and his twelve guards. The riders arrived at the execution site less than a mile west of Berryville in Beemer's Woods on Grindstone Hill. The time was 0400 on 7 November. The guards prepared to implement Mosby's directive that four of the prisoners were to be shot and three hung — to match the style of execution of his Rangers.

The Rangers' were experts in conducting raids, not executions. One of the condemned, Private George Soule, per his request, was provided an opportunity to pray. As he knelt, the private was able to slip off the rope that held him. Leaping to his feet, he slugged Thompson in the face and escaped into the nearby dark woods.

Galvanized by the escape, the Confederates hastened to finish their work. Two of the prisoners were each shot in the head and arm. A third Ranger placed his pistol to the head of Corporal Charles E. Marvin only to have it misfire. Taking a lesson from Soule's success, Marvin knocked his would-be executioner to the ground and disappeared. The final three men had nooses placed around their necks and were placed on mounts. A quick whip to each of the horses completed the effort.

The following morning a local resident discovered the execution site. Remarkably, he also discovered the two men shot, still alive, though one would lose most of his eyesight and the second his arm.

As it so happened, Mosby was not at all disturbed by the fact two of the condemned had escaped. As he wrote later, "It was not an act of revenge, but a judicial sentence to save not only the lives of my own men, but the lives of the enemy. It had that effect. I regret that fate thrust such a duty upon me; I do not regret that I faced and performed it."

In response to an earlier raid by Colonel William Powell's cavalry division on 7 November through Markham, Piedmont, Rectortown, Upperville, and Paris, Mosby dispatched Montjoy and Company D on the 15th for a raid along the Valley Pike between Newtown and Winchester. Having captured twenty men and their mounts, the Rangers withdrew the following day.

En route the unit dispersed as Rangers began to head home. The company was down to thirty men and just west of Berry's Ford when a detachment of Blazer's Scouts surprised them. One Ranger was killed as the remainder scattered. Montjoy rallied his men a mile or so to the east at "Vineyard," the home of one of Jeb Stuart's officers. But the Scouts offered no quarter and continued to press. Another Ranger was killed, five wounded, and two captured. The remaining Rangers made their way to the Shenandoah River and safely crossed the ford, leaving their pursuers behind. The second of two engagements between the two antagonists had once again gone to the Scouts.

Until now, Mosby had, for most intents and purposes, ignored Blazer and his Scouts. Though a nuisance, they were too small a force to significantly affect his operations, which had been focused on Sheridan in the valley and the Manassas Gap Railroad. But now, with Sheridan having reduced his numbers and with the Manassas Gap Railroad being dismantled along much of the line for it was no longer needed, Mosby now decided to deal with Blazer once and for all.

The evening following the skirmish at Vineyard, Mosby met with Captain Dolly Richards. Assigning him Companies A and B, Mosby ordered his commander to locate the Scouts and "wipe Blazer out! Go through him." To support Richards' efforts, Mosby dispatched two Rangers that evening to see if they could scout out Blazer's current location.

The one hundred Rangers of Richards' task force rallied at Bloomfield early the next morning. Mosby's two scouts arrived to inform Richards that Blazer was on a raid toward the Allegheny Mountains. Not convinced about the accuracy of this information, Richards rode with five Rangers to Snicker's Gap. At Snickersville, a sympathizer informed the Rangers that Blazer had been seen making his way toward Hillsborough, the bluecoats having previously passed through his village earlier that morning. This new information directly contradicted that which Richards had been told earlier.

Dispatching two Rangers to scout toward Hillsborough, Richards returned to his main body at Bloomfield to bring them forward. Moving through Snicker's Gap, the Rangers forded the Shenandoah River as a heavy rain fell. Northeast of Berryville, Richards camped in the woods. Allowing no campfires, the Rangers slept the best they could as they lay wet, cold, and miserable in the downpour. During the darkness, a scout located Richards to report that Blazers camp had been located near Kabletown.

Up before dawn, the Rangers made their way to the reported campsite. At first light, they attacked the bivouac only to find it deserted. But the fires were still burning and unopened bundles of newspapers lay on the ground. They were somewhere close at hand. Richards detailed two of his Rangers to locate the Yankees. If anyone could find the Scouts, he was convinced John Puryear and Charles McDonough could. These two men had the reputation of knowing no fear. They were "brevet-outlaws who accompanied [the Rangers] only by the tolerance of the Colonel." McDonough, in particular, even had a reward offered by the Federals for his apprehension. If anyone were to flush the Yankee Scouts, these two men were the ones.

The flushing did not take long. Riding into Kabletown, Mosby's two men encountered a small group of horsemen in gray uniforms. Disdaining caution, the two Rangers allowed the men to approach. The men were from Blazer's Scouts and, before they could react, the two Rangers were fired upon. Puryear was quickly captured but McDonough was able to gallop out of town under a hail of lead. Locating Richards, McDonough reported the situation.

Hoping to catch Blazer in an ambush should he advance, Richards moved back toward the river and placed his men below a cliff, near the home of Albert Davis. An hour later, Blazer and some of his men halted at the Davis residence. Moving around the house, one of the Scouts caught sight of the Rangers and the small group of Union cavalry swiftly rode off to join the main body between Myerstown and Kabletown.

Blazer arrived to find one of his officers, Lieutenant Cole, interrogating Puryear, attempting to gain information about the whereabouts of his comrades. Puryear's reputation as a tough man was well earned and he revealed nothing despite being clubbed with the butt of a rifle and threatened with hanging.

Having learned nothing from their captive, Blazer gathered his sixty-five-man company and moved toward Myerstown. Meanwhile, Richards had circled south of the village, coming to a halt a mile out of town along the road to Myers' Ford. Deploying his men in a hollow two hundred yards south of the road to their front, Richards warned his men not to "fire a shot or raise a yell until you hear shooting in the front. Don't shoot until you get close to them, among them."

With the trap set, he now needed to offer some bait. Moving forward with his brother, Thomas, Richards waited in a stand of trees for Blazer's approach. Suddenly, just as the van of the Scouts appeared before them on the road, Ranger David "Graft" Carlisle, drunk and feeling the effects, galloped up beside the two Rangers, drew his revolver, fired a shot at the approaching cavalry, turned, and spurred his horse to quickly gallop back to his waiting comrades.

Richards rode back to his men, probably wanting to shoot the drunk Carlisle himself, but instead needed to change his plans, for the Blazers were dismounting and preparing for a fight as they filed off into the woods. Realizing that it would be foolhardy to advance across an open field against a prepared enemy, Richards ordered Lieutenant Hatcher to withdraw in the open with his Company A to give the appearance that the entire Ranger detachment was leaving.

As experienced a cavalryman as Blazer was, he did not know the size of the force he was facing. Falling for the ruse, he ordered his men to remount and pursue. While the Scouts broke from the treeline, Company B charged from the depression in which they'd hidden.

The Confederate charge was close range and Spencer rifle and Colt revolver fire crisscrossed the field. As Company B slammed into the front of Blazer's formation, Company A circled and hit the Federal flank. Though Blazer's men "fought desperately," the Rangers pressed, finally forcing the Scouts to break and scatter.

Fleeing back toward Myerstown, Blazer rallied some of his men and continued to offer resistance, fighting from behind houses as Richards pursued his vanquished foe. Overwhelmed once again and, for the most part ignoring their commander's orders, the Federal Scouts broke and ran, this time fleeing towards the small village of Rippon.

Having fought his way out of Myerstown, Captain Blazer rode after his men. In hot pursuit of the Yankee commander was an eighteen-year-old Ranger named Sydnor Ferguson. The race was left to the horses and it was the Ranger who had the finer steed, a thoroughbred named Fashion. Overtaking the captain on the outskirts of Rippon, Ferguson rose up in his stirrups and knocked the Federal officer off his horse and to the ground with a blow to the head from his pistol.

Meanwhile, leading the pursuing Confederate Rangers into Rippon was John Puryear. With Richards' earlier charge, the prisoner and his captives found their roles quickly reversed. Slugging his guard, Puryear swiftly assisted his comrades' attack on the Scouts. Joining in the pursuit of the fleeing bluecoats, Puryear borrowed a pistol from John Foster and set out in search of his chief nemesis, Lieutenant Cole.

In the village, Puryear found Cole as he was surrendering to John Alexander. Riding up to the officer who was dismounted, Puryear leveled his pistol at the man only to have Alexander intercede on Cole's behalf, telling Puryear, "Don't shoot this man; he has surrendered."

Puryear objected, informing Alexander "The rascal tried to hang me this morning."

When queried by Alexander if the accusation was true, Cole pleaded for his life, crying "Oh save me!"

Puryear's response was to tell Cole, "Yes, I will save you," and pulled the trigger. As the lieutenant lay dying, the Ranger jumped from his saddle and burst into tears.

The actual number of casualties inflicted was never accurately determined. Sheridan put the number of Scouts killed at sixteen while Confederate reports placed the losses as high as twenty-two. Prisoners were reported to be from eleven to greater than thirty. Ranger losses were one killed and five wounded.

Though the final Union figures may have been in dispute, there was one thing for certain. Blazer and his Scouts had been destroyed as an effective combat force, though they would not officially be disbanded until 17 July 1865. The Union captain's capture attracted the attention of the Rangers, for he had earned by his action and conduct the respect of the Confederates. Exchanged as a prisoner in early 1865, Blazer would rejoin his regiment in the Shenandoah Valley and eventually be an attendee at the negotiations between Mosby and the Union at the close of the war. His captor, Sydnor Ferguson, was among Mosby's escorts at these sessions and, when the two adversaries recognized one another, they "hugged each other like long lost brothers." Blazer would eventually die from yellow fever in 1878.

From 20 to 27 November, Mosby conducted a series of raids into Loudoun County and the Shenandoah Valley. Company-sized or larger, these raids operated independently of each other, gathering one hundred prisoners and nearly two hundred and fifty mules and horses. Ranger losses, with one exception, were placed at six men captured.

Unfortunately for Mosby and his men, the one exception was Captain Richard Montjoy. It occurred during a skirmish outside of Leesburg between Montjoy's company and a thirty-six-man Union detachment called the Loudoun Rangers. Having dispersed the Federals, the Confederate Rangers gave chase. Montjoy, while pursuing a Federal, was struck in the head by an unaimed bullet fired over the fleeing man's shoulder. It was reported that "every man of his company who witnessed the tragedy reined in his horse voluntarily and groaned."

Montjoy was carried to Leesburg where he died a few hours later. With a combat record the equal of anyone in the battalion, his loss to Mosby's Rangers was a tremendous blow. Buried in Warrenton, his tombstone bore the inscription "His death was a costly sacrifice to victory. He died too early for liberty and his country's cause, but not too early for his own fame."

With little time to feel the loss, Mosby organized his seventh company in Fauquier the day following Montjoy's death. Company G was basically a reorganization of the artillery company that had been disbanded on 2 November following the capture of Mosby's four cannon artillery battery. Dolly Richards' twice-wounded brother, Thomas W. R, was Mosby's selection for command. Richards' lieutenants were John N. Murphy, W. Garland Smith, and John Puryear. Mosby, upon informing Puryear of his appointment, explained to him the parameters of his commission. "Puryear, I am going to make you a Lieutenant for gallantry. But, I don't want you to ever command any of my men." As understood by most of the men, "Mosby wanted Puryear to fight for him, but not to think for him."

The 28th of November would prove to be a most "red-letter" day for Mosby, for his men, and for his Confederacy for reasons other than the activation of a new Ranger company. Unfortunately for all concerned, to the west a solid column of Union cavalry were making their way from the valley and through Ashby's Gap to destroy the very base of Mosby's operations in Loudoun County. The bill owed by the citizens of Mosby's Confederacy had just come due and Sheridan was riding to collect it.

Though Mosby's operations had proven to be nothing more than an annoyance to him, Sheridan had, for the most part and with only the exception of Blazer's Scouts, ignored the partisan Rangers while he focused on the destruction of Early's army and the Valley. But with his strategic victory now complete and Grant's urging to clear "out that country so that it will not support Mosby's gang," Sheridan could no longer ignore Mosby.

Sheridan issued detailed orders for the large-scale raid on the 27th. Assigning the mission to the command that had suffered the most at the hands of Mosby and his Rangers, Major General Merritt and his First Cavalry Division were ordered to raze all within the territory bordered by the Manassas Railroad to the south, the Potomac River to the north, the Shenandoah River to the west, and the Bull Run Mountains to the east.

Departing at 0700 on the 28th, the three brigades of Merritt's division, 3,000 cavalry, cleared Ashby's Gap, and proceeded into their individually assigned sectors. Passing through the countryside, livestock was gathered as barns, corncribs, outbuildings, and crops were torched. Flames flickered throughout the night and smoke rose during the day. By 1 December, the region, as Sheridan had ordered, had been made a "desert." The people of Upper Fauquier and Loudoun Counties were made to pay dearly "for being part of Mosby's Confederacy," with the accumulations of a lifetime turned to ashes.

Facing such an overwhelming number of enemy, Mosby and his men could do little but observe from the fringes as the "burning raid" continued. Strong picket forces secured the flanks of Merritt's brigades and regiments denying the Rangers easy openings through which they could attack. Out of frustration, Mosby countered with a series of raids into the valley from the 3rd to the 11th of December but they achieved little in terms of results.

Mosby's request to reorganize into two battalions was approved in early December. Along with this approval came his promotion to colonel on 9 January 1865, with a date of rank of 7 December 1864. The 43rd Battalion was reorganized into a regiment with Lieutenant Colonel William H. Chapman and Major Dolly Richards assigned as battalion commanders. Upon Mosby's return to Fauquier County, he assigned Companies C, E, F, and G to Chapman and Companies A, B, and D to Richards.

Mosby's luck almost ran out before he reached the New Year. On the cold evening of 21 December 1864, he was dining in the home of some Fauquier County friends as the sleet fell outside. While he ate, a three-hundred-man Union cavalry detachment quietly surrounded the house. As a Federal corporal rode into the yard, he observed a small man dressed in gray pass a window in the house. The corporal fired his pistol through the pane of glass striking the man, Mosby, in the abdomen.

Seriously wounded for the third time, Mosby fell to the floor, blood flowing heavily. Still maintaining a presence of mind, he removed his jacket with the colonel's insignia and hid it under a bureau. Questioned by a drunk Union major, Mosby gave him a false identity. Not knowing who they had, the cavalry quickly departed believing they'd left the man lying in his blood to die of his wounds. Mosby decided not to oblige and by March had recovered enough to climb back into the saddle.

As the new year progressed and the Confederacy's cause moved into its final waning moments, Mosby continued to have his men conduct scouts, gather information, and skirmish with the significantly superior Union forces. During one such scout on 30 March, five Rangers were making their way towards Berryville when they spotted two Federal soldiers running into a barn. Charley Wiltshire galloped forward, followed closely by George Gill. Pulling up to the barn door on his mount, Wiltshire demanded the Yankees surrender. The reply of "Never!" was immediately followed by a shot from Lieutenant Eugene Ferris of the 30th Massachusetts Infantry. Wiltshire tumbled from his horse with a bullet in his neck. The barn door was then kicked open and out stepped Ferris and his orderly. A quick shot from Ferris dropped Gill from his horse before he could fire.

With Ferris securing Wiltshire's mount and the orderly his own, the two Federals were confronted by the remaining three Rangers as they galloped into the barnyard, John Orrick, Robert Eastham, and Bartlett Bolling. Ferris smoothly engaged all three, wounding both Orrick and Bolling in the exchange of gunfire. Despite their wounds, the two Rangers remained seated and joined Eastham in the pursuit of the fleeing Yankees. Even with a bullet in his chest, Bolling was able to ride down the orderly and drag him to the ground. Ferris was also ridden down but was able to avoid a swing from Eastham's revolver and outdistance the Rangers in another horse race. While both Wiltshire and Gill would die from their wounds, Lieutenant Ferris would be awarded the Medal of Honor for his efforts that day.

The Confederacy was in dire straits. Mosby had received a letter from Lee dated 27 March that directed Mosby's regiment to guard the Piedmont region from Gordonsville northward to Fauquier and to cover the Blue Ridge Mountain gaps into the Shenandoah Valley. Mosby's task was to guard a large segment of territory that had once been one of the most strategically vital sections of not only Virginia but also the entire South. Unfortunately, Mosby did not have the men nor the resources to cover such a vast region.

On 5 April, he organized his eighth and final company at North Fork Church in Loudoun County. A majority of the unit's fifty volunteers had served with the Prince William Partisan Rangers, which had been disbanded just a few months prior on 4 December 1864. For commander,

Mosby had selected George Baylor, who had fought with Stonewall Jackson's Brigade in the early part of the war. Mosby had wanted Baylor in his command and it was felt by many that Company H had been formed to reward Baylor with a captaincy. The company's lieutenants were Edward Thompson, Jim Wiltshire, and B. Franklin Carter, Jr.

Resorting back to his previous tradition, Mosby deployed the newly formed command, ordering Baylor "to go out and see what he could do." Riding out about 0200 the following day, Baylor and his men rode to the Shenandoah River and attacked the Loudoun Rangers' camp. This Federal unit was only a shadow of its former self and was quickly overrun and annihilated with the capture of forty-seven prisoners.

On 9 April, Baylor and his company, along with some members of Company D, rode into Fairfax County to attack a wagon train. Their timing was off, though, for the train had already arrived safely within the Union lines. The Rangers bivouacked northeast of Manassas Junction at a farm. Much to Baylor's regret, for he must have failed to post sentries, he and his men were surprised by an attack at sunrise by the 8th Illinois Cavalry. Baylor, his three lieutenants, and a handful of veterans remained to fight a rearguard action as the company's newer recruits fled with the first shot fired. Casualties were light for no one was killed and only five Rangers were captured as the Union cavalry followed the retreating Confederates to the Bull Run battlefields. As the Yankees halted their pursuit near the battlefields, Lieutenants Carter and Wiltshire each fired one final departing shot. Those two rounds would prove to be the last rounds fired by Mosby's Rangers in the Civil War.

Mosby learned of Robert E. Lee's surrender to Ulysses S. Grant at Appomattox Court House on 9 April 1865, a day or two after the event, while reading the Baltimore American newspaper. Mosby was still not prepared to surrender, though, as long as Major General Joseph E. Johnston's army remained in the field in North Carolina and he had no orders from his commander, General Lee.

Following a series of correspondence and meetings with Federal officials, Mosby met his assembled officers in Paris on 20 April at 1030 and rode to Millwood to meet with Major General Winfield S. Hancock's representative, Brigadier General George H. Chapman in a brick house and tavern owned by J. H. Clarke. Chapman and Mosby sat at a small mahogany table surrounded by fourteen Union and nineteen Confederate officers. Chapman refused to consider any new terms or truce extensions that had been considered previously.

It was then that Ranger Hern, who had unknowingly ridden to the meeting without Mosby's knowledge, burst through the door and into the crowded parlor where the meeting was being held.

"Colonel," exclaimed Hern, "the damn Yankees have got you in a trap; there is a thousand of them hid in the woods right here. Let's fight 'em Colonel. We can whip 'em."

Controlled and standing up slowly, Mosby placed his hand on his revolver.

"If the truce no longer protects us, we are at your mercy; but we shall protect ourselves."

No one moved or spoke. Years later, one of the Union observers in the room wrote, "Every partisan was well prepared for instant death and more than ready for a desperate fight. Had a single pistol been discharged by accident, or had Mosby given the word, not one Yankee officer in the room would have lived a minute."

Without further word, Mosby turned and walked through the door followed by his Rangers. At their horses, he said, "Mount and follow me." At a gallop, he led them east, toward the towering Blue Ridge Mountains. As they disappeared in a swirl of dust down the dirt road, the Yankees left behind were unaware of the fact that they were observing the historic last ride of an organized detachment of Mosby's Rangers.

Mosby's final muster was the following day, 21 April 1865. An early morning rain had created a thick fog that hung "like a pall over the face of the country," as remembered by Ranger James J. Williamson. The location was Salem, Virginia, and the time was noon. Mosby arrived a little late but clean-shaven. With the truce ended and an extension no longer an option, Mosby was unwilling to subject his men or his Confederacy to any more hardships for a cause that was now dead.

The regiment was formed by company west of the village and in a field south of the Rectortown Road. Eight companies properly aligned on parade, posted in accordance with their organizational dates. All told, there were scarcely two hundred Rangers.

Mosby rode forward, opposite of Company A. Slowly, he trooped the line, passing in a final review, inspecting his valiant warriors who had endured the best the Union could throw their way. Before Colonel John Singleton Mosby stood the battle-tested and unbroken representatives of the one Southern battalion that had, according to General Halleck, beat "the armies of the enemy."

Returning to his original starting point in front of Company A, the colonel of the regiment wheeled his horse back to the center of the formation. Halting between his two battalion commanders, William Chapman and Dolly Richards, Mosby remained quiet as his brother and regimental adjutant, Lieutenant William H. Mosby, read a prepared announcement.

> Soldiers! I have summoned you together for the last time. The vision we have cherished of a free and independent country, has vanished, and that country, is now the spoil of a conqueror. I disband your organization in preference to surrendering it to our enemies. I am now no longer your commander. After association of more than two eventful years, I part from you with a just pride, in the fame of your achievements, and grateful recollections of your generous kindness to myself.
>
> And now at this moment of bidding you a final adieu accept the assurance of my unchanging confidence and regard.
>
> Farewell.
>
> John S. Mosby Colonel

A "profound silence" enveloped the ranks as Mosby's brother read the words, to be followed with three wholehearted cheers for their 'former' commander. The finality of their war efforts was before the Rangers and many were reluctant to embrace it initially. Gradually, though, as farewells were offered, the men began to depart.

At the edge of Rectortown Road, Colonel Mosby waited to shake the hand of each of his men in heartfelt thanks for their dedication and service to him and their cause. As remembered by James Williamson, the "Gray Ghost's," as Mosby had come to be known in the South, iron facade gave way and he "cried like a child. It was the most trying ordeal through which we have ever passed."

Service in Mosby's Rangers demanded a price be paid, and that price was usually in blood. Though precise figures will never be attainable, it is believed that 35 percent to 40 percent of the command were casualties of the war with at least eighty-five men killed, mortally wounded, or executed. At least one hundred men were wounded and 477 captured. Of those captured, sixteen are known to have died in captivity. Interestingly enough, despite all the hardships and all the adversity, only twenty-five members of the battalion deserted. Surely such a low figure under such adverse circumstances is a testimonial to Mosby's style of leadership and his command philosophy.

On 30 May 1916, at the age of eighty-two, John Singleton Mosby passed away in Washington, D.C., the capital of his former enemies.

Interred in Warrenton beside his wife and deceased children, it was only fitting that, not far away, just down the slope, rested the remains of Richard Montjoy.

CHAPTER 15

World War II

Upon going ashore at Sorrento, an officer approached a Ranger in uniform ask-ing, "Do you know where I can find Colonel Darby?" A slow grin crossed the face of the husky soldier as he answered, "You'll never find him this far back."

As told by General William H. Baumer

The Second World War saw the dawning of the modern Ranger organiza-tion.

In the spring of 1942, the U.S. Army Chief of Staff, General George C. Marshall, sent Colonel Lucian K. Truscott, Jr., to London to arrange U.S. participation in British Commando raids against German occupied Europe. In that U.S. ground forces had yet to engage German soldiers, Marshall intended to have men selected from across a broad spectrum of units gain combat experience alongside their British allies. These soldiers would be trained by the commandos and participate in combat opera-tions under British command. Once trained and exposed to combat, the U.S. soldiers would be reassigned to their original units with new, inex-perienced soldiers sent to replace them. This rotation of trained and inex-perienced troops would lead one to believe that the original intent in regards to the Rangers was *not* to create a unit of unique and highly skilled light fighters, which it would ultimately become.

On 26 May 1942, the newly promoted Brigadier General Truscott rec-ommended to the Chief of Staff that an American unit be organized along similar lines as the British Commandos. Wanting a unit similar in capabil-ity as the British Commandos, General Marshall authorized the formation and activation of a U.S. Army commando-type organization. Upon his return, Truscott conveyed to Major General Russell P. Hartle, commanding general of the U.S. Army Northern Ireland Forces and U.S. Army V Corps, Marshall's directive to organize the new unit as quickly as possible.

On 1 June, Major General James E. Chaney, commanding general of the U.S. Army Forces British Isles, forwarded a letter titled, "Command Organization," to Major General Hartle. In this letter, Chaney provided guidance for the organization of an American "commando unit for training and demonstration purposes." This was to be "the first step in a program specifically directed by the Chief of Staff for giving actual battle experience to the maximum number of personnel of the American Army." The selection criteria for volunteers specified that only fully trained soldiers of the best type were to be accepted. Organized in Northern Ireland, the battalion-sized unit would be attached to the British Special Services Brigade for tactical control and training. The U.S. 34th Infantry Division would provide logistic and administrative support.

During one of his trips to Washington, D.C, Truscott had discussed with then Major General Dwight D. Eisenhower—who was the chief of Operations Division War Department General Staff—the possibility of activating a U.S. commando-type unit. Eisenhower's recommendation was to use a select a name that was not closely associated with British special forces. After some thought, Truscott decided that, in honor of Rogers' Rangers, the official designation of the unit would be the 1st *Ranger* Battalion.

The legendary William Orlando Darby was selected to command the 1st Ranger Battalion. Darby—previously Hartle's aide-de-camp and newly promoted—was given a free hand to organize, man, and equip his battalion. On 7 June, a letter to the 1st Armored Division, 34th Infantry Division, and other major commands was sent from Hartle, informing them of the Ranger Battalion's formation. Authorized to choose volunteers from any military unit then in Ireland, Major Darby began the selection process on 8 June when he began to interview his first officer volunteers. By 10 June, he had selected twenty-nine.

The selection of enlisted men was conducted over a ten-day period beginning 11 June at Carrickfergus, Northern Ireland. Unfortunately, by 15 June, of the 575 volunteers who had been interviewed, 104 were judged to be unacceptable and returned to their units. Consequently, Darby found it necessary to send six boards of officers on a recruiting tour to raise additional volunteers.

The 1st Ranger Battalion was formally activated on 19 June 1942 on the parade field at Carrickfergus with a strength of twenty-nine officers, 488 enlisted. The battalion was organized into a headquarters company and six line companies. The line companies consisted of two platoons, each platoon having two assault sections and a 60-mm mortar section. The Rangers were lightly armed with M-1 rifles, .30-caliber machineguns, which would be replaced by Browning Automatic Rifles (BAR), 45-caliber submachineguns, and 60-mm mortars at platoon level. The lightness of their weapons was to enhance their mobility.

Fully manned and equipped by 28 June, the 1st Ranger Battalion moved to the British Commando Depot at Achnacarry, Scotland, where they would remain until 31 July. Training was tough, stressful, and as realistic as possible: assaulting positions under directed live fire, swimming ice-cold rivers, and cliff climbing — all with full pack, numbing road marches for time, beach-landings, basic soldiering skills, and unarmed combat. These were only a few of the many ordeals the new Rangers endured under the guidance and supervision of the British Commandos.

From the beginning, Darby strongly emphasized a concept that is still very much alive within the Ranger organization today: the buddy system. Allowing the soldiers to choose their own buddies, Darby required these small groups to work in pairs. They would eat, perform details, and train as a team. It is a concept that has stood the test of time and combat.

The commando training was designed to be physically demanding and to condition the Rangers to think and to act quickly. It also required them to face the possibility of personal injury, for such realistic training had its costs. By 17 July, one Ranger had drowned and either bullets or hand-grenade fragments had wounded another three. Four hundred of the six hundred Ranger volunteers survived the intense commando training.

On 1 August, most of the Ranger Battalion moved to the vicinity of Argyle to train with the Royal Navy on amphibious operations for a month while a select group of six officers and forty-four enlisted men were attached to Numbers 3 and 4 Commandos and the Canadian 2nd Division for a raid on the European continent.

The raid was launched on 19 August 1942 with an amphibious assault on the English Channel port of Dieppe, France, located on the upper Norman coast approximately 105 miles northwest of Paris. The attack was poorly planned and badly executed. The port was heavily defended with 88-mm cannon in fortified positions on cliffs overlooking the beach, machinegun pillboxes, and top-quality, well-entrenched troops. No preassault air or sea bombardment had been planned and the rocky, shingled beach immobilized the attackers' tanks and seriously impeded dismounted movement. With only a two-to-one ratio of attacker to defender—in contradiction to the 'rule of thumb' three-to-one minimum, the assaulting Allied forces suffered horrendous losses and were decisively defeated. Overall the attack cost the Canadian Division seventy-five percent of its force killed, wounded, or captured within six hours. Dieppe was a national disaster for Canada.

Sprinkled among the British Commando units, the fifty Rangers became the first American soldiers to fight the Germans on land in the Second World War. Despite the overwhelming odds, the Rangers who fought at Dieppe lived up to the highest expectations and won the admiration of their seasoned and more experienced Commando comrades with whom they fought side by side. Ranger losses for this operation were two officers and four enlisted men killed, seven wounded, and four captured—an American loss of thirty-four percent. The raid at Dieppe proved to be the only operation in which the Rangers would fight under the auspices of the British.

The Ranger Battalion moved to Dundee on 3 September to take part in a three-week training exercise, rehearsing attacks against coastal positions. Having completed their training at Dundee, the Rangers moved to the vicinity of Glasgow on 24 September where they were attached to the 1st Infantry Division. The battalion's personnel authorization at this point was twenty-six officers and 452 enlisted men. Headquarters and Headquarters Company's strength was set at eight officers, seventy-four enlisted men. Each of the six line companies—'Able' through 'Fox'—were authorized three officers, sixty-three enlisted men. The line companies were composed of a company headquarters, which included a command section, two mortar sections, and two platoons. Each platoon was authorized one officer, twenty-five enlisted men, a platoon headquarters, and two sections composed of eleven soldiers each.

Departing England in October, the 1st Ranger Battalion's official entry into the war occurred on 8 November 1942, as part of Operation Torch—the invasion of North Africa. The initial mission was to seize two batteries that threatened the landing sites north of Arzew, Algeria. Companies A and B made a direct assault on the smaller fortification by attacking straight into the harbor. The remainder of the battalion landed four miles to the northwest and attacked the major fort of Batterie Superieur from the rear. Concentrating their 81-mm mortars—which they had brought in lieu of their 60-mm's—on the objective, the fort quickly fell with the loss of only one Ranger killed in action (KIA).

Despite their uniqueness, the 1st Infantry Division's commanding general opted to commit the Rangers to conventional infantry operations within fourteen and a half hours of their setting foot on North African soil. On 9 November, Company E in support of the 16th Infantry Regiment captured the town of LaMacta while Company C assisted Combat Team (CT) 18 secure the town of St. Cloud on the 10th, an action that cost three Rangers KIA.

Following Arzew, the 1st Ranger Battalion did not see combat for nearly three months. During February and March 1943, the battalion was involved in several major actions. On 11 February, Companies A, E, F, and a battalion headquarters element, all under the command of Lieutenant Colonel Darby, conducted a night raid against Italian front-line positions near station de Sened in central Tunisia. The successful raid resulted in an estimated seventy-five Italian casualties, ten POWs captured, and the destruction of one antitank gun and five machineguns. Ranger losses were one KIA and twenty wounded in action (WIA).

During the period 16 February to 1 March, the Ranger Battalion conducted patrols from their defensive positions south of Bou Chebka. Several skirmishes with Italian and German forces resulted in six enemy KIA, sixteen POWs captured, and the destruction or capture of six wheeled vehicles. Ranger losses were one missing in action (MIA).

Major General George S. Patton, Jr.'s II Corps was tasked with the mission of supporting Field Marshal Bernard Montgomery's Eighth Army attack along Tunisia's east coast. Part of that support required II Corps to capture Gafsa to serve as a logistical base for the Eighth Army. Once again attached to the 1st Infantry Division, the Rangers attacked Gafsa in support of Combat Teams 16 and 18 on the evening of 13 March. Lightly defended, the town quickly fell with no Ranger casualties.

The ease of the operation indicated that the enemy had withdrawn from the immediate area of operation. Allied intelligence indicated two thousand Axis troops were positioned at the town of El Guettar with additional forces located at Djebel el Ank. At 0200 on 17 March, Darby was ordered to conduct a reconnaissance in force toward El Guettar to gather information and to reestablish contact with the enemy. The intelligence reports proved to be wrong for the Rangers found El Guettar undefended.

Rapidly occupying the town, the battalion extended its search for the enemy and located them astride the Gafsa-Gabes road at Djebel el Ank Pass. Shortly thereafter, 1st Infantry Division received a warning order that it was to attack along the Gafsa-Gabes road and take the high ground east of El Guettar on 20 March. In order to accomplish this mission, the division had to first secure the Djebel el Ank Pass.

An unsupported frontal attack against the prepared and heavily defended pass was out of the question. Instead, the plan called for the Ranger Battalion to infiltrate the enemy lines and attack the defenders' position from the rear in conjunction with a frontal attack by the 26th Infantry Regiment. Having been provided the time to properly recon the area, the Rangers mapped a tortuous ten-mile route through the heavily mountainous terrain.

Late on the evening of 20 March, Lieutenant Colonel Darby led his 1st Rangers and an attached 4.2-inch mortar company along the infiltration route. Burdened by the weight, the mortar company quickly fell behind. Having safely arrived at their attack positions without being detected, the Ranger Battalion waited until first light when, shortly after 0600, they launched their assault—without the mortars that were still slowly moving forward.

With covering fires being provided by the machineguns and rifles of a support element, the remainder of the battalion swarmed down on the unsuspecting and completely surprised Italian defenders. The hail of bullets, grenades, and thrusts of fixed bayonets proved too much. Within twenty minutes, the north side of the pass was secured and the infantry regiment was entering the pass. With the just recently arrived 4.2-inch mortars, direct and indirect fires were focused on the southern side of the pass. Still needing to secure the pass against the direct fire of some enemy machineguns, Darby ordered one company to take out the automatic weapons. Descending to the floor of the pass and dashing across the open area to the base of a wall on the south side, the Rangers slowly fought their way up the ridge in a skirmish line formation to secure the far side.

By 1120, most of the enemy resistance in the area had been cleared and the Ranger Battalion was ordered to move to secure the high ground beyond Bou Hamran. Overall, the 1st Ranger Battalion and 26th Infantry Regiment captured more than 1,000 prisoners. Ranger losses were only one officer wounded. By 1610 that afternoon, the battalion had reverted to division reserve and was bivouacked at El Guettar.

Unfortunately, the Germans launched a counterattack forty-eight hours later and recovered the pass taken the morning of 21 March. Called upon to fight as conventional infantry, the 1st Ranger Battalion suffered three KIA and eighteen WIA near Djebel Berda during the period 23 to 27 March. For their action at Gafsa, Djebel el Ank, and El Guettar, the 1st Ranger Battalion was awarded a Distinguished Unit Citation.

The next few months saw a dramatic change to the Ranger Battalion's organization. The first occurred on 14 April 1943, when Darby recommended to General Eisenhower the activation of two additional Ranger battalions to support the Sicily invasion. Approving the recommendation, Eisenhower forwarded the request to General Marshall. On 19 April, Marshall authorized the activation of the 3rd and 4th Ranger Battalions to be manned by an additional fifty-two officers and 1,000 enlisted soldiers. These three battalions would be designated "Ranger Force." Unfortunately, Darby's request for a regimental headquarters for this force was denied on 29 April "without further comment."

Using members of the 1st Battalion as cadre, the 3rd and 4th Ranger Battalions were activated. Major Herman W. Dammer, the 1st Ranger Battalion's executive officer, was selected to command the 3rd Ranger Battalion and provided Companies A and B of the 1st Battalion to assist with building the new unit. Captain Roy A. Murray, Jr., the former F Company commander, was selected to lead the 4th Ranger Battalion and provided Companies E and F for his nucleus. Darby retained command of the 1st Ranger Battalion, which kept Companies C and D. In that the request for a Ranger Regimental Headquarters had been denied, Darby 'simply' attached the 3rd and 4th Battalions to the 1st and remained a battalion commander with the duties and responsibilities of a regimental commander.

The second significant change dealt with organic indirect fire support. Authorized 60-mm mortars by TO&E and having employed 81-mm mortars during Operation Torch, Darby felt there was a need for heavier indirect fire support and his request for the 83rd Chemical Battalion and its 4.2-inch mortar unit to be attached to Ranger Force was approved.

Spearheading Patton's Seventh Army amphibious landings on 10 July 1943 after only six weeks of training the new regiment, Darby's 1st, 3rd, and 4th Ranger Battalion Ranger Force landed as the lead elements of Operation Husky, the invasion of Sicily. The 1st and 4th Ranger Battalions—designated "Force X" and attached to Major General Omar Bradley's II Corps—made an opposed landing at Gela.

Force X captured the town and then defended it against a German and Italian armored counterattack. Darby personally played a part in the defense of the city when Italian tanks temporarily penetrated the Rangers' defenses. Borrowing an antitank gun, he destroyed one tank. Later, he was seen riding on the top of a second tank trying to open its hatch to grenade the crew. For his heroism at Gela, Darby was awarded the Distinguished Service Cross.

TO FIGHT WITH INTREPIDITY...

Meanwhile, the 3rd Battalion, attached to Major General Lucian Truscott's 3rd Infantry Division, conducted an opposed landing approximately fifteen miles west of Licata and remained attached to the 3rd Infantry Division as it moved inland. As the Seventh Army beachheads expanded, the 3rd Infantry Division was directed by Patton to conduct a "reconnaissance in force." The 3rd Infantry Division's plan of attack had elements of the 7th Infantry Regiment securing the city of Favara by daylight on 15 July. The 3rd Ranger Battalion passed through the 7th's front lines around 1900 that evening and advanced by foot along Highway 122, the Favara-Agrigento road.

The Rangers encountered their first opposition around midnight when they come upon an Italian roadblock at the junction of Highways 122 and 118, just north of Agrigento. Attacking at 0030, the Rangers quickly overran the enemy position and secured the surrounding heights near Highway 118 by 0130. While there were no Ranger casualties, they did capture 165 Italian prisoners who had to be escorted back to Favara and turned over to the 7th Infantry Regiment.

Following a few hours sleep, the Ranger Battalion resumed its march at 0600 toward the town of Montaperto, located on a hill overlooking a valley that led into the port of Porto Empedocle. Just 200 yards beyond Highway 118, an Italian motorized column of ten motorcycles and two troop-laden trucks was spotted on its way to Agrigento. Already having the high ground, the Rangers prepared a hasty ambush that was initiated with total surprise and deadly effect. The ambush proved to be exceptionally one-sided as many Italian soldiers were killed and forty captured. Again, there were no Ranger casualties.

Continuing their mission, the Rangers entered Montaperto around 0800. From their vantage point at Montaperto, the 3rd Battalion observed four Italian artillery batteries. Seizing the opportunity, Major Dammer engaged them with his 60-mm mortars and automatic weapons. The artillery pieces quickly fell to the Americans.

From Montaperto, the Rangers moved to Hill 316 to prepare their attack down the valley to the port. During their movement, they took occasional machinegun and sniper fire as they captured the Italian artillery command element for the valley. Unfortunately, the only Ranger to be killed during the entire operation, Lieutenant Raymond F. Campbell, the Company F commanding officer, was cut down in an assault on a machinegun position.

Dammer's plan of action was to split the battalion into a two-pronged attack along parallel avenues of advance down a draw into the port city. Though this violated the principle of mass and unity of command, he believed the risk was justified, for it provided him a maneuver element should one of the two groups become heavily engaged. Events would prove him right.

Taking command of the three companies advancing along the east side of the draw and leaving the remaining three companies under the command of his executive officer to advance along the west side, Dammer commenced the attack at 1420.

Moving forward, the Ranger elements on the west side found themselves heavily engaged by determined resistance coming from behind a walled cemetery and by German forces manning coastal defense and antiaircraft positions. Meeting much less resistance on the east side, Dammer's force fought its way into the city. The port was cleared and secured by the Rangers by 1600. Patton had his port and the Rangers had captured a total of 675 Italians and ninety-one Germans during the day's events. Mission complete.

Reuniting, the Ranger Force was augmented by the 39th Infantry Regiment and employed as conventional infantry. Maintaining the 1st and 4th Battalions as a reserve, the force attacked around the western end of the island on a drive to Palermo. At Menfi, the 3rd Ranger Battalion was attached once again to the 3rd Infantry Division to continue the drive to cut off the enemy's retreat between the northeastern end of Sicily and Italy and to assist Patton's movement to Messina, which was secured on 17 August. Immediately upon its capture, the entire Ranger Force assembled at Palermo to begin preparation for the invasion of Italy.

Darby's experience with enemy armor in Gela—and his background as an artilleryman—convinced him of the need to supplement his light force with an anti-armor capability. Subsequently, Darby increased the force's organic firepower with the creation of a Ranger cannon company equipped with four 75-mm guns mounted on halftracks. The new company was formed at Corleone after the battle for Sicily was completed and was ready for use during the invasion of Italy.

On 1 August, all Ranger Battalions had been redesignated Ranger Infantry Battalions. Nine days later, Darby once again made an attempt to obtain a regimental headquarters for the Ranger Force. Endorsed by Patton, Darby's request was forwarded to Eisenhower. On 3 September, the request was once again disapproved without comment.

Operation Avalanche found Ranger Force landing in advance of the Fifth Army's invasion at Mairori, Italy, a location 20 miles west of Salerno. Attached to the British X Corps, the Rangers achieved total surprise prior to daylight on 9 September. After securing the town and destroying nearby coastal defenses, the Ranger Infantry Battalions quickly moved inland and seized the critical Chiunzi Pass by midmorning.

Unfortunately for the Rangers, the main invasion force failed to obtain its initial day objectives. To further compound the Ranger Force's problems, even once the beachhead was established, the Fifth Army was slow to breakout. Consequently, the anticipated two-day Ranger mission of holding the pass lasted more than two weeks. Subjected to repeated German counterattacks and sustained artillery fire, Darby's Rangers held the strategic terrain until relieved by X Corps units on 28 September.

While the 1st and 3rd Ranger Infantry Battalions were awarded the Distinguished Unit Citation for their actions at Mairori and Chiunzi Pass, the cost was high. Not equipped or organized to sustain continuous conventional battle, the Ranger Force suffered twenty-eight killed, sixty-six wounded, and nine missing in action — nearly 20 percent of a Ranger Infantry Battalion's authorized strength.

Following a nearly uneventful drive on Naples, the Ranger Force found itself employed in a conventional infantry role on the Winter Line for nearly a month and a half. Enduring bitter winter mountain fighting near San Pectro, Venatro, and Cassino, the Rangers' heavy losses were repeated. During a week's time, which ended on 27 November, the force suffered more than seventy casualties.

Fortune did eventually smile the Rangers' way when, on 16 January 1944, the Ranger Force and its attached units were designated the 6615th Ranger Force (Provisional). As a result, a Regimental Headquarters element was authorized that provided Darby a staff and a greater degree of control over the three Ranger Infantry Battalions. Having been promoted to colonel on 11 December, Darby now had his title of regimental commander.

To break the stalemate on the Italian peninsula, the Allies developed a plan that called for an amphibious landing at Anzio that would threaten the rear of the German Winter Line and force them to displace northward. Withdrawn to rest, refit, and prepare for this invasion, Ranger Force rehearsed for the operation on 17 January as part of a 3rd Infantry Division exercise. While observers were favorably impressed with the Rangers' spirit, élan, and enthusiasm, they were significantly concerned with noted violations of doctrine and combat techniques. Companies made excessive noise during night movements, moved while flares were being fired thus giving away their location, and were failing to reconnoiter likely ambush sites or take local security precautions. The high casualty rate on Sicily had taken its toll, thus leading to a serious deterioration of the Rangers' fighting skills. Time had not been allocated to properly train Ranger replacements to a suitable standard, as noted in Murray's correspondence, and the Rangers would soon pay a heavy price as a result.

The invasion at Anzio commenced before dawn on 22 January 1944. Once again leading the way, the 6615th Ranger Force (Provisional) — reinforced with the 509th Parachute Infantry Battalion and H Company of the 36th Combat Engineer Regiment — seized the port facilities, reduced enemy defensive positions, and secured the beachhead for follow-on forces. In that the local defenses were composed of two undermanned German coast-watching battalions that had been deployed to Anzio from the Winter Line for some R&R, the Rangers encountered little resistance. By midnight of that first day, Major General John Lucas' VI Corps had landed 36,000 men and 3,200 vehicles.

Unfortunately, Lucas failed to exploit his advantage. Cautiously moving inland for a distance of eleven miles during the next five days, VI Corps provided the Germans the time and the opportunity to concentrate their forces. On 28 January, General Mark Clark urged Lucas to act more aggressively. On 29 January, VI Corps finally published a field order outlining a major attack.

Having anticipated the corps' order, Truscott's 3rd Infantry Division had issued its own order on 28 January. Darby's Rangers would cross the line of departure (LD) at 0100 on 30 January to seize and to hold the town of Cisterna and its vital road junctions until relieved. The Ranger Infantry Battalions were replaced on the line the morning of 29 January, and the battalion commanders met with Darby at 1800 later that evening to discuss the plan. The intelligence annex to the division order noted that "[i]t does not now seem probable that the enemy will soon deliver a major counterattack involving units of division size; on the other hand, the enemy will probably resort to delaying action coupled with small-scale counterattacks in an effort to grind us to a standstill."

While the 3rd Infantry Division Intelligence section (G2) was optimistic and believed that the Rangers would encounter little in the way of opposition, Darby's headquarters believed this optimism was misplaced. Soldiers of the Hermann Goering Panzer Division had been taken prisoner in the Cisterna area. Historically, this division's presence indicated significant reinforcements and preparations for a counterattack. Consequently, the Rangers were of the opinion that enemy resistance at Cisterna had the potential to be considerable.

With Darby directing the attack from the Regimental headquarters' location near the LD, the 1st Ranger Infantry Battalion advanced across the LD at 0100 on 30 January as planned. Fifteen minutes after the 1st Battalion cleared the LD, the 3rd Ranger Infantry Battalion followed in support of the 1st. The terrain between the LD and Cisterna was flat farmland with little cover or concealment. Moving along a previously reconnoitered route, the 1st and 3rd Battalions used a drainage ditch that provided cover and concealment to avoid enemy detection.

The 4th Ranger Infantry Battalion, led by an eight-man minesweeping party, crossed the LD at 0200 and advanced on the Conca-Isola Bella-Cisterna road toward Cisterna. Sweeping for mines and securing the route, the battalion was to be followed by the Ranger Cannon Company, a platoon of the 601st Tank Destroyer Battalion, and the 83rd Chemical Battalion — the Rangers organic heavy mortar support.

At 0248, a series of events occurred that did not bode well for the 1st and 3rd Battalions. Four radio operators that were to have accompanied the 3rd Battalion reported themselves lost to the regimental headquarters. Soon thereafter, the 3rd Battalion reported that there had been a break in contact with the 1st Battalion halfway to the objective. Compounding that problem was a break in contact within the 1st Ranger Infantry Battalion itself. Approximately a half-mile ahead of the 3rd Battalion, the 1st had split in two, with three companies remaining in place and three continuing to advance. The inexperience of the replacement Rangers was beginning to show.

Quickly assessing the situation and taking command of the 1st Battalion's rear element, Captain Charles Shunstrom sent a runner back to find the 3rd Battalion. Having located the lost 3rd, the runner returned to report that a German tank round had killed its newly assigned battalion commander, Major Alvah Miller.

Despite the brief engagement, no general alarm appeared to have been raised about the presence of the Rangers. Cautiously moving toward the objective, the 1st and 3rd Battalions sought to avoid detection. Though they passed close by German positions, and enemy patrols crossed in front and on both sides, the Ranger presence seemed to remain undetected as daylight approached.

Continuing to crawl through empty trenches, the lead Ranger element reached a flat field on the southern edge of Cisterna. Roughly triangular in shape and a thousand yards distance, the Rangers began running toward Cisterna in an attempt to reach the town's outskirts prior to daybreak. Approximately 600 yards outside of town, they passed through a German bivouac and killed a large number of the surprised enemy with bayonets and knives.

Clearing the bivouac site, the Rangers crossed the remaining four hundred yards to the town's edge only to be met by overwhelming fire from the town. Having detected the Rangers' units moving northward approximately a mile south of the triangular field, the Germans had prepared their surprise welcome. Stopped in their tracks, the Rangers returned fire as best they could from a position astride a road leading into Cisterna.

Following closely behind the three lead companies of the 1st Battalion were the 3rd Battalion and the remaining three companies of the 1st. Stopped three hundred yards short of the embattled lead elements by two tanks, the follow-on elements were able to destroy the tanks with bazookas. Moving forward, Shunstrom was able to reestablish contact with the 1st Battalion's commander, Major Jack Dobson, another commander new to the Rangers.

Meanwhile, on the Conca-Isola Bella-Cisterna road, the 4th Ranger Infantry Battalion attempted to reinforce its sister battalions but met heavy resistance. Stopped short of Isola Bella by heavy tank, self-propelled gun, automatic weapon, and small arms fire, the 4th continued its efforts to reduce the roadblock. Unable to communicate with the 1st or 3rd Battalions, Darby realized that it was critical to the survival of the lead battalions that the 4th get through. Unfortunately, Darby, the 4th Ranger Infantry Battalion, and supporting 3rd Infantry Division units were fought to a standstill. Finding itself surrounded by that afternoon, the 4th Battalion would not be relieved until the next day. The lead Ranger Force was on its own.

Outnumbered, outgunned, and now commanded by captains, the 1st and 3rd Ranger Infantry Battalions continued the fight throughout the morning of the 31st. Three German tanks appeared behind the 1st and 3rd Battalions' position and were quickly destroyed by bazookas. But the realization had sunk in. The Ranger Force was surrounded. Confined to a perimeter three hundred yards in diameter, the Rangers were deluged by a storm of automatic and small arms fire. Ranger attempts to escape the encirclement and German attempts to overrun their position were met with unrestrained ferocity on both sides.

Two hours later and still continuing to hold on, the Rangers found themselves running low on ammunition. Three companies held in reserve within the battalion's perimeter allocated half of their ammunition to the companies on the perimeter.

Growing in strength as the Rangers were being bled dry, the Germans threw the newly arrived 2nd Parachute Lehr Battalion into the fray.

Armor, antiaircraft batteries, and artillery in direct fire mode rained destruction down on the entrapped Rangers.

Shortly after noon, approximately the same time that the 4th Ranger Infantry Battalion realized that all hope of assisting its sister battalions had vanished, a dozen captured Rangers were marched forward toward the center of the Rangers' position by German paratroopers with armored personnel carrier support in an attempt to gain the Rangers' surrender. Ranger marksmen shot two of the escorting German paratroopers. Retaliating by bayoneting two of the Ranger prisoners, the group continued to move forward. Two shots again rang out, two Germans fell, and two Rangers were bayoneted. Rangers—mostly those new to combat or the unit—began to surrender and join the advancing German group.

With the group of Ranger prisoners now numbering eighty, the advance continued toward the center of the American position with the German guards shouting they would shoot the prisoners if the remaining Rangers did not surrender. The surrounded Americans fired on the group for a third time, accidentally hitting some of the prisoners along with a few Germans. The gradual surrender of individual Rangers continued despite the attempts of more resolute Rangers to stop those offering to surrender by threatening to shoot them.

Recognizing that the end was near, the surviving Rangers began disassembling their weapons, burying or scattering key parts, and destroying communications equipment. The last man to speak with Colonel Darby from Cisterna was the sergeants major of the 1st Battalion, Robert Ehalt. He informed Darby that the 1st Battalion commander was wounded, the 3rd Battalion executive officer dead, and German tanks were closing in. Concluding his conversation with "So long Colonel, maybe when it's all over I'll see you again," Ehalt destroyed the radio and continued to fight for a while longer with the few Rangers left before finally surrendering.

Broken into smaller and smaller units of resistance, some Rangers continued to fight it out only to be captured or annihilated in detail. By the end of the day, the 1st and 3rd Ranger Infantry Battalions had ceased to exist, having been completely annihilated. Of the 767 Rangers who reached Cisterna, only six made it back to American lines, the remainder were either killed or captured.

The senior German commander in Italy, General Field Marshal Albert Kesselring, had assessed the situation correctly. Recognizing Lucas' cautious nature, Kesselring had concentrated considerable strength in Cisterna area of operation in preparation for a German counterattack on 2 February. Even worse for the Rangers, he also anticipated the American attack on Cisterna and took measures to defeat it by reinforcing its garrison with elements of the Hermann Goering Panzer Division on the evening of 29 January.

Despite their destruction, the Ranger Force extracted a heavy price for their eradication, inflicting over 5,500 German casualties and seriously disrupting the planned German counterattack on the beachhead, thus forcing its execution back by two critical days. This additional forty-eight hours proved to be the difference for the American forces, for the German counterattack failed by only the narrowest of margins as American artillery batteries were forced into the direct fire mode over open sites and clerks and cooks were pressed into service as infantrymen to repel the German counterattack. Had the Ranger attack on Cisterna been any less forceful and unwavering, the U.S. VI Corps could have conceivably found itself conducting another Dunkirk. The Rangers' great sacrifice had thwarted Hitler's "Push the Allies into the sea!" directive.

The battle at Cisterna proved to be the beginning of the end for Darby's Ranger Force. After helping to turn back the German counterattack of 4 February, and a later one on 19 February, the Ranger survivors were assigned to conduct a scouting and patrolling school outside of Civitavecchia, Italy, for the Fifth Army. On 6 May, approximately 150 veteran Rangers of long standing were returned to Camp Butner, North Carolina, and remained there until the 1st and 3rd Ranger Infantry Battalions were inactivated on 15 August 1944 and the 4th Ranger Infantry Battalion on 26 October. Newer Rangers, those who had yet to earn the privilege or justification of being returned to the United States, were assimilated into the 1st Special Service Force. For their services, the 1st Ranger Infantry Battalion received the Presidential Unit Citation for El Guettar and Salerno while the 3rd Ranger Infantry Battalion was awarded the Presidential Unit Citation for Salerno.

As for Colonel Darby, he briefly commanded the 179th Infantry Regiment during the German counterattack at Anzio. In April 1944, he was assigned for one year to the Operations Division of the War Department General Staff in Washington, D.C, reviewing and evaluating the effectiveness of infantry training. At his request, Darby's Washington tour was followed with an assignment to the 10th Mountain Division, fighting in Italy, as the assistant division commander. While visiting the front in Torbole on 30 April 1945, a shell fragment from a German 88-mm gun killed him.

The timing of Darby's death was sadly ironic. German forces had agreed to surrender unconditionally in Italy effective at noon, 2 May. Furthermore, his name appeared on a list to be submitted to President Truman of nominees for promotion to brigadier general the day he died. Secretary of War Henry L. Stimson recommended to the President that Darby's name be retained on the list in recognition of his outstanding combat record. The President concurred and on 15 May 1945, Darby was posthumously promoted to brigadier general, the only Army officer to be posthumously promoted to general officer rank during the entire war.

Following the departure of Darby's Rangers from England to the Mediterranean, there continued to be a desire for a Ranger-type organization that could conduct raids on Fortress Europe. Theater headquarters authorized the organization of a new Ranger Infantry Battalion in September 1942 to replace the deployed 1st Rangers.

On 20 December, the 29th Provisional Ranger Infantry Battalion commanded by Major Randolph Milholland was formed. Manned by volunteers from the 29th Infantry Division, the battalion underwent rigorous training at Tidworth Barracks, England, and at the Commando Training Depot. Completing amphibious assault training in February 1943 at Bridge Spean and having won the admiring respect of both Lord Lovat and the approval of Brigadier General Norman Cota, the 29th Infantry Division assistant division commander, the 29th Battalion was attached to the Number 4 Commando at Dartmouth for six weeks.

Lord Lovat commanded the Number 4 Commando and was considered the elite of the elite. He was a legend in his own time. During the raid at Dieppe, his legend had only grown even greater as his Commandos moved forward against overwhelming odds destroying German fortifications. When orders came to withdraw, he refused to leave behind his dead. Unable to bring them down the cliffs in the hasty retreat, he ordered gasoline to be poured over the bodies to burn them. Scots never leave their dead behind.

After conducting three joint raids on the Norwegian coast, the battalion moved to Bude, Cornwall, in May, and then to Dorlin House, Scotland, in July. The battalion participated in a fourth raid on Ile d'Ouessant—Ushant Island—off the tip of Brittany. The small number of Rangers accompanying the Commandos acquitted themselves very well and killed three German soldiers in the process. Moving to Dover in August, the battalion was deactivated at Okehampton, Devon, on 18 October 1943 and its soldiers returned to the 29th Infantry Division when it was determined to be no longer needed with the pending arrival of the 2nd and 5th Ranger Battalions from the U.S.

The two other European Theater Ranger Infantry Battalions, the 2nd and 5th Ranger Infantry Battalions, were officially designated the Provisional Ranger Group on 6 May 1944. Under the command of Lieutenant Colonel James Earl Rudder, these two battalions—referred to by some as "suicide squads"—had their baptism of fire on the beaches of Normandy on D-Day, 6 June 1944, as part of Operation Neptune, the amphibious phase of Operation Overlord.

Hitler's Atlantic Wall of Fortress Europe stretched a total of 2,400 miles along the coast of the English Channel. Field Marshal Erwin "The Desert Fox" Rommel, former commander of the Afrika Korps, commanded the Normandy sector of the coastline.

The 2nd Ranger Infantry Battalion had been activated on 1 April 1943 at Camp Forrest, Tennessee. With the quick turnover of the unit's first four battalion commanders, the organization did not begin to solidify as a unit until the arrival of Rudder in June 1943. Training moved at a swift pace: Fort Pierce, Florida, in early September; Scout Raiders School 17 September; followed by Advanced Tactical Training at Fort Dix.

On 21 November, the battalion sailed for England. Quartered in Bude, they planned but did not execute some recon raids with the Number 4 Commando. An intense training cycle run by the Number 4 Commando ensued. In preparation for their upcoming mission, the Rangers rehearsed amphibious invasions on the Scottish coast against a fortified beach defended by wire, beach obstacles, and anti-assault landing boat devices. The amphibious training was followed by a rotation through the British Assault Training Centre in April. Finally, on 5 May, the 2nd Ranger Infantry Battalion linked up with the 5th Ranger Battalion to conduct joint cliff scaling training exercises with ropes, grapples, and extension ladders.

The 2nd's mission was the toughest, most desperate, and dangerous mission of any of the D-Day assaulting units: three of its companies, D, E, and F, were to land seven kilometers west of the right flank of Omaha Beach on a narrow strip of beach at the base of Pointe-du-Hoc—has also been spelled Pointe-du-Hoe—scale the 120-foot sheer cliffs under heavy enemy fire, cross the mined and obstacled top, and destroy six 155-mm cannon located in open, reinforced concrete casemates. Noted Lieutenant General Omar Bradley of Lieutenant Colonel Rudder, "Never has any commander been given a more desperate mission."

The remainder of the Ranger force would wait offshore under the command of newly promoted Lieutenant Colonel Max Schneider. If the assault force under Rudder took possession of Pointe-du-Hoc, the code phrase "Praise the Lord" would be transmitted and the force under Schneider would move by boat to the Pointe to reinforce the position. If the message was not received by 0700, Schneider's force would move to the Dog Green and Dog White sectors of Omaha Beach, move through the Vierville Draw, and proceed overland to assist their fellow Rangers at the Pointe.

Pointe-du-Hoc had been the focus of an intense Allied air and sea bombardment for weeks. It was key terrain. From its location, the heavily entrenched but wheel carriaged 155-mm cannon had a range estimated to be 25,000 meters that allowed them the opportunity to place fires along the full lengths of both Omaha—fourteen miles distant—and Utah—ten miles distant—beaches. This would not only wreak havoc on Allied ground troops as they disembarked from their assault boats but such range would provide the defending Germans an opportunity to engage larger troop and equipment transports farther out to sea.

What was believed at the time to be the coup-de-grace was delivered by the battleship U.S.S. *Texas* when it delivered salvo after salvo of 14-inch rounds on the target during the predawn hours of 6 June shortly after an 0600 aerial bombardment by eighteen medium bombers of the U.S. Ninth Air Force. The cumulative total of explosives delivered against Pointe-du-Hoc was calculated to be more than ten thousand tons of explosives—the equivalent of half the tonnage of "Little Boy," the nuclear bomb that would be dropped by the *Enola Gay* B-29 Superfortress bomber on Hiroshima, Japan, 6 August 1945.

H-Hour was finally set for 0630, just past extreme low tide, on the 6th of June. From the start of the operation, things did not go as planned for the 2nd Ranger Infantry Battalion. Loaded aboard ten Landing Craft, Assault (LCA) landing craft crewed by British seamen—the British equivalent of U.S. Landing Craft, Vehicle and Personnel (LCVP)—the force struggled against the high seas. Changes to the boats' configuration made the transit across water even more difficult. Light armor had been added to the gunwales and sides of the boats and, while this increased the Rangers' survivability against enemy fire, it also increased the weight of the boats thus resulting in a lower draft.

Riding low in the water at slower than designed speeds, the boats began to take on water soon after departing the transport area as water washed over their sides. The force began to take losses even before the coastline came into view. The boat carrying the D Company commander was swamped, depositing him and twenty of his soldiers into the cold, numbing channel waters where they tread water for a couple of hours prior to being rescued. A little farther on, one of the supply boats sank and the second was forced to jettison over half its cargo in order to remain afloat.

At 0630, the *Texas* lifted her fires from the Pointe at the moment the Rangers were to be touching down at the cliff's base. Unfortunately at 0630, Rudder, in the lead assault craft, came to the realization that his boat's coxswain was headed toward Pointe-de-la-Percee, four kilometers off target on the Omaha Beach side of du-Hoc. Fighting a heavy tidal current and running a gauntlet of German fire from dug-in positions, the tiny invasion force slowly paralleled the beach at the cost of one of their four DUKWs — a 2.5 ton 6x6 cargo carrier that could make five-knot speeds in moderate seas and 50 mph overland — sunk by a 20-mm shell.

More critical than the loss of the DUKW was the impact on their time schedule, for they were thirty-five minutes off the landing time. The plan called for the Rangers to hit the base of the objective just moments after the *Texas* lifted her heavy suppressive fires that were planned to drive the Germans into the protection of underground bunkers. It was hoped that the Rangers could scale the cliff before the defenders could reoccupy their defensive positions. Unfortunately for Rudder and his men, that was not to be.

The original plan called for the three D Company LCAs to land on the west side but, because of the navigation error and the loss of one of the D Company boats, Rudder elected to have all nine LCAs land side by side on the east side of the Pointe. The enemy fire was intense as the Rangers approached. Machinegun and cannon fire enfiladed the assaulting force from reoccupied German positions along the edge of the cliff. Two destroyers, the U.S.S. *Satterlee* and H.M.S. *Talybont*, moved from their stations offshore after observing what was happening to the attacking Rangers. Providing 5-inch gun, 40-mm, and 20-mm fire support, these two Navy ships were able to drive some of the defenders from the cliff's edge.

The beach was only ten meters wide at the point of attack and was, literally, losing ground with each passing minute as the tide rose. Composed of shingle and not sand, the beach would be completely submerged come the tide's peak. Additionally, the heavy concentration of fires against the cliff had resulted in huge chunks of soil being knocked to the cliff's foundation. Clay based, these soils only served to make the shale rock slipperier. There was one silver lining, though. The soil accumulation at the base was over twenty feet high in some areas thus providing the climbers an added lift.

The Rangers had a number of inventive devices to assist their scale to the top. Unfortunately, much of that special mountain climbing equipment did not make it to the shore having been lost or jettisoned at sea. Of the equipment that did make it, the adverse weather conditions seriously impacted on its ability to function as designed. One device that did make it to the beach was a twenty-five meter assault ladder. These donated extension ladders from the London Fire Department were mounted on the DUKWs. Try as they would, though, the three surviving DUKWs were unable to obtain a foothold on the clay-covered shale from where they could extend their ladders. Despite the rolling effect, however, one DUKW was able to extend its ladder while afloat. Heroically, Sergeant William Stivison climbed to the top of the ladder, from where he began to engage the enemy on the cliff with his machinegun. Swaying widely back and forth in a forty-five degree arc to both sides of vertical—the ladder basically serving as a huge moment arm that threatened to sink the DUKW—the ladder had to eventually be brought back down.

Another plan called for steel grapnels to be fired from the LCAs. Fired just prior to each LCA touching down, three rocket-propelled grapnels trailing either a rope ladder, plain three-quarter-inch rope, or toggle ropes exploded from the deck of the boat and arced their way toward the cliff. Attached to each grapnel was a burning fuse lit just prior to launch to make the Germans believe that the grapnels were some type of exploding device that should be avoided. The Rangers watched with great apprehension as the water soaked lines heavily played out behind the rockets. Though a majority of grapnels failed to reach the cliff, at least one from each boat did.

Unfortunately for the Rangers, a second problem was encountered in regard to the bombardment of Pointe-du-Hoc. Bombs and shells that had fallen short had created craters underwater. Unseen because they were submerged by the rising tide, these craters swallowed many a Ranger as he unloaded the ramp of his boat. One Ranger, Lieutenant Kerchner, was resolved to be the first Ranger to hit the beach from his boat. Jumping into what he believed to be a meter of water with a shout of "OK, let's go," the lieutenant found himself literally in over his head as he leaped into a large shell hole. Noting their lieutenant struggling to remain afloat, the men following deboated to the sides and advanced to shore hardly getting their feet wet.

Each Ranger company's strength, on average, was approximately seventy men per company, only half that of a traditional infantry company. One of the first assault craft to make it to the Pointe's beach was Colonel Rudder. Disembarking from their beached boats, Rudder's men assaulted across the gradually narrowing strand of land to the base of the cliff. Taking heavy machinegun fire from a position located on their left flank, the Rangers quickly lost fifteen, dead or wounded. Reaching the ropes, the Rangers began their arduous climb up the suspended rigging.

The Rangers made the climb with various degrees of success and difficulty. For some of them, the climb proved to be much less difficult than their practice climbs back in England. For others, wet and clay-covered ropes required a number of efforts to successfully negotiate.

Not anticipating an attack on their position from the sea, the German defenses facing the Rangers were the weakest. As the Rangers climbed, the Germans tossed grenades over the cliff and cut three or four of the ropes. Ranger Browning Automatic Rifle (BAR) fire from below and continued supporting fires from the U.S.S. *Satterlee* drove many of the defenders from the cliff's edge. Within five minutes of starting the climb, the first Rangers were secure on top to be followed in another ten minutes by the bulk of the fighting force.

At approximately 0730, the message "Praise the Lord" was broadcast from Pointe-du-Hoc, indicating that the Rangers had successfully scaled the cliffs. With less than two hundred Rangers left to drive on with the attack on top of the cliff, Colonel Rudder's signal to his floating reserve, A and B Companies, 2nd Ranger Infantry Battalion, and the 5th Ranger Battalion to reinforce at Pointe-du-Hoc was transmitted fifteen minutes too late. The reserves had moved on to assault Omaha at 0715 in accordance with their established contingency plans.

The top of the cliff was like nothing the Rangers had ever seen before. Having studied in great detail maps, sketches, and aerial photos of the objective, they were amazed to find "just one large shell crater after the other." Large pieces of concrete, blown off the reinforced casements, were strewn about the area.

Each platoon had a specific mission and despite the losses, despite the heavy concentration of defensive fire, and despite the intermingling of units, they each moved out as rehearsed and without being ordered to do so. For once, the shell holes turned out to be an asset to the Rangers, for the craters provided immediate cover and concealment for them. Ignoring the machinegun and 20-mm cannon fire directed at them, the Rangers moved through the shell craters and German trenches toward the six heavy gun casemates. Closing on their mission objective, they were stunned to find that the 'guns' were, in reality, telephone poles. Fresh tracks running inland indicated that the six weapons had been recently removed.

Undaunted and unfazed by the turn of events, the Rangers continued to move inland in small groups toward their second objective—the hard surface road that linked the towns of Vierville and Grandcamp. Intent upon establishing a roadblock across the road to prevent German reinforcements from moving to Omaha Beach, the Rangers encountered heavy resistance in the vicinity of the outer perimeter of Pointe-du-Hoc. The Pointe was a fort and the landside perimeter was heavily defended with machinegun emplacements, barbed wire entanglements, and antipersonnel minefields. By the time D Company was able to establish a blocking position across the road, only twenty Rangers were left combat-effective out of the seventy who had loaded on the assault boats.

Though the Rangers had swept across the objective and established a roadblock along the Vierville and Grandcamp road, the situation was far from stabilized. A battalion aid station was established in a two-room concrete emplacement and Ranger wounded were swiftly overwhelming its capacity. Movement above ground was still nearly impossible so the Rangers stuck to the trenches. Germans, moving by underground passages, continued to snipe and quickly disappear. Individuals and small groups carried on the fight, with both sides taking prisoners.

Yet to be silenced was the machinegun strong point on the eastern edge of the German position that had caused so many casualties during the initial attack across the small beach below. Ordered by Rudder to eliminate it, Lieutenant Elmer "Dutch" Vermeer moved forward with a small patrol. Moving through shell holes, Vermeer encountered a patrol from Company F determined to accomplish the same mission. Unfortunately, as both patrols continued to move forward, the craters disappeared, leaving flat, open space of nearly three hundred yards to assault across.

Realizing that their losses would be heavy, Vermeer prepared to move forward in a frontal attack just as Rudder ordered the patrols to hold their position. Lieutenant Eikner, the colonel's communications officer, had brought with him an old First World War signal lamp with shutters. Having lost their naval shore-fire-control party to a short round earlier and having lost all other means of radio communications, Eikner would attempt to contact the *Satterlee* by Morse code and have the ship train its five-inch guns on the pesky machinegun position. Locating enough dry-cell batteries to get the device working, he established two-way communications with the destroyer. Shortly thereafter, the *Satterlee* blew the machinegun position away with a direct hit.

Despite the support, the Rangers still found themselves in a very tight position. They were cut off from the sea as intense German fires still prevented any additional support ships from landing. They were still cut off by land, as Allied forces had not yet been able to force the Vierville Draw on Omaha Beach. They had no radio communications, other than the old lantern, for all of their equipment had either been lost, destroyed, or damaged. And they had sustained over 50 percent casualties. They were completely isolated.

To top matters off, the British cruiser H.M.S. *Glasgow* had fired a short marker round that struck in the vicinity of Rudder's command post (CP), knocking him senseless, killing one, and wounding another. Recovering quickly, Rudder angrily went hunting for snipers only to be shot in the leg. Fortunately for the Rangers and despite the pain, the Force commander continued to direct his unit's defense. Vermeer concisely stated Rudder's contribution to the operation. "He was the strength of the whole operation."

At the roadblock, the fighting continued with much of it at close quarters. Companies D and E had the roadblock perimeter established by 0815 with a force of thirty-five Rangers. Twelve Rangers from Company F joined them fifteen minutes later. Patrols were immediately sent out to reconnoiter the area.

Following heavy tracks of the missing artillery pieces for nearly 250 meters down a dirt road, Sergeants Leonard Lomell and Jack Kuhn abruptly stopped. They had located the six missing cannons. Well camouflaged and prepared to fire on Utah Beach, the weapons were stocked with piles of ready ammunition but no gun crews. Having apparently moved away from the guns during the heavy pre-invasion bombardment out of fear of having their own ammunition stocks hit, the one hundred Germans that constituted the crews were only now beginning to form across an open field approximately a hundred meters away. They appeared to be in no hurry, for they had to wait until the observation tower on Pointe-du-Hoc was recaptured in order to place accurate and adjusted fires on the beachheads.

Never hesitating, Lomell secured some thermite grenades Kuhn was carrying and moved to the guns. The grenades were placed in the traversing and recoil mechanisms of two of the guns. Then, prior to withdrawing, he destroyed the sighting mechanism of a third. Racing back to the roadblock, Lomell and Kuhn collected more thermite grenades, which they were able to place in the traversing and recoil mechanisms of the remaining three guns.

At the same time, a patrol led by Sergeant Frank Rupinski stumbled across a huge stockpile of ammunition south of the gun battery's location. Using explosives, Rupinski destroyed the ammunition dump. By 0900, word was quickly sent back to Rudder by messenger that both the guns and ammunition were destroyed. Mission complete: the first United States forces to accomplish their mission on D-Day.

For the next forty-eight hours, the Rangers were relatively on their own and still isolated. Armed with nothing more than BARs and 60-mm mortars, the force did receive some reinforcements in the form of a platoon of Rangers from Omaha Beach. Led by Lieutenant Charles Parker, the twenty-three soldiers arrived at 2100 that evening with an additional twenty POWs in tow. During the afternoon of the 7th, a landing craft was able to remove the wounded and prisoners of war as well as bring reinforcements of twenty Rangers of the 5th Battalion from Omaha Beach.

The siege of Pointe-du-Hoc continued as the Germans attempted to retake the fortified area with a series of counterattacks throughout the 6th of June and into the next day. But, despite their desperate situation, the Rangers held. By the end of the battle on 7 June, having fought nonstop for two days without relief, only 25 percent of the original force — fifty Rangers — were still capable of fighting.

Some historians claim that the mission was all for naught, that the unit scaled the heights and secured the Pointe at such a terrible cost for nothing. That claim cannot be substantiated. While the guns were not located and destroyed on the cliff, they were located in the vicinity and were prepared to fire on the struggling and jammed beachheads. Their added weight to the fray below could have been significant. At the worst, it would have proved devastating to Omaha Beach — just in terms of morale alone. At the best, many more Allied troops and much more equipment would have been lost than that lost by the attacking Rangers. Regardless of their eventual location, the guns still could not have been located and destroyed prior to their opening fire without the Rangers scaling the cliffs.

Ten years later, during the reunion at Normandy, Colonel Rudder returned with his son to revisit the site. At the base of the Pointe, he looked up the towering cliff and asked, "Will you tell me how we did this? Anybody would be a fool to try this. It was crazy then, and it's crazy now."

As Companies D, E, and F prepared to take Pointe-du-Hoc, the remainder of the 2nd Ranger Infantry Battalion, A, B, and C Companies, maintained position in the channel. Companies A and B waited with the 5th Ranger Battalion for word from Rudder's Rangers at Pointe-du-Hoc. C Company was prepared to land at H+03 minutes in sector Dog Green of Omaha Beach on the far right flank of the assaulting units, only two minutes after the initial landing of Company A, 116th Infantry Regiment.

The 116th Infantry Regiment was a Virginia National Guard unit and the success of C Company's mission depended significantly on A/116th Infantry crossing the beach and securing the Vierville Draw at the start of the invasion. Unfortunately for the C Company Rangers, A/116th Infantry company was virtually annihilated prior to crossing the beach.

Approaching Dog Green in six LCA assault boats at H+1, A Company was initially engaged by shore batteries 5,000 yards from the beach. No casualties were sustained until LCA 5 received a direct hit at 1,000 yards and six infantrymen drowned. LCA 3 took a hit at one hundred yards, killing two more soldiers outright and drowning another twelve as the boat sank. At 0636, the remaining boats dropped their ramps. Water depth ran from chest height to over one's head. Machinegun fire swept the entire length of the amphibious line. Even lightly wounded soldiers drowned as their heavy soldier's load drove them under the waves. Survivors crawled along the water's edge, attempting to obtain some sort of concealment from the churning foam. Fifteen minutes after the first ramp had dropped, A Company had ceased to exist as an effective fighting force. Within thirty minutes, nearly two thirds of the unit, including all officers and most NCOs, was either killed or wounded.

Immediately behind A/116th in two LCAs and unable to see any of the carnage on Omaha, the Rangers of Company C felt rather confident that they would meet little resistance at the water's edge—considering all of the air and sea bombardment that had transpired earlier. This confidence soon transformed itself into consternation as they realized they were off course and about to be the first to assault the section of beach they were about to land on. Moments later at 0645, the Rangers hit the shore at the far western edge of Omaha Beach, out of position just west of the Vierville Draw.

More than two kilometers from the nearest supporting troops, the Rangers were isolated and on their own. But, they were not alone for, as the first LCA's ramp dropped, the German defenders opened up with a lethal concentration of rifle, machinegun, mortar, and artillery fire. Machinegun fire ripped through the thin-skinned boat and across the water, killing many of the first who had just entered the water. With little chance of survival exiting the front of the boats, many Rangers elected to jump over the sides. Loaded down with rifles, grenades, ammunition, radios, bedrolls, and personal gear, many of the Rangers from the first LCA found themselves sinking below the waves of the channel, for they were unfortunate enough to have had their LCA hit a sand bar some distance from the shore's edge. Mortar and artillery rounds created large geysers of water as they targeted the second LCA, which was hit three times by artillery fire.

Struggling through—or under—the water, individual Rangers fought through the channel surf and heavy German fires toward the water line, hoping to attain safety at the base of a bluff a few hundred meters inland. Many did not make it. Dead Rangers lay everywhere, in the destroyed LCAs, floating in the water, rolling on and off the beach as the surf ebbed and flowed. Others were strung across the beach from the water's edge to the bluff. Sergeant Walter Geldon was one of those soldiers. Lying on the beach, Geldon died the day of his third wedding anniversary. Sixty-eight

C Company Rangers embarked on the two LCAs; only thirty-one fatigued men made it across the beach to the cliff. Behind them were nineteen dead and eighteen wounded. C Company's initiation to combat in the Second World War had resulted in fifty-five percent casualties and the company had yet to fire a shot!

For those Rangers who survived and made it to the base of the cliff, exhausted, their stringent, demanding, and repetitive training took effect. As grenades rolled down the cliff from overhead and impacting mortar rounds walked their way toward the base, the company commander, Captain Ralph Goranson, and his two platoon leaders, Lieutenants William Moody and Sidney Salomon, began to rally their troops. To stay where they were meant eventual destruction. The Vierville Draw had not been secured and was heavily defended. The only viable alternative was to scale the ninety-foot cliff overhead.

Having landed with some specialized climbing equipment, the two platoon leaders and Sergeants Julius Belcher and Richard Garrett quickly moved down the cliff where they located a crevice. Inserting their bayonets to establish handholds, the four Rangers used their highly honed climbing skills to scale the bluffs. From the top, toggle ropes were dropped for the remainder of the company to follow. Company C became the first Omaha Beach assault unit to reach the high ground.

The company's mission was to move west, away from the draw. But Goranson elected to send a patrol to attack the Germans, securing the draw in an attempt to provide an exit off the beach for the trapped invasion forces. Centered on a Norman stone farmhouse from which the Rangers were being engaged, the German defenses consisted of numerous pillboxes, 20-mm cannon, and a maze of communications trenches. Leading the patrol, Lieutenant Moody kicked in the farmhouse door, killed an officer, and began to move through the trenches when he was killed by a round through his forehead.

Lieutenant Salomon moved forward to continue the clearing operation. At one point, Sergeants George Morrow and Belcher located one of the machineguns that had placed such devastating enfilading fires on their company as they had tried to disembark earlier on the beach. Incensed and infuriated, Belcher openly charged the position. Kicking in the pillbox's door, he tossed in a white phosphorus grenade and proceeded to shoot each German as he abandoned the position in burning agony.

Throughout the day, the battle just west of the draw raged as a stalemate. Unlike the Utah Beach area, airborne forces had not been inserted behind the beachhead to block reinforcements. Consequently, the Germans were able to continuously bring fresh troops into the area through their trench network to reoccupy those areas cleared by the Rangers. With his only reinforcements being a section of soldiers from the 116th Regiment landing a kilometer off course, Goranson was too weak to totally pry loose the defenders and his force was too few in number to secure the areas he did clear. To further compound their troubles, the Company C Rangers found themselves on the wrong end of some 20-mm and 5-inch gunfire support when Navy destroyers fired on the cliff positions without realizing that the Rangers had scaled the heights.

To many Rangers, it seemed as if the day would never end. Isolated and without radio communications, the Rangers and a few 116th soldiers continued the fight that gradually provided attacking elements the opportunity to force the Vierville Draw.

Though C Company never started, much less completed, its mission, its firefight at the Vierville Draw proved to be critical for it redirected reinforcements and fires that would otherwise have been directed at the force on "Bloody Omaha." Burial party reports recorded that sixty-nine German and two American dead were located in the vicinity of the stone farmhouse and its defensive trench network.

While the 5th Ranger Battalion's experience was less dramatic, it was certainly not without its own difficulties. Activated at Camp Forrest, Tennessee, on 1 September 1943, the 5th's training started 14 September. Following a plan of instruction similar to the 2nd's, the battalion trained in Florida and New Jersey prior to deploying to England early January 1944. Arriving in Liverpool on 18 January, the 5th Rangers continued to follow the same schedule as the 2nd Rangers: cliff assaults and the British Assault Training Centre.

The 5th Rangers and the two attached Ranger companies from 2nd Battalion rode the channel tides waiting for Rudder's message from Pointe-du-Hoc. Schneider waited until the appointed time of 0700 for the "Praise the Lord" message. The time came and went but the Ranger continued to hold his position. Finally, at 0715, he could delay no longer. The flotilla of twenty LCAs turned to make their run at the beach.

Fifteen minutes later, the message came. But it was too late. The Ranger reserves were committed. Companies A and B in five LCAs, five minutes in advance of the lead 5th Battalion elements, hit the beach first on the boundary between Dog Green and Dog White, just east of the Vierville Draw.

Omaha Beach was the main seaborne effort of the American Army. Situated centrally on the Normandy invasion front, nearly double the number of forces were targeted here than were targeted at the other U.S. objective of Utah Beach. Omaha Beach was unlike any other in the region. Stark cliffs ranging in height from 100 to 170 feet commanded much of the water's edge. A shingle embankment about eight feet high and extending approximately fifteen feet inland lay just above the high water mark. This embankment rose, on average, at a steep rate of one vertical foot for every six feet traversed. This ratio, combined with the fact that the shingle was basically composed of four- to six-inch-diameter "pebbles," created a serious obstacle to both wheeled and tracked vehicles. The only positive aspect about the shingle was that it did provide cover and concealment to those caught on the beach by the withering and unrelenting enemy fire.

The beach itself was two hundred yards deep at the center and tapered off to become quite narrow at each end. Along the rear of the beach was a masonry seawall that ran in height from four to eight feet. The combination of seawall and cliff made the four exit points of D-1 (Vierville Draw), D-3, E-1, and E-3 key terrain that needed to be seized if vehicular traffic was to move off the beach. Vierville Draw, in particular, was the most critical of the four since it was the only paved route and provided the shortest access to a coastal highway that ran parallel to the beach.

Recognizing the criticality of the draws, the Germans constructed twelve heavily fortified positions along the heights overlooking Omaha Beach, concentrated on the four beach exits. The vast majority of gun positions were selected to bring nearly the entire extent of the beaches under enfilading fire. Wing walls were installed to hide muzzle flashes. While these walls limited the weapon's ability to fire at targets offshore, they did not limit the weapon's ability to target landing craft closing on the shore. Ultimately, these walls proved to be an excellent investment of resources, for they significantly hindered the ability of supporting naval ships to target and destroy the strongpoints.

Air and sea preparatory bombardment had been minimized along the coast prior to the invasion as a tradeoff to achieve surprise. The plan, though, did call for one massive sea and aerial bombardment to commence at 0600, just thirty minutes prior to H-Hour. Moving into position, a force composed of two battleships, four light cruisers, and twelve destroyers commenced their shore bombardment ahead of time at approximately 0530 when the battleship U.S.S. *Arkansas* was spotted and engaged by a German shore battery.

Conditions and intelligence were less than perfect, though. Smoke and haze prevented spotter planes from accurately locating targets and, despite the intense analysis of aerial photographs, many of the fortified positions defending the draws were not identified as targets. The final naval prep fires were delivered by specially modified Landing Craft, Tanks (LCT). As the assault craft approached in the final ten minutes prior to H-Hour, each of these LCTs launched approximately 1,000 five-inch rockets at the shore. Within that ten-minute interval, over 10,000 rockets impacted on Omaha.

Unfortunately, a similar degree of success at Omaha Beach was not achieved by aerial bombardment. Weather conditions made altitude bombing by heavy bombers of the U.S. Eighth Air Force exceptionally difficult that morning. Unduly concerned with dropping large amounts of ordnance on advancing assault craft, the air command elected to delay by a few seconds the release point over Omaha. The end result was a saturation bombing approximately three miles inland—with not a single bomb placed on the defenses.

Intelligence failures played one final crucial role for the assault forces on Omaha Beach. Reports indicated that only one reinforced battalion of the German 716th Infantry Division was defending both the Omaha and Utah Beach sectors. The defenders were believed to be of minimum quality and standard with no reserves available for local counterattacks.

Unfortunately for the attacking force, this assessment was in total error. An experienced German infantry division, the 352nd, had been moved to the coast early that spring and assigned a sector that was inclusive of Omaha Beach. The net result was a doubling of forces in the area, a soldier of higher standard, improved command and control, and a mobile reserve positioned only five miles from the beach. This ominous oversight nearly led to defeat for the Americans attacking Omaha.

During the approach of the two Ranger companies of the 2nd Battalion, the beach at this location appeared to the seabound observer to be free of the ravages of war. In reality, though, armor and infantry units from the initial waves were bogged down at the water's edge. Not knowing this, the A Company commander Captain Dick Merrill, called out, "Fellows, it's an unopposed landing." How wrong he was.

As the ramps dropped, the German defenders opened fire, unloading on the disembarking Rangers with a heavy concentration of fire. The fires were intense and some Rangers took nearly thirty minutes to struggle through the water to reach the beach. The percentage of casualties they incurred were almost as great as those of the 29th Infantry Division's lead element, the 116th Infantry Regiment, which had been severely mauled and eliminated as an effective combat force.

Offshore, Schneider observed the overwhelming struggle and carnage faced by the 2nd Ranger Infantry Battalion companies. Realizing that the landing effort had been "a disaster," he elected not to wastefully throw his battalion away. Ordering the remaining fifteen LCAs to move east down the coastline, he found a quieter, relatively speaking, sector of Dog Red and commenced his assault — undoubtedly saving many Ranger lives in the process.

The 5th Battalion landed at 0745 on a sector of beach strewn with the wounded and dead of 116th Regiment assault teams. Leaderless, unorganized, and shell-shocked, the first wave assault teams had been under constant and heavy fire since 0630 and were gripped by fear. Across the beach toward the seawall, four hundred and fifty men of the Ranger Infantry Battalion ran. Of that total, four hundred and forty-four safely made the dash.

The 5th Battalion's Ranger Chaplain was Father Joe Lacy. The evening prior, he had advised his flock, "When you land on the beach and you get in there, I don't want to see anybody kneeling down and praying. If I do, I'm gonna come up and boot you in the tail. You leave the praying to me and you do the fighting." The next day, while the Rangers fought, the good father moved about the shoreline, hauling the dead, dying, and wounded from the water to protected positions where he could either provide comfort or tend to last rights.

Enemy resistance had greatly exceeded expectations. By 0830, all landings at Omaha Beach were halted and Lieutenant General Omar Bradley was seriously considering redirecting the follow-on forces to one of the other beachheads. Over 5,000 soldiers were trapped on the beach with nearly 50 percent of them lying wounded or dead on the shore. Body parts — headless torsos, arms, legs — floated in the surf. Groups of exhausted, confused, and frightened soldiers huddled wherever they could find some cover or concealment. Equipment was stacked on the waterfront and vehicles that were not already hit and burning were immobilized with nowhere to go, inviting targets for the ranging mortar and artillery rounds.

Though it would seem at that moment that the Allied war had been lost on Omaha Beach, there was American resistance and movement. Tanks of the 741st Tank Battalion, the first to arrive at Omaha, put up a stiff fight despite their inability to get over the shingle at the beach's edge. Caught between rising waters and German anti-armor fires against their exposed positions, the tankers continued to engage the overwatching enemy pillboxes until either taken out of action by a hit or flooded out by the incoming tide. Individuals and small groups bypassed the heavily defended beach exits and began to move directly off the beach by moving straight up the bluffs. Bravely moving onward, these courageous soldiers passed "many dead bodies, all facing forward."

Realizing that the situation was critical and that his forces must clear the beachhead, the assistant division commander of the 29th Infantry Division and first general officer to the beach, Brigadier General Norman D. Cota, set about moving his troops inland. Cota served as an inspiration to all who saw him on that bloody day. Shortly after arriving on the beach, he gathered a group of men and led them through a mortar barrage across the beach and up the bluff. Reaching the top of the bluff at a point midway between St. Laurent and Vierville and meeting some resistance, Cota organized his group into fire and maneuver teams that drove the German defenders to flight.

Progressing along a dirt road that ran parallel to the beach, the general moved through and secured the town of Vierville. On the western edge of the town, he dispatched a twenty-three-man patrol of Rangers that had joined him in the direction of Pointe-du-Hoc. Encountering stiff resistance, the Rangers' movement was nearly stopped until Cota moved forward to assist the Ranger platoon leader Lieutenant Parker, with the disposition of his element. This group of Rangers would be the group that'd link up with the 2nd Battalion at Pointe-du-Hoc around 2100 later that evening.

Needing to get back to the beach, Cota moved to the Vierville Draw accompanied by his aide and four riflemen. Still heavily defended by German troops, the draw had just finished being pounded by the *Texas's* secondary armament of 5-inch batteries when Cota's small group arrived to find German troops quickly moving from their bunkers and reoccupying their positions. Observed and fired on by some of the defenders, Cota's group was able to capture five German prisoners who showed them a safe passage through the minefields of the draw that allowed all to safely reach the beach.

Under constant machinegun and sniper fire from the bluffs, Cota continued to move about the beachhead, ordering, cajoling, herding, and reorganizing units, telling his soldiers, "Don't die on the beaches, die up on the bluff if you have to die, but get off the beaches or you're sure to die." Moving from group to group, he came across one of his sons' West Point classmates, Captain Raaen, commander of the 5th Ranger Battalion Headquarters Company (HHC). Directed to Schneider's command post (CP), the general commented to Raaen, "You men are rangers and I know you won't let me down."

Locating the Ranger Infantry Battalion's CP, Cota remained standing. Schneider stood to speak with the general. Cota asked of the men around him, "What unit is this?"

Schneider replied, "We're Rangers, sir!"

With that, Cota yelled, "Rangers, lead the way off this beach before we're all killed." Thus was born what would eventually become the official motto and mantra of the 75th Ranger Regiment: *"Rangers Lead the Way!"*

As events would have it, the Rangers were in the final stages of preparation to break out of the beachhead when Cota arrived at their location. Moving forward, Corporal Gale Beccue of B Company and an accompanying private, shoved an M-1A1 bangalore torpedo — a five-foot section of steel tube filled with TNT and amotal — under some barbed wire to blow a gap in the obstacle.

Lieutenant Francis W. "Bull" Dawson was tossed on top of a barrier wall by some of his men. Charging through more wire, Dawson destroyed a machinegun nest, cleared trenches of German defenders, and secured prisoners. The lieutenant's efforts inspired the rest to follow. For his actions, Dawson would be awarded the Distinguished Service Cross.

Having breached the main German defenses on the beach, the Rangers then advanced up the bluff, encountering little opposition along the way. However, the push was not without its moment of levity. For a brief period, members of the Headquarters Company donned their chemical protective mask in belief that the heavy smoke from a brush fire might be gas. The cure nearly turned out to be greater than the "disease," for some men nearly suffocated, having forgotten to pull the plug on the front of the mask that allowed air to circulate through it to breath.

Cresting the top, Schneider deployed his battalion to the left and right flanks and dispatched a unit to move four miles down the road to seize Vierville. To the front lay open fields and a maze of hedgerows from which German machineguns took the Rangers under fire. The failed aerial bombardment earlier that morning would prove to be costly to the attackers. Breaking up into smaller assault groups, the Rangers and other members of the 116th Infantry Regiment whc had also made it to the top had to move forward across intermittently open ground to engage and to outflank the enemy defensive positions. The breakout from Omaha Beach had begun.

Finally, on D+3, the 5th Ranger Infantry Battalion linked up with its sister battalion at Pointe-du-Hoc. Though not as heavy in relation to other assault elements at Omaha, the 5th Rangers suffered 23 KIA, 89 WIA, and 2 MIA — 25 percent casualties — during the first five days of fighting in Normandy.

Following Normandy, the two Ranger Infantry Battalions were committed as conventional infantry to help reduce the defenses of the port city of Brest in September and to clear the Crown and La Conquet Peninsulas. This operation cost the 5th Rangers an additional 24 KIA, 111 WIA, and 2 MIA.

In December 1944, the 2nd Ranger Infantry Battalion deployed to the Heurtgen Forest, Germany, and seized Hill 400 overlooking the Schmidt and Roer dams that previous regular infantry attacks had failed to secure. During the Battle of the Bulge, the battalion primarily conducted defensive operations. In January 1945, they trained replacements at Schmidthof, Germany. February found them crossing the Roer River attached to the 102nd Cavalry Group. Conducting security mission through April, they moved to Czechoslovakia in May to find themselves in Dolreuth at the war's end. Having been awarded the Distinguished Unit Citation and the Croix de Guerre, the 2nd Ranger Infantry Battalion was deactivated at Camp Patrick Henry on 23 October 1945.

With the war in Europe coming to a close and Allied forces advancing rapidly, the 5th Ranger Battalion, under the command of Lieutenant Colonel Richard Sullivan, found itself being used for long-range patrols and other conventional infantry operations such as providing security to the 12th Army Group Headquarters in October and November. During the first eighteen days of December, while attached to the 6th Cavalry Group, the battalion suffered an additional 18 KIA, 106 WIA, and 5 MIA clearing towns. Seriously weakened by its cumulative losses of experienced Rangers, the 5th Ranger Battalion was gradually becoming an undermanned and depleted light infantry battalion. January 1945 once again found the battalion conducting security missions, but the 5th's luck would soon change for the better with the tasking of the only true Ranger-style mission of their existence.

On 22 February 1945, elements of Major General Walton H. Walker's XX Corps crossed the Saar River in the Serrig and Taben areas. In a move designed to quicken the bridgehead's expansion by encouraging a German withdrawal, Walker tasked the 5th Ranger Battalion on 23 February to infiltrate deep behind enemy lines and establish a blocking position on the critical Irsch-Zerf road. This mission would prove to be the last major combat mission of any Ranger Infantry Battalion in the Second World War.

The Rangers were released from the 3rd Cavalry Group at 1200 on 23 February and immediately attached to the 94th Infantry Division. The Rangers set about planning the mission. Minus B Company, the battalion assembled in Weiten to draw extra ammunition, antitank mines, and rations. Marching two miles to Taben-Rodt to link up with B Company, the battalion found itself under artillery fire around 1815. Two rounds landed on Company A, resulting in twenty-four Ranger casualties.

Departing the town at 2200 amidst sporadic and harassing indirect fires to cross the river by footbridge, the battalion assembled a half mile northeast of the crossing site at 2230, still within friendly lines. Unfortunately, several more Rangers had become casualties of artillery fire during the march.

The Ranger Infantry Battalion crossed the American lines at 2345 and moved forward of the 94th Infantry Division's sector. Though their route would take them through what was called the Waldgut Hundscheid forest, the Rangers were not as concealed as they wanted to be. German forests characteristically were crisscrossed by numerous trails that were seldom more than a few hundred yards apart. Despite the cover and concealment of the trees and despite the nighttime conditions, the Rangers stood a good chance of being detected by enemy patrols.

As the lead company closed on the first checkpoint about a mile and three quarters southwest of the objective, it was subjective to light small arms and machinegun fire. Several Rangers fell wounded. This engagement would be the first of four skirmishes that would mark the infiltration phase of the 5th Rangers' movement.

At 0145, the battalion's strength was further reduced when two B Company platoons became separated from the main body. Halting at a checkpoint around 0630 and establishing a perimeter defense, Lieutenant Colonel Sullivan waited for the two platoons to catch up with the formation. The wait did no good, for the only group to show up was an enemy patrol. Capturing several of the enemy soldiers after a brief firefight, Sullivan quickly sent a reconnaissance patrol to find a safe route out of the area to the northeast. The patrol returned at 0815 and the battalion continued its advance with its prisoners in tow.

Despite the reconnaissance, the battalion was once again subjected to small arms fire from small groups of Germans. Ignoring the fire, the Rangers came within sight of the north edge of the Waldgut Hundscheid around 0930, approximately a mile southwest of the objective. After a brief halt, the unit continued its movement to the northeast. Five hundred yards later, Company D encountered stiff resistance. The company proceeded to outflank the defending Germans with one of its platoons and, following a short firefight, captured several prisoners. In the engagement, the Rangers suffered two more WIAs.

Though it was possible to continue to the objective along a concealed route through the woods, Sullivan elected to avoid the forest route and proceed east to cross a half-mile wide open area that was to the north, under the cover of darkness. Having been engaged during the infiltration on four occasions, stealth was the least of his worries at the moment. The open route was shorter and would save time.

Company A led the battalion across the open expanse. Knowledge of the Rangers' presence in the sector appeared to be sorely lacking, for a German artillery officer, a medical officer, and several enlisted soldiers casually drove into the area and were immediately captured.

As they advanced, the Rangers methodically checked a cluster of houses near the center of the clearing and found them unoccupied. As the final unit, B Company, crossed the field, machinegun and small arms fire erupted from a medium-sized farm dwelling at the edge of the woods, called the Kalfertshaus, and a nearby pillbox. A patrol was dispatched to deal with the menace. It accomplished the mission but, unfortunately, sustained a KIA in the process. Outposting the houses in the open and having captured twenty-three prisoners, the battalion set about preparing to spend the night just south of the objective.

At 2340 that same evening, just as the Rangers were settling in for the night, Task Force Riley, a subordinate unit of Combat Command B (CCB), passed through the 94th Infantry Division, captured Irsch, and continued its drive toward Zerf against strong German resistance.

The Rangers began their final push to the objective at 0600 on 25 February. Confronting only light resistance and capturing more prisoners, the battalion closed on the objective by 0830 and began to prepare their defensive positions. The location presented some serious problems, though, for it was a poor defensive position. The blocking position was set in a narrow strip of woods that extended north from the Waldgut Hundscheid forest and intersected the Irsch-Zerf road. The intersecting of the road with the woods was described as "the cleft in the wood line." Toward the west, the road sloped away approximately thirty yards to the front of the positions the Rangers would take in the woodline for cover and concealment. To the northeast and south stretched woods that provided a tempting avenue of approach for a dismounted attack. Only the position facing east, toward the town of Zerf, provided suitable fields of fire.

Having no other choice than to make the best of the situation, Sullivan set about establishing his perimeter. E Company was located to the north and was responsible for placing antitank mines on the Irsch-Zerf road and for covering them with fire. D and F Companies secured the east side, facing Zerf. Company C secured the west side. Company A was set up on the south side, where it could keep the Kalfertshaus under observation. In that B Company was still missing its two platoons, the remaining members of that company guarded the prisoners in a barn near the center of the perimeter.

Apparently still unaware of the proximity of the Rangers, German elements continued to attempt traversing the road. Shortly after 1200, E Company captured a tank destroyer and destroyed it on the road with a bazooka to serve as a roadblock. Later a halftrack was destroyed when it detonated one of the antitank mines located on the road and a group of German walking wounded was taken prisoner.

Organized German resistance to the Rangers did not begin until around 1545 — about the same time TF Riley was entering Zerf from the north — with the initiation of an intense artillery bombardment of their position. Immediately following the artillery prep was a two-pronged dismounted infantry attack along the covered and concealed routes offered by the forest. Company A was attacked by about two hundred infantry from the south while Company E had to face nearly four hundred infantry from the northeast. Though both assaults were repelled, it proved necessary to reinforce Company E with a platoon from Company F. The company commander and sixteen Rangers of Company B who had been guarding the prisoners filled the gap left in Company F's line.

An interrogation of eight enemy POWs identified the attacking unit as the 136th Regiment, 2nd Mountain Division. Having suffered heavily throughout the war, the regiment was seriously battle-fatigued. Though ordered to continue attacking the Rangers "to the last man," many of the 136th's soldiers preferred capture to death. The POW total by the end of the day was 135 captives.

Having expended large quantities of ammunition during the infiltration and defense of the objective, the Rangers found themselves running low. At 1620, an attempt was made to resupply the battalion by air but German antiaircraft weapons in the area forced the resupply plane to maintain an altitude of 1,500 feet above ground level (AGL). Though the drop was attempted, the majority of the parachuted containers landed outside of the Rangers' defensive perimeter. Without resupply or relief soon, the battalion faced the possibility of running out of ammunition and of being overrun.

Throughout the night of 25 February, the Rangers continued to improve their positions. At 0300 the next morning, a German force estimated at four hundred strong, attacked E Company's position. Members of the Kampfgruppe Kuppitsch — or provisional task force — the attackers were an assortment of miscellaneous administrative units, convalescent companies, and new recruits. Lacking unit cohesion, training, and any weapons heavier than rifles and machineguns, the provisionals compensated with spirit and intense indirect fire support.

Hard-pressed, Company E was reinforced by the A Company commander and twelve of his Rangers. Accepting heavy losses, the Germans continued to apply the pressure, forcing the Rangers 100 yards from their positions. Only after the Americans called artillery in on their own overrun positions did the German force disengage. While capturing twenty-five more German prisoners, the Ranger head count indicated fourteen Rangers missing and believed captured.

Throughout the remainder of the early morning hours, intense artillery fire fell on the Rangers' position. As the morning wore on, the intensity decreased and finally stopped altogether. A quiet descended upon the battlefield. At 1155 on the 26th, Combat Command B reached the Rangers as the American mechanized force was driving on Zerf from the west. CCB was able to meet the Rangers' most immediate needs: ammunition, water, food, and radio batteries.

Having evacuated the wounded Rangers and secured the seventy-five enemy prisoners found on hand, CCB continued its movement east while the Rangers remained in their blocking position throughout the night. A dense fog arrived the next morning, as did a disoriented group of two hundred Germans. Seizing the initiative, the Rangers caught the enemy in a hasty ambush. Many of the Germans were killed. Realizing the futility of continuing the fight caught in a kill zone, the remaining one hundred and forty-five survivors threw down their weapons and surrendered.

Later around midday, the battalion was joined by the two lost platoons of B Company. Having returned to American lines after their break in contact, the two Ranger platoons had joined an armor unit and fought as conventional infantry alongside its tanks during the push to Zerf.

The final Ranger casualties were inflicted on the battalion by artillery fire that fell sporadically on the unit until mid-afternoon. Finally, at 1500 on 27 February, nearly four days after crossing the LD, the 94th Infantry Division relieved the 5th Ranger Battalion.

This action by the 5th Ranger Battalion in the vicinity of Zerf, Germany, is considered to be one of the most successful Ranger operations of the war. While infiltrating a battalion-sized element through enemy territory, securing the objective, and fighting off repeated attacks, the 5th Rangers killed 299 German soldiers and took 328 prisoners during an operation that lasted four days. The Rangers suffered approximately ninety casualties. The 5th's performance during that time significantly contributed to the collapse of the German front west of Zerf.

Despite this authentic Ranger operation success, the 5th Rangers were to finish the final two months of the war fighting as conventional infantry conducting routine combat missions, guarding prisoners, and imposing military government in and around Bamberg, Erfurt, Jena, Gotha, and Weimar. In April, General George S. Patton tasked the unit with the mission of escorting 1,000 Germans through the Buchenwald death camp. The German surrender found the battalion in Ried, Austria.

The 5th Ranger Battalion fought for eleven months from the beaches of Normandy to the country of Austria. Along the way, they lost 115 KIA, 552 WIA, 25 MIA, and two known POWs. But the enemy paid an extremely heavy price for the 5th Rangers killed an estimated 1,572 soldiers and captured 4,541 POWs. Finally, on 2 October 1945, after being awarded the Distinguished Unit Citation and Croix de Guerre for Normandy and the Presidential Unit Citation for Zerf, the 5th Ranger Infantry Battalion was deactivated at Camp Miles Standish, Massachusetts.

In the Pacific Theater of Operations, the 6th Ranger Infantry Battalion had its beginning in the 98th Field Artillery Battalion. Activated in January 1941 at Ft. Lewis, Washington, the 98th served in New Guinea and was at Port Moresby as part of the Sixth Army. The Sixth Army commander was Lieutenant General Walter Krueger.

In 1943, shortly after taking command of the Army, Krueger had created an elite force, patterned after the Navy's Underwater Demolition Teams (UDT) that conducted reconnaissance and special missions behind enemy lines. Designated the Alamo Scouts, these small teams of one officer and six enlisted men garnered nineteen Silver Stars, eighteen Bronze Stars, and four Soldier's Medals without suffering a single casualty during a nine month period.

Significantly impressed, Krueger decided to create a larger force to accomplish the same type missions as the Alamo Scouts but on a grander scale. Furthermore, it was decided that the new unit would be created from the 98th Field Artillery Battalion, thus making the 6th Rangers the only World War II Ranger Infantry Battalion to carry the lineage of a previous unit.

To command the new unit, the general selected Lieutenant Colonel Henry A. Mucci, a 1936 United States Military Academy graduate. Arriving in Port Moresby in April 1944, Lieutenant Colonel Mucci assumed command of the 98th. On 25 September, the 98th Field Artillery Battalion was redesignated and reflagged as the 6th Ranger Infantry Battalion. Men who did not want to be Rangers were encouraged to transfer to allow the unit to be manned exclusively by volunteers. Those who remained underwent a rigorous training program similar to the one that Darby's Rangers had undergone.

The 6th Ranger Infantry Battalion's initial baptism of fire was the invasion of the Philippines. Starting on 17 October 1944, three days prior to the actual landings on the main island of Luzon, the 6th Ranger Infantry Battalion landed on three strategic islands that guarded the entrance to Leyte Gulf to destroy Japanese communications facilities and weapons emplacement. Company D and part of HHC landed on Sulvan Island. The bulk of the battalion—all of those elements not landed on the other two islands—landed on Dinagat Island. The next day, 18 October, B Company and the remaining elements of HHC landed on Homonhan Island. Following some minor security missions, the Ranger Infantry Battalion landed on Luzon on 10 January 1945 only to spend the next two weeks guarding the Sixth Army's headquarters.

American and Allied POWs had been on Krueger's mind for a long time. Aware of a POW camp at Pangatian, five miles east of Cabanatuan and thirty miles behind enemy lines, Krueger commenced planning the liberation of the camp as his army entered central Luzon.

Liberating the POW camp would be a significant challenge to whoever was assigned the task. Deep behind enemy lines, the camp was situated on a major supply route (MSR) with Japanese units moving only at night along the route to avoid American airpower. Such movements would complicate the night activities of infiltrating units. Japanese tanks also used the roads in the area and there were reports of high-density Japanese troop concentrations in the nearby town of Cabu and Cabanatuan City. Additionally, the compound itself also served as a transit camp for units passing through.

In that the Japanese had already evacuated many of the prisoners from the camp, Sixth Army headquarters grew concerned for the welfare and safety of the remaining POWs, many of whom were survivors of the "Bataan Death March," and so emaciated and wasted away as to be referred to as "ghost soldiers." Fearing that they would be moved north or worse executed, to prevent their liberation, Krueger assigned the difficult mission to the 6th Ranger Infantry Battalion.

Mucci's task organization for the mission consisted of himself, Company C, 2nd Platoon of Company F, two teams of Alamo Scouts, and four combat photographers. The total strength of the assembled force was eight officers, 120 enlisted men.

The planning and preparation phase of the operation was exceptionally thorough. Aerial photographs, in addition to map and ground reconnaissance, were used. Officers and enlisted soldiers were familiarized with the routes, rendezvous points, and location of the camp. The Army Air Corps would provide air cover. Intelligence updates would be relayed by Sixth Army to the Rangers, who would carry an SCR 694 radio specifically for that purpose.

The Ranger uniform would be fatigue without rank or insignias and soft caps. Riflemen would carry either the M-1 rifle or M-1 carbine. The weapons section would carry BARs. Most NCOs carried a Thompson submachinegun and .45-caliber pistol. While Mucci was armed with only a .45-caliber pistol, most officers augmented that pistol by carrying a rifle. In addition to their personal weapons, each man carried a minimum of two bandoleers of ammunition, a trench knife, and two hand or rifle grenades.

Both Alamo Scout teams departed the base camp on the afternoon of 27 January. From there, they marched to a guerrilla headquarters at Guimba. Native guides would lead them to Platero three miles north of the objective. After linking up with the local guerrillas at that location, the Scouts would keep the prisoner compound under surveillance, determining the number of Japanese guards, their routines, and the location of the prisoners. That intelligence would be furnished the Rangers when they arrived in the area.

Having completed their preliminary planning and needing to wait until they got closer to the target to complete the plan, Mucci's force departed its base camp at Calasiao at 0500 on 28 January by truck. Detrucking at Guimba to link up with native guides, the force departed that location by foot and marched five miles to the east to a guerrilla camp in the vicinity of Lobong. Upon their arrival, a guerrilla force of eighty men led by Captain Eduardo Joson joined the Ranger force. Concerned about skirmishing with Communist Huk guerrillas operating in the area, Joson secured the camp with twenty of his men and sent the vast majority of the remainder out along Mucci's flanks to prevent the force from being ambushed during its movement.

Marching east through open grasslands and rice paddies, the force, approximately 188 strong at this point, crossed into enemy territory after dark about a mile south of Baloc. Fording the Talavera River around midnight and crossing the Rizal Highway around 0400, the force arrived at Balincarin at 0600 on the morning of the 29th, having completed the fourteen-mile march from Lobong without a single incident.

Mucci linked up with the two Alamo Scout commanders, Lieutenants Thomas Rounsaville and William Nellist, who had departed from the base camp on the 27th, to learn that the Scouts were not finished with their reconnaissance. Shortly thereafter, the local guerrilla area commander, Captain Juan Pajota, and his force of approximately ninety armed and one hundred and sixty unarmed men joined the Rangers and Scout commanders in Balincarin. The size of the force was now up to 438.

The current situation was not good. Heavy concentrations of Japanese troops were in the area. Considerable traffic was passing in front of the camp and two to three hundred enemy soldiers were bivouacked just a mile north of the compound on Cabu Creek. To top it off, there was a minimum of one Japanese division four miles to the south at Cabanatuan City. Convinced by the intelligence that a delay was prudent, Mucci postponed the raid for twenty-four hours.

Continuing to plan, the Rangers settled in. The Company C commander, Captain Robert W. Prince, and the guerrilla leader Pajota, arranged for the guerrilla force to provide all around security of the village. Coordination was made to assemble a carabao-cart train large enough to carry two hundred liberated POWs and food needed to be prepared along the return route to feed 650 men.

The guerrillas passed instructions to the civilians within their area. Chickens had to be penned and dogs tied and muzzled to prevent disturbances as the force moved by. Civilians north of the Cabanatuan City-Cabu highway were requested to detain any outsiders who wandered into their area until after the raid. And, for the safety of those living in the vicinity of the objective, they were told to leave but to do so at intervals so as not to alert the Japanese.

Flanked by Joson's and Pajota's guerrillas for security, Mucci's Rangers departed Balincarin shortly after 1600 for the two-and-a-half-mile trip south to Platero. The Alamo Scouts joined the force halfway to Platero to provide a situation report (SITREP). Verifying the previous reports, the Scouts added that another division-sized force was heading toward Bongadon from the southwest. The decision to delay the assault had proven to be a wise one.

Platero's inhabitants warmly greeted the Rangers when the force entered the town at dusk. While most of the force rested, the officers and NCOs planned the operation and transformed a one-story wooden building into a makeshift hospital. Having the time, the Alamo Scouts and guerrillas continued to recon.

The final report the recon elements returned with was very detailed. The compound was on the south side of the Cabanatuan City-Cabu highway. Measuring 600 by 800 yards, it was enclosed by three barbed wire fences, four feet apart and six to eight feet high. Less formidable barbed wire fences compartmentalized the compound. The prisoners seemed to be housed in buildings in the northwest corner. An eight-foot-high gate secured with a heavy-duty lock barred the main entrance to the camp. A building inside the compound was believed to house four tanks and two trucks. One sentry stood guard at the gate in a well-protected shelter. Three twelve-foot-high guard towers were occupied, as was a pillbox with four heavily armed soldiers inside. Seventy-three Japanese soldiers guarded the stockade. At 1100 that morning, an additional one hundred and fifty soldiers entered the compound apparently to rest. Traffic on the nearby highway was light and the nearest outside threat came from the eight-hundred-man force supported by tanks and trucks at Cabu.

The plans were completed. The attack would commence at dusk. Surprise was essential. Every member of the force was briefed as to his assigned mission. The Alamo Scouts had the camp under continual surveillance and civilian runners to maintain communications between the Scouts and the main body, if necessary.

Mucci departed Platero with a force numbering 375 men for the objective on 30 January at 1700. Only the SCR 694 radio crew had been left behind with several armed villagers to provide security. Unknown to Mucci was the fact that Pajota had a second force of four hundred armed guerrillas and four .30-caliber machineguns for additional support. Half of this force would be allocated to support his blocking position; the other half was to serve as a reserve for Joson's roadblock. Pajota's rationale for not sharing this information was quite simple. He preferred to deploy these additional men in his best judgment without having to discuss the issue with Mucci.

The force advanced for a half mile along a well-concealed, narrow dirt trail that pierced the tall grass and bamboo to the Pampanga River. At this point, the force split into three separate elements with Pajota and Joson leading their men across the river and to their blocking positions.

Pajota's forces were to cut the phone lines linking the camp to the outside just prior to the attack and to establish a roadblock three hundred yards northeast of the compound at the highway bridge over the Cabu Creek with the mission to stop any reinforcements from getting to the camp from Cabu. Strengthened by the additional two hundred men he had sent ahead and his four .30-caliber machineguns, Pajota was able to cover the highway, the bridge, and likely river-crossing sites. Given that it was the dry season, the low water level of the creek provided a number of potential crossing sites. Additionally, an ambush was set up on the far side of the creek and a time bomb — one of several delivered by an Ameri-

can submarine — had been placed under the far end of the bridge and set
to go off ten to twenty minutes after the assault started.

Joson's guerrillas, in the meantime, had moved eight hundred yards
southwest of the compound to establish a roadblock on the main highway to stop any reaction elements that might come out of Cabanatuan
City. Attached to the guerrillas was a six-man bazooka team from 2nd
Platoon, Company F to provide anti-armor protection. Backing Joson up
was the two-hundred-man reserve that Pajota had secretly provided.

After the departure of Pajota and Joson, Mucci led the main body
across the river for the two-mile march to the objective. High grass concealed the first mile of their approach. At 1800, the main body broke from
the tall grass to find a shrubless, treeless, flat, and barren rice paddy
before them.

2nd Platoon, Company F, whose missions were to kill the guards at
the rear of the compound, destroy a pillbox at the northeast corner of the
compound, and prevent Japanese elements from moving into the prisoners' stockade, split from the main body and moved east. A half mile later,
the platoon followed a streambed that would conceal its movements to
the east fence of the compound.

Company C's tasks were critical. 1st Platoon's mission was to breach
the front gate of the compound and kill the Japanese guards in several
known locations. Once that was accomplished, a platoon section would
advance on the building housing the tanks and trucks and destroy it with
bazooka fire. 2nd Platoon's mission was to follow the 1st Platoon through
the breach to secure and evacuate the prisoners.

Looking across the wide-open expanse before him, Prince led his two
platoons forward another five hundred yards just to the point where the
compound's watchtowers could be seen on the horizon. Assuming that
"if he could see them, they probably could see us," Prince had his Rangers, the combat photographers, medics, the Alamo Scouts, and several
guerrillas drop to the ground and begin crawling. It would take the Rangers seventy-five minutes to cover the one-mile distance.

At 1840, a P-61 Black Widow night fighter approached the compound. One of Pajota's recommendations, the aircraft would provide a
diversion and possibly distract the Japanese guards from observing the
Rangers' movement forward as they kept their eyes skyward. Flying over
the bridge and prison camp twice at an altitude of two hundred feet AGL,
the fighter then departed the area on the prowl for enemy troops caught
on the road.

Prince and his group completed their crawl approximately twenty-
five minutes after Black Widow's departure from the area. Having

arrived at a drainage ditch opposite the main gate of the compound and across the highway, the group waited for the assault to begin.

2nd Platoon, Company F, was still on the move while Company C waited in its attack position. Moving through a large culvert under the highway, the platoon advanced toward the back of the compound in a five-foot ditch that ran to the compound's east fence. At one point as the platoon was passing a guard tower, a sentry raised his weapon as if prepared to fire in the direction of the 2nd Platoon. Fortunately, the guard apparently convinced himself it was nothing, lowered his weapon, and went about his business. The unit was finally in position by 1925.

In that the 2nd Platoon had the greatest distance to cover, Mucci selected the platoon leader, First Lieutenant John F. Murphy to commence the assault on the objective. Though the attack was to be initiated at 1930, Murphy took some additional time to ensure his platoon was properly emplaced and prepared. Finally, at 1945, Murphy raised his rifle and, aiming at an open window in the nearest barracks, pulled the trigger. The assault on the compound occupied by nearly 223 enemy soldiers had begun.

Small arms, automatic weapons, and grenades quickly followed. A lone sentry at the front gate was the target of so many weapons that his upper torso literally disintegrated under the hail of lead. Within thirty seconds, all pillboxes, guard shacks, and towers were neutralized.

Staff Sergeant Theodore R. Richardson of Company C led the charge across the highway. Blowing the lock off the front gate with his .45-caliber pistol, he continued to advance into the compound. Bazooka sections moved to the central portion of camp and destroyed two trucks and a corrugated metal tank shed, but no tanks were found as had previously been reported.

As the Rangers were storming the compound, Pajota found himself with his hands full at the bridge. With the Rangers' opening shots, the guerrillas opened fire on a Japanese battalion in bivouac approximately three hundred yards beyond Cabu Creek. The Japanese attempted to counterattack in a piecemeal fashion and were continually repelled with heavy casualties. The time bomb blew a gap in the bridge and the four machineguns killed a significant number of Japanese as they attempted to cross the shallow river. Pajota's men were even able to destroy two Japanese tanks and one truck.

Twelve minutes after the opening round, enemy resistance had pretty much ceased to exist in the compound and the Rangers began moving the POWs out of the camp, carrying many of them on their backs. The Rangers suffered their first casualties of the operation when three light mortar rounds were fired in the vicinity of the front gate. Six men were wounded with Alamo Scout Rounsaville and the battalion surgeon, Captain James C. Fisher, among the casualties. Unfortunately, Fisher would die from his wounds prior to reaching friendly lines.

After a second sweep of the facilities for any stragglers, Prince fired one red flare into the sky signaling that the withdrawal was to begin. Unknown to Prince, a scared British civilian POW had hidden in the latrine during the assault. Luckily for him, Filipino guerrillas rescued him later that evening. Tragically, another POW died of an apparent heart attack as he was being assisted out of the compound.

The last Rangers to withdraw from the objective were six men from Company F. Brought under fire, Corporal Roy Sweezy turned to return fire only to be hit in the chest with automatic weapons fire. Dying minutes later, he and the fatally wounded Captain Fisher were the only Ranger KIAs of the operation.

Most of the Rangers and the liberated POWs were at the Pampanga River by 2030. A total of forty-five minutes had elapsed. By 2045, these men were across the river. Prince fired the signal flare for the roadblock positions to withdraw. For Joson, that was relatively simple, for he had not fired a single shot in defense of his position. Undoubtedly, any idea to attack his position was probably squelched at 2000 when a P-61 providing air cover for the operation strafed and destroyed a Japanese convoy heading toward Cabanatuan City and the roadblock from San Jose. Quickly withdrawing, Joson deployed half his men to Platero for local security while the remainder of his force would provide flank security for the Ranger column when it left Platero.

Still battling a determined Japanese foe, Pajota was unable to withdraw as planned as indicated by the signal flare. The fight at the roadblock continued until 2200 when the exhausted and seriously mauled Japanese battalion ended their assaults against Pajota's position. At the cost of not even one serious casualty, Pajota's force had rendered nearly combat-ineffective an eight-hundred-man battalion. Conducting an orderly withdrawal, Pajota took up as rear guard on the Pampanga to prevent any pursuit of Mucci's column. All told, a total of 250 Japanese soldiers had been killed during the attack and defense of the road blocks.

The mission was not yet complete for the liberated POWs needed to be returned to friendly lines. Carabao carts were awaiting at the south bank of the Pampanga River as requested. The column moved to Platero where it stopped to reorganize, eat, and tend to some of the more seriously sick or wounded. Those ex-POWs who could walk departed for Balincarin at 2100 under Ranger escort and were soon followed by the remainder of the column.

At Balincarin, there was more food and water as well as an additional fifteen carabao carts to be added to the twenty-five already on hand. Captain Fisher would die in Balincarin of his wounds.

The column departed Balincarin at midnight and moved on to Matoas Na Kahey where it arrived at 0200 on 31 January. Again, there was food and water and eleven more carabao carts. The column departed at 0230 with fifty-one carts stretched along a column a mile and a half long.

Just beyond Matoas Na Kahey lay the Rizal Highway. Not only did the column have to cross this danger area but, because of the peculiar terrain features along the highway, the column had to enter the road at one point to the north and exit it at a point one mile to the south! Given the length of the column, two thirds of it would be exposed and vulnerable on the highway at one point.

1st Platoon, Company C, was tasked to provide crossing site security. Armed with a bazooka and antitank grenades, one of the platoon's sections established a roadblock four hundred yards northeast of the column's entry point. A second, identical section, established another roadblock 3,000 yards to the south. The column took over an hour to clear the highway, amazingly completing the maneuver by 0430 without being discovered.

The column halted for a rest stop at a small village around 0530 then quickly moved on. Communications with the forward base at Guimba had been nonexistent throughout the operation despite the SCR 694 radio that had been lugged around. Repeated attempts to establish communications had failed.

At 0800, the column arrived at the small town of Sibul. Food and water were again provided with an additional twenty carabao carts thrown in for good measure. During the halt, radio contact with Guimba was again attempted. This time communications were established. Ambulances and trucks were requested to meet the column, which resumed its march to freedom shortly after 0900.

Technician 5 Patrick Marquis, on point and several hundred yards forward of the column, was halted by a Sixth Army reconnaissance patrol at about 1100. With the requested ambulances and trucks just a short distance away, the former POWs were at the 92nd Evacuation Hospital in Guima within an hour, mission accomplished for what would become known as the most daring raid in U.S. military history. Later, as the rescued prisoners made their way back to the United States, tens of thousands of Americans turned out to cheer the men on as they passed below the Golden Gate Bridge.

The Cabanatuan prison camp raid was an overwhelming tactical success. The raid liberated 511 American and Allied POWs and resulted in an estimated 523 Japanese casualties at a cost of two Ranger KIA and ten WIA. General Douglas A. MacArthur stated that the raid was "magnificent and reflect[ed] extraordinary credit to all concerned."

Lieutenant Colonel Mucci was awarded the Distinguished Service Cross for planning, implementing, and leading the raid. The Silver Star was awarded to all American officers and the Bronze Star was awarded to all American enlisted men, all Filipino officers, and all Filipino enlisted men who participated in the raid. It must further be noted that the mission's success would have probably been highly unlikely had it not been for the Filipino friendship and support provided both going to and returning from the objective.

Unfortunately for the 6th Ranger Infantry Battalion, the prison raid proved to be their one and only major combat operation. Relegated to providing security for Sixth Army headquarters, conducting reconnaissance patrols, searching for Japanese stragglers, and eliminating small pockets of enemy resistance, the battalion suffered only one additional KIA and three WIA for the remainder of the war. The battalion departed on 15 September to serve as part of the occupational forces in Japan. Having been awarded the Presidential Unit Citation and the Philippine Presidential Citation, the 6th Ranger Infantry Battalion was inactivated 20 December 1945 in Kyoto, Japan.

A seventh Ranger-style unit was never officially designated a Ranger Infantry Battalion but it certainly had the earmarks of one. In September 1943, as the result of the Quebec Conference of August 1943, the United States agreed to the formation of a long-range penetration unit to spearhead the Chinese Army in the Burma area of operation. Activated on 8 January 1944 as 5307th Composite Unit (Provisional)—code name Galahad—the unit, better known as Merrill's Marauders in honor of its commander, Brigadier General Frank D. Merrill, was a regimental-sized unit organized and trained for operations deep behind enemy lines in Japanese-held Burma. They were the first U.S. ground combat force to meet the enemy on the Asian continent in the Second World War.

Burma, now officially called Myanmar, is a mountainous region with deep valleys and major river networks. Most of Burma receives heavy rainfall, with some regions receiving up to two hundred inches a year. Almost 50 percent of the region is covered with thick, broad-leaved evergreen rain forests and nearly impenetrable strands of bamboo. Mud, high humidity and temperatures, monsoons, leeches, mosquitoes, and mites made this region an extremely difficult one in which to operate.

A call for volunteers for "a dangerous and hazardous mission" brought a response from more than 2,900 soldiers. Preliminary training was secretly conducted in the jungles of India starting in early November 1943. The unit departed from India for Ningbyen, Burma, in late January and marched the final 150 miles to arrive 21 February. From this march was coined the name "Merrill's Marauders."

The Marauders were especially noted for their ability to quickly move over seemingly impassable terrain. Organized into three battalions, two teams each battalion, for a total of six combat teams of four hundred men each, and a rear echelon logistic headquarters of six hundred men, the Marauders, in concert with Chinese troops of the 22nd and 38th Divisions, began a series of operations on 24 February against Japanese units, supplies, and lines of communications designed to recover northern Burma and to clear the way for the construction of a vital road. A Staging Area Detachment operating out of Dinjan, India provided air resupply. Unit supplies and equipment were transported on the ground by seven hundred mules and horses of two Quartermaster pack troops.

Advancing along the Ledo Road, the unit conducted numerous raids against the enemy. In five major and thirty minor engagements, they marched over 1,000 miles through extremely dense and almost impenetrable jungles and defeated the veteran soldiers of the Japanese 18th Division—conquerors of Singapore and Malaya. As effective as they were in their missions, however, the Marauders' casualties mounted as the enemy and disease took their toll.

The Marauders continued their operations and attacked an airfield at Myitkyina on 17 May 1944, an objective of significant tactical importance to the allied Burma campaign, for it was the only all-weather strip in northern Burma. Moving quickly, the force surprised the Japanese and seized the airfield in a daring and brilliant daylight attack. Unfortunately, the assault against the town itself met heavy resistance that dragged on for months. Under siege, the town of Myitkyina finally fell on 3 August. For their outstanding performance during this operation, the 5307th Composite Unit (Provisional) was awarded the Distinguished Unit Citation. Later, in November 1966, the award was redesignated as the Presidential Unit Citation.

Having been promised relief, the Marauders' morale and cohesion deteriorated as they remained on the line. Periods of rest and improved rations failed to maintain, much less restore, strength and endurance. A subsequent inspector general report stated that there was "an almost complete breakdown of morale in the major portion of the unit." Physical and mental exhaustion continued until utterly worn-out and depleted, this most heroic unit was relieved and consolidated on 10 August 1944 with the 475th Infantry Regiment.

Galahad's accomplishments had been achieved at a horrendous human cost. Out of the original fighting force of 2,830 officers and men who set out on their first mission on 24 February, only 1,310 of them reached the objective at Myitkyina airfield. By the time the town itself was taken, Merrill's Marauders had been reduced to some two hundred undernourished, diseased, and exhausted men. Merrill himself had been evacuated a few weeks earlier after a heart attack.

The 475th was assigned as part of the 5332nd Brigade (Provisional) "Mars Task Force." In November and December 1944, the 475th assisted the Chinese 22nd Division near Si-u and attacked to restore positions near Mo-hlaing, establishing contact on 15 December with the British 36th Division. On 3 and 4 February 1945, the regiment fought its last battle at Loi-kang Ridge.

The 475th itself was deactivated in China on 1 July 1945. On 21 June 1954, the 475th numerical was shortened and redesignated the 75th Infantry Regiment. Activated later that year on 20 November on Okinawa, the 75th Infantry Regiment assimilated the equipment of the 29th Infantry Regiment. Though it would be inactivated once again on 21 March 1956, *this infantry regiment would serve as the forefather of today's 75th Ranger Regiment.*

CHAPTER 16

Korean Conflict

It is fatal to enter any war without the will to win it.

General of the Army Douglas MacArthur

During the early stages of the Korean Conflict, the Eighth Army command found itself impressed by the effectiveness of infiltrating North Korean specialized small units. Needing a unique small unit of its own to patrol a small salient north of the Pusan Perimeter called the Pohang Pocket—a reentrant into the perimeter—the Eighth Army assigned the task of organizing a commando-style unit to its G3 who passed it along to Colonel John H. McGee, head of G3 Miscellaneous Division.

Afforded only seven weeks to select the personnel, organize and train the unit, and armed only with a copy of the Table of Organization and Equipment (TO&E) used by Ranger companies near the end of World War II, Colonel McGee flew from Korea to Camp Drake, Japan, on 8 August 1950 to begin soliciting and interviewing potential candidates for the new unit. Based on a recommendation, the colonel sought out a 1949 West Point graduate, Second Lieutenant Ralph Puckett, while at the Replacement Depot. Puckett immediately volunteered for the Rangers for he "wanted to be with the best."

When informed that the only officer slot left to fill was that of commander—a captain's position—Puckett answered that he would "take a squad leader's or rifleman's job" if it would secure his assignment to the unit. Not only did this warrior spirit get him assigned to the Ranger unit, it also earned him that commander's position. Unknown to Puckett at the time, two of his classmates, Second Lieutenant Charles Bunn and Second Lieutenant Barnard Cummings, Jr., had been selected as platoon leaders

and had been the ones to recommend to McGee that Puckett be interviewed.

Puckett, fresh out of Infantry Officer Basic Course (IOBC) and airborne school, began to form his combat command. Assisted by the depot
commander, Puckett and his two platoon leaders scoured personnel files
and conducted personal interviews to select the final Ranger candidates.
Demonstrated motivation, just as it had been for Puckett's selection as
company commander, proved to be a major discriminator.

Gathering those potential Rangers who made the initial cut into a
group, the new commander made a general announcement to all: anyone
not willing to volunteer for anything dangerous could leave the room
immediately. Two thirds of the recruits remained and the final individual
interviews were conducted to select the seventy-four enlisted soldiers
who would be assigned, in addition to the three officers. The results were
relatively surprising. While all company members were volunteers, the
unit could not be defined as elite as a function of soldiers selected. Most
selected were average soldiers, either service personnel with little or no
Infantry training assigned to support units in Japan or unassigned
replacement infantrymen on their way to Korea. Few had any combat
experience.

Formally designated the 8213th Army Unit (AU), the Eighth Army
Ranger Company (8ARC) was officially established by Eighth Army General Order Number 237 on 25 August 1950. Organizing the company into
two thirty-six-man platoons—consisting of a headquarters element, two
assault sections and a special weapons section—and a five-man company
headquarters element, Puckett drew equipment at Camp Drake in accordance with the TO&E that Colonel McGee had provided. Armed with M-
1 carbines and rifles, pistols, two M-1C sniper rifles, four light machineguns, two BARs, two 60-mm mortars, and two 3.5-inch bazookas, the
8ARC departed Japan by ship on 1 September and arrived at Pusan on 1
September—the first Ranger unit deployed to the Korean conflict.

The Rangers moved to Kijang, a small village northwest of Pusan,
where a training camp dubbed "Ranger Hill" had been prepared by Colonel McGee. In that North Korean guerrillas were still active in the area,
the 8ARC had to establish and maintain a 360-degree defense of the hill,
as well as conduct training. Focusing on the basic infantry fundamentals
of shoot, move, and communicate, the intense training cycle commenced.
As the weeks progressed, the Rangers grew to learn how to overcome
physical exhaustion, mental fatigue, and the fear of possible bodily
injury. MacArthur's amphibious invasion at Inchon removed the initial

mission objective of the Eighth Army Ranger Company and the Eighth Army's need for a unique small unit to patrol the Pohang Pocket.

Despite only five and a half weeks of the allocated seven weeks of preliminary training, it was proposed that the company be assigned to combat duty effective 11 October. Colonel McGee's final statement in a deployment memorandum was a recommendation to the commanding general "[t]hat the combat value of this Company immediately be studied with the view of either expanding it into a Ranger Infantry Battalion or deactivating the Company." This comment would prove to be exceptionally insightful and lead to the establishment of more Ranger units in the future.

The decision was made. The company was attached to the 25th Infantry Division, IX Corps, for anti-guerrilla operations and was ordered to move no later than 12 October. On the 10th, the three newly promoted first lieutenants of the Eighth Army Ranger Company departed Ranger Hill with an advance party to link up with the 25th Infantry Division.

The United Nations' rapid push north, across the 38th parallel, resulted in the bypassing of many smaller enemy pockets of resistance. By the time the Ranger company linked up with the 25th Infantry Division on 14 October, the division had been heavily engaged in an anti-guerrilla campaign that had already accounted for 1,500 killed or captured enemy soldiers. Linking up with the division's Reconnaissance Company at Taegu, Lieutenant Puckett was informed that two companies, his Ranger and the Reconnaissance, had been assigned the mission of clearing a sector around the village of Poun.

On 11 October, Puckett moved to Poun to establish a base of operations and to begin coordination with the Reconnaissance Company. Reorganized — to accommodate the additional ten South Korean soldiers — and supplied, the remainder of the Ranger company arrived at Poun on 14 October to commence operations.

The company sector was divided into two areas of operation. The 1st Platoon under Lieutenant Bunn would move to a nearby village; the 2nd Platoon, under Lieutenant Cummings, would operate from Poun. Continuous day and night sweeps were to be conducted, ambushes were to be initiated along known and suspected routes of enemy passage, roadblocks established with the Reconnaissance Company, and prisoners captured, if possible.

The Ranger company's combat initiation proved to be a rather smooth transition as the platoons went about their missions. 1st Platoon captured twelve enemy soldiers during one incident and, on a few occasions, engaged in firefights with retreating enemy elements that normally had little stomach to fight. 2nd Platoon, meanwhile, was able to conduct a few ambushes. In one such engagement against a nine-man patrol, they killed eight enemy soldiers within the first minute of the ambush and captured the lone survivor.

Throughout this shakedown period, Lieutenant Puckett continued to stress and emphasize learning from one's mistakes. Rotating between platoons, he would require each platoon to conduct detailed debriefings after each operation. These reviews assisted the unit's refinement of their standing operating procedures (SOP), patrolling techniques, and immediate battle drills—especially those that focused on immediate action to enemy contact.

Periodically, mostly for training purposes, Puckett would also conduct company-sized operations. During one such mission, a fifteen-man North Korean patrol blundered upon the Rangers during one of their rest periods. The resulting firefight ended with six enemy dead and one prisoner. By the end of October, the area had been pacified enough to turn over anti-guerrilla responsibilities to the local South Korean police forces.

Moving north, the 25th Infantry Division was once again tasked with eliminating enemy units that had been bypassed in the Masan-ni/ Uijongbu region. On 3 November, the Ranger company was ordered by division to close on Kaesong. The Eighth Army Ranger Company arrived the next day; a force of three commissioned officers, sixty enlisted soldiers, and ten ROK enlisted soldiers.

The Ranger company was attached to Task Force Johnson on 10 November along with the 2/35th Infantry Regiment and the 25th Infantry Division's Reconnaissance Company. The task force's mission was to sweep and clear a triangular area bounded by the villages of Uijonbu, Tongduchon-ni, and Shiny-ri. The company's two platoons moved out at dawn on 13 November and, initially, encountered no resistance. The next day, while teamed with a company from the 35th Infantry and approaching the outskirts of Uijonbu, the 2nd Platoon engaged a North Korean patrol of fourteen soldiers on a narrow trail. The Rangers killed two of the enemy and the remainder scattered.

On 14 November, the task force was ordered to move farther north. Leading the advance, the Ranger company cleared mines and provided flank security for the armored elements of the task force as they convoyed along the constricted route. Finally, on 18 November, the task force was ordered to break contact and return to an assembly area in the vicinity of Kumcheon.

Forced to march on foot back to their base in Kaesong in near-zero temperatures on the night of 18 November, the Ranger company arrived to find that they had been placed under the operational control (OPCON) of Lieutenant Colonel Welborn "Tom" Dolvin, commander of the 89th Medium Tank Battalion, who was forming a task force as part of the Eighth Army's final push north. Moved by truck, the Ranger company linked up with the armored task force on 22 November.

Despite serious indicators of Communist Chinese involvement in the conflict throughout the months of October and early November, Eighth Army resumed the offensive on 24 November 1950. The 25th Infantry Division's center zone of attack was to be spearheaded by Task Force Dolvin. During the task force's planning phase on 23 November, the Rangers conducted reconnaissance patrols out to 5,000 meters forward of Dolvin's position. No contact was made.

Task Force Dolvin crossed the line of departure (LD) at 1000 on the 24th with the Rangers in the center of the formation. Task organized with and riding on the top of a tank platoon, the company had only moved for a short distance before coming across two American soldiers of the 8th Cavalry Regiment—a unit that had been severely mauled by Chinese forces on 1 November—who had been captured and released. The Rangers relayed information regarding twenty-eight other seriously wounded American prisoners who had been abandoned by their Chinese captors. Later that afternoon, another task force element located the wounded Americans.

Continuing their movement, the company moved on its objective, Hill 222. Closing on the hill, the force was engaged by Chinese defenders. Swiftly dismounting the tanks, the Rangers formed two assault elements with its platoons and began to fire and maneuver toward the hill under First Lieutenant Puckett's command. The Rangers' first KIA, Private First Class Joseph Romero, was brought down when he led the rush as point man for 2nd Platoon across a rice paddy toward a far embankment. Though seriously wounded, he continued to provide covering fires until he died. Supported by 1st Platoon and continuing the assault, the 2nd Platoon was just cresting the embankment when friendly fire from the supporting tank platoon killed two Rangers and wounded three others. Running back across the exposed paddy and unable to communicate to the "buttoned-up" tanks through their external telephones, Puckett mounted the tank to inform the platoon leader to stop firing.

The hazard of friendly fire removed, the 2nd Platoon continued the tough climb under hostile fire, sweeping and clearing the objective hilltop. Casualties and near-zero evening temperatures reduced the Ranger company's strength to fifty-one combat effectives. With the tanks remaining at the base of the hill, the Rangers formed a defensive perimeter on the hill, attempting to dig fighting positions in the frozen ground.

The task force resumed its attack the next morning. Reinforced now with an entire tank company, the Ranger company again rode mounted on the tops of the tanks. The mounted detachment immediately began encountering enemy resistance as soon as they advanced from their attack position from behind a hill. Under mortar, machinegun, and small arms fire, the small force stopped approximately eight hundred yards from the base of their objective, Hill 205. Receiving fires from their right flank, the tanks halted and buttoned-up as the Rangers dismounted in preparation to cross the open and frozen rice paddy before them.

Unfortunately for Puckett and his Rangers, the holed up tankers were not returning fire. Again, unable to communicate through the use of external sound powered phone on the closest tank because he could not get the frozen or damaged box opened, Puckett jumped on the tank's deck and banged on the tank commander's (TC) closed hatch with the butt of his M-1 rifle. Cracking the hatch slightly and peering out, the TC cowered inside as Puckett, exposed to enemy fire on the outside, berated him and his fellow tankers in no uncertain terms for their lack of support. In response to the tanker's explanation that they had only a couple of inches of steel to protect them, the Ranger lieutenant reminded him that he and his Rangers were significantly worse off with only an eighth of an inch of cloth. Apparently realizing how ludicrous his argument had been, the tanker began to fire.

Supported by indirect artillery and direct tank fires on the objective, Puckett's company fired and maneuvered across the objective as enemy fire from high ground in the vicinity was suppressed by close air support (CAS) called in by Dolvin. Reorganizing and consolidating on the objective with a 360-degree defensive perimeter and crew-served weapons sighted on likely enemy avenues of approach, the Rangers found that their strength had been reduced by nine more soldiers—six American and three ROK casualties.

Satisfied with his defensive positions, Puckett walked back to the task force command post to coordinate his artillery fire support plan. While there, he also evaluated the overall tactical situation based on the battalion operations officer's (S3) map overlay. What he saw, he did not like; his company, sitting on the very top of the hill, had both flanks exposed. There was a several kilometer gap between the Rangers and the nearest friendly units.

Continuing to dig in, the Rangers prepared for the inevitable Chinese counterattack that they knew would take place later that night or early morning. Battle-weary, the misery continued as the temperatures continued to drop. At 2100, the unit listened to a firefight in the distance, not knowing that swarming Chinese forces had just overwhelmed a friendly platoon.

An hour later, a mortar barrage cascaded on the Rangers' positions — the opening bell to an overwhelming sequence of Chinese attacks. Lifting their fires, the Chinese ground assault against the Rangers commenced with the blowing of whistles and the blasting of bugles. Swarming up the hill amid a storm of hand grenades, the Chinese attack was welcomed by the Rangers with an overwhelming fusillade of small arms and grenade fire of their own. Firing preplanned missions and illuminating the hill's slopes, of which the front and rear were quite steep, with flares, Puckett directed the Rangers' defenses.

The accurate direct and indirect fires decimated the assaulting Chinese formations. By 2350, the Ranger company commander was able to report to the task force that the attack had failed and the Rangers still held the hill. The attack was not without cost, though. Additional Rangers had fallen in defense of Hill 205 and Puckett himself had been wounded by a shard of grenade shrapnel that had pierced his thigh. The American tank company, located to the rear at the base of the hill were unable to fire a single shot in support of the Rangers throughout the course of the battle.

Throughout the next three hours, the Chinese launched four additional human wave attacks against the Ranger position. While concentrated direct and indirect fires took their toll of the attacking enemy, there were moments when the Rangers' perimeter was breached. The "spirit of the bayonet" was very much alive as it was used by the Rangers to secure these breaches. Moving about the perimeter checking the status of his men and injecting himself at the point of decision, Puckett steadied his men and directed his command's defenses, calling in artillery fire "danger close" to place a high explosive wall of steel significantly closer to their positions than the doctrinally recommended 600 meters.

The sixth, and final, Chinese blow directed at Hill 205 was launched at 0230 as a battalion-sized force directed their main effort at Puckett's exposed right flank. Already significantly hampered by casualties and shortages in ammunition, the Rangers were unable to react quickly enough to this overwhelming threat. Led by mortar fire and hand grenades, the enemy breached 2nd Platoon's sector and proceeded to begin overrunning the Ranger defenses. Artillery was not available for it was firing a mission in support of another heavily engaged infantry company.

Inside a foxhole, on his knees and continuing to call for artillery support, a tremendous blow to his feet, butt, thigh, and arm stunned Puckett. A mortar round had impacted and detonated in the foxhole. A moment later, he suffered similar wounds from the detonation of a second round.

In the hole with him were Cummings and Corporal James Beatty. The resulting blasts killed Cummings and seriously wounded Puckett.

The Chinese had finally overwhelmed the Rangers' position. Isolated Ranger elements continued to fight against the staggering odds as Puckett, still conscious, reported his unit's situation to the task force. With the enemy shooting and bayoneting Rangers in their foxholes, survivors sought their escape from the hill. Failing to leave a wounded comrade behind, many surviving Rangers assisted their injured buddies off the hill. The unit's after action account noted a number of heroic actions taken that night.

> Moving about the fire-swept terrain, Sergeant John Diliberto organized his men for the withdrawal and started them on their way to more tenable positions. As he proceeded to fall back himself, he observed two of his comrades lying wounded on the exposed terrain. Without regard for his personal safety, he returned to the helpless men and dragged them both to safety as the enemy overwhelmed the defense perimeter.

Another Ranger, Private First Class David L. Pollock, upon observing that the company commander had been seriously wounded and was unable to move, fought his way to Puckett's position, where the Ranger commander was crumbled on his hands and knees just outside of the foxhole and unable to move. With the assistance of Private First Class Billy G. Walls, Pollock grabbed Puckett, who had suffered his third wound of the evening, and dragged him down the hill, gathering other Ranger survivors, avoiding capture, and killing along the way a Chinese machine-gun crew setting up their weapon.

During this escape, when Walls asked at one point if he was all right, Puckett retorted, "Yes, I am all right! I'm a Ranger!"

Placed on the back of a tank at the bottom of the hill, Puckett was evacuated to the task force's aid station. Hospitalized because of the severity of his wounds until November 1951, Puckett never returned to command the Eighth Army Ranger Company.

Another of Puckett's men, Ranger Bill Kemmer, realizing that his Ranger buddy, Ted Jewell, was not at the bottom of the hill, returned to the top of Hill 205 to aid his wounded friend down the hill to safety.

Other Rangers were not so fortunate. Ranger Merrill Casner, seriously wounded by grenade fragments and unable to move, watched one of the few black Rangers in the unit, Private First Class Wilbert W. Clanton, charge with only a bayonet in hand a group of enemy soldiers only to be cut down by their fire. Casner himself had the muzzle of a rifle placed against his head and a shot fired. Fortunately for him, the resulting injury was not serious enough to prevent him from making his way back to friendly lines later that morning after the Chinese had departed the hill.

Some Rangers still wanted to continue the fight despite the odds. Surviving the annihilation of his squad, Ranger Merle Simpson escaped to Private First Class Harland Morrissey's squad, screaming a warning about the advancing Chinese. Initially ordering his men to "Fix Bayonets!," Ranger Morrissey realized that discretion was the better form of valor when he noted the staggering number of enemy cresting the hilltop.

Ordering his men to "get off the hill," Morrissey led his squad's withdrawal while four brave Rangers—Sumner Kubinak, Librado Luna, Alvin Tadlock, and Ernest Nowlin—sacrificed their lives by remaining behind to form a rear guard providing covering fires. Three other Rangers were cited for gallantry, sacrificing their lives by remaining in position, firing at the enemy with fierce determination as their comrades fell back: Private First Class Harry Miyata, Private First Class Roger E. Hittle, and Private First Class Robert N. Jones. These seven men, Clanton, and two others would receive the Bronze Star for Valor.

At the base of Hill 205 that night, the Ranger company senior non-commissioned officer (NCO), First Sergeant Charles L. Pitts, assembled and reorganized the Ranger survivors. Unfortunately, dawn of the 26th found only one commissioned officer and twenty-one enlisted soldiers present for duty.

The blow that nearly annihilated the Eighth Army Ranger Company was part of a 500,000-man Chinese offensive opened on Thanksgiving Day that surprised, staggered, mauled, overwhelmed, and broke United Nations units all along the front. Entire divisions were encircled and had to fight their way through Chinese roadblocks and ambushes established along main escape routes. The 25th Infantry Division was forced to fight a series of delaying actions. In order to save Task Force Dolvin from destruction, reserves under the command of the assistant division commander, Brigadier General Vennard Wilson, had to be committed to save not only the task force from being destroyed but to also assist the 25th's withdrawal to an area nine miles north of Kunu-ri.

In recognition of their heroic stand on Hill 205 against a force estimated to be a 600-man battalion, twenty of the forty-seven Rangers of the Eighth Army Ranger Company present for duty that night were awarded a Distinguished Service Cross—Puckett, five Silver Stars—Pollock, Walls, Morrissey, Diliberto, Cummings, and fourteen Bronze Stars with "V" device.

On 5 December 1950, Captain John P. Vann assumed command of the Rangers at the direction of the 25th Infantry Division's commanding general, Major General William B. Kean. Having served in the G4 section (Logistics) of the 25th, Captain Vann was able to quickly reconstitute the company's equipment losses and increase its personnel strength in accordance with the TO&E of the Airborne Ranger companies being trained in the U.S.

With a newly authorized strength of five officers and 107 enlisted soldiers, the Eighth Army Ranger Company expanded from two to three platoons, with First Lieutenant Bunn still retaining his original assignment as 1st Platoon Leader. The unit's firepower was increased with the addition of a 57-mm recoilless rifle and a heavy machinegun in each platoon.

The new TO&E also alleviated one of the Ranger company's most significant problems: logistical support. In that the company headquarters' element was only composed of the first sergeant, a company clerk, and a supply corporal, the company had depended on other units to provide it with mess and transportation assistance for food, water, ammunition, supplies, and even transportation of prisoners. Logistical assets were added in the form of two jeeps, a two-and-a-half-ton cargo truck, a mess team, and a communications section.

In that the vast majority of replacements generally lacked the individual skills or physical fitness necessary to serve in a Ranger unit, a training program was once again implemented to bring these replacements up to the Ranger standard. Identified now as an Airborne Ranger unit, training also included practice parachute landing falls (PLF) from the back of the moving two-and-a-half-ton truck. Seasoned Ranger veterans were selected and placed in leadership positions. Unfortunately, mission requirements necessitated the Rangers' deployment only three days into the training cycle.

Attached to a Turkish Brigade in support of the 25th Infantry Division on 13 December, the Ranger company received on 16 December its first combat mission since its heroic stand against overwhelming odds on Hill 205. Ordered to conduct reconnaissance and combat patrols on the twelve-mile-by five-mile island of Kanghwa-do, the Ranger company's mission was to inform higher headquarters if North Korean forces attempted to use the island as a staging base for raids behind Eighth Army lines on the mainland.

During their two-week deployment on the island, the Ranger company established a series of outposts, swept the island and its shores with ground and sea patrols, conducted cross channel reconnaissance to the mainland, and assisted with the evacuation of 4,500 island civilians to the mainland. On 28 December, the Rangers were relieved.

With the start of a massive new Chinese offensive on New Years Eve 1950, the Eighth Army was once again forced to abandon Seoul and to withdraw just south of the city of Suwon. In reserve and operating out of Chonan, the 25th Infantry Division ordered the Ranger company to conduct anti-guerrilla patrols in the vicinity of Nonsan.

Arriving at the town on 8 January, the mission provided the Rangers the opportunity to conduct refresher training as it performed its rear area security missions. Commencing platoon-sized patrols the next day, the movements proved relatively uneventful until the afternoon of the 12th. Having made contact with an enemy force in a small village, the 2nd and 3rd platoons, under the overall command of the company executive officer Lieutenant Glenn Metcalf, broke contact after a ninety-minute firefight. Returning along the same trail and through a narrow defile they had traveled previously—a significant tactical mistake and contrary to Rogers' Rangers Standing Orders—the unit was ambushed around 1400 as it prepared to take a short break along a river .

Opening fire with machineguns, the enemy immediately killed two Rangers as they crossed a frozen rice paddy at the end of the defile and wounded several others. From a ditch alongside the trail, the Rangers returned fire against a force estimated at approximately one hundred enemy soldiers. Despite repeated attempts, the Rangers were unable to recover the two Ranger dead. The three Ranger lieutenants provided supporting fires with machineguns to cover the Rangers' bounding overwatch-type withdrawal. With casualties totaling two killed and nineteen wounded, including both platoon leaders, the Ranger force linked up with the company's vehicles to depart the area.

Returning the next day reinforced with two ROK infantry companies, Captain Vann and his Rangers conducted a sweep of the ambush site and local villages. Finding sixty men hiding in one village, Vann had them taken prisoner. As the prisoners were being escorted out of the village, an enemy guerrilla element opened fire. While most of the enemy prisoners escaped in the ensuing skirmish, seven guerrillas were killed. Aggressive patrolling by the Ranger company continued in this area until the end of the month.

As part of a major Eighth Army counterattack launched against the Chinese on 25 January, the 25th Infantry Division recaptured the city of Suwon on the 26th. By 30 January, the Eighth Army Ranger Company had been reassigned missions and assumed security for the 25th Infantry Division's main command post.

Continuing to punch northward, the 25th Infantry Division tasked the Ranger company with a series of missions conceived to capitalize on the light unit's infantry, reconnaissance, and night fighting skills. Other than a few limited engagements, however, the patrols proved to be rather routine. On 14 February, Captain Vann passed command to his executive officer, Captain Charles Ross, who would retain command of the company until its inactivation.

By the 19th, the 25th Infantry Division's advance north brought them to the banks of the Han River. The Eighth Army's counter-offensive plan, Operation Killer, called for the 25th Infantry Division to send strong patrols across the Han River to harass the enemy. Crossing the frozen river by foot in the vicinity of Sachon-ni village at 2135 on 20 February, the Ranger company, reinforced with an infantry platoon from the 27th Infantry, was challenged then fired on by enemy machineguns while still on the ice.

Illuminated by bright moonlight, the dark-uniformed Rangers clearly contrasted with white snow and ice. Luck was on their side, though, for not a single Ranger was hit. While the lead element, the 3rd platoon, moved to the enemy side of the river, the remainder of the Rangers withdrew to the friendly side as the enemy fire died down. Having lost the element of surprise, Captain Ross decided to scrub the mission and ordered the 3rd platoon to return. The enemy opened fire again as the platoon stepped out on the ice. Unable to provide covering fires out of fear or hitting their own men, the Ranger company had to watch the platoon cross the ice on their hands, knees, and bellies. Despite the heavy enemy small arms fire, the unit suffered no casualties.

On the 22nd, the Rangers moved ten miles south of their position to the village of Polli where they began an intense four-day training period focused on raids and waterborne operations. Moving to a staging area close to the Han River on the 26th, the Ranger company was tasked to prepare a platoon sized patrol for a raid across the river against the village of Yangsuri. This raid, as well as others, was being conducted to gather information and prisoners in support of the Eighth Army's Operation Ripper — the final counteroffensive to be launched 7 March to restore the 38th parallel.

The 2nd Platoon was assigned the mission with Captain Ross accompanying the group. At 2200 on the 28th, the platoon's initial assault force of six two-man boats entered the water with the 1st Platoon prepared to provide covering fires, if necessary . Unfortunately for their occupants, three of the boats were unable to negotiate the swift current swollen with

huge chunks of ice and overturned halfway across. Luckily, the six soldiers in these boats were able to cling to their overturned rafts and return
to the friendly shore for a second, successful, attempt. The other three
boats, including Captain Ross', secured the far side while the remainder
of the platoon in eight-man assault rafts paddled across.

Quickly organizing and moving out on the far shore, the platoon
moved to Yangsuri. Contrary to the division's intelligence update, no
enemy soldiers or equipment were found. Expanding their search an
additional mile inland, the Rangers still failed to make contact with the
enemy. The patrol was completed by 0330 with their return across the
Han.

Still needing intelligence, the division's next assignment for the Rangers was to search the railway tunnels north of Yangsuri. Ross selected the
1st Platoon for this mission. Departing the shore at 2105 on 1 March, the
water movement proved even more difficult for the 1st Platoon than it
had for the 2nd Platoon just days prior. The swift current and blocks of
floating ice again made the movement extremely challenging. Finally,
halfway across the river, a large sheet of ice was encountered. The ice
proved too thin to walk on and too thick to push the boats through. The
patrol had to be canceled.

While the Eighth Army pushed north on the 7th of March with its
counteroffensive, the Ranger company conducted refresher training in its
assembly area. Attached to the all black 24th Infantry Regiment on 12
March, the Rangers conducted day and night reconnaissance patrols to
the regiment's front. Having met limited contact with the enemy, the
Eighth Army Ranger Company reverted to division control on the 17th in
preparation for a behind enemy lines combat mission.

With the securing of the high ground northeast of Seoul, the 25th
Infantry Division needed to seal the road and rail line running northeast
out of Seoul through Pupyong-ni to deny the enemy an avenue of escape.
The Rangers' mission was to infiltrate seven miles to Pupyong-ni to
establish blocking positions and ambush sites along this egress route.

Having been allocated some artillery priority of fires and CAS, the
Ranger company—minus one platoon—infiltrated along its route of
advance in squad-sized elements on the morning of 19 March. Rendez-
vousing at a specific location, the company elements linked up at 1525
and occupied a hide position within the objective area. Around 2100, the
Rangers moved forward to their blocking and ambush locations. Maintaining a high degree of alert for the next five hours, the Rangers encountered no enemy forces. Departing the area of operation (AO) between
0100 and 0200, the Ranger force exfiltrated back and safely conducted a
passage of lines through the 24th Regiment at 0500.

As the 25th Infantry Division continued to advance the final two weeks of March, the Rangers found themselves being used in more conventional infantry roles. OPCON to the 24th Infantry Regiment, the Rangers found themselves once again setting up blocking positions, conducting screening operations, and securing the regimental command post.

Shortly thereafter, the 8ARC was assigned a mission that properly utilized their unique capabilities. Ordered to infiltrate six miles north of Changgo-ri to conduct a raid on the village and to determine enemy strength and dispositions, Captain Ross and his Ranger company crossed the LD at 2200 on 27 March 1951. Arriving in the vicinity of their objective around 0100 and finding that they were located on the wrong side of the town, Captain Ross elected to initiate the raid from that position.

Forming an assault line, the Rangers stealthily moved into town, holding their fire until fired upon. Encountering an enemy outpost, the Rangers engaged the enemy in a general firefight. Two and a half hours later, with their reconnaissance probe complete, the Rangers withdrew at 0340 as they called an artillery strike in on the town to break up a Chinese counterattack. The company successfully exfiltrated back through the 35th Regiment's lines shortly before 0500. The Rangers' detailed information significantly benefited the 35th's attack on Changgo-ri the following day.

Just hours after their return, the Eighth Army Ranger Company was assembled. Captain Ross informed the unit that it had just completed its last mission and that the company was to be disbanded. General Orders Number 172, issued on 27 March by Headquarters Eighth Army state: "Eighth Army Ranger Company, 8213th Army Unit is discontinued in Korea effective 28 March 1951." On 31 March 1951, the 5th Airborne Ranger Company, a unit formed and trained in the United States, was officially attached to the 25th Infantry Division to replace the Eighth Army Ranger Company.

Interestingly enough and despite their example, the Eighth Army Ranger Company is not officially considered to be part of the proud lineage of the 75th Ranger Regiment. In that the company was a temporary Table of Distribution & Allowances (TDA) unit and not an official TO&E organization activated by the Department of the Army (DA), it is not regarded by Army regulation to be part of the official Ranger heritage. Unofficially, though, its place in Ranger lore is assured. Fittingly, Colonel (Ret) Ralph Puckett, a member of the Ranger Hall of Fame, was designated an honorary Colonel of the 75th Ranger Regiment in 1996.

On 29 August 1950, shortly after having returned to the United States, Army Chief of Staff General J. Lawton Collins directed the formation of "marauder companies" on an experimental basis, noting that, "One of the major lessons to be learned from the Korean fighting appears to be the fact the North Koreans have made very successful use of small groups, trained, armed and equipped for the specific purpose of infiltrating our lines and attacking command posts and artillery positions."

Directing one company per infantry division, General Collins ordered the companies to be organized into three platoons of three ten-man squads. A minimum number of logistic and administrative personnel would keep the company's total strength to a maximum of 113 men: five officers and one hundred seven enlisted men. Volunteers for the first company were drawn from the 11th and 82nd Airborne Divisions — volunteers had to be airborne-qualified. It is reported that the call for volunteers brought in over 5,000 paratroopers from the 82nd alone.

On 15 September, Colonel John G. Van Houten was personally selected by the Army Chief of Staff to command the new Ranger Training Section and to prepare a detailed program of instruction six weeks in duration. On 22 September, an official Department of the Army memo authorized the establishment of the Ranger Training Center at Harmony Church, Fort Benning, Georgia.

Prior to Korea, there had only been one effort to establish a formal Ranger School. During World War II in January 1943, a Second Army Ranger School was started at Camp Forrest, Tennessee. Having only completed two two-week cycles of training for the newly formed 2nd Ranger Infantry Battalion, the school was closed on the orders of Army Ground Forces. The command's rationale was based on a belief that taking soldiers from their units would prove to be disruptive to that unit's training. Based on the 1st Ranger Infantry Battalion's successes, though, it was determined that there was a real need for an additional Ranger Infantry Battalion to be employed in the invasion of Europe. Hence, the 2nd Ranger Infantry Battalion on 11 March 1943.

The Ranger Training Center began operating on 2 October 1950, when it initiated training for the first four Airborne Ranger Companies to be trained there. Needing qualified instructors, Van Houten selected a number of volunteers who had served and fought with the original Ranger Infantry Battalions, the First Special Service Force, or the Office of Strategic Services (OSS) during the Second World War.

The Ranger recruits were placed through an intense and extensive training cycle that included small unit tactics, demolition training, cold weather training, mountaineering, low-level parachute jumps, and river-crossing operations. To replicate realistic combat conditions, the training was designed to be extremely stressful by limiting food and sleep and by conducting continuous operations, normally at night.

During this formative period, the Chief of Staff also solicited ideas and recommendations from the Commander-in-Chief Far East Command, General of the Army Douglas MacArthur. Concurring with the Ranger Company concept, General MacArthur informed the Chief of Staff about the formation and training of the Eighth Army Ranger Company. In that the 8ARC employment was going to be similar to that envisioned of the Ranger Training Center's Ranger companies, MacArthur promised to forward the results of the 8ARC's tactical employment and combat performance to be used by the Chief of Staff as an initial basis for testing the organization and future utility of Ranger companies in Korean operations.

The first four Airborne Ranger companies to graduate from the intensive six-week course established by the Ranger Training Command did so on 13 November 1950. At their graduation, the Rangers were awarded a small, yellow-on-black RANGER arc tab insignia to be worn on the left shoulder of their uniform. Though the yellow color of this tab would eventually be changed to gold and later become coveted and recognized by military units worldwide, most of the early graduates were disappointed. They had expected a white and red on black insignia similar to the scrolls of the World War II Ranger Infantry Battalions. Consequently, many Korean War Ranger veterans purchased copies of the Second World War Ranger Infantry Battalion scrolls, removed the letters BN, then sewed in white thread the letters CO. It was this modified scroll that many of the early Ranger School graduates wore on their uniforms.

Note: Today, the Ranger scroll is worn by members of the 75th Ranger Regiment. For all soldiers who have graduated from the U.S. Army Ranger School, the black and gold Ranger Tab is awarded to be worn on the left shoulder of each graduate's uniform.

Augmented by graduates of the 3rd Ranger Infantry Company (Airborne) to bring the unit up to strength, the 1st Ranger Infantry Company (Airborne) departed the United States on 25 November, quickly followed on 9 December by the 2nd and 4th companies—the 4th having also been filled out by personnel of the 3rd.

The 1st Ranger Infantry Company (Airborne) entered the war executing a daring feat of land navigation when it penetrated nine miles behind enemy lines to destroy an enemy complex that was later identified as the 12th North Korean Division headquarters. Caught by surprise and unsure of the American force's size, two North Korean regiments quickly withdrew from the area during the raid. The 1st Ranger Company would eventually go on to earn two Distinguished Unit Citations.

Ranger Training Command retained the remainder of the 3rd Ranger Company at Fort Benning, where it was refilled with replacement volunteer parachutists from the 11th and 82nd Airborne Divisions to begin training a second time with the second cycle of four companies: 5th, 6th, 7th, and 8th Companies. With the six-week course expanded to eight weeks, this cycle of Rangers began their training on 26 November. Completing the regularly scheduled training on 13 January 1951, these companies were required to undergo an additional four weeks of mountain and winter warfare training at Camp Carson, Colorado, immediately following their Ranger graduation. Some companies were even required to conduct an additional third phase of training at Eglin Field, Florida, following Camp Carson.

Much of this new training came in handy, especially for the 8th Ranger Company. Known as the "Devils," the 8th had a thirty-three-man platoon engage in a firefight while on patrol forward of friendly lines with two Chinese reconnaissance companies. The Ranger platoon suffered two KIAs and three WIAs while inflicting over seventy dead on the two Chinese companies.

In that the Department of the Army's original intent was to assign one Airborne Ranger company per infantry division in Korea, the first three companies were attached to the 2nd Infantry, 7th Infantry, and 1st Cavalry Divisions.

The 2nd Ranger Infantry Company (Airborne was unique in that it was an all-black unit. The company was formed from volunteers of the 505th Parachute Infantry Regiment and the 80th Anti-aircraft Artillery Battalion of the 82nd Airborne. Originally designated the 4th Ranger Company, it was redesignated the 2nd Ranger Infantry Company (Airborne prior to graduation. Attached to the 7th Infantry Division, the 2nd Ranger Company was initially used in conventional infantry missions, primarily plugging gaps on the line and assaulting Chinese Communist positions.

In late February 1951, though, the company found itself attached to the 187th Airborne Regimental Combat Team (ARCT) along with the 4th Ranger Infantry Company (Airborne). On the morning of 23 March 1951, the 2nd Company Rangers conducted the first combat parachute jump ever made by American Rangers with an assault onto Drop Zone (DZ) North near Munsan-ni to assist cutting off retreating enemy forces north of Seoul. Quickly securing the DZ for the 2nd Battalion, 187th Regimental Combat Team, the 2nd Company Ranger proceeded to fight its way to their primary objective, Hill 151, where it was dug in by nightfall. These two Ranger companies remained attached to the 187th ARCT until 4 April.

One of the 2nd Ranger Company's most notable engagements took place in May 1951, when a Chinese force seized Hill 581, key terrain in the 7th Infantry Division sector. Having been assigned the mission of retaking the hill, the 2nd Rangers assaulted the objective. Sustaining only six casualties, the Ranger force was able to seize the hill and inflict over 150 casualties on the enemy, with sixty of those casualties being KIAs.

Later that night, the Chinese counterattacked. Despite their overwhelming numbers, the Chinese assault was defeated, leaving an additional sixty dead on the battlefield. Ranger losses were ten wounded.

The arrival of the second Ranger cycle in late February found the potential for two Ranger companies to be assigned to the 25th Infantry Division — its Table of Distribution and Allowances unit, the Eighth Army Ranger Company, and the 5th Ranger Infantry Company (Airborne), authorized in accordance with Department of the Army TO&E. In that only one Ranger company per division was authorized to draw jump pay and most members of the Eighth Army Ranger Company were not jump-qualified, the decision was made to disband them on the 28th of March 1951. To lessen the blow, jump-qualified members of the 8ARC were afforded the opportunity to volunteer for duty with the 187th Airborne Regimental Combat Team stationed in Korea.

Having endured Ranger School for two complete cycles of training, the 3rd Ranger Infantry Company (Airborne) was assigned to the 3rd Infantry Division during the first week of April 1951. Its initial introduction to combat was a true baptism of fire. Attached to a company of tanks on 11 April and spearheading the 3rd Infantry Division's advance north toward the town of Yonchon, two of the Ranger company's platoons found themselves caught in the open rice paddies of a long valley under heavy enemy small arms and mortar fire when their armor support withdrew. Fixing bayonets, the two platoons attacked forward using bounding overwatch to provide alternating supporting fires.

As they approached the enemy's positions located on a ridge at approximately two hundred yards' distance, two tanks came forward to assist. Supported by fires from these two tanks and the second platoon, the first platoon conducted a bayonet charge amid a shower of Chinese grenades. Fighting hand-to-hand through the Chinese trenches, "Bloodynose Ridge" was captured at a cost of forty-three of the ninety-seven attacking Rangers.

Fourteen Department of the Army authorized Ranger Infantry Companies (Airborne) — in addition to two TDA Ranger companies in Korea — were eventually formed between August 1950 and February 1951 (Note: See Appendix E). In due course, six of these TO&E Ranger companies were attached to six divisions within the Eighth Army during the Korean War.

The 10th and 11th Ranger Infantry Companies (Airborne) were composed of National Guardsmen from the 45th Infantry Division (Oklahoma) and the 40th Infantry Division (California) respectively. Both Ranger companies were inactivated in Japan while enroute to Korea.

By July 1951, the situation in Korea had stabilized to the point that major commands felt there was no longer a need for so specialized a force as the Rangers. One major argument against retaining such an elitist force was that they drained quality troops from regular army units. "If there's only one guy in a regular unit squad who wants to fight, he's needed there to influence the other men; this same guy, went the logic, was the one who would join a Ranger unit, thus leaving the squad bare of inspiration."

This "elitist" argument has been advanced since the formation of the very first Ranger-style unit prior to the Revolutionary War. Unfortunately for the divisions still left fighting in Korea after the Ranger companies were disbanded, they still found a need for these specialized units.

Though the final Ranger company was deactivated 1 December 1951, the U.S. Army command saw a continuing need for Ranger training. In January 1952, the Ranger Training Command that had been established for the Korean War was inactivated and immediately reconstituted as the Ranger Department of The Infantry School (TIS).

The Ranger Department's mission was — and continues to be, relatively speaking — to train selected officers and NCOs in a course of instruction on Ranger tactics. Upon successful completion of this course, these newly qualified Rangers would return to their parent organization to serve as instructors. The overall objective of this training was to raise the standard of training in all combat units. This course was the birth of the current U.S. Army Ranger School program.

A second 'birth' that began with the Korean Conflict was the Ranger "Black Beret." Conceived of in 1951 by then Captain Charles "Pete" Spragins, commander of the 10th Ranger Infantry Company (Airborne), while training with the 11th Ranger Infantry Company (Airborne) at Camp Carson, Colorado, the beret's color was symbolic of much of the Ranger training and combat which took place in the hours of darkness. The Ranger Training Command at Fort Benning, Georgia, evaluated and endorsed the black beret for Ranger use but its official authorization in accordance with regulations by the Department of the Army would not be forthcoming for more than another two decades.

CHAPTER 17

Vietnam Conflict

"You know you never defeated us on the battlefield," said the American colonel.
The North Vietnamese colonel pondered this remark a moment. "That may be
so," he replied, "but it is also irrelevant."

Conversation between Colonel Harry G. Summers, Jr.
and Colonel Tu, North Vietnamese Army, 1975

As the Cold War lengthened in the late 1950s, NATO nations felt there was a need for small units to conduct passive, deep penetration intelligence gathering missions at corps levels and higher. From this need was born the Long Range Patrol (LRP) or Long Range Reconnaissance Patrol (LRRP) unit—both LRP and LRRP designations were used similarly and considered interchangeable—trained and equipped to infiltrate enemy lines by ground, air, or water. From well-concealed observation posts or as a function of point, area, or route reconnaissance, they were intended to report enemy movements. Stealth and reconnaissance were the mission of the LRRP, not direct combat.

The first such unit, the U.S. Army Surveillance Unit, Europe, was organized on 1 July 1958. The unit was task organized with fire-control radar, observation aircraft, ground-surveillance radar, counter-mortar radar, and mobile photographic instruments. Man-portable Atomic Demolitions Munitions (ADM) added a new nuclear dimension to tactical warfare. The infiltration of such weapons required airborne-qualified men who could parachute into an area of operations, scout forward to their objective, and fight as infantry when required.

During early 1960, the Seventh Army addressed the feasibility of such units with its two corps, V Corps and VII Corps, forming a special

291

patrol company. In September 1960, two experimental eighty-man scouting companies in support of V and VII Corps confirmed the effectiveness of long-range reconnaissance patrols during exercise Winter Shield II. Based on that success, United States Army Europe (USAREUR) approved in March 1961, the formation of two corps-level reconnaissance patrol companies.

Prior to these LRRPs—which would ultimately lead directly to Ranger companies—and following the inactivation of the Korean War Ranger companies, the only unit to be designated "Ranger" at that time was the 180-man Provincial Ranger Platoon, 1st Battle Group (Airborne, 505th Infantry Regiment, 8th Infantry Division from 1959 to 1961. Each company was authorized 166 paratroopers. Their missions were to conduct deep infiltrations on special tasks that included the placement of T-4 Atomic Demolitions Munitions and the identifying of enemy targets for Army tactical nuclear delivery systems.

Both of these companies were activated on 15 July 1961 with V Corps' U.S. Army Long Range Reconnaissance Patrol Company (Airborne) based at Wildflecken. This unit was later moved near Frankfurt. This provisional company was organized under Table of Distribution (TD) 3779 and, having no specific numerical designation, was known as the "Victory Lerps." The Victory Lerps were assigned the mission of patrolling the Coburg, Bad Kissingen, Bad Hersfeld, and Fulda corridors from the Iron Curtain into West Germany.

The second company was activated in Nellingen in support of VII Corps. Organized under TD 3780. This company was referred to as the "Jayhawk Lerps" and patrolled the Furth and Hof corridors.

Early in the 1960s, there was a growing need for an updated field manual on Ranger training and operations. In January 1962, the Department of the Army responded with the publication of a new manual. Within this manual, Ranger operations were defined as "overt operations by highly trained infantry units, to any depth into enemy-held areas, for the purpose of reconnaissance, raids, and general disruption of enemy operations." At a minimum, such units would be required to conduct air-mobile operations, establish and execute ambush and roadblock positions, climb cliffs, conduct extended operations, conduct small-unit waterborne operations, and employ anti-guerrilla techniques.

As the nuclear scenario continued to grow in Europe with the deployment of additional and improved systems, the decision was made to transform the two USAEUR provisional companies into regular active duty components. Inactivated on 15 May 1965, the companies' men and materiél were transferred to form Company D of the 17th Infantry Regiment and Company C of the 58th Infantry Regiment. These companies would practice combat reconnaissance operations in the mountains, conduct river-crossing operations across the German highlands, rehearse deep penetration missions, as well as parachute from C-130 cargo aircraft into an objective area.

In 1968, the two companies were relocated to the United States as part of troop reduction agreements with the Soviets. Though Company D was moved to Fort Benning and Company C to Fort Riley, they were both still attached to V and VII Corps, prepared to return to the European continent in the event of hostilities.

The third LRRP company to be activated was Company E, 30th Infantry Regiment at Fort Rucker, Alabama. This LRRP unit was assigned to the Aviation Center and School to provide the student pilots with a trained aggressor force for escape and evasion and "hot" landing zone exercises. The LRRP aspect of the company was lost as it played a more combative, aggressor role. In 1969, never having truly performed as an LRRP unit, the company was reorganized as an airborne rifle company.

In support of U.S. military operations in Vietnam, units designated as Long Range Reconnaissance Patrols (LRRPs) were officially sanctioned and authorized. Field forces and division-sized elements activated an Infantry Company (LRP). Each company had a total of 118 soldiers assigned with a headquarters section and two reconnaissance platoons with eight six-man patrols. Two of the companies, Company E of the 20th Infantry Regiment and Company F of the 51st Infantry Regiment, were each nearly twice the authorized strength at 230 soldiers and four reconnaissance platoons.

Separate brigades activated infantry detachments (LRP). These detachments had a total of sixty-one soldiers assigned with a large headquarters section and a single reconnaissance platoon. Eventually, eleven companies—this number does not include Company E, 30th Infantry Regiment, that was used as a training resource in Support of the Aviation Center and School—and four detachments—this number does not include the 70th Infantry Detachment that was deactivated in Hawaii prior to the 11th Infantry Brigade's deployment to Vietnam with the 23rd American Division—were activated and deployed with combat units. They would eventually earn one Presidential Unit Citation, three Valorous Unit Citations, two Meritorious Unit Commendations, eleven Vietnamese Gallantry Cross Unit Citations, and six Vietnamese Civil Actions Unit Citations.

Unfortunately for the LRP units, even though they would eventually become the founding units of the Rangers, there initially was no heritage or lineage to bind the separate companies and detachments. Since its formation in 1952, the Special Forces, had been without a lineage. To rectify this shortcoming, they had been granted the lineage and honors of the 1st through 6th Ranger Infantry Battalions and the 1st Special Service Forces of the Second World War. Thus, on 15 April 1960, the 75th Infantry Regiment with the lineage and honors of Merrill's Marauders and the 475th Infantry Regiment were selected as the lineage for the new LRRP organizations.

On 1 February 1969, most of the active army LRRP companies and detachments were deactivated as LRRP units and reactivated as companies of the 75th Infantry Regiment. Unfortunately, a regimental headquarters would not be activated until 1984. The reorganization probably proved to be the most cost-effective transition the army has ever performed. In essence, on that date the army simply redesignated all LRP units "Ranger" and renamed them "Ranger Companies," though the ARNG LRP units would retain their original LRP designations. The detachments still retained their original unit strength of sixty-one soldiers—the same number of soldiers Company E, 75th Infantry Regiment would have during its second tour in Vietnam. Companies C, D, and H of the 75th Infantry Regiment would field 230, 198, and 198 soldiers respectively.

With the redesignation of the LRPs to 75th Infantry Regiment companies in 1969, additional Army Reserve National Guard (ARNG) Ranger-style companies were organized: Alabama's Company E, 200th Infantry Regiment in 1969; Puerto Rico's Company E, 65th Infantry Regiment in 1971, and Delaware's Company A, 259th Infantry Regiment, also in 1971. Two ARNG Ranger companies were inactivated and reconsolidated. In March 1971, Indiana's Company E (Long Range Patrol), 151st Infantry Regiment consolidated with Company D (Long Range Patrol), 151st Infantry Regiment while Michigan's Company E (Long Range Patrol), 425th Infantry Regiment was consolidated with Company F (Long Range Patrol), 425th Infantry in February 1972.

The Ranger companies in Vietnam were deactivated during the period 1969 to 1972 as the units they were attached to were deactivated or returned to the United States as part of Vietnamization, though Company O (Arctic Ranger), 75th Infantry Regiment would be reactivated in 1970 for duty at Fort Richardson, Alaska, for a short period of time.

While in Vietnam, the 75th Infantry Regiment companies were deco-rated with four Valorous Unit Awards, one Meritorious Unit Commenda-tions, fifteen Vietnamese Gallantry Cross Unit Citations, and nine Vietnamese Civil Actions Unit Citations.

In 1960, counter-guerrilla forces of South Vietnamese Army light infantry Ranger companies were created. Referred to as Biêt-Dông-Quân or BDQ, a significant number of Ranger-qualified officers and NCOs served as advisors to the Army of the Republic of Vietnam Ranger units throughout the duration of the war—nearly 2,000 in total.

At its inception, the BDQ was composed of eighty-six companies. By 1965, they had been reorganized into battalions. Graduation from the South Vietnamese Ranger course was a "real world" combat operation with those who returned alive graduating. Overall, there were a total of eight BDQ regimental sized groups with twenty-two battalions—each assigned five U.S. Ranger-qualified officers and NCOs—by the time the United States' advisors were phased out by the end of March 1973.

Though they were supposed to operate only in an advisory capacity, there were those situations that thrust some Ranger advisors to the fore-front. On 4 April 1970, Sergeant First Class Gary L. Littrell found himself the only unwounded American Ranger advisor left after a surprise mor-tar barrage by the 28th North Vietnamese Regiment struck the 23rd ARVN Ranger Battalion in their defensive positions on top of Hill 763 in Kontum Province. An attempted helicopter extraction of the wounded Americans by Littrell failed as the helicopters could not penetrate the small arms fire to land near the Ranger NCO, who was standing in the open, exposed, holding a strobe light. Securing the wounded, Littrell pro-ceeded to direct close air support throughout the night and into the next morning.

The light of dawn was met with another heavy mortar barrage against the besieged RVN battalion. Littrell moved about the perimeter administering first aid, directing fires, and moving casualties. A resupply helicopter was able to make it into the LZ around 1000. Littrell loaded the three wounded American Ranger advisors on board along with some ARVN Rangers as another American Ranger, Specialist 5 Raymond Diet-erle, disembarked from the helicopter with ammunition.

For the remainder of the day, the two Ranger advisors moved about the perimeter, calling in air strikes, adjusting artillery strikes, and encour-aging their South Vietnamese Ranger compatriots. The pressure against the perimeter grew along with the night. Sapper probes were driven back by indirect, aerial, and small arms fire.

The morning of 6 April opened with a North Vietnamese Army (NVA) attack that was repelled. Throughout that day, the NVA continued to rain heavy weapons and mortar fire down on the beleaguered force while the two American Rangers continued to make their rounds of the perimeter, shoring up the Vietnamese's spirits. At 0630 the following morning, another firestorm of explosive volleys swept the hilltop. A massed assault staging in the woods was met by helicopter strikes directed by Littrell at the point of attack. Despite the air strikes, the human-wave attack a half hour later nearly breached the perimeter. Only a stoic defense by the fatigued defenders and the advisors' bravery repelled the charge.

The Rangers were able to hold against a series of attacks that night. Finally, at 1030 on 8 April, the depleted and exhausted battalion was ordered to withdraw down the hill, through the jungle, across the Dak Poko River, to reach the 22nd ARVN Ranger Battalion. The two Ranger advisors set about organizing the movement, redistributing ammunition, and seeing that the dead and wounded were brought along.

The battalion moved out at 1100, under the command of the dazed ARVN battalion executive officer who proceeded to move down the wrong spur of the hill—despite the warning of the two American Rangers—and closer to the enemy position. At the bottom of the hill, the executive officer incredulously halted his formation for a five-minute tea break.

Immediately, the battalion was inundated with mortar fire. Littrell was able to establish radio contact with the 22nd ARVN Ranger Battalion and direct counter-fires against the enemy mortars. Requests for gunship support brought the word that none was immediately available, which prompted the battalion executive officer to panic and run. Seeing their commander flee, the remainder of the South Vietnamese Rangers began to scatter, leaving their dead and wounded behind.

With a "Come on, partner, let's hat up," Littrell grabbed Dieterle and slowly gathered up the dispersed Rangers. With the remnants of the battalion regrouped, the two Rangers proceeded to lead the formation through the jungle for several hours toward the proper objective. As the North Vietnamese pursued, the Rangers directed mortar fires "danger close" to keep the enemy at bay. During the repulse of one assault, Littrell and his partner were knocked to the ground by the force of 500-pound bombs the senior Ranger had called in nearby.

Directing the fight through two ambushes, the Americans continued to lead, cajole, and drag the ARVN soldiers along. At the last ambush site, Littrell stopped to assist three wounded Vietnamese Rangers. Carrying the most seriously wounded one on his back, Littrell ended up dragging the other two behind him and across the Dak Poko River as they held on to his web gear and were led to safety by Littrell with the remainder of the battalion.

Total losses for the ARVN Ranger Battalion were 218 casualties and nineteen MIA. For conduct above and beyond the call of duty, Sergeant First Class Gary L. Littrell was awarded the Medal of Honor.

Also of note was the Special Forces Operational Detachment Alpha-41 (Ranger) of the 46th Special Forces Company. This detachment served to instruct the Royal Thai Army Ranger School at Lopburi and was the only unit in the United States Army to be designated both Special Forces and Ranger. All of the unit's members were Ranger-qualified graduates of the Ranger School, with many having served as instructors in the U.S. Army Infantry School.

Another training organization was Company B (Airborne Ranger), 1st Battalion, 29th Infantry Regiment that was attached to the Infantry School to test airborne tactics and equipment. They were also to serve as aggressors in the early and mid-1970s in support of the Ranger Department.

By the end of United States involvement in Vietnam in 1973, Companies A and B of the 75th Infantry Regiment were the only two active duty Ranger/LRRP companies still in existence. Following the Arab-Israeli Yom Kippur War later that same year, it was determined that there was a strategic need to have a mobile, light infantry unit that could deploy anywhere in the world on a moment's notice to handle specialized missions. Companies A and B would be deactivated in late 1974 to provide the manning slots necessary for the activation of the 1st and 2nd Battalions (Ranger) of the 75th Infantry—and ultimately 75th Ranger—Regiment.

On 25 January 1974, the 1st Battalion (Ranger), 75th Infantry Regiment was activated and stationed at Fort Stewart, Georgia. Its sister battalion, the 2nd Battalion (Ranger), was activated 1 October 1974 at Fort Lewis, Washington.

Four ARNG LRRP/Ranger units—Company E, 65th Infantry Regiment; Company D, 151st Infantry Regiment; Company A, 259th Infantry Regiment; and Company F, 425th Infantry Regiment—were also activated during this time period. Eventually, however, Company A, 259th Infantry Regiment was disbanded in 1974, Company D, 151st Infantry Regiment was disbanded in 1977, and Texas Company E, 65th Infantry

Regiment was disbanded in 1980, to be replaced by Company G, 143rd Infantry Regiment.

* * * *

In early 1966, the commander of U.S. Military Assistance Command Vietnam (MACV), General William C. Westmoreland, ordered that each division and separate brigade in country form a long-range patrol detachment to increase each unit's reconnaissance capability. What follows is an account of their history.

Company C (Airborne Ranger) 75th Infantry Regiment

I Field Force

The American military had divided South Vietnam into four corps level tactical zones: Zone I was north along the Demilitarized Zone, Zone II was in central South Vietnam, Zone III was the Saigon capital region, and Zone IV was the Mekong Delta. The U.S. Army's zones of responsibility were III and IV. I and II Field Force Vietnam were created by the army to exercise control over these two regions. The field force concept was created for those missions within each zone that carried beyond the traditional corps combat missions, to include pacification, restoration, and advisory functions.

On 12 September 1967, Company E (Long Range Patrol), 20th Infantry (Airborne) was activated at Phan Rang in Ninh Thuan Province under the command of Major Dandridge M. Malone. The nucleus of the new company was the "Reconnaissance Nomads" LRRP Platoon of the 1st Brigade, 101st Airborne Division. To augment the platoon and to fill the authorized manning slots, soldiers originally designated for the 18th Military Police Brigade were diverted. The unit's designation soon came to be known as "Typhoon Patrollers" after the code name of the I Field Force Headquarters.

The company was placed OPCON to the 4th Infantry Division on 15 October and deployed to the division's base at Camp Enari in Pleiku Province. There, the company's training began in earnest. By 23 December, the four platoons of the command were declared combat-operational.

The first deployment of the Typhoon Patrollers teams proved to be exceptionally disappointing. OPCON to the 1st Brigade, 101st Airborne

Division, Company E, 1st Platoon was — contrary to doctrine — deployed by the brigade as an extra rifle platoon. While fighting their way through the Bao Loc region on 19 December, both the platoon leader and a squad/team leader were killed in action. The company's 2nd Platoon was later rotated in support of the 1st Brigade from 26 December through 5 January but they, also, were misutilized and employed as conventional infantry.

Despite these initial problems, things began to improve quickly for Company E. Fifteen indigenous Montagnard tribal warriors were integrated into Company E to improve on the company's native scouting abilities. On 30 December, the 3rd Platoon supported the 4th Infantry Division's actions near Cambodia, in addition to providing reconnaissance support in the Plei Trap Valley around the Special Forces Camp Djereng. The intensity of the Typhoon Patrollers' missions continued and by the end of January 1968, they had conducted seventy-eight patrols and reported thirty-one observations.

One significant advantage the company had, not only over the enemy but also over most other American long-range patrol detachments and companies, was a large number of qualified canine handlers. As a result of this skill, their patrols would routinely employ scout dogs. During one such February patrol west of Pleiku and around Fire Support Base Oasis, a German Shepherd dog named Nick halted as the team was moving through the dense jungle, and perked his ears.

Acknowledging the dog's alert, the team moved to concealed positions. Shortly thereafter, they heard voices. When four NVA soldiers came into view, the patrol opened fire from their hasty ambush locations, killing two, wounding and capturing the others.

Moving from the ambush site, the team was once again alerted by Nick. Believing there may be a larger number of enemy approaching as a result of the previous engagement, the patrol's concerns were soon confirmed when Nick started to act jumpy. Almost outflanked by a superior enemy force, the patrollers needed to call in gunships for additional support. Running low on ammunition, the team finally requested to be extracted. Team member Specialist 4 Dave Seidel spoke for all of the team when he stated that "when it comes to spotting Charlie before he sees us, this dog's the best thing we've got going for us."

Company E continued to field patrols throughout central Vietnam during the winter, averaging fifty combat reconnaissance patrols a month. In addition, teams also trained other units on rappelling and reconnaissance as well as conducting joint reconnaissance missions during Operation Bath from 12 March to 5 April. The monsoon season in central South Vietnam set-in during May. By June, the region was under siege from low clouds, dense morning fog and rainy drizzle, and heavy afternoon thunderstorms. From February through July, the company conducted 306 patrols with 262 observations. Enemy casualties were 117 killed by direct fire while the patrollers suffered five KIA and thirty-three wounded.

During this time, the company was also conducting the training at the Duc My ARVN Ranger Training Center. The high standards of the American company cadre soon drew the wrath of the South Vietnamese high command on 28 July when only twenty-two of 121 South Vietnamese soldiers graduated the course. Furthermore, the company was accused of selecting the cream of the crop and accepting them into their own ranks. Unable to resolve their differences, the company was relieved of its instructor duties at the ARVN Ranger Training Center.

In September 1968, Company E was placed OPCON to the 4th Infantry Division to provide reconnaissance support along the tri-border front of western Kontum Province. On 10 October, the company headquarters and two of its platoons were moved to support the 173rd Airborne Brigade with reconnaissance patrols along Highway 19 from the highland city of Pleiku to the central South China Sea ports.

The company was not reconstituted as a single entity until 11 December when they stood down for two weeks at An Khe to train and recondition their teams. From August 1968 until the end of January 1969, the Typhoon Patrollers had conducted an amazing 320 patrols with 232 sightings. Their losses during this time were two KIA and thirty-nine wounded.

On 1 February 1969, Company E (Long Range Patrol), 20th Infantry (Airborne) was deactivated to serve as the nucleus of Company C (Airborne Ranger), 75th Infantry Regiment, which was activated the same day. Without missing a beat, the "Charlie Rangers" immediately began to conduct field operations.

During the period 4 to 22 February, three of the company's platoons rendered reconnaissance support to the 9th Division of the Republic of Korea (ROK) in the Ha Roi region. From 26 February to 8 March, two of the Ranger platoons assisted the Phu Don Province advisory campaign. Support of the 4th Infantry Division during Operation Hines lasted until 28 March while an additional one or two platoons worth of Rangers were assigned reconnaissance-security tasks along the ambush-prone sections from Mang Yang Pass to An Khe of Highway 19.

Charlie Ranger support shifted in late April to the 173rd Airborne Brigade, where Company C (Ranger) assisted Company N (Ranger) in the Binh Dinh Province during Operation Washington Green. Concurrently with Operation Washington Green, Company C also fielded a platoon in the Ia Drang Valley for a week, followed by a two platoon deployment in support of the ROK 9th Division in the To Hop-Ba Cum region in late May. Two platoons would remain with the ROK Division through mid-July.

On 21 July, the Ranger company was deployed to the southern region of Zone II to support Task Force South in its efforts to eradicate Viet Cong (VC) strongholds along the II and III Corps Tactical Zone boundary. Company C remained OPCON to Task Force South until 25 March 1970. During the course of their assignment in this area, the Rangers averaged twenty-seven patrols a month.

The Rangers were able to reap a large harvest of intelligence and wreak considerable damage to the enemy along the Corps Tactical Zone boundary. One such patrol, Ranger Team 23 under the command of Staff Sergeant Hendrick Greeneword, was inserted into the rugged jungle along the boundary on 14 September 1969. While their first night was uneventful, the Ranger team discovered a well-used and littered trail the following afternoon. As the team was considering the ambush possibilities, a group of fifty NVA infantrymen were observed marching up a gully from a nearby stream. Minutes later, another fifty-man group of soldiers was observed following behind.

Greeneword radioed his platoon leader, Lieutenant Richard Grimes, who was orbiting overhead in an O-1 Bird Dog reconnaissance aircraft. Grimes immediately ordered the dispatch of an airmobile reaction force and directed his team on the ground to refrain from calling in air strikes unless compromised. The team remained concealed in the thick underbrush as they observed the enemy company stop and rest in a grassy clearing approximately thirty feet from their location. The NVA soldiers cleared their weapons and inserted newly issued magazines. Seemingly intent on remaining at the location for the evening, many of the enemy soldiers dispersed to the edge of the clearing to cut foliage and twigs upon which to rest, some coming within inches of the hidden Rangers.

Circling nearby hills were Air Force F-100 fighter-bombers and army helicopter gunships, unable to move in yet because of the close proximity of the Rangers to the enemy. Then, as the airmobile reaction force of nine UH-1 Huey and four escorting Cobra gunships passed directly overhead, the enemy below began to scatter and make for the stream from which they'd marched.

Despite their proximity, Greeneword immediately called in the close air support and gunships. Released to attack the objective, the helicopters and jets pounded the retreating enemy formation with machineguns, rockets, and bombs. Caught in the open, the NVA found the effects devastating.

Some of the enemy tried to make it back up the ravine, moving in the direction of the Rangers, only to be engaged by rifles, an M-60 machinegun, and grenades thrown by Greeneword's men. When the smoke cleared, fifty-eight enemy soldiers lay dead with numerous blood trails leading into the jungle. Following a quick search through the bodies for additional intelligence information, the team was extracted, having suffered no casualties.

The company was split on 1 February 1970 with two platoons moving to Tuyen Duc Province. By 6 March, the company was reassembled and moved to the city of Pleiku on 29 March, where they were placed OPCON to the 7th Squadron of the 7th Cavalry for whom they conducted thirty-two patrols. On 19 April, the company was relocated to An Khe where it was OPCON to the 3rd Battalion, 506th Infantry Regiment to operate in the Mang Yang Pass region of Binh Dinh Province.

On 4 May 1970, the Ranger company was attached to the 4th Infantry Division in support of Operation Binh Tay I, the invasion of Cambodia. By 24 May, the Charlie Rangers were released from the 4th Infantry Division and withdrawn from Cambodia. Within four days, though, the company was rushed to Dalat to assist with defending against an NVA push toward that city.

The remainder of May, June, and July was a whirlwind of operations in Binh Dinh, Pleiku, Tuyen Duc, Binh Thuan, and Lam Dong Provinces. Interestingly enough, because of all the redeployments, the company only conducted sixty-five days of tactical operations during the ninety-two-day period.

On 26 July, the Ranger company was once again in support of the 173rd Airborne Brigade in Binh Dinh Province during Operation Washington Green. August found the Rangers attempting to locate and destroy the Viet Cong (VC) Khanh Hoa Provincial Battalion. A conflict, though, arose between the Americans and the ROK, who claimed the area of operation fell within their region of responsibility. The issue was not resolved before it was overcome by events with the discovery of a major Communist headquarters in the Secret Base Area 226 in Central Highlands. OPCON once again to the 173rd Airborne Brigade on 17 August, the Ranger company provided reconnaissance assistance.

From that point on until late April 1971, the Charlie Rangers remained OPCON to either the 173rd Airborne Brigade or the 17th Aviation Group. With the inactivation of I Field Force in April, Company C (Ranger) was reassigned to the Second Regional Assistance Command. By 15 August, the company was reduced to a brigade-sized Ranger element with an assigned strength of three officers and sixty-nine enlisted men. Two months later, the company was stood down on 15 October. Ten days later, on 25 October 1971, Company C (Airborne Ranger), 75th Infantry Regiment was inactivated.

Company D (Airborne Ranger) 75th Infantry Regiment

II Field Force

The III Corps Tactical Zone was 10,000 square miles of South Vietnam's industrial, logistical, and political heartland. Encompassing the nation's capital of Saigon, this zone's tactical responsibility fell to II Field Force. The II Field Force reassigned the 173rd Airborne Brigade's LRRP platoon prior to the brigade's departure from Corps Tactical Zone III to the field force to serve as the foundation for Company F (Long Range Patrol), 51st Infantry (Airborne.

Activated on 25 September 1967, Company F was commanded by Major William C. Maus. Replacements were diverted to bring the "Hurricane Patrollers," based on II Field Force's call sign, to its authorized strength of 230 men.

Company F proceeded to undergo a carefully planned and phased training program that commenced on 8 October. Declared combat-ready and fully operational on 2 December 1967, Company F was formally tasked to work with the support of Troop A, "Red Horse" 3rd Squadron, of the 17th Cavalry.

The Hurricane Patroller's first major combat operation was in response to the Tet-68 Offensive on 31 January 1968. In support of the 199th Infantry Brigade, the unit's teams conducted an intense reconnaissance and interdiction campaign north of the Bien Hoa base in the "Catcher's Mitt" region. Penetrating the enemy's staging area, the patrols were able to ambush, disrupt, and hinder the NVA and VC operations during their campaign, which lasted until the end of March.

Following Tet and throughout the spring of 1968, the reconnaissance company operated in a large arc around the South Vietnamese capital.

From May to mid-July, Company F supported first, the 3rd Brigade of the 101st Airborne Division and then the 199th Infantry Brigade during Operation Toan Thang with most team missions being conducted northeast of Saigon around long Binh or Phuoc Vinh.

During the period from April through June, the reconnaissance company conducted 250 patrols with 284 observations. As a result of 115 engagements, the teams killed by direct fire forty-eight enemy soldiers and captured four prisoners while suffering twenty-nine wounded in return. Unfortunately for the teams, these battlefield casualties, combined with unit administrative and rotational losses, forced the company to reduce team size from six to five soldiers each.

On 18 July, the Troop A air cavalry troops and Company F were assigned as part of a joint reconnaissance force with Red Horse aerial Troop D and the 36th South Vietnamese Ranger Battalion. This recon regiment conducted "reconnaissance-in-force" and screening operations east of Saigon in the vicinity of the Bien Hoa installation. In August, this ad-hoc regiment was augmented with D Troop (Tank), E Troop (Mechanized) of the 11th Armored Cavalry Regiment and the Special Forces 1st Battalion, 3rd Mobile Strike Command.

On 11 August, Company F was assigned the mission of conducting a separate operation to monitor the boggy and marshy infiltration routes west of Saigon that extended from the Pineapple Plantation region outside of the capital to Cambodia. Also reconned were the Yam Co Dong and Song Yam Co Rivers. The area proved to be a very active region and the Hurricane Patrollers conducted 241 patrols from August through October. The teams had 193 observations and killed 125 enemy soldiers by direct fire while suffering three KIA and forty-eight wounded.

Following a brief rest, refurbishment, and an Annual General Inspection (IG), the company was deployed on 13 August to War Zone D, northeast of Bien Hoa. OPCON to II Field Force G3 (Operations) instead of the G2 (Intelligence), the company primarily conducted combat patrols rather than reconnaissance operations. Observed enemy units that were too large to directly engage were targeted for fighter-bomber close-air-support attacks or B-52 bombing sorties.

The company was redeployed south of Rang Rang on 23 December 1968 where it was officially "inactivated" to allow for the deployment of the Indiana National Guard's Company D (Long Range Patrol), 151st Infantry. Though inactivated, Company F was not disbanded, for it became the Provisional II Field Force Vietnam Long Range Patrol Company (Airborne). Within a short period of time, though, a majority of the personnel were either transferred to the 3rd Brigade, 82nd Airborne Division or to the 1st Brigade, 5th Infantry Division.

The Provisional Long Range Patrol Company was inactivated on 15 February 1969, having conducted an additional 208 patrols and eighty-two sightings from November through January. Direct fire engagements resulted in twenty-seven dead enemy soldiers and six friendly KIA, in addition to thirty-five wounded.

On 13 May 1968, Company D (Long Range Patrol), 151st Infantry Regiment was called into federal service. Volunteering for duty in Vietnam, it would prove to be the only National Guard unit to serve overseas during that conflict. Following an extensive six-month preparatory training program in the United States, the National Guard company's deployment required the deactivation of a similar unit to remain within the authorized troop limit ceiling. Hence, the inactivation of Company F (LRP) of II Field Force .

Company D arrived at Camp Atterbury East in Long Binh in late December 1968. II Field Force developed a very careful and detailed training program implemented by both the 199th Infantry Brigade and the Provisional II Field Force Vietnam Long Range Patrol Company (Airborne) to acclimate the Indiana Guardsmen with Vietnam and the operational requirements within III Corps Tactical Zone.

By 23 January 1969, the company was declared operationally ready. Nine days later, their Long Range Patrol identifier was redesignated to read "Ranger." Though the MACV commanding general, General Creighton Abrams, was not enamored with the idea of having to replace his battle-experienced reconnaissance team with an untested and inexperienced group of guardsmen, political requirements dictated that the new unit remain intact and not be infused with combat-experienced soldiers at critical leadership levels with personnel transfers.

As a compromise to the II Field Force and MACV commander's requests, Westmoreland authorized the former Company F (LRP) commander, Major George W. Heckman, to command in "parallel" with the National Guard commander, Captain Robert Hemsel. While Hemsel remained in command of the unit, giving commands, he in essence served as Heckman's executive officer, taking orders from the senior officer. In addition, as the unit was attrited through casualties and transfers out, regular army soldiers would be transferred in to fill the slots.

With this new guidance in effect, the Indiana Rangers began their first combat patrols on 8 February in War Zone D and eastern Bien Hoa Province. Employed for screening and long-range saturation patrols, the Rangers conducted 573 patrols in this area from February through July.

The teams reported 134 observations while killing seventy-six NVA and VC soldiers by direct fire.

One of the most unusual patrols in the annals of Ranger history occurred in April 1969. The team had settled into their patrol site around 1800 when Specialist 4 Loren Dixon observed a large gray mass in the underbrush about twenty-five feet from their perimeter. Before anyone could react, the gray mass broke for their position.

Screaming "Elephant!," Dixon warned the team as the pachyderm charged at full speed straight for Lieutenant Eric T. Ellis and Specialist 4 H. C. Cross. Throwing themselves to opposite, sides, the two Rangers each unloaded a full twenty-round clip of 5.56 mm from their M-16 rifles. Apparently unfazed, the elephant continued to thunder forward through the position.

The patrol continued to scramble. Unable to sidestep the behemoth in time, Specialist 4 Ken Bucy found himself coiled in the elephant's trunk. With a mighty flick, the Ranger was raised overhead and thrown to the ground. The remainder of the team opened fire with their rifles and a machinegun as the elephant moved to stomp on Bucy's head.

The rounds began to take their toll and the elephant fell to its knees. Just then, a baby elephant broke from the other side of the perimeter and made off into the brush. Rising to her feet, the mother pachyderm gathered enough strength to disappear after its offspring.

August and September found the Indiana Rangers' area of operations inundated by torrential rains of the monsoon season. Commencing on 5 September, Company D's zone of reconnaissance was considerably reduced in size and the Rangers were reassigned for close-in patrolling for the Bien Hoa Tactical Command. By 26 October, the company had dropped below 60 percent of authorized strength.

A little less than a month later, on 20 November 1969, the Indiana Rangers departed Vietnam for demobilization back in Indiana. In their place, Company D (Ranger), 75th Infantry Regiment was activated under the command of Major Richard W. Drisko. The new "Delta Rangers" were then placed OPCON to the 3rd Squadron, 17th Cavalry.

The Rangers' zone of operation encompassed the Indian Rangers' old area of operation, in addition to western War Zone D in Long Khanh and Bien Hoa Provinces and the northeastern section of the Catcher's Mitt. Primarily focusing on combat patrols and ambushes, the Delta Rangers also performed various reconnaissance patrols. On 8 February 1970, Company D found itself released from the 17th Cavalry and placed OPCON to the 199th Infantry Brigade in the eastern portion of the

Catcher's Mitt and southwestern region of War Zone D. By 18 March, the company was returned to II Field Force control to train reconnaissance members of the South Vietnamese 18th Division and to patrol the Nhon Trach district.

The Delta Rangers commenced stand-down procedures by the end of March. During its Vietnam service, the company conducted 458 patrols with seventy sightings of enemy activity. Sixty-five engagements resulted in eighty-eight enemy killed by direct fire and the capture of three prisoners. In exchange, the Rangers suffered two KIA and twenty-four wounded. On 10 April 1970, the Delta Rangers of Company D (Ranger), 75th Infantry Regiment were inactivated.

Company E (Ranger) 75th Infantry Regiment

9th Infantry Division

Prior to the 9th Infantry Division's deployment to Vietnam in early 1967, Major General George S. Eckhardt, the division commander, arrived in-country for an orientation tour of the combat theater. Noting the use of long-range patrol units by other deployed divisions, Eckhardt ordered the formation of a similar reconnaissance platoon for the 9th upon his return to Fort Riley, Kansas. Organized under the command of Captain James Tedrick, the provisional division Long Ranger Reconnaissance Patrol (LRRP) Platoon, otherwise known as the "War Eagle Platoon," and its forty members reported to Panama in November 1966 to train at the Jungle Warfare School. The platoon shipped to Vietnam in January 1967 with the division.

The division's area of operation was primarily in the Mekong Delta, the Rung Sat Special Zone, and the lowlands south of Saigon. Initially deployed east of Saigon to Bear Cat-Long Thanh while its base camp, Dong Tam, was constructed with fill from the My Tho River at a site five miles west of My Tho in Dinh Thong Province, the division's area of operations was extremely flat, dissected by canals, rivers, and a multitude of tributaries. Extensive marshes and vast swamp forests ranged the region, usually well flooded during the rainy season from May through October. Exceptionally fertile and heavily populated, much of the area was referred to as the "rice bowl of Asia" with rice being sown, transplanted, and harvested from July through February. As events would later prove, the dense population would make clandestine movement difficult while the vegetative growth would provide excellent ambush opportunities.

The year-round exposure to water had a significantly detrimental impact on not only the patrollers but also on the division for, by the fourth month of deployment, nearly 75 percent of all infantrymen had some form of tropical infection. Immersion injuries were common and would often result in a soldier not being able to put a boot back on once taken off. Bacterial infections resulted in boils and skin ulcers. Fungal infections such as ringworm would cover large tracts of the body while other non-disease ailments, such as leech infestations, blisters, and heat rash, were common occurrences. These afflictions, and the ease of being observed, forced the division to limit the length of patrols to a maximum of forty-eight hours. Even these relatively short patrol durations could result in soldiers becoming combat-ineffective quickly.

The LRRP platoon began combat operations in the March–April time frame with some reconnaissance and surveillance missions. By June, the decision was made to expand the platoon to a full company-sized element of 119 soldiers. The new 9th Long Range Patrol Detachment (LRPD) was formalized on 8 July 1967. In consideration of terrain and weather operating conditions, the operational tempo of the LRPD was regulated, allowing the detachment to progressively pace training and operations. Though paced, the detachment did conduct forty-three reconnaissance patrols during June and July with the primary purpose of these missions being to provide surveillance on the VC Base Areas of 302 in lower Long Khanh Province and 303 in the Hat Dich Secret Zone.

Division emphasis was given to fully manning the detachment. Full manning was achieved in October, at which time the unit's status was reported as fully operational. LRPD patrols were assigned to support 2nd Brigade during Operation Coronado, in addition to 1st Brigade during Operation Akron. Detachment teams also supported Operation Riley. One of the detachment's more unique missions was to support the Mobile Riverine Force within the Mekong Delta. In support of the Riverine survey teams, the assigned LRPD teams would assist with the gathering of vital river data.

To enhance the detachment's reconnaissance capability, division intelligence began to assign native South Vietnamese Army scouts for linguistic support. Unfortunately, many of these scouts took issue with the hard work and dangers encountered. Innovatively, the detachment's operations sergeant hired three Hoi Chanhs—former Viet Cong and North Vietnamese prisoners who had agreed to work for the Americans in exchange for their freedom—for cash. The hard currency proved to cement the deal as the Hoi Chanhs served as dedicated and resilient scouts.

The division commander, Major General George C. O'Connor, activated Company E (Long Range Patrol), 50th Infantry on 20 December 1967. Absorbing the LRPD detachment, the new company called themselves the "Reliable Reconnaissance" in concert with the division's Vietnam nickname of "Old Reliables." The LRPD's six-man patrols were restructured as eight-man patrols. New volunteers were sent to the MACV Recondo School for training. Unfortunately, Company E suffered its first fatality at the course.

As their final graduation exercise, MACV Recondo School customarily deployed a class's final patrol into a hostile region for exposure to realistic combat conditions. Student Team 3, under the leadership of Special Forces Sergeant First Class Jason T. Woodworth, was compromised and involved in a firefight on the morning of 3 January 1968. Following a request for extraction, a Huey flew to the pick-up point and arrived around 0815. As the bird hovered, the team members, with the exception of Specialist 4 Kenneth R. Lancaster from Company E and Specialist 4 Kozach, clambered aboard.

While Kozach waited for another lift, Lancaster, unknown to anyone, apparently attempted to ride out with the first group, grabbing hold of the helicopter's skid as it began to rise from its hover. Unseen by anyone in the aircraft until they'd reached an altitude of 1,000 feet, Lancaster lost his grip and fell before he could be pulled aboard. An extensive search through the jungle below was conducted, but his body was never located. Though it could be, unfortunately, safely presumed that he had been killed from the fall, Lancaster remains the only reconnaissance member from the 9th Infantry Division's Vietnam era to be still classified as missing in action.

To gain experience and training in the Mekong Delta environment, Company E began to conduct joint operations with Navy SEALs—SEa, Air, and Land teams—in January. Designated as SEAL-ECHO missions, the joint teams were inserted by a variety of different means from Navy patrol craft to helicopter to conduct "aquabush" attacks to block the waterway or to seize prisoners. The program proved to be so effective it was extended to run throughout the year.

The reconnaissance team's association with the Mobile Riverine Force was not changed as a result of the unit's new designation. Reliable Reconnaissance patrols continued to assist with terrain analysis and hydrographic tasks, avoiding direct combat whenever possible. One of the patrol's priorities was to direct and guide the nightly movement and positioning of artillery barges by reconning shore conditions, sandbars, and other potential water obstacles.

In February, Company E was authorized to utilize any personnel available from the Provincial Reconnaissance Unit (PRU) of the Central Intelligence Agency's Project Phoenix program. A controversial CIA program initiated in 1967 and run by future CIA director William Colby, Phoenix was designed to identify and "neutralize"—by capture or death—Viet Cong cadre, propagandists, and tax collectors found within the peasant population. Though its degree of success was suspect during the war, senior North Vietnamese leaders noted after the war that the program's elimination of tens of thousands had been exceptionally destructive and significantly hampered operations in the South.

Hardened anticommunist troops, PRU personnel proved to be a tremendous asset to the reconnaissance teams with their innate knowledge of Viet Cong operating methods and their high esprit. The company was able to receive nine PRU scouts who were able to operate with their teams on a periodic basis.

During the three months from February to April, Company E teams killed seventy-four Viet Cong by direct fire while only sustaining three KIAs themselves. The next three months from May to July, found the company teams operating deeper into the Mekong Delta and involved in heavy fighting within the Plain of Reeds. Late July and August found some reconnaissance teams accompanying U.S. Marine advisors and the South Vietnamese 5th Battalion into the rough U Minh Forest along the western coast while other teams waded through the dense foliage and waste-deep mud of Tan An within the Song Vam Co Tay. Additionally, two eight-man teams were positioned on Navy river patrol boats on the Song Dong Nai while a third team of ten men were assigned the task of patrolling west of Route 15 just south of Saigon.

Company E experimented with the concept of employing snipers with their patrols. In July, two expert marksmen from the Fort Benning Army Marksmanship Training Unit, Staff Sergeants Aprail Gapol and Richard D. Rebidue, were attached to a patrol operating outside of Tan An. Armed with national Match M-14 rifles modified to mount commercial Redfield adjustable-range telescopes, the two sergeants took up a nighttime sniper position. As a group of fifteen Viet Cong approached in the vicinity of Highway 4 a few hours later, the two snipers began to engage the group while they were still over four hundred yards away. Only five of the VC escaped the crosshairs of the two sergeants.

Convinced of the utility of such experts, the 9th Infantry Division established a division sniper school under the direction of the two Benning snipers. Given the geography of the division's area of operation, snipers would prove to be a very effective weapons system in the spacious region. Soon, every team would have at least one sniper-qualified soldier on the team.

To counter the tide of enemy supplies along the waterways from Rung Sat Special Zone and Go Cong into Long An Province, Company E developed a new tactic called the "Parakeet" flight—a play on words with the larger platoon sized "Eagle" flights developed and employed by Special Forces. These flights consisted of a four-man recon element on a UH-1 Huey helicopter. The flights would conduct an aerial surveillance over water and land nearby if it noted anything needing further investigation. Once on the ground, the four-man detachment would move to the water's edge, wave the suspicious vessel over to beach, and board for a thorough search.

Reliable Reconnaissance continued its patrols throughout the Mekong Delta during the fall of 1968, with the majority of patrols focused on Dong Tam. In addition, the mission with the Navy river patrol and the Mobile Riverine Force continued to be supported as before. Despite the difficulty of securing helicopter support, Company E was still able to conduct 202 patrols during the three-month period of August to October. Seventy-one contacts were made with the enemy resulting in forty-seven enemy dead by direct fire and twenty-six prisoners.

As winter progressed, the Company E headquartered at the main division base at Dong Tam. One team continued to provide support to the Navy at Nha Be while two eight-man recon teams were provided to each of the three brigades for direct support. The remaining teams were maintained under direct company control.

For the most part, the Viet Cong were not inclined to fight and remained concealed during division sweeps. To counter this tactic, infantry battalions would deploy with a recon team attached, which would be clandestinely left behind following the battalion's departure. Patrols noted that the region would soon come "alive" with enemy activity following the perceived departure of the American troops. Air and artillery strikes would quickly show them the error of their ways. With the deployment of these stay behind teams, the American command was able to obtain valuable intelligence they would not otherwise be able to observe.

Company E closed out the last three months of its existence from November 1968 to January 1969 with 217 patrols and 102 enemy engagements. During those engagements, they were credited with killing eighty-four enemy by direct fire and with capturing eleven prisoners.

Company E (Long Range Patrol), 50th Infantry was inactivated on 1 February 1969 with the activation of Company E (Ranger), 75th Infantry Regiment. Referred to as either the "Riverine" or "Echo" Rangers, the company continued to be headquartered in Dong Tam and consisted of eleven reconnaissance teams, six men each. Two Ranger teams supported the 1st Brigade at Fire Support Base Danger in Dinh Thong Province. 2nd Brigade Mobile Riverine Force in Kien Hoa Province was supported by three Ranger teams as was the 3rd Brigade based at Tan An in Dinh Thong Province.

Two special tactical techniques were employed by the division Rangers, one old and the other new. Third Brigade continued to fly the Parakeet flights that were considerably strengthened from those that tested the original concept. Deployed with a full six-man Ranger team versus the previous four-man partial teams, the flights were also escorted with two Cobra gunships for immediate suppressive fire support.

Meanwhile, within the 1st Brigade's area of operation, it was proving to be extremely difficult to locate and suppress the enemy's secret supply lines. To deal with their frustration, the teams reverted from intelligence gatherers to hunter-killer teams. While one Ranger team would attempt to lock enemy soldiers into an engagement, the other two Ranger teams, waiting on standby, would be deployed to maneuver in support of the engaged Ranger team. Unfortunately, the main problem with this tactic was that it employed all three of the brigade's Ranger teams on a single raid.

From February to April, the Echo Rangers conducted 244 patrols with 134 reported observations. During 111 direct fire engagements, the Rangers were credited with killing 169 Viet Cong and capturing five prisoners. Turnover and injuries were impacting the unit hard, though. Not only did the Riverine Rangers have to deal with the normal impact of the personnel rotation policy and other administrative impacts, but the immersion foot, bacterial, and fungal infections further exacerbated the problem. Worse yet, was the issue that despite the inability of those injured to perform field duty, they still had to be carried as part of the unit's organizational structure. Thus, replacements could not be requisitioned for them until they were actually transferred out of the Ranger company.

The division was notified of its redeployment to the United States on 12 June 1969, the first major U.S. Army unit scheduled to depart. Selected to remain behind to secure the approaches into Saigon from the southwest was the "Go Devil" 3rd Brigade, which was established on 26 July as an independent command.

Commencing in July, just weeks after the notification, the Rangers were assigned the task of assisting with the defense of Dong Tam base as the remainder of the division focused on the redeployment home. To commemorate the event, Company E Rangers temporarily renamed themselves the "Kudzu Rangers," after the operational code word for the close-in defense of Dong Tam.

The Rangers were released from this conventional infantry role by 3 August and consolidated at Tan An. A major issue concerning the Ranger company was still unresolved. Company E was scheduled to depart Vietnam as part of the division by 12 August. This would leave the 3rd Brigade with limited reconnaissance capability. The Department of the Army, on the other hand, would not reconsider the redeployment schedule, fearing political repercussions.

Having anticipated the problem earlier, U.S. Army Vietnam headquarters had begun to work its way around the issue with a published General Order 2434 on 6 July that created a provisional brigade Ranger company as of the 20th of July. Company E (Ranger) personnel and equipment were transferred to form the new command. Though it had a personnel strength of zero, Company E (Ranger) was logged out as having departed Vietnam on 12 August. On 23 August, the "Ranger Company" was formally inactivated. In addition, the 3rd Brigade was placed OPCON to the 25th Infantry Division in September with the final departure of the 9th Infantry.

The inactivation of Company E did not affect the brigade's provincial Ranger company, which continued with its patrols. A month later, on 24 September, U.S. Army Pacific General Order 705 reactivated Company E (Ranger) and reassigned the unit to 3rd Brigade, 9th Infantry Division as of 1 October that year.

The "new" Ranger company was organized with two platoons but manning problems decreased the total number of teams per platoon to two each. During the wet season, though, there was little for the reconnaissance teams to do, for the Viet Cong usually stopped military activities to assist with the rice harvest, and, generally, they could not be distinguished from the ordinary villagers.

With the onset of winter in December, the Rangers employed Hoi Chanhs to assist with the spotting of enemy activity and the conduct of nighttime ambushes. By spring, two additional teams were manned to bring the company's total number to six. May and June of 1970 found the 3rd Brigade participating in the Cambodian invasion. As an "economy of force" measure, Company E remained behind to secure the Long An Province. During the six-month period of January to June 1970, the Rangers were credited with killing ninety-three Viet Cong by direct fire and the capture of two prisoners. Ranger losses were two K1A and twenty-eight wounded.

With the brigade's return in June, the Rangers became more actively involved with the implementation and integration of remote electronic surveillance and radar systems. On 15 September, having been notified of its impending demobilization, the Rangers ceased combat activity and redeployed to Di An base camp. The unit's final ceremony was held on 28 September. Company E (Rangers), 75th Infantry Regiment was officially inactivated, technically for the second time, on 12 October 1970.

Company F (Ranger) 75th Infantry Regiment

25th Infantry Division

In March 1966, the "Tropical Lightning" Division, the 25th Infantry, deployed to Vietnam. Based in Cu Chi, the division would conduct most of its operations in the Tay Ninh, Binh Duong, and Hau Nghia Provinces. The area of operations were smooth lowlands consisting of swamps, light woodland and rubber tree plantations, strips of jungle, and cultivated fields. Overall, the terrain was very favorable to guerrilla warfare.

In June 1966, Major General Frederick C. Weyand, the division commander, directed the formation of a provisional Long Range Reconnaissance Patrol (LRRP) contingent. Three officers and thirty-eight enlisted soldiers manned the contingent named "Mackenzie's Lerps." The name was derived from the LRRP's administrative attachment to the 4th Cavalry, whose nickname was "Mackenzie's Raiders," named after Colonel Ranald Slidell Mackenzie who had been a mercilessly proficient former commander of the regiment during the 1870 to 1882 Indian frontier time period.

Though declared operationally ready on 30 June 1966, the LRRP cadre underwent three weeks of training at the MACV Recondo School while the remaining members conducted only four combat patrols during the month of July. The unit continued to expand in size and gain experience from August through October as they conducted thirty patrols. Not only was the operating range of the patrols expanded, but the unit also underwent a four-day Special Forces water infiltration program during this period.

OPCON to the division intelligence section, Mackenzie's Lerps were assigned missions to either conduct anti-ambush or point reconnaissance patrols or to screen the flanks of mechanized or dismounted infantry sweeps. In support of Operation Gadsen, a divisional invasion of War Zone C in February 1967, the Lerps played a significant combat reconnaissance role in the division's success.

During the three months of February to April, Mackenzie's Lerps conducted thirty patrols throughout the division's area of operations. Spring and summer of 1967 found the 3rd Brigade of the 9th Infantry Division operating independently within the Central Highland's region. In support of the brigade's operations, the LRRPs found themselves involved in seven major operations as they pushed through jungles, waded through rice paddies, searched caves, and patrolled the beaches.

Bearing a grudge usually proved fatal, which was exemplified on a particular patrol on 30 May 1967. Unfortunately for the five-man patrol, one of its members had extended his Vietnam tour to, by his own words, "even the score" for the death of his twenty-two-year-old sister, who had been killed in Cu Chi during a mortar attack. Having sworn to kill one Viet Cong for every year of her life, the soldier had achieved a confirmed kill count of eighteen prior to this mission. Though court-martialed and reduced in rank for unbecoming conduct in regard to his personal vendetta, he had been maintained in service as a LRRP because of the scarcity of qualified personnel.

Soon after the patrol's insertion, radio communications were lost around 2030 that evening and never reestablished. A reaction team was later deployed and the location of the team's last stand on a hillside, which took place about 0300, was found the next morning.

Around the shattered site strewn with spent 5.56-mm and 7.62-mm shell casings and near grenade blast impressions were discovered the bodies of two of the patrol members. Blood trails and thrashed vegetation indicated the three other team members had probably been wounded and dragged off. Those three men remain missing in action. Though the exact circumstances of the team's final moments are unknown, it is conceivable that the one team member's desire for revenge involved his teammates in a death struggle that was beyond their resources and capability to handle.

With the monsoon season's commencement in May, the activities of Mackenzie's Lerps were reduced with the limited patrol schedule providing an opportunity to conduct training for their newly recruited volunteers. In October, the new division commander, Major General Fillmore K. Mearns, authorized the expansion of the Lerps into a Long Range Patrol Detachment. Its association with the 3rd Squadron, 4th Cavalry was formalized with the squadron commander issuing the detachment its missions. And, with its increase to 118 soldiers, the detachment gained some additional flexibility with the organization of two team-sized "ambush groups" and four team-sized "stay-behind" groups.

The detachment developed a few new techniques and implemented some old tried and true ones. One new insertion technique was referred to as "tailgating," which was a method of deployment from the rear exit of an armored personnel carrier as it passed down hedgerow-lined jungle avenues that provided concealment to the inserted patrollers.

Stay-behind groups, on the other hand, deployed with regular infantry and remained behind obscurely to survey. These types of missions usually proved to be very successful, for the Viet Cong were much less vigilant when they believed there were no American troops in the area.

The detachment's recon teams found themselves working with Vietnamese Provincial Reconnaissance Unit (PRU) scouts from 18 November to 23 December to locate and explore a massive tunnel complex during Operation Atlanta. Essentially composed of two tunnel networks, the system served as a major underground infiltration route through what was known as the "Iron Triangle." The tunnels proved to be so long and complex, one PRU recon team traveled for three days and nights as it scouted a five-mile branch of the network.

Mackenzie's Lerps were inactivated and absorbed into Company F (Long Range Patrol), 50th Infantry, upon that unit's activation on 20 December 1961. Given the unit's call sign of "Cobra" and its mission as division reconnaissance, Company F acquired the new name of "Cobra Lightning Patrollers." The company fielded two platoons with seven six-man teams each, many of whom took the opportunity to attend the MACV Recondo School soon after the formation of the new company.

With few exceptions, combat reconnaissance elements of both sides rarely encounter, much less engage, each other on the field of battle, for reconnaissance elements, by definition and as a matter of survival, would prefer to avoid combat whenever possible. One major exception to this norm occurred late in the afternoon of 29 January 1968 when a Cobra Lightning patrol was inserted into the northern edge of the Ho Bo Woods to locate and report enemy movement within the area. Coincidentally, the vanguard of a Viet Cong column marching toward Saigon in preparation for the start of the Tet-68 Offensive and composed of the elite 272nd Regiment Reconnaissance Company was moving through the woods.

The initial contact between the two reconnaissance elements occurred at 1645 and quickly escalated. Automatic rifle and machinegun rounds streaked through the dense jungle foliage with hand grenades following behind. Each move by one to maneuver was deftly met with a counter-move by the other. As the American team radioed for reinforcements by the aero "Rifles" platoon, the Viet Cong called up the lead companies of their column.

Each side received specific orders from their higher headquarters. As the Americans were ordered to hold their ground until more reinforce-ments arrived, the Viet Cong were directed to shield from observation and interference the change in direction of the main regimental column around the engagement area. The Viet Cong's position became more dif-ficult to accomplish with the arrival of the 2nd Battalion, 27th Infantry "Wolfhounds" during a daring dusk air assault.

Under considerable pressure, the dug-in VC engaged the newly arrived Wolfhounds, attempting to prevent them from linking up with the beleaguered LRP team and the aero platoon nearly three hundred yards away. As the reinforcing American troops charged through the hail of fire, the tenacious VC reconnaissance soldiers continued their deter-mined resistance, ambushing and delaying with great skill whenever and wherever possible. Division intelligence reports would later describe their ammunition supplies as seemingly "limitless."

The ferocity of the battle began to diminish somewhat as the reinforc-ing battalion finally linked up with the aero platoon and LRP team. Around the Americans lay sixty-four dead recon VC. All preferred death to surrender. Only one seriously wounded VC soldier who could no longer fight nor flee was taken prisoner.

As to who was the victor, it is all relative. It would be claimed that the LRP team accomplished its mission, encountering the lead elements of the enemy column and holding its ground until reinforcements arrived. But a stronger claim could probably be made for the VC recon element who, through their sacrifice, were able to shield the main column's move-ment, enabling the regiment to reach its Tet-68 Offense attack positions.

Following Tet, the main focus of the Cobra Lightning Patrollers was to prevent the weakened Viet Cong from regrouping, replenishing, and rearming. In addition to their traditional long-range patrols, the Cobras were tasked to perform the more mundane close-in roving security about the division's main base camp at Cu Chi. Part of their tasking was to secure a wooden bridge that led to the Filhol Plantation. Night ambushes were also scheduled as part of the routine.

Overlooking and dominating much of the division's area of operation was a huge solitary slab of granite jutting from the agricultural plain named Nui Ba Den, "Mountain of the Black Virgin." Nearly 3,200 feet high and located fifty miles northwest of Saigon, the mountain's craggy and boulder-strewn slopes were honeycombed with caverns and tunnel networks. While the Americans maintained a helicopter sustained communications complex on its peak, the Viet Cong controlled its hillsides.

Security of the communications site was maintained by periodic reconnaissance sweeps of the slopes below. In July, a Cobra Lightning team led by Sergeant Willard R. Ethridge conducted one such sweep. Air landed on the peak, the patrol began what was supposed to be a forty-eight-hour descent down the mountain.

The first day went well, with the six-man team cautiously maneuvering its way down steep pathways, over and around immense rocks. Nearing the bottom of the mountain on the second day, the team observed a large group of Viet Cong blocking their exit path. Maneuvering around the VC was not an option. Moving back up their trail and down in another direction, the patrol observed another group of VC on this alternate route. A third similar movement met with the same results.

Having found themselves trapped on the hillside, the team moved to a more secure location where they uneasily drew together for the night. The third day found similar efforts thwarted just as they'd been the day prior. Unfortunately, one of the team's members, Specialist 4 Miller suffered a serious leg injury from a falling rock. A second man suffered heat exhaustion. With two men injured, out of food and water, and blocked at every turn by detachments of Viet Cong, Ethridge moved his men to a rocky gulch and radioed for help.

Company F responded by directing two recon patrols operating in the area to the trapped team's location. Unfortunately for Ethridge and his men, these two teams were quickly engaged in a firefight by machine-gun nests concealed in rock crevices and narrow cave entrances and were unable to advance beyond the mountain's base. Rocket-propelled grenades (RPG) fired down on their positions finally forced each of the two relief teams to withdraw to safety.

The two teams reassembled and, reinforced by additional Cobra team members, attempted, once again, to make their way up the hill. Though the twenty-five men were able to gain a foothold two hundred yards up the slope, the fighting was extremely sharp among the rocks and the platoon soon had to cease movement for the night. The dawn of the fourth day found them totally unable to move, pinned down as they were by the VC's fires.

The besieged team's plight was growing steadily worse. With no supplies or water, wounded men on hand, the relief force pinned down, and the enemy now searching the rocks all about them for their location on a cliff 1,200 feet above the level terrain below, the situation was somewhat dire. While the terrain prevented normal helicopter extraction, a Huey medical evacuation helicopter attempted to lower a hoist to extract Miller. Despite the gunship support of two Troop D Cobras that rocketed and machine-gunned the hillside, the enemy were able to fire from relatively secure positions within the shelter of rock outcrops every time an attempt was made to lift the injured soldier out.

Overhead, a Cayuse light observation helicopter piloted by Warrant Officer Stephen R. Patterson and accompanied by the Troop D commander, Major Fred R. Michelson, surveyed the scene below. Michelson radioed for more fire support and soon an additional two Cobras from the 25th Aviation Battalion, two Huey gunships, and two Air Force tactical fighter-bombers were on station assisting the original two Cobras with suppressive fires.

As menacing storm clouds gathered in the afternoon, a second Medevac approached the trapped team's location in an attempt to extract Miller. As the Huey was maneuvering in, a sniper's round shattered the helicopter's radio and the storm clouds erupted into a violent tropical thunderstorm. The heavy rain reduced visibility and prevented any other helicopters from hovering near the team's location and forced the aircraft to return to Tay Ninh.

With dusk moving in by the time the storm moved off, Major Michelson, two Huey gunships, and Patterson's Cayuse observation helicopter arrived back on the scene to attempt a resupply of the stranded team and to give the hillside one final good blasting prior to departing for the evening with the hope the team could survive until their return the following morning. As the gunships sprayed the slope with rocket and machinegun fire, Patterson maneuvered his aircraft as close to the cliff as was safely prudent while Michelson leaned out on a skid prepared to throw a bag full of food, water, and radio batteries onto the team's ledge. The effort failed as the bag bounced off the rocks and fell over the cliff into a Viet Cong base camp far below.

Realizing the men were now in a real dilemma, Patterson noted a large boulder on the cliff that was just wide enough for him to place one skid of his helicopter on. Hovering over, he placed the toe of his right skid on the rock to serve as a reference point to maintain stability against the bad updrafts. Miller was quickly passed over to Major Michelson. Lifting off, Patterson immediately flew back to Tay Ninh where the injured soldier was dropped off along with Major Michelson to save weight and to make room on board.

Returning to the cliff, Patterson performed the dangerous maneuver again, precariously balancing the aircraft's skid on the rain-slick rock. The aircraft's blades swung dangerously close to a large tree nearby as Patterson struggled to keep a level hover while Sergeant Ralph J. Hosey and Private First Class Roger F. Van Rensselaer leaped from the edge of the cliff onto the tiny helicopter's skid. With only the loss of a few small trees to the helicopter's blades, the two men were quickly transferred to Thy Ninh and dropped off.

Despite the darkness, Patterson elected to return a third time to extract the final three men. In the dark, the pilot searched the dark mountainside for the cliff, inadvertently flying over the Viet Cong base camp and being sprayed with automatic weapon's fire. Finally locating the men, he perched on the boulder for the third time. Loaded with their equipment and rucksacks, Ethridge and Specialist 4 Joseph Hitchens jumped on the observation helicopter first. The last person left was Private First Class Merilan Henry, who'd volunteered to board after the first two. Though the bird looked full to him already and Patterson was struggling to keep the aircraft level with the additional weight on one side, Henry did not hesitate and just dove for the chopper. With his feet on board, his body hanging over the side, his right hand in a death grip on the pilot's chair, and his squad leader holding on to his left hand, Henry safely made it back to Tay Ninh. The valor and personal sacrifice made by some of the pilots associated with the reconnaissance detachments and Ranger companies could not be better exemplified than that displayed by Warrant Officer Stephen R. Patterson.

As the Viet Cong's "Third Offensive" took shape around Tay Ninh, Company F was ordered to conduct surveillance and harass their efforts. Following the defeat of the VC attack, the teams reverted to routine patrols along the upper Siagon River, inside the Ho Do and Boi Loi Woods, and around Trang Bang.

Patrol skirmishes had the potential to lead to significant losses of aircraft. On 5 November, one such patrol by a recon team started with the "innocent" ambush of an isolated boat traversing a canal in the Ho Do

Woods. As a precautionary move, the Troop D aero rifle platoon was inserted to assist with the team's extraction. The patrol's extraction went without incident but, when the helicopters returned to lift the platoon, the Viet Cong surprised the Americans with heavy machinegun and rocket propelled grenade fires. Two of the five Hueys were shot down over the landing zone in flames. Two others managed to gain some altitude but were unable to return to base and crashed. Only the fifth heavily damaged bird flown by a wounded crew was able to make it back.

Company F, 50th Infantry was deactivated and absorbed into the activation of Company F (Rangers), 75th Infantry Regiment on 1 February 1969. The three field platoons were organized with three or four eight-man teams with teams 11 through 14 supporting the 1st Brigade in Tay Ninh Province, teams 21 through 23 supporting the 2nd Brigade and teams 31 thru 33 supporting the 3rd Brigade, both in Hau Nghia Province. A minimum of one sniper was assigned with each team.

Referred to as either the "Fox" or "Tropical" Rangers, the Ranger teams began the spring in support of the division's counteroffensive against enemy encroachments toward Saigon. Later, during June, their reconnaissance secured information that assisted with the defeat of another attempted enemy attack against Tay Ninh. In October, the Rangers' mission was switched from reconnaissance to combat patrols as they were placed OPCON to the division operations section by the direction of the division's new commander, Major General Harris W. Hollis.

For the six-month period from November 1969 until April 1970, the Ranger company was placed in direct support of the 3rd Brigade. Conducting their combat reconnaissance missions against the An Ninh infiltration corridor, the Ranger company accomplished, on average, ninety missions per month. During this period, they were credited with approximately 100 enemy killed by direct fire.

At times, the Rangers' own reconnaissance reports would serve as the catalyst for further missions. On 2 April 1970, the 3rd Brigade commander, Colonel Olin E. Smith, directed two Ranger teams to investigate observations of sizable Viet Cong groups infiltrating back into the Renegade Woods. A thirteen-man force composed of Ranger teams 38 and 39 was assembled under the command of First Lieutenant Philip J. Norton with Sergeants First Class Colin K. Hall and Alvin W. Floyd assisting.

The patrol was inserted by Troop D Hueys at 0835 that morning into a landing zone with two large bomb craters near a bend in the South Vam Co Dong River, each crater being nearly thirty feet across and fifteen feet deep. Initially taking shelter in the craters, the patrol began to move across the LZ toward a woodline in the direction of a destroyed village named Ap Ben Dinh. They had not moved too far before they were engaged by an enemy light machinegun. The initial rounds wounded Sergeant Fred B. Stuckey, ripped the M-16 weapon out of the hands of Specialist 4 Donald E. Purdy, and severed the handmike cable to Norton's radio. Despite his wounds, Stuckey assisted Purdy with suppressing the machinegun nest with a shower of hand grenades.

To the experienced Rangers, a machinegun only indicated one thing: the presence of a large force. As he ordered gunfire support from the overhead Cobras against the treeline, the lieutenant began to maneuver Team 39 forward behind the Cobra runs while Floyd and his Team 38 provided covering fires. Team 39 made it to the eastern edge of the woods before encountering stiff opposition.

Team 38 followed at a distance and secured some cover in one of the bomb craters. Cover was a relative term, for the team quickly came under fire from rockets and machineguns. Casualties began to mount quickly as Floyd and Sergeant Michael F. Thomas were killed and Specialist 4 Donald W. Tinney mortally wounded. Compounding the team's difficulty was the fact that the rocket that killed Floyd also destroyed the radio, thus severing any communications with the outside.

Recognizing the severity of his situation and the fact that his force was now split, Norton ordered his team to fall back and to reconsolidate with Team 39 in the crater, where they would form a defense. Hall and Sergeant Charles P. Avery provided the opportunity by destroying a machinegun nest and eliminating a rocket crew with grenade and rifle fire. Avery was seriously wounded during the exchange.

As the team retreated, Norton grabbed the dying Tinney and dragged him back with him. In the crater, the lieutenant was able to salvage enough from both the patrols' damaged radios to place one into operation. With radio communications restored, Norton was able to hear only bad news. Not only was there not a reaction force available to reinforce their position, but the Cobras overhead had to withdraw for they were now out of ammunition.

The patrol was not totally abandoned, though, for the light observation helicopters refused to leave despite the fact they, too, were out of ammunition. Instead, they remained to "buzz" and harass the enemy troops with "dry" runs as they attempted to form for a charge against the entrapped American force on the ground.

The patrol formed a 360-degree perimeter defense and repelled repeated probes against their position. Soon, though, the patrol was down to just their M-16 rifles for defense. The only M79 grenade launcher had jammed very early in the battle after firing only one round, leaving

249 rounds remaining. At the crater, one of the two M-60 machineguns jammed, leaving the second weapon to fire all of the remaining rounds. By 0920, the Rangers' situation was beginning to look very bleak as they were down to the last rounds for their individual weapons, a number of which were beginning to malfunction also.

Completely surrounded, under fire from every direction, nearly out of ammunition, and strapped with casualties already totaling two dead, one dying, and six wounded, the surviving and conscious Rangers prepared for the final assault that would not be long in coming. Calmly, they still went about their business, engaging the enemy with what they had remaining.

Overhead, realizing the dire straits of the Rangers' situation, were Warrant Officer 1 James Tonelli and Captain Philip Tocco in their UH-1H Huey. Intrepidly and unexpectedly, the pilots and crew thundered down onto the darkened, fire-swept field, frantically signaling for Norton to get his men aboard. As the crew chief and door gunner, Specialist 5 Charles E. Lowe, placed heavy suppressive fires into the treeline from his mounted M-60 machinegun, the Rangers began to scramble and stagger to the aircraft, dragging their wounded with them but forced to leave their two dead behind. A second door gunner, Private First Class Richard K. Adams, a former Tropical Ranger himself, leaped from the aircraft and assisted the exhausted Rangers by taking and placing Tinney aboard. Taking rounds, overloaded with fifteen personnel, exceeding maximum torque specifications, and experiencing serious vertical vibration, the Huey was somehow able to clear the trees at the edge of the LZ and make its way back to base.

When the aircraft was examined later by Bell Aircraft Company technical experts, they "expressed utter amazement that [the Huey] was still able to fly" given the damage and conditions it was forced to operate under. As for Teams 38 and 39, a subsequent airmobile operation and mechanized sweep of the area indicated that the two teams had accidentally encountered the firmly dug-in forces of the 271st Viet Cong Regiment.

As the Ranger company entered the spring, they were assigned the task of training selected South Vietnamese units as part of a division project initiated by MACV titled "Progress Together Campaign." This assignment proved to be burdensome and a detraction from their primary function of reconnaissance, which still needed to be conducted in support of the division. Though some of the Ranger teams would deploy in May with the division during the Cambodia invasion, most of the teams remained behind in an economy of force measure.

In late June 1970, the Rangers' mission was readjusted as the primary emphasis once again became reconnaissance and combat patrolling was relegated to a secondary function. Overall command of the company was transferred from the brigades to the division, as the Rangers grew more involved with the placement and operations of ground sensors and radar. Finally, in November 1970, the division, with the exception of the 2nd Brigade at Xuan Loc, was alerted for redeployment to the United States.

Reorganized on 8 November as a separate Brigade, the 2nd was task-organized with a reduced Company F (Ranger) of sixty-two men for support. The brigade's area of operation encompassed all of Bien Hoa Province, northern Phuoc Thy Province, and southern Long Khanh Province. The primary focus of the Ranger operations was surveillance and interdiction of enemy lines of communications. Finally, on 5 March, notification was received that the Ranger company was to be disbanded as part of the redeployment from Vietnam. The final company and award formation was held the next day. On 15 March 1971, Company F (Ranger), 75th Infantry Regiment was officially inactivated.

Company G (Ranger) 75th Infantry Regiment

197th Infantry Brigade; 23rd Infantry Division (American)

The 197th Infantry Brigade arrived in Vietnam in August 1966 and was assigned to Tay Ninh Province in the southern region of Vietnam. Early operations clearly indicated a need for a specialized long-range reconnaissance detachment (LRRD) that was organized on 2 January 1967 at the direction of the brigade commander, Brigadier General Richard T. Knowles. The hardships and hazards of the duty and the unwillingness of commanders to approve the transfer of some of their best soldiers made recruiting difficult. By 31 January, only thirty of the sixty-seven authorized slots had been filled.

As with most of the newly formed LRRPs, the unit's higher headquarters was the brigade intelligence section. Administrative and logistical support were provided by Troop F, 17th Cavalry. The unit became known as the "Burning Rope" Patrollers. The nickname was an interpretation of the brigade's shoulder patch. Following the detachment's organization, it underwent an intensive and condensed training cycle of reconnaissance and small unit patrolling tasks.

Sergeant Anthony Mazzuchhi led one of the Burning Rope Patrollers' initial missions. Following their insertion into their area of operation, his six-man team heard noises behind them as they began to cross a large open area. Ordering his men to return to the woodline, Mazzuchhi prepared a hasty ambush. Minutes later, three Viet Cong soldiers made their way along the trail. The ambush was initiated and the three VC were quickly eliminated. Realizing the three men may have been the point men for a larger formation, Mazzuchhi ordered the team back into a tight defensive perimeter, called for artillery fire, and requested an extraction. Later, a sweep through the area would indicate that the indirect fires that the team had vectored in had decimated a platoon of VC.

In late February, the 196th pushed into War Zone C with several other major units in Operation Junction City. During April, the brigade redeployed to Chu Lai, along the northern coast and thirty miles from Da Nang. The brigade would remain at this location for the remainder of its Vietnam service, first as part of a provisional-sized organization referred to as "Task Force Oregon," then later as part of the 23rd, American, Division. Though the 196th Infantry Brigade commander, Brigadier General Frank H. Linnell, attempted to retain his Burning Rope Patrollers detachment, his efforts proved to be unsuccessful with their transfer to the newly formed division LRRP detachment by November.

From May to October, the detachment averaged nearly eight patrols a month for a total of fifty patrols through the six months. The pace, losses, and rotations had a serious impact on the small unit. To maintain unit integrity, patrols, which originally had fielded six members, were going to the field with only four. Four Rangers was not a satisfactory number, though, and the detachment commander, Lieutenant Frank Pratt, reconfigured the team organizations to seven men each. This reorganization proved to provide the minimum number of men per team in the field but there was a cost associated with it, for it also reduced the total number of available reconnaissance teams and the number of patrols conducted each month.

In June 1967, following the 196th's deployment to Chu Lai, a patrol led by Sergeant Michael W. Daniels was inserted on a small, heavily forested hill to serve for three days as an observation post. Later that day, the team heard shots fired from an adjacent knoll. Believing that another team under the command of Corporal William Davis was signaling them, Daniels' team discharged some rounds in the air to acknowledge the signal. Not long afterward, Daniels and his men soon realized that the other team was under attack as the sounds of firing increased. As night fell, a helicopter extracted Davis' pressured team.

Daniels was now in a quandary. Having mistakenly discharged their weapons, the team realized they had compromised their own position and would probably be attacked next. These fears became reality soon after the sun set as their position began to take on scattered rifle fire. With extraction not an option until the next morning, Daniels had his team prepare their defense as they placed trip flares around their tiny perimeter and called in artillery salvos to detonate in the woods around them.

At approximately 2115, light from two handheld flashlights were spotted in the trees. A handheld flare fired by Private First Class Mark Brennan illuminated a number of enemy soldiers in a draw nearby. Too close for indirect fires, the VC were engaged by small arms fire from the LRRP team. Distracted and engaged with the enemy in the ravine, the small detachment would have found itself outmaneuvered and under heavy fire if not for the sharp vigilance of Private First Class William Connor. Despite the darkness, he had observed an enemy squad making its way up the hill by another ravine. Grabbing his M-60 machinegun, Connor ran through some sporadic gunfire to deliver some heavy fires into the approaching squad. A third enemy assault was suppressed on the far side of the hill.

Two UH-1 Huey helicopter gunships arrived overhead to provide suppressive fires on the flare-lit hilltop. One of the gunships was hit with return fire. Wounded, a gunship's door gunner fell back into the bird, his M-60 machinegun continuing to fire, spewing rounds across the hilltop. Fortunately for the team defending below, none of them were hit by the errant friendly fire.

Daniels called in more artillery to stop another VC charge but he soon knew the situation had grown indefensible. As the team members withdrew down the hill, the VC swarmed across the top. Though the VC could be heard searching the hilltop, they never did venture below. At dawn, Daniels and his five men were safely extracted.

Task Force Oregon reorganized as the American Division by order of Westmoreland on 25 September 1967. Headquartered in Chu Lai, the American was assigned an operational area that encompassed Quang Tin and Quang Ngai Province, as well as part of Quang Nam Province. Operating within this region were NVA and VC forces under the command of Military Region 5, which dominated much of the South Vietnamese population between Cam Ranh Bay and Da Nang. The terrain varied with rice-cultivated lowlands along the east coast, hilly and overgrown tropical forests in the center, and multi-canopied jungle to the west. For the most part, the enemy avoided major engagements within this area, opting to work, instead, with small detachments.

On 22 November, Major General Samuel W. Koster, the division commander, activated the Americal Long Range Patrol Detachment (Provisional). Lacking an intrinsic patrolling organization of its own, the division transferred the Burning Rope Patroller detachment to their command to serve as the nucleus for the new organization. In late December, the 11th Infantry Brigade arrived from Hawaii to join the 196th and 198th Infantry Brigades to round out the division.

As a separate brigade for U.S. Army Pacific, the 11th had been authorized its own long-range detachment, the 70th Infantry Detachment. Unfortunately, with the brigade's redeployment to Vietnam, the detachment was deactivated in Hawaii on 19 December.

In Vietnam, just a day following the 70th's inactivation in Hawaii, the provisional Americal Long Range Patrol Detachment was formalized as Company E (Long Range Patrol), 51st Infantry. The detachment's first commander was Captain Gary F. Bjork. Organized in accordance with the prescribed 118-man division-level long-range patrol company, Company E was placed through a severe and demanding training program.

Upon completion of their training, Company E began to routinely conduct patrols throughout their area of operations. Though resistance was light, obstacles, mines, and booby traps hindered their movements to some degree. During the summer of 1968, teams deployed as part of Operation Wheeler-Wallowa into the Antenna Valley and Que Son Valley regions where they met significantly greater resistance.

On 1 February 1969, and in accordance with an Army directive, Company E was inactivated and Company G (Ranger), 75th Infantry Regiment was simultaneously activated with the personnel and resources of Company E. Referring to themselves as the "Golf" Rangers, in reference to the phonetic alphabet pronunciation of the letter "G," the company was organized in accordance with the authorized 118-man authorization. Within the company, each Ranger team was named after a state.

On 18 March 1969, the regions formally operated in by the Americal Division and the 2nd ARVN Division were merged. The 23rd's area became a joint American-Vietnamese responsibility and Ranger Company G was directed to build two demonstration teams to show how U.S. and ARVN soldiers could work together. Though each of the two teams only had two ARVN Rangers assigned, they proved a valuable asset and were assigned lead and trail positions within the patrol. This was the most dangerous position within the team, for the point and rear guard were the most likely positions to make enemy contact first. The purpose of placing them there, though, was to use their innate ability to discern friend from foe for these ARVN Rangers could tell the difference between a civilian and an enemy soldier just by the sound of their walking through the jungle.

The Americal Division Reconnaissance Zone was often referred to as the "Suicide Zone" for it extended from the interior mountains to the remote and isolated Laotian border. Having already had two garrisons destroyed by regimental-sized NVA assaults, even the U.S. Army Special Forces had abandoned the region. Facing such adversity, the Americal Rangers planned reconnaissance missions within the area that were limited to twenty-four hours between insertion and extraction. Longer missions would only expose the teams to eventual compromise and destruction.

Staff Sergeant Robert J. Pruden commanded ranger Team Oregon. On 14 November 1969, he and his team were conducting a road surveillance west of Duc Pho when they ambushed a ten-man Viet Cong patrol, killing a number of the enemy prior to withdrawing and being extracted from the area. Four days later, Pruden and his team—composed of Sergeant Danny L. Jacks, Specialist 5 John E. Shultz, Specialist 4 John S. Gaffney, Specialist 4 James R. Gromacki, and Specialist 4 Robert B. Kalway—volunteered to return to the same valley road to conduct another ambush and to capture a prisoner.

Inserted on a hill, the team moved into some rice fields and established two three-man positions alongside the road. Depending on the direction of travel of their intended prisoner, one team would make the capture while the other team provided rear security. As they were preparing the ambush site, a twelve-man VC patrol approached. Ceasing all movement, the Rangers watched quietly as the patrol moved through their ambush site.

With the patrol's departure, the preparations continued. Unfortunately, six VC spotted one of the Rangers as he crawled forward to emplace a claymore mine along the trail. The member was pinned down by rifle fire from these six as the team began to take additional fires from an enemy force closing in from the opposite direction near a road bend.

Seeing one of his men cut off and exposed and the enemy closing in, Pruden realized that his team was in a precarious and critical situation. Leaping onto the trail from his concealed position, Pruden charged toward the road bend firing his CAR-15. Startled by this unexpected assault, the VC shifted their fires from the Ranger trapped in the road to the Ranger charging their way. Hit and knocked to the ground, Pruden rose and continued forward to be hit a second time.

Falling along the edge of the trail, the Ranger paused long enough to slap in another magazine, his first clip having killed four of the enemy and wounded several others. Rising to his feet once again, Pruden's efforts so unnerved the remaining VC that they fled from behind the berm they had been firing from. As they withdrew, though, they fired some departing shots, hitting the charging Ranger a third time.

Having engaged and defeated the second approaching enemy element while Pruden was attacking on the other end of the trail, the team closed in on their fallen leader to find him on the ground only fifteen feet from the enemy's previous position with five bullet wounds in the chest and abdomen. Amazingly, the fallen Ranger was still conscious. With a hasty defensive perimeter thrown around him by the team members, Pruden, despite the overwhelming pain, forced himself to remain conscious and even attempted to call in the air support and an immediate extraction for his team, though he could barely speak above a whisper by this time.

As his breathing became more difficult, team members attempted to keep the sergeant resuscitated with mouth-to-mouth. Temporarily regaining some strength, Pruden asked the status of his team members and quietly reiterated his orders to the team that they were to be extracted. Moments later he lost consciousness and died just minutes before the arrival of the extraction helicopter.

With his gallantry, intrepidity, inspirational leadership, and personal self-sacrifice, Pruden's actions had led to the defeat of two flanking enemy squads and the safe return of his five team members. For conduct above and beyond the call of duty, Ranger Staff Sergeant Robert J. Pruden was posthumously awarded the Medal of Honor.

Throughout 1970, the Ranger company averaged nearly sixty patrols per month. In August, patrols were assigned the additional task of shielding the national election campaign along the coastal region against any attempts to disrupt by the NVA or VC. As the war stretched into 1971, the Rangers found themselves increasingly involved in supporting the acquisition of data through electronic means such as ground surveillance radar (GSR) or line sensor strings by emplacing, securing, and maintaining such systems. On 14 September 1971, Company G (Ranger) ceased combat activity and commenced to stand down for deactivation that took place on 1 October.

Company H (Airmobile Ranger) 75th Infantry Regiment

1st Cavalry Division

In September 1965, the army's first airmobile division, specifically designed for the war in southeast Asia, the 1st Cavalry Division, deployed to Vietnam. Heavily equipped with helicopters, the division was one of the most responsive and flexible divisions of the war. For the first eighteen months of the cavalry's deployment, the aerial scouts and aero-rifle platoons of the 1st Squadron, 9th Cavalry, provided reconnaissance.

Despite the capabilities of this unit, which were considerable, there did prove a need, over time, for a specialized patrol to conduct ground reconnaissance, especially in early 1967 in support of Operation Pershing. The operation was an extended search and destroy campaign that covered an operational area of 1,032 square miles in the southern Quang Ngai Province, as well as the northern and eastern portions of Binh Dinh Province.

The division Long Range Reconnaissance Patrol (LRRP) element was activated on 2 February under the command of Captain James D. James. The unit's nickname was the "Pershing Lerps," named after the operation they had been raised to support. The unit was organized with two teams, one in support of the 1st Brigade in the An Lao Valley, the second in support of the 2nd Brigade in Kim Son Valley.

In April, the LRRP detachment was attached to the division intelligence section and expanded into the provisional 1st Cavalry Division Long Range Patrol Detachment (LRPD) with an authorized strength of 118 soldiers. Additionally, the detachment was augmented with eighteen South Vietnamese scouts and eighteen Montagnard tribal warriors. To enhance their skills, twenty detachment members attended the MACV Recondo School from August through October. By November, all of the divisions Recondo school slots were reserved solely for detachment volunteers.

The Pershing Lerps proved to be a valuable resource for division intelligence with numerous sightings of NVA and VC elements. During the final two months of the year, the Lerps, operating out of three bases at Landing Zone Uplift, Landing Zone English, and Phan Thiet conducted a total of 105 patrols with over 350 sightings of enemy personnel.

One of the Pershing Lerps' most successful patrols occurred toward the end of Operation Pershing on 5 December 1967 by a team inserted to search the mountains of the lower Suoi Ca Valley a day earlier. Late that afternoon, the patrol observed and engaged three Viet Cong, who were, contrary to the norm, wearing green uniforms. Killing one and capturing the other two, the team was extracted. Under interrogation, the prisoners revealed that the small party were high-ranking members of a VC delegation from the Binh Dinh provincial communist headquarters. The soldier who had been killed was a battalion executive officer while one of the captives was a senior VC intelligence captain who had just recently completed a two-year program of study in the Soviet Union. Over time, the division was able to obtain a great deal of information from the intelligence officer.

Company E (Long Range Patrol), 52nd Infantry was activated on 20 December 1967 outside of An Khe at Camp Radcliff. The Pershing Lerps were transferred to this new command, which was known as the "First Team Patrollers," after the division's moniker, "The First Team." By January 1968, reconnaissance teams from Company E were in direct support of all the brigades along a widely separated front. Command and control would prove to be somewhat difficult for the company commander, though, for he could only exercise marginal control of his teams while they were stationed with the various brigade command posts and held under tight brigade control.

Additionally, these teams were improperly employed at times as they performed sentinel, listening post, and observation post duties around the command post or forward fire support bases. Administrative support and training was also difficult as a result of the company being dispersed to the brigades. The separation and mission requirements allowed for only eight slots a quarter to the MACV Recondo School.

The company was scattered throughout the division area of operation when the Viet Cong surprise Tet offensive of 1968 struck South Vietnam. While only a few teams could be released to monitor and interdict North Vietnamese supply lines leading into the Quang Tri and Hue battlefields, nine teams were deployed to monitor Viet Cong activity in the Cay Giep, Nui Mieu, and Crescent Mountains to secure Binh Dinh Province. The company also maintained perimeter security around Camp Radcliff.

In March, the division prepared to launch a counteroffensive to the Tet-68 Offensive. For the first time, all of the Ranger teams were assembled in one place as Company E assembled at Camp Evans. Assigned the mission of scouting the mountains of central and eastern Quang Tri Province for suspected enemy strongholds, Company E fielded sixty-one patrols from May through July. During that time, the LRRP teams had ninety-eight separate observations, killed twenty-eight NVA regulars by direct fire, and suffered five killed in action (KIA) and four wounded.

The company's tough pace continued from August through September but the NVA and VC had reduced their degree of activity. Though Company E deployed sixty-six patrols during this two-month period, they only had fifty-two observations of enemy activity and twenty-two enemy dead as a result of direct fire.

Recognizing that dispersing the company as it had been earlier would only exacerbate his problems of having a well-trained, responsive reconnaissance detachment, the division commander, Major General Forsythe, resolved the issue on 18 October 1968 by consolidating the company under the operational control (OPCON) of the 1st Squadron, 9th Cavalry. Despite some initial growing pains, the centralization decreased redundancy within the company and led to an increased number of teams that could be fielded. Teams were properly employed for the missions for which they had been trained. With the aviation support available from the squadron, the LRRP teams received more timely intelligence from the aerial scouts, quicker insertions, and more expeditious reinforcement from the aero-rifle platoons.

In late October, the division found itself relocated south to assist with the screening of the Saigon approaches. As a result, Company E became the only Army reconnaissance unit to transfer between zones in the Vietnam conflict by sea. Boarding the Landing Ship-Tank, LST-532 *Chase County*, at Tan My, the company took a week's trip through the South China Sea to arrive at the Newport docks in Saigon for disembarkation on 5 November.

The division's mission was to conduct reconnaissance and surveillance missions along the principle NVA and VC routes leading from Cambodia to Saigon. To support this mission, the First Team Patrollers were tasked to work against previously identified NVA resupply routes. Adjusting to the new terrain was not easy, for the coastal valleys and mountains they had grown used to were now miry swampland, jungle plains, and interior rice fields.

Not only was the terrain different, but so were the tactics employed by the enemy. To keep their ranks on line during a sweep through an area, the NVA would often fire shots as signals. The timing of the shots would decrease as the gap between enemy units closed. To disrupt the maneuver, scouts would call in artillery fire to obstruct the formations and to drown out the sound of the rifle shots.

During another patrol, it was discovered that the VC were using a dog to discern their trail. Following the close canine encounter, LRRP teams began to routinely carry black pepper to cover their tracks by spreading it behind them periodically as they moved.

Another big change for the First Team Patrollers was the number of noncombatants and livestock in the area. Moving without being observed or without giving oneself away by frightening an animal was nearly impossible. Locals watched patrols closely, and it was nearly impossible to tell if they were friendly or enemy.

Periodically, a patrol would find itself unexpectedly within a well-camouflaged bunker complex. Usually, the patrol would just continue to move through cautiously but, on those few occasions when the enemy spotted the patrol, they usually gained time to react while the enemy clacked bamboo shoots together as an alarm.

Prisoners were a coveted commodity by patrols on reconnaissance missions and, at times, some individuals would go to extreme measures in an attempt to obtain one. On 13 December 1968, Recon Team 39, led by Staff Sergeant Ronald J. Bitticks, was inserted approximately four miles northwest of Phuoc Vinh to locate enemy forces reported to be in the area. Moving through thick bamboo the team made its way to a well-used trail. Informed by his point man, Sergeant Edward Malone, that two NVA soldiers were walking in their direction, Bitticks decided the opportunity was right to snatch a prisoner.

Jumping from his concealed position onto the trail, Bitticks landed in front of the startled soldiers and yelled in Vietnamese that they should surrender. A few seconds later, as their surprise wore off, the two NVA soldiers reached for their weapons. Bitticks opened fire first, killing one as the second managed to escape.

With their position compromised, Bitticks and his men headed back into the jungle, forced to advance slowly or give themselves away as they thrashed through the dense underbrush. Nearly three hundred meters later, they stumbled across the trail again, for it made a sharp 90-degree turn back toward them. Barely able to see ahead because of the dense growth, the team observed several large groups of VC.

As Bitticks radioed for air support, the VC dispatched some small search parties, one of which encountered the hiding team. The three-man VC party was quickly killed but a heavy volume of fire against the team position from every direction immediately followed these deaths. Marking their position with a smoke grenade, the team attempted to hold out, surrounded and outnumbered, as two Cobra gunships made repeated strafing runs against the advancing enemy ranks. Each gunship pass brought a pause to the team's dire straits as the enemy's weapons were raised skyward in an attempt to bring down the helicopters.

The battle continued for over two hours. At one point, the VC were able to get a machinegun within twenty-five feet of the patrol's position. Its presence was announced with a swath of heavy-caliber bullets shredding the bamboo all around them. Coordinating with their overhead support, the team was finally able to break out of their encirclement behind the strafing runs of three gunships.

Making their way to a small clearing in the jungle that would serve as a PZ, Bitticks and Sergeant Howard Fatzinger III began to frenziedly cut down trees with their machetes to clear a large enough area for the extraction helicopter to land as the remainder of the team held off the pursuing enemy and the gunships continued to place suppressive fires from overhead. The fires proved to be enough to discourage any further attempts to overrun their position. By that evening, Team 39 was safely extracted.

Effective 1 February 1969, Company E was deactivated and Company H (Airmobile Ranger), 75th Infantry Regiment was activated. The men and equipment of Company E formed the nucleus of this new Ranger company. The company remained OPCON to the 1st Squadron, 9th Cavalry Regiment headquartered at Phuoc Vinh. As the Tet New Year of 1969 approached, the Cavalry Rangers heightened their patrol activity and noted an increased willingness on the part of the enemy to engage their patrols.

The Rangers intensified their efforts to gather intelligence throughout March, focusing on prisoners and documents. Much of the documentation carried by the enemy was hidden, especially sewn in clothes. Hasty searches could miss such valuable information. Consequently, Rangers began to strip the enemy dead and return with the dead's clothing for military intelligence to search.

As part of their psychological war effort, Cavalry Rangers would leave a wooden nickel on the body of the stripped enemy. The nickel had an Indian head on one side and the unit's identification on the reverse and its purpose was to plant fear into the minds of the enemy, forcing them to move in larger groups. According to many cavalry soldiers, the token seemed to serve its purpose.

Enemy activity picked up as the end of March 1969 approached. Patrols observed large numbers of enemy bicycle-mounted units and vehicular traffic. Cyclist units without accompanying security were prone to Ranger ambushes. Attempts were made to block vehicles with antitank mines emplaced in the road or trail. Rangers received detailed training on minefield emplacement. For these patrols, a combat engineer would usually accompany the Rangers as the seventh man of the patrol to record the mined area for future reference. Each minefield emplaced usually consisted of four M7A2 antitank mines with a kicker block of C4 placed underneath.

In April and May, Company H participated in Operation Montana Scout/Montana Raider. To support this operation, the Rangers conducted surveillance along infiltration routes and conducted ambushes on almost a routine basis during April as only small groups were making their way across the battlefield. Activity increased in early May as reinforcements were moved into the area to support attacks against three division fire support bases. Long columns of bicycles and oxcarts with heavy loads were routinely observed by Ranger patrols at night and dealt with appropriately by directed artillery fire. The movement of large enemy formations gradually tapered off as the month came to a close.

From May through July, the 1st Cavalry and Company H interdicted a major North Vietnamese offense directed against Saigon. During this time period, the Cavalry Rangers conducted 328 patrols. These patrols resulted in 143 enemy sightings and 118 team engagements. Combined Ranger and aerial fires resulted in 128 NVA killed. Ranger casualties were six KIA and forty-two wounded.

Field duty was not the only thing in a Ranger's life that proved to be dangerous. Training also had its moments. As part of a special demonstration for the commanding general, a Ranger team led by Sergeant Stanley J. Lento had been selected. Outfitted and equipped for a patrol, the team was to march onto a stage in single file, make a right face, and place a sign at their feet that listed all of the equipment and munitions they were carrying.

On 24 July, Lento conducted a final thirty-minute rehearsal. With his team in formation, he directed them to align their equipment. As Specialist Archie H. McDaniel, Jr., removed his rucksack, at least one, and possibly two, of his Claymores inside detonated. The explosion killed McDaniel, Lento, and the assistant team leader, Sergeant Paul J. Salminen. Specialist 4 Charles M. Steele suffered a punctured chest wound while the remaining two team members, Sergeant James W. Kraft and Specialist 4 Fred R. Doriot suffered head wounds. The detonation also caused a fire that burned down half of the building they were rehearsing in.

An Explosive Ordnance Disposal (EOD) team conducted a detailed investigation. The results of their investigation, though, clearly indicated that the team members had apparently taken every necessary safety precaution. Trip flares and hand grenades were so well taped to their belts that the tape on both sides of the handle had to be cut away in order to remove the grenades. An additional layer of protection was added with the wrapping of each pin in tape. The Criminal Investigation Division (CID) was also called in to determine if there might have been any foul play involved. Again, just as with the safety inspection, no reason to suspect criminal intent was found. The cause of the explosion that wiped out Lento's team was never determined.

As daytime movement of enemy personnel abated, nighttime ambushes by the Rangers received greater emphasis. One such ambush was conducted by team 41 on 26 June 1969 at a trail intersection on the Adams Road infiltration route near Song Be. The team prepared their ambush near a recently used bunker complex and began their wait. Later that evening, the team leader, Staff Sergeant Guy R. McConnell, observed the approach of three flashlights followed by the silhouettes of twelve enemy soldiers. The Rangers initiated their ambush by opening fire on the lead and trail elements. Their fire forced the remaining soldiers into a second kill zone covered by six Claymore and M-14 mines that completed the job.

More NVA troops made their way to the area, attempting to overwhelm the five-man Ranger team. The battle continued throughout the night as the Rangers repelled a number of enemy charges with the assistance of gunships and illumination support. To mark their location for the overhead aircraft, Specialist Kenneth E. Burch held up a strobe light, only to be shot in the arm for his effort. To maintain communications, the team radioman, Specialist Germany, stood up to improve the signal transmission, shielding the radio with his body. Though severely wounded in the side, Germany succeeded in restoring and maintaining radio communications.

Team members also sacrificed for each other. When a grenade landed within the perimeter, Staff Sergeant McConnell scooped it up and was wounded as he threw it away from his comrades. Specialist Leerburg was seriously wounded when he knocked Private Taijeron aside after his weapon had jammed during an exchange with some enemy soldiers who had closed on the team's position. By dawn and despite their wounds, the team was still intact and subsequently reinforced by cavalry elements.

For the remainder of the year, the 1st Cavalry continued to screen the border region between Vietnam and Cambodia. In December, Company H participated in Operation Dong Tien. This operation was an exercise in partnership between the 1st Cavalry Division and the South Vietnamese Airborne Division. The Cavalry Rangers worked closely with their South Vietnamese Airborne counterparts until 22 April 1970, teaching American patrolling and communications techniques.

As they trained, the Rangers also continued to conduct field operations, seeking out enemy routes of infiltration. From February to April, Company H conducted ninety-five patrols and made forty-seven observations of enemy troop movement,

In May 1970, the 1st Cavalry found itself involved in the Cambodian invasion with Company H (Airmobile Ranger) serving as the advance element for both the cavalry and the South Vietnamese Airborne Division. Despite the hostile fires and adverse weather conditions, the company successfully performed its critical ground surveillance missions.

From 1 May to 30 June, the Cavalry Rangers conducted fifty missions in Cambodian territory. These missions resulted in thirty-eight major enemy sightings and numerous enemy killed by both direct and indirect fires.

During the Cambodian invasion, Ranger Team 52 was seriously mauled during an extended engagement. Having received orders to search between the Vietnamese border and O'Rang, Cambodia, the team was lifted into an advanced outpost in Cambodia on 14 June. While at the outpost, the team leader was medically excused because of an infected foot. Staff Sergeant Deverton C. Cochrane arrived as the replacement for the team leader on 15 June. As Cochrane arrived, the assistant team leader was also being medically excused from the patrol for an eye infection. Specialist 4 Carl J. Laker was designated the assistant team leader later that evening. Rear scout Staff Sergeant Dwight D. Hancock, radioman Sergeant Ronald M. Andrus, and another replacement, medic Specialist 4 Royce D. Clark rounded out the remainder of the team.

Following a recon overflight of the LZ, the team was inserted on high ground at 1645 on the 16th. Radio communications were established and the team moved to a point three hundred yards into the jungle, where they were to spend the night. The next morning, the team discovered an empty NVA position full of flares and ammunition. As the patrol continued to move, they were drenched by a tropical storm. While the rain fell, the team located a small bunker complex on top of Hill 717 around 1535.

Deciding to wait until later to call the report in, Cochrane continued to move his men down the far side of the forested hill. At approximately 1730, Cochrane moved to the edge of woods along an open field. Believing he heard voices, the team leader had just started to assume a crouched position when a burst of machinegun fire swept through the trees from a position in the woods directly across from the field. Hit, Cochrane dropped to the ground. Andrus radioed in that they had contact but the signal was never received for they were in low ground and their PRC-25 only had the short whip up.

Clark saw the head of an NVA soldier pop up from some distant shrubbery and placed three rounds into the enemy. Hancock threw hand grenades until the North Vietnamese ceased firing. During the brief respite, Laker ordered Andrus to bring him the radio and for all of them to move farther back into the woods. Laker moved to recover Cochrane but was shot in the head, just above the left eye, by a sniper and collapsed on Hancock. Andrus was shot in the chest as he affixed the long antenna to the radio. Moments later, the radio was destroyed as a number of rounds impacted on it. Clark was hit by a round that shattered his thigh.

Hancock desperately tried to locate the team's URC-10 emergency survival radio among the dead and wounded Rangers but could not. Picking up Clark, Hancock carried the wounded soldier while Andrus, seriously wounded himself, provided covering fire from the rear. Moving back into the heavy underbrush, the three Rangers halted to allow Hancock to administer first aid. With no ability to establish communications and being the only one not seriously wounded, Hancock proceeded to conceal the two wounded Rangers with leaves and vegetation.

Leaving his rifle and ammunition behind with the wounded for personal protection, Hancock struck out unarmed cross-country to seek help. Moving from tree to tree and greatly assisted by a heavy fog and rain, Hancock traveled for miles, passing North Vietnamese camps, guards, and machinegun positions without much trouble. Hancock finally reached an American outpost near Fire Support Base David later that evening, having to first convince the sentries not to shoot him.

At daybreak the next morning, 18 June, Hancock returned to the skirmish site with a reinforced search team of Rangers and Cavalrymen. While Clark and Andrus were located, neither Cochrane nor Laker was ever found. The official inquiry would rule that Laker was in fact dead and would be carried as KIA. In that no one was able to verify conclusively whether or not Cochrane had actually been killed, he would be carried as MIA.

In July, the 1st Cavalry withdrew from Cambodia back to South Vietnam. Though the division was still in a war zone, political pressure led to the Cavalry Rangers being ordered to terminate missions immediately upon direct contact with enemy forces. Later, in April 1971, the 1st Cavalry's redeployment to the United States began. From the period 27 March to 2 April, Company H was reduced to seventy-three authorized and attached to the separate 3rd Brigade. The Brigade's area of operation included both Binh Thy and Long Khanh Provinces and some additional territory that encompassed a total of 3,000 square miles. Based at Bien

Hoa, the Ranger company conducted surveillance operations to identify enemy avenues of approach.

From June 1971 until its withdrawal from Vietnam to the United States, Company H was composed of Teams 71 through 79. In December, the 3rd Brigade was assigned the task of guarding the Saigon-Long Binh logistical complex. Surrounded by "rocket belts" from which the NVA or VC fired rockets, the Rangers spent the remainder of their time in country patrolling these pockets.

On 9 June 1972, the final Cavalry Ranger casualties were suffered when an enemy rocket or command-detonated bomb went off during a sweep through an enemy bunker and command complex near Tan Uyen. Killed in the explosion were the team leader, Sergeant Elvis W. Osborne, Jr., and his radioman, Specialist 4 Jeffrey A. Maurer. The team's secondary radioman, Specialist 4 Donald E. Schellinger was also wounded but he and his three other team members were able to fight their way clear from the complex and make it to a PZ for extraction. This engagement proved to be one of the last significant Ranger engagements of the Vietnam War.

On 27 June, Company H was reassigned from the 3rd Brigade to the "Garry Owen" task force of the 1st Battalion (Airmobile), 7th Cavalry. Military operations were halted by mid-July. On 15 August 1972, Company H (Airmobile Ranger), 75th Infantry Regiment was officially deactivated as the last Army Ranger unit in Vietnam.

Company I (Ranger) 75th Infantry Regiment

1st Infantry Division

The 1st Infantry Division completed its deployment to Vietnam in October 1965. Its area of operation throughout the war would be the territory west and north of Saigon and included the main road that connected Saigon with Cambodia, Highway 13.

In April 1966, the Division Commander, Major General William E. DePuy, formed a provisional division Long Range Reconnaissance Patrol (LRRP) unit called the "Wildcats." By late April, Wildcat teams were called upon to support Operation Birmingham in northern Tay Ninh Province. Rappelling into the heavy jungle along the eastern bank of the Cai Bac River and the Cambodian border, the teams had to abort their missions early when all were quickly detected by numerically superior Viet Cong forces.

Later, in June, the teams deployed to the field in support of Operation El Paso. It was in support of this operation that the LRRP suffered its first KIA, Sergeant Rudolph A. Nuñoz, as they were conducting a scout near the Special Forces Camp at Loc Ninh.

On 28 September 1967, Major General John H. Hay, Jr., the 1st Infantry's commanding general, received authorization to formalize his Wildcat Lerp organization. Hay took an active interest in this new unit, ensuring that it upgraded and expanded to its authorized strength of 118 men. The new organization was identified as the provisional 1st Infantry Division Long Range Patrol Detachment (LRRD). Headquartered at Lai Khe, it was OPCON to the division intelligence section.

The unit was declared operational and fully combat capable in late October. Initial LRRD patrols were deployed around Bu Dop and Loc Ninh to reconnoiter reported NVA and VC concentrations. The detachment remained in the region for the remainder of the year, locating caches and scouting west of Highway 13 into the Michelin Plantation.

Teams had to be prepared to handle any and all circumstances, especially when the tables were turned. On 24 October, a five-man reconnaissance team under the command of Sergeant Edward Davis was inserted near War Zone C. From an overnight position, the team observed VC soldiers passing their position around midnight. At dawn the next morning, the team followed the enemy trail. After stalking the enemy for a number of hours, the team moved to their designated extraction point only to be surprised and subjected to heavy small arms fire from a large VC unit.

Davis and his men killed seven of their ambushers before being forced into a nearby rice field. The radioman, Private First Class Wilber J. Latin, called for and received gunship support that prevented the pursuing VC from overrunning their exposed position. A Huey braved the fire and courageously extracted the team.

The 1st Infantry Division Long Range Patrol Detachment was deactivated on 20 December 1967 and Company F (Long Range Patrol), 52nd Infantry was activated in its place. Its call sign was "Danger Forward Reconnaissance" to show the relationship between it and the division command post, call sign "Danger Forward." The teams were numbered sequentially and prefixed with the code designation of "Remote Trails" — signifying Recon Team (RT). Interestingly enough, the unit's first official detail was three days later, when it provided part of the sixty-man honor guard for President Lyndon B. Johnson's Vietnam visit on 23 December.

The company's reconnaissance missions began in earnest during January 1968 when division intelligence assessments indicated there would be a major rocket and ground attack launched by at least a regimental-sized element against the division's base camp at Phu Loi where the major percentage of division aviation assets were staged. In anticipation of this attack, Hay withdrew Company F from the field and posted them around all major division bases, to include Phu Loi.

At approximately 2005 on the evening of 31 January, a patrol manning a forward observation post (OP) outside Phu Loi noted a force of approximately twelve enemy soldiers advancing toward their location. The patrol leader, Sergeant Ronny O. Luse, reported the site and set about preparing an ambush.

But the group of VC turned prior to entering the ambush's kill zone and moved into the far woods. This proved to be rather fortuitous for the small patrol, for an hour later they watched with amazement as an entire battalion of VC emerged from the woodline and made their way across the rice paddies.

Based on Luse's report, division ordered him and his men to withdraw as a division artillery battery of 105-mm howitzers rained rounds down upon the advancing enemy battalion. Fused to spray shrapnel from air-bursts, the volleys shredded the ranks and forced the VC to take shelter in the adjacent village of An My, unable to advance any farther.

As a result of their attentiveness, Luse and his men had detected the lead battalion of a three-battalion attack force that was to initiate the Viet Cong's Tet-68 offensive against the 1st Infantry Division. Later, following a significant tactical defeat on the battlefield following their Tet offensive, the Viet Cong withdrew their seriously depleted units to regroup. Subsequently, patrols noted the significant decrease in all types of enemy movement.

One of the most unique extractions occurred in June. Having been inserted in the area referred to as the Catcher's Mitt, a four-man reconnaissance patrol under the command of Sergeant Robert P. Elsner had just left the concealment of the jungle to cross a rice paddy at night when Specialist 4's William Po Cohn, Jr., and Gerald W. Paddy both indicated they thought they had observed movement at the edge of the darkened woodline across the paddy. With a starlight scope, Elsner confirmed the presence of enemy personnel.

Caught in the open, the three men and the assistant team leader, Sergeant David M. Hill, attempted to low-crawl back to the cover and concealment of the jungle but were spotted and immediately fired on. Pinned down, Elsner radioed for gunship and artillery support. As the gunships arrived overhead, Elsner fired flares over the enemy troops while the

NVA concentrated their fires against the circling aircraft and massed their forces on the ground. Realizing that they were just moments away from being overwhelmed and annihilated, Elsner radioed that his patrol was about to be overrun.

Suddenly, an AH-1G Cobra gunship peeled off and defiantly swooped into the center of the rice paddy between the NVA and Elsner's men. Swiftly, the four patrol members seized anything attached to the aircraft that they could safely grasp. The attack helicopter proceeded to lift off with two men wrapped around the skids, one man laying on a small wing, and the fourth clinging to a rocket launcher. The incident proved to be the only Cobra extraction of the entire war .

Throughout the summer and into the fall, Company F conducted a variety of intelligence gathering and screening operations. In November, Company F was OPCON to the 1st Brigade, which was operating in one of the most hazardous areas of South Vietnam. Under the command of Captain Allen A. Lindman, the company had been tasked to observe enemy movements east of the Thi Thinh River between slices of Viet Cong occupied territory referred to as the "Trapezoid" and the Long Nguyen Secret Zone.

On 20 November, Lindman deployed four teams of six men each to observe enemy activity. Inserted between 1500 and 1530, each team reported observing enemy activity within an hour of their insertion. RT 3 was inserted in the northernmost area of the region to be reconned near the stream junction of the Suoi Ho Da and the Rach Thi Thinh. Soon after their arrival, the team was engaged by fifteen Viet Cong and subsequently extracted.

RT 5 was inserted near the center of the recon area, south of the village of Ap Bo Cang and near the Rach Thi Thanh where they spotted a company of seventy-five heavily armed Viet Cong. While they observed the first column of seventy-five soldiers, a second column of the same size passed in another direction on the other side of the patrol. In the distance, they could see dogs, chickens, and water buffalo, and hear female voices. There was no doubt in their minds that the area was heavily occupied by VC forces planning to stay. Later that evening, the team was extracted.

RT 10 was inserted along the Rach Thi Thanh. Following a skirmish with four VC, the team was extracted later that evening.

The last patrol, RT 9, was inserted in the southern portion of the recon area. This team was also extracted at dusk following an engagement with a fifteen-man VC patrol.

Later that evening, Lindman recommended against inserting any more teams within the region the following day. All four patrols had confirmed the area was saturated with VC. The 1st Brigade commander and executive officer supported his recommendation. The division intelligence section insisted, however, that two new teams should be inserted into the area to verify the reports of the previous day, which they were skeptical of.

Regardless of his misgivings, Lindman did as ordered and selected RT 4 and RT 11 for the assignment. At 0830 on 21 November, Lindman and his two team leaders conducted an overflight of the area with Chief Warrant Officer 2 David R. O'Dell, the pilot who would fly the mission. Later that day, RT 4 was inserted at 1143.

Returning to Lai Khe, O'Dell waited as the six men of RT 11 loaded and then flew them to the area reconned by RT 5 just the previous day. At 1205, the helicopter landed at the preselected field, a rice paddy dominated with heavy jungle along its borders. With the last patrol member out and the helicopter just beginning to lift, the first enemy rounds began to strike the Huey with one of them striking O'Dell in the leg. At a later inquiry, the right door gunner stated he was under the impression that the patrol did not realize it was under enemy fire yet, for as the last man off loaded, he looked back at the gunner with a puzzled expression on his face. When the gunner motioned for him to get down, the scout squatted for a few moments in the paddy then stood up to move away.

Despite his wounds and the damage inflicted on his Huey, O'Dell managed to get the craft airborne and, with both door gunners firing away, executed a sharp left turn in the bullet-riddled helicopter. Just prior to his communications being destroyed, he was able to transmit that the landing zone (LZ) had been "hot." With a stream of aviation gas gushing from his punctured fuel cell, O'Dell was able to skillfully pilot his crippled bird back to Lai Khe.

At the LZ, the team had moved from the aircraft to the nearest treeline. Upon reaching cover, the team leader proceeded to orient himself with map and compass. As he was doing so, several rocket-propelled grenades suddenly exploded within their position. Some dead and some wounded, the six team members were knocked to the ground as a platoon sized element of VC emerged from their ambush, firing, advancing, and shooting each team member as they overran the team's position.

Above the LZ flew a command helicopter carrying the brigade executive officer, Lieutenant Colonel Duddley T. Bunn, the Troop D commander, Major Robert H. Haley, and Captain Lindman. Having monitored the communications and observed the action below, the officers attempted to raise the team on the radio. All efforts proved to be unsuccessful, though. Haley ordered their helicopter closer to the ground where they were able to pick up a brief radio transmission from a team member.

"We're in contact! Get us out of here! Get us out of here!"

Unable to determine the team's exact location, Haley withheld requesting gunship support or the reinforcement of his aero-rifle platoons. Efforts to obtain a situation report (SITREP) were only met with silence as the command Huey circled the LZ attempting to establish radio or visual contact. Suddenly, a very muffled transmission was received.

"This is Eleven....They're all dead....They're all dead.... I'm dying." It would prove to be RT 11's final message.

Incredibly, there was a sole survivor. Left for dead with a bullet wound in the chest and a "double tap"—an infantry term used to indicate an execution-style shot at a wounded enemy in the back of the head—Private First Class Comyers managed to painfully crawl to the edge of the rice paddy. There, approximately five hundred yards from the insertion point, he was able to later signal a rescue helicopter with a handheld mirror.

Shortly after the incident, the division conducted an official inquiry into the disaster. Haley's position was that better radio discipline would have made the difference.

"If they had said, 'We're in contact, direction of fire is in a certain heading, we are popping smoke to identify our position location,' I could have immediately started gunship runs in the area, laying down suppressive fire, and could have started my backup slick [helicopter] into the area to extract these men." The inquiry concluded that there was no culpability for the division intelligence section, for the mission was deemed a "calculated wartime risk." The official record was to show that RT 11's demise was due to its own negligence.

Company F did not have to bear the RT 11 tragedy for long. On 1 February 1969, Company I (Ranger), 75th Infantry Regiment, was activated by the directive of the division commander, Major General Talbott. Along with the Ranger company's activation came the inactivation of Company F. As with the other activations, the men and equipment of Company F were transferred to Company I. Phonetically, the company was called India Rangers, but it was also referred to on occasion as the "Iron Rangers" in association with the brigade it supported the most, the 3rd, or Iron, Brigade.

There was also a third label attached with the unit, provided by its minority members. This alternative name was "Bro Rangers." "Bro" was not only black slang for "brother" [comrade], but it also served as the initials for the Big Red One 1st Infantry Division, in reference to the design of its shoulder patch. The Ranger company's teams were numbered 1–8 for the first platoon and 909–916 for teams of the second platoon. Combined teams were assigned double-digit number sequences.

The Ranger unit's first mission was in Support of Operation Toan Thang. The operation's objective was to clear and pacify the Binh Duong Province. The India Rangers' task was to field reconnaissance patrols into the Easter Egg, the Heart-Shaped Woods, the Iron Triangle, the Long Nguyen Secret Zone, the Mushroom, and the Trapezoid. Working extensively with the 3rd Brigade, Company I would continue to monitor NVA and VC movements within these dangerous areas of operation for the remainder of their activation.

The Rangers' close association with a traditional infantry brigade also had its drawbacks, for there was a tendency to employ the specialized reconnaissance teams in more conventional roles. One such role was to have them establish static night ambushes at predetermined sites or conduct close-in security sweeps in the vicinity of forward fire support bases. Both of these missions decreased the team's flexibility and increased their probability of being detected by a more alert enemy wary of the area around known American positions.

On 20 February 1969, eight teams were inserted to monitor enemy movements and to provide security to forward fire support bases. Team 3 was one of those teams. Positioned as an advance division outpost near Highway 13 near the boundary of Binh Long and Binh Duong Provinces and in the vicinity of Ap Bau Bang, Team 3 was located just outside Fire Support Base Thunder II. Led by Specialist 4 Raymond Cervantes, Jr., the patrol made its way through the thick jungle to the Song Be.

Nearly an hour into the mission, the point man, Specialist 4 Michael P. Cannon, heard some movement and faint coughing adjacent to the patrol. Simultaneously, the assistant team leader and trail man, Specialist 4 Daniel R. Wiggins, heard movement to the patrol's rear and soon observed the silhouette of an enemy soldier. With hand signals, Cervantes motioned for his team members to move quickly to their preselected extraction point, a marshy clearing in the Suoi Ong Bang tributary of the Song Be.

Arriving at the extraction point, the team established a hasty defensive perimeter just inside the woodline that included the emplacement of claymore mines. The team's pace man, Specialist 4 Robert D. Law, provided rear security. Despite their efforts, a VC unit had trailed the Ranger team and a brief firefight erupted as the two units clashed at the edge of the field.

While the Rangers fought a delaying action, gunships arrived overhead, strafing and rocketing the attacking enemy ranks. Having achieved a temporary lull in the battle, Cervantes had his men detonate the Claymores and withdraw into the jungle stream. Radioman Private First Class Bill G. Powell requested an immediate extraction. Surprisingly, despite the fact the unit had been compromised, their higher headquarters denied the request based on the facts that the team was no longer under fire, none were wounded, and night was quickly approaching.

As the night progressed, Cervantes led his team farther down the stream, through the dense jungle. They left the stream at a point where it emerged from the jungle and crossed an open tract of swamp. Halfway across the clearing was a small footbridge that crossed the Suoi Ong Bang. When informed of the structure, headquarters instructed the team to keep it under surveillance.

Moving to the bridge, the team established a defensive perimeter from which they observed throughout the day and into the evening of the 22nd. No activity had been observed until a little past 2000, when the Rangers spotted three VC soldiers moving on the far side toward the bridge. Two were armed with AK-47s. The third was carrying a light machinegun. Because of the VC's heightened awareness from the engagement the day prior and their proximity to an American firebase, the team was soon spotted by the three enemy soldiers who dropped to the ground and commenced firing. The Rangers responded with all weapons on automatic and the detonation to their front of three Claymores. Though wounded, all three of the VC continued to fight, throwing fragmentation and gas grenades at the Ranger position. Cervantes called in artillery and gunship support in anticipation of the arrival of enemy reinforcements.

During the initial exchange, Law moved to the right flank of the team's position to obtain a better sight picture of the prone enemy soldiers. Without warning, a grenade landed near grenadier Specialist 4 Robert A. Rossien and Powell. Unhesitatingly, Law threw himself on the grenade, shielding his teammates, and absorbing the full blast of the explosive device. The remaining Rangers killed all three of the VC soldiers and, following a search of their bodies, were safely extracted. For conduct above and beyond the call of duty, Ranger Specialist 4 Robert D. Law was posthumously awarded the Medal of Honor.

The North Vietnamese Army launched a second Tet offensive on 23 February 1969, which included attacks against the division's base installation. Tied in close to the installations, the Rangers suffered some heavy losses. In March, the Rangers were able to shift their focus to longer ranged patrols in the Trapezoid and Michelin Plantation regions. On 1 April, Company I was officially attached to the 3rd Brigade and would remain that way for the remainder of its existence in Vietnam. During May and June, the Rangers' primary missions were bomb damage assessments (BDA) of B-52 Arc-Light bombing sorties — planned carpet bombings of specified areas where everyone or everything within the area was given an almost 100 percent probability of being killed or destroyed.

From August to October, the Rangers participated in Operation Toan Thang, assisting with the emplacement of a "protective umbrella" across the eastern and northern reaches of War Zone D and Binh Duong Province. As part of this umbrella, the Rangers were heavily involved with the emplacement of sensor fields to serve as electronic screens.

In late October, the Ranger company began conducting reconnaissance operations north of Lai Khe and observed the Song Be Corridor along Highway 13 and the Long Nguyen Secret Zone. On 15 December 1969, Company I (Ranger) was alerted along with the 1st Infantry Division for redeployment to the United States. In March 1970, the Ranger company was ordered by the division commander, Brigadier General John Q. Herrion, to cease combat operations and to stand down effective 7 March. On 7 April 1970, Company I (Ranger), 75th Infantry Regiment was officially inactivated.

Company K (Ranger) 75th Infantry Regiment

4th Infantry Division

The 4th Infantry Division completed its deployment to Vietnam in September 1966. The division's area of operation was in the western Central Highlands in the vicinity of Pleiku. Their mission was to secure Vietnam's tri-border region with northern Cambodia and southern Laos. Relative to other division areas of operation, the 4th's was larger and more remote than any other in Vietnam. The geography of the region consisted of jungle-covered mountains, scrub forests, and wild grasslands. Tropical forests complete with plateaus and rolling wooded plains were bisected with numerous hunting and logging trails and seasonal streams that served the enemy well as infiltration routes.

On 1 November 1966, the division commander, Major General Arthur S. Collins, Jr., authorized a divisional Recondo program to be established at brigade and battalion level. In January 1967, division Recondo teams were fielded during Operation Sam Houston. Numerous lessons in reference to tropical mountain operations were learned from this exercise. In particular, helicopter extractions proved to be most difficult. Having to combat dense fog, low cloud ceilings, and rainy weather, the teams soon realized that the colored smoke from flares or grenades quickly dissipated in the thick haze of mist or rain. In most instances, the smoke failed to penetrate the towering double—and triple—canopied forests.

An alternative choice to smoke was the Special Forces technique of "breaking squelch." With the keying of a radio hand-mike every fifteen seconds, aviators could follow the brief signals with the aircraft's homing device to within a few hundred yards of the patrol's position. The search could then be narrowed by smoke, mirrors, or signal panels—or, in the worst case, by a quick radio confirmation that the helicopter was overhead.

Another significant lesson learned was the fact that North Vietnamese soldiers could track the Recondo units should they run across their trail. To combat this trailing, the teams learned to vary their routes, zigzagging, weaving back and forth, or even doubling back to surprise the trailing unit. Also, as a result and concurrent with Operation Sam Houston, the decision was made to implement a division sniper course. In addition, three specialized Recondo countermeasures patrols—one per brigade—were formed and trained to eliminate enemy sentries, officers, and couriers.

The concept of "Hawkeye" teams was also implemented, founded on the noted success of similar Special Forces teams. Each of these teams paired two division Recondo members with two Rhade tribesmen. Doctrinally, the Recondo teams were trained for trail watching, terrain analysis, and screening. Hawkeye teams, on the other hand, were to be employed as stay-behind forces. With innate terrain and hunting mastery, the Hawkeye teams were to observe hidden enemy facilities, vector artillery and aerial gunship support, and evade pursuit to successfully exfiltrate back to friendly lines. Eventually, the distinction between the two types of teams blurred as each became proficient with the other's tasks.

Each infantry brigade of the 4th Infantry Division was authorized a sixty-two man reconnaissance platoon. Each platoon was organized into a headquarters section, eight Recondo teams, and three Hawkeye teams. All of the platoons were fully operational in time for the division's Operation Francis Marion in early April. In June, the provisional 4th Infantry Division Recondo Detachment was authorized. Activated to supplement the brigade reconnaissance platoons, the Recondo detachment was identical to the platoons it was to assist with the exception that it had no headquarters section. Its higher headquarters was the division intelligence section.

The division's area of operation stretched the Recondo and Hawkeye team surveillance screen thin, even with the addition of the new detachment. Consequently, the division's teams routinely operated at distances far greater than those experienced by other divisional long-range reconnaissance units in Vietnam.

On 12 June 1967, a five-man reconnaissance team from the 2nd Brigade had the opportunity to feel just how lonely it could be in the tri-border region. For a number of days, the team had occupied an observation point on a mountaintop overlooking the Ia Ayun, transmitting valuable intelligence reports of the NVA traffic in the river valley below. Unknown to them, they had been detected and an NVA force had stealthily climbed the steep mountainside to within grenade range. At 2000, the NVA attacked.

The team leader, Specialist 4 Russell Oliver, quickly radioed to have his team extracted. Higher headquarters' response to Oliver was to "hold on," for it was believed the small team could hold off a company of NVA from their vantage point. Oliver's response to that suggestion was "If you wait until morning to get us out of here, there won't be anyone here." To emphasize their dire predicament, the radioman, Specialist 4 Joseph F. Camper kept his radio keyed as he was interrupted during his SITREP by the enemy's third attack wave.

As the sky darkened, Air Force C-47's lit the surrounding countryside with flares. Propeller-driven A-1E Skyraiders finally arrived to provide aerial gunfire support during the NVA's fourth assault. When queried by the forward air controller as to where the patrol wanted the close air support (CAS), Camper informed him to "Feel free to do anything!"

As the propeller-driven Skyraiders strafed and rocketed the mountainside below them, the NVA attack faltered on the edge of the summit. In response to headquarters' request about the results of the CAS, Camper's reply was to ask "Where's the ship to get us out of here?" Finally, three hours after the attack had commenced, the team was safely extracted from their position. Camper's final official action of the day was to order a concentrated barrage of 155-mm artillery against the NVA infantrymen swarming over their newly gained possession.

While reptiles were certainly abundant in the tropics of Southeast Asia, there usually was little interaction between man and beast. During Operation Francis Marion, an incident involving Staff Sergeant Charles L. McKee's team proved to be the exception to that rule. Having successfully completed their mission, McKee and his team had moved to their designated PZ for extraction and were waiting for the helicopter when a seventeen-foot python and its serpent family writhed past the stationary American patrol and made their way toward an NVA platoon that had suddenly appeared in front of the team's location just prior to the arrival of the helicopter. The team was aboard and the helicopter lifting off before any shots were fired by the NVA. McKee credited the NVA delay to the snakes, which must have made their way into the platoon's position.

The 4th Division Recondo and Hawkeye teams achieved considerable success during Operation Francis Marion. During the operation period of 6 April to 11 October, the teams completed 555 missions and made 366 sightings. Ninety NVA and VC soldiers were killed in eighty-two patrol engagements. Only one American was KIA. The reconnaissance and Hawkeye teams closed out the year by participating in Operation Mac-Arthur and completing an additional 143 patrols and reporting another 45 sightings.

Company E of the 58th Infantry (Long Range Patrol) was activated on 20 December 1967 with the 4th Division Recondo Detachment serving as its nucleus. The company was referred to as "Echo Fifty-Eight." The operational readiness of the new unit was postponed by the Viet Cong Tet-68 offensive that struck Pleiku, Kontum, and Ban Me Thout in the 4th Division's area of operation.

In January 1968, the new division commander, Major General Charles P. Stone, initiated a program with the 23rd Vietnamese Division to teach patrol techniques to its strike company members. Thirty Vietnamese soldiers were integrated into Company E to train from 23 April to 21 June. The initiative did not go over well with the Americans, for there was a definite lack of interest on the part of the South Vietnamese soldiers. A second class only contained conscripts. Following difficulties with the third class, a halt was finally called to the test in November.

A number of Company E teams operated in the rugged western mountains of Kontum Province from 24 May to 21 June in support of the 1st Brigade Task Force Mathews. Working closely with Special Forces Project Omega, the teams assisted in turning aside an NVA division advance against the Special Forces Camp Ben Het with their reconnaissance and direct B-52 bombing runs against identified targets. Their reports proved to be critical in directing thirty-nine Arc-Light sorties in front of Camp Ben Het and Camp Dak To and an additional eleven Arc-Light missions near Dak Pek.

Arc-Light missions were quite possibly the most destructive and conventionally devastating operation of the war. In September of 1968, a Company E team had the opportunity, not by choice, to see one up close and personal. Led by Specialist 4 Emory Spraggins, the three-man team was inserted close to the Laotian border just outside the beleaguered Special Forces outpost of Dak Seang. The mission was to clear a landing zone by destroying two trees that were standing in the way. It was to be a forty-eight-hour mission at most.

Moving through thick jungle, rain, and fog, the team located the field and packed high explosives in the roots of the trees. The team opted to delay the detonation until the extraction helicopter was on station. Given the number of VC in the area, the men saw no reason to draw any attention to themselves. Heavy rains prevented helicopters from using the LZ as planned for the next four days. By the sixth day, out of food and subsisting on rainwater, the team was prepared to detonate the trees when a radio transmission instructed them to clear the area immediately.

Spraggins and his two teammates, Specialist 4 Harold Thompson and Private First Class Mike Overturf moved out across a dense, sloping jungle that these team veterans called the worst terrain they'd ever been in. Crossing a swift-running jungle stream, the team was ordered to keep moving throughout the night, for a B-52 Arc-Light mission had been targeted for their area. The team members were growing too exhausted to care but the persistent yelling over the radio kept them going. To stay together and to keep pressing each other to drive on, the men tied ropes between them as they continued to fight the jungle vines, foliage, and underbrush that had torn their uniforms to shreds.

In the daylight of the next day, the three men could move no more. Collapsing on a steep hillside, they radioed that they could go no farther. Heeding headquarters' advice to take cover, the team sought refuge and cover between the roots of a six-foot-thick hardwood tree. The ground heaved, shook, and trembled as the men huddled under their ponchos while the bombs detonated in the distance.

Overturf was to recall, "The whole sky turned red. We could hear things flying over our heads."

Eight days into their patrol, the team weakly continued. Climbing to the top of another mountain, the team stumbled into a North Vietnamese bunker complex. The smell of rice was in the air and the men knew the enemy could not be far away. Spotting some tools and Vietnamese pith helmets, they loaded up with as much of the gear as they could find to serve as camouflage—given that their uniforms were in tatters—and safely made it back into the jungle without raising an alarm.

Parched, dehydrated, and delirious with hunger and fatigue, the men struggled on. Finally, Overturf looked up and spotted a head. It was an American patrol that now had the three-man team in its sights. Realizing that they were still dressed as NVA following their escape from the bunker complex, Overturf threw off the enemy helmet and began to yell, "Don't shoot! I'm a Lerp! I'm a Lerp!"

Safely linked up, the team was escorted by the friendly patrol to the forward lines of an infantry company located on a rain-drenched summit. The team's odyssey did not end here, however, for the company they had just "joined" had been unable to secure supplies and the adverse weather had grounded all helicopter flights. The company and the Lerp team would have to continue to march.

For two more days, as infantrymen began to pass out around them from lack of sleep and overwhelming fatigue of their equipment loads, the three Lerps continued to move through the rain. Finally, after a full week, the rain stopped and the team was airlifted back to Dak To, having conducted the longest division mission on record. As Spraggins noted, "Somehow, it [the record] didn't seem to matter."

Lack of experience had a significant effect on Team 28, which was inserted on 20 October near Ban Me Thuot to perform a three-day surveillance mission. Though Private First Class Dickie W. Finley was the team leader, he had little training or experience beyond his regular infantry training and one year in service. Moving through an upland plateau forest, the five-man team moved into an overnight position from where the night passed without incident.

Reconning and observing during the day, the team returned to the position it had occupied the previous evening. Around 1900, Finley radioed his platoon leader, Captain Donald E. Connerville, to report enemy activity in the area. Ordered by Connerville to relocate, Finley and his men elected to remain in their current position instead. Thirty minutes later, Finley had the radioman, Private First Class Robert E. Hamby submit a false report that the team had completed the ordered relocation.

For the next hour, the team sent a constant stream of frantic reports about enemy trails throughout their area, noises all around them, and the observation of a flashlight. Finley called for artillery support at 2030 and thirty minutes later requested an extraction in that contact had been made with the enemy. Ten minutes later, the team reported they were running low on ammunition. By 2100, Finley reported that all ammunition had been expended.

The extraction helicopter arrived soon thereafter, hovering over what the pilot thought was a deep pond but which was, in reality, a shallow pool. The five men of Team 28 bunched up around the starboard side of the aircraft, clambering to get loaded. In that the helicopter was in a hover, its oscillation made boarding the aircraft difficult. Hamby made it on by being shoved from behind, as Private First Class Bernard C. Pisarcik pulled himself onto the cabin floor.

The aircraft had been hovering for approximately three minutes when the pilot asked his door gunner, "Are we up?" Claiming later that one of the team members told the pilot to take off, the gunner replied, "I think so," to the pilot's second question of, "Is everyone on board?" Specialist 4 Gerald O. Hancock, who was halfway on board, scrambled to pull himself farther into the aircraft as it lifted from the PZ.

Pisarcik yelled to Hamby, "Where are the other two guys?" as the aircraft gained altitude. Looking out and down, Hamby saw Finley hanging from the skid. Turning to Pisarcik, Hamby yelled, "Finley's on the skid!" Peering out the door, Pisarcik saw nothing but an empty skid and trees far below. Pisarcik screamed at the pilot that he'd left two men behind at the same time the door gunner was announcing that a man had fallen from the aircraft.

Circling back, the pilot returned to a different location than the one he'd extracted the three team members from. Having exited the aircraft and noting that this was not the same LZ, the team members reboarded the Huey, telling the pilot "This is the wrong field." In response, the pilot circled the woods momentarily and then returned to Ban Me Thuot.

The following morning, an extensive ground search was initiated at dawn. The body of Specialist 4 Luther A. Ghahate, the assistant team leader, was located along the helicopter's flight path and gave testimony to the fact that the soldier had fallen from a great height. Captain Connerville located the team's night location later that afternoon, along with evidence that indicated the team had not redeployed as ordered or reported.

The division convened an official inquiry into the event. The board of inquiry concluded that the patrol panicked the night of 22 October and probably had encountered no one during their one and a half hour "firefight" with a phantom force. It was also ruled that the helicopter crew had departed improperly, not having assured that everyone was on board. While it was presumed that the team leader had fallen from the skid and most likely died as a result, Private First Class Finley remains missing in action.

Company K (Ranger), 75th Infantry Regiment was activated on 1 February 1969 under the command of Captain Reuben H. Siverling. The deactivated Company E, 58th Infantry, provided the nucleus of the unit. Known as the "Highlander" or "Killer" Rangers, the Ranger company did not operate at full authorization until the brigade reconnaissance platoons were integrated into the company. All told, the Company E reached their authorized field strength of 220 men.

Consolidation of the divisional reconnaissance assets with the Ranger company was not completed until 6 October, at which time the unit was placed OPCON to the division operations section. Administrative and logistical support was retained with the 1st Squadron, 10th Cavalry. The company had a fifty-three-man headquarters section and three field platoons. Each platoon contained a headquarters section, five five-man patrol teams and five six-man Hawkeye patrols with the sixth man being a local scout. The Ranger teams were identified with an alphanumeric of R1 through R27.

Shortly after its reorganization and consolidation, the Ranger company had an opportunity to demonstrate its capabilities. As a major battle grew in An Lao Valley, the 4th Infantry found itself having to withdraw and commit its 2nd Brigade from north of Pleiku. This displacement left a crucial stretch of Highway 19A uncovered. Anticipating that the NVA would attempt to take advantage of the situation, the division commander, Major General Pepke, deployed the Highland Rangers to screen the unsecured sector.

Twelve Ranger teams and a control headquarters staged from Special Forces Camp Plei Mrong, located near Highway 19A. The teams rotated regularly with eight of the teams always on patrol to the west of the highway along the NVA avenues of approach.

The 24th NVA Regiment began to move toward Highway 19A on 12 October. Moving east from the Chu Goll-Pa mountain region, the regiment took advantage of the adverse weather that kept the American aircraft grounded. Despite the clouds, rain, mist, and fog, the Rangers detected the regiment as it neared the highway. For four days, the Rangers tracked, harassed, and directed artillery and air strikes at the enemy columns. Supply parties were ambushed and stragglers were killed.

Having been provided the warning time he needed, Pepke ordered the 2nd Battalion, 8th Infantry Regiment (Mechanized), to Camp Plei Mrong. As the 24th NVA Regiment emerged from the mountains, this armored force met it. Defeated, the NVA regiment withdrew toward Cambodia. The detailed surveillance and persistent tactics of the Killer Rangers had paid great dividends for the division.

In mid-February 1970, the Highland Rangers found themselves a vital part of the prisoner rescue attempt, Operation Wayne Stab II. Intelligence indicated that American prisoners were being kept in an identified jungle compound. The Ranger company was consolidated and the mission launched on 16 February. As the 1st Brigade ringed the suspected area with three swift battalion-sized airmobile operations, the Rangers air-assaulted into the compound.

The attack occurred a little before noon. A brief skirmish with a small enemy force led to the release of one captive who reported that the other captives had recently been moved. It was believed that South Vietnamese staff officers of the 22nd Division had compromised the mission and informed the VC, who had broken down into small groups and left a large series of mechanical booby-traps and punji-stakes behind to hinder pursuit. And hinder they did. By evening, eleven helicopter sorties were needed to evacuate the large number of Rangers wounded by the devices.

The search widened as the Americans continued their pursuit. Teams rappelled into LZ's cleared through triple-canopy by large bombs. Scout helicopters and scout ships from the 7th Squadron, 17th Cavalry swept across the rugged terrain. An ambush by the 2nd Battalion, 35th Infantry on 19 February killed ten enemy soldiers and captured a female nurse. The Rangers were redeployed to vainly pursue the heavy blood trails of the escaped enemy. Despite all the effort to the contrary, the VC guards were able to slip through the security net with their prisoners.

On 19 March, the division attacked the enemy Base Area 226 in central Binh Dinh Province in Operation Eichelberger Black. As the enemy withdrew before the American advance, the division reduced the size of the attacking force to a single brigade. Company K's participation was also reduced accordingly to a single platoon. Unfortunately, this single platoon found it difficult to effectively screen the flanks and van of the advancing brigade.

The steep ridges and dense jungle of Base Area 226 made for difficult times. The hills were honeycombed with caves and tunnels while the trees limited the availability of landing and pick-up zones. A unique Ranger tactic was able to minimize both these difficulties. Teaming up with combat engineers of the 4th Engineer Battalion, the Company K Rangers organized and trained three joint rappelling teams. During nearly every afternoon, one of these exceptionally proficient Ranger-Engineer teams would rappel into a preselected location to clear a landing zone or to destroy a cave and tunnel complex. Their task completed, they'd be extracted the following morning. The teams were exceptionally beneficial to the brigade's missions and were continued until the operation's conclusion on 24 April.

Company K did not participate in the invasion of Cambodia on 5 May. While the division deployed in support of the cross border invasion, the Rangers of Company K remained behind to serve as an economy of force measure to secure Binh Dinh Province during the division's absence. The personnel situation continued to hamper the company's effectiveness. During the nine months from November 1969 to July 1970, the unit suffered ten KIA and forty-seven wounded. And, while 291 new recruits were received during that time, more were lost through the attrition of transfers, rotations, and emergency leaves.

As the war began to wind down for the division, Company K was redeployed to the division's main base, Camp Radcliff, to provide security as the line battalions prepared to depart. From 26 September to 10 October, Company K supported a 2nd Brigade sweep of the Tiger Mountains, operating as a conventional infantry line company. The Highland Rangers were ordered to stand down two days later on 12 October but would continue to conduct limited operations until 22 November. The Rangers were mustered for a final review on the morning of 26 November for an awards ceremony conducted by the division commander, Major General Burke. Company K (Ranger), 75th Infantry Regiment was officially inactivated on 10 December 1970.

Company L (Airborne Ranger) 75th Infantry Regiment

101st Airborne Division

The 1st Brigade of the 101st Airborne Division disembarked at Cam Ranh Bay in South Vietnam on 29 July 1965. Deployed as part of a national effort to forestall a Viet Cong insurgency victory, the brigade realized early that there was a need for better mission tailored and trained ground reconnaissance units. To overcome this deficiency, the brigade's three infantry battalions were directed to reorganize their Headquarters and Headquarters' Company (HHC) jeep recon and antitank platoons into combat reconnaissance elements. From this directive, the 1st Battalion of the 327th Infantry assembled the "Tiger Force," the 2nd Battalion of the 327th Infantry formed the "Hawks," and the 2nd Battalion of the 502nd Infantry established the "Recondos."

The Tiger Force of the 1/327 Infantry best exemplified the new combat reconnaissance teams. With their name derived from an old call sign of the jeep and antitank platoon, the Tigers, were the idea, design, and result of the personal involvement of the battalion executive officer, Major David "Hack" Hackworth, who was a highly decorated Korean War raider who had commanded the Wolfhound Raiders of the 27th Infantry Regiment and who went by the call sign "Steel Five." First Lieutenant James Gardner commanded the platoon.

The platoon was organized into long-range patrol teams that were resourced and tasked to "look for trouble." Much to their pleasure, the unit was provided a great deal of experimental and classified equipment to test during their patrols to include Starlight night observation devices (NODs) and chemical man-packed personnel detectors designated "People Sniffers." During its initial year of existence, the Tiger Force participated in a number of heavy engagements, at times sending fifteen-man patrols with as many as eight M-60 machineguns looking for enemy ambushes to blow away.

One of the Tiger Team's most interesting, and amusing, missions took place in early 1966 when a newly assigned Second Lieutenant, Dennis Foley, was directed by Hackworth to lead a fifteen-man patrol on a naval infiltration to conduct an ambush along the coastal foothills south of Phan Rang. Though technically in command by function of rank, the green lieutenant, based on the battalion executive officer's directive, was wise enough to allow his exceptionally experienced senior noncommissioned officer, Platoon Sergeant Philip Belden, to guide him. Most frustrating for the new lieutenant about to lead his first combat patrol was the fact that he had been hit with dysentery and had uncontrollable diarrhea. The young officer would soon learn that his illness would be the least of his concerns.

Following their final precombat inspection, the patrol loaded onto a two-and-a-half ton truck with a sandbagged truckbed—to minimize the effects of anti-vehicular mines—and, escorted by two gun jeeps, made its way on a long trip to a South Vietnamese naval base. Consisting of little more than a few shacks and a dock, the base was relatively empty except for a few Vietnamese sailors who looked like little boys. Two American advisors were at the port but they were not involved with the mission nor spoke the language and quickly departed upon the patrol's arrival. A Vietnamese Army interpreter scheduled to join Foley and his men never arrived.

The Americans were unable to effect a dialogue with the navy men and saw little at the "base," other than a thirty-foot-long dilapidated, motorized sampan that looked as though it had already seen its last days at sea. With little else to do, the patrol members searched for food and water, to conserve what they were carrying for the patrol. Having to settle for beer because there was no drinking water available, the men lay about in the hot sun, partaking of their Bier LaRue. The Vietnamese navy boys giggled like kids as the Americans sizzled in the sun and got a buzz from their beer.

As dusk loomed, one of the sailors approached the patrol, pointing to the men and then to the sampan. Incredulously, Foley realized that their ride had been there all along. The Americans boarded the boat and observed the four-man crew make ready for sea, without performing a single pre-inspection of the vessel. An abundance of squawking and crazed hand gestures finally resulted in the Americans finding locations on the cramped vessel that seemed not to be in the way of the crew.

The craft, which they nicknamed the *Asian Queen*, set sail with two bamboo boats tied to a line in trail. The little boats would serve as the means of delivery to the beach once they arrived offshore, just outside of the breakers. The primary boat was powered by a little engine that appeared as though it had once been in a jeep or a generator. It had no muffler and the exhaust consisted of a hole in the manifold that emitted sparks and a great deal of noise. To keep the engine from dying, the crew had to routinely rev it up, which resulted in a spectacular display of bright red, blue, and yellow flame. Light and noise discipline obviously meant very little to the sailors.

The vessel bobbed, weaved, and pitched as it struggled to make its way through the surf to the calmer open water beyond. The Americans labored to hold on, finding little to grab on the deck of the craft. The helmsman, who weighed no more than ninety pounds, fought with the well-worn tiller that was connected to the rudder to keep the boat pointed into the waves. As a series of large swells smacked the boat and moved it sideways, the helmsman nearly found himself flung off the deck and into the sea.

While the sea was slapping the helmsman around, it was also getting the best of Foley and his men; who should have forgone the beer. Seasickness had grown rampant among them and within thirty minutes, nearly all of the men had vomited over the side.

Once past the rough surf of the breakwaters, the ride grew a bit smoother. The sun had settled and the boat was slowly making its way along when three of the crew began to make issue of something out to sea. Before any of the patrol members could stop him, one of the Vietnamese sailors pulled out a flashlight and focused a strong beam of light at an object approximately twenty-five meters off port. It was the boat's tiller. It had fallen off the boat's little deckhouse where one of the sailors had placed it during his rest.

With no other way to steer the vessel, someone needed to retrieve the tiller and the sailors were arguing among themselves as to who that would be. Finally one of the sailors stripped and dove into the black water. Cheered on by the whistles, cheers, and screams of encouragement from the other crewmembers, the sailor returned to the side of the boat with the six-foot tiller in tow. All Foley and his men could do most probably was look at each other and think to themselves, "Can you say 'Compromised'?"

As the sailors somehow navigated to the debarkation point, the patrol pulled the two small boats in and prepared to board them. As fate would have it, and despite all the adversity they'd faced, lady luck was still not on their side. While lowering a 60-mm mortar base plate from the deck of the larger vessel into the thin-skinned craft below, one of the team members lost his grip on the lowering rope with a pitch of the sampan. The heavy metal base punched a hole through the bottom of the bamboo boat and it quickly sank.

At nearly the same moment, the second boat was preparing to meet a similar fate. An M-60 machine-gunner had just stepped into the one remaining craft when he lost his balance. Struggling to maintain his footing, the bipod of the weapon ripped a gouge in the thin material. Within a minute, the second of the two craft was history, making its way to the floor of the South China Sea.

The loss of the two boats prompted another vigorous round of jabbering and hand waving from the Vietnamese crew as they tried to figure out what to do next. Finally, one of them indicated that they would take the sampan through the waves to land the patrol on the beach. As the boat putt-putted its way into the surf, the seas grew rougher and the men grew sicker. Foley, hammered with dysentery, diarrhea, seasickness, and still vomiting over the side, was nearly looking forward to being put out of his misery by any VC they might encounter once they hit the beach.

As the craft neared the beach, the swells gave way to waves that crashed upon the shore in a turbulent and violent churning of spray and foam. With the surf pounding and the noise of the vessel's unmuffled engine rising above the din of it all, the members of the Tiger Team clung for dear life to anything they could grasp. Suddenly, the hull of the *Asian Queen* ground into the sandy bottom of the beach, bringing the little boat to an abrupt halt. Those on the bow were flung into the surf, as others rolled off the deck, over the side. As the remaining men on board scrambled to secure their gear, a large wave lifted the rear of the beached boat as it crashed across the open deck flinging the remainder of the crew into the water.

Miraculously, there were no enemy waiting in the treeline of the beach and the men were able to assemble as the little boat's crew fought against the waves to successfully wrestle their stranded vessel, with much more additional noise, from the coast's grip. Soaked, covered with sand, and already exhausted, Foley and his men moved to a point within the treeline where Belden would take an inventory of their equipment losses.

As Foley staggered into the defensive perimeter of the team, he incredulously realized that they had just completed the first, and "easiest," leg of their mission. Now, it was time to find Charlie. Welcome to Vietnam and the world of the long-range reconnaissance patrol.

The Tiger Team's commander, First Lieutenant James Gardner, who was due to be reassigned within a few days because of an impending promotion, was killed in action shortly after the successful return of Foley and his men from their amphibious odyssey. The fateful day was 7 February 1966 and the Tigers were the lead element for Task Force Hackworth, a slice of the battalion that was conducting a search and destroy mission in the vicinity of the city of Thy Hoa at a village called My Canh II. Enemy contact had already been made by other American elements in the area of operation.

Moving across an open field against what was initially believed to be no more than a squad-sized element, the Tigers suddenly found themselves under a withering hail of automatic weapons fire. Over a dozen of the Tigers fell as they were left with no other alternative than to charge straight ahead, into the machinegun nests.

Having penetrated the enemy's perimeter, the small group of survivors gathered in a communications trench, caught in the vicious crossfire of machinegun fire from a minimum of three bunkers. Unknowingly, they had stumbled into the perimeter of a heavily armed, well equipped, and dug-in North Vietnamese Army battalion, a major element of the elite 95th NVA Regiment. Now it was up to the Tigers to get themselves out of their predicament so Hackworth could call in artillery, gunships, and close-air support to pulverize the enemy positions.

Having secured Foley's two fragmentation grenades to add to his own, Gardner rose to his feet without another word and began to run up the trench toward the first enemy bunker scarcely fifty meters away. With M-16 rounds and profanities blazing from his weapon and his lips, the lieutenant charged as the concentrated enemy fire kicked up mud, dirt, and debris all about him. Repeatedly struck, Gardner heroically continued to rise to his feet, first destroying one bunker with a grenade, then a second bunker, despite having sustained additional wounds from one of his own grenades being tossed back at him. The third bunker cut him down moments after the second one was eliminated.

Unknown to many at the time, the young lieutenant had been killed on his birthday. For conduct above and beyond the call of duty, First

Lieutenant James Gardner was posthumously awarded the Medal of Honor.

With the intense pressure of the fires mitigated for the moment, Foley, now the Tigers' commander, coordinated with Hackworth the fire support necessary for a breakout back to their lines. Bent over and running as quickly as their exhausted bodies would allow them, the Tigers made their way along the communications trench and broke across the field. Despite the heavy fire directed at them from the flanks and rear, all of the surviving men attempting the breakout made it back.

Losses had been exceptionally heavy, though, for the Tigers—nearly all of the men were casualties, either having been killed or wounded. Amazingly, shortly after their near annihilation, the team was back on the line and conducting patrols later that evening.

In need of a reconnaissance element at higher headquarters, the brigade commander, Brigadier General James S. Timoth authorized the formation of a long-range reconnaissance patrol (LRRP) platoon at Bear Cat-Bien Hoa in December 1965. Based on their wide-ranging activities throughout Vietnam, they were referred to as the "Reconnaissance Nomads" and were organized into nine six-man teams. The platoon was assigned in January 1966 to the Thy Hoa region in support of Operation Harrison. In early April, the brigade deployed south along the coast to Phan Thiet. Designated as Operation Austin, the movement assigned the Nomads the mission of securing small landing zones for subsequent infantry battalion air assaults with an on-order mission of performing reconnaissance tasks ahead of the battalions once deployed.

In support of this operation, there occurred a rather humorous event that other units tried to claim as their own. As one of the Nomad teams was conducting a reconnaissance, attempting to locate a reported Viet Cong headquarters, it stumbled across an enemy training camp with a class in session. Surprised by the Americans, the class quickly scattered with some assistance from the LRRP team. Gathering potential intelligence material, the team sent back the class lecture placards for translation. As events would show, the subject matter of the class that had been surprised was "Beware of American Long Range Patrols."

With the conclusion of Operation Austin and following a small respite, the LRRP platoon moved west into Kontum Province in support of Operation Hawthorne. Their patrols assisted with the identification and location of the 24th NVA Regiment, which was pounded by B-52 bomber raids and infantry battalion air-assaults. Following Operation Hawthorne, the Nomads patrolled Phu Yen Province and returned to Phan Rang in February 1967.

The next two months found the LRRP actively in support of Operation Farragut throughout Lam Don, Ninh Thuan, and Binh Thuan Provinces. On 30 March, they reconsolidated for the commencement of Operation Summerall in Khanh Hoa Province. With the conclusion of Operation Summerall on 29 April, the Nomads redeployed to Quang Ngai Province, where they not only conducted their reconnaissance missions, but they also successfully planned and executed two airmobile raids to capture specific enemy personnel in the Song Ve Valley.

Early July 1967 found the platoon deployed in a more conventional infantry role occupying blocking positions in the vicinity of Route 1 between Sa Huynh and Dien Truong as combat engineers swept the highway for mines and obstacles. Upon completion of this mission, the Nomads returned to what they did best and conducted reconnaissance patrols until the end of August in Quang Ngail and Quang Tin Provinces. In September, the platoon was ordered back to Phan Rang in preparation for the activation of Field Force patrol company, Company E (Long Range Patrol), 20th Infantry (Airborne), of which the Nomads would form the nucleus.

With the Nomads no longer assigned to the airborne brigade and the bulk of the 101st Airborne Division soon to deploy to Vietnam, the division commander, Major General Olinto M. Barsanti, had a problem. His solution was to authorize the activation of a new provisional Long Range Patrol Company created from the staff of the division's home station Fort Campbell Recondo School. Following an intensive training cycle for select teams involving Ranger School instruction, Australian Special Air Service instruction, and swamp-conditioning patrols with the 9th Infantry Division in the Mekong Delta, the fifty-man unit finally found itself consolidated late December in Vietnam.

The Department of the Army authorized the 101st to officially activate on 10 January 1968 a 118-man parachute recon company. Formally designated Company F (Long Range Patrol), 58th Infantry (Airborne), the "Screaming Eagle Patrollers" was organized at Bien Hoa airbase. The former Fort Campbell Recondo School cadre formed the nucleus of the new command but, from the start, Company F was known as a "hard luck" outfit, through no fault of their own. Having lost the 1st Brigade's LRRP Platoon to the Field Force, there were few combat-experienced men to fill the new company's slots. In light of this fact, the company was initially assigned to the outlying provincial capital of Song Be to serve as traditional infantry security.

The company began to redeploy by sections on 21 January from Song Be to Bien Hoa, from where it would be airlifted to rejoin the division in

northern South Vietnam. The company found itself split between Song Be
and Bien Hoa when the Viet Cong Tet-68 offensive was launched. Company F quickly found itself enmeshed in major engagements at both city
locations.

After the Tet offensive was defeated, the company was finally airlifted and reconsolidated in the I Corps Tactical Zone. Unfortunately,
even this redeployment did not provide them the opportunity to initiate
the necessary reconnaissance training they required for the commanding
general quickly assigned them the mission of securing the 101st's new
base camp outside the city of Hue, Camp Eagle. For the next two months,
the company's morale continued to sag as they conducted their mundane
taskings under adverse weather conditions with inadequate support.

Their fortunes began to change in May when the company was
released from its security mission and assigned to the division intelligence section. The first reconnaissance patrol by the company finally
occurred on 4 May with the insertion of a six-man team under the leadership of Lieutenant John W. Gay, Jr., in support of Fire Support Base Birmingham. The patrol only lasted two hours, though, for they were
extracted soon after killing three North Vietnamese soldiers.

The number of patrols gradually grew, as did the length and duration, until they were patrolling as far west as the A Shau Valley on the
Laotian border. In June, a platoon from the elite *H__-Báo,* "Black Pan-
ther," strike company of the South Vietnamese 1st Division was attached
to the American LRP Company. After a weeklong familiarization program, two of the Vietnamese scouts were joined with four American
LRPs to create a joint team. Six teams, in total, were so organized.

The combination of American and South Vietnamese scouts resulted
in some very successful missions, including one of the very first under
the leadership of Staff Sergeant James M. Johnson. Inserted in the vicinity
of Song Be River, Johnson and his five team members reconnoitered the
river until they ran across a well-used, but hidden, trail. Further explora-
tion revealed that the trail was part of a larger network that branched off.
Each branch ended at a large tree overhanging the river from where bamboo log rafts could be loaded. In essence, they had discovered an enemy
river port.

The patrol continued to follow the main trail as it made its way up a
steeply inclined hill. Making their way up the hill by grasping on to boulders and vines, the patrol observed a hut located on top of the hill. Fortunately, it was empty, for a further study of the structure led to the
discovery that a lower level had been dug below the hut, complete with

firing ports that dominated the trail they had just climbed. Another similar hut was located farther along the ridge.

The patrol continued beyond the hut to find a deserted North Vietnamese camp with another thirty huts. The men soon realized that the camp had not been deserted very long, for they found damp enemy uniforms hanging over vine clotheslines. Quickly withdrawing from the area, Johnson radioed in a report of their discoveries. Some returning NVA soldiers spotted Johnson and two of his men when they attempted to observe the camp from a different direction.

Following a brief exchange of fire, Johnson and the patrol pulled back into the brush as NVA soldiers rapidly began to overrun the area looking for the interlopers. On the radio, Johnson requested fire support and an extraction. Within minutes, two Cobras were overhead pinning the enemy soldiers down with mini-gun and rocket fire. With the appearance of Air Force fighter-bombers, Johnson directed them to place their napalm canisters along both sides of the trail leading into the camp. With the heat of the flames on their backs and the screams of the dying and burning enemy in their ears, the six men raced to their extraction point to be safely lifted out.

Despite successes such as Johnson's patrol, the joint venture between the American and Vietnamese armies was canceled on 19 July when the Vietnamese division commander demanded the return of his scouts. The company continued to have problems as their new company commander, Captain James G. Shepard, stepped on an antipersonnel mine just three days after assuming command and had to be medically evacuated. On 3 October, the operational control of the reconnaissance company was transferred to the 2nd Squadron, 17th Cavalry, which immediately shifted the emphasis from passive reconnaissance to more active combat scouting.

With this shift in emphasis, though, the casualties began to mount. On 19 November, the company suffered a catastrophic engagement. On that day, one of its twelve-man patrols initiated an ambush, killing nine of ten members of the targeted North Vietnamese patrol, with the lone survivor managing to escape the kill zone. Unknown to the patrol, while they were searching the bodies of the dead for any intelligence information, the survivor was linking up with reinforcements.

Having completed their search, the American patrol was making its way to the extraction point when the point man was engaged by heavy enemy fire and killed. Quickly realizing that they were outnumbered, the patrol formed a hasty defensive perimeter and returned fire. In response, the North Vietnamese detonated a directional mine against the compact defensive circle. Four men were killed, seven wounded.

With every team member either dead or wounded, the team's annihilation seemed certain unless they were immediately reinforced. Responding to the encircled team's desperate calls for assistance were two of Company F's teams and the aero-rifle platoon of the 2nd Squadron. Arriving in time to prevent the enemy from overrunning the badly mauled unit, the reinforcements were able to assist with the extraction of the patrol but only at the cost of an additional thirteen Americans seriously wounded.

Subsequently known as the "Black November" mission, the incident only added to the company's bad luck reputation. Worse yet was the fact that having just recently been assigned to the cavalry, where the terminology for company was troop, Company F soon became know as "F Troop." This proved to be an embarrassing and humiliating moniker for the company soldiers, for "F Troop" was the title of a popular 1967 situation comedy that depicted a comical, ridiculous, and undisciplined horse cavalry company in the old American West of the 1870s. Overall, F Company performed 124 long-range patrols with fifty-four sightings and a total of sixty-two confirmed NVA and VC killed.

The activation of the 75th Infantry Regiment Companies (Ranger) could not have happened at a more auspicious moment for the men of Company F. With the activation of Company L (Airborne Ranger) and the deactivation of Company F, 58th Infantry on 1 February, the title of F Troop was a thing of the past. With the actual activation ceremony occurring at Camp Eagle on 13 February 1969, the new unit went by either "Lima" or "Airborne Eagle" Rangers. The company maintained the designation of "airborne" even though the division was no longer on jump status and had been redesignated as "Air Assault." Within the unit, teams were designated after automobiles, countries, and cities. While the 2nd Squadron, 17th Cavalry, supplied administrative and tactical support, the company received its missions from the division intelligence section.

In May 1969, the new division commander, Major General John M. Wright, Jr., designated a divisional reconnaissance zone adjacent to the Laotian border. The zone's intent was to serve as a buffer between enemy enclaves in Laos and the populated regions of coastal Vietnam. For the remainder of their service in the war, the Airborne Eagle Rangers would conduct a significant number of patrols within this designated region.

Operations within this zone proved to be challenging from a number of different perspectives. Geographically, landing and pick-up zones were usually covered with elephant grass eight to twelve feet tall. Sometimes the height of the grass would prove to be so deceptive that helicopters would hover too high during an insertion, causing Rangers to mistakenly jump eighteen to twenty feet to the ground, resulting in some serious injuries.

The enemy was also a challenge beyond the normal difficulties associated with them. Aware of the presence of American reconnaissance teams as a result of increased air and radio traffic, the North Vietnamese Army would usually deploy counter reconnaissance groups to seek out and engage the clandestine Rangers. Weather, also, seriously impacted on operations, especially between November and January during the monsoon season.

In November, the Rangers assigned NVA turncoat Kit Carson Scouts to their teams to enhance the unit's overall capability. In January 1970, the company's focus was shifted for the month from the reconnaissance zone to the Da Krong Valley and the She Sanh plain. In May, the operations tempo was increased in an effort to determine the degree of buildup of fresh NVA forces and patrols were launched deep into the jungles of Ruong Ruong Valley. The month of July was dominated by a number of heavy engagements, one of which resulted in six of the eleven team members being wounded. The North Vietnamese fared much worse, though, for they lost an entire platoon to aerial gunships in the exchange.

An additional resource made available to the division intelligence section and the Eagle Rangers were an array of elaborate electronic sensor devices. In that the sensors in the reconnaissance zone were rather remote, Air Force aircraft had to be relied on to relay the transmissions. The employment of these devices assisted with a prolonged reconnaissance campaign by the Rangers from August to December in the Ruong Ruong, Spear, and A Shau Valleys.

Monsoons seriously impacted on Ranger operations from mid-November to January 1971. In February, the Lima Rangers were once again focused on the reconnaissance zone to observe any attempt by the enemy to move against South Vietnamese forces during their Operation Lam Son 719 invasion of Laos. A month later, the Rangers shifted emphasis to harass the North Vietnamese unit that had overrun Fire Support Base Ripcord.

Another shift in focus led to a disastrous engagement for the Rangers on 23 April 1971, when the six-man Ranger team, Cubs, was inserted into the eastern rim of the A Shau Valley. Emplaced to establish a ground radio relay for another team's raid on an enemy-held bridge, the Cubs had mistakenly been inserted in a landing zone that had just been used a few days previously for a false insertion. With enemy attention having already been drawn earlier to the area, the Ranger team's arrival was immediately compromised. Before the Americans could elude the fires, team leader Specialist 4 Marvin A. Duren was hit twice. Carrying their wounded teammate to a field located on the spur of nearby Hill 809, the Rangers radioed for a medical evacuation.

Two 17th Cavalry helicopters were the first to respond. Both aircraft were hit by heavy weapons fire as they attempted to land at the field. One of the Hueys, carrying a Ranger team leader, Staff Sergeant William R. Vodden, was riddled with gunfire and crashed on the ridge. The bird's commander, Captain William Cullum, was killed. Captain Lewis J. Speidel, the pilot, was badly burned. The crew chief and door gunner, Private First Class Clarence D. Allen and Specialist 4 Brian H. Plahn, were seriously wounded. The second Huey, while also seriously hit, was able to maintain flight to the valley floor where it was forced down and its crew safely rescued.

At the site of the first crash, Vodden, relatively unwounded, was able to extract himself from the wreckage of the helicopter and assume control of the Ranger team on the ground. Looking back at the downed aircraft, Vodden observed Plahn staggering across the open field. When the door gunner collapsed in the open, Vodden directed his men to provide covering fire as he ran to Plahn's side. Reaching the injured crewman and attempting to stand up with him, Vodden was shot in the leg and knocked down the ridge.

A medical evacuation helicopter flown by Warrant Officer 1 Frederick Behrens of the 326th Medical Battalion was able to land unopposed to extract Plahn and the wounded Duren. The pilot bravely returned to the field to conduct a night extraction around 2000. The five remaining Rangers of the team scrambled on board but before the Huey could begin to lift off a concentrated volley of heavy weapons fire tore through the thin-skinned aircraft. Ranger Specialist 4 Johnnie Sly and crew chief Specialist 5 Michael Bunner were instantly killed as the destroyed UH-1 settled to the ground. Swiftly, the survivors raced for the treeline, where they established a small defensive perimeter to wait out the darkness.

Dawn of the next morning arrived with Cobra gunships overhead placing suppressive fires into the forest surrounding the open field. Unfortunately, the gunships initially believed that the survivors were within the destroyed aircraft in the field. Consequently, they were firing all along the perimeter of the woods where their rounds accidentally mortally wounded the assistant crew chief, Specialist 4 David P. Medina. Seeking to elude the friendly fire, the group broke from its concealed position and made for the downed Medevac helicopter. A trio of men, Lieutenant Roger Madison and two Rangers, Sergeant Fred W. Karnes and Specialist 4 Steven N. MacAlpine were pinned down separately in the field when they tried to retrieve a radio.

The day progressively worsened as additional reinforcements attempted to extract the trapped survivors. A six-man Ranger team led by the Ranger company Commander, Captain David H. Ohle, and elements of the 17th Cavalry's Troop D attempted to reach the site by climbing the ridge. Intense fire, though, prevented much maneuvering. To make matters worse, NVA snipers were firing from concealed positions in the trees at the survivors trapped in the open field. The medic, Specialist 5 Robert F. Speer, was killed. Behrens was hit in an arm and both legs while Ranger Private First Class Issako F. Malo was shot through the hip.

About the only bit of good that occurred on the hill that day for the Americans was a sprint by Ranger Private First Class James A. Champion. Braving enemy fire, the Ranger safely made it to the site of the first downed Huey to find Speidel and Allen both wounded but alive. Champion remained with the men to protect them through the night.

As darkness descended, the three men trapped in the open in the field, Madison, Karnes, and MacAlpine, were able to dodge a hail of bullets as they scrambled from the field and made their way through the woods to link up with the stalled reaction force and Captain Ohle. While the three men briefed Ohle, Behrens and Malo were painfully trying to drag themselves out of the open and into some cover and concealment on the western side of the landing zone. Behrens was unable to keep the same pace because of the more serious extent of his wounds and soon lost contact with Malo, who crawled ahead and was never seen nor heard from again.

Malo was not the only man to disappear during this engagement. Daybreak of the third day, 25 April, found Speidel and Allen still alive but in desperate need of water. Champion informed Allen that he would look for water. These were the last words spoken by the Ranger. Moving from the wreckage of the downed Huey to the edge of the ridge, Champion suffered the same mysterious fate that befell Malo for he was, also, never seen again.

Ohle and the reaction force finally broke through the enemy's resistance around noon and advanced across the landing zone. As they swept across the field, they located Behrens, seriously injured but still alive. Vodden was also discovered alive, disabled with his wounded and fractured leg on the slope of the ridge. Speidel and Allen were also secured. Overall, the mission resulted in five American dead, two missing in action, six wounded, and the loss of three UH-1 Huey helicopters.

The 101st received orders to prepare for its redeployment to the United States in mid-July 1971. As the division prepared to stand down, the Rangers were kept active, averaging nearly twenty reconnaissance missions a month from July through October to prevent any surprise attacks as the division reduced its scope of operations. The Airborne Eagle Rangers received their stand-down orders on 24 November, at which time they ceased combat operations. Of the company's eighty-eight personnel, many were reassigned to the 1st Cavalry Division Rangers who were still to remain in country. Finally, on 25 December 1971, Company L (Airborne Ranger), 75th Infantry Regiment, was officially deactivated.

Company M (Ranger) 75th Infantry Regiment

199th Infantry Brigade

The 199th Infantry Brigade, the "Redcatchers," arrived in Vietnam in December 1966 and were assigned the task of defending the east region of Saigon from Long Binh. Having no organic long-range patrol assets, the brigade was allowed to siphon sixty-one select personnel from the II Field Force's Company F (LRP), 51st Infantry Regiment, to form on 20 December 1967 the nucleus of its own 71st Infantry Detachment (Long Range Patrol).

The detachment was declared fully operational a month later, just at the start of the Tet-68 offensive. For four months, the detachment conducted ambush and reconnaissance operations in the Long Binh and Bien Hoa localities. With the conclusion of the Tet campaign by the end of May, the 199th Infantry Brigade and the 71st Infantry Detachment were redeployed to secure an extensive marshland region, referred to as the "Pineapple" plantation, southwest of Saigon. Based at "Horseshoe Bend," the detachment routinely ran patrols through the elephant grass clearings and rice paddies.

The detachment conducted operations in this region for over a year, during which it was reorganized into a Ranger company by the end of January 1969. Company M (Ranger), 75th Infantry Regiment was formally activated on 1 February. Known either as the Mike or Redcatcher Rangers, the company worked in close coordination with Troop D of the 17th Cavalry.

The new company was relocated to Fire Support Base Blackhorse in Long Khanh Province northeast of Saigon. The region encompassed sparsely populated rubber plantations, vast jungles, and the hardened, well-trained, highly disciplined, and more professional enemy soldiers of the 33rd NVA Regiment and the 274th VC Regiment. The Rangers launched a campaign along the Dong Nai and Lga Nga Rivers and in the rain forests north of Dinh Quan and northeast of Trang Bom to locate the NVA and VC strong points, supply bases, and infiltration routes.

Operations against enemy base camps were not without their perils. During the second day of a patrol led by Sergeant David Reeser's Team Bravo in September 1969 in the vicinity of the Dong Nai River, the Rangers located a dozen camouflaged bunkers in a lush tropical forest. Moving his team 300 yards from the objective, Reeser ordered Specialist 4 Lou Garland to climb a tree to observe and adjust fires as the sergeant prepared to call in an artillery strike.

No sooner had Garland climbed the tree than he abruptly scampered back down to report to his teammates that a group of twenty enemy soldiers was headed in their direction. Quickly setting a hasty ambush of Claymore mines, the team moved back into a covered and concealed position to await the enemy's arrival.

The ambush was initiated with the detonation of the Claymore mines, which were instantly followed by M-16 rifle and M79 grenade launcher fires. Initially repelled, the surprised enemy withdrew, established a base of fire with their machineguns, and began to maneuver against the Ranger team. Close air support arrived in the form of an OV-10 Bronco observation aircraft and F-100 fighter-bombers. Reeser tossed a smoke grenade to identify their position while the Bronco flew low, taking small arms fire, to identify the objectives for the fighter-bombers. As enemy reinforcements attempted to move forward, the F-100s and subsequently arriving Cobra gunships bombed, rocketed, and strafed the area.

The engagement lasted three hours as the Rangers defended their position and the air cover pounded the area around them. Out of ammunition and smoke grenades to mark their location, the embattled team was resupplied with a fresh case of 5.56-mm ammunition for their M-16s dropped by a light observation helicopter that courageously skimmed the treetops against enemy fire. The resupply and overwhelming air support eventually forced the enemy to withdraw and allow for the extraction of the Ranger team.

The Ranger campaign against the 33rd and 274th Regiments continued unabated. By early February 1970, the Rangers had interdicted such a vast number of supply routes that the Viet Cong were reduced to eating roots and bananas. The NVA regulars of the 33rd withdrew altogether from the Long Khanh Province. Despite their withdrawal from the province, though, the 33rd NVA Regiment was hounded by the Mike Rangers into Binh Thy Province.

In mid-July, the Redcatcher Rangers' base of operations moved to Fire Support Base Mace in Binh Tuy Province. Prepared to pursue the NVA deeper into their territory, the Rangers were forced to cease combat operations on 9 September to commence stand-down procedures. On 12 October 1970, Company M (Ranger), 75th Infantry Regiment was officially inactivated.

Company N (Airborne Ranger) 75th Infantry Regiment

173rd Airborne Brigade

The first major U.S. Army unit to deploy to Vietnam was the 173rd Airborne Brigade on 5 May 1965. The brigade's initial reconnaissance resources were motorized jeep and aero-scout platoons of Troop E (Airborne) of the 17th Cavalry Regiment. It was not until nearly one year later on 25 April 1966 that the brigade commander, Brigadier General Paul F. Smith, ordered the creation of a provisional brigade Long Range Reconnaissance Patrol (LRRP) platoon with a total of nine six-man reconnaissance teams, which was attached to Troop E.

The team's missions were purely reconnaissance in nature. In August, the supported Operation Toledo led to Gia Ray in Phuoc Tuy Province and Operation Waco in November in upper Bien Hoa Province. In January 1967, the LRRPs conducted bomb damage assessments (BDA) in support of Operation Cedar Falls in the Iron Triangle. During this period, the teams also began to expand on their missions as they searched tunnels and conducted night ambushes.

Though airborne-qualified, no LRRP team participated in the brigade's sole combat jump of the Vietnam war on 22 February during Operation Junction City. While some individual team members were able to obtain credit for a jump, pathfinders and not the reconnaissance platoon performed the drop zone duties. In June, the brigade shifted its area of operation and focused in the Central Highlands, assisting the 4th Infantry Division during Operation Greeley.

Not all reconnaissance members received the ultimate recognition that they so richly deserved. On 17 August, Staff Sergeant Charles J. Holland and his team were inserted to conduct a trail surveillance mission. With no observations on the first day, Holland moved to another point on day two to watch a trail intersection. Around noon, several groups of enemy soldiers were observed moving along the main trail.

As Holland was coordinating by radio for an artillery strike, the team's rear security man, Specialist 4 Robert E. Brooks, quietly signaled to the team that he heard movement to their rear. Before they could move, an attack was initiated against the Americans with heavy volumes of enemy fire from three different directions. Brooks was wounded during the initial burst of fire, as was Specialist 4 James Gowen, who suffered a head wound. Holland directed Sergeant Chester A. McDonald to lead the team to the base of the hill while the team leader covered the detachment's rear.

Reaching the bottom of the hill with no further losses, the team was soon rejoined by Holland. Though the enemy had temporarily ceased maneuvering to develop the situation, they still continued to fire. The team was in a serious predicament, for the radioman had been unable to retrieve his radio prior to their withdrawal.

Holland then proceeded to calmly order McDonald to move to an extraction point while he remained behind to divert the enemy's attention from the main group. As the team raced across an open grassy field, their leader, Staff Sergeant Holland, charged up the hill toward the team's original position, firing his weapon.

Holland's diversion proved to be enough. The team made it to another ridge where they were able to signal a helicopter for extraction with the use of a smoke grenade, only forty-five minutes after the initial contact. A sweep of the area the following day located the team leader's body. With his equipment partly cut off, numerous wounds inflicted, and mangled vegetation all around, it was determined that Holland had made a heroic stand before being killed in a hand-to-hand struggle. Staff Sergeant Holland's courage and personal sacrifice for his team should certainly have warranted the posthumous awarding of the Medal of Honor.

In October 1967, at the directive of the MACV commander, General William C. Westmoreland, the platoon was manned to 229 hand-picked paratroopers and reassigned as Company F, 51st Infantry in support of II Field Force Vietnam. As a result, the brigade needed to create a new provisional reconnaissance platoon from scratch. Though not fully reconstructed or properly trained, the new LRRP platoon initiated operations in the Dak To region on 12 November with eight missions and five enemy killed by direct fire. Interestingly enough, the platoon's intelligence haul for the day proved to be very considerable. So much so, that it was awarded the Presidential Unit Citation for its actions that day.

Effective 20 December 1967, the brigade received authorization to organize the 74th Infantry Detachment (Airborne Long Range Patrol) with two officers and fifty-nine enlisted assigned. Not actually activated until 5 February 1968, the detachment became known as the Cochise Raiders to commemorate their nearly exclusive use in Operation Cochise.

Headquartered near Bong Son at Landing Zone English, the Raiders were initially fielded mixed teams of American paratroopers from the brigade and South Vietnamese scouts from the 22nd Division. To help support the 173rd's reconnaissance mission requirements, Company E (Long Range Patrol), 20th Infantry) from I Field Force Vietnam conducted patrols in the An Khe and Tuy Hoa Phu Hiep regions thus allowing the Raiders to focus on their counterinsurgency campaign in Binh Dinh Province as part of Operation Cochise.

The Raiders' aggressive style resulted in a high number of field losses. During one such patrol on the morning of 13 November 1968, the five-man Team D, led by Staff Sergeant Laszlo Rabel, was established in a defensive perimeter on the steep slope of a wooded mountainside overwatching the Nuoi Luong River. Hearing the sounds of enemy movement, Private First Class Arthur F. Bell signaled Sergeant Cameron T. McAllister a warning while the radioman, Specialist 4 Paul L. Desmond, was shaken by Specialist 4 Stephen Fryer from underneath his poncho where he was monitoring the PRC-25.

As the men tensely waited, the jungle grew very quiet. When queried, Fryer indicated that he had seen one enemy soldier but it appeared as though he had left the area. Rabel and McAllister decided to check out the sheer drop-off to their front. Rabel began to move, ducking under a tree limb, when a grenade bounced into the tight, clustered perimeter striking a rock. Unhesitatingly, Rabel immediately pounced on the grenade, smothering its detonation and shielding his teammates from injury or death with his own body. Mortally wounded, Rabel rolled downhill.

The other team members sprang into action, detonating their emplaced Claymore mines. They then recovered the dying sergeant's body and successfully broke contact prior to reaching their extraction point. The sergeant never regained consciousness and died eight hours later. For conduct above and beyond the call of duty, Ranger Staff Sergeant Laszlo Rabel was posthumously awarded the Medal of Honor.

On 1 February 1969, the 74th Infantry Detachment was inactivated and incorporated into the activation of Company N (Airborne Ranger),

75th Infantry Regiment. The assignment of 75th Infantry led to some confusion within the brigade for there was, in addition to the Rangers, a combat tracker dog platoon with the 75th Infantry designation. To add further confusion, I Field Force required the brigade to render personnel and equipment support to its Company C (Ranger) corps level unit.

By 9 February, Company N, though only maintained at its former detachment level size of sixty-one soldiers, was declared fully operational and deployed in advance of the anticipated Tet-69 offensive in Binh Dinh Province. Inserted into eight different regions, the Rangers conducted over one hundred reconnaissance missions, with 134 enemy sightings. While the missions only resulted in thirty-four NVA killed by direct fire, the Rangers were instrumental in directing indirect fires and for preventing the enemy from massing forces to attack urban populations within Binh Dinh Province. By 26 March, the campaign against the NVA was complete.

For the rest of its wartime service, Company N remained in northern Binh Dinh Province, primarily conducting reconnaissance missions. In support of Operation Washington Green for over one year from November 1969 to December 1970, the company was expanded to a full company complement of 128 Rangers to meet mission requirements. The additional personnel were secured from new recruits who could be molded and trained rather from more experienced soldiers who might have developed bad habits. To help augment the expansion, new equipment such as remote firing devices to detonate Claymores from up to 1,000 yards' distance, personal seismic detectors to detect motion created by vehicles and personnel, and concussion grenades to assist with the capture of prisoners were tested and incorporated into the unit's operational plans.

One such prisoner patrol led by Sergeant Santos A. Matos on 12 November 1969, had set up an initial ambush site with Claymore mines. When two unarmed North Vietnamese officers approached, Matos indicated for his men to cover him while he attempted to capture one of them alive. Just as the sergeant stepped on the trail and placed one of the officers in a headlock, an armed group of five NVA appeared on a second trail that also led into the ambush kill zone.

Maintaining his hold on the prisoner, Matos proceeded to level his M-16 rifle and engage the five enemy soldiers. Rather than kill his prisoner, as most of the Rangers would have been inclined to do, the sergeant dragged him out of the area and broke contact with the encountered patrol. The prisoner proved to be so indebted for having had his life spared and for the subsequent treatment he received, that he led the

Ranger company to a long-hunted enemy hospital complex. Within four days, the complex was located and destroyed.

Even with the expansion to a full company, the Rangers were unable to maintain an effective screen of the brigade's area of operation. Consequently, they were supplemented with raider team personnel from Company E, 3rd Battalion, 503rd Infantry Regiment. It was one of these raider teams, the eight-man Team 3 that would score the largest single direct fire casualty total on the enemy. Initiating an ambush with Claymore mines, the team killed twenty-three NVA outright and mortally wounded two others. This same team would kill four Viet Cong officers, to include the Deputy Viet Cong Commander of Binh Dinh Province, nine days later on 10 October in a well-orchestrated ambush in revenge for the targeted death of the 3rd Battalion, 503rd's battalion commander, Lieutenant Colonel John J. Clark on 2 June 1970. During a search of the bodies, a citation was found on one of the bodies describing that officer's actions in the killing of Clark.

The brigade and its Rangers returned to active combat operations in January 1971 following twenty months of pacification security. In support of these operations, the Rangers conducted screening operations and bomb damage assessment from artillery and aerial strikes.

They also participated in prisoner rescue attempts. On 19 February in Operation Greene Lightning, four eight-man Ranger teams were inserted to block and search for a reported Dron River prisoner compound. Following a heavy spraying of riot control chemical agent, two of the protective-mask wearing teams, rappelled through the triple-canopy jungle only to find after a lengthy and very thorough search that there was no enemy prisoner compound in the area.

Though conventional infantry were usually deployed to block enemy reinforcements from closing in on a battlefield, the Company N Rangers found themselves being deployed in the later years of the war to perform such missions as a result of their expertise and greater dependability. During a weeklong engagement against entrenched NVA regulars on Cui Cung Chap, the brigade ordered the Ranger company to seal off the western periphery of the Suoi Ca Valley.

Late in the afternoon of 6 April, Ranger Team Lima found itself quickly surrounded by enemy forces shortly after its insertion. Throughout the day, night, and early morning hours of the following day, Specialist 4 Michael Bowerrun, the team's radioman, saved the team from annihilation as he directed a steel wall of artillery around their encircled position.

That same morning, Staff Sergeant Juan S. Borga led a combined two Ranger Team detachment to destroy a column of NVA rocket troops. Another team of Rangers under the command of Staff Sergeant Walter Solgalow ambushed and destroyed a second enemy column and captured two prisoners. Other teams located and destroyed enemy command and logistics complexes prior to the battle's termination on 9 April.

During the commands of the two previous brigade commanders, Brigadier Generals Hubert S. Cunningham and Ray Ochs, the black berets unofficially worn by Vietnam Rangers had been banned by the airborne general officers out of concern that it would undermine the camaraderie of the brigade's paratroopers. At this time, the Army only officially recognized two berets to be worn by "elite" troops: the maroon beret by those paratroopers assigned to an airborne unit, and the "Green Beret" of the Special Forces.

Following this battle at Cui Cung Chap, this policy against Ranger berets was overturned by the new brigade commander, Brigadier General Jack MacFarlane, in recognition of the Ranger company's heroic contribution to the brigade's mission. During a formation of the Ranger company, MacFarlane personally fitted the first black beret on Private First Class George L. Miner, the unit's guidon bearer.

Routine reconnaissance patrols always had the potential to develop into something significantly more dangerous, as Team Bravo, now led by Staff Sergeant Solgalow, found out on 29 May 1971. Inserted into the dangerous Suoi Ca Valley during the afternoon, the six-man team quickly moved 150 yards through the dense jungle to establish a listening post. Upon hearing Vietnamese voices nearby, Solgalow had the team move to investigate.

Sergeant Terry Ziegenbein, the point man, was cautiously moving when, to the American's surprise, three enemy soldiers suddenly stepped into view. Almost face-to-face, the American recovered first and quickly killed all three with an automatic burst of fire from his M-16 rifle. Immediately, from the high ground to their front, the American Rangers came under heavy machinegun fire.

Quickly scurrying behind a small embankment, the patrol returned fire and lobbed grenades. Attempts to withdraw from their position were met with heavier concentrations of fire. In response to their calls, a reaction force from the 2nd Battalion, 503rd Infantry was dispatched. Despite their best efforts, though, the infantry company's advance was halted only a few hundred yards from the trapped Rangers' position after having suffered serious casualties.

As darkness approached, the Rangers moved to hide themselves in the dense foliage of the jungle. As torrential rains fell, groups of NVA searched for the concealed Rangers with flashlights and electric lanterns. At one point, enemy soldiers walked within a foot of Private First Class Chris Simmon's head. As dawn arrived, the enemy called off their vain search and the battle with the stalled reaction company resumed its full intensity.

Unknown to the Rangers, they had initiated an engagement with a significantly superior force and the infantry company's option to maneuver was, in reality, a non option, for every movement resulted in more casualties. Mass artillery or aerial bombardment had to be ruled out because of the close proximity of the trapped Rangers. Finally, after the hours continued to roll by and the threat of additional enemy forces arriving growing, the Rangers were ordered to move from their position, regardless of losses.

Low crawling, the six men began to slither their way past enemy battle positions. Having radioed ahead their intentions to dash across an open field toward the infantry company's perimeter, the first three Rangers made the wild run and were safely within the company's formation before the surprised enemy could react and without being mistakenly fired on by their compatriots. Following a delay, the final group of Rangers were also able to surprise the enemy with their dash.

But this time, there was a casualty as four rounds hit Specialist 4 Don Bizadi. Lying in the open field, Bizadi was unable to move. Through the hail of gunfire, Solgalow made his way to the wounded Ranger's side. Despite the danger, the team leader applied dressings to stem the flow of blood and then dragged Bizadi the remaining distance to safety.

Staff Sergeant Solgalow's mission would prove to be the last major Ranger engagement for the company in Vietnam for shortly thereafter, the Airborne Brigade received instructions in July to prepare for its return to the United States. Finally, during a solemn ceremony on 25 August 1971, Company N (Ranger), 75th Infantry Regiment was inactivated.

Company O (Airborne/Arctic Ranger) 75th Infantry Regiment

3rd Brigade, 82nd Airborne Division/U.S. Army Alaska

Considered the premier combat division of the army, the 82nd Airborne Division constituted a significant part of the rapid strategic response capability of the United States, and was thus excluded, for the most part, from duty in Vietnam. In response to an appeal by General Westmoreland for the release of a brigade to combat the Tet-68 offensive, the 3rd Brigade of the 82nd Airborne was airlifted from Fort Bragg to the Hue-Phu Bai region in northern South Vietnam as a temporary emergency measure. With no organic reconnaissance elements, the three battalions of the brigade formed long-range reconnaissance companies from their jeep, recon, and antitank platoon elements.

In late October 1968, the brigade relocated to the Saigon region of the Tan Binh and Hoc Mon districts. Needing greater and more dedicated reconnaissance resources, the brigade activated at Camp Red Ball, northeast of Saigon, the 78th Infantry Detachment (Airborne Long Range Patrol) on 15 December under the command of Lieutenant William E. Jones. Given the density of the population, the urban terrain, and the unwillingness for the Viet Cong to wage open warfare after their Tet offensive losses, the 78th's mission was not an easy one to carry out.

The difficulty of the region and the subversive nature of the enemy were readily apparent during one patrol along the Nha Be River. During a village search of a small store run from her home, a fifty-year-old woman — later identified as a leading Viet Cong spy and tax collector — was found to be in possession of United States Government documents that listed the names, identification numbers, and other personal data of the majority of officers and NCOs assigned to MACV headquarters.

Following her apprehension, the patrol returned to establish an ambush in the vicinity of her village along the Nha Be River. Later that evening, they observed in the moonlight a large debris field of flotsam drifting slowly downstream. Though no one was observed on or near the tangled mass, the patrol, on a hunch, fired into the center mass of the debris field with their machine-guns and M79 grenade launchers. While the M-60 rounds produced no results, the impact of a grenade in the center initiated a huge detonation followed by a number of secondary explosions. Unknowingly, the patrol had fired upon and destroyed a major Viet Cong ammunition resupply package.

The 78th Detachment was inactivated and absorbed into the activation of Company O (Airborne), 75th Infantry Regiment on 1 February 1969. Titled the "All-American Rangers" after the double A of their division shoulder patch, the company would never consist of more than fifty soldiers throughout the remainder of their wartime service.

Declared operational on 1 March under the command of Captain Peter A. Donald, the company conducted routine reconnaissance missions along the periphery of the brigade's area of operation. Little activity was noted in the region and only six enemy soldiers were killed by direct fire from May through July because of the difficulty of firing within populated regions. Much of the diminished enemy activity in the region was attributable to the Rangers' efforts as they restored stability and security to the area through their constant patrolling.

By the end of July, the Ranger company was involved in the establishment of an elaborate battlefield surveillance system of electronic sensors, radar, and night observation points around the Capital Military District Command. Following expanded areas of operation into the Phu Hoa and Iron Triangle Districts, the company received word to stand down on 17 September. Company O (Airborne), 75th Infantry Regiment was officially inactivated on 20 November 1969.

Unlike any of the other Ranger companies of the Vietnam era, Company O was reactivated once again upon the discovery of the immense oil fields along Alaska's northern coast at Prudhoe Bay. The oil reserves were of national strategic importance and there was significant concern in regard to their security against potential sabotage from the former Soviet Union. U.S. Army Alaska insisted on a strike force that could respond quickly, even under the most adverse of weather conditions, if the Prudhoe Bay oil reserves were threatened. In response, Company O (Arctic Ranger), 75th Infantry Regiment was reactivated on 4 August 1970 at Fort Richardson. Directly subordinate to U.S. Army Alaska, the Ranger company was known as the "Arctic Rangers" and wore the gold-starred, growling polar bear patch of the Alaska command as their insignia.

Authorized 216 soldiers, the unit's first commander, Major George A. Ferguson, Jr., worked to train and equip his command. Organized into three platoons, each capable of operating from its own remote base camp, the company was equipped with long-range communications gear and snow machines. By mid-December 1970, the command was declared fully operational.

Subsequent winter exercises proved just how adverse and brutal Alaskan winter operations could be. During one exercise, code-named Ace Band, the true nature of arctic warfare was made relevant as the routine temperature remained around -30 degrees, tearing exposed skin that came in contact with exposed metal and cracking the metal on weapons. Communications were disrupted or terminated by the aurora borealis while radio batteries only lasted for five minutes' worth of transmission. Fierce winds and snow blizzards assaulted the soldiers as they attempted to conduct a march in snowshoes, forcing them to transfer to skis and ropes to be towed behind the snowmobiles. The exercise proved to be a supreme test of human endurance that the Arctic Rangers were able to overcome.

Following an airborne training course, fifty-seven of the Alaskan Rangers parachuted on the frozen Beaufort Sea on 18 February 1971, conducting the first military airborne operation on the polar icecap. Less than a month later on 4 March, 135 Rangers parachuted onto an ice-sheet 130 miles north-northwest of Point Barrow, Alaska.

Interestingly enough, press releases announced that the main purpose of the Rangers and their training was to aid in the possible search, rescue, and recovery of crashed transpolar aircraft, rather than their true mission, which was to protect the exposed oil fields. On 29 September 1972, the Alaskan command, faced with strength reductions, deactivated for the last time Company O (Arctic Rangers), 75th Infantry Regiment.

Company P (Ranger) 75th Infantry Regiment

1st Brigade, 5th Infantry Division (Mech)

In July 1968, the "Red Devil Brigade," the 1st Brigade (Mechanized) of the 5th Infantry Division, arrived in Vietnam. They were to be the last major unit deployed in the conflict. Based in Quang Tri, the brigade's area of responsibility ran along the Demilitarized Zone. On 15 December 1968, the brigade activated the 79th Infantry Detachment (Long Range Patrol). Despite the activation, the detachment never reached operational status, for it was converted while still in training to Company P (Ranger), 75th Infantry Regiment on 1 February 1969.

Known as the "Red Devil Rangers," Company P was declared combat-ready in March. Averaging twenty-six patrols a month, nearly two thirds of the patrols were sent beyond the brigade's area of operation into the reconnaissance zone that ran along the Laos border. Those patrols inserted into the reconnaissance zone were normally assigned six-kilometer "patrol box" squares with a duration of five days. Standard operating procedures (SOP) had the teams establishing an ambush on the last day and initiating contact prior to extraction.

During their short existence, the Red Devil Rangers were able to accomplish a mission that the Special Forces had been unable to accomplish in six years. Considered "the most wanted Viet Cong guerrilla leader in Quang Tri Province," Nguyen Quyet was targeted by the Rangers of Company P. Inserted on a ridge eight miles southwest of Quang Tri in the Ba Long Valley, a Ranger heavy sniper team settled into their position and waited.

The senior marksman observed an individual hunched over with a cap pulled down over his face and collar turned up carrying an M-16 rifle and moving briskly from a treeline along a creek bank. At a distance of twenty yards, the sniper killed him. Based on a pinkie finger missing from his right hand, the target was later identified as Quyet. As a result of this success that eliminated Quyet's leadership, the province's previously undefeated Viet Cong guerrillas ceased effective combat operations within the Quang Tri region.

The Mechanized Brigade was alerted on 12 June 1970 of its redeployment to the United States. The Red Devil Rangers commenced stand-down procedures on 23 July. On 31 August 1971, Company P (Ranger), 75th Ranger was officially inactivated.

CHAPTER 18

Formation of the 75th Ranger Regiment

Never forget: the Regiment is the foundation of everything.

Field Marshall Wavell

Upon the completion of the Arab-Israeli Yom Kippur War in 1973, the Pentagon grew concerned about the United States' strategic ability to quickly move well-trained infantry forces to any spot in the world. Even though the 82nd Airborne Division was considered "light," it still required a tremendous amount of airlift capability to get it to the fight. In the fall of 1973, General Creighton Abrams, Chief of Staff of the United States Army, issued a charter for the formation of the 1st Battalion (Ranger), 75th Infantry Regiment.

> The battalion is to be an elite, light, and the most proficient infantry in the world. A battalion that can do things with its hands and weapons better than anyone. The battalion will contain no "hoodlums or brigands" and if the battalion is formed from such persons, it will be disbanded. Wherever the battalion goes, it must be apparent that it is the best.

The 1st Battalion (Ranger) was ordered activated on 25 January 1974, with an effective date of 31 January. Initially, Fort Stewart, Georgia, was considered home. In 1978–1979, the battalion moved to Hunter Army Airfield (HAAF) in Savannah, Georgia. To initially man this battalion and to serve as its nucleus, the men and equipment of Company A, 75th Infantry of the 1st Cavalry Division were transferred and the company eventually inactivated on 19 December 1974. The new battalion was assigned the heritage of the Vietnam era Company C Ranger.

The 2nd Battalion (Ranger) was activated on 1 October 1974 and stationed at Fort Lewis, Washington. The men and equipment of Company B, 75th Infantry of the 5th Infantry Division Mech were transferred and the company deactivated on 1 November 1974. This second battalion was assigned the heritage of Company H (Airmobile Ranger), 75th Infantry Regiment.

In 1975, the Ranger black beret became only the third officially sanctioned U.S. Army beret. Literally centuries of lineage and battle honors were symbolized by the unique Ranger beret. Though little more than a dark piece of cloth to some, to those who serve as Rangers, the beret is representative of personal courage and selfless sacrifice. It is a symbol to be *earned*, not *issued*.

Unfortunately, the uniqueness of this distinctive symbol was impinged upon in 2001 when the Chief of Staff of the United States Army, General Eric K. Shinseki made what was believed by many to be a misguided decision of having the black beret issued at large in an attempt to raise moral within the United States Army. When asked why the Ranger's *black* beret, Pentagon spokeswoman Martha Rudd was reported to have stated that the decision was based in part on *fashion* and that "it is the only color that goes with the Army uniform." A sad, and insulting, justification for the demise of such a cherished symbol.

Following the invasion of Grenada during Operation Urgent Fury, the most recent Ranger battalion addition, the 3rd Ranger Battalion, 75th Ranger Regiment was reactivated on 3 October 1984 and stationed at Fort Benning, Georgia, with its World War II heritage to serve as its lineage.

To control the three Ranger battalions, a regimental headquarters was needed, thus leading to the formation and activation of the 75th Ranger Regiment on the same day as the activation of the 3rd Battalion. The overall Regimental strength is approximately 2,000 Rangers. Each 580-man battalion consists of three 152-man line companies and a battalion Headquarters and Headquarters Company (HHC). Each line company has three line platoons and one weapon's platoon. Weapon's strength for each battalion is sixteen 84-mm Ranger Antitank Weapon's Systems (RAWS), six 60-mm mortars, twenty-seven M-240G 7.62-mm machineguns, and fifty-four 5.56-mm Squad Automatic Weapons (SAW).

General John Wickham, Chief of Staff of the Army, provided the first colonel of the Ranger Regiment—though technically and officially titled the third after the ceremonial commanders Rogers and Darby—Colonel Wayne A. Downing, the following guidance on 10 May 1984 (author *ital* added):

The Ranger Regiment will draw its members from the entire Army ... after service in the Regiment ... *return these men to the line units of the Army with the Ranger philosophy and standards.* Rangers will lead the way in *developing tactics, training techniques, and doctrine* for the Army's light infantry formations. The Ranger Regiment will be deeply involved in the *development of Ranger doctrine.* The Regiment will experiment with new equipment to include off-the-shelf items and *share results with the light infantry community.*

In the 1990s, another Chief of Staff of the Army, General Gordon R. Sullivan, would develop his own charter for the Ranger Regiment with the following (author *ital* added):

The 75th Ranger Regiment sets the standard for light infantry throughout the world. The hallmark of the Regiment is, and shall remain, the discipline and esprit of its soldiers. It should be readily apparent to any observer, friend or foe, that this is an awesome force composed of skilled, dedicated soldiers who can do things with their hands and weapons better than anyone else. The Rangers serve as the connectivity between the Army's conventional and special operational forces.

The Regiment provides the National Command Authority with a potent and responsive strike force continuously ready for worldwide deployment. The Regiment must remain capable of fighting anytime, anywhere, against any enemy, and *WINNING.*

As the standard-bearer for the Army, the Regiment will recruit from every sector of the active force. When a Ranger is reassigned at the completion of his tour, he will imbue his new unit with Regiment's dauntless spirit and high standards.

The Army expects the Regiment to lead the way within the infantry community in modernizing Ranger doctrine, tactics, techniques, and equipment to meet the challenges of the future.

The Army is unswervingly committed to the support of the Regiment and its unique mission.

As previously noted, Special Operations had been granted the lineage and honors of the 1st through 6th Ranger Infantry Battalions of World War II in 1960. However, with the formation and activation of the Special Forces Operations Command, the lineage and honors of the Second World War Ranger Battalions, the Korean Conflict Rangers, and the Vietnam Conflict Rangers were rightfully transferred on 3 February 1986 to the 75th Ranger Regiment.

CHAPTER 19

Iran: Operation Eagle Claw (Desert One)

Any damn fool can write a plan. It's the execution that gets you all screwed up.

General James F. Hollingsworth

Denigrating the U.S. as the "Great Satan," a mob of militant followers of the Ayatollah Khomeini stormed the American Embassy in Tehran on 4 November 1979 and took sixty-six Americans hostage. The revolutionaries released thirteen of their captives and offered to free the remaining prisoners if the United States returned the former Shah of Iran, Mohammed Pahlevi, to stand trial for what they described as crimes against the state—crimes for which he had already been found guilty and condemned to death. The United States refused the demand and, in response, imposed economic sanctions.

Months passed with no progress in regaining the hostages' release. Finally, it was determined that it was a matter of national honor as well as moral and political obligation to conduct a military operation to rescue the remaining fifty-three captives. The mission went to Colonel Charlie A. Beckwith. A veteran of Korea and Vietnam, "Chargin' Charlie" was a hardened Green Beret and Ranger who was considered to be the premier U.S. expert in unconventional warfare.

Colonel Beckwith was commander of 1st Special Forces Operational Detachment-Delta (1SFOD-D) more commonly referred to as "Delta Force," a secret—at the time—elite team of commandos who were specifically trained in a number of antiterrorist tasks, one of which was to surreptitiously infiltrate target areas dressed in civilian clothes and free hostages from buildings.

The concept for Delta had been approved 2 June 1977. Since then, Colonel Beckwith had planned, organized, trained, and commanded the elite unit. Eventually, a small group of volunteers from the Ranger—after much "turf" fighting—and Special Forces communities were selected to serve as the nucleus for this unique antiterrorist organization. By the summer of 1979, Delta and Ranger units had learned to interface smoothly and assist each other in joint operations. Now, they were to put their skills to the test.

On 11 April 1980, President Carter authorized the rescue mission to be conducted thirteen days later, on the 24th. The mission called for a group of 130 Delta soldiers, Rangers, drivers, and translators to be inserted into the Iranian desert by a support force of fifty pilots and air crewmen. Six C-130 Hercules transports were to lift the men, their equipment, and helicopter aviation fuel from the Egyptian air base at Qena to the island airfield of Masirah off the coast of Oman for a refueling stop.

From there, the force would fly to a secret landing strip in Iran, designated "Desert One." Located 265 nautical miles from the hostages held in Tehran, this site would be secured by the Rangers. Eight Sea Stallion RH-53D helicopters launched from the aircraft carrier U.S.S. *Nimitz* on station in the Arabian Sea would join them.

Refueled at Desert One by C-130s carrying fuel bladders, the helicopters would depart prior to dawn to transport the assault force of 120 men to a remote mountain hideaway designated "Desert Two" located fifty miles from Tehran. After their departure, the remaining Ranger security element and aircraft would sterilize and depart Desert One and return to Qena.

Later that evening, the commandos would clandestinely depart Desert Two and drive in vans and trucks to Tehran to storm the American Embassy compound at around 2300 to free the hostages. Approximately forty minutes after the assault commenced, the helicopters would arrive from their hide site, about fifteen miles from Desert Two, to load the freed hostages and the commando force either in the vicinity of the embassy compound or a nearby soccer stadium.

Two AC-130H Spectre gunships would be on station overhead to interdict any Iranian mobs on the ground and to prevent any Iranian Air Force aircraft from taking off at a nearby airfield. Crewed by five officers and nine enlisted men, the Spectre is loaded with sophisticated computers, surveillance equipment, and detection devices that can, with exceptional precision, pinpoint and target objectives hidden by cloud or darkness. The plane normally flies at an altitude of 6,000 to 10,000 feet in a 30-degree bank turn. It is armed with two 20-mm Vulcan cannons that can fire 2,500 rounds per minute, two six-barreled 7.62-mm Gatling machineguns, each capable of firing from 4,000 to 6,000 rounds per minute, a 40-mm gun, and a 105-mm M-102 cannon that can fire up to eight forty-pound shells every minute out the left side paratrooper door.

As the assault was commencing by the Delta team at the embassy compound, eighty Rangers would be airlifted from Qena to an isolated desert airstrip at Manzariyeh. Located thirty-five miles south of Tehran, this airstrip was part of an unoccupied former bombing range and had an asphalt paved runway that would be secured by the Rangers and used by C-141 Starlifters. Withdrawing from the embassy compound to the airstrip by helicopter, the Delta commandos and hostages would load the Starlifters. Then they, along with the helicopter crews, drivers, translators, and DOD agents—select individuals who were operating in Tehran in support of the rescue attempt—would depart for Qena, mission complete.

Once the other elements were lifted out, the Rangers would collapse their perimeter and fly out themselves. Delayed demolition charges would ensure the destruction of the helicopters left behind.

At least, that's how the plan was to work in theory. A later investigation concluded that the operation was "a high-risk operation with little margin for mistakes or bad luck." Unfortunately for Colonel Beckwith and the United States, "Murphy's Law"—"if something can go wrong, it will go wrong"—was flourishing and thriving on 24 April 1980.

Captain David L. Grange commanded C Company, 1st Battalion, 75th Rangers. Ultimately referred to by the Rangers as Operation Eagle Claw, Grange and his men commenced training for the mission in September–October of 1979 when their efforts began to focus on more urban-type scenarios. The training intensity increased as the months passed with rehearsals involving room clearing and casualty extraction.

They were introduced to new techniques and equipment, to include the UH-60 Black Hawk and the quick insertion technique known as "fast-roping"—a technique by which a fully combat-loaded Ranger snaps a sixty to ninety-foot rope attached to the helicopter to a carabiner around his waste and jumps out, controlling his descent with the rope gripped between his boots below and his gloved hands above. Under the command of Grange, the C Company Rangers also implemented a strange physical training regimen that included pulling C-130 transports down the Hunter Army Airfield—HAAF—runway, pushing two-and-a-half-ton cargo trucks, and conducting long litter runs with mock casualties.

Needing a break from the normal routine, Grange planned an operation that required his men to scour the local bars in and around Savannah in search of a "suspect." Dressed in paramilitary outfits consisting of black fatigue blouses and blue jeans tucked into jungle boots, carrying weapons, and on foot, the men worked their way through the taverns, with some getting somewhat drunk along the way, before locating their quarry in a small bar on Tybee Island.

Entering the bar, the Rangers opened up with M-16 rifles and an M-60 machinegun firing blanks. According to reports, the locals were not amused and the police were summoned. Grange was somehow able to keep his men, and himself for that matter, out of jail. For the remainder of the morning, Grange moved the men of his command to his house, which was considered to be somewhat of a landmark surrounded with concertina wire, "defended" by sandbagged fighting positions, and further marked with a large Ranger Tab suspended over the entrance to the yard.

After a couple of false starts, the mission was launched from the United States on 20 April when Colonel Beckwith's Delta departed Fort Bragg, North Carolina, by air to Qena, Egypt. At the same time, eighty-three Rangers of Grange's C Company, 1st Battalion (Ranger), 75th Regiment departed Hunter Army Airfield near Savannah, Georgia, also enroute to Qena, Egypt, to link up with Delta and to finalize plans. Uninformed and having been directed not to speculate nor to talk with any members of the other Ranger companies about the mission, the C Company Rangers were surprised to find themselves hours later, after one brief stop, in Egypt.

Remembering their arrival, Ranger medic Sergeant Sisk recalled the overwhelming heat that embraced them as the tailgate of their aircraft was lowered. On the ramp stood Sergeants Major Walter Shumate, who looked at the Rangers and stated, "Men, you've heard of bum fuck Egypt. Welcome to bum fuck Egypt."

The Rangers disembarked, drawing cots, a mosquito net, and a case of C-rations per man and set up in an old MiG fighter hangar. They competed with an overwhelming population of flies for each bite of their rations amidst the large amounts of human feces that surrounded the hangar area. The company remained relatively hidden during the day and trained at night out of concern for Soviet satellites passing overhead. In their vicinity, the Rangers observed a large group of civilians with long hair and beards, some just lying around while others made up demolition charges.

The longhaired civilians were Delta operators. The Delta commandos that comprised the embassy compound assault teams were dressed in nondescript, civilian clothes to aid their movement by vehicle to the compound and to assist their escape and evasion (E&E) should the operation unravel. Each man, when loaded with weapons and his ruck, weighed approximately 270 pounds. A small U.S. flag was sewn on each jacket sleeve and covered with tape, to be removed once the assault against the compound began.

On 24 April, the majority of the ground force, to include a detail of Rangers, boarded two C-141s and flew to Masirah Island. Later that evening, they departed for Desert One. At 1930 on the deck of the U.S.S. *Nimitz*, eight Sea Stallions crewed by Marines rose in formation and began their fateful six-hundred-mile flight to Desert One under radio listening silence.

Two hours into the flight across the desert, Helo 6 had a cockpit warning light, a BIM — blade inspection method — that indicated a possible rotor blade failure and a potential loss of nitrogen within the hollow blade. Setting down to inspect, the pilot decided not to chance continued flight. This proved to be an unfortunate and, probably, unwarranted decision, for later investigation revealed that in some 38,000 flight runs of the Sea Stallions not one crack had been found in a rotor blade, despite three BIM signals. Removing all classified material, the crew abandoned the aircraft and departed in Helo 8, which had landed next to the stricken helicopter.

Down to seven helicopters, the formation next found itself flying unexpectedly into a giant, blinding dust cloud referred to in the region as a *haboob*. An hour later, the widely separated aircraft broke clear of the dust storm. Unfortunately, an hour later they found themselves right back in a second cloud that was thicker than the first. Two hundred miles across and reaching an altitude of 6,000 feet, there was little the pilots could do but continue to fly through it. The investigation would later show that operational security and extreme compartmentization had prevented the pilots from seeing the weather annex of the OPLAN or even speaking with weather team meteorology officers. As a result of this super-secrecy, the pilots found themselves flying through a phenomenon they had not been briefed about.

As the pilots struggled through the storm, an alarm signal in Helo 5 indicated a motor that operated a blower for cooling air to the aircraft power supply had overheated and failed thus rendering navigation and flight control systems inoperative or erratic. Loss of flight instruments, poor visibility, vertigo, and a range of mountains that had yet to be crossed convinced the aircraft commander to abort and return to the *Nimitz*.

Unknown to the aircrew at the time, because of radio listening silence, was the fact that Helo 6 was down or that in a few more minutes they would have broken into the clear. To add insult to injury, the problem was allegedly traced to a crewmember who had placed a flak jacket and duffel bag over the cooling vent of the motor, thus causing it to burn out. Now the number of helicopters was down to six—the exact minimum deemed necessary by Beckwith to conduct the mission.

Beckwith's EC-130E arrived at Desert One at approximately 2200. With him was the on-scene commander for the desert rendezvous, Colonel Kyle, USAF. Rangers deployed to establish security and a road watch while Delta support personnel prepared to receive the soon to be arriving helicopters. The Ranger road watch team had no sooner off-loaded a jeep and spread out when a large Mercedes bus drove up to the field. Stopping only after shots were fired over the bus, the forty-five distressed Iranians were unloaded from the bus and secured.

Minutes later, another approaching vehicle was spotted, a small fuel truck. Failing to halt, the vehicle was set afire by an antitank rocket fired by a Ranger. Quickly exiting the burning truck, the driver ran a hundred yards back to a pickup that had moved into the perimeter undetected. In a blaze of rubber and tossed sand, the pickup with its two passengers escaped in a hail of bullets.

Despite the activity, Colonel Beckwith did not fear that the mission or site had been compromised, for he theorized those who had escaped were gas smugglers and had probably mistaken his rescue force for local police on patrol. To believe otherwise, would probably have forced Beckwith to abandon the site.

Within two hours of the team's arrival at Desert One, two MC-130Es had landed, discharged their passengers and equipment, and departed. Four other MC-130Es, including three loaded with aviation fuel, had landed and were parked. Fuel hoses were routed in preparation for the helicopter refueling operations that would commence with the arrival of the Sea Stallions.

The first helicopter arrived at the site fifty-five minutes behind schedule. With the arrival of each Sea Stallion, the deafening noise and blasts of swirling dust increased. Out of concern that an engine might not restart once shut down, the decision was made for all C-130 and RH-53D engines to remain running. The dust and noise seriously hindered personal recognition between key officers and made voice communications exceptionally difficult, even within an aircraft itself.

Finally, the last two helicopters arrived, nearly an hour and a half late. But, with their arrival, the mission's fate had been sealed, for one of the last two aircraft had sustained a crippling mechanical malfunction.

Two hours after their departure from the *Nimitz*, Helo 2 received an indication that its secondary stage hydraulic system was defective. Fluid had leaked out and the pump froze. With no backup, the next hydraulic failure would prove to be catastrophic.

The task force leaders rejected the option of flying the aircraft with only one operational system. With the mission now down to only five operational helicopters, Beckwith recommended that the mission be aborted. Asked if he would reconsider continuing with only five helicopters, Beckwith was quick to reply with the obvious: "There's just no way."

This was a decision that had been made long before the actual event ever arrived, even though he was reputed to admit a few years later that he could have run the raid with as few as two helos. Never having trusted in the reliability of helicopters, Beckwith's point was rather easy to see. If the force had lost three of eight helicopters just flying to Desert One, how could one safely assume no more would be lost in the assault itself? At the White House and to his credit, President Carter endorsed Beckwith's decision. "Let's go with his recommendation."

The task now at hand was to close up Desert One and get everyone safely back to Egypt. Unfortunately, that was not meant to be. At approximately 0200, while maneuvering to top off with fuel from a C-130, the Helo 3 pilot became disoriented in the great swirls of dust created by his engine and that of the C-130. Moving left, then right, the helicopter banked and crashed into the refueling C-130, creating a mammoth fireball in the desert night that caused fuel and debris to rain all about.

From the side troop doors of the stricken C-130, thirty-nine soldiers tumbled or were carried out while other soldiers risked their lives to rescue several unconscious men trapped on the ground near the raging inferno. The five Air Force crewmen in the C-130 cockpit as well as three Marines in the helicopter perished in the intense flames. Four Army soldiers suffered serious burns.

Believing the force was in imminent peril and not realizing that he was leaving classified and sensitive material behind, Colonel Kyle ordered all helicopters immediately abandoned and for the entire force of Delta, Rangers, and support personnel to load on the remaining C-130s. Equipment was jettisoned from the C-130s to make room for the extra bodies that had not been originally planned on the manifest.

Thirty minutes after the crash, the first C-130 was lifting off. Located on the third and final C-130 to depart around 0300, Colonel Beckwith's plane experienced the only stroke of good luck during the entire mission. While picking up speed down the runway and partially airborne, the Hercules hit a three-foot-high embankment. The aircraft's nose jerked almost straight up and then dropped hard. Bouncing on the ground, the pilot gave the plane more power and somehow, miraculously, managed to get the aircraft back into the air.

Left behind at Desert One were five serviceable helicopters, weapons, communications equipment, secret documents and maps, as well as fifty-three hostages in Tehran, a nation's honor, and its pride. A second mission was never attempted. Having served as hostages for 444 days, the fifty-three Americans were released on 20 January 1981, just minutes after Ronald Reagan was sworn in as President of the United States.

What went wrong? Why had the rescue attempt been such a disastrous and humiliating failure? The subsequent investigation found a number of faults with the planning and execution of the mission, especially at the senior level. The command framework at Department of Defense level was weak and poorly used, denying the rescue force access to valuable resources. Operational security was enforced too zealously, preventing critical coordination. Unity of command and task force cohesion were not always clearly defined or emphasized. There was an absence of a clear-cut chain of command with tightly defined responsibilities. There had never been a full dress rehearsal conducted by all task force members to include soldiers, C-130, and helicopter crews. And the abandonment of the fully operational helicopters clearly indicated an absence of detailed plans for contingency operations.

Fortunately, some good did come of this failure. In that the investigation found that a significant number of high-level errors had been made in decision-making and planning, a major shakeup of the nation's Special Operations Forces (SOF) was initiated. Additionally, a counter-terrorist task force was established in addition to the formation of a special operations advisory panel. Future operations would prove the value of these changes and of Delta's worth.

CHAPTER 20

Grenada: Operation Urgent Fury

The mark of a good military unit is versatility in combat situations, not simply the ability to memorize and execute a set piece.

Lieutenant General Arthur S. Collins, Jr.

On 25 October 1983, United States Army Rangers, as part of a seven-nation task force, led the invasion of the tiny Caribbean island of Grenada. The Executive Order to execute Operation Urgent Fury was issued at 1654 on Saturday, 22 October. Admiral McDonald, commander of the Atlantic Command, was directed to "conduct military operations to protect and evacuate U.S. and designated foreign nationals from Grenada, neutralize Grenadian forces, stabilize the internal situation, and maintain peace." The task force was designated Joint Task Force (JTF) 120 under the command of Vice-Admiral Joseph Metcalf, III.

The Joint Special Operations Command (JSOC) had been alerted the day prior on 21 October and had already assembled under the command of Major General Richard Scholtes Task Force (TF) 123 which consisted of Army Ranger, Navy SEAL, Air Force Combat Control Teams (CCT), and the Army 1SFOD-D – "Delta." In that the Ranger Battalions specialized in airfield seizures – "takedowns" – the 1st Battalion was assigned the Point Salines Airfield and the securing of the True Blue medical school campus occupied by U.S. citizens at the eastern end of the runway. The 2nd Battalion was assigned the mission of taking Pearls Airport.

A combined SEAL and CCT detachment was to infiltrate the Salines area the night of 23–24 October to emplace radio navigational beacons for the airborne invasion force that was to arrive in the early morning hours of 25 October. A second SEAL team was directed to secure a new, large transmitting station at Beausejour in the St. George region, while a third team was tasked to secure the Government House. Delta was assigned the mission of conducting a nighttime helicopter air-assault on the prison at Richmond Hill.

Little was known about the enemy they faced, no tactical intelligence, or details of locations. Military maps of the island did not exist and much of the planning was based on an old, outdated British 1:50,000-tourist map of the region. Black and white photocopies of this map were distributed for planning purposes.

The defending force was called the PRA and was believed to be 1,200 strong with an additional 2,000 to 5,000 militia and 300 to 400 armed police to draw on. Soviet antiaircraft 12.7-mm machineguns and eighteen ZSU-23 37-mm cannons were in the inventory, as were eight BTR-60 Armored Personnel Carriers (APC). There were a small number of 75-mm antitank recoilless rifles and 82-mm mortars.

The defenders had no combat aircraft, helicopters, or ships. They had no radar detection systems. In addition, there were approximately forty Cuban military advisors and 635 armed—though mostly older—Cuban construction workers on the island and there was no way to determine whether they would involve themselves in the fight or not. Overall, though, despite the limited intelligence available, it was believed that the PRA had minimum military capability against a well-equipped and trained force and that the Cubans were unlikely to offer much in the way of resistance.

With little time to properly plan, initial objectives and missions quickly changed. The decision was made on 23 October to let a Marine Amphibious Unit (MAU) secure the northern portion of the island to include Pearls. From both Ranger Battalions, 600 Rangers would land or drop, depending on the conditions encountered at the airfield on Salines. 1st Battalion, in addition to securing the airfield and True Blue, would also reinforce the sixty Special Operations soldiers in the St. George area of operations with fifty to sixty Rangers while the 2nd Battalion would attack the PRA base at Calivigny. H-Hour was set for 0200 on 25 October though this would be changed the very next day to 0500 on 25 October.

Major General Scholtes at JSOC headquarters, Fort Bragg, briefed Lieutenant Colonel Wesley Taylor, commander of the 1st Battalion (Ranger), 75th Infantry Regiment, at Camp Hunter-Ligett, Georgia, and Lieutenant Colonel Ralph Hagler, commander of the 2nd Battalion (Ranger), 75th Infantry Regiment at Fort Lewis, Washington, on the morning of 22 October. Scholtes informed each battalion commander of his unit's objectives in addition to the fact that they would only be able to deploy with 50 percent of their unit's authorized strength for there were not enough air force crews trained for night-time C-130 operations to deploy the full two battalions.

Following the general's briefing, the two Ranger commanders immediately returned to their units to commence planning. During their absence, the 2nd Battalion (Ranger) had been alerted for an exercise deployment at 0900 on 22 October. Deploying from McChord Air Force Base, the 2nd Battalion arrived to marshal at Hunter Army Air Field, Georgia, at 1400 on 23 October. There, they linked up with the 1st Battalion (Ranger), who had been alerted for the same exercise at 0500 that morning. Though rumors were rife, there was no knowledge, yet, that the operation was anything other than a training exercise.

The fact that the two Ranger Battalions would not be able to deploy intact was not a fact that would sit well with any commander, especially to commanders of units that rely heavily on personnel, since they were so lightly armed to begin with. With C Company assigned as part of the Special Operations package and, in essence, out of the picture, Taylor was able to select A Company, under the command of Captain John Abizaid and B Company, under the command of Captain Clyde Newman, in total, each with a strength of 150 Rangers. An additional fifty men were selected to form two battalion headquarters cells. Given that he had three complete companies to work with, Hagler directed that each of his commanders, Captains Francis Kearney, Thomas Sittnik, and Mark Hanna of A, B, and C Companies respectively, select their best men only with fifty to eighty men from each. Like the 1st Battalion, Hagler manned two battalion headquarters.

Having been informed by Scholtes during their brief that the 2nd Battalion (Ranger) was to secure Pearls Airfield, Hagler's next surprise was announced during the afternoon of 23 October when he was informed that the Marines now had that mission and that he was to follow the 1st Battalion into Point Salines, assist with the securing of the airfield, and conduct a follow-on mission to attack Camp Calivigny. Given that Calivigny was twelve kilometers from Point Salines, Hagler was to march in the dark, without the aid of reliable maps, to be in position to launch the attack against an unknown enemy no later than dawn.

Changes continued to occur as the Rangers planned that Monday, 24 October. The SEALs initial attempt to infiltrate into Point Salines on the evening of 23–24 October had failed. Now, in an attempt to allow them a second try, H-Hour was pushed back on three hours to 0500, thirty minutes before dawn. The 2nd Battalion now had to not only drop in daylight but also conduct a field march in daylight and attack Calivigny in daylight.

The Air Force 1st Special Operations Wing would transport the Rangers to their drop zone. With two MC-130Es — aircraft that carry precision navigation and terrain-hugging equipment for deep-penetration and low-altitude night operations — leading the way, the 1st Battalion (Ranger) would be carried on five C-130s. The 2nd Battalion (Ranger) was also allocated five C-130s for their lift. Five AC-130H Spectre gunships from the 16th Special Operations Squadron out of Hurlburt Field, Florida, were assigned for fire support.

Leading the air armada was to be a group of Pathfinders. Free-fall specialists, the group would parachute over Point Salines around 0330 on the 25th from a reconnaissance C-130 aircraft flying overhead. Once on the ground, they were to radio the airborne Ranger Battalions with a status on the runway, as to whether the Rangers would be able to air land or would have to jump. In addition, they would mark the drop zone with lights. Their follow-on mission was to conduct a reconnaissance of the True Blue facilities.

An hour after the Pathfinders and thirty minutes prior to the arrival of the main Ranger force, A Company, 1st Battalion, loaded on the two lead MC-130s, would arrive to clear the air strip. The decision as to how to arrive, air land on the runway in the transport or parachute, would be made at the last minute based on the best available information at that time. Taylor and the remainder of the 1st Battalion in their five C-130s would then drop and secure the Salines runway from Hardy Bay, east. Following close behind would be Hagler's five C-130s to drop and secure the Salines runway west of Hardy Bay. With completion of their follow-on missions at True Blue and Calivigny, and the arrival of the 82nd Airborne Division, it was believed the Ranger force would be completed by noon, after which they would return to their home stations. There is an old adage that the best of plans do not survive the first shot and Grenada would prove to be no exception.

During the evening of 24 October, as Taylor was having a final word with his Rangers, the first seven MC-130s and C-130s arrived. Much to his consternation, Taylor learned that the 1st Special Operations' and the Rangers' flight schedules differed by two hours and the 1st Battalion — along with two heavy equipment operators of the 618th Engineering Company (LE)(ABN) of the 82nd Airborne — needed to load immediately. A frantic rush to organize for loading ensued. Only twenty-five minutes late, the first MC-130 with A Company Rangers roared down the runway at 2130. Even more annoying to the battalion commander, though, was the fact that the aircraft had arrived at HAAF without hatch mounts for antennas. Consequently, Taylor was left with no option other than communicating to his men through the aircrew's radios.

Cramped within the aircraft, the Ranger leaders huddled up front as they reviewed their missions. In red nylon seats along the sides of the aircraft, the Ranger rank and file waited, trying to find some comfort and get some sleep during the long flight packed like sardines in a can. In the middle of the cargo bays were gun jeeps, motorcycles, ammunition and medical supplies, and AH-6 and MH-6 Little Bird Special Operations helicopters of the 160th Special Operations Aviation Regiment (SOAR), often referred to as "Task Force 160" or the "Night Stalkers."

The Little Birds were Hughes 500 helicopters. Painted black with no identifying insignia, they could be transported in a C-130 by doing nothing more than securing the rotor blades with a safety restraint. A multi-mission helicopter, the Little Bird carried a crew of two but also had space for four fully equipped soldiers. It could be outfitted with a wide variety of weapons packages, including two TOW antitank missiles, 2.75-inch rockets, a minigun, or a .30-caliber chain gun. Specifically designed for night operations, the aircraft was equipped with infrared night-flying equipment. For self-defense, the helicopter had armor protection, self-sealing fuel tanks, and infrared suppressers to minimize heat-seeking missile vulnerability.

As the Rangers approached, the commanders continued to receive updates, though all were not necessarily timely or accurate. A half-hour after departure, Taylor was informed that the runway was definitely blocked. At 2320, the report was passed that enemy movement had been observed near True Blue. At 0030, Taylor had learned that the SEALs' insertion to Point Salines had failed for a second time. By 0130, the battalion commander made the decision to direct Abizaid and his men in the two lead MC-130s to jump.

At 0330, the reconnaissance C-130 was over the port and the Pathfinder team jumped at 2,000 feet AGL. Once on the ground, the Pathfinders confirmed that heavy equipment was blocking the runway. Realizing that the mission before the A Company was greater than he could accomplish within the allocated thirty minutes, Taylor directed at 0400 that everyone chute-up for a jump.

With only an hour left until H-Hour, the Rangers hastened to perform an in-flight rigging, the most difficult task of an airborne operation when performed within the restricting confines of a combat-loaded transport. Even though Taylor had received confirmation from the air force that the message had been transmitted to the other aircraft in his battalion, the message had not been clearly understood by the last three aircraft, numbers five, six, and seven, of his formation.

In transport number five, Taylor's battalion executive officer, Major Jack Nix, anticipated the jump and directed his men to rig their chutes. Shortly after he'd issued that order, though, the Air Force loadmaster erroneously announced the Rangers would be air landing. Amidst much cursing, the chutes were taken off, gathered, and moved forward out of the way.

A little while later, the same loadmaster reappeared, yelling, "Only thirty minutes fuel left. Rangers are fighting. Jump in twenty minutes!" Both the sixth and seventh C-130s had received similar messages and now the chaotic race was on to rerig for a combat jump. Little time remained and there was no time to follow proper Jump Master Procedures Inspections (JMPI). Employing the buddy system, teams composed of two Rangers assisted each other to place, adjust, and attach the main chute over their battle harnesses, secure the reserve chute, attach large, heavily laden ruck-sacks to their D rings, and attach weapons cases to the left side of the body; all while everyone else in the cramped aircraft was fighting to do the same. Later studies would clearly indicate the soldier's load was in many cases quite excessive, with men carrying over 1,000 rounds of ammunition and some ruck-sacks weighing greater than 120 pounds.

Troubles continued to grow for the airborne assault elements. Fifteen minutes out, the lead MC-130 reported a navigational equipment malfunction that prevented their locating the drop zone in the dark. It also so happened that the two lead aircraft were passing through a rainsquall and the lead pilot felt it was not safe to change positions with the tail aircraft.

As a consequence of the MC-130 problems, Scholtes, who was also in the air in a command EC-130, pushed back H-Hour another thirty minutes to 0530 and directed the two MC-130 aircraft with the A Company Rangers to abort their first run and come in behind the battalion formation, both actions infuriating Taylor. Not only had he been forced to depart two hours earlier than planned, now he was jumping his battalion in ahead of his designated runway-clearing unit. To finish off events, Taylor then learned, as he was attempting to reform the remaining five aircraft, that the Rangers on three of them were still struggling to rig for the coming jump. Upon learning of their problem, he directed them to racetrack until all of the Rangers were properly rigged.

It was 0531 when Taylor's aircraft began the final approach. Almost daylight, the sky was partly cloudy and the winds were a blustery twenty knots. As the aircraft approached on a straight and level flight at 500 feet and 150 knots, a PRA searchlight locked onto Taylor's plane from the western end of the runway. Any thought of surprising the enemy had certainly vanished by this time.

From an altitude below the minimum safety altitude of 500 feet AGL—which prompted some Rangers to remove their reserve chutes for there would have been little opportunity to employ it should the main chute fail—Taylor, his headquarters group, and a platoon from B Company exited on the green light at 0534. Rapidly following each other out the side troop doors of the aircraft, the T-10 chutes opened overhead as the C-130s continued down the drop zone. A 12.7-mm four-barrel antiaircraft machinegun opened up, spewing green tracers across the sky. With the final Ranger unloaded, the C-130 dove for the deck and pulled out, unhit, approximately 100 feet above the sea.

Taylor watched in frustration as the pilots of the next two aircraft—taking heavy machinegun fire—were forced to abort their drops. With only forty-odd men on the ground and totally exposed to view and fire from the surrounding low hills two hundred meters north of the runway, Taylor called in the two orbiting Spectre gunships for support, thus requiring the troop transports to remain clear of the area.

As communication was being established, the platoon from B Company began to clear the runway of vehicles, obstacles, and debris. Tankers, bulldozer, trucks, and drums were scattered about and stakes had been pounded into the ground with wire strung between them. While some vehicles were found to still have keys in their ignitions, others had to be hot-wired to start. For fifteen minutes, the Rangers cleared the field without a shot being fired in their direction. One operator was able to start a bulldozer and use it to flatten the stakes and push aside the drums.

At 0552, one of the two A Company MC-130s approached in a hail of tracer fire—and amid later reports that a Ranger officer had drawn a weapon to ensure the aircraft continued on course—and dropped all but seven of its paratroopers, those remaining on board unable to get out prior to "red light" and the end of the drop zone. With these additional men on the ground, Taylor ceased clearing operations and moved into a covered position south of Hardy Bay.

A gaggle of C-130s surrounded the southern end of Grenada as the planes jockeyed for position or waited for the 1st Battalion Rangers to finish chuting up, the pilots always mindful that they needed enough fuel remaining to fly the forty-five minute route to Barbados. By 0634, the remainder of A Company was on the ground, having assembled at their alternate point having discovered a machinegun nest located at their primary. The airborne operation continued to drag on until the final Battalion (Ranger) was on the ground at 0705.

With the last of Taylor's men on the ground, it was now Hagler's turn. To avoid confusion and to minimize the risk of intermingling the units, he and his men had been forced to wait until all 1st Battalion elements were on the ground. Minutes after the 1st's last pass, the 2nd Battalion (Ranger) arrived overhead in a tight five-plane formation to jump into space at 0707.

By 0710, all of Hagler's Rangers were safely on the ground with only two exceptions. One of those exceptions was Specialist 4 Harold Hagen, who broke his leg executing his parachute-landing fall (PLF) on the runway. The second exception was Specialist 4 William Fedak, whose static line became entangled as he exited the door, making him a "towed jumper." Fortunately for him, the air force loadmasters were able to safely retrieve him into the aircraft, shaken but not injured. By a stroke of amazing and God blessed luck, the American force was on Point Salines without having suffered a single casualty inflicted by enemy action.

On the ground, the 1st Battalion (Ranger) moved out to conduct its missions. A Company crossed the tarmac of the runway without a shot being fired and continued to advance on the village of Calliste. During their movement into the village, the Rangers suffered their only KIA in securing the runway when an M-60 machine-gunner, Private Mark Okamura Yamane, was struck by a round in the neck after calling out in Spanish for an enemy group who were holed up in a school to surrender. Sergeant Manous Boles then proceeded to lead an attack against the entrenched enemy by driving a captured dozer followed by his squad up the hill toward the school.

A Ranger platoon arrived at the True Blue campus around 0730. Though there was a brief engagement between the Rangers and a PRA guard detail at the main gate, the campus was secured in fifteen minutes as the PRA fled north into the hills. This part of the operation proved to be a bona fide success, for one student had been harmed, none taken hostage, and the Ranger platoon had suffered no casualties.

There did prove to be one major problem, though. The Rangers found less than half the total number of students than they'd expected. As events would have it, the remainder was at a campus called Grand Anse, a site that had not been considered in the plan of operation.

On the runway, B Company had been tasked to clear and to secure the control tower and the hills beyond the terminal. For a brief moment, an engagement flared in the vicinity of the Cuban camp but those defenders were soon on the run, leaving behind one dead and twenty-two prisoners. Having secured the fuel storage tanks on the high ground six hundred meters northeast of the terminal, the Rangers were able to look down into the Cuban mission headquarters at Little Havana and observe two mortars being prepared to fire. Bursts by the Rangers from a captured 12.7-mm machinegun quickly encouraged them to reconsider their actions and scattered the crews. Both A and B Companies of the 1st Battalion, worked to consolidate their positions and by 1000, Calliste and the fuel tank hill were secure.

An unfortunate incident occurred shortly after 1000 when two Ranger motorcyclists mistakenly headed for the Cuban mission compound from the terminal. Riding through the valley, the two Rangers came under heavy fire and were both wounded and knocked off their cycles. The members of B Company, 1st Battalion, who had observed the scene, were unable to secure the men because of their exposed positions. Eventually, the overwatching Rangers sealed off the area with sniper fire by mid-afternoon as surrender negotiations were underway and evacuate the wounded men.

Because of the nature of their drop, the 2nd Battalion (Ranger) had been able to assemble quickly and, meeting little resistance, briskly cleared the runway area west of Hardy Bay. A Company moved into the partially completed terminal buildings and up into the old Cuban camp where a small cache of abandoned weapons were found. B Company cleared the narrow strip of land south of the runway towards Point Salines. C Company cleared the low hills from the north down to Canoe Bay. Both Hagler and Scholtes knew that Calivigny would not be secured that day.

The region around Point Salines airfield had been secured. Within four hours of the first drop, the aircraft that had flown in the Rangers were refueled and landing on the airstrip to off load their vehicles and supplies. Scholtes arrived to establish his headquarters near the terminal. Black Hawks and Little Birds of TF 160 laggard, refueled, and rearmed. By 1045, soldiers from the Caribbean members of the Organization of Eastern Caribbean States (OECS), Jamaica, and Barbados were arriving. The first C-141 Starlifter to arrive at 1405 brought with it the initial contingent from the 82nd Airborne Division.

Another very unfortunate incident, similar to that which befell the two Ranger motorcyclists, occurred following the landing and off loading of the Ranger C-130s. Gun Jeep Team 5 of A Company, 1st Battalion, and under the command of Sergeant Randy Cline, reported to their company commander soon after the team's arrival on the island. Directed to take his five-man team to secure a road junction two hundred meters north of the True Blue campus just forward of the company's position, Cline and his men missed spotting the campus, which was hidden in a shallow point below ground level. Realizing they were not in the right location, Cline attempted to match the terrain and trails around them with those found on the map. But the map was of little help, for it did not reflect the majority of trails in the area. Continuing to search for the intersection, the team drove well into an area still held by a PRA company.

The PRA company had established an ambush site eight hundred meters northwest of True Blue. Cline and his team had already driven through it once but the enemy had not reacted. Turning around, Cline and his men were not so lucky the second time. Concealed in bushes and shallow trenches, the PRA opened with a heavy volume of fire at close range on the swiftly moving jeep. Though surprised, Cline and his fellow Rangers were able to return fire with their M-16 rifles and the jeep's M-60 machinegun, killing at least one of their ambushers. But the remaining ambushers were able to destroy the Rangers' vehicle and kill Cline and three of his fellow Rangers—Privates Marlin Maynard, Mark Rademacher, and Russell Robinson. The only Ranger to escape the ambush was Private Timothy Domick, who was able to make his way back to his company despite his wounds. These four Rangers and Yamane would be the only Rangers killed in Grenada.

The Special Operations Command had a unique role to play in the first day of the invasion. The Special Ops mission against the transmitter station at Beausejour, Government House, and Richmond Hill Prison began on 23 October with the alert of the Task Force (TF) 160 aviation support team at Fort Campbell, Kentucky. With no briefing, maps, details, or destination, nine UH-60 Black Hawks were loaded the next day onto three C-5A Galaxy transports from Dover and flown to Pope Air Force Base, North Carolina, adjoining Fort Bragg. There, a total of 100 men from SEAL Team 6, C Company, 1st Battalion (Ranger), and Delta operatives joined the men of TF 160. Together, the joint force flew to Barbados.

The last C-5A arrived at Grantley Adams Airport at 0330 on the 25th. It would prove to be impossible to offload, assemble, and check out the Black Hawks, as well as brief all of the participants in the forty-five minutes that remained if they were to depart, fly, and hit their objectives at H-Hour—0500 that morning.

Despite the handicap, the group drove on. SEAL Team 6 was split with half the group assigned to take Beausejour in two Black Hawks. Another two Black Hawks would take the remainder of the team to secure Government House. The five remaining Black Hawks would take the Ranger company and Delta team members to secure Richmond Hill Prison.

Still relatively ignorant of details or terrain, the nine helicopters and their passengers lifted off for the short flight at 0530. By that time, the invasion had already commenced, with the Rangers parachuting on Point Salines and the Marines storming ashore at Pearls. Night and surprise were no longer their ally. Seventy-five minutes late, the SEAL team reached their first objective at the Beausejour transmitter building just a few hundred meters from the beach. The insertion went smoothly and by 0630 the five soldiers guarding the site were quickly overwhelmed and the station secured.

Events would not remain that way for long, though, and the SEALs came under some intense direct and indirect fire from an approaching counterattacking mobile force supported with an APC and mortars. Unable to obtain close-air support and with casualties mounting, the SEAL team was forced to abandon the station, leaving the tower to be destroyed by the guns of the U.S.S. *Caron*. Hiding until dark, the team then swam out to sea to link up with the U.S. Navy destroyer.

The Government House operation also provided a few dicey moments with the SEALs having to undergo a siege for nearly a day. They were eventually able to secure the facility the following morning having suffered no injuries to the team members.

The same could not be said for the prison raid where all hell was breaking loose and nothing was going as planned. For starters, the location of the prison and the terrain surrounding it were not as briefed. The prison had been constructed on the spine of a high ridge with vertical slopes covered with dense foliage. Walls at least twenty feet high and topped with barbed wire and watchtowers encircled the compound. The only way into the prison was for the Black Hawks to hover over it and allow the Rangers to fast-rope in.

Unfortunately, there was one unanticipated dilemma that made such an approach exceptionally dangerous. Unknown until their arrival at the prison, there was a fort, Fort Frederick, which sat on a ridge only 300 meters across the valley to the east. The ridge was higher and the fort dominated the prison below it by at least 150 feet. And, in actuality, it was not the fort itself but the two antiaircraft guns within it that would make life for the airmen, Rangers, and Delta miserable. The prison, itself, was a tough enough objective to get into without the overwatching—and unanticipated—heavy weapons.

Flying in low over the valley, looking for anywhere safe to put the ground forces down, the Black Hawks were easy targets as the fort's guns fired either level or from above the aircraft. Unescorted and with Spectre

AC-130H gunships engaged elsewhere with the commencement of the invasion, the small force was on its own. As the pilots attempted to evade the fires and locate a place to put the force down, bullet holes appeared through the aircraft's fuselage, striking both troops and crew, splattering blood and bone everywhere. After the first run through the valley, the flying machines were holding up better than the wounded men they carried inside.

On the second run, the pilot of the fourth Black Hawk, Captain Lucas, who had already suffered a wound to the right arm on the first go-around, was killed when five rounds fired from above smashed through the windshield and struck him in the head and chest. Though suffering a grazing wound himself, the copilot, Chief Warrant Officer 2 Paul Price, was able to maintain control of the seriously damaged and burning aircraft.

The assault aircraft scattered with many of the UH-60s heavily damaged and full of wounded men. Price flew south towards Point Salines, escorted by a second Black Hawk, as he struggled to keep the battered helicopter airborne, realizing that to crash-land at sea would probably mean death for many of those seriously wounded in the rear. Unable to maneuver, Price was forced to fly over the PRA base at Frequente. Hit again, the Black Hawk quickly began to lose altitude as the controls locked. The UH-60 crashed around 0640 just on top of Amber Belair Hill with such force that the helicopter broke in half and the main rotor blades fell over the cliff in the water and rocks below.

Moments later, the aircraft burst into flames. Despite the intensity of the flames, the severity of the impact, and the number of machinegun rounds that had passed through it, all but Lucas survived. Price and the remainder of the crew, Warrant Officer 1 Jon Ecker, Sergeant Gary Minerve, and Specialist 4 Loren Richards, were able to escape the inferno, as were the wounded Rangers in the back.

Despite the downed aircraft's proximity to the American fleet and the knowledge of their situation, the dead and injured would not be evacuated until after 1000 that morning. Incredibly, it has been reported that the Navy allowed two administrative issues to hinder combat operations. The first issue was in regard to allowing Army helicopters to land on ships. Because the Black Hawk pilots were not certified or properly trained to land on ships, they were waved off as they attempted to land with their wounded Rangers.

Even more incredulous, the second issue revolved around the question of refueling funding. In that the Navy did not have the necessary funding to pay for refueling Army helicopters, they refused to do so. Though the certification requirement was eventually waived for wartime and emergency situations and the funding accounts between services were put in abeyance during combat, needless pain and suffering was inflicted on U.S. soldiers because of this serious lack of common sense and peacetime bureaucracy.

In closing and regarding this chapter of the invasion, there are those who have claimed that the invasion's records were falsified and did not reflect the losses incurred on this mission. Those who have personally reviewed the operational records, believe and state otherwise.

The last major action of the day occurred around 1530, when an armored force of three BTR-60s attempted to move through 2nd Platoon, A Company's sector, firing toward the runway. The Rangers reacted at once, countering with small arms, machinegun, light antitank weapons (LAWs), and a 90-mm recoilless rifle. The lead BTR slammed to a halt, shifted its gears into reverse, and proceeded to crash into the second BTR. Following two misses with their antitank weapons, the Rangers finally hit and disabled the first two APCs. The crews abandoned their vehicles leaving two dead behind. The third BTR rapidly turned around and fled with the assistance of a LAW impacting on its rear door. An AC-130H Spectre gunship spotted the vehicle and destroyed it.

The day closed with the official initial day losses for the Rangers placed at five dead and six wounded.

With the departure of Scholtes and his Special Operations Forces the afternoon of the 26th, Metcalf, at 1900, placed the two Ranger battalions OPCON to the 82nd Airborne Division's commanding general, Major General Trobaugh. While Trobaugh was aware of this fact, Hagler did not learn of it until three and a half hours later. Taylor, on the other hand, did not learn of it until 0630 the next morning, nearly a full twelve hours later.

Concerned for the welfare of the medical students still unsecured at Grand Anse, the Pentagon was able to creatively establish communications within the students' compound with the assistance of Mark Barettella, a ham radio operator located inside Grand Anse. Metcalf directed that the facility was to be seized by nightfall of the 26th. The task fell to Hagler and the Rangers of his 2nd Battalion with an approved recommendation to employ Marine helicopters for the mission.

An air-assault force composed of Marine CH-46s "Sea Knights" covered by USAF AC-130H Spectre gunships and Marine Cobra attack helicopters was quickly organized. While all three of the Ranger battalion's companies were assigned for the mission, each would be no larger than fifty men in strength. Navy A-7 Corsairs, a Spectre gunship, two Marine Cobras, and an assortment of naval, artillery, and mortar indirect fire support would be directed at suspect enemy locations prior to the air-assault.

Following the preparatory fires, thirteen CH-46s would approach the objective. Each company would be allocated three of the aircraft with A and B Companies cordoning and securing the campus from any PRA interference. C Company would locate the approximately 230 American students and faculty and escort them to the final four CH-46s that would extract them from the beach to Point Salines where they would be flown by C-130 to Barbados and then on to Charleston, South Carolina, by C-141. The Rangers would withdraw in reverse order of their arrival.

Unknown to the American military at the time, an additional two hundred or more Americans were spread out around the Grand Anse campus with the majority living in communities on Lance-aux-Epines peninsula, and area between True Blue and Calivigny on the south coast. As events would eventually play out, the potential danger and possibility of these unknown and unsecured Americans being taken hostage were greatly diminished by the preemptive strikes of the United States on those forces most likely to do the hostage taking.

In total, nineteen helicopters prepared to depart from Port Salines around 1600 to make the short six-kilometer flight. Lifting off with their Ranger complements, the CH-46s failed to keep formation, thus intermingling the Ranger companies. Five minutes after lifting off, the preparatory fires commenced. The fires continued until the CH-46s were twenty seconds out. Missing the beach in front of the campus, the first three helicopters set down nearly five hundred meters away in the midst of sporadic small arms fire. One helicopter was abandoned for a while after its rotor blades were damaged striking a palm tree. Subsequent waves of choppers set down to evacuate the students and Rangers. The remaining helicopters set down in various spots and, following a few moments to reorganize the scattered companies, the Rangers set about their task collecting the American noncombatants and placing them aboard the waiting helicopters.

With the civilians safety extracted, a yellow smoke grenade was thrown on the beach to signal the Rangers' withdrawal. During this extraction, another CH-46 fell victim to a palm tree but, this time, the damage was too extensive and the machine had to be abandoned. Overall, the mission had been accomplished in twenty-six minutes with the only casualty, other than the one destroyed and one damaged helicopter, being a Ranger wounded by a piece of mortar shrapnel.

Unfortunately, there was one bit of potentially bad news when it was realized that an eleven-man flanking guard had been left behind in the withdrawal. Unable to get a helicopter to return for the Rangers, radio contact was established with the men. In that they did not have the 82nd's call signs or frequencies, the men did not wish to approach the airborne positions in the dark and be shot by friendly fire. Opting for an alternate method, the Rangers rummaged through the badly shot up and abandoned CH-46 in the surf. Finding three inflatable rubber boats, the patrol set about trying to inflate them only to find that two of them were too badly damaged. The third boat was serviceable, though two of the men had to swim alongside because they and all their equipment could not fit inside. For hours, they battled the tide and current, using their helmets and weapon butts as paddles. Eventually spotted by a helicopter, they were rescued by a Navy destroyer around 2300 that evening. Despite this one "snafu," and if one overlooks the pilot errors that were not the Ranger's doing, the Grand Anse mission is a clear example that Ranger forces do not necessarily require continuous rehearsals in order to successfully execute an assigned mission.

The final mission left for the Rangers was Calivigny. Directed by the JCS to secure the camp by the evening of the 27th, intelligence organizations claimed it was the center of Cuban military efforts on the island, as well as the central training base for the spread of subversive military activities within the region. Estimates placed the garrison strength at 600, including Soviet advisors. A full-scale battalion attack was ordered.

The planning time line was once again exceptionally short. With H-Hour set at 1630, the Rangers and supporting aircrews only had an hour to brief and to coordinate for the mission. Basically, though, the plan was simple. Flatten the camp with a half hour's worth of preparatory fires and then charge in on Black Hawks to secure the site.

Hagler had four companies at his command. His own A, B, and C Companies, and C Company of the 1st Battalion recently returned from the near disaster at Richmond Hill Prison. Each company would be allocated four UH-60s. Following the preparatory fires, the battalion would attack in four company waves, with each flight of four helicopters closing on the objective, just above the water at 100 knots per hour, to climb rapidly above the cliffs to set the Rangers into the camp. A and C Companies would secure the southern end of the camp and sweep on line through the remains. B Company would be inserted in the southeast and destroy a suspected antiaircraft gun position. C Company, 1st Battalion, would arrive last and be held in reserve.

The overall commander of the mission, Colonel Scott, and Hagler briefly flew by the objective prior to commencement of the preparatory fires and were surprised to note they could observe no activity in or around the camp. Despite this observation, Scott elected to commence with the massive prep fires that had been planned at 1600 with seventeen 105-mm howitzers.

Positioned at Point Salines, the cannon fired a total of 510 rounds at Calivigny, 8,000 meters distant. Unfortunately, the guns of the 82nd Airborne's artillery proved, with the exception of a single round, to be totally ineffective as each round fell short into the sea. Later, it was determined that the batteries had misplotted not only their position by 700 meters, but they also had inaccurate coordinates for Calivigny. From the air, neither Scott nor Hagler were able to adjust the fires, for they had no method by which they could coordinate with the fire support officer. The five-inch cannon fire from the destroyer, U.S.S. *Moosbrugger* and fires from a supporting Spectre proved to be somewhat more effective, hitting a fuel and ammo point that resulted in huge secondary explosions.

Close-air support soon arrived to give it a try. Pushing back the attack by fifteen minutes to allow the aircraft time to work, the A-7's flew eight sorties against the camp. Significantly more successful than the artillerists, by the time the aircraft flew off, there was little left as recognizable in the camp.

The four flights of Black Hawks, each loaded with approximately fifteen Rangers, roared in across the waves and settled for the objective. Coming in rapidly behind each other, the first UH-60 set down safety and in the proper location to discharge its passengers but smoke and flames from the destroyed camp masked some of the area. The following two Black Hawks of that flight overshot their marks and landed farther in the camp. The second aircraft had just begun to discharge passengers when the pilot of the third Black Hawk lost control and crashed into the landed second bird. Upon seeing what was happening, the fourth Black Hawk attempted to veer away but damaged its tail rotor in the maneuver. Unaware of the damage, the pilot attempted to lift off but immediately spun out of control and crashed.

Within twenty seconds and without a shot being fired, three UH-60s had been destroyed. Worse yet was the fact that the Rangers who had disembarked from the first Black Hawk were exposed to the scattered debris and the spinning blades of the trailing damaged and destroyed aircraft. While no one in the downed birds was killed or injured, three of the exposed Rangers from the first bird were killed and another four seriously wounded. Killed were Sergeant Eric Slater and Specialist 4s Joseph Lannon and Sebastian Greiner. A Ranger medic, Sergeant Stephen Trujillo, would receive the Silver Star for his bravery that day and be credited with saving the lives of several of his Ranger buddies. In an unusual and exceptionally unique gesture, the young sergeant would receive his award from President Ronald Reagan before a joint session of Congress.

Despite the death and destruction about them, A Company regrouped and continued their mission as the remaining three companies safely touched down to conduct theirs. A sweep of the camp resulted in the discovery of no enemy bodies or wounded. The travesty of it all was that the mission had been all for naught. The barracks and camp had been empty. That night, the Rangers camped in the ruins of Calivigny before withdrawing the next day.

The two Ranger battalions were redeployed to their home stations by C-141 on 28 October. Both units touched down at Hunter Army Airfield on 29 October before the 2nd Battalion (Ranger) continued on with its journey to Washington state. Total tosses for the two battalions were ten dead — five of whom were accidental — and ten seriously injured — five of whom were also accidental. Reports and claims of additional, unreported losses, have never been substantiated nor documented.

While Grenada proved not to be a stellar operation for the United States Armed Forces, neither was it a failure, for the President's objective — of securing the American students — had been achieved. Significant mistakes were made by every branch and component of service, however. Fortunately, numerous valuable lessons were also learned that would pay handsome dividends in future conflicts. To ensure a more coordinated special operations effort in the future, the Special Operations Command (SOCOM) was established. This action was soon followed by the 3rd Ranger Battalion's activation on 3 October 1984, as well as the activation of the 75th Ranger Regiment headquarters on the same date.

CHAPTER 21

Panama: Operation Just Cause

*What the American people want to do is fight a war without getting hurt.
You cannot do that any more than you can go into a barroom brawl without
getting hurt.*

LTG Lewis "Chesty" Puller

President George Bush authorized the invasion of Panama by U.S. forces shortly after midnight on 20 December 1989 in an effort to capture General Manuel Antonio Noriega, the Panamanian dictator, and bring him back to the U.S. to face drug-smuggling charges. The plans for this invasion, designated Operations Plan 90-2, previously code-named "Blue Spoon," had been completed by the second week of October. Under the overall command of the U.S. Southern Command commanding general, General Maxwell Thurman, Lieutenant General Carl Stiner, commander of the XVIII Airborne Corps, was selected as the warfighting commander of Joint Task Force South.

Among a vast number of other missions to be conducted throughout Panama on the morning of the invasion, OPLAN 90-2 directed "Task Force Red," the 75th Ranger Regiment, to conduct an airborne assault on the Omar Torrijos International Airport and Tocumen Military Airfield complex with the 1st Ranger Battalion and C Company of the 3rd Ranger Battalion—designated as Task Force Red-Tango—simultaneously with a jump by the remainder of the regiment against the Rio Hato base camp—designated as Task Force Red-Romeo. The ready brigade of the 82nd Airborne Division, over 2,000 paratroopers strong, was to jump forty-five minutes after the Rangers' seizure of Torrijos-Tocumen Airport and conduct battalion-sized air-assaults against Fort Cimarron (home base of the

413

200 soldiers of the Battalion 2000), Tinajitas (home base of the PDF 1st Infantry Company), and Panama Viejo (home base of the PDF 1st Cavalry Squadron).

In preparation for the attack, the 75th Rangers executed a rare Mod-4 — battalion-level — regimental-sized exercise on 14 December. Code named "Sand Flea," the exercise was a rehearsal of a large airfield take-down that was practiced at the air force's special operations base at Hurl-burt Field in the Florida panhandle. Detailed, large scaled-models of each objective had been created. The exercise also involved fire support rehearsal with Spectre and Little Bird aircraft. Two companies from the 101st Airborne Division served as the "opposing force" enemy on the objectives. So real was the exercise, the Rangers would realize later that the names of the objectives for the rehearsal were the same names of the objectives secured during the actual operation.

Official notification to the Rangers about the impending invasion occurred at 1600 on 17 December with a call from the Joint Special Operations Task Force commander, Major General Wayne A. Downing, to the Ranger Regiment commander, Colonel William F. Kernan, at Fort Benning, Georgia. In turn, Kernan alerted his three battalion commanders, Lieutenant Colonel Robert Wagner of the 1st Ranger Battalion at Hunter Army Airfield, Georgia, Lieutenant Colonel Alan Maestas of the 2nd Ranger Battalion at Fort Lewis, Washington, and Lieutenant Colonel Joe Hunt of the 3rd Ranger Battalion at Fort Benning, Georgia. From the battalion commanders, the alert passed to their men.

Late in the evening on 17 December, Hunt and his C Company commander, Captain Alfred E. Dochnal, were briefed about the upcoming operation. The deployment cycle, formally referred to as C-Day, commenced at 0100 on Monday, 18 December. Early that morning, Dochnal and his company departed Fort Benning in a convoy of buses on a six-hour road trip to link up a Hunter Army Airfield with the 1st Ranger Battalion. Arriving at Hunter around 0800, the company was met by the 1st Ranger Battalion commander, who began the necessary planning and coordination between his battalion and the newly attached company.

Though the assembled Rangers had been originally informed this was little more than another training exercise, the truth began to dawn on them as informed platoon leaders spread the word. Platoons and squads continued to plan and coordinate throughout the day. By late afternoon, though, the weather had turned exceptionally adverse as a winter storm of rain, sleet, and wet snow gripped the southeastern coast of the United States. The Rangers continued to toil in the open as they went about their work in 20-degree temperatures — a stark contrast to the 90 + degrees and

100 percent humidity they would soon be experiencing in Panama. As the weather worsened, the Rangers grew more wet, cold, and miserable as they formed along the runway's tarmac at Hunter to draw live ammunition, the final act of the day that removed any doubt the operation was just another exercise.

With the completion of rigging their rucksacks, the Rangers underwent "sustained airborne training" — prejump — during which time they rehearsed their actions upon entering and exiting an aircraft and how to react in an emergency. Most found their final meal before loading their planes, fried chicken, a bit of a disappointment. Following the meal, the Rangers boarded for a 1900-hour takeoff.

From Hunter, the sixteen aircraft of Task Force Red-Tango departed. Seven C-141s transported the 1st Ranger Battalion while four C-130s transported C Company, 3rd Ranger Battalion, along with the remaining 1st Ranger Battalion elements. Normally for airborne operations, C-130s carry no more than sixty-two paratroopers but, for Just Cause, these four aircraft were crammed with more than seventy Rangers each. In addition to the eleven troop transports, the air armada included five C-141s carrying vehicles, additional supplies, and equipment.

Completely exhausted from the day's preparation, many of the Rangers fell asleep. Two hours out from green light, word was received that the operation had been compromised and the Panamanians were aware of the Ranger's imminent arrival. For most of the Ranger leaders, they were only surprised that they had not been compromised much earlier, given the magnitude of the overall operation.

H-Hour, the time of the actual attack, was set for 0100 on 20 December. There were three reasons Stiner selected this time. One reason was to allow SEAL Team 6 to attack their targets at high tide. Another reason was to provide a minimum of four hours of darkness in which to fight, providing the technologically superior American forces a significant combat advantage. The last, and maybe most important reason of all, though, was to accommodate a 2245 hour Brazilian commercial flight into the Torrijos International Airport during the evening of the 19th. The early morning attack would hopefully commence after the civilian passengers had picked up their luggage and made their way through customs and departed the airport. Unfortunately, this was not to be, for it would soon be reported that while the commercial airliner was on the ground and deserted, it had arrived late and the approximately 398 passengers and crew were still within the terminal.

At 0100 on 20 December, after a seven hour flight, the airborne assault on Torrijos-Tocumen Airport commenced with an AC-130H Spectre and two AH-6 Little Bird helicopters of the 160th Special Operations Aviation Regiment (SOAR) - TF 160 (TF 160) engaging and suppressing the airport's military facilities. The rules of engagement for all of the American forces, both ground and air, were strict and required precision, as the preparatory fires were directed at two air defense guns, the 2nd Rifle Company's barracks, the command and control communications building, and two identified guard posts.

Three minutes later at 0103, according to plan, 732 Rangers of the 1st Ranger Battalion task force exited seven C-141 Starlifters and four C-130 Hercules transports 500 feet AGL over the objective. The 1st Ranger Battalion's targets were Objective Tiger—the Fuerza Aérea Panamena (FAP)—Panamanian Air Force barracks to the north that were assigned to A Company, Objective Pig—the barracks of the 2nd Infantry Company in the center of the airfield—and the Tocumen control tower that were assigned to C Company, and Objective Bear—the main airport terminal south of center that was assigned to the attached C Company, 3rd Ranger Battalion. In addition, B Company was assigned the mission of securing the perimeter of Condor, preparing the runway for follow-on air landings, and, on order, securing Objective Hawk—the Ceremi Recreation Center in the La Siesta Military Resort Hotel that was a potential hideaway for Noriega or his Dignity Battalions.

The vast majority of the Ranger task force landed on the concrete runway or on the tarmac surrounding the Torrijos main terminal. The final aircraft to drop, though, the fourth C-130, was caught in a wind shear that forced its load to be dropped into twelve-foot-high elephant grass approximately one hundred feet from the runway. Overall drop casualties were light with fifteen Rangers suffering a variety of torn knee ligaments and broken feet or legs.

Unknown to the American command, their primary target was in Task Force Red-Tango's area of operation. As the Rangers exited their aircraft overhead, Noriega and his aides, who were lodging at the Ceremi Recreation Center, hurriedly scrambled into and departed in two small hatchback cars. B Company had quickly assembled and was in the process of establishing a hasty roadblock at the entrance of the military airfield when the two vehicles approached.

Traveling without the aid of their headlights, Noriega's vehicles seemed to appear out of nowhere. The Rangers fired on the two vehicles, striking and disabling the lead car. The second car, containing Noriega, was able to avoid capture and escaped. The Panamanian dictator would eventually give himself up two weeks later on 3 January to U.S. federal drug enforcement agents after seeking asylum in the Vatican embassy.

Despite this isolated incident at the airfield's entrance, security along the southern edge of the airfield was quickly established by B Company. With the perimeter secured, the company began to prepare the runway for the transports that would be landing later that morning. The following day, they would execute their on-order mission and secure the Ceremi Recreation Center.

The seizure of Tocumen was nearly a flawless operation. With the southern security established, A Company quickly overwhelmed a handful of FAP personnel who elected to fight and secured the FAP barracks and their nearby aircraft. Part of C Company's objective, the 2nd Rifle Company's barracks had been leveled and completely destroyed by the Spectre gunship. Unfortunately, none of the members of that company had been inside. Undeterred, the Ranger company quickly secured the barracks area, killing those Panamanian soldiers in the area who resisted and holding as Prisoners of War (POW) the remainder.

The second phase of their mission, the securing of the control tower, met stiffer resistance. As they began to surround the tower, the Rangers received some sniper fire. A Ranger medic, Private First Class James W. Markwell, was shot and killed. He would be the only Ranger to die during the seizure of Torrijos-Tocumen Airport. By 0210, twenty-five minutes later than planned, the 1st Ranger Battalion's objectives on the Tocumen military airfield were cleared and secured.

South of the 1st Ranger Battalion, C Company, 3rd Ranger Battalion, was involved in considerably more action. Quickly assembling, the majority of the company had reached their initial objectives within the first fifteen minutes of the assault. The 3rd Platoon had moved to clear the fire station north of the terminal, which was composed of a large rectangular building with two enclosed tunnel-travels jutting out of its side running to a rotunda that housed a number of aircraft access gates. South of the terminal, 2nd Platoon was to clear a small Eastern Airlines baggage area, establish an overwatch position, and then, on order, assault into the terminal. 1st Platoon's mission was to initially secure the entrance way into the Torrijos Airport then move to clear the terminal's restaurant.

As 3rd Platoon closed on the fire station, one of the fire trucks moved out from the garage. A squad leader directed warning shots to be fired in front of the vehicle. Deterred by the 5.56-mm tracer rounds cutting the air just feet before him, the vehicle driver did a sharp U-turn and drove the truck back into the garage. Inside the station, the platoon found fifteen firemen whom, through an interpreter, they were able to convince to surrender without another shot being fired.

With the fire station secured, the platoon continued on to the main terminal. Shots rang out from the northern rotunda, shattering glass, as the platoon moved across the tarmac. The Rangers scattered under the hail of gunfire. Sergeant Reeves, Specialist Eubanks, and Private First Class William Kelly located some maintenance stairs and entered the terminal.

Inside, the three Rangers observed two PDF soldiers—who must have fired the shots—run into a women's restroom. The PDF soldiers had started the fight and the Rangers decided they were going to finish it in what would become one of the strangest five-minutes' worth of close-quarters combat experiences in the annals of Ranger history.

Electing to finish the enemy off with one move, Reeves pulled the pin on a grenade and kicked the restroom door in, only to find a second closed door just inside. With only seconds to spare, he tossed the grenade into the middle of the concourse as he and his men jumped for cover. The detonation blew out what remained of the windows and created a huge hole in the floor.

Gathering themselves, the three-man Ranger assault team led by Reeves proceeded to charge through the two doors, through which only one man could fit at a time. Surprisingly, all was quiet when Reeves burst through the second door into the darkened room. Seeing nothing to his right, Reeves was just starting to look towards the stalls on his left when he caught movement out of the periphery of his eye. One of the PDF soldiers was standing on the toilet of the stall closest to the door.

Before Reeves could fire or react, he was struck by three rounds from the enemy's AK-47, fired only three feet away. With two hits to the shoulder, one through the collarbone, and powder burns covering his face, Reeves was knocked to the floor. As he lay on the floor seriously wounded, Reeves was pounced on by the second of the PDF soldiers. Believing he was about to die, Reeves closed his eyes only to be startled and relieved when the enemy soldier and his compatriot quickly disappeared to the rear of the bathroom. Fighting mad and unable to use his right arm to grip his M-16 rifle, the sergeant attempted to grip a grenade with his left but he was unable to move his arm enough to get at the grenades in his hip pocket.

Having heard the shots, Eubanks and Kelly crawled on their hands and knees into the dark facility to grab their wounded squad leader. Bullets ricocheted off the walls and floor as one of the PDF jumped out in the open to fire at the Rangers. Three shots bounced off Kelly's Kevlar helmet as they pulled Reeves to safety.

Outside of the restroom, the two Rangers sat the wounded Ranger up against the wall as Eubanks attended to the sergeant's wounds the best he could. Caring little about his wounds and wanting the two PDF soldiers dead, Reeves assisted the two with the development of another plan of attack.

Their plan of action was to start with the toss of another grenade into the room. Opening the second door that had stymied Reeves the first time, the two unwounded Rangers tossed a grenade into the left side of the restroom. Mirrors were shattered and glass flew everywhere with the detonation, but the two enemy soldiers had moved to the far side of the restroom, seeking shelter by the stall partitions located there.

Eubanks and Kelly realized that grenades were not the solution. They needed another plan and quickly realized that only a personal, face-to-face confrontation would accomplish the mission. Eubanks quietly entered first with Kelly covering the opposite side of the wall. Creeping along the wall as quietly and concealed as possible, Eubanks soon spotted the two PDF soldiers towards the rear of the room.

Raising his weapon and placing one of the enemy in the sights of his Squad Automatic Weapon (SAW), the Ranger pulled the trigger only to have the weapon malfunction as it failed to chamber a 5.56-mm round. To add insult to injury, the machinegun's barrel fell off as a result of the locking lever having become unsecured. Compromised by the noise, Eubanks had three rounds fired at him from a pistol. The bullets whistled by his head, high and left as he scrambled from the room.

Back out in the concourse, Eubanks grabbed and loaded Reeves' M-203 grenade launcher and secured a second hand grenade. Tossing the hand grenade into the room with the intent to stun the enemy, Eubanks and Kelly rushed through the door and opened fire with their weapons. When they ceased-fire, the two Americans incredulously heard the PDF cursing the Rangers and the United States in Spanish.

Understanding and able to speak a little Spanish, Eubanks told the two PDF soldiers to lay down their arms and surrender. With each offer to surrender, one of the enemy soldiers would poke his head around the far corner and yell at Eubanks, "Fuck off!" The third such humorous effort to retort found one of the PDF poking his head out a little too far, for Eubanks was able to fire a single round through the taunter's neck. The wounded Panamanian dropped his weapon and crumbled to his knees. Eubanks screamed at him to lie face down but the babbling and dazed PDF soldier was not listening. M-203 in hand, Eubanks grabbed the wounded soldier by the back of his shirt and pushed him to the floor.

Neither Eubanks nor Kelly saw the second PDF soldier behind a stall door. Lunging for Eubanks' weapon, the second enemy soldier struggled for the grenade launcher as the wounded soldier on the floor rolled over and attempted to pull a pistol from his waistband. Eubanks and Kelly were able to kick the wounded soldier out a window where he bounced off a ledge onto the tarmac twenty-five feet below.

Having somehow survived the plunge, the PDF soldier's luck finally had run out, for he had fallen in front of a Ranger M-60 machinegun position. Refusing to halt as ordered, he was finally killed with a burst of 7.62-mm rounds.

Inside the bathroom, however, the struggle still ensued. Able to get both hands on Eubanks' weapon, the remaining, though wounded, enemy soldier attempted to wrestle the weapon away from the Ranger rather than shoot him with it. Enraged, Eubanks pushed the Panamanian against a urinal and began to kick him repeatedly, screaming for Kelly to shoot the man. Kelly's shot to the arm was immediately followed by two more to the head that finally brought the action within the airport restroom to a close.

For their actions in the terminal, Eubanks and Kelly were awarded the Bronze Star for heroism while Reeves was awarded the Army Commendation Medal (ARCOM) for his contribution to the effort.

From south of the terminal, 2nd Platoon advanced on the baggage handling area. Noting activity in the facility, the platoon shot the lights out in the structure and rushed in to find four Panamanians whom they quickly made prisoners. Forming a half-moon perimeter defense, the platoon waited while 1st Platoon secured the entrance to the airport and then cleared and secured the restaurant where they detained eighteen other Panamanians without a shot being fired.

1st Platoon continued its advance into the terminal, entering the ground floor through the terminal's main entrance. Along the way, they had detained an additional thirty people they'd encountered in a rental car facility just outside the terminal. A sweep of the terminal's ground floor netted another forty people. With eighty-eight detainees on hand, including the initial eighteen, the 1st Platoon Rangers established a holding area. As they did so, the first of the 376 passengers from the Brazilian airline began to emerge from their hiding places around the terminal.

Meanwhile, outside the terminal, 2nd Platoon was directed to enter and clear the remainder of the building. While they were waiting, three mortar rounds impacted close by. They did not need much more additional incentive to enter the terminal. Inside the building, 3rd Squad was engaged by five PDF soldiers as the Rangers made their way up the escalators to the second floor. Retreating into the customs police office, the five enemy soldiers began to burn files behind the closed metal door thought to link Noriega and other PDF officers to drug operations. As smoke billowed from beneath the door as more files and furniture were added to the blaze, the PDF soldiers blindly fired rounds through the door in an attempt to drive off the Rangers.

Having been informed by the squad leader that their demands for surrender had been answered with gunfire, Dochnal directed the Ranger squad leader to "deal with" the situation. Two magazines of 5.56-mm were fired at the door but the lighter and smaller rounds lacked "punch" and failed to penetrate the metal, unlike the heavier and more powerful PDF 7.62-mm AK-47 rounds. Finally, a hand grenade was detonated at the bottom of the door, forcing a one-foot gap. A second grenade was rolled through the gap into the middle of the office. The blast killed the five PDF soldiers but it also contributed to the raging inferno inside, which activated the overhead sprinkler system.

In the meantime, the platoon's 1st Squad had advanced to the third floor where they heard women crying. A quick search failed to locate the people. Finally, upon hearing "Don't shoot. We're civilians," the Rangers looked over a ledge to the ground floor below to spot hundreds of civilians. As the 1st Squad directed from above the gathering of the civilians below, the 3rd Squad, fresh from the customs police office on the second floor, arrived at ground level to escort the civilians back outside of the terminal.

But before all of the passengers could be escorted out, however, one of the women screamed. She had, for some reason, given her baby to another woman and now she was not going to leave without the child. In a huge terminal that was on fire, the Rangers did not have a clue as to where to look. One English-speaking Panamanian civilian did inform the 2nd Squad leader that he had observed a woman and a baby enter a baggage claim area around the corner on the ground floor. What he did fail to mention, though, was the fact that nine PDF soldiers had grabbed the woman and child, along with some other civilians, to serve as hostages.

A fire team was quickly dispatched to secure the woman and child. Kicking in a door, two Rangers entered the baggage claim room. Fortunately, they were equipped with PVS-7 Night Vision Goggles and were able to quickly spot a number of enemy soldiers armed with AK-47s within the dark room. Two women were being held on the other side of the room at gunpoint and the baby was crying.

Informed of the situation, Sergeant Anderson, the squad leader, brought the Panamanian who had identified the room forward. At the prodding of the squad leader, the Panamanian was directed to warn the PDF soldiers inside to drop their weapons and surrender. Only one enemy soldier did so. The remainder responded that they had hostages and were staying where they were. The squad leader sought additional guidance from his company commander.

The hostage crisis was just one more item added to a long list of things that were not going well in the terminal. As the fire burned, Dochnal was constantly being updated as the number of detainees grew . To handle the new situation, Dochnal called in a heavy broadcast and civil affairs team that tried to convince the soldiers inside to release the hostages and surrender, but to no avail.

A PDF colonel volunteered to assist with the effort. While the colonel opened a dialogue with the soldiers, a Ranger team broke into a room next door to take up positions. One Ranger, Sergeant Michael Smith, landed on top of an unseen PDF soldier after being fired upon and vaulting over a conveyor belt. With a weapon pointed at his head the PDF soldier surrendered but the remaining PDF soldiers in the other room opened fire. This proved to be the last straw for Dochnal.

Approaching the door, the Ranger company commander got the enemy's attention. He proceeded to tell the Panamanians inside, "If you don't come out, I'm just going to kill you. You've got five minutes to come out or I'm just going to kill you." The standoff was over three minutes later as the remaining PDF soldiers dropped their weapons, walked out of the room, and lay on the floor. Behind them, uninjured, walked the woman with the baby. The time was approximately 0500. By 0700, the 82nd Airborne Division relieved C Company, 3rd Ranger Battalion of responsibility for the terminal

By dawn, all of the Ranger objectives on Tocumen and Torrijos had been cleared and secured. In addition to the fifteen injured on the jump and the death of Markwell, only eight other Rangers, including Reeves, were casualties. Thirteen PDF soldiers had been killed with an undeterminable number wounded. Overall, fifty-four PDF soldiers were captured, including thirty at the international terminal

The 82nd Airborne Division's deployment for Operation Just Cause was not as smooth an event as Task Force Red-Tango's, for the same storm that had hit the 1st Ranger Battalion prior to its departure had struck the airborne division at Fort Bragg even harder. With each plane forced to de-ice at least twice prior to departure, the twenty-eight pax ("passenger") C-141s at Pope Air Force Base were forced to deploy in three separate waves.

Leading the paratroopers was another flight of twenty-eight C-141 heavy-drop aircraft that had been flown out of Pope with their loads and out of the storm's path, the day prior. Arriving overhead at 0155 and flying exceptionally low, the pilots dropped nearly 60 percent of their tanks, vehicles, artillery, and supplies deep into the elephant grass and swampland nearly 300 yards from the runway. While the heavy drops were on target—to keep from blocking the main runways—the marshiness of the area had been an unplanned obstacle.

The first eight pax aircraft from Bragg dropped at 0211. As some of these paratroopers descended into the midst of still on-going Ranger operations, Wagner had his heavy broadcast team use handheld megaphones and loudspeakers to tell the "All Americans" that they were among U.S. Rangers and directed them to their assembly areas. Though there were a few reported 'blue on blue' shootings, there were no casualties as a result. The subsequent two drops took place at 0330 and 0430. It was a testimonial to the Rangers' performance that the 82nd paratroopers did not have to engage a single member of the PDF as they assembled and deployed to their objectives.

Despite the 82nd's arrival and contrary to what they may have thought, all was not over for the Rangers of Task Force Red-Tango. Dawn of the 20th found one major objective on Stiner's list yet to be achieved. The PDF headquarters at La Comandancia in Panama City had yet to be taken by Task Force Bayonet. Late that morning, Stiner ordered the compound cleared and any remaining PDF resistance eliminated. The task fell to C Company of the 3rd Ranger Battalion. Though the Ranger company had just completed its arduous mission at Torrijos International Airport, La Comandancia was the mission it had specifically trained for nearly one year to execute.

Plans for the final assault were quickly drawn up and coordinated. Dochnal issued his company "frag" order to his platoon leaders from a spot overlooking the Carcel Mondelo and the La Comandancia. Preparatory fires commenced at 1500 as Sheridan Reconnaissance tanks of the 82nd Airborne's 3rd Battalion, 73rd Armor Regiment, fired ten 152-mm rounds into the central headquarters building. A Light Armored Vehicle (LAV) fired in excess of 100 25-mm rounds into the building to deter sniping. Arriving late at 1545, two AH-64 Apaches attacked the rear of the building with Hellfire missiles and 2.75-inch rockets. Unfortunately, the rockets missed, detonating against nearby buildings instead and starting a number of fires. It was later noted that, despite the direct fires from Spectre gunships, the Sheridans, the LAV, and the Apache helicopter gunships, the damage inside the building from these prep fires was minimal.

C Company of the 1st Battalion, 508th Infantry (Airborne) Regiment had the supporting task of clearing the fourteen buildings located within the walled compound and behind the main headquarters building. With the prep fires completed, the Airborne company went about its business, breaching the wall and securing the secondary buildings.

As the Airborne company was accomplishing its mission, the Rangers cleared and secured the Carcel Mondelo Prison, directly across the street from the La Comandancia headquarters building, with its 1st Platoon. The platoon proceeded to blowout the back door of the prison's gymnasium, which led directly across the street to the La Comandancia's front gate. The company's 2nd and 3rd Platoons established positions around the block from which they would launch into the objective.

With 2nd Platoon M-203 gunners suppressing the second floor with 40-mm grenade rounds and other teams suppressing the third floor to deter snipers, the final assault commenced around 1550 with a Ranger running through the blown door and across the street as fellow Rangers provided covering fires. Sliding open the gate, the intrepid Ranger blew the front glass doors off the headquarters building through which the Ranger company poured.

First in, 2nd Platoon deployed to the left and rear of the building while the 3rd Platoon did the same to the right. The squads began a methodical search of the building on each floor . Other than some sniper fire into the headquarters building and compound from nearby apartment buildings, the Rangers encountered no PDF soldiers within the building, which was secured by 1700. The only casualty inflicted during the clearing operation would be the shooting and killing of a naked man waving a pistol as he ran out of a building straight for a Ranger security position. At 1900, the Rangers were relieved by C Company, 1st Battalion, 508th Infantry (Airborne) Regiment.

The 2nd Ranger Battalion had just returned to Fort Lewis from the exercise in Florida the morning of the 17th. Eight hours after release amidst the expectation of half-days and four-day weekends for the next two weeks, the Rangers found themselves recalled around 2000. Repalletizing their rucksacks and combat deployment (CD) bags, the Rangers drew their weapons and went to sleep. At 0545, they were awoken and trucked to McChord Air Force Base where they loaded C-141s that immediately departed. Four hours later, the battalion arrived at Lawson Army Airfield, Georgia, in the vicinity of Fort Benning, to link up with the 3rd Ranger Battalion. Lawson was to serve as their remote marshaling base (REMAB) as Hunter had for the 1st Ranger Battalion.

Lieutenant Colonel Joe Hunt's 3rd Ranger Battalion had been alerted and recalled under the pretext of a training exercise hours prior to his being briefed the evening of 17 December. Confined to the barracks area, the Rangers of his command speculated about the upcoming mission.

Select leaders and section chiefs were let in on the mission to allow them to plan and to prepare their operations orders (OPORDER). With the departure of C Company early the next morning to support the 1st Ranger Battalion, the 3rd Ranger Battalion was left with A and B Companies with which to go to war. On the 18th, they moved to Lawson.

Task Force Red-Romeo's objective was Rio Hato, home base to the 6th and 7th PDF Rifle Companies—considered the best fighting units in the PDF—and located approximately sixty miles southwest of Panama City on the coast of the Gulf of Panama. Intelligence estimates placed the combined two-company strength at 440 soldiers with an additional fifty-man engineer platoon. It was also believed that there were up to 250 cadets at the Panamanian noncommissioned officers (NCO) Herrera-Ruiz Academy. The facilities at the airfield included two company and one platoon barracks, a communications center, a training center, two motor pools, an ammunition supply point (ASP), a medical dispensary, and the operations complex for the 4,380-foot long runway. Noriega's beach house, Farallon, was located nearby.

Estimates indicated a wide variety of weapons capability. For mobility, there were three V-300 and sixteen V-150 armored cars and fifteen motorcycles. Three ZPU-4 14.5-mm quad barrel air defense guns and at least forty-two machineguns could provide antiaircraft fires. Heavy direct fires existed in the form of nine bazookas, four recoilless rifles, and up to 200 RPG-7 rocket-propelled grenades. Indirect fires could be provided by at least twenty-three mortars. Overall, the mission facing the Rangers was not an easy one.

Designated "Area of Operations Eagle," or AO Eagle, Rio Hato was divided into two different operational regions for each attacking Ranger battalion. The southern portion was assigned to the 2nd Ranger Battalion and included the 6th and 7th Company compounds—Objectives Cat and Lion. The two companies of the 3rd Ranger Battalion were to secure the northern sector of Eagle to include the NCO academy, the camp headquarters, the airfield operations complex, the motor pools, the communications center—Objectives Dog and Steel—and the ammunition supply point at the far northern end of the runway. Additionally, the battalion was to clear the runway for air landing operations to follow and cut the Pan American Highway that ran through the area.

The weather at Lawson Airfield turned as bitterly cold and adverse as it did at Hunter. Housed in a tent city, the Rangers assembled in the Airborne School hangars just hours prior to their departure, where they began the demanding task of rigging their chutes, conducting Jump Master Pre-Inspections (JMPI), and organizing the chalks—having the soldiers line up in the order they would load the aircraft and jump. They were bathed in red light to keep external surveillance to a minimum.

Rangers walked down vast rows of opened ammunition crates, drawing live ammunition, hand grenades, and anything else they wished to jump into combat. Morphine, a controlled substance, was distributed to the medics. Chaplains moved about the airfield conducting small services for the Rangers. Observers noted that the Rangers "did not seem frightened or anxious, just very aware of what was about to happen and confident of their abilities."

The weather continued to worsen and the freezing rain continued to fall. Miserable, the Rangers sat or stood exposed to the elements. Chicken soup and cookies were provided and heavy wool blankets issued to ward off the chill. Prior to loading and departure, the regimental commander, Colonel Kernan, spoke to his assembled Rangers as they stood in mud and slush. Reminding them of the rehearsals they had so successfully and confidently completed just days prior, the senior Ranger promised them all that "We're going down there with everybody here and we're coming back with everybody here."

Tired, soaked, chilled, and apprehensive, the Rangers entered the aircraft "loose-rigged" in their chutes and packed themselves into the heat and humidity of one of the thirteen assigned pax C-130s. The flight, which included two heavy-drop C-130s, departed soon thereafter. During the long flight, a five-gallon water can served as a "field expedient" latrine and was passed up and down the heavily packed isles of the transports.

As the Ranger task force neared Panama, the Rangers elbowed each other awake and prepared to stand up to hook up their parachute static lines to the anchor line cables at six minutes out. Following the final jump command of "Sound off for equipment check," each planeload of Rangers proceeded to recite the memorized and honored lines of the Ranger Creed.

The attack on Rio Hato commenced simultaneously with the assault on Torrijos-Tocumen. But instead of opening up with overwhelming firepower against the barracks, two F-117A Stealth fighters flown from Nellis Air Force Base at Tonopah, Nevada, flew over the airfield at 0100. Each carried a 2,000-pound bomb with a time-delay fuse that was to be dropped on the 7th Company headquarters and next to the 6th Company headquarters. Stiner had made the decision, over Downing and Kernan's strong objections, to minimize "collateral damage" and not destroy the base and kill Panamanian soldiers on a large-scale basis. As a compromise, he opted to stun the enemy instead by having the Air Force deliver the two one-ton bombs near their facilities.

The method of delivery was determined by the Air Force who selected the newest aircraft in their inventory. Embarrassingly, and contrary to future missions, the two aircraft were off the mark with their first wartime deliveries. The lead Stealth, having arrived on target without precise targeting information, dropped his payload 160 meters northwest of its intended point of detonation. The second Stealth, following the first's lead, dropped his bomb between the two company buildings. Overall, though, the fact that they both missed — or had not been targeted for the barracks — would prove to be relatively irrelevant for the airborne assault had reportedly been compromised hours earlier and none of the PDF soldiers were located in the buildings.

A contingent composed of an AC-130H Spectre gunship, two AH-64 Apache attack helicopters, and two AH-6 Little Bird helicopters belonging to TF 160, opened fire on preselected targets immediately upon the detonation of the second Stealth's bomb. For ninety seconds, machine-gun, cannon, rockets, and Hellfires lit up the sky as they impacted a wide variety of targets, especially the ZPU-4 air defense guns.

The airborne force approached north to south from over the Gulf of Panama to be greeted by tracer rounds fired skyward. Despite the fires, three minutes after the initiation of the Stealth's attack, the green light of the lead C-130 came on and the first of 837 Rangers exited the blackened aircraft at 500 feet AGL, though not all Rangers were able to exit on the first pass with the DZ so tight.

The antiaircraft fires were heavy and, for the moment, unsuppressed as the Spectre and helicopters had to cease-fire and withdraw while the paratroopers were in the air. Eleven of the thirteen pax transports were hit as they over flew the objective. The two heavy-drop birds followed close behind to deliver their eight pallets loaded with jeeps, motorcycles, and supplies.

Inside one C-130, a 7.62-mm bullet penetrated the skin of the aircraft and struck Staff Sergeant Rich Wehling of B Company, 3rd Ranger Battalion, above his flak jacket and in the back, as he was shuffling to the door. As he staggered forward and fell to the floor, the Ranger behind him cut his static line, pushed him aside, and continued to lead the remainder of the chalk out the door into the Panamanian night air.

Found tangled up in parachute deployment bags by the C-130 load-masters after the drop, Wehling regained consciousness. Having been called back to the rear of the transport, the aircraft's pilot, Colonel McJunkins, began to apply first aid.

When asked by the colonel, "How do you feel?" the Ranger's response was "Mad, sir."

Surprised by the reply, the pilot asked why, to which Wehling remarked, "I didn't get to jump with my buddies."

Back at Rio Hato, Wehling's fellow Rangers found themselves in a 360-degree firefight on the ground. The 2nd Ranger Battalion's section of the drop zone was rough and at least a few of the Rangers found themselves caught in a tree landing. Metal pickets with barbed wire were located in the northern sector and there were hot power lines running down the middle of the area. One Ranger who was unable to avoid the power lines was Kernan, the regimental commander. As he approached the ground, he passed through some power lines and became hung up on a fence. His chute, tangled in the overhead wires, caught on fire. Suspended ten feet above the ground, the colonel released his harness and climbed down as his burning parachute shorted out the wires and cut off all electricity to the camp. As he would note later, his was the "lightest landing at Rio Hato."

One Ranger, Private First Class John Price of the 2nd Ranger Battalion was killed when his chute malfunctioned. Thirty-five other Rangers were injured on the jump, including the 2nd Ranger Battalion commander who suffered a broken foot. Another Ranger officer, Captain Steven G. Fogarty, suffered two broken ankles. Staff Sergeant Richard J. Hoerner landed in the middle of a road. As he struggled to get his parachute harness off, Hoerner observed an enemy vehicle rapidly approaching his location. Unable to get his M-16 rifle out of its M-1950 weapons case in time, the vehicle sped by him, catching his partially inflated chute. Slammed to his back, the Ranger was dragged for nearly one hundred feet before he could pop the cable loop assemblies of his risers. Back on his feet, the Ranger set about gathering up the equipment that had been dropped as he was dragged after the vehicle before he making his way towards the assembly.

On the ground, the Rangers found an alert and dispersed PDF who, while not well organized, were all over the place, firing at the Rangers as they discarded their chutes. As the Rangers moved to assemble, two things kept them from firing on each other in the dark. One was the word, "Bulldog," which was used as a sign/countersign. The other was the distinctive ragtop camouflage of their Kevlar helmets, which the Rangers wore to differentiate themselves from some of the PDF who also wore the American-style helmet.

The Rangers of A and B Companies, 3rd Ranger Battalion, moved to their objectives. One three Ranger group composed of Lieutenant Loren Ramos, Staff Sergeant Wayne Newberry, and Specialist Oler thought they would find a twenty-five-foot-high stone structure at the main gate, but found, instead, a two-story arched structure with several rooms at ground level and a castle-like top. Worse, still, was the fact that there was a .50-caliber machinegun located on the structure and it was engaging them as they moved toward it.

The Rangers made it safely to the gate. Just as two of the Americans had stepped into the road to assault one of the rooms, one of them pushed the other back off the road and to safety as a V-150 armored car sped by them down the entrance road with the Rangers firing at the receding target. As the vehicle vanished along the Pan American Highway, the Rangers turned their focus once again back to the job at hand, eliminating the machinegun, killing two of its crew, and clearing the gate structure.

As other Rangers fanned out to the northwest toward the ammunition supply point, Staff Sergeant Olivera jumped into a ditch to avoid some incoming small arms fire. Unfortunately for him, two PDF soldiers were in the ditch, one of whom immediately shot and seriously wounded the Ranger in the shoulder and chest. Literally cheering over their success, the two enemy soldiers proceeded to cut off the American's patches as war trophies, including the Ranger scroll on his left shoulder. Obviously hoping to leave him dead, one of the Panamanians fired a pistol pointblank at his head. Prior to departing, they then wrapped a black bandanna that read *Machos del Monte,* "Men of the Mountain," around his rifle and departed the area.

Fortunately for Olivera, the executioner's bullet had been deflected enough by the sergeant's Kevlar helmet to only ricochet off his skull and exit from behind the Ranger's left ear. He regained consciousness around 0600. Unable to move either his arms or legs initially because of the large amount of blood lost, the sergeant was eventually able to move enough to contact a rescue team with a portable radio secured from his rucksack.

In the southern portion of the airfield, A and B Companies of 2nd Ranger Battalion had to laboriously move building-to-building, conducting room-to-room sweeps as they did. A Company worked its way through the NCO Institute while B Company, the main effort, cleared the complexes of the 6th and 7th Rifle Companies, a mission it had spent considerable time training for. As the Rangers pressed, the PDF would abandon the building, hiding in the broken terrain, ambushing the Rangers as they advanced to the next building. Specialist Philip Lear was killed in the attack on the barracks.

Though a tense situation, the Rangers did not fire or toss grenades indiscriminately. During the sweep of one barracks building, a Ranger recognized that there were unarmed PDF within. Taking a chance, he-entered a room without prepping it to find 167 cadets, ages fourteen to eighteen, cowering inside.

C Company, which had been held in reserve, dispatched a small force of Rangers prior to dawn to secure the Farallon beach house. Encountering a detachment of bodyguards that fired on the Rangers from the rooftop, the Rangers opted not to waste much time or effort in trying to coax the enemy out. Firing a LAW, they proceeded to blow away the front door. The guards fled, to be captured later at one of the Ranger blocking positions.

On the ground, Kernan and his regimental headquarters, "Team Black," were located in a recreation center on the north end of the airfield from where they coordinated the various supporting fires and served as the task force's liaison with Stiner. Seven minutes ahead of schedule, one hour and fifty-three minutes into the operation, Kernan reported the airfield secure and authorized the first air land of soldiers and supplies. The hard fight had cost the Rangers four KIA, two of whom, Staff Sergeant Larry Barnard and Private First Class Roy Brown, were killed by Spectre friendly fire as they assaulted a sniper position halfway down the west side of the runway. Twenty-seven other Rangers were wounded in battle. In exchange, the PDF suffered thirty-four dead, an unknown number wounded, and 362 taken prisoner along with forty-three detained civilians.

Hunt and his 3rd Ranger Battalion of Rangers air-assaulted into the town of David to secure the Malek Airfield at 1000 on 25 December. Located in the Chiriquí Province, the little town was fifty miles from the Costa Rican border. Within the hour, the attack on the small airfield was completed and the facility seized. The Rangers would not be relieved until the following night early in the morning of the 27th.

Task Force Red-Romeo's final mission occurred on 28 December when the two companies of 3rd Ranger Battalion assaulted Camp Machete, a penal colony on Coiba Island. The small island was located south of Chiriquí Province in shark-infested waters. In addition to the penal colony that held Panama's least redeemable criminals, the island also served as the base for a PDF jungle training school.

The Rangers arrived to secure all the prisoners who had broken free from their locked cells. Hostile guards were rounded up and flown off the island. The next day, the Rangers were relieved by elements of the 7th Infantry Division.

CHAPTER 22

Persian Gulf War:
Operation Desert Shield/Storm

First we're going to cut it off; and then we're going to kill it.

General Colin Powell, Chairman of the Joint Chiefs
(In reference to the Iraqi Army)

On 2 August 1990, Iraq invaded Kuwait in the Persian Gulf. Mobilizing a force of over 539,000 American and 270,000 Coalition troops, the United States, under the auspices of the United Nations, began the "liberation of Kuwait" at 1840 EST on 16 January 1991. Following thirty-seven days of intense, high-tech air bombardment, Desert Saber, as the ground phase was termed, was launched on 23 February. Lasting only four days until 27 February, ground forces killed an estimated 150,000 Iraqi soldiers — depending on whose numbers you accept — and captured tens of thousands of others.

In support of this operation, B Company and 1st Platoon of A Company — with a section from their weapons platoon — deployed from the 1st Ranger Battalion on 12 February 1991 to conduct pinpoint raids and quick reaction force missions behind enemy lines, searching for SCUD, surface-to-surface, missile sites, destroying communications sites, and submitting reports on enemy troop movements.

The team redeployed to their home station on 6 April 1991.

CHAPTER 23

Somalia: The Creed in Action

The choice of death or dishonor is one which has always faced the professional fighting man, and there must be no doubt in his mind what his answer must be. He chooses death for himself so that his country [or comrades] may survive, or on a grander scale so that the principles for which he is fighting may survive.

Lieutenant General Sir John Cowley

Most recently, Ranger forces were committed to Somalia in support of ongoing peacekeeping operations. Throughout the history of the United States, Rangers have always stood ready to answer our nation's call to arms. In 1993, they were once again called into harm's way in support of the United Nation's efforts to establish order in the African nation of Somalia.

For years, the world had watched as a bitter civil war between six rival clan factions destroyed Somalia and brought about a famine that was killing tens of thousands of innocent people a month. The country's capital, the once beautiful port city of Mogadishu, lay in ruins from five years of civil war. Under the directive of the clans, roving bands of "technicals"—teams of Somali fighters in small trucks with mounted heavy weaponry—controlled all movement of goods into and throughout the country. Clan chiefs—warlords—hoarded food and medical supplies, dispensing them only to their supporters, thus denying basic sustenance to the vast majority of the population.

Death and misery escalated, all caught on tape and transmitted about the world by CNN. Drought compounded the famine. By the summer of 1992, over 300,000 had perished during the preceding eighteen months. The United Nation's efforts at simple famine relief failed miserably, with the technicals stealing most of the earmarked supplies. The U.N. Secretary General, Boutros Boutros-Ghali, appealed for military assistance from member states and began the United Nations Operation in Somalia (UNOSOM). A token force and lack of U.S. involvement ensured failure, as was stunningly displayed in late July 1992, when two U.N. relief planes were stopped and looted on the Mogadishu Airport runway by clansmen and technicals.

On 16 August, President Bush authorized Operation Provide Relief, a small airlift with an equally small support base. The first sorties by C-141Bs and C-130s began on 28 August. Though the operation was able to deliver large quantities of supplies to the famished nation, the limited scope of involvement was tantamount to dropping it off at the doorstep. Within hours of each delivery, the chieftains had secured all the items for their own use. Despite the deliveries, hunger and dissension in the region were on the increase.

By November 1992, Operation Provide Relief had proven to be no more successful than the previous U.N. efforts. Civil war and famine continued to take its toll. Nearly a half million Somalis were dead, up to a million more would die from hunger if the status quo were maintained, and almost one million had fled the country. The Somali struggle threatened to spread throughout Africa like cancer.

General Colin L. Powell, Chairman of the Joint Chiefs of Staff (JCS), and the Joint Chiefs had been opposed all along to military intervention in the region. There were too many questions and too few answers. But in late 1992, following the defeat of President George Bush in the national election, the chiefs and their chairman changed course, stating to the National Security Council (NSC), "If you think U.S. forces are needed, we can do the job."

Having anticipated such a contingency, the JCS had prepared an operational plan. The President's request for one more operation to tie up loose ends prior to his retirement was going to be honored by the JCS, who also knew that, as the Commander-in-Chief, the President could have ordered it done anyway.

Powell's "combat model" was employed: while the mission would be limited to humanitarian relief for the Somalis, overwhelming force would be used to crush or frighten off any armed resistance. The orders were issued to U.S. forces on 25 November. On 3 December, the U.N. Security Council passed Resolution 794, authorizing under Chapter 7 of the U.N. Charter, the use of U.N. force to defeat a threat to international security, "to restore peace, stability, and law and order with a view to facilitating the process of a political settlement under the auspices of the United

States." A great void appeared between that which the United States intended and that which the United Nations directed, for while the U.S. was committed to a limited peacekeeping role, the U.N. Resolution had the world body going after bigger game—peace*making*.

This change in objective was so serious, the Italian mission refused to comply and was believed to have made a secret deal with Mohamed Farrah Aidid, the main Somali War Lord, to protect their personnel. In the end, they stood accused of compromising the U.N. goal by transmitting intelligence on military operations to Aidid by radio.

In the early morning hours of 9 December, elements of the Marine Fleet Recon and Navy SEALs tactically made their way to shore, near the port of Mogadishu, to be met by a distracting mob of journalists, cameramen, and bright lights. Referred to as "Operations Other Than War" (OOTW), the force had strength to bring organization and relief to the people of Somalia as part of UNOSOM II. A total of 25,426 American soldiers, seamen, and airmen—designated Unified Task Force (UNITAF)—were assigned to Operation Restore Hope with nearly 16,000 serving on the ground in Somalia.

One of the greatest challenges of UNITAF was trying to figure out who the "bad guys" were. Nearly everyone had weapons and vast numbers of the populace walked and drove about with them displayed. Security for the U.N. force meant taking the weapons or ensuring the Somalis kept them out of sight. Disarming an aggressive populace with a significant warrior heritage, even partially, is an incredibly complicated and laborious process and one guaranteed to get mired down in petty details and potentially incessant, tragic mistakes. Fortunately, wise policies and common sense resulted in some semblance of order and the blackness of starvation being lifted. UNITAF began to redeploy on 4 May 1993, the Bush initiated operation successful.

President William J. Clinton was now in the Executive Mansion. But many knew the order in Somalia was only an illusion. The warlords had lain low, waiting for the American-led U.N. coalition to depart. Once gone, the clans would rule again. The American/UN operation had only been a temporary measure with no final solution.

With the departure of UNITAF, the United Nations' effort, under the command of Turkish Lieutenant General Cevik Bir, began to work on the nation-building effort with a mix of 28,000 U.N. soldiers, which included 4,000 Americans. This nation-building was authorized under another U.N. Resolution, number 814, that directed the U.N. commander in

Somalia to begin "rehabilitating political institutions and the economy and promoting political settlement and national reconciliation."

Bir's deputy was U.S. Major General Thomas M. Montgomery. Montgomery had little staff and even worse, little force at his disposal. Elements of the 10th Mountain Division—a brigade headquarters, a light infantry battalion task force, an aviation battalion task force, and a combat service support unit—were in-country to serve as a Quick Reaction Force (QRF) in support of U.N. forces. Unfortunately, they only numbered 1,200 combat troops and, there was no armor. For attack helicopters in the aviation battalion, there were only upgraded Vietnam-era AH-1F Cobras, which had limited night-fighting capabilities. The QRF remained solely under U.S. command, reporting directly to Montgomery. They did not wear the blue U.N. berets sported by the other foreign units in Somalia.

Unfortunately, militia leaders saw these humanitarian nation-building actions—and the combat forces associated with them—as a threat to their power and the situation quickly deteriorated as the warring tribes shifted their aggressive attentions from each other to the United Nations forces. Mohamed Farrah Aidid—"Aidid" in Somali means "one who tolerates no insult"—was one of the warring chieftains and head of the Habr Gidr clan. His militia, the Somali National Alliance (SNA), was more disciplined than most. In an interview, Aidid blamed the U.N. forces for interfering in the internal affairs of his country and for blocking his clan's succession to power. "We intend to rule" was his edict.

Anti-U.N. and anti-American rhetoric gave way to full-blown violence on 5 June when Aidid, forewarned by sources in U.N. headquarters, ambushed a careless and lightly armed Pakistani force preparing to seize his pirate radio station. The ambush killed twenty-four and wounded fifty-three, including three American WIA from the QRF who deployed to cover the Pakistani withdrawal. A decisive point had been reached.

On 6 June, the U.N. Security Council—with U.S. sponsorship and approval—passed Resolution 837, calling for the apprehension "for prosecution, trial, and punishment" of those responsible for the ambush and to use "all necessary measures" to install United Nations authority "throughout Somalia." It was determined that Aidid and his SNA were responsible for the ambush and a plan was developed to bring about his capture. The warlord had become a serious obstacle to the U.N.'s efforts of trying to establish a Somali coalition government to prevent famines similar to that of 1992 from happening again.

A request for additional firepower was approved by the administration and four AC-130H Spectre gunships were dispatched on 9 June. The precision 105-mm, 40-mm, and 20-mm cannon and night-fighting capability would be of significant benefit. On June 17, an arrest order was issued by the United Nations and, as a result, Aidid went into hiding deep within Mogadishu.

Actions to "apprehend" Aidid commenced at 0400 on 12 June when the four Spectres destroyed his radio Station while QRF Cobras destroyed four other SNA targets. Ground troops secured other sites. The following night, the Spectres destroyed Aidid's compound, which served as his headquarters and home.

The night of 14 June had the Spectres hammering the home of the warlord's deputy, Osman Ato, with the Cobras destroying an additional target later that day with TOW — Tube-launched, Optically tracked, Wire-guided — antitank missiles.

Early on 17 June, a multinational effort was undertaken to destroy the block on which the Aidid and Ato houses sat in what was referred to as a "decapitating strike." Before light, the Spectres circled, warning the citizenry with leaflets, searchlights, and loudspeakers as they obliterated surrounding technical roadblocks. Italian tanks and Royal Moroccan mechanized elements moved in around 0545 to isolate the area. Two Pakistani infantry battalions followed to assault the housing complexes.

The effort was going well for the Pakistanis, but for the Moroccans on the perimeter things were heating up. Street demonstrators began to come out in force, shielding heavily armed militia. Heavy weapons began to fire from rooftops. At 1030, the Moroccan regimental commander was killed when a recoilless rifle destroyed his command vehicle. The crowds surged forward but the Moroccans held on, firing into the mob. French reinforcements with tanks arrived around 1130 to stabilize the situation, the crowds melting away before the show of force.

Though Clinton declared that "the military back of Aidid [had] been broken," Aidid did not seem to pay any attention to that declaration from the world's most "powerful" man. In that tradition of history's finest insurgents and rebel fighters, Aidid realized that with such declarations he did not need to win; he only needed to survive to gain victory.

On 2 July, his men attacked an Italian checkpoint, killing three and wounding twenty-four. Retribution for Aidid's attack of 2 July — an event that would eventually culminate in the Ranger's pitched battle on 3 October — began on the morning of 12 July with a U.N. effort to cut off the head of Aidid's organization. A sizeable group of the Habr Gidr's tribal elders had gathered on the second floor of a large building referred to as the "Abdi House," so named after Aidid's interior minister, Muhammed Hassan Awale (aka Qeybdid).

Inside, seated on rugs in the center of the room, were the senior representatives of the clan: religious leaders, professors, former judges, and even a poet. Standing behind them, around the wall, were younger clansmen. All told, there were approximately ninety men in the room — though no Aidid, who was still in hiding.

Those attending were some of the most influential men in the clan and thus, some of the most influential in all of Somalia. There were those who wanted more blood but there were also those, more moderate, who were businessmen and understood the need to resolve the outstanding issues by cooperating with the United Nations, and thus the United States.

The attack caught the group by complete surprise. From a distance, four QRF Cobra gunships — part of a seventeen-helicopter assault group that had encircled the building — stood off and pounded the second floor of the Abdi House with sixteen TOW missiles — each carrying a fourteen-pound shaped charge explosive warhead — and minigun fire. In front, a ground force from the QRF fast-roped in from hovering Black Hawks, and rushed into the burning building to secure prisoners. The attack resulted in the deaths of over twenty of the attendees, though there are those who claim the number was as high as seventy-three.

Previous raids had been announced with loudspeaker broadcasts before the relatively benign assaults had occurred. The 12 July attack was a clear escalation of the United Nations' effort to bring peace and stability to the nation. Meant to get Aidid's attention and to place additional pressure on him and his group, it unknowingly did more than that. Feeling that war had already been declared against them, the clan declared war against the United Nations and the United States in particular, for they owned the death-dealing Spectres and Cobras. Even worse, the clan militias and hired guns roaming the streets ceased fighting among themselves and turned to engage a common enemy.

Unfortunately following this raid, there was a general consensus that Aidid's resistance had been broken and that the need for the Spectre gunship's minimized. Consequently, to serve as an enticement for Aidid to negotiate, the United State's administration decided to redeploy the Spectres out of country. While all were led to believe that the aircraft were moved back to the States, they were, it's been reported, just repositioned to the bordering country of Djibouti, a tiny nation just north of Mogadishu at the southern entrance of the Red Sea. There they would remain, under the operational control of the commander of the soon to arrive Task Force Ranger.

U.N. intelligence estimated that Aidid's SNA militia was composed of 1,000 regulars, though the actual number may have been closer to 12,000. Even if the number were closer to 6,000 than 12,000, it was still a formidable force when one considered it was operating at home and could be quickly augmented with "irregular" volunteers, since it seemed nearly every male in Somalia owned his own weapon—the preferred favorite being a 7.62-mm Soviet-made AK-47 assault rifle. For these men, and many others, strife and fighting were the norm, and the warrior was the noblest individual within Somali society.

U.N. ambassador to Somalia, U.S. Admiral (Retired) Jonathan Howe, eventually requested 1st Special Operational Detachment-Delta—the premier three-squadron U.S. counter terrorism unit known as Delta Force to the public—to assist in Aidid's capture. Though there were the soldiers of the QRF in support, they, as with most purely combat elements, were not skilled in the "snatch-and-grab" tactics necessary to capture Aidid.

Howe had initially requested the deployment of the elite unit soon after the 5 June Pakistani attack. The request was taken under consideration and members of the unit began to train early that summer for such a mission. An assessment team dispatched to Somalia in June submitted a report indicating that the warlord could easily be captured in the streets. Some leaders were not so easily convinced. Powell, for one, was skeptical of the nation-building efforts in Somalia. After all, it was a tribal nation that had lived that way for centuries. No exertion or series of actions on the part of the United Nations or the United States would create a democracy there overnight, or even in the near future. Generals Downing and Hoar were the others who also recommended against employing Delta to "get" Aidid. Downing was convinced that surprise had already been lost and that using Delta would get really tricky.

Aidid's "war" against the United States continued and on 8 August, a command-detonated mine killed four QRF Military Police in an HMMWV—High-Mobility Multi Wheeled Vehicle, referred to as "Humvees" or "Hummers." Two weeks later on 22 August, a mortar attack against the QRF airfield wounded six and damaged some U.S. Army aircraft.

Howe asked again for the Delta unit and its associated support elements. President Clinton approved the request to send in the specialized unit. "Mission Creep" had commenced.

The U.S. deployed Task Force Ranger, a 450-man force composed of approximately sixty men from the one-hundred-and-fifty-man Squadron C of 1st Special Forces Operational Detachment-Delta located at Fort Bragg, North Carolina; B Company (Reinforced), 3rd Ranger Battalion,

75th Ranger Regiment from Fort Benning, Georgia; and support helicopters from the Army's 1st Battalion, 160th Special Operations Aviation Regiment (SOAR)—the world's finest night fliers known as the "Night Stalkers," stationed at Fort Campbell, Kentucky. Commanding Task Force Ranger was Major General William F. Garrison, a combat veteran and former commander of Delta.

Task Force Rangers' advance party—with Garrison disguised as a lieutenant colonel—departed Fort Bragg on 22 August with the main body of personnel and equipment arriving onboard six C5B Galaxy transports on 26 August. The task force set up base on the shore of the Indian Ocean at the Mogadishu Airport on the far southern end of the city. On the 29th, they were welcomed with a mortar attack on the airfield.

The operation was to be conducted in three phases: Phase I, lasting until 30 August, was to get set up; Phase II, lasting until 7 September, would focus exclusively on locating and capturing Aidid; and Phase III—in the event Phase II failed—the focus would shift to Aidid's command structure with the intent of forcing the warlord to take a more active and open role with his forces.

Frustration quickly set in for the task force as their target had last been spotted 28 July. The problem facing the American effort was the fact that Mogadishu was a perplexing, convoluted web of interlocking family and kin, a base of support into which Aidid could vanish for a lifetime, much less for just a few months. To make matters more difficult, while the task force's specialty was night operations, the Joint Special Operations Command (JSOC) controlled Intelligence Support Activity (ISA) Somali agents that served as human intelligence (HUMINT) sources in the city were fearful of venturing into Mogadishu's menacing streets after nightfall.

This aversion by the agents to move about during times of reduced visibility seriously impacted on the task force's mission. Not only could the Task Force not readily obtain 24-hour-a-day real-time intelligence but more critical was the fact that their operations would have to be executed during hours of daylight on some missions, thus seriously limiting surprise and stealth, two significant strengths of light forces.

In spite of these handicaps, Task Force Ranger attempted to seize and to maintain the initiative by planning and launching a number of raids. The first mission, launched in twelve helicopters at 0300 on 30 August, had the force mistakenly arresting eight Somali United Nations Development program contract workers. Besides the embarrassment, one critical advantage that had been on the task force's side since their arrival in-country was lost with the blown raid: surprise. Until the raid, there had only been suspicions that Delta and the Rangers had been deployed. Now that fact had been confirmed and the effort had gained them nothing in return.

On 7 September, the force moved to Phase III and expanded its target list to include six of Aidid's top lieutenants and staff. A snatch on 14 September again proved to be in error when they mistakenly captured General Ahmed Jilao, a U.N. ally and the head of the new Somali police agency. On 18 September, they just missed grabbing the SNA financier and Aidid's chief munitions supplier, Osman Ato.

The task force's hard work finally paid off on 21 September with the daylight attack on a convoy of cars. Captured inside one of the vehicles was Ato, the man who had slipped through their fingers just three days prior. The next week, the task force conducted two raids against pirate SNA radio transmitters, knocking them out of operation.

Aidid continued to be defiant even as the task force attempted to track him down. On 5 September, his forces killed seven Nigerian soldiers and captured one. On 9 September, QRF Cobras had to respond to keep an embattled Pakistani outpost from being overrun. Two days later, in retaliation for the deaths of women and children killed in the crossfire on 9 September, SNA-incited crowds killed four CNN employees. On the 13th, the QRF was involved in its first major firefight during a cordon-and-search mission near Benadir Maternity Hospital. SNA snipers opened up first and were soon followed by rocket-propelled grenades (RPG), seven of which were fired at the QRF trucks. Following the initial shock of the attack, the QRF repelled the attack and withdrew with three wounded. On 15 September, Aidid's snipers killed two Italians within their fortified camp.

The most brazen attack took place just after midnight on the 24th, when QRF headquarters was informed of a mortar attack on the airport located two miles away. A Black Hawk, piloted by Chief Warrant Officer Dale Shrader, was launched at 0130 as a spotter craft to direct U.S. mortar and Cobra counter fire. Cruising along at 130 feet, looking for the enemy firing position, the helicopter took an RPG round impact or near airburst in the cabin. Though RPGs have a self-destruct mechanism that detonates the warhead at a distance of 900 meters, some were said to have been tampered with to detonate in the air at shorter ranges, thus making them viable anti-aircraft weapons.

With the Black Hawk burning, Shrader struggled to set it down in a controlled crash. Hitting hard, the tail broke off and the on board fuel tanks burst into flames. Shrader and his copilot, Chief Warrant Officer

Perry Alliman, barely cleared the blaze. Their three crewmen in the rear died in the flames.

Forced to engage the enemy with their pistols, the two men were able to hold out until picked up by a patrolling armored car from the United Arab Emirates. C Company of the QRF suffered three wounded as they recovered the three badly burned bodies left in the aircraft.

The pattern of confrontations was escalating and Montgomery knew he did not have the necessary firepower to handle a full-scale engagement. Consequently, he solicited the return of the AC-130H Spectre gunships to Somalia. In addition, he requested armored vehicles—M1A2 Abrams tanks and M2 Bradley Infantry Fighting Vehicles. Powell endorsed the requests. Out of political expediency and a desire to not send the wrong message, however, the Secretary of Defense, Les Aspin, ignored the request, electing not to act on it "in the context of an evolving policy" that now focused on a political solution.

Despite his activities and successes, Aidid was feeling the pressure, having sent a letter to former President Carter appealing to him to intercede with the current American administration on his behalf. Informed of the request, Clinton ordered the renewal of negotiations to solve matters peacefully. Howe agreed and was returning by plane from a meeting on the peace initiative when he was forced to circle the city while waiting to land. *It was a late Sunday afternoon, 3 October, the nine year anniversary of the reactivation of the 3rd Ranger Battalion, 75th Ranger Regiment and "The Battle of Mogadishu' was underway in the streets below.*

Though Task Force Ranger had finally been successful with a mission, there was an inherent problem, for within that success a noted pattern had been set. They had developed a template approach to conducting their operations to cut down Somali reaction time, a pattern that was initiated with ISA recon and confirmation of target that quickly led to fast-rope insertion of Delta grabbers and Ranger security, to be followed by a rapid extraction by vehicle convoy. Total time at the target was not to exceed thirty minutes. One SNA senior leader, Colonel Ali Aden, stated, "If you use a tactic twice, you should not use it a third time." The Somalis had the tactics and timing down and it would soon come back to haunt the task force.

The seventh and final mission of Task Force Ranger commenced at approximately 1300 on 3 October when a Somali agent passed word that a number of Aidid's lieutenants, including two of the six on the expanded target list — Muhammed Hassan Awale and Omar Salad Elmi — would be meeting later that afternoon. A Little Bird had been dispatched to observe the agent through a telescopic lens from a distance. The agent stopped his vehicle in front of a house, raised and lowered his hood, and then drove away. The aerial observer marked the spot on his street map.

The mark was in the vicinity of the Olympic Hotel — a white, five-story building that served as a landmark since it was one of the few large buildings left intact in the city. Hawlwadig Road, intersected by narrow dirt alleys, ran in front of the hotel and was one of the few paved roads in the city. Across Hawlwadig, one block north, was — what would turn out to be — the ultimate target house, a two-sectioned building with two stories in the front, three stories in the rear, and a flat roof on both. L-shaped, the structure had a small courtyard enclosed by a high stonewall.

Just three blocks to the west of the hotel was the Bakara Market, the most heavily armed region of Mogadishu. This area was known by soldiers as "the Black Sea" and was referred to as real "Indian country" by Garrison when briefed of the target location. Earlier, he had stated, "If we go into the vicinity of the Bakara Market, there's no question we'll win the gunfight, but we might lose the war." This final mission, by those words, would seem to have been a self-fulfilling prophecy.

Despite the known risks, the code word "Irene" was transmitted, initiating the operation. Previously, President Clinton had been briefed on each mission in advance. This one would be different, though, for it was a target of opportunity that required the mission to be executed quickly, Thus, neither the President nor his staff were aware of the ongoing operation at the time of execution.

The assault force was formidable — though, as events would prove later, not formidable enough — and consisted of seventy-five Rangers and forty Delta soldiers onboard an air armada of sixteen helicopters. Wearing desert camouflage battle dress uniforms (BDU) and flak vests, the Rangers had elected to travel light, leaving behind bayonets, canteens, and night-vision devices (NOD) — believing this was to be a quick daylight operation. Communications would be transmitted in the clear, meaning they would not be encrypted and could thus be monitored by the Somalis with the proper equipment — meaning military surplus or off-the-shelf commercial scanners.

The Delta and Ranger assault force would be inserted by four MH-6 and six MH-60 Black Hawks with four AH-6J Little Birds providing close air support. The Little Birds were a special version of the egg-shaped observation OH-6 helicopter. Tiny, quick, and highly maneuverable, the bubble-front choppers were an exceptional asset. The AH-6Js (Attack Helicopter-6) were armed with miniguns and Hydra 70-mm rocket system. The MH-6s (Military Helicopter-6) carried benches mounted on the outside skids on which Delta operatives rode.

The Black Hawks employed by the Night Stalkers were MH-60A and MH-60L models. The former were UH-60s with Forward Looking Infrared Radar (FLIR) installed; the latter had not only the FLIR but upgraded engines and weather radar as well. For ease of movement and greater visibility, the pilot's and copilot's doors were removed. The SOAR also operated "K" models that had an aerial refueling boom, long-range tanks, and satellite communications capabilities, in addition to the other items found on the "L" models. All of the TF 160 Black Hawks were configured to burn any type of aviation fuel.

A combat search-and-rescue (CSAR) MH-60 with a special team onboard—in essence a flying reserve that was capable of more than just routine search and recovery—stood by while the air mission commander, Lieutenant Colonel Tom Matthews, the SOAR commander, and Lieutenant Colonel Gary Harrell, Squadron C commander, call sign Romeo 64, circled the operation 3,000 feet overhead in a command-and-control MH-60, also referred to as a "C2 Bird." A Navy P-3 Orion aircraft—with a Magnetic Abnormality Detector (MAD) onboard that was most likely being used to hunt large weapons caches rather than submarines—and a MH-60K were also nearby prepared to videotape and photograph the action for after action review and intelligence gathering purposes.

In that the target area was too confining and too dangerous to land helicopters to extract the prisoners—"precious packages"—and assault force, a fifty-two-man Ranger ground element—including some Delta operatives and Navy SEALs from SEAL Team Six—led by the 3rd Ranger Battalion and ground force Commander, Lieutenant Colonel Danny McKnight, call sign Uniform 64, was to deploy from the airport on a three-mile journey in direct support of the operation. The twelve-vehicle convoy was composed of seven Kevlar-lined and ballistic-doored armored Humvees mounted with MK-19 grenade launchers or .50-cal machineguns, two cargo Humvees, and three five-ton cargo trucks. All of the vehicles were lined with sandbags to minimize small arm fires and fragmentation. In addition, the cargo trucks had "walls" constructed with dirt-filled wooden ammunition crates along the flatbed sides.

The helicopters lifted off at 1532 after a thirty-seven minute delay, for it was discovered that their target house actually lay a block west of that identified, for the agent had been too afraid to stop directly in front of the objective. Taking a circuitous flight from their staging base just three miles away from the objective and moving low and fast over the ocean's breakers, the aircraft made a dash over the city, with the MH-6s carrying four Deltas, two to a side, on their external benches. With the aid of the aerial surveillance, Garrison and his staff in the Joint Operations Center (JOC) command post, located in a dilapidated building in U.S. Army Headquarters at the Mogadishu Airport, followed the operation as two AH-6's flying advance guard buzzed the target house at 1543.

The AH-6 sweep indicated nothing abnormal. Rapidly landing on Hawlwadig Road in a billowing swirl of rust-orange dust, a group of six helicopters, composed of four MH-6 Little Birds and two Black Hawks, inserted forty Delta soldiers, under the command of Captain Scott Miller on the road in front of the building.

The external troop carrying MH-6s made their runs first. The lead aircraft, Helo 1 code named Star 41, determined that it was unable to land in the tight area and fast-roped its operatives in. Helo 2, seeing that its landing zone (LZ) was tight also, landed on the far side of an intersection.

The combined downdrafts of Helo 1 — that had landed in an intersection following the disembarkation of its load — and Helo 2, however, created such a brownout that Helo 3 was forced to do a racetrack. Helo 4, the trail bird, did not hear Helo 3's transmission that it was going around. It continued to the LZ, using the building to the left and some wires directly across the front as reference points.

Adding their own dust to that which already existed, Helo 4 quickly found itself in a total blackout. From a hover, the helicopter set straight down. Thinking that they were still in a hover, the left side team dumped its rope and conducted the world's shortest fast-rope on record — approximately three inches in distance. As Helo 4 took off and exited the billowing cloud of dust and dirt, it realized that it had passed directly over Helo 3, which was landing just a few feet away.

Following the four Little Birds, the two Black Hawks fast-roped their charges in twelve Deltas each. Once safely offloaded, the teams stormed the target building with team leader, Sergeant First Class Matthew Rierson, coordinating the roundup.

Simultaneously, sixty Rangers, under the command of Captain Mike Steele, call sign Juliet 64, company commander of B Company, 3rd Ranger Battalion, were to be inserted into the objective to establish a security perimeter between the four corners of the target's city block. The four Black Hawks, each armed with two six-barreled 7.62-mm miniguns capable of firing 4,000 rounds per minute in each door, and carrying fifteen Rangers each, approached their designated insertion points. The Rangers aboard were armed with 5.56-mm M-16A2 assault rifles, 5.56-mm M-249

Squad Automatic Weapons (SAW), 40-mm M-203 grenade launchers—attached under the barrel of the M-16, the 7.62-mm M-60 machinegun—affectionately, or derogatorily, referred to as the "Pig" depending on one's perspective and experience with the weapon, M-72 Light antitank Weapons (LAW), and a various assortment of grenades. The 5.56-mm ammunition were green-tipped, armor-piercing rounds with tungsten carbide penetrator cores—excellent for punching holes in metal but given that they maintained their shape passing through soft human tissue rather than expanding like a mushroom and tearing out large pieces of muscle and flesh, they lacked "stopping" power.

Chalk One, under the command of First Lieutenant Larry Perino, 3rd platoon leader of B Company's 1st Platoon, and carrying the company commander, Captain Steele, fast-roped in a street intersection one block west on Hawlwadig Road. Chalk Two fast-roped in the northeast corner under the command of First Lieutenant Tom DiTomasso, B Company's 2nd Platoon leader. Chalk Three, under the command of Sergeant First Class Sean Watson and part of Perino's platoon, fast-roped into the southwest corner on Hawlwadig Road.

To the northwest, Super 67 with Staff Sergeant Matt Eversmann's Chalk Four—DiTomasso's platoon—was inserted a block north of its proper position on Hawlwadig Road. Compounding that problem was the fact that the mission's first casualty was suffered when eighteen-year-old Ranger Private Todd Blackburn ended up unconscious, bleeding from his nose, ears, and mouth, on the dirt road beneath the whirling blades of the Black Hawk high above, having jumped and failed to secure a firm grasp of the rope, resulting in at least a forty-foot plummet to the ground. The chalk's medic, Private Second Class Mark Good, immediately began to administer first aid to the seriously injured Ranger.

The mission's "precious cargo," twenty-four prisoners, including the two primary men they had sought, had been quickly captured and secured with their hands behind their backs with plastic "flex-cuffs" by the Delta operatives who called at the twenty-minute mark for McKnight's twelve vehicle convoy to make its way to their location. Having departed from the Mogadishu Airport upon lift-off of the helicopters, the convoy had taken twelve minutes to negotiate the narrow streets of Mogadishu to arrive at its holding position behind the Olympic Hotel, about 200 meters from the target, with the lead vehicle, having made a wrong turn, ending up as the trail vehicle. Other than the serious injuries sustained by Blackburn, an incident of near fratricide when a group of Rangers mistakenly fired on some Delta operatives on the target roof, who, in turn, were firing at a Somali sniper, and some intermittent but steadily increasing fire from Somali gunmen, the operation went off exactly as planned.

Overhead, though, the airborne commanders saw a different scene evolving as growing crowds of armed Somalis poured into the streets, erecting barricades and moving in the direction of the task force's objective clearly marked by the helicopters circling overhead. The smoke from burning tires, rising black against the sky, signaled not only for the Somali gunmen to muster, but it also signaled the start of the most vicious firefight ever experienced by an American force since the days of Vietnam. The Somalis knew the script and now was the time to change the story's ending.

Mogadishu was in chaos and its inhabitants, united against a common enemy—probably for the first time in decades—swarmed through the streets in search of vengeance as militiamen with megaphones shouted, "Come out and defend your homes." Those knowledgeable about American tactics knew that a column of vehicles would have to extract any force fast-roped into the Bakara Market area. Thus, the preparation of roadblocks and ambushes were the orders of the day.

The ground convoy moved from its position to pick up the prisoners in front of the building. Three blocks away, Eversmann radioed his platoon leader, Lieutenant Perino, requesting that a Humvee be dispatched to pick up the injured Ranger—Blackburn—who needed proper medical attention immediately for his internal wounds. When informed by the lieutenant that no vehicle could be dispatched, Eversmann had Blackburn placed on a compact litter and directed two of his sergeants, Casey Joyce and Jeff McLaughlin, to assist Good and a Delta medic, Sergeant First Class Bart Bullock, in transporting the young private to the convoy.

With the four men posted at each corner of the litter, the litter team began to run down the street, bent over, Bullock with an IV in hand that was feeding the precious liquid into Blackburn's arm. Taking fire, the team would place the litter down and return fire every few steps. Their movement was too slow and too dangerous.

Realizing the need to bring a vehicle to them, Joyce volunteered to secure a Humvee and began running on his own down Hawlwadig Road toward the convoy. The first vehicle he encountered was a cargo Humvee with a group of Delta soldiers and Navy SEALs. A quick explanation from Joyce had the vehicle's driver back in the Humvee and racing a block up the road to where the remainder of Joyce's group was waiting.

With Blackburn safely aboard, the Humvee returned to the main convoy while the litter team ran back down the road to their chalk. Understanding the gravity of the injured Ranger's condition, McKnight authorized the SEALs' vehicle to transport Blackburn to the American compound. In that the vehicle was unarmed and relatively unarmored, McKnight ordered Staff Sergeant Jeff Struecker and his two armored Humvees, one armed with a .50-caliber machinegun and the other with a Mark 19 40-mm automatic grenade launcher, to escort the SEAL vehicle.

Struecker's had originally been the lead vehicle that had taken a wrong turn. But this time, he knew where he was going and had mapped out a simple route. The problem was, the Somalis were not about to cooperate. Barricades had been erected and roadblocks emplaced. Armed street fighters roamed within crowds of civilians, masking their presence behind these supposed non-combatants until they opened fire. The intensity of the incoming fire increased as the little three-vehicle convoy pressed on, bypassing obstacles or ramming through them, shots coming from all directions, down every street and alley, and from windows and rooftops.

In the lead vehicle, Struecker directed Sergeant Dominick Pilla, his M-60 machinegunner, to engage targets to their right while the .50-cal concentrated to the left. Shortly thereafter, a simultaneous exchange between Pilla and a gunman resulted in a bullet to the sergeant's forehead, striking just below his Kevlar helmet, killing him instantly, splattering blood and brain matter about the vehicle.

Demands for a situation report (SITREP) about Pilla's condition finally forced Struecker to transmit over the radio the words he did not want to acknowledge: "He's dead!" With that declaration, all radio traffic ceased for a number of very long seconds as the confirmation of the task force's first KIA began to sink in.

The three vehicles continued to move, albeit very slowly, for despite the intensity of the firing, there was a swarm of Somalis in the road. Relatively harmless flash-bang grenades were tossed in front of the vehicles and the .50-cal fired overhead in only moderately successful attempts to disperse the crowds. When a slow-moving pickup truck loaded with people hanging all over it refused to move aside or speed up, Struecker had his driver push it off the road. Dazed, bloodied, and twenty minutes after their departure from the target area, the little convoy finally passed through the gates of the American compound.

Back at the target site, the situation was growing worse at nearly an exponential rate with all elements, especially those on the perimeter taking heavy fire. Incredibly, crowds of locals still made their way through the streets, complicating the efforts of the Rangers and Delta teams to adhere to their restrictive rules of engagement (ROE) that prevented them from firing on seemingly unarmed and noncombative civilians. Such restraints were proving exceptionally difficult to follow as armed men jumped out from among the crowds, firing their weapons, and jumping back into the security of the masses while others hid behind women, firing their weapons either from between a woman's legs or from under her arms. Other gunmen fired from the prone position, children in front and sitting on top of them, serving as human shields.

Minutes later, though, there were even more serious concerns as a call from Chief Warrant Officer 4 Clifton P. Wolcott, the pilot of the lead assault Black Hawk, designated Super 61, reverberated from the Task Force's speakers. *"Six-One's going down. Six-One's going down."*

Within moments of this call, the task force's nightmare began as rifles, hand grenades, and RPGs were fired or thrown from nearly every building window, doorway, rooftop, and corner in sight. During the course of Task Force Ranger's four-month campaign, Aidid's militia recognized that the U.S. task force's most significant asset was speed and mobility as represented by the variations of UH-60 Black Hawk helicopter. A plan needed to be developed to negate this advantage.

The raid of 3 October, deep within their own territory, provided the militia the opportunity to implement a strategy of massed firepower in the form of rocket-propelled grenades—with a range of accuracy of 300 meters versus moving targets—against low-flying helicopters. U.S. commanders had considered this strategy a possibility and a detailed, complex "downed aircraft" drill had been conducted just three days after the shoot down of the 10th Mountain's Black Hawk. While a number of "kinks" were worked out with the drill, the task force clearly realized that there was a continued need to rehearse and revamp CSAR actions in the future.

However, despite the successful use of an RPG against an airborne target, it was still believed to be a relatively infeasible anti-helicopter defense system. The fact that not a single TF 160 helicopter had been hit to date, by either a bullet or an RPG, might have added to this ultimately proven false belief. Later, in a perverse and morbid sense of irony, it would be recalled that it was Walcott's Super 61 Black Hawk that had served as the "downed" aircraft during the CSAR drill.

Mobilizing quickly upon notification of the raid's objective, SNA militia forces rapidly converged on the vicinity of the Olympic Hotel with a huge arsenal of RPGs they had been stockpiling for months—a significant failure of U.S. intelligence to detect. The militia put their plan into effect. At around 1610, the first RPGs started to fly. In less than ten minutes, one Black Hawk alone was the target of ten to fifteen RPGs.

Finally, at 1620, forty-eight minutes into the raid, the Somali strategy paid off. Having safely inserted his chalk of Rangers earlier, Black Hawk Super 61, piloted by Wolcott and co-piloted by Chief Warrant Officer 3 Donovan L. Briley, was hovering 75 feet AGL and searching for Somalis who could threaten the objective, when it was hit in the tail rotor by an RPG round fired by a gunner kneeling in an alley below.

Three blocks west of the crash site, the Rangers of Chalk Two in the northeast corner of the objective watched in stunned disbelief as a puff of smoke appeared near the Super 61's tail rotor and the aircraft began to shake violently. The blades began a difficult counter-rotation as Wolcott struggled to keep the seriously crippled eight-ton bird under control. Approximately 300 meters northeast of the task force's assault objective— about four city blocks—Super 61 crashed on the roof of a house located within a walled compound. The Black Hawk fell to earth on its left side, its top wedged against the remains of a wall in a narrow alley, its nose to the ground. Within, Wolcott and Briley, lay dead, the five others aboard—two crew chiefs, a Delta medic and two Delta snipers—lay injured.

Having rehearsed the possibility of an aircraft going down, the task force quickly implemented three contingency plans: provide cover with a nearby CSAR Black Hawk, Super 68, deploy the main body of Task Force Ranger from the objective to the crash site, and alert the Quick Reaction Force from the 10th Mountain Division to deploy from its location at the Somali National University to the Mogadishu Airport, from where it could launch to support CSAR missions.

On the ground at the objective, DiTomasso, whose Chalk Two element was closest to the crash site, immediately radioed Captain Steele, requesting permission to depart the perimeter and move to the location of the downed Black Hawk. Steele, unable to break through the radio traffic to higher headquarters to make himself heard, ordered his platoon leader to proceed to the downed Black Hawk with half his force, leaving behind seven men, including an M-60 machinegun crew and an M-203 grenade launcher under the command of Sergeant Ed Yurek to continue perimeter security of the objective. DiTomasso had to run to catch up with his men, who had already set out at a trot without him.

Meanwhile at the Super 61 crash site, two dazed survivors quickly extracted themselves from the wreckage. The second, Sergeant Jim

Smith—one of the Delta snipers—emerged from the shattered aircraft armed with a rifle. Immediately moving about to defend the crash site, Smith quickly shot and killed one Somali gunman and set about engaging a group of others while taking a bullet in his left shoulder. Though wounded, the sniper was able to return to the downed Black Hawk to extract his injured partner, Staff Sergeant Daniel Busch. Smith then positioned Busch with his SAW and .45-caliber pistol against a wall only to see his friend suffer a serious wound to the abdomen, just below the plate of his bulletproof vest, as they continued to valiantly defend their position.

The Star 41 MH-6 Little Bird piloted by Chief Warrant Officer 3 Karl Maier courageously set down on the five to eight degree slope of a nearby alley called Freedom Road that was so narrow the rotor blades barely cleared the walls of two stone houses. Smith appeared next to the window of the Little Bird's copilot, Chief Warrant Officer 4 Keith Jones, mouthing the words, "I need help," for he was unable to be heard above the disturbance of the rotary blades overhead. While Maier held the controls in one hand and provided covering fire with his personal weapon in the other, Jones ran after Smith to the downed Super 61.

Within moments of Jones' departure, Lieutenant DiTomasso was nearly shot by a startled Maier when the Ranger turned the corner of a building to find the grounded Little Bird before him. With the lieutenant were his men, each having just completed the terrifying run of over three blocks, bullets boring down the alleys from every direction.

DiTomasso sent his small patrol to secure the downed helicopter's perimeter and to assist Smith and Jones, who were dragging and carrying the critically wounded Busch uphill to Star 41. Opening a small back door in the aircraft, Jones placed Busch onboard and then assisted Smith inside. With Jones once again seated, Maier applied power and climbed for a quick flight back to the American compound. But, for Busch, it would not be quick enough. His wound would prove to be fatal.

Eight minutes after Super 61 going down, the CSAR Black Hawk, carrying fifteen members of a highly trained combat search-and-rescue unit composed of Delta—including a captain and sergeant's major—and Air Force Para Rescue, commonly referred to as PJs (Para Jumpers), was hovering over Freedom Road, approximately seventy meters around the corner from Wolcott's aircraft. Doctrinally, it would be the CSAR commander who'd find himself in charge at the site of any downed aircraft.

Fourteen of the men had fast-roped in before the fifteenth man, Air Force PJ Technical Sergeant Tim Wilkinson, noticed that the team had forgotten to take their two medical kits. Waiting until the last man had exited the ropes on his side thirty feet below, Wilkinson tossed the kits out the door and jumped for the rope.

Exposed too long as a result of the delay, the CSAR bird took an RPG round on the left side, behind one of its two engines. The whirling blades overhead whistled, damaged by shrapnel. The pilot, Chief Warrant Officer Dan Jollotta, radioed the command bird that they'd been hit and had to withdrawal from the action.

However, a yell on the aircraft's intercom from one of Jollota's crew chiefs brought to his attention that there were still people on his ropes. Dangling below was not only Wilkinson, but below Wilkinson was another team member, Master Sergeant Scott Fales. Fighting his natural instinct to extract the aircraft as it began to lurch from side to side, Jollotta eased back into his hover providing the additional seconds necessary for the two men to complete their descent. This action undoubtedly spared both men from serious injuries and quite possibly death.

Peering through the swirling brown dust cloud generated by their rotary downdraft, the crew chiefs observed and reported the two men clear. Ordering the ropes cut, Jollotta eased back on his stick, pulling up and away from the insertion point. Trailing a thin gray haze of smoke, the mortally wounded aircraft started to make its way back toward the airfield three miles away. Fighting his controls the final mile of his approach, Jollotta was able to execute a rolling crash landing, hitting hard on the right landing gear but keeping the Black Hawk upright and intact. Having suffered no casualties, the crew immediately switched to a backup aircraft and headed back toward the fight.

Hesitating for a moment to orient himself, Wilkinson gazed around the area, unable to spot either the crash wreckage or his teammates. What he did spot were the two medical kits still lying in the middle of the street. Running out to grab them, he continued to run, rounding a corner to the left and stumbling upon the downed Black Hawk. His teammates, who had arrived only moments before, had already set up a tight defensive perimeter around the crash site along with DiTomasso and his small team.

The bodies of several Somalis were scattered close about with others visible in the distance. Two Somalis strayed into the area and were shot. Bullets began to fly through the area, the Somalis being careful, for the most part, to stay outside of hand grenade range. Fales, stretching up in an attempt to peer inside the right side of the aircraft, was hit in the left calf and moved to the rear of the bird. Up front and on top of the wreckage was one of the aircraft's survivors, Delta medic Sergeant James McMahon, pulling Briley's lifeless body out of the cockpit.

Further examination of the aircraft's interior found the whole frontend of the Black Hawk folded onto the remains of Wolcott, trapping him in his seat from the waist down. The real problem now became how to get the body out, for there appeared no easy way to reclaim it. Abandoning their aviation comrade was not an option for the Rangers or Delta.

As Wilkinson checked the interior of the wrecked helicopter—not sure how many crewmen remained given that a Little Bird had spirited some away—searching for classified material, weapons, and any other sensitive equipment, he discovered one of the crewmen, the left side gunner Staff Sergeant Ray Dowdy, still in his seat and buried under a large pile of debris. A Delta medic, Sergeant First Class Bob Marby, made his way into the wreckage to assist but not before Wilkinson had freed the trapped gunner.

A fusillade of bullets ripped through the skin of the aircraft with the three men inside. All three men were hit—Wilkinson in the arm and face, Dowdy had the tips of two fingers shot off, and Marby in the hand. Pulling up the Kevlar floor panels, Marby propped them up where the bullets had entered. Then, to avoid any additional exposure, the two medics tunneled out from the left troop door, bringing Dowdy out with them.

A casualty collection point was established around the bent tail of the aircraft where Fales had moved. Subsequent trips back into the bird resulted in the bulletproof mats being brought out and placed around the collection point. Hunkering down behind the mats, Fales traded rounds with gunmen in the alley while the two medics patched up the three survivors of the crash—including Dowdy's right side partner—who were all now consolidated at the tail.

From the northern end of the Mogadishu Airport in the American compound, the soldiers and airmen stood in awe observing in the distance the massive fireworks display of rockets, RPGs, and tracers. Streaking across the sky, these lethal rounds sought out the helicopters, hoping to bring down another victim.

It did not take long for the situation to dramatically worsen when an RPG claimed that second victim less than twenty minutes after the first. Overhead, Chief Warrant Officer 3 Michael Durant in Super 64 had been directed to take Super 61's orbital spot over the target area opposite Super 62, piloted by Chief Warrant Officer Mike Goffena. Durant was in the process of making his fourth or fifth racetrack at rooftop level when his Black Hawk shuddered from the detonation of a grenade against the rear rotor. From behind Super 64, Goffena observed large chunks of material rupture from Durant's gearbox as oil blew from the exposed engine rotor in a fine mist. Goffena quickly radioed Durant, informing him that he'd taken an RPG in the tail.

A scan of the instrument panel by Durant indicated that all readings still fell within equipment operating parameters. Knowing that the Black Hawk had been designed to fly without oil for a limited time, he felt confident that he could bring the crippled aircraft back to the American compound at the airfield that he could see in the distance — only a four-minute flight to the southwest. Ordered by Lieutenant Colonel Matthews in the C2 bird circling above to withdraw from the fight, Durant pulled out of his orbit and headed southwest with Goffena trailing in Super 62 for the first mile of the journey. Suddenly, just as Goffena was preparing to return to the fight, the rotor and three feet of the tail assembly of Durant's aircraft disintegrated. *Super 64 was going down.*

With the center of gravity shifted, the aircraft began to spin rapidly to the right, nose lunging down. The severity of the rotations intensified as the Black Hawk corkscrewed toward the ground, Durant struggling for control as his copilot, Chief Warrant Officer 4 Raymond A. Frank, raised his arms overhead to throw the switches on the craft's two engines in an attempt to cut power. Seconds before impact, Durant radioed, "Going in hard! Going down!" as the nose of the bird rose just enough to level off the aircraft, impacting on top of a frail shack. As the dust from the crash settled, Goffena was able to report that the aircraft had remained upright, having come to rest amid a cluster of makeshift tin huts, thus increasing the odds that there would be survivors aboard. A low pass by Super 62 confirmed the movement of at least three of the four downed airmen.

The time was 1640 and Super 64 was down in a neighborhood called Wadigley, 1500 meters southwest of Super 61's location. The task force's ultimate nightmare had been realized and the American command-and-control system was stretched to the breaking point. One bird down was bad enough but Task Force Rangers' contingency plans could cover such an event. A second Black Hawk down, though, had never been seriously considered. Now that this improbability was a reality, the only task force elements available were already committed to battle. For the moment, at least, Durant and his crew were on their own as Goffena watched a slowly growing mob of Somalis close in on the fresh kill.

But Goffena was not about to abandon his mates on the ground. Onboard were his two crew chiefs manning the aircraft's two miniguns. In addition, there were three Delta snipers, Master Sergeant Gary Gordon, Sergeant First Class Randy Shughart, and Staff Sergeant Brad Hallings. On one run after another, Goffena brought the Black Hawk down to the deck on a low sweep, employing his blade wash and door gunners to dispel the gathering mob while the Delta snipers searched and eliminated any identified RPG gunners. Small arms rounds penetrated the thin skin of the aircraft, increasing in intensity with each gun run.

Additional aircraft arrived to assist Goffena with the close air support and crowd suppression. Repeated calls by the pilots for ground assistance were met by repeated assurances that a hastily assembled ground convoy located only two miles away at the American compound would soon be on its way.

Having been directed to load his two dozen prisoners aboard one of the five-tons and consolidate his forces at the Super 61 crash site, McKnight's nine-vehicle convoy had not even begun to move before Durant's Black Hawk was shot down a mile south of the convoy's position. New orders directed McKnight to move to Wolcott's aircraft to provide what assistance they could and then move on to Durant's.

Incoming fire grew in intensity as the convoy struggled to find its way through the narrow, smoke- and lead-filled streets of the city. High overhead, the command-and-control bird tried to direct the movement of the wheeled vehicles—marked with large fluorescent-orange panels on top to assist identification.

Communications delays proved to be deadly, for commands from above to turn left or right were not received by McKnight until the lead elements of his convoy had passed the intended spot. Consequently, they were consistently turning on the wrong roads. There also proved to be one additional significant disadvantage to directing the fight from above. The airborne commanders could not adequately see the pounding the convoy was taking. What at first was believed to be a simple task—movement to the crash sites—would eventually prove to be impossible.

Contrary to the initial plan to return to the American compound following the securing of the captives, McKnight was directed to move his convoy in support of those troops located at the first crash site. Unfortunately, all hell broke loose before the vehicles even had begun to move when the convoy lost its first vehicle, a five-ton, to multiple RPG hits in front of the target building. Fortuitously, the vehicle was empty at the time, its crew dismounted and pulling local security.

Casualties began to mount steadily as the column pulled out and began to try making its way through the deadly streets to the site. Wounded were gathered and placed in the eight remaining vehicles—six Humvees and two five-tons—during periodic halts. Injured gunners manning the M-60 and .50-caliber machineguns and Mark 19 grenade launchers traded places to keep the heavy weapons operating and the convoy popped smoke to mark its location.

The airborne command-and-control elements directed McKnight to take another route, which brought him right back to a location just a block north of the target house—the very same location where they had loaded the prisoners. As luck would have it, this proved to be most fortuitous for Staff Sergeant Eversmann and the eleven other remaining men of Chalk Four. Pinned down by enemy fire since the start of the mission, Eversmann was reported to have acknowledged a directive from a Ranger officer to move though he apparently knew he would be incapable of doing so with only four or five men still able to fight. Cut off, unable to maneuver, and left behind, these Rangers were most fortunate, indeed, and Eversmann most certainly knew it as he loaded his battered and bloody men aboard the vehicles that had most fortuitously returned to their location.

With the members of Chalk Four safely mounted, the convoy continued to move only to find each dirt crossroads a virtual shooting gallery. Intersections were crossed one vehicle at a time. Every member of the convoy who could fire a weapon, including the drivers, engaged gunmen in the alleyways, on rooftops, and in windows.

Somalis were everywhere. A fifteen-man group of gunmen ran along a parallel road, pursuing the convoy and placing heavy fire at each intersection the Americans passed through. For Task Force Ranger, the rules of engagement were changing. For over an hour, the hard-fought battle had been waged, the sites, sounds, and smells of the conflict permeating the city. Forewarned, there could be only two types of people caught in the area of operation: fools or those desiring to be part of the fight. Both types presented serious problems for the Americans as supposed noncombatants began to actively participate or were seemingly willingly used as human shields. In either case, they came to be seen as part of the problem, and could consequently, under the given set of circumstances, be defined as combatants.

Back at the target house following McKnight's departure, those left behind to move dismounted to the crash site were encountering equally stiff resistance. The remainder of DiTomasso's Chalk Two were ordered to move first and to make their way to the lieutenant's location. That proved to be much easier said than done. With the sounds of a raging firefight rising in the distance, the seven men began to move east along a ten-meter-wide alley. Warned to stay away from the walls, which served as funnels for bullets, the patrol moved down the dirt road. The patrol began to take heavy fire as gunmen sprayed their automatic weapons from doorways, windows, and around corners. The Rangers laid suppressive fires north and south as they leapfrogged through each intersection.

Turning a corner three blocks later, the patrol, without having taken a casualty, linked up with the remainder of their chalk, which had established a small perimeter. DiTomasso was hunkered down behind a Volkswagen with the newly arrived patrol's leader, Yurek, when the "Bug" began to rock from the impact of heavy caliber machinegun rounds passing through it fired from a large tripod-mounted gun located in an alley. Taking a LAW, Yurek fired, only to have his round impact short. Unslinging his M-203 grenade launcher, his aim with this weapon proved to be significantly more accurate as the heavy machinegun and its crew were tossed aside by the explosion of the 40-mm round.

The men of the CSAR team watched as the Rangers from Chalk Two moved into position around the downed Black Hawk, relieved to know their numbers were growing, for the action around them was steadily increasing as rounds ricocheted all about. Some of the shots were coming from the vicinity of a clump of trees about twenty meters away. As one Ranger hosed the area down with 5.56-mm fire from his SAW, a CSAR member and some Rangers tossed hand grenades, one of which was tossed back after the others had exploded — its pin pulled but a safety clip that rested on the handle had not been "flicked" off. The grenade's detonation seriously wounded the CSAR man.

Steele had intended to conduct an orderly foot movement from his location to the crash site in conjunction with McKnight's vehicular movement from the target building. With Chalk Two either already at the site or on the move, the Ranger company commander had directed Chalk One under the leadership of Lieutenant Perino to lead the movement through the alleys, followed by Delta and trailed by Chalk Three. Chalk Four on the far corner of the perimeter — and a greater distance away than originally planned — was ordered to close on the group — an order that was acknowledged by the Chalk leader but much tougher to carry out. Miller's Delta operatives fell in with the Ranger movement.

Unit integrity did not last long, though, and began to disintegrate within two blocks of movement as Miller and his men, feeling the need to advance at a more rapid pace against the withering small-arms and RPG fire, began to strike out on their own, believing that staying alive meant moving quicker through the streets and alleys. Confused, some of the Rangers moved from their assigned chalks to join the faster paced Delta movement.

On the surface, command and control, integral to the efficiency and effectiveness of any combat unit, appeared to have broken down. But, such lack of control was not totally the case, nor should it have been totally unexpected. For those who have experienced such intensive close-quarters combat, such moments are nothing less than sheer terror, as so movingly displayed on the screen during the opening minutes of Steven Spielberg's movie, *Saving Private Ryan.* In 'combat reality,' commanders can reasonably expect to exercise command and control prior to contact and again on consolidation. As for the moments in between: even if a commander were able to issue orders during such a movement, he most likely would not be heard or—if he is—be listened to as a function of the intensity and effectiveness of the enemy. Tempo and cohesion of the unit during such times are left to the initiative of NCOs—who stepped up exceptionally well during this engagement—and individuals. To a significant extent in the alleys of Mogadishu, such initiatives proved successful.

The dismounted force moved east until meeting up with Freedom Road. A Delta team with some Rangers in tow, led by Sergeant First Class Paul Howe, were the first to round the corner of the wide dirt road and head north on a down slope to the crash site only two blocks away. For many, it would be the longest two blocks of their lifetime.

As they rounded the corner, the first RPG fired at the dismounted group impacted on a wall close by, knocking some of the men off their feet and wounding one with shrapnel on his left side. Seeking shelter, Howe kicked in the door of a one-room house. The team filed in to treat their wounded comrade, reload, and recover for a moment from the laborious run with heavy equipment that had left them breathing hard and sweating profusely. A quick examination of the wounded man found him still fit to fight.

Trailing in the group behind Howe was Lieutenant Perino. Sergeant Mike Goodale was hit in the upper right leg, necessitating the need to move him off the street and into a courtyard as the bullets and RPGs flew along the road and alleys. Some Delta men soon joined them.

Steele led the last group to turn onto Freedom Road and he felt time was quickly running out to link up with the convoy ground unit—not knowing that McKnight and his men were being hammered and not waiting at the crash site as originally planned. The convoy, though, was not the captain's primary concern at the moment. His sixty Rangers were, and he was relatively clueless as to the location of the majority of them.

Steele and his radiotelephone operator (RTO), Sergeant Chris Atwater, were facedown in the dirt, watching the last of the Deltas from the first group advance through the intersection. Suddenly, one of the men, Sergeant First Class Earl Fillmore, went slack, his black hockey-style helmet recoiling up as a bullet exited his head. He was dead before he hit the ground. The Delta following Fillmore stopped to grab the KIA but he, too, was hit in the neck after a few short steps. A third Delta assisted the wounded man with the recovery. Undoubtedly, the realization struck those around the intersection for the first time that they were in great peril.

Casualties mounted in the vehicles as the lost convoy fought its way through the city, the unarmored five-tons, in particular, serving as large, inviting, and extremely vulnerable targets for RPG rounds. Periodically, the slow-moving convoy would be seen to the west by those at the Super 61 location, passing within a block or two of the crash site. Some of the convoy's drivers were also aware of their close proximity to the downed aircraft but made no effort to relay this information to McKnight, who was in the lead vehicle, a Humvee.

In their haste to leave the target site, few if any of the other members of the convoy had been informed of the change in plan to close on the crash site. Thus, those who saw the downed Black Hawk never realized until much later that they were looking at their new mission objective.

Up front, McKnight, having sustained wounds to his arm and neck, was desperately trying to follow the directions of those circling overhead, who were now endeavoring to steer the convoy clear of potential problem sites. Periodically, the column of vehicles would make a dogleg left or right but to no avail. Neither the crash site nor relief from attack was found. On one occasion, to the disbelief of many in the convoy, they made a U-turn on a narrow street—the five-tons having to perform a three- or four-point backing maneuver to turn around—returning through a storm of heavy fire they had just successfully run.

The vehicles of the convoy were beginning to prove to be more of a liability than an asset. Lightly armored and constantly forced to stop and take on casualties, the vehicles made inviting targets. Worse yet, the Rangers were not trained for such a task. They were dismounted warriors and had little experience with convoy procedures. Their inexperience continually showed as they stopped at intersections or just beyond, forcing those behind to remain exposed. At the halt, those who were still mobile dismounted the vehicle to secure the column, resulting in more casualties that had to be placed on the vehicles.

Manning the .50-cal on the convoy's trail Humvee was Sergeant Lorenzo Ruiz. Like many of the other Rangers who were originally assigned to the convoy, he had removed the Kevlar plates from his flak vest for additional comfort while seated in the vehicle. He paid for this comfort with his life as a bullet penetrated the unarmored nylon of the vest, entering his lower right chest and exiting out his back.

Soon after Ruiz was gunned down, the convoy made another halt. Dismounting to secure their vehicle, Sergeant Casey Joyce and Specialists Aaron Hand and Eric Spalding quickly found themselves in a vicious firefight at the end of an alley. Sprinting from the trail vehicle, SEAL Petty Officer (PO) John Gay placed some suppressive fires down the alley, allowing the seriously exposed Hand to egress back to his vehicle.

Joyce was across the alley, behind cover, placing efficient and effective fires against the enemy. A short automatic weapon's burst fired down on the kneeling Ranger from a window above, though, caught the unsuspecting sergeant in the back. Despite the heavy fires and the risk involved, Specialist Jim Telscher was able to make his way to Joyce and drag him back by his shirt and vest to the vehicles. A quick examination showed that a round had passed through the top upper back of the vest, where the vest had no armored plating, and passed through his torso, exiting his abdomen. Tragically, the wound would prove to be fatal.

Racing to the front of the stalled convoy, Rierson, the senior Delta NCO present, spoke briefly with McKnight, finally learning what it was they were trying to do and where they were trying to go. Moving back down the column, he conveyed that information to each vehicle. It was then that the realization had set in with some of the men that they had actually passed the site.

The order to continue to press on with the mission was passed on to McKnight along with an additional set of directions. Shortly thereafter, McKnight rounded a corner and encountered a roadblock. The column stopped and the men deployed to provide local security as a tremendous volume of fire inundated them. Two more Rangers went down from wounds, and were dragged back to their vehicles.

Remounting, the Americans once again began to move just as they were hit with a barrage of RPG rounds. The second vehicle in line, a Humvee, caught one of the rounds as the grenade penetrated the light armored skin just in front of the gas cap. Detonating inside the vehicle, the round blew through some sandbags within the interior, ejecting Delta Master Sergeant Tim Martin, Telscher, and Private Adalberto Rodriguez from the rear of the still moving vehicle.

Black smoke filled the Hummer from small fires lit inside as the vehicle came to a halt. Rodriguez, tossed approximately ten meters from the vehicle, was struggling to his feet when he was accidentally run over by the five-ton that had been following them, its driver momentarily dazed and disoriented by another RPG detonation. Martin had been leaning against the sandbags inside the vehicle and the main force of the blast had passed through his lower body, practically tearing the master sergeant in half. Soldiers again scrambled from their vehicles to secure the three men on the ground and the other wounded and stunned men still left in the destroyed Humvee. Seriously wounded, Rodriguez would survive his injuries; Martin, though still alive, would not.

Farther back in the convoy, Private Ed Kallman, driving a Hummer, was waiting for another vehicle preceding him to clear an intersection when he caught sight of a smoke trail heading right for him. The RPG impacted against the vehicle's door just opposite the young driver, the resulting detonation knocking Kallman out. Regaining consciousness just a few seconds later, he resumed his driver's position and pressed the accelerator to the floor. The vehicle responded and raced through the intersection. Fate had intervened on behalf of Kallman and all those aboard his vehicle, for the driver's window had been rolled down. The combination of the lightly armored Kevlar door and the reinforced glass window inside had proven to be enough to defeat the penetrating capability of the RPG.

With the attempt to deploy a second ground element to Durant's crash site — Staff Sergeant Struecker's convoy — the situation grew even more confused for McKnight as the command-and-control elements attempted to direct two independent ground forces to two independent crash sites. Repeatedly, the battalion commander would receive instructions directing him to the second site when, in reality, he was still searching for the first. Back in the column, the Delta medic, Sergeant First Class Don Hutchingson, was providing medical attention to those wounded while Rierson maintained communications with the Little Birds, relaying updates and calling in close air support.

Finding themselves in a relatively nonlethal environment for the moment, McKnight halted the convoy, and reviewed their situation with some of the column's senior NCOs. A quick SITREP to Romeo 64 brought an insistent response pressing McKnight to move to the first crash site. But McKnight knew that the situation for his men was worse at that moment than the situation they probably would find at the location of the downed bird. He already had more dead and wounded with him than the other two crash sites combined, and if he did not get his most serious casualties back, there would be more dead. What vehicles he had left were barely running and he was low on ammunition.

In addition to all that, he was still lugging around the prisoners. Though one had been shot dead and a second one wounded, the Somalis obviously were being very careful and not intentionally firing on the captive's vehicle. The convoy had made a gallant, though fruitless, effort to assist their downed comrades. Frustrated and enraged at their inability to find the crash site, McKnight realized it was now time to return to base.

Seven seriously battered vehicles remained: five Humvees and two five-tons. McKnight's Humvee still led, followed by a second Humvee—a cargo vehicle lacking heavy gun capability, dragging its rear axle and being pushed along by one of the five-tons. Gay's Humvee was running on three flat tires, while a fourth, Kallman's, had all four flat, in addition to a large hole in the driver's door from the RPG.

Encountering ambush after ambush, the survivors fought to remain alive. A Mark 19 automatic grenade launcher atop a Humvee pumped round after round of deadly, accurate fire into second-story windows at the hands of Specialist James Cavaco. As he turned and began to engage targets down an alley to his left, he took a round to the back of the head, just under his Kevlar, killing him instantly. His body was pulled down and Delta Sergeant Paul Leonard stepped up to take the vacated position. Minutes later, a bullet passed through the vehicle, striking Leonard in the left leg and taking off much of it behind and below the knee. With a tourniquet in place, the resolute sergeant remained in the turret and continued to place exceptionally accurate and devastating fires on the enemy.

Another gunner, Private First Class Tory Carlson, manning a .50-cal, was also hit in the leg as he laid down suppressive fires. Wounded in the right knee, he initially felt great fear and found it difficult to breathe. Then, as he realized it was not he but his buddies who mattered, his fear passed and he once again placed the machinegun into operation.

In the second of the two five-tons, Private First Class Richard Kowalewski, commonly referred to as "Alphabet," continued to drive despite a wound to the shoulder. Private First Class Clay Othic was struggling within the confined space of the vehicle's cab to apply a pressure dressing to Kowalewski's wound when an RPG round entered the vehicle from the left side, severing the driver's left arm and embedding itself in his chest, killing the young Ranger instantly. Failing to detonate, the two-foot-long rocket with fins protruded from under the stump of the missing appendage.

Continuing to move, Kowalewski's driverless truck rear-ended the vehicle in front, the remaining five-ton that was carrying the precious cargo, causing that truck to veer into a wall. Again, the convoy halted to assess the situation and to gather casualties. Incredibly, Othic and Hand, the other man in the cab, suffered only minor injuries. Kowalewski's body was moved to the rear of the vehicle with the RPG round still imbedded in his body. Hand recovered the missing arm. Uncertain as to what to do with it, he placed it inside the cargo pockets of his pants, feeling it would be wrong to leave it behind. The convoy once again moved on with a new driver in Kowalewski's vehicle.

The group finally encountered something they recognized, a four-lane road that led to the K-4 traffic circle and their home base. Gay's Humvee was now the lead vehicle with one Ranger KIA and eight wounded in back. A wounded Delta sergeant was in the front, stretched out between the SEAL and his driver. Encountering the last of what seemed to have been an infinite number of roadblocks, this final one was constructed of fifty-five-gallon drums that had been placed across the road amid other debris and set ablaze.

Fearful that his vehicle would not be able to start again should he stop—having been hit by dozens of rounds and running on its tire rims—which the vehicle is designed to do but certainly not under these most adverse of circumstances, Gay ordered his driver, fellow Navy SEAL PO Homer Nearpass, to ram the roadblock. Their luck held as they breached the obstacle, going over and through the flames. Behind, the remainder of the convoy followed as Gay led them to the K-4 circle.

At the Mogadishu airfield, American soldiers, sailors, and airmen gathered, listening to the firefight on the radio and the downing of both Wolcott's and Durant's Black Hawks. Some were eager to "move to the sound of the guns," while others felt a great deal of trepidation and anguish—especially those who had already braved the violent streets of Mogadishu once and had lived to tell about it. To feel such overwhelming fear was not at all unreasonable given the set of circumstances these men had faced. If courage is defined as action in the face of that fear, then all participants were courageous that day.

Word soon spread that Staff Sergeant Struecker's two shot-up gun vehicles along with an additional two Humvees and three five-ton flatbed trucks were to make an attempt to reach Durant's crash site. As the rescue team of Rangers, Delta, cooks, clerks, and other volunteers began to assemble, a Delta sergeant took Struecker aside, offering some sage advice about washing down his blood-splattered vehicle. "If you don't, your guys are going to get more messed up. They're going to get sick."

One Ranger in particular, Specialist Dale Sizemore, watched Struecker and his men prepare to depart. Dressed in a T-shirt and athletic shorts, the young Ranger had injured his elbow a few days prior. With a cast on his arm, he was not only unable to deploy on the day's raid, he was manifested to depart on a flight for the United States later that evening. Informing Struecker that he was going to join the convoy, Sizemore ran back into the hangar, putting on his BDUs while searching for stray gear such as Kevlar and flak vest. Grabbing his SAW, the specialist returned to the vehicles, his pockets bulging with extra ammunition, his shirt unbuttoned and boots unlaced. Sizemore's response to Sergeant Raleigh Cash's directive that he could not deploy with a cast on was to cut it off.

When confirmation was received that McKnight and his men were returning to the compound, the hastily assembled convoy of men and vehicles began to deploy to Durant's location less than two miles away. Taking a left turn out of the compound's back gate, Staff Sergeant Struecker's lead vehicle had traveled no farther than eighty meters when all hell broke loose as the seven vehicle convoy—two Hummers in the front, two to the rear, and the three five-tons in the center—came under heavy fire. At point, Struecker's Humvee was the primary target as an RPG round scraped across the top of his vehicle, continuing on to detonate against a concrete wall just a short distance away. The force of the explosion raised one side of the heavy vehicle clear off the ground.

Struecker very quickly realized that continued movement forward along this route would invite disaster, especially for those lying exposed on the flatbeds of the five-tons. A quick order to his driver had the vehicle backing into the second vehicle in column, which backed into the third. This sequence of events was repeated until all the vehicles had reversed back into the safety of the compound.

Seeking another route from the C2 bird circling above, Struecker led his small command back out the gate, making a right instead of a left turn, and found themselves encountering a large roadblock composed of wire, dirt, and large chunks of concrete. The .50-cals in the convoy opened up, laying down suppressive fires. Beyond the roadblock, Struecker could see a concrete wall that surrounded the immense ghetto in which Durant's Black Hawk had fallen.

A quick assessment of the situation virtually eliminated all their options at this location. While his Hummers could traverse the roadblock, the five-tons could not, and even if he were able to get his force on the other side of the obstacle, the wall itself served as an additional barrier with no points of passage in immediate view.

Struecker's request to those overhead for a third route was met with the response that there was no other route. Unwilling to concede defeat, the sergeant continued to press for a way until it was revealed that the only option left available was for the convoy to make its way around the city and come in from the rear. Struecker accepted the option.

Soldiers dismounted, providing 360-degree local security and engaging targets as the vehicles—the five-tons in particular—struggled to turn-around in the narrow street, ramming into walls as they moved back and forth. With the convoy finally turned around, the security elements remounted and they all began to make their way along a road that ran southwest through the city, with only a few bursts of fire directed their way. From one rise on the road, they could actually see Durant's crash site only a quarter of a mile away—not knowing that five of the valiant defenders, including two Delta snipers inserted earlier—were already dead and that the sixth, Durant, having suffered a serious beating at the hands of an angry mob, was now a captive.

They continued on their route, eventually arriving at the K-4 traffic circle. The scene they came upon at K-4 was shocking. Before them were the smoking and bleeding remnants of McKnight's convoy that had arrived at the circle just moments before, the broken-down cargo Hummer still being pushed by a five-ton. Struecker and his men were even more stunned to find the shot-up vehicles overloaded with dead and wounded Rangers.

For McKnight and his men, who had expected a serious fight at the circle, the sight of Struecker's relief column approaching them was a godsend. Struecker and his men quickly encircled the battered force, setting up security. The transfer of the dead and wounded from the most heavily damaged vehicles began as the cargo Humvee and Gay's vehicle were abandoned and destroyed.

In the midst of the transfer, there was a bright flash followed by an explosion as an RPG detonated under one of Struecker's Humvees. The force of the explosion blew the vehicle into the air but it landed back on all four wheels, undamaged, and still fully functional as demonstrated by its .50-cal, which quickly eliminated a Somali gunner in a tree.

Though they had less than a mile to travel, the return trip was not easy as the combined force—Struecker's element pulling rear security—exchanged fire with everything they encountered along the way, pouring heavy volumes of fire in all directions and down every alleyway. Then, just blocks from the compound, quiet, as the Somali guns fell silent and the Americans entered a different world, as large crowds slowly rambled through open-air markets.

The masses parted, allowing the embattled convoy to slowly make its way through the gate of the compound. Unbelievably, as they traversed the final one hundred meters, the Somalis all turned to face the Americans and proceeded to applaud.

The time was approximately 1730 and McKnight and his men were finally secure—though, unfortunately, one of the convoy's survivors, First Class Matt Rierson, would be killed a short time later by a mortar attack against the airfield that would also wound twelve others. Within the compound, personnel surrounded the vehicles to find wounded

Rangers piled on top of dead ones, who were on top of live Somali prisoners, who were on top of Somali dead.

Some of the dead Rangers' eyes were wide open, the fear still somehow captured in them. Others had a look of peace. Kowalewski still had the unexploded RPG round stuck in his chest. After his body had been carefully off loaded from the vehicle, a bunker had to be built around it out of fear the warhead would detonate.

The convoy's cost had been steep: four KIA, numerous wounded, and three dead prisoners. Yet the battle was still in full swing and the grim reaper still had a price to exact. For the moment, at least, the ninety-nine men scattered in groups around the site of Super 61 were on their own.

Hours earlier, the air commander had rejected the requests of his four MH-6 Little Bird copilots that they be inserted on the ground to defend Durant and his three crewmen. Two additional requests to be inserted from the Delta snipers on Goffena's Black Hawk, Gordon and Shughart, were also denied. Finally, a third request by these two NCOs was approved after it was learned that Struecker's convoy, upon which the command's hopes had rested, had been forced to turn back.

Upon hearing the news, Gordon, the team chief, expressed his satisfaction with the decision with a smile and a "thumbs up." Moving to the back of the aircraft with Shughart, they set about making their plans. Though the intent of the insertion was to have the two men — each armed with only his sniper rifle and a pistol — provide first aid, establish a defensive perimeter, and secure the site until the arrival of a rescue force, all concerned knew that death was awaiting the two Delta NCOs below in the streets of Mogadishu for no rescue force would arrive in time before the growing number of enemy personnel observed closing in on the crash site overwhelmed them. An eyewitness would later state, "Anyone in their right mind wouldn't have done what they did."

But Gordon and Shughart also knew that the four wounded men below would have no chance of survival without additional support. At a later ceremony, Master Sergeant Gordon's widow, Carmen, spoke of why she believed her husband did what he did. "Gary went back to save his fellow soldiers, not to die there. Gary was one hundred percent Ranger. He lived the Rangers' creed every day. He knew that he had a chance. He and Shughart wouldn't ever have gone out there trying to be heroes."

The first insertion failed as debris and small arms fire made a landing difficult. Finding a second site in a small clearing approximately one hundred meters from Super 64, Goffena employed the blade wash of his Black Hawk as it hovered five feet above the ground to knock down a fence. Gordon tripped and fell as he ran for cover. Shughart, in his haste to disembark, forgot to disconnect his safety line and had to be cut free of the aircraft as it began to ascend.

The swirling debris, noise, and confusion of combat disoriented the two snipers. Crouched in the open field, Shughart motioned to Goffena their confusion as to which direction to move. The pilot brought his aircraft back down, leaned out the window, and pointed the way to Super 64 as one of his crew chiefs tossed a smoke grenade in the direction of Durant's bird. The last sight of the two intrepid soldiers as Super 62 lifted off to hover overhead with covering fires was of both men signaling a thumbs up as they began to fight their way under intense small arms fire through a dense maze of shanties and shacks to the downed Black Hawk.

In the wreckage of Super 64, all four crewmen had survived the crash. Durant, knocked out by the impact, regained consciousness to find the femur of his right leg broken and a large sheet of tin punched through his shattered windshield and draped over him. Frank had his left tibia broken. Both pilots had sustained back injuries. Unable to move, Durant secured his German MP-5K 9-mm rifle and prepared to defend himself from his seat as the copilot crawled from the wreckage out the opposite side.

Just as Frank moved out of his view, Durant was surprised and relieved by the arrival of Gordon and Shughart. Undoubtedly, a rescue team had arrived and their trial by fire would soon be over. Calmly reaching in, the two Delta men gently lifted and carried the injured pilot outside of the right side of the aircraft to a nearby tree. Behind him, the front end of his aircraft was wedged tightly against a tin wall, which the pilot covered with his weapon. Staff Sergeant William Cleveland, nearly comatose and covered in blood from the waist down was placed near Durant.

Gordon and Shughart moved to the left side of the chopper to extract the remaining crew chief, Staff Sergeant Thomas J. Field. Frank, having exited the cockpit from his left seat, joined the two Delta sergeants engaging the approaching militia and defending the exposed side of the downed helicopter.

Unknown to any of the six men at the site, Maier and Jones were once again on the ground with their Little Bird, personal weapons drawn, only one hundred and ten meters or so away. Having done what they could for Wolcott and his crew at the first crash site, they had set down to see what they could do for Durant and his men. Goffena circled above, observing Gordon and Shughart moving about the site and realized that the two Delta men would not be able to move the wounded men the distance necessary to link up with Star 41. Reluctantly, after a five-minute wait and a brief by Goffena of the crew's condition, Maier and Jones, fuel running precariously low, were forced to lift off to refuel.

Fate intervened again twenty minutes into Super 64's fight when Super 62 took an RPG round in the cockpit that knocked out the copilot and amputated the door gunner's leg. With the windshield knocked out, the right side of the aircraft blown apart, and the number-two engine destroyed, Goffena was still able to miraculously nurse Super 62 back in the direction of the airfield. Unable to make it to the flight line, he skillfully conducted a controlled crash landing in the dock areas, undoubtedly saving the lives of his crew.

With their air cover gone, Gordon and Shughart were on their own, facing an overwhelming number of Somali militia advancing on the wreckage of Super 64. Automatic weapons of the defending Americans covered all approaches to the downed aircraft and a multitude of Somali bodies littered the entire area.

But time—and luck—were soon to run out on the gallant defenders. An exchange of gunfire brought a shout of anger and pain from Shughart on the far side of the wreck. Durant never heard from him again.

Moments later, Gordon moved to the right side of the aircraft, searching for ammunition and asking the dazed, confused, and painfully wounded pilot if there were any weapons onboard. Searching the interior, Gordon returned with the crew chiefs' M-16s in hand.

Reality—and probably a sense of hopelessness—finally struck the wounded warrant officer when the sergeant asked him what the support frequency was on the survival radio. With a sickening and nauseous feeling, Durant realized that such a question only meant one thing: the two Delta men had arrived at the site on their own, with no other support. There were no other rescue team members!

Following Durant's brief explanation of procedure, Gordon established radio contact, requesting immediate help. The reply, as it had been before his insertion, was that a reaction force was en route to their location. With that, the Delta sniper gathered his weapons and moved back around to the left side of the aircraft to engage the advancing militia.

Out of ammunition, Gordon returned once again to the wreckage, looking for anything to fight with, only to find very little. Gordon handed a loaded CAR-15 automatic rifle to Durant, whose own 9-mm weapon was either out of ammunition or jammed. Telling him "Good luck," Gordon made his way back to the far side armed only with a pistol.

At the nose end of the aircraft, Durant observed two Somalis trying to climb over. A short burst from the automatic rifle caused them to quickly disappear. Another Somali tried to crawl over the wall. Durant shot him, as he did a second man trying to crawl around a corner. Off in the distance, less than a mile and a half to the south, Durant could hear the throaty roar of .50-caliber machineguns as Struecker's rescue convoy tried to deploy from the vicinity of the American compound.

Without warning, there was a hail of small arms fire on the left side of the Black Hawk, lasting for nearly two minutes, as a force of over a dozen concealed men focused their concentrated fires on the one remaining defender on the left side. Gordon's shout of pain was soon followed by silence.

The crowd surged across the clearing, descending on the four Americans who lay before them on the exposed side of the Black Hawk, one of whom was still alive, shouting and waving his arms as the mob grabbed his limbs, struggling to tear his and the other three bodies into pieces. Within a short time, the lifeless bodies of the Americans were being joyfully paraded and drug naked through the streets.

On the far side of the aircraft, his weapon empty, and a loaded pistol strapped to his side but forgotten, Durant placed the rifle across his chest, folded his hands over it, and waited to die. The crowd rushed around the tail of the aircraft, assailing Durant and the body of his crew chief lying beside him.

High above, the cameras aboard the surveillance helicopters recorded images of "indigenous personnel moving around all over the crash site." Nearly two hours after the aircraft had gone down, the fierce and deadly battle for Super 64 was over, all defenders and crew dead with the exception of Chief Warrant Officer 3 Durant, whose life would be spared to serve as a hostage and whose eleven days of captivity, pain, and affliction, were just commencing.

AUTHOR'S NOTE: Official records and their Medal of Honor citations reflect that Shughart was the first one killed in action with Gordon being killed just prior to Durant's capture. Subsequent interviews with Durant indicate that the official reports may have reversed the roles of the two Delta NCOs. Each Delta team member had a weapon designed and modified to his personal specifications — usually an M-14 or CAR-15. Based on the description of the weapon he was handed, it seems that Durant was provided Gordon's rifle as a final defense. It is doubtful the sniper would have handed over his own personal weapon and fought with another.

Durant had also indicated that he'd met Shughart before, during an air mission prebrief, and he did not recognize the man who stood before him that day of the battle. Records, though, indicate it was Gordon who had attended the prebrief in question, and thus it was Shughart he had not seen before. While the truth may never be known with certainty — though the audio tape of the final transmission from Super 64 would most probably indicate who died first — it is nearly irrelevant, for both of these courageous and professional soldiers fought and died as a team attempting to defend their fellow comrades in arms.

The casualties continued to mount in the vicinity of Super 61. Two Ranger gunners working an M-60 machinegun, Private First Class Peter Neathery and Vince Errico were each hit in the right arm. Lying on the ground behind a tin hut, Steele and another of his officers, Lieutenant James Lechner, were on the radio and failed to note Delta Sergeant Norm Hooten, who was trying to warn them from across the way when they began taking fire.

Steele was able to make it into the courtyard from which Hooten beckoned, and to which the previously wounded Goodale had been moved, but Lechner was not so lucky, suffering a bone-shattering wound to the leg as he tried to scramble from behind the shed. Delta medic Sergeant First Class Bart Bullock and a second man dashed out to bring the wounded man back to the courtyard for treatment.

On the radio again, Lieutenant Colonel Harrell — who was, by default, the 'ground commander' as a result of McKnight's predicament — answered Steele's strong demands for immediate support from McKnight's convoy and extraction in the command bird high above the fray.

"I understand you need to be extracted. I've done everything I can to get those vehicles to you, over."

Steele's weary response was, "Roger, understand."

From the doorway of the courtyard, Steele motioned for more of his men to join him. Eventually, he ended up with a courtyard full of wounded men.

A block up the road, several small groups of Rangers and Delta had linked up with those defending the downed Black Hawk who still found themselves caught in a kill zone targeted by AK-47s and RPG rounds. Eventually an L-shaped perimeter was established that included the intersection of the crash. At the destroyed aircraft itself, the CSAR team continued to gather casualties as well as work to recover the trapped body of the dead pilot. Air cover continued to be provided by the Little Birds and Black Hawks but the pilots' fires were restricted with so many of the enemy mixed in among the friendlies scattered about.

Howe was looking for a location to get his men off the street. With the assistance of a second man, he broke through a gate securing a narrow courtyard between two houses in the vicinity of Lieutenant DiTomasso and his men. Inside one of the houses, they found a family cowering in the corner of a room. Following a quick search, their hands were secured and they were moved to a side room.

Miller, who had finally caught up to the fast moving Howe, and the rest of the Delta team settled into the courtyard and houses. Miller, who had been monitoring the progress of McKnight's badly mauled column, knew it would be a longer than anticipated wait until those at the crash site, now cut off and surrounded, were rescued.

Farther back along Freedom Road, the Rangers of Perino's Chalk One continued to move forward, creeping along the walls, searching for the position that offered the advantage of being able to see and to not be seen, thus allowing them to eliminate targets with the risk of minimum exposure to return fire. Others, unable to find such positions, risked exchanging shots by exposing themselves. During one such exchange, Ranger Specialist Jamie Smith, standing behind a tin shed, took a round from a volley of gunfire that ripped through the shack" The bullet severed his femoral artery in the upper thigh. On the street, others lay wounded. Over half of Perino's thirteen men, eight in total, were casualties.

Perino and Sergeant First Class Kurt Schmid pulled the seriously wounded Smith into a compound off the street. An examination of the wound found a gaping hole in the Ranger's upper leg and blood everywhere. As Schmid began his treatment, the lieutenant radioed Steele to inform him that he could go no farther. "We have more wounded than I can carry," he informed his commander. Steele, though, wanted his unit concentrated in the vicinity of the wreckage and thus directed his subordinate to push on.

Perino was able to establish contact with DiTomasso, who was located across an alley from Super 61 in a stone house. Unable to confirm the position verbally, DiTomasso popped a red smoke grenade, revealing in the darkening sky that he was only fifty feet or so away from Perino.

Fifty feet or fifty miles. It was the same either way for Perino and his men. He did not have the resources to move his wounded through the crossfire to link up with DiTomasso. In response to Steele's insistence that he move forward to assist, Perino replied, "Look, sir, I've got three guys left, counting myself. How can I help him?" Faced with that logic, Steele relented, directing the lieutenant to occupy and defend the building at his current location.

It was nearly 1700 and the fight had "only" been ongoing for an hour and fifteen minutes, yet during that time two Black Hawks had been shot down, two others had been seriously crippled, a lost and misdirected convoy was being severely mauled, and the dismounted rescue force was scattered about, itself now needing to be rescued. The situation only continued to grow progressively worse.

In Perino's courtyard, the medic had his hand in Smith's leg, trying to stem the flow of blood. Because the wound was so high on the leg, a tourniquet could not be applied. Clamps and hemostats could not be placed on the artery either. The only option left was direct pressure with fingers placed within the leg, pressing directly against the ruptured artery.

Steele relayed Perino's request for a Medevac to higher headquarters, though it proved to be exceptionally tough to be heard with all of the ongoing events generating their own radio traffic. Headquarters' reply was of no help. The current situation precluded any relief effort. Placing another helicopter in the caldron of the Super 61 area of operation was not an option at that moment, or any time in the foreseeable future.

At the Super 61 crash site, the beat up and exhausted soldiers grew concerned as the sun set. Exceptionally well versed and trained as night fighters, the force found itself without its technological edge, having left its night vision devices — both for personnel and weapons — behind. Without that advantage, they all knew that whatever the night was to bring, it could not be dealt with as effectively as it could have been with the NODs.

As darkness fell, Wilkinson received a radio transmission requesting his assistance with Private First Class Carlos Rodriguez, who had a round strike him in the buttock, pass through his pelvis, and exit from his upper thigh. Picking up his medical kit, he braved the fires in the open street, rushing from his place of relative security inside the downed Black Hawk to the courtyard across the street where Miller had set up his command post. With the use of wads of gauze and pneumatic pants, he was able to stop the bleeding.

Wilkinson's only problem now was that the IV he'd just hooked up was his last. There were more but they were back at the downed aircraft with his wounded partner, Fales. Back out into the open he dashed, to the Black Hawk. Gathering up a load of the fluid, he once again defied the fires, making it through the lead hail without being hit. A request by Wilkinson to have the seriously wounded Ranger extracted was met with just a look from Miller that indicated there was nothing more that could be done for the time being.

After nightfall, the pace of the Somali attacks slackened noticeably until all grew quiet. Lights flickered in the city, indicating that life still existed beyond the limits of the task force's defensive perimeter. Fires were burning back in the vicinity of the target house. The helicopter gunships were still in the air, as they would be all night, periodically making runs when targets exposed themselves. Later, unconfirmed reports would indicate that pilots and crewmen—under the supervision of the regiment's flight surgeons—were offered the option of taking amphetamines to keep them awake and alert. Meanwhile, on the ground, ammunition was running low and many of the men were parched, having left their canteens behind, believing they'd be in and out, mission complete, within an hour.

Those across the street from Miller's compound were ordered to fall back through the intersection, into the courtyard. During the withdrawal, Specialist John Stebbins was badly wounded by the explosion of an RPG round that nearly took his head off. Later, two RPG rounds struck the building occupied by Miller and his men, starting several front-room fires. The smoke and fumes filling the house forced all but the wounded and medics attending them out for a time before they reoccupied the structure.

In early evening, a Black Hawk made a daring run to deliver ammunition, water, and medical supplies into an area that had already seen two helicopters shot down and two others hit and heavily damaged. Hovering over the intersection within the defenders' perimeter, the resupply helicopter took numerous small arms hits and deftly avoided RPG fire as all supplies were pushed out. A Delta volunteer crewman was added to the growing list of casualties with shrapnel wounds to the face and shoulders. The aircraft just barely made it out and back to the airfield, the fifth Black Hawk to be destroyed that day.

Within the area were ninety-nine men—nearly evenly split between Rangers and Delta—who had moved off the streets and hunkered down in four houses, the Black Hawk's wreckage, and associated courtyards. Farthest away was Steele with nearly thirty Rangers, some Delta, and nearly every automatic weapon from the blocking force at his location.

At the crash site, Miller repeatedly requested Steele's assistance in consolidating their forces. Even though the two company commanders shared the same FM net, Steele never once spoke directly with Miller. When informed that Miller was unable to make contact with Steele by

FM, one of the Delta team leaders at the Ranger's location offered his MX communications set to Steele to speak with Miller, only to have Steele refuse to take it.

Overhead, having heard Miller's requests, Harrell agreed that the force should consolidate on the crash site, thus providing greater defensive fires and making it easier for the gunships to do their job. Steele indicated he would make the attempt. However, upon hearing the news, Sergeant First Class Sean Watson, the leader of Chalk Three, told his commander he needed to reconsider. Five wounded men would have to be moved. Two were serious, each requiring to be transported by a four-man litter team. The body of Fillmore had to be carried. Then there was the issue of just getting out of the door. On the other hand, the courtyard and building were easily defensible with the force they had. Upon reflection, Steele agreed with his senior NCO, informing Harrell that he would not be able to move with the casualties he had. Harrell left it to the two commanders on the ground, unwilling to make a decision either way.

After seeking communications and coordination with Steele for over two hours, Miller finally gave up. Still needing men to reinforce his perimeter, Miller ordered the Delta men with Steele to close on his position. Though aggravated, Steele did not attempt to stop the men. The Delta men lined up and the first four rushed out the door into the darkness. The area lit up as weapons opened up from everywhere. Seconds later, the four men were soaring back through the door, landing in a tangled heap. Later, during early morning darkness, the Delta team was able to slip out and safely make their way to Miller's location.

At the Black Hawk, a hole was blown through the wall against which the wreckage rested to gain access to the stone house occupied by Miller on the far side, allowing all the wounded and dead — with the exception of Wolcott, whose body was still trapped — to be transferred into the adjacent space.

Less than fifty meters away in another courtyard, Wilkinson, Perino, and others were trying to save Smith's life, each taking his turn applying pressure to keep the punctured femoral artery closed. He needed immediate medical attention and he was not going to get it lying in the dirt of the courtyard. Perino transmitted the request to Steele, who radioed Harrell. The Lieutenant Colonel's response was not encouraging, noting how badly the resupply helicopter had been pounded in less time than it would take for a grounded Medevac to load casualties.

Harrell pressed the issue with headquarters, though, informing them that there would be more KIAs from WIAs if the two men in question, Smith and Rodriguez, were not extracted soon. Another helicopter would not be risked, command replied. Steele's two seriously wounded men would just have to wait until the QRF made it to their location, which they estimated would be within the next hour. Shortly thereafter, the news was broadcast over the command net that James Smith, the son of a retired Lieutenant Colonel Vietnam veteran Ranger, had bled to death from his wounds.

Close air support was stellar, with those on the ground knowing full well they owed their lives to their aviation comrades, for no one there doubted they'd have been overrun without their gun runs. Helicopter crews flew nearly nonstop for almost eighteen hours as Matthews rotated the AH-6Js and his remaining Black Hawks over the primary objective, breaking them off only to rearm and to refuel.

A five-word phrase was indelibly etched in the minds of all who listened on the radios: "Where do you want it?" To that question, the answer from Miller or the CSAR captain was usually to place it "Danger close" — as close as twenty feet of a friendly position.

Even when equipment failed, the crews quickly reacted. During one approach, a lead helicopter detected the launch of an RPG from a position 700 meters distant. The pilot "sparkled" — targeted — the gunner with his laser and passed it off to a trail bird. Accepting the target, the trail attempted to engage with his minigun, which malfunctioned. Quickly switching over to rockets, the pilot killed the gunner. Overall time of engagement was three to five seconds.

During the course of the battle, the aircraft cycled through the Forward Arming and Refuel Point (FARP) up to a dozen times each. Armed during that time with eighty-seven rockets and 64,000 rounds of 7.62-mm minigun ammunition, the gunships would fire sixty-three rockets and 48,000 rounds into the engagement area. Over 12,500 gallons of fuel were pumped.

As the hours marched into darkness, Miller and the CSAR captain continued to maintain their perimeter around the downed aircraft. When they were not working CAS and suppressive fires, they were cross leveling and running supplies between their positions. Working together, they had no issue as to who was in "command."

Support on the ground also continued to push. In the "door" as the QRF was C Company, 2nd Battalion, 14th Infantry Regiment (2/14 Infantry) — the "Golden Dragons." Having heard of the first Black Hawk being shot down, the ready company of the QRF received word at 1629 to deploy to the airfield to reinforce Task Force Ranger. Needing to skirt

around Mogadishu's SNA neighborhoods, C Company deployed in sixteen vehicles to the airport from their university location—which was
two miles west and in the southern part of the city—by a long, secure
route that skirted to the south, reaching the Ranger compound at 1724.

Again, another flaw in the Task Force Ranger plan became glaringly
obvious at this point: Their planning was not integrated with the 2/14
Infantry mission. Garrison reported through the Commander-in-Chief
Central Command to the NCA. Montgomery, who controlled the QRF,
reported along a U.N. chain of command. Thus, there was no one
involved with the QRF who was knowledgeable about the Task Force
Ranger missions. Such a lack of integration had not been an issue during
the first six missions, for the QRF was not needed. Now that it was, 2/14
Infantry needed to first deploy to the Rangers' compound to be briefed on
its mission prior to heading out into the streets of Mogadishu. This was
time that could ill afford to be lost.

Lieutenant Colonel Bill David, battalion commander of 2/14 Infantry
and the ground commander of the QRF—which also had elements of the
1/87 Infantry assigned to it—arrived with C Company and met with
Major General Garrison. Attached to Task Force Ranger, David was
directed by Garrison to retrieve Durant's downed aircrew. David, given
the enemy and the city he was to face, knew the effort required a force
much more significant in size than what he currently had on hand.
David's request to bring up the remainder of his battalion was not met
with a great deal of enthusiasm. Time was of the essence and Garrison
was hoping speed would substitute for David's lack of firepower. Little
Bird and QRF Cobra gunship support were promised.

As David developed and issued his plan, a patchwork force of Task
Force Ranger headquarters soldiers—cooks, clerks, staff—scrambled
aboard six Humvees. Not quite sure where they were going, only knowing their comrades needed help, they preceded David's convoy by a few
minutes. David departed at 1747 with his company in column with seven
Kevlar-armored Hummers and nine sandbag-lined five-ton cargo trucks.

The six Ranger vehicles in front and sixteen QRF vehicles to the rear
moved north at a good clip of thirty miles per hour despite the fire they
had started to take as soon as they pulled out of the gate. Just north of the
K-4 circle, at 1754, all that changed. Direct fires increased dramatically
and a Ranger Humvee veered off the road and started to burn. A second
Ranger vehicle was hit. The column slowed and began to close up on the
lead vehicles.

Tracers were flying everywhere, as were RPGs, with estimates of up
to 200 or more being fired during this segment of the engagement. The
150 men in the convoy dismounted. From the airfield, observers saw

black smoke rising from the vicinity of K-4. The radio net grew eerily quiet. Though badly outnumbered, the Americans were very fortunate, for the Somalis proved to be rather lousy shots, wounding only two of David's men.

The aircrews of TF 160 found it difficult to provide accurate fires for the force. Not accustomed to working with their type of aircraft and support, the QRF had to have it explained during the course of engagement how to mark and adjust for fires. Communication was reestablished at 1815 when David frustratingly reported that they could move no farther.

The QRF unit continued to fight until 1821, at which time they were ordered to withdraw. Even with the support of A Company 2/14 Infantry and the QRF Cobras, it took David nearly an hour to break contact after an expenditure of over 40,000 rounds of ammunition and hundreds of grenades. Clearly, a larger, stronger, and armored force would be required to break through to the trapped Rangers.

The QRF's second effort involved the use of a heavy armor force composed of a platoon of four Pakistani American-manufactured M-48 tanks and two companies of Malaysian mechanized infantry consisting of twenty-eight Russian-built BRDM wheeled armored personnel carriers (APC)—all painted the U.N. color of *white*. David augmented his original company with another 150 men from his A Company. An additional composite unit of approximately fifty Rangers in four Humvees under McKnight—ambulatory survivors from the lost convoy—Delta, and SEALs, joined the rescue force, which now totaled well over 425 men.

Humvees and five-tons were added to the convoy until it totaled seventy vehicles in all. David charitably called the entire procedure a "mess." Others called it a "three-ring circus." No matter what it was called, it was, in reality, the only rescue force in town.

The effort took over four hours to put together. In that blackout drive would be used—a tactical lighting system on vehicles that did not use the large head or tail lights—operators had to be found who knew how to drive with NVGs. And, while the U.N. allied officers spoke English, their men did not, which resulted in delay as instructions had to be translated.

Then there was the issue of David having to explain to the Malaysians that it was their APCs he needed, not their soldiers. They would be replaced, with the exception of the driver, the track commander, an assistant, and a machinegunner, by his Alpha Company and whoever else could squeeze inside the rear of the vehicles—approximately nine Americans per carrier.

David's plan—developed on the hood of a Humvee, flashlight in hand—was to lead with the four Pakistani tanks, fight their way to a midway point between the two crash sites and then split his column in the two directions. There was only one problem with the plan: The Pakistani tank commander had been directed by his headquarters not to lead the attack.

The QRF deployed at 2324 from New Port, a facility a few miles up the coast from Task Force Ranger's base and the site that had been used to affect the linkup between the multinational forces. As to who would lead, a compromise had been reached with the Pakistanis regarding the deployment of their tanks. Initially, they would lead along what became known as the "Mogadishu Mile" to the K-4 circle and a bit beyond, punching through any roadblocks or ambushes encountered along the way. Shortly thereafter, the APCs mounted with the 10th Mountain's Alpha Company would pass through and lead the remainder of the way.

The convoy was hit within five minutes of its departure by intermittent fires. Lieutenant Ben Matthews of 2/14 Infantry was riding in the lead Pakistani tank. The ferocity of the ambushes increased dramatically as the two-mile long convoy neared the Black Sea neighborhood, compelling Matthews to cajole the lead tank to continue on. Behind the tanks, inside the unfamiliar APC vehicles, the American light infantry could hear the rising storm of gunfire and explosions outside, small arms fire pinging off the armored surfaces and RPG rounds, hitting at the wrong angle to penetrate, deflecting off the sloped armor. The convoy pressed on, firing thousands of rounds of ammunition as they crashed through barriers and ambushes. Finally, though, the lead tank would advance no more.

The two lead APCs moved forward and pressed the attack. Disoriented and unsure of the route, the lead vehicle made a wrong turn followed by the second APC. The lead APC was quickly hit in the front by an RPG, bringing it to a burning halt. Inside the disabled vehicle, half a squad of infantrymen began to bail out as the second APC came to a halt. Inside that vehicle, the dim, red lights went out, leaving the enclosed American infantry in the dark. The platoon leader, Lieutenant Hollis, was aboard and ordered his men to dismount.

To make matters worse, the squad was stranded in a communication dead zone, unable to radio the main convoy that was now passing them by to continue the rescue. The men blew a hole through the wall of a nearby building and began to move in but not before Specialist Cornell Houston took a round in the leg.

The squad was trapped inside, caught in the midst of a serious firefight with encircling gunmen. Houston was hit again, this time in the chest by a sniper. This wound would prove to be fatal, causing the specialist to die a few days later in an American medical facility in Germany.

Outside, in the still smoking APC, a wounded Malaysian had been left behind. Opting to take the mission on himself rather than sending one of his other men, Corporal Richard Parent successfully made the run to the vehicle himself, dragging the wounded man back with him.

Somewhere in the city, a chained prisoner in a darkened room, Durant could hear the progress of the QRF as the convoy battled its way forward—machinegun fire, Mark 19 grenade launchers, rockets. At one point of the engagement, several APCs rolled by outside of his building— perhaps the two lost APCs? For a moment, he thought it might be a rescue attempt as an intense gunfight exploded outside. But those sounds faded quickly as the battle moved on.

With the two APCs heading in the wrong direction, the Pakistani tanks found themselves in the lead once again. Shrugging off RPGs and small-caliber rounds, the tankers were coerced to slowly press on, halting at times to fire. Approaching another flimsy barricade, the lead Pakistani tank driver refused to drive over it, thinking it was salted with antitank mines. Threats from the American lieutenant failed to budge him.

The convoy halted and the American soldiers dismounted. The 10th Mountain deployed from the vehicles, establishing local security while others began to disassemble the obstacle with their bare hands, under heavy fire. The convoy remained at a stop for over half an hour taking fire.

Incredibly, mobs of people were still making their way about, pressing to move closer. When warning shots overhead failed to disperse them, a few shots into the crowd would convince them of the necessity to do so.

Along a wall, Specialist Phil Lepre was preparing to move a few meters to get a better aim at a building from which shots were being fired. Ordering Private James Martin to move forward and place supporting fires from the position he was leaving, Lepre had only moved forward a few steps before Martin was hit and sent sprawling on his back. He had taken a bullet in the forehead. Martin would prove to be the final American soldier killed or mortally wounded in combat during that fateful battle.

At the release point following the obstacle breach, the convoy split into the two main 10th Mountain companies. A Company, commanded by Captain Drew Meyerowich, continued to move north until they were five hundred meters short of the American perimeter around Wolcott's crash site. C Company, under the command of Captain Michael Whetstone, moved west to the site of Durant's Black Hawk but was forced to stop just short of the location, unable to go any farther.

Delta Sergeant First Class John Macejunas gathered a small group of men and continued to press on by foot. A sweep of the wreckage showed there was nothing other than blood to be found of the men who had fought so valiantly there. The group remained in the area long enough to ensure the destruction of the downed aircraft by well-placed thermite grenades and then moved back with the remainder of the company, per David's directive, to secure Hollis and his men who were still trapped in the vicinity of their two destroyed APCs.

At the first crash site, Miller, Steele and their men could hear the heavy gunfire in the distance, the brilliant glow of the guns and explosions illuminating the black sky of the city to the south. The area around Super 61 had been relatively quiet for some time now. There were a few shots here and there and periodically, a Somali would wander into the crash site only to be shot. Just to keep any thoughts of massing and rushing the site out of the enemy's head, Little Birds would swoop down from time to time, unleashing rockets and a streak of tracers from their miniguns.

The distant roar and thunder of the column advancing north intensified, its men firing in every direction, at everything, as they moved. The word soon came from command that the 10th Mountain would soon be there. The Rangers and Delta at the site pulled back from the windows, not wanting to become fratricide casualties as the QRF stormed in. To minimize the possibility of an accidental clash, flashing strobe lights were emplaced to identify their locations.

Steele's location on Freedom Road was the farthest south and thus the closest to the advancing rescue force. Around 0155, Steele heard the vehicles in the vanguard of the half mile-long column turn onto Freedom Road. The images of dismounted soldiers soon appeared closing in on their building.

Steele's men called out, "Ranger! Ranger!"

"Tenth Mountain Division," came the reply in return. Linkup had been accomplished.

The combined group still had four hours of work ahead of them as they struggled to extract Wolcott's body from the crumbled remains of his aircraft. A rescue saw that had been brought along specifically for the task was ineffective, its blade dulling on the Kevlar-lined cockpit. Finally, the realization set in that they would literally have to tear the helicopter apart. Chains were attached to the front of the Black Hawk and a Humvee began to pull and separate the nose of the aircraft.

As this four-hour contest of man against machine continued, the wounded were assisted to the APCs parked in the center of the road—an inviting target to any roving RPG gunner that, fortunately, never seized the opportunity. Unable to see out of the vehicles and unaware of the efforts taking place to recover the pilot's body, some of the men began to grow restless as the wait intensified.

The recovery team's persistent efforts finally paid off and the warrant officer's body was freed. Gathering the body, the crew's personal weapons, one minigun, and classified documents, the force torched the wreckage with some thermite grenades.

But the rescue column now had another problem: there were too many people to ride in the limited number of vehicles available. Space within each vehicle had been fully utilized by the force on the way in. Now, on the way out, there were an additional ninety-nine men to accommodate, some dead, many wounded.

Though exhausted, those who were still ambulatory in Task Force Ranger found that they had to remain dismounted, once again braving the fires as they made their way down the dawning streets of "Mog." The men departed the area the same way they had arrived—under intense fire. Running, leapfrogging through intersections, placing heavy fires down alleyways, the force only suffered one additional casualty, Sergeant Randy Ramagliea, as the main body fought its way toward their destination, the Pakistani compound that had been set up as a field hospital. A smaller group that had separated ended up in New Port.

The true horror of combat was readily apparent and on display at the Pakistani compound, a converted soccer stadium. Doctors, medics, and nurses performed triage on the mangled, brutalized, and bloody bodies that lay about covered in remnants of military uniforms. Men cried and hugged each other, glad to see a friend alive. Others cried at the sight or memory of a comrade killed in action. Some just sat, completely exhausted, numb, looking off with that "thousand-mile stare" many veterans talk of, but few within this group had ever seen or even experienced until this day. Steele would later learn that a third of his company had been killed or wounded.

Though seriously mauled, the fight was not out of Task Force Ranger. Many of the Delta operatives had departed the compound as soon as possible to make their way back to their hangar, where they were already preparing for any follow-on mission—cleaning weapons, restocking ammunition, and replacing lost and damaged equipment.

Even those Rangers who were badly wounded still had fight left in them. Specialist Rob Phipps lay on a cot in the field hospital badly battered and bruised, his back and legs heavily bandaged. Steele stood over the wounded man, placing his hand on the Ranger, telling him he would be all right. Recognizing his company commander through blood red eyes, Phipps reached up, grabbing the captain's arm.

"Sir, I'll be OK in a couple of days. Don't go back out without me."

How can the American people not treasure such dedication and personal sacrifice by its youth?

Officially, the raid of 3 October—which came to be known by many of the participants as "Black" or "Bloody Sunday" and the "Battle of the Black Sea," and by those in Somalia as "Ma-alinti Rangers," "The Day of the Rangers"—came to a close around 0700 on 4 October with the return of the final Task Force Ranger and Quick Reaction Force (QRF) elements.

Given the savagery of the battle, "Task Force David" had suffered 'moderate' American casualties: two KIA and twenty-two WIA. Malaysian casualties were one KIA and seven WIA while Pakistani losses were two WIA. Casualty figures were much more severe for the 120-man Task Force Ranger who suffered seventeen KIA—six of which were from B Company—fifty-seven WIA, and one MIA—Durant—during the course of the fifteen-hour firefight. All told, nineteen brave Americans were killed in action that day or would eventually succumb to their mortal wounds:

> Chief Warrant Officer 4 Raymond Frank
> 160th Special Operations Aviation Regiment (SOAR)
> Chief Warrant Officer 4 Clifton Wolcott
> 160th Special Operations Aviation Regiment (SOAR)
> Chief Warrant Officer 3 Donovan Briley
> 160th Special Operations Aviation Regiment (SOAR)
> Master Sergeant Gary Gordon
> 1st Special Forces Operational Detachment - Delta
> Master Sergeant Timothy Martin
> 1st Special Forces Operational Detachment - Delta
> Sergeant First Class Earl Fillmore
> 1st Special Forces Operational Detachment - Delta
> *Sergeant First Class Matthew Rierson
> 1st Special Forces Operational Detachment - Delta

Sergeant First Class Randy Shughart
     1st Special Forces Operational Detachment - Delta
Staff Sergeant Daniel Busch
     1st Special Forces Operational Detachment - Delta
Staff Sergeant William Cleveland
     160th Special Operations Aviation Regiment (SOAR)
Staff Sergeant Thomas Field
     160th Special Operations Aviation Regiment (SOAR)
Sergeant Cornell Houston
     2/14th Infantry Regiment, 10th Mountain Division
Sergeant James Joyce
     3rd Ranger Battalion, 75th Ranger Regiment
Sergeant Lorenzo Ruiz
     3rd Ranger Battalion, 75th Ranger Regiment
Corporal James Cavaco
     3rd Ranger Battalion, 75th Ranger Regiment
Corporal James Smith
     3rd Ranger Battalion, 75th Ranger Regiment
Specialist Dominick Pilla
     3rd Ranger Battalion, 75th Ranger Regiment
Private First Class Richard Kowalewski
     3rd Ranger Battalion, 75th Ranger Regiment
Private First Class James Martin
     2/14th Infantry Regiment, 10th Mountain Division

*NOTE: Generally, losses for Task Force Ranger have been placed at
     eighteen KIA but do not include Sergeant First Class Matthew
     Rierson killed shortly after 3 October that lead some to state a
     loss of nineteen KIA.

Relatively speaking, Somali militia losses were staggering, with
United States and Somali sources placing them at nearly 500 killed—
though a special U.S. envoy a few days after the battle believed the actual
number to be closer to 1,000. The number of wounded was over 1,000.
Certainly, though, all the casualties were not attributable to American
weapons, considering the number of RPGs—claimed to be more than
1,000—fired. How many Somali fatalities and casualties were the result of
RPGs detonating outside of the engagement areas and of militia small
arms fratricide? No one will ever know.
     In 1997, former Chairman of the Joint Chiefs of Staff Colin L. Pow-
ell—an advisor who had sat in on all of the President's policy meetings
on Somalia—stated in an interview, "Bad things happen in war. Nobody

did anything wrong militarily in Mogadishu. They had a bad afternoon. No one expected a large number of soldiers to get killed. Is eighteen a large number? People didn't start noticing in Vietnam until it was 500 a week."

The world awoke on the morning of the 4th to a most barbaric sight: bodies of American soldiers being defiled. Broadcast by CNN, film footage of exuberant Somalis celebrating around and on the burnt hulk of Durant's Black Hawk gave way to a shot of a body, the remains of what was believed to be Durant's crew chief, Staff Sergeant Bill Cleveland, being dragged through the street at the end of a rope, the corpse kicked, poked, and prodded. People were noting that a body count of "500" was no longer the threshold.

Half a world away in a hotel room in San Francisco, President Clinton watched the images, horrified and angered, demanding to know who made the decision to undertake the mission and why he had not been informed.

In Mogadishu, members of the task force gathered by a set, watching the morbid spectacle. Delta and Rangers waited for the word to launch again to secure the bodies. They knew where the remains were. TF 160 pilots just wanted to go and mow down the cheering crowds. Fearing the cost in terms of local lives, the commanders — unfortunately — decided not to make the effort.

Later that evening, American helicopters began to fly over Mogadishu, broadcasting messages to their captured comrade whom they knew was still held a prisoner somewhere below.

"Mike Durant, we will not leave you."

"Mike Durant, we are with you always."

"Do not think we have left you, Mike."

Hearing the messages, Durant felt some encouragement.

The following day, 5 October, A Company, 3rd Ranger Battalion, arrived in country to augment the battered task force, remaining until 23 October.

Despite the humiliation of having dead American soldiers publicly desecrated, despite the reports that Aidid had been struck a mortal blow, despite the reports that Aidid's supporters were fleeing the city, despite the fact that the Somali arsenal of RPGs was at or near complete depletion, and despite the fact that other influential Somalis were offering to dump Aidid as a peace overture, the President and his staff had lost the will to pursue anything further in Somalia. For President William Jefferson Clinton, nineteen obviously was too "large" a number."

The former U.S. Ambassador to Somalia under President George Bush, Robert Oakley, was dispatched to deliver the news: all efforts to capture Aidid would be called off and Task Force Ranger would be reinforced and stay on as a show of military resolve but would be withdrawn by March 1994. By Oakley's visit, all the badly mutilated bodies of those killed at the Super 64 site had been turned over. Only one major issue remained — the release of Durant, alive.

In that Aidid was still in hiding, Oakley met with the warlord's clan on 8 October and delivered President Clinton's message. When informed that the President wanted Durant released with no conditions, the warlords informed Oakley that there would need to be a trade for the sixty to seventy clansmen that Task Force Ranger had already captured. Oakley offered to relay their request to the President for his consideration but there would be no guarantee.

Durant needed to be released soon and, to assist the clan with its decision, the former ambassador offered a bit of friendly advice.

When the decision is made to launch a rescue mission for the missing pilot, "*the minute the guns start again, all restraint on the U.S. side goes. Once the fighting starts, all this pent-up anger is going to be released. This whole part of the city will be destroyed, men, women, children, camels, cats, dogs, goats, donkeys, everything.*"

The message and advice were delivered to Aidid, who quickly turned over the pilot — along with a Nigerian POW captured during Aidid's 5 September attack — on 14 October.

The United States, the world's one true Superpower, had quit. The courageous sacrifice made by the members of Task Force Ranger was for a cause that proved to be totally unessential to their Commander-in-Chief. Not only had their mission been called off the very next day just as it was within their grasp to achieve success, all of their previous efforts also went for naught, as the President accepted Oakley's recommendation in support of the clan's request and ordered the release several weeks later of all those detained after their capture by Task Force Ranger. In hindsight, eighteen turned out to be an exceptionally huge number.

In a letter drafted by hand in the days proceeding the battle and delivered to the President and Secretary of Defense through the House National Security Committee, the Task Force Ranger commander, Major General William F. Garrison, wrote thirteen brief paragraphs in which he reported about the mission and its results. Paragraph 1 read: "The authority, responsibility, and accountability for the Op rests here in Mog with the TF Ranger commander, not in Washington." The general had displayed that one aspect of character that seems to be eluding many national leaders today. By his own hand, the "buck" stopped with him.

The best of America's fighting elite had performed incredibly well in the face of such overwhelming adversity. Older, more experienced, and most, if not all, Ranger School graduates, even the Rangers had to admit the "D-boys," as the Delta operatives were called, were, with few exceptions, virtual killing machines. The small number of Navy SEALs and Air Force PJs involved also performed most admirably.

Within the Ranger ranks, which was by a large margin the majority of the force, all performed their duties, but some performed much more ably than others. Understanding that most of the junior enlisted Rangers ranged in age from seventeen to nineteen and many were not Ranger School graduates, it is not surprising that a relative few of the younger men found it difficult to perform under such adverse, self-testing, and life-altering circumstances. The fact that some men did not fight with considerable bravery does not denigrate them, nor does it make them cowards. In the words of one participant, "All gave some, but some gave all."

Nor does the questioning of their conduct indicate a criticism of that conduct. Those who were not there should never be so brazen as to imply that they or anyone else would have performed better. However, given the Ranger's elite status, there are lessons to be learned and questions need to be asked to provide these special forces every opportunity and advantage available in future engagements.

Much has been made about this "failed" raid that did achieve the stated mission objective of capturing the two Aidid lieutenants. Unfortunately, there were flaws at the strategic, operational, and tactical levels that contributed to the final casualty figures. The raid certainly failed at the strategic level for the strategic objective as it should have been defined by national policy was never clearly stated. Deploying elite combat forces such as the Rangers and Detachment-Delta to conduct a city-wide manhunt is not exactly one of their mission essential or war-fighting tasks. Intelligence underestimated the tenacity of the enemy, the status of the warrior within the Somali society, and the pride associated with that warrior heritage. Worse yet, was the failure to realize that the U.N. focus on the SNA and the warrant to arrest Aidid were, in the minds of Somalis, de facto declarations of war that forced them to act accordingly.

Operationally, there were a number of very critical errors. One of the most egregious was the lack of a designated chain of command that included both Major Generals Montgomery and Garrison. Unity of command would have brought the QRF into the Task Force Ranger planning phase, thus preventing the waste of a considerable amount of time spent on the behalf of the QRF planning and preparing for rescue operations that they were on the hook to execute but didn't have a clue about what was involved. This lack of integration also seriously impacted Task Force David's ability to coordinate close-air support with TF 160 aircraft during the QRF's first deployment attempt, thus prompting the rescue force's withdrawal back to the American compound and further delay.

AUTHOR'S NOTE: Contrary to the analysis of others, to include an earlier review of this author, there seems to be less of an issue about unity of command at the tactical level than some may claim. Though there were three independent company grade commanders on the ground — Miller, Steele, and the CSAR captain — the issue of "command" was, in the end, a non-issue. The rationale was quite simple: all were in touch with the senior ground commander at all times — first McKnight, then Harrell. A lieutenant colonel "trumps" a captain *every* time. If there were command issues, they were a result of a failure to communicate or for the senior commander to make a command decision. It was not the result of a lack of clarity regarding the chain of command.

In addition to command and control operational breakdowns, there was another critical operational failure and that was in the realm of intelligence. The failure to note the stockpiling of RPGs and to realistically take into account the downing of the 10th Mountain Black Hawk late in September — despite the downed aircraft rehearsal — proved, ultimately, to be a fatal — and deadly — interlaced oversight.

The deadliest error, though, proved to be the lack of armor or Spectre support. There are four proponents to combat power: firepower, maneuver, protection, and leadership. Unfortunately for Task Force Ranger, leadership was about the only thing they had available to them for contingency operations. Having been denied armor support by the Clinton administration, the Quick Reaction Force had to initially rely on their own wheeled, soft-skinned vehicles to secure the downed aircraft. As events so clearly proved, American combat power was not tailored to meet the threat. Consequently, American soldiers lost their lives or were wounded while the U.S. command had to borrow the needed combat power from Malaysian and Pakistani forces to augment the Quick Reaction Force. Some may claim this is hindsight. Others would refer to it as "protecting the force."

Though the task force's commander, Major General Garrison, testified before the Senate Armed Forces Committee that it was unlikely that armor and AC-130H Spectre gunships would have saved lives, an exceptionally strong and objective argument can be made that they would indeed have saved many. The contention that the Spectres would have made no difference seems to be readily refuted by the fact that four of these aircraft performed quite well during the period 9 June to 12 July. Why then, if these heavy weapon's platforms were stationed nearby in Djibouti and still under Garrison's operational control, were they not brought in for support that fateful evening when Task Force Ranger needed every bit of suppressive fire it could muster? Total flight distance was only 680 miles or so as the "crow flies" and, thus, only a few hours away.

> NOTE: Sadly, one of the four AC-130H Spectre's, Jockey 14, would crash-land on 14 March 1994 200 yards off the Kenyan coast, near the town of Malindi. Operating in support of ongoing operations in and around Mogadishu at the time, eight of the fourteen crewmen aboard were killed in the crash.

As for armor, the statement that Mogadishu was another Chechnya is not valid. Chechen rebels were much better trained and equipped than the Somali militia. Armed with heavy antitank weapons and powerful antitank mines—in addition to being well trained and well led—the former Soviet Republic rebels were able to make short work of the ill-trained, ill-equipped, and ill-led third-rate Russian units sent to subdue them.

Urban combat offers the opportunity to implement three different attack profiles against the weakest parts of an armored vehicle: side, rear, and top. As a consequence, tactical doctrine calls for dismounts to lead in a city environment with armor providing covering and supporting fires. The Russians failed to execute to standard. Furthermore, old-style Soviet BMPs or BRDMs were not designed to defeat RPG rounds. Poorly maintained and obsolete T-55 tanks with fatigued armor and limited dismounted infantry support were able to be defeated by either heavy weapons, command-detonated or tilt-rod mines, or multiple RPG shots directed against the weakest part of the vehicle.

Those who profess that armor would have made no difference based on the "Chechen model" should not confuse American military might against a poorly trained militia armed with low-tech weaponry and the results of a tired and worn out Russian Bear against a very capable, heavily armed, relatively well-trained, highly disciplined, paramilitary organization. The U.S. M2 Bradley Infantry Fighting Vehicle is specifically designed to defeat RPG rounds with its sloped armor, onboard weapons systems, and armored tread skirts, as demonstrated during live-fire demonstrations during the IFV's development. Its 25-mm chain gun with armor piercing rounds and M-240G 7.62-mm coaxial gun are mounted in a 360-degree revolving turret that can be fired in a nearly vertical position—a significant advantage in urban combat. An M-2 .50-caliber machinegun and three firing ports on each side of the vehicle to house shortened versions of the M-16 provide additional offensive and defensive firepower. The TOW launcher is just icing on the cake to take out any hardened targets. Combined with its optics for long-range viewing and night-seeing capabilities, the vehicle makes for the best mechanized urban fighting vehicle in the world.

As for the combat loaded seventy-ton M1A2 Abrams main battle tank, its unique Chobham armor is designed to defeat any round fired with the exception of the latest Russian main battle tank or another Abrams—as was unfortunately demonstrated in the Gulf War. Armor skits provide a very narrow window of opportunity for a mobility kill. An RPG probably wouldn't even put a dent in the behemoth much less stop or kill it. As for firepower, a 120-mm cannon, a M-240G 7.62-mm coaxial machinegun, a turret-mounted 7.62-mm M-60 machinegun, and an M-2 .50-caliber machinegun would make it the biggest gun on the street. And, if there is anything the militia in Somalia were impressed by and respected, it was big guns—the bigger the gun, the greater their respect and subsequent apprehension.

The respect that the Somalis had for armor had already been demonstrated. Recall the incident on 17 June, when a Somali mob interaction that day—a harbinger of events to occur on 3 October—was stabilized by the show of force exhibited by light tank and APC reinforcements. One can only begin to imagine the impact an American Main Battle Tank would have had.

In the end, the debate of whether armor would have made a difference is really unarguable. Without a doubt American armor would have made a world of difference and prevented the loss of many of those eighteen KIA. The proof was literally on the streets of Mogadishu that day and early morning when the lightly armored convoys of McKnight, Struecker, and David were able to make it back with all or most of their thin-skinned vehicles—despite overwhelming number of RPGs. Kallman's experience of surviving a direct hit on his Humvee and still being able to drive away cannot be ignored. Nor can the RPG blast beneath one of Struecker's Humvees at the K-4 circle that didn't affect the vehicle in the least.

Even the old BRDMs in the multinational rescue effort survived RPG hits, with the exception of the lead two, which took a wrong turn and found themselves isolated and vulnerable to close in assault. As for the M-48s, the only "force" stopping these tanks was the timidity of the drivers to punch through roadblocks. RPGs were of no consequence to them.

Therefore, considering the survivability of much less capable vehicles on the hostile streets of Mogadishu, how can anyone claim that an American-trained platoon of Abrams with a company of Bradleys would not have made a difference? Such equipped units are pure combat power — firepower, maneuver, and protection — especially in the harsh urban environment of Mogadishu. They would have been unstoppable, crashing through any barrier thrown before them, as the significantly less capable Humvees were able to do. They would have been responsive and easily employed to travel and fight at night if necessary. Should there have been a lucky mobility kill, it would have been a simple process to hook the disabled vehicle up to an operable Abrams or Bradley with a tow bar — which would have already been in place for the operation — to drag the immobile vehicle along. American armor would most probably have been able to get to both crash sites in time to save the lives and limbs of many of the trapped warriors, had they been stationed only two to three miles away as part of the QRF.

Armor, even in an urban environment, especially this particular urban environment, would have proven to be an invaluable resource. Unfortunately, the main problem with many officers schooled for so long primarily in light infantry tactics is that they are not fully knowledgeable of armor capabilities. While armor has some obvious disadvantages, it also has a number of tremendous advantages that, when used properly with dismounted infantry, can make for a powerful and exceptionally capable urban combat force.

The analysis of the operation also indicates some tactical flaws. For sheer simplicity, a review of Rogers' Rangers Standing Orders shows a "violation" of three of the nineteen principles:

Rule #1: Don't forget nothing: The force left NODs and water behind, believing the raid would be quick. Yet it was past 1530 when the raid was launched — not much of a window of daylight left should anything go wrong.

Rule #4: Tell the truth about what you see and what you do-don't ever lie to a Ranger or officer: It has been reported that SSG Eversmann, leader of Chalk 4, was unable to obey an order to move though he acknowledged that he would do so. Only by luck and accident were he and his men discovered by Lieutenant Colonel McKnight when he drove by the squad's position with his convoy. If it weren't for the fortuitous moment, there would most likely have been an additional twelve Rangers added to the KIA total.

Rule #11: Don't ever march home the same way: The intent behind this rule is to ensure one takes a different route to avoid a possible ambush. Can also be interpreted as never conduct an operation the same way twice; avoid following the same template.

There were also serious communications deficiencies. The inability of the Delta and Ranger units to effortlessly communicate with each other and the transmitting of information in the clear—not "green" or encrypted—proved to have been an Achilles heel rather than a strength. For the strongest and most technologically advanced military force in the world, this seems inexcusable. Surprise, stealth, speed, and flexibility are paramount to the survival of these elite and lightly armed special forces. Such units cannot afford time nor can they afford confusion and yet, because of the poor communications process and system in place, they lost time and had mass confusion. Considering the microtechnology accessible today—already reflected in the communications gear carried by each Delta operative—the financial and material resources available to the United States, and the criticality of the missions assigned the Ranger Regiment, there is absolutely no reason why each Ranger going into a mission is not outfitted in a fashion similar to the Delta operative. The advantages in terms of the military accomplishment of national objectives more than compensates for the minimum financial costs associated with such equipment.

It is said Japan had "Victory Disease" after what it considered to be a successful attack at Pearl Harbor. The Israelis would later formulate "The Concept," believing that no Arab nation, or even group of Arab nations, would have the audacity to attack them following their stunning victory in the 1967 "Six-Day War"—only to have the 1973 "War of Atonement" shatter that misplaced belief—and almost the State of Israel.

Success and victory breed complacency and America had a touch of the same in Somalia based on our successes of Grenada, Panama, Operation Desert Storm, and the Iraqi Kurdish Operation Provide Comfort. This "disease"—or even hubris, false pride—has a way of getting those who have it into trouble, no matter how great they may—or believe themselves—to be. The United States had the disease on 3 October 1993 and paid for it—or rather nineteen of its finest did.

Amazingly, though, despite the mistakes, despite the misapplication of military force and resources, it almost worked! America was close to meeting its objective, if that objective was to remove Aidid from the political and military equation. Task Force Ranger had Aidid on the ropes. Unfortunately, just at the moment the U.S. needed the greatest of intestinal fortitude, the President of the United States cut and ran, thus making the personal and professional sacrifices of all in vain.

Sadly, Howe would later admit Task Force Ranger soldiers "had many opportunities to eliminate [Aidid]. That's not our job. We're trying to arrest him." Maybe, based on the outcome of our experience in Somalia, some thought should be taken in the future to make eliminating such an individual "our job." *At times, it's best to make it personal, if you are looking to get someone's attention.*

Setting aside the issues of why, how, and what if, as a country what unfortunately appears to have been lost in the national debate is the heroism and valor of these soldiers. We, as a society, have failed to appreciate the personal sacrifice of these men. These members of the profession of arms did not ask to be placed in a situation that put them in harm's way. They did not ask to be placed in a situation that found them significantly outnumbered, outgunned, and deep within enemy territory. They did not ask to be placed in a situation that required them to suffer wounds and death in defense of their comrades.

While they did not ask for any of these hardships, they endured them anyway in a demonstration of incredible bravery and devout professionalism. They endured because of dedication. They endured because of responsibility. They endured because it was their duty. They endured because they believed in the Creed. They endured because many wore the coveted black and gold Ranger Tab on their left shoulder.

For their actions that day the two Ranger-qualified Delta snipers, Master Sergeant Gary I. Gordon and Sergeant First Class Randall D. Shughart, were posthumously awarded the Medal of Honor in a White House ceremony on the morning of 23 May 1994, where it was reported that Sergeant First Class Shughart's father, Herb Shughart, refused to shake the President's hand. Later that day, the two Rangers were enshrined in the nation's Hall of Heroes at the Pentagon.

Regrettably, when competing against the burial of Mrs. Jackie Kennedy Onasis later that afternoon, the few square inches of newsprint and the couple of minutes of television sound bites dedicated to their monumental sacrifice were a great disservice to them and their families. They deserved so much better. These American heroes were faced with the choice of death or dishonor—as they saw it. Their standards of dedication, responsibility, and duty left them with no other option but to knowingly choose that which had a nearly 100% probability of death.

Their choice should not be so easily dismissed nor forgotten. Facing overwhelming forces deep within enemy territory, the ground and air members of Task Force Ranger more than held their own against such incredible odds. "I will never leave a fallen comrade to fall into the hands of the enemy." The Rangers and Delta never agonized over their decision to remain with the body of the dead pilot. Though the Ranger force could have fought their way out to a more secure site, bringing their wounded with them, that alternative would have meant leaving their dead comrade behind for Aidid's jackals to tear apart.

In May of 1941, the staff of British Admiral Sir Andrew Browne Cunningham recommended that the Royal Navy abandon British ground forces on Crete in order to protect the Royal Navy's ships. The admiral resoundingly dismissed their recommendation.

"It takes the Navy three years to build a ship. It would take three hundred to rebuild a tradition."

Rangers live by their own tradition, their own ethic, their own Creed. Though some may question their remaining at the crash site, others understand that the Ranger Creed is a function of tradition, of sacrifice, and not of arithmetic. True to their Creed, the members of Task Force Ranger who secured the wreckage of Super 61 remained at the crash site to retrieve the body of a fallen comrade rather than to abandon it, allowing it to fall into the hands of the enemy while Master Sergeant Gordon and Sergeant First Class Shughart most likely knowingly and willingly sacrificed their lives in the defense of Super 64. There are those who question the judgment of risking lives on the behalf of those who have already given theirs. For those who question, they will never understand the pride and loyalty intrinsic with being a Ranger.

For an article published in the August 1, 1994, edition of *U.S. News & World Report*, Master Sergeant Gordon's widow was asked to write a letter to her children on a topic she believed to be important to their development. Mrs. Carmen Gordon elected to write to her two children about "Responsibility" and what it meant to their father. Among that which she wrote was the following:

> I hope that in the final moments of your father's life, his last thoughts were not of us. As he lay dying, I wanted him to think only of his mission to which he pledged himself.... He chose the military, and "I shall not fail those with whom I serve" became his simple religion.

No man or woman will read that piece and not feel a tugging at the heart, a swelling in the eyes, and a greater appreciation for the term "responsibility." Master Sergeant Gordon's widow is a true soldier's wife, the epitome of class, who understands what it means to be a Ranger.

Beyond the human tragedy of the lives lost, bodies maimed, and families devastated, there is a reverberating legacy of Mogadishu that has, and will continue, to resonate on a national, and even global, scale for years to come — or at least until the United States learns and implements the lessons learned that have been bought and paid for by the blood of valiant American warriors. A manifestation of this legacy was exhibited during an interview with ABC News on 28 May 1998 by Osama bin Laden, who noted:

We have seen in the last decade the decline of the American government and the weakness of the American soldier who is ready to wage Cold Wars and unprepared to fight long wars. This was proven in Beirut when the Marines fled after two explosions. It also proves they can run in less than 24 hours, and this was also repeated in Somalia.

Bin Laden's citing of Somalia was premeditated, relevant, and quite revealing. Not only did it serve as an allegory of the terrorist's disdain for and derision of America's military will, it also traced the terrorist bombings of the Khobar Towers in 1995, the U.S. Embassies in Tanzania and Kenya in 1998, and the U.S.S. *Cole* in 2001 directly back to the U.S. decision to pull out of Somalia after suffering a relative handful of casualties, just as victory was in its grasp. Given that pusillanimous decision, it took little to convince non-conventional adversaries that an exceptionally productive way to drive out the United States or to gain an advantage is to kill Americans.

American resolve in terms of world opinion was and continues to be in question as a result of the actions taken following that fateful day in Mogadishu. Also in question are the attitudes of our national and military leaders, as well as the functionality of American troop deployments. Since 3 October 1993, "force protection" has served as the byword of all American leaders, for all deployments. Unfortunately, the current definition of "force protection" has taken on a distorted, and nearly perverted, perspective that has become synonymous with "playing it safe."

Bearing a "zero defect" mentality that means career termination if there are casualties, American soldiers and Marines to swagger about in full "battle rattle" — Kevlar helmets and flak vests — while timid leaders require the minimization of contact and exposure to ensure that no one gets hurt. A noble cause, particularly from the soldier's perspective, for sure, but a tactic that leads to, and perpetuates, the convictions and actions of cowards such as bin Laden. It is a tactic that leads to large numbers of American dead hunkered behind imaginary Maginot and Bar Lev Lines as we leave the offense to our enemies. It is a tactic, a Faustian bargain, which can lead United States forces into long-term occupations, enforcing false, constricted borders, all of which are not in the national interest.

Who is to blame for this situation? While it is easy to blame the senior American leaders, by and large it is the American public who should bear much of the burden. Enamored by the overwhelming success of the United States Armed Forces during the Gulf War, captivated by the "video game" approach to combat that high-tech weaponry demonstrates, and given a false expectation that all combat is sterile and impersonal, the American public has lost touch with the reality of modern combat. Modern conflict is not all overwhelming success, high-tech, and impersonal. Modern conflict is overwhelmingly brutal, "in your face," and very personal. And, it's about time that the American public lowered its expectations from the virtual realm to worldly reality and learn to realize, and to accept, that every once in a while there will be bloody noses. There will be, to paraphrase Colin Powell, the potential for a few "bad days." Force protection is force *projection*, and as the world's superpower, the United States should begin to act its status.

American society will generally accept the fact that United States soldiers will be placed in harm's way and even killed in various regions of the world as implements of national policy *when there seems to be a good reason for the fight.* Was there, in Somalia, a good reason to fight? There were no vital national interests at stake for U.S. security was not an issue. With hindsight, it would seem that America's involvement was purely an altruistic effort to bring order and stability to a region that was suffering the loss of tens of thousands of innocent victims in a brutal civil war. From a purely moral and ethical point of view, that could be a good reason to fight. The end seemed to justify the means.

But there was just one, obtrusive, trifling concern never fully addressed by America's leaders — nor questioned by the media — and that was one, singular and unmistakable fact. Many of those apparent innocent 'victims' did not care for U.S. or U.N. help. Many of those victims, in fact, were more inclined to spit upon the very forces attempting to protect them — a display of scorn that a large number of the populace carried out.

Somalia was and still is a country, not a nation. Its society, if one can call it that, can feel nothing for the greater good given how their most simplistic world focuses on nothing beyond the family unit, food, and basic survival. To build a country from the outside is doable; to create a nation, however, that must come from within. True peacemaking and nation building require more of the beneficiaries than of the benefactors. More importantly, the beneficiaries must want the same adaptation of assistance that the benefactor is offering to provide. Such was, and continues to be, not the case in Somalia.

Why, then, is it deemed incumbent on America to step in and sacrifice the blood and lives of its warriors in a philanthropic attempt to provide assistance to beneficiaries who lack the will, ability, and desire to sustain such efforts? *Ultimately, the greatest lesson learned from Somalia needs to be the realization and acceptance of the fact that when a nation's people do not give a damn about their country or their own quality of life, neither should the people of the United States.*

History is replete with examples of defeated armies that attempted to force those who believe power is derived from the barrel of a gun into giving up those ideals in pursuit of some abstract concept titled nation-state legitimacy. It didn't work for empires in centuries past and, as demonstrated on 3 October 1993, such a concept still does not work.

> *Throughout the war, you were always in my mind. I always knew if I were in trouble and you were still alive, you would come to my assistance.*
>
> General Sherman in a letter
> to General Grant after the Civil War

CHAPTER 24

Ranger Lessons Learned

Those who cannot remember the past are condemned to repeat it.

George Santayana

The term "Elite" throughout history has made many a leader cringe for there has always been a price associated with that term and the cost has invariably been the best men and resources at the expense of the traditional line units. Since the advent of the modern Ranger during the Second World War, the United States Army also cringed as it transitioned through cycles of activating and disbanding such units.

With the formation of the 75th Ranger Regiment in 1984, it seems that the military, as a war-fighting institution, has finally come to grips with the realization that such organizations are an integral part of not only our success on the tactical battlefield but are also the cutting edge of our strategic force projection capability. In addition, despite the dedication of men and resources to the 75th Ranger Regiment and the Ranger Training Brigade, there has been a significant "return on investment" regarding the spread of the Ranger ethos and warrior spirit throughout the Army as a whole—in keeping with Wickham's directive to Colonel Downing, the First 'modern' Colonel of the Regiment but Third Colonel after the ceremonial titles conferred upon Robert Rogers and William O. Darby—to *return these men to the line units of the Army with the Ranger philosophy and standards.* That has happened, and the United States Army is a much greater institution as a result of the Ranger philosophy and standards.

Some Significant Lessons Learned from Ranger Operations

The need for Ranger units. There are those who will argue that there is nothing Rangers can do that cannot be done by good conventional infantry. Given the correct set of circumstances, such as full manning, continuity, adequate training, and proper resources, there may be some validity to that argument. The counterpoint to that argument, though, is that conventional infantry rarely operate under the best set of circumstances. Attrition and the routine tasks associated with traditional conventional warfare preclude these infantry units from devoting time and resources to more specialized operations of the type conducted by the Rangers. Even Darby's Ranger Battalions were unable to fulfill conventional infantry roles and execute specialized missions without sustaining horrendous casualties — and they were better trained and prepared for those specialized missions than any conventional infantry unit would be. If special units such as the Rangers are not held in reserve for specific and unique missions, there would be no assurance that, when the missions are necessary, there would be any unit capable of accomplishing them. Given the short-notice pace of execution as experienced during World War II, and more recently in Grenada and Panama, only exceptionally well-trained and cohesive units such as the Rangers are likely to successfully accomplish high-risk missions.

The more Rangers look like conventional infantry, the more likely they are to be committed in conventional infantry roles. As the firepower of lightly armed Ranger units increased with the addition of anti-tank units and heavy mortars during the Second World War, the more these units grew to resemble conventional infantry units. This "look" led to deployment of Darby's Ranger Force, 1st, 3rd, and 4th Ranger Battalions, in areas such as Salerno and the Winter Line in Italy. This created a vicious cycle, for with the Rangers' commitment as traditional infantry, the casualty list grew, the replacements grew scarce and less trained, which eventually led to even greater losses over time.

Ranger units need time to replace and retrain losses. Inexperienced and untrained replacements dilute and weaken the cohesion and effectiveness of specialty units. During World War II, both the 5th Ranger Battalion at Zerf and the combined 1st and 3rd Ranger Battalions at Cisterna suffered excessively heavy losses as a result of having to commit untrained and unseasoned Ranger replacements in specialized operations before they were ready. With the establishment of the U.S. Army Ranger School and the dispersion of school and regiment trained personnel throughout the Army, there currently exists a dependable source of Ranger-trained replacements should the need ever arise.

Surprise is critical to the success of light forces. Ranger units traditionally go into combat against well-defended objectives with what they can carry. To attack a well entrenched, alert enemy would have nearly suicidal implications such as the 2nd Ranger Battalion's daring seaborne assault against Pointe-du-Hoc at Normandy. On the other hand, complete surprise such as that achieved by the 3rd Ranger Battalion at Porto Empedocle or the 6th Ranger Infantry Battalion Cabanatuan prison camp raid can result in victory at nearly no cost in lives.

Full mission rehearsals must be conducted with all involved elements. The failure to conduct "full dress rehearsals" can lead to disasters similar to that experienced by Detachment-Delta and C Company, 3rd Ranger Battalion at Desert One. The relatively smooth and coordinated operations experienced by the 75th Ranger Regiment during their Operation Just Cause airborne assaults serve as the model for all future joint operations to emulate.

Contingency planning. The Rangers' greatest strengths also create their greatest weaknesses. While stealth and shock may successfully get Rangers to the objective, once they wear off, it's up to the lightly armed infantry to get themselves out. When deep in enemy territory, surrounded at every turn by hundreds of potential enemy safely entrenched behind cover and concealment, it is critical to have plans that provide them the combat power they would then lack — protection and survivability. No matter how well trained or how tenacious, light arms, limited mobility and lack of armor protection lead to significant difficulties and casualties, as experienced by Task Force Ranger in Mogadishu.

Interestingly enough, if one carefully reviews the Rangers' history, there is not a single example at team, squad, platoon, company, battalion, or regiment level of any Ranger operation that was not carried out in an aggressive and dedicated manner. Even when directed by higher headquarters to execute missions that were poorly planned or poorly coordinated, the Rangers never shirked their responsibility even when the odds or circumstances were totally confused or overwhelmingly against them.

By anyone's standards and in accordance with General Abrams' charter, the Ranger battalions of the 75th Ranger Regiment are the most elite and proficient light infantry in the world. As long as they continue to focus on the charter and to keep in mind the lessons learned of the past, the Regiment will remain capable "*of fighting anytime, anywhere, against any enemy, and winning.*"

Appendix A

The 'Truth' Behind Rogers' Rangers Standing Orders

The Ranger Handbook, SH 21–76, published by the Ranger Training Brigade of the United States Army Infantry School, states the following, in part, in regards to the Standing Orders of Rogers' Rangers: "Ranger techniques and methods were an inherent characteristic of the frontiersmen in the colonies, but Rogers was the first to capitalize on them and incorporate them into a permanently organized fighting force. His "Standing Orders" were written in the year 1759. Even though they are over 200 years old, they apply just as well to Ranger operations conducted on today's battlefield as they did to the operations conducted by Rogers and his men." There are three sentences in that quote. The first is true, the second is false, and the third, based on the second, is inherently misleading.

On 14 September 1757, Rogers' 'Ranging School' was officially authorized. Its first group of students were British Cadet volunteers. To structure his training, Rogers drafted twenty-eight tactical rules which came to be known as "Rogers' Rules of Discipline." In 1765, he would have them published as part of his French and Indian War Journals. His rules, as written, were detailed, comprehensive, and exceptionally insightful for the period. They proved to be so insightful, as a matter of fact, that they are still very much applicable to today's modern battlefield. The "Rules of Discipline" were truly a brilliant discourse on unconventional scouting and skirmishing and a very sound argument could be made that they constitute the first military field manual written on the North American continent.

So, then, where did the more succinct and entertaining "Roger's Standing Orders" come from? As noted previously in this work, Robert

501

Rogers served as the role model for Kenneth Roberts' protagonist in the 1936 novel *Northwest Passage*. Within the written conversation between the fictitious characters Langdon Towne and Sergeant McNott, in which McNott is explaining to Towne what a Ranger must know, one can find the foundation for the wording of what were to become the "Standing Orders." There should be no doubt that Kenneth Roberts' fictional conversation was predicated on Robert Rogers' Rules of Discipline.

This passage from the novel apparently struck a cord with an officer assigned to The Infantry School as a doctrine writer for the 1960 version of Field Manual (FM) 21–50, *Ranger Training and Ranger Operations*. Within this FM was an appendix on Ranger History that included a paraphrased version of the novel's passage attributed to Rogers and titled "Standing Orders." A year or two later, a review of the reprinted *Journals of Major Robert Rogers* by The Infantry School led the staff to question the validity of "Roger's Standing Orders." Despite an attempt on the part of the school to clarify the record, their efforts proved fruitless. Rogers' Standing Orders had become part of lore and legend.

AUTHOR'S NOTE: The author is indebted to Major William H. Burgess III in regards to background on the questionable history of Roger's Standing Orders. In an article titled *The Real Rules of Discipline of Major Robert Rogers and the Rangers* printed in the July-August 1993 edition of *Infantry* magazine, Burgess wrote of the discrepancy between the Rules of Discipline and the Standing Orders.

Appendix B

Rogers' Rules of Discipline

I.   All Rangers are to be subject to the rules and articles of war; to appear at roll call every evening on their own parade ground, each equipped with a firelock, 60 rounds of powder and ball, and a hatchet, at which time an officer from each company is to inspect them to see that they are in order, so as to be ready to march at a minute's warning; and before they are dismissed the necessary guards are to be chosen, and scouts for the next day appointed.

II.   Whenever you are ordered out to the enemy's forts or frontiers for discoveries, if your number is small, march in single file, keeping far enough apart to prevent one shot from killing two men, sending one man or more forward, and the like on each side, at a distance of 20 yards from the main body, if the ground you march on allows it, to give the signal to the officer of the approach of an enemy, and of their number, etc.

III.   If you march over marshes or soft ground, change your position and march abreast of each other to prevent the enemy from tracking you (as they would do if you marched in single file) until you get over such ground, and then resume your former order and march until it is quite dark before you encamp. Camp, if possible, on a piece of ground that gives your sentries the advantage of seeing or hearing the enemy at considerable distance, keeping half of your whole party awake alternately through the night.

IV.   Some time before you come to the place you would reconnoiter, make a stand and send one or two men in whom you can confide to seek out the best ground for making your observations.

V.   If you have the good fortune to take any prisoners, keep them separate until they are examined, and return by a route other than the one you used going out so that you may discover any enemy party in your rear and have an opportunity, if their strength is superior to yours, to alter your course or disperse, as circumstances may require.

VI. If you march in a large body of 300 or 400 with a plan to attack the enemy, divide your party into three columns, each headed by an officer. Let these columns march in single file, the columns to the right and left keeping 20 yards or more from the center column, if the terrain allows it. Let proper guards be kept in the front and rear and suitable flanking parties at a distance, as directed before, with orders to halt on all high ground to view the surrounding ground to prevent ambush and to notify of the approach or retreat of the enemy, so that proper dispositions may be made for attacking, defending, etc. And if the enemy approaches in your front on level ground, form a front of your three columns or main body with the advanced guard, keeping out your flanking parties as if you were marching under the command of trusty officers, to prevent the enemy from pressing hard on either of your wings or surrounding you, which is the usual method of savages if their number will allow it, and be careful likewise to support and strengthen your rear guard.

VII. If you receive fire from enemy forces, fall or squat down until it is over, then rise and fire at them. If their main body is equal to yours, extend yourselves occasionally; but if they are superior, be careful to support and strengthen your flanking parties to make them equal with the enemy's, so that if possible you may repulse them to their main body. In doing so, push upon them with the greatest resolve, with equal force in each flank and in the center, observing to keep at a due distance from each other, and advance from tree to tree, with one half of the part ten or twelve yards in front of the other. If the enemy pushes upon you, let your front rank fire and fall down, and then let your rear rank advance through them and do the same, by which time those who were in front will be ready to fire again, and repeat the same alternately, as occasion requires. By this means you will keep up such a constant fire that the enemy will not be able to break your order easily or gain your ground.

VIII. If you force the enemy to retreat, be careful in pursuing them to keep out your flanking parties and prevent them from gaining high ground, in which case they may be able to rally and repulse you in their turn.

IX.   If you must retreat, let the front of your whole party fire and fall back until the rear has done the same, heading for the best ground you can. By this means you will force the enemy to pursue you, if they pursue you at all, in the face of constant fire.

X.   If the enemy is so superior that you are in danger of being surrounded, let the whole body disperse and every one take a different road to the place of rendezvous appointed for that evening. Every morning the rendezvous point must be altered and fixed for the evening in order to bring the whole part, or as many of them as possible, together after any separation that may occur in the day. But if you should actually be surrounded, form yourselves into a square or, in the woods, a circle is best; and if possible make a stand until darkness favors your escape.

XI.   If your rear is attacked, the main body and flanks must face about the right or left, as required, and form themselves to oppose the enemy as directed earlier. The same method must be observed if attacked in either of your flanks, by which means you will always make a rear guard of one of your flank guards.

XII.   If you determine to rally after a retreat in order to make a fresh stand against the enemy, by all means try to do it on the highest ground you come upon, which will give you the advantage and enable you to repulse superior numbers.

XIII.   In general, when pushed upon by the enemy, reserve your fire until they approach very near, which will then cause them the greater surprise and consternation and give you an opportunity to rush upon them with your hatchets and cutlasses to greater advantage.

XIV.   When you encamp at night, fix your sentries so they will not be relieved from the main body until morning, profound secrecy and silence being often of the most importance in these cases. Each sentry, therefore, should consist of six men, two of whom must be constantly alert, and when relieved by their fellows, it should be without noise. In case those on duty see or hear anything that alarms them, they are not to speak. One of them is to retreat silently and advise the commanding officer so that proper dispositions can be made. All occasional sentries should be fixed in a like manner.

XV.   At first light, awake your whole detachment. This is the time when the savages choose to fall upon their enemies, and you should be ready to receive them.

XVI.   If the enemy is discovered by your detachments in the morning, and if their numbers are superior to yours and a victory doubtful, you should not attack them until the evening. Then they will not know your numbers and if you are repulsed your retreat will be aided by the darkness of the night.

XVII.   Before you leave your encampment, send out small parties to scout around it to see if there are any signs of an enemy force that may have been near you during the night.

XVIII.   When you stop for rest, choose some spring or rivulet if you can, and dispose your party so as not to be surprised, posting proper guards and sentries at a due distance, and let a small party watch the path you used coming in, in case the enemy is pursuing.

XIX.   If you have to cross rivers on your return, avoid the usual fords as much as possible, in case the enemy has discovered them and is there expecting you.

XX.   If you have to pass by lakes, keep at some distance from the edge of the water, so that, in case of an ambush or attack from the enemy, your retreat will not be cut off.

XXI.   If the enemy forces pursue your rear, circle around until you come to your own tracks and form an ambush there to receive them and give them the first fire.

XXII.   When you return from a patrol and come near our forts, avoid the usual roads and avenues to it; the enemy may have preceded you and laid an ambush to receive you when you are almost exhausted with fatigue.

XXIII.   When you pursue any party that has been near our forts or encampments, do not follow directly in their tracks, lest you be discovered by their rear guards who, at such a time, would be most alert. But endeavor, by a different route, to intercept and meet them in some narrow pass, or lie in ambush to receive them when and where they least expect it.

XXIV.   If you are to embark in canoes, or otherwise, by water, choose the evening for the time of your embarkation, as you will then have the whole night before you to pass undiscovered by any enemy parties on hills or other places that command a view of the lake or river.

XXV.   In paddling or rowing, order that the boat or canoe next to the last one wait for it, and that each wait for the one behind it to prevent separation and so that you will be ready to help each other in any emergency.

XXVI. Appoint one man in each boat to look out for fires on the adjacent shores, from the number and size of which you may from some idea of the number that kindled them and whether you can attack them or not.

XXVII. If you find the enemy encamped near the banks of a river or lake that you think they will try to cross for their security when attacked, leave a detachment of your party on the opposite shore to receive them. With the remainder, you can surprise them, having them between you and the water.

XXVIII. If you cannot satisfy yourself as to the enemy's number and strength from their fires and the like, conceal your boats at some distance and ascertain their number by a patrol when they embark or march in the morning, marking the course they steer, when you may pursue, ambush, and attack them, or let them pass, as prudence directs you. In general, however, so that you may not be discovered at a great distance by the enemy on the lakes and rivers, it is safest to hide with your boats and party concealed all day, without noise or show, and to pursue your intended route by night. Whether you go by land or water, give out patrol and countersigns in order to recognize one another in the dark, and likewise appoint a station for every man to go to in case of any accident that may separate you.

Appendix C

Rogers' Rangers Standing Orders

1. Don't forget nothing.
2. Have your musket clean as a whistle, hatchet scoured, sixty rounds powder and ball, and be ready to march at a minute's warning.
3. When you're on the march, act the way you would if you was sneaking up on a deer. See the enemy first.
4. Tell the truth about what you see and what you do. There is an army depending on us for correct information. You can lie all you please when you tell other folks about the Rangers, but don't ever lie to a Ranger or officer.
5. Don't ever take a chance you don't have to.
6. When we're on the march we march single file, far enough apart so one shot can't go through two men.
7. If we strike swamps, or soft ground, we spread out abreast so it's hard to track us.
8. When we march, we keep moving till dark, so as to give the enemy the least possible chance at us.
9. When we camp, half the party stays awake while the other half sleeps.
10. If we take prisoners, we keep 'em separate till we have had time to examine them, so they can't cook up a story between 'em.
11. Don't ever march home the same way. Take a different route so you won't be ambushed.
12. No matter whether we travel in big parties or little ones, each party has to keep a scout 20 yards ahead, 20 yards on each flank, and 20 yards in the rear so the main body can't be surprised and wiped out.

13. Every night you'll be told where to meet if surrounded by superior force.

14. Don't sit down and eat without posting sentries.

15. Don't sleep beyond dawn. Dawn's when the French and Indians attack.

16. Don't cross a river by a regular ford.

17. If somebody's trailing you, make a circle, come back onto your own tracks, and ambush the folks that aim to ambush you.

18. Don't stand up when the enemy's coming against you. Kneel down, lie down, hide behind a tree.

19. Let the enemy come till he's almost close enough to touch. Then let him have it and jump out and finish him up with your hatchet.

Appendix D

Battle Honors of Rogers' Rangers

BATTLE	DATE
Isle of Mutton	29 September 1755
La Barbue Creek	21 January 1757
First Defense of Ft. William Henry	19–23 March 1757
Freshwater Cove	8 June 1758
Second Siege of Louisbourg	9 June–26 July 1758
Ticonderoga Falls	6 July 1758
Marin's Defeat	8 August 1758
Fort Frontenac	27 August 1758
The Three Battles	7 March 1759
Louisbourg Woods	1 June 1759
Beaumont	30 June 1759
St. Joseph	30 June 1759
Point Levis Woods	1 July 1759
L'Ange Gardien	8 July 1759
Langlande's Ambuscade	8 July 1759
Rogers-Campbell Maneuver	12 July 1759
Hazen's Post	15 July 1759

Ticonderoga Bridge	22 July 1759
Siege of Ticonderoga	23–26 July 1759
Montmorenci Ford	25 July 1759
St. Francis Raid	13 September–1 November 1759
Point Levi	24 February 1760
Old Lorette	March 1760
Second Siege of Quebec	28 April–17 May 1760
Pointe Au Fer	6 June 1760
Fort Ste. Therese	11–20 June 1760
Pointe Platon	18 July 1760
Siege of Fort Levis	18–25 August 1760
Siege of Isle Aux Noix	19–27 August 1760
Varennes	1 September 1760
Detroit	13 September–29 November 1760
Etchoe Pass	10 June 1761
Capture of Dominica	6 June 1761
Morne Tortenson	24 January 1762
Morne Grenier	27 January 1762
Defense of Detroit	29 July–November 1763
White Plains	28 October 1776
Fort Washington	16 November 1776
Defense of Fort Independence	18–23 January 1777
Defense of Castine	11 August 1779
Siege of Fort Anne	10–11 October 1780
Fort George	11 October 1780
Ballstown	13 June 1781

Appendix E

Korean War Ranger Units

RANGER INFANTRY COMPANY (ABN)	ACTIVATION DATE	UNIT ATTACHED	DUTY STATION	INACTIVATION DATE
Eighth Army Ranger Company (8213th AU)	25 Aug 50	25 Infantry Division/IX Corps	Korea	28 Mar 51
Eighth Army Raider Company (8245 AU)	12 Nov 50	3ID/8227AU-Special Activities Group	Korea	1 Apr 51
1st	28 Oct 50	2 Infantry Division	Korea	1 Aug 51
2nd	28 Oct 50	7ID/187ARCT	Korea	1 Aug 51
3rd	28 Oct 50	Ranger Tng Cmd 3ID/I Corps	Ft Benning, GA Korea	1 Aug 51
4th	28 Oct 50	1st Cav Div 187ARCT/1st Marine Div	Korea	1 Aug 51
5th	20 Nov 50	25ID/I Corps	Korea	1 Aug 51
6th	20 Nov 50	7th Army	Kitzingen, West Germany	1 Dec 51

7th	20 Nov 50	Ranger Tng Cmd	Ft Benning, GA	5 Nov 51
8th	20 Nov 50	24ID/IX Corps	Korea	1 Aug 51
9th	5 Jan 51	3rd Army	Ft Benning, GA	5 Nov 51
10th	5 Jan 51	45ID	Camp Polk, LA	15 Oct 51
11th	5 Jan 51	40ID	Camp Cook, CA	21 Sep 51
12th	1 Feb 51	5th Army	Camp Atterbury, IN	27 Oct 51
13th	1 Feb 51	2nd Army	Camp Pickett, VA	15 Oct 51
14th	1 Feb 51	4ID	Camp Carson, CO	27 Oct 51
15th	1 Feb 51	3rd Army	Ft Benning, GA	5 Nov 51

Appendix F

Vietnam War

Regular Army Long Range Patrol Companies & Detachments[1] Activate Ranger Companies

LRP Co/ Detach	Activation Deactivation	Command HQ	Ranger Company	Activation Deactivation	Command HQ
Co E 30th Inf (Rifle Co)	23 Aug 66 1 July 78 ⇒16 Jan 69	Aviation Center & School	Co C 509th Inf (Pathfinder)	1 July 76 Present	AC&S 101st Abn Div (Air Asslt)
Co D 17th Inf	15 May 67 21 Feb 69	V Corps	Co A 75th Inf	21 Feb 69 19 Dec 74	197th Inf Bde/ 1st Cav Div
Co C 58th Inf	15 May 67 10 Feb 69	VII Corps	Co B 75th Inf	10 Feb 69 1 Nov 74	5th Inf Div (Mech)
Co E 20th Inf	25 Sep 67 1 Feb 69	I Field Force	Co C 75th Inf (Airborne)	1 Feb 69 25 Oct 71	I Field Force
Co F 51st Inf	25 Sep 67 26 Dec 68	199th Inf Bde (Lt) (Sep)	Co D 75th Inf (Airborne)	20 Nov 69 10 Apr 70	II Field Force
Co E 50th Inf	20 Dec 67 1 Feb 69	9th Inf Div	Co E 75th Inf	1 Feb 69 23 Aug 69	9th Inf Div
			Co E 75th Inf*	1 Oct 69 12 Oct 70	3rd Bde (Sep) 9th Inf Div

515

Co F 50th Inf	20 Dec 67 1 Feb 69	25th Inf Div	Co F 75th Inf	1 Feb 69 15 Mar 71	25th Inf Div
Co E 51st Inf	12 Dec 68 1 Feb 69	AMERICAL (23rd Div)	Co G 75th Inf	1 Feb 69 1 Oct 71	AMERICAL (23rd Div)
Co E 52nd Inf	20 Dec 67 1 Feb 69	1st Cav Div (AirMobile)	Co H 75th Inf (AirMobile)	1 Feb 69 15 Aug 72	1st Cav Div (AirMobile)
Co F 52nd Inf	20 Dec 67 1 Feb 69	1st Inf Div	Co I 75th Inf	1 Feb 69 7 Apr 70	1st Inf Div
Co E 58th Inf	20 Dec 67 1 Feb 69	4th Inf Div	Co K 75th Inf	1 Feb 69 10 Dec 70	4th Inf Div
Co F 58th Inf	10 Jan 68 1 Feb 69	101st Abn Div (AM Aug68)	Co L 75th Inf (Airborne)	1 Feb 69 26 Dec 70	101st Air Mobile Div
71st Inf Det	20 Dec 67 1 Feb 69	199th Inf Bde (Lt) (Sep)	Co M 75th Inf	1 Feb 69 12 Oct 70	199th Inf Bde (Lt) (Sep)
74th Inf Det	20 Dec 67 1 Feb 69	173rd Abn Bde (Sep)	Co N 75th Inf (Airborne)	1 Feb 69 25 Aug 71	173rd Abn Bde (Abn)
78th Inf Det	15 Dec 68 1 Feb 69	U.S. Army Vietnam	Co O 75th Inf (Airborne)	1 Feb 69 20 Nov 69	3rd Bde 82nd Abn Div
			Co O* 75th Inf (Artic)	4 Aug 70 29 Sep 72	U.S. Army Alaska
79th Inf Det	15 Dec 68 1 Feb 69	U.S. Army Vietnam	Co P 75th Inf	1 Feb 69 31 Aug 71	5th Inf Div (Mech)
70th Inf Det	19 Dec 67 15 Jan 68	11th Inf Bde (Lt) (Sep)	Inactivated assignment	prior to 11th to American	Inf Bde's Division

*Second Tour

[1] Note: Co E (LRP) was activated in 1968 at Ft Benning but never manned. In addition, four Army National Guard LRRP units were also formed from disbanded ARNG airborne infantry battalions. Companies D and E (LRP) of the Indiana 151st Infantry Regiment were formed in 1967; Companies E and F (LRP) of the Michigan 425th Infantry Regiment were formed in 1968. Company D (Long Range Patrol), 151st Infantry Regiment was the only reserve component infantry unit to serve in Vietnam. Federalized on 13 May 1968, it trained at Fort Benning and shipped to Vietnam on 29 December 1968 and returned 20 December 1969. It was attached to II Field Force and replaced Vietnam LRP Company (Provincial) that had been briefly active 1968/1969.

Appendix G

75th Ranger Regiment Lineage & Honors

CAMPAIGN PARTICIPATION AWARDS, DECORATIONS, & CAMPAIGNS		
WORLD WAR II	**KOREA**	**VIETNAM**
Algeria-French Morocco (with Arrowhead)	UN Defensive	Advisory
Tunisia	UN Offensive	Defense
Sicily (with Arrowhead)	CCF Intervention	Counteroffensive
Naples-Foggia (with Arrowhead)	1st UN Counteroffensive	Counteroffensive, Phase II

Anzio (with Arrowhead)	CCF Spring Offensive	Counteroffensive, Phase III
Rome-Arno	UN Summer Full Offensive	Tet Counteroffensive
Normandy (with Arrowhead)	299 Turkey Shoot	Counteroffensive, Phase IV
Northern France	Bloody Nose Ridge	Counteroffensive, Phase V
Rhineland	Korean Advisory	Counteroffensive, Phase VI
Ardennes-Alsace	Combat Jump-Munsan Ni	Tet 69/Counteroffensive
Central Europe	Chipyong Ni	Summer-Fall 1969
New Guinea	Majori-Ri	Winter-Spring 1970
Leyte (with Arrowhead)	Sang Wi Ryang	Sanctuary Counteroffensive
Luzon	CQ4594	Counteroffensive, Phase VII
India-Burma	Objective Sugar	Consolidation I
Central Burma	Hwachon Dam	Cease Fire

ARMED FORCES EXPEDITIONS

Grenada (with Arrowhead)
Panama (with Arrowhead)

AWARDS AND DECORATIONS

Presidential Unit Citation (ARMY), Streamer embroidered EL GUETTAR

Presidential Unit Citation (ARMY), Streamer embroidered SALERNO

Presidential Unit Citation (ARMY), Streamer embroidered POINTE DU HOC

Presidential Unit Citation (ARMY), Streamer embroidered SAAR RIVER AREA

Presidential Unit Citation (ARMY), Streamer embroidered MYITKYINA

Presidential Unit Citation (ARMY), Streamer embroidered HONG CHON BATTLE

Presidential Unit Citation (ARMY), Streamer embroidered CHIPYONG YI

Presidential Unit Citation (KOREAN), Streamer embroidered KOREAN GOVERNMENT (7)

Presidential Unit Citation (ARMY), Streamer embroidered VIETNAM 66–68

Valorous Unit Award, Streamer embroidered VIETNAM I CORPS AREA

Valorous Unit Award, Streamer embroidered BINH DUONG PROVINCE

Valorous Unit Award, Streamer embroidered FISH HOOK

Valorous Unit Award, Streamer embroidered III CORPS AREA 69

Valorous Unit Award, Streamer embroidered III CORPS AREA 71

Valorous Unit Award, Streamer embroidered THUA THEIN-QUANG TRI

Meritorious Unit Commendation (ARMY), Streamer embroidered VIETNAM 68

Meritorious Unit Commendation (ARMY), Streamer embroidered VIETNAM 69

Meritorious Unit Commendation (ARMY), Streamer embroidered VIETNAM 69–70

Meritorious Unit Commendation (ARMY), Streamer embroidered PACIFIC AREA

Valorous Unit Award, Grenada (1st and 2nd Battalions)

Joint Meritorious Unit Award, Operation Just Cause

Joint Meritorious Unit Award, Operation Desert Storm

Appendix H

Ranger[1] Medal of Honor Recipients

I would rather have that medal than be President of the United States.

President Harry S. Truman

NAME	RANK	DATE	UNIT
Nett, Robert P.	First Lieutenant	14 Dec 1944	Commander, Company E, 305th Infantry Regiment
Millett, Lewis L. Sr.[2]	Captain	7 Feb 1951	Commander, Company E, 2nd Battalion, 27th Infantry Regiment, 25th Infantry Division
*Porter, Donn F.	Sergeant	7 Sep 1952	Company G, 14th Infantry Regiment, 25th Infantry Division
Mize, Ola L.	Sergeant	10–11 Jun 1953	Company K, 15th Infantry Regiment, 3rd Infantry Division
Marm, Walter J.	Second Lieutenant	14 Nov 1965	Company A, 1st Battalion (Airborne), 7th Cavalry, 1st Cavalry Division (Airmobile)
Dolby, David C.	Staff Sergeant	21 May 1966	Company B, 1st Battalion (Airborne), 8th Cavalry, 1st Cavalry Division (Airmobile)

Ray, Ronald E.	First Lieutenant	19 Jun 1966	Company A, 2nd Battalion, 35th Infantry Regiment, 25th Infantry Division
Foley, Robert F.	Captain	5 Nov 1966	Commander, Company A, 2nd Battalion, 27th Infantry Regiment, 25th Infantry Division
*Sisler, George K.	First Lieutenant	7 Feb 1967	HHC, 5th Special Forces Group (Airborne), 1st Special Forces
Zabitosky, Fred M.	Staff Sergeant	19 Feb 1968	5th Special Forces Group (Airborne), 1st Special Forces
Bucha, Paul W.	Captain	16–19 Mar 1968	Commander, Company D, 3rd Battalion, 187th Infantry Regiment, 101st Airborne Division (Air-Assault)
*Rabel, Laszlo	Staff Sergeant	13 Nov 1968	74th Infantry Detachment (Airborne LRRP) 173rd Airborne Brigade
Howard, Robert L.	Sergeant First Class	30 Dec 1968	5th Special Forces Group (ABN), 1st Special Forces
*Law, Robert D.[3]	Specialist 4	22 Feb 1969	Company I (Ranger), 75th Infantry 1st Infantry Division
Kerrey, J. Robert	Lieutenant (j.g.)	14 Mar 1969	SEAL Team 1
*Doane, Stephen H.	First Lieutenant	25 Mar 1969	Company B, 1st Battalion, 5th Infantry, 25th Infantry Division
*Pruden, Robert J.[4]	Staff Sergeant	20 Nov 1969	Company G (Ranger), 75th Infantry 23rd Infantry Division (American)
Lemon, Peter C.	Specialist 4	1 Apr 1970	Company E, 2nd Battalion, 8th Cavalry, 1st Cavalry Division (Airmobile)

Littrell, Gary L.	Sergeant First Class	4 Apr 1970	Advisory Team 21 (Airborne Ranger) US Military Assistance Command, Vietnam
Lucas, Andre C.	Lieutenant Colonel	1–23 Jun 1970	Commander, 2nd Battalion, 506th Infantry, 101st Airborne Division (Air-Assault)
*****Gordon**, Gary I.	Master Sergeant	3 Oct 1993	US Army Special Operations Command, Special Detachment-Delta, Task Force Ranger
*****Shughart**, Randall D.	Sergeant First Class	3 Oct 1993	US Army Special Operations Command, Special Detachment-Delta, Task Force Ranger

*Posthumously

[1]Soldiers either assigned to a Ranger unit or a graduate of the U.S. Army Ranger School.

[2]Earned his Ranger Tab in 1958.

[3]First U.S. Army Ranger to be awarded the Medal of Honor while assigned to a U.S. Army Ranger unit.

[4]Only graduate of the U.S. Army Ranger School to be awarded the Medal of Honor while serving in a Ranger unit.

Appendix I

Medal Honor of Certificate

MASTER SERGEANT GARY I. GORDON

THE UNITED STATES OF AMERICA

TO ALL WHO SHALL SEE THESE PRESENTS, GREETING:

THIS IS TO CERTIFY THAT
THE PRESIDENT OF THE UNITED STATES OF AMERICA
AUTHORIZED BY ACT OF CONGRESS MARCH 3, 1863
HAS AWARDED IN THE NAME OF THE CONGRESS

THE MEDAL OF HONOR

TO

MASTER SERGEANT GARY I. GORDON
UNITED STATES ARMY

FOR

CONSPICUOUS GALLANTRY AND INTREPIDITY AT THE RISK
OF HIS LIFE ABOVE AND BEYOND THE CALL OF DUTY
IN ACTION WITH THE ENEMY

IN MOGADISHU, SOMALIA

GIVEN UNDER MY HAND IN THE CITY OF WASHINGTON
THIS 23rd DAY OF May 19 94

SECRETARY OF THE ARMY

PRESIDENT OF THE UNITED STATES OF AMERICA

Bibliography

PUBLISHED WORKS:

Adkin, Mark, *Urgent Fury: The Battle for Grenada*, Lexington Books, Lexington, Massachusetts, 1989.

Ambrose, Stephen E., *D-Day June 6, 1944: The Climatic Battle of World War II*, Touchstone Book, Simon and Schuster, New York, New York, 1994.

Bass, Robert D. *Swamp Fox: The Life and Times of General Francis Marion*, Henry Holt and Company, 1959.

Beckwith, Colonel (Ret) Charlie, *Delta Force*, Harcourt Brace Jovanovich, New York, New York.

Berger, Sid, *Breaching Fortress Europe*, Kendall/Hunt Publishing, Dubuque, Iowa, 1994.

Bolger, Colonel Daniel, P. *Savage Peace: Americans at War in the 1990s.* Presidio: Novato, California, 1995.

Compton, *Compton's Interactive Encyclopedia*, Compact Disk, Edition 1997.

Darby, William O., Baumer, William H., *We Led the Way: Darby's Rangers*, Jove Book, Presidio Press, San Rafael, California, 1980.

Donnelly, Thomas, *Operation Just Cause: The Storming of Panama*, Lexington Books, Macmillan, Inc, New York, New York, 1991.

Dupuy, R. Ernest, *The Encyclopedia of Military History From 3500 B.C. to the Present*, Hero Books Partnership, Harper & Row, Publishers, New York, New York, 1986.

Eighth Army Ranger Company Association, *The Eighth Army Ranger Company from August 1950–March 1951* (Bound Manuscript).

Faust, Patricia L. *Historical Times Illustrated Encyclopedia of the Civil War*, Harper & Row, Publishers, New York, 1986.

Flanagan, Edward. *Battle for Panama: Inside Operation Just Cause*. Brassey's Inc, Maxwell Macmillan, Inc: New York, 1993.

Flint, Roy K. *The American Civil War*, Department of History, United States Military Academy, West Point, NY, 1980.

Foley, Dennis, *Special Men: A LRP's Recollections*, Ivy Books, Ballantine Books, Publishers, New York, New York, 1994.

Freeman, Douglas S. *Lee's Lieutenants: A Study in Command.* Charles Scribner's Sons: New York, 1944.

Goodes' World Atlas, Rand McNally & Company, Chicago, 1997.

Graham, James. *The Life of General Daniel Morgan of the Virginia Line of the Army of the United States*, Derby and Jackson, New York, 1856.

Grant, Ulysses S. *Memoirs*. Great Commanders Collectors Reprints, Inc: Pennington, New Jersey, 1996.

Gray, David, *The First Rangers in Korea: The Eighth Army Ranger Company in Combat August 1950–March 1951* (Master Thesis).

Hackworth, David, *About Face: The Odyssey of an American Warrior*, Simon and Schuster, New York, New York, 1989.

Johnson, James M. *Militiamen, Rangers, and Redcoats: The Military in Georgia, 1754–1776*, Mercer University Press, Macon, Georgia, 1992.

Karnow, Stanley, *Vietnam: A History*, Penguin Books, Publishers, New York, New York, 1984.

Landau, Alan and Frieda, *Power Series: Airborne Rangers*, Motorbooks International, Publishers, Osceola, Wisconsin, 1992.

Lang, George. *Medal of Honor Recipients, Vols. I & II*. Facts on File, Inc: New York, 1995.

Leach, Douglas Edward. *Arms for the Empire: A Military History of the British Colonies in North America, 1607–1763*, The Macmillan Company, New York, 1973.

Lee, Robert E. *The Great Commander's: Lee ... Wartime Papers, Volumes One & Two*, Collectors Reprints, Inc., Pennington, NJ, 1996.

Rottman, Gordon, *US Army Rangers & LRRP Units 1942–1987*, Osprey Publishing, London, 1987.

Ryan, Cornelius, *The Longest Day: June 6, 1944*, Simon and Schuster, Inc, 1959.

Ryan, Paul, *The Iranian Rescue Mission: Why It Failed*, Naval Institute Press, Annapolis, Maryland.

Stanton, Shelby L., *Rangers at War: LRRPs in Vietnam*, Ivy Books, Ballantine Books, Publishers, New York, New York, 1992.

Time/Life Books. *Spies, Scouts, and Raiders: Irregular Operations*, Time/Life Books, Inc, 1985.

Wert, Jeffry D. *Mosby's Rangers*, Simon and Schuster, New York, 1990.

OFFICIAL DOCUMENTS/PUBLICATIONS:

Army Historical Series, *American Military History,* Center of Military History, United States Army, Washington, DC, 1989.

Bjorge, Gary, *Merrill's Marauders: Combined Operations in Northern Burma in 1944,* extract of US Army Military History Exchange paper, June 1994.

Chief of Staff, US Army, Comments dated 3 May 1996.

Harrison, Gordon, *US Army in World War II: European Theater of Operations – Cross Channel Attack,* Center of Military History, United States Army, Washington, DC, 1989.

King, Michael, *Leavenworth Papers: Rangers – Selected Combat Operations in World War II,* Combat Studies Institute, Fort Leavenworth, Kansas, 1985.

Loescher, Burt G., *The History of Rogers' Rangers, Volume I, The Beginning: Jan 1755–April 6, 1758,* San Francisco, Self Published 1946, United States Military Academy Special Collection.

Loescher, Burt G., *The History of Rogers' Rangers, Volume II, Rogers' Rangers – The First Green Berets, The Corps & The Revivals, April 6, 1758– December 24, 1783,* San Mateo, California, Self-Published 1969, United States Military Academy Special Collection.

Loescher, Burt G., *The History of Rogers' Rangers, Volume III, Officers and Non-Commissioned Officers,* Burlingame, California, Self-Published 1957, United States Military Academy Special Collection.

National Historical Society, *War of the Rebellion Official Records of the Union and Confederate Armies,* Historical Times, Inc, Ann Arbor, MI, 1985.

Ranger Training Brigade, *Ranger Handbook* SH 21–76, United States Army Infantry School, Fort Benning, Georgia, July 1992.

Ranger Training Brigade, *Ranger Pamphlet,* United States Army Infantry School, Fort Benning, Georgia, 1978.

Reimer, Dennis J. General, Chief of Staff, U.S. Army. *USNS Shughart Naming Ceremony* comments dated 3 May 1996.

Special Operations/Low-Intensity Conflict, Office of the Assistant Secretary of Defense, Memorandum, dated 4 November 1993.

JOURNAL/NEWSPAPER PUBLICATIONS:

Army Times,
    "Army Silent on Anti-Sleep Drugs."
    Adelsberger, Bernard. "Commanders: Armor Could Have Saved Lives," May 23, 1994, p. 18.

Adelsberger, Bernard. "Ranger Parents: Who Made Somalia Decisions," May 23, 1994, p. 18.

Peterson, Donna. "General Said to Take Blame for Failed Raid," November 8, 1993, p. 8.

Donnelly, Tom. "Rangers in Somalia: Anatomy of a Firefight." December 1993, p. 14.

Krawczyk, Stephanie. "Recognizing the Heroes of Somalia," April 11, 1994, p. 8.

"Remembering Mogadishu," 12 October 1998.

Franke, Major Henry G. "Somalia Mission: Finishing What Was Started" (Commentary).

"The Soldiers: Where some of them are now," 12 October 1998.

"Timeline of Events," April 10, 1995.

Beckwith, Charlie, *Somalia's Needless Deaths*, Dec 1993.

Boston Globe, "Film of Somalia Gunfight Shows It Was Not a Rout," US Says, November 3, 1993, p. 2.

Infantry Magazine, Burgess, William H. III. "The Real Rules of Discipline of Major Robert Rogers and the Rangers," The Infantry School, Ft. Benning, Georgia, pp. 12–14.

Military, Smith, James, "In Memory of Ranger Smith," May 1994, pp. 11–13.

Military History, "The Medal of Honor," March 1997.

NCO Journal, United States Army Sergeants Major Academy, Ft. Bliss, Texas.

New York Newsday, Sloyan, Patrick J. "Brave Beyond Call of Duty," March 22, 1994.

New York Times, "Fateful Decision: Staying to Guard Pilot's Body," October 24, 1993.

Newsweek, Joyce, Larry E. "'Unfortunate Losses' Have Names," April 11, 1994, p. 12.

Paraglide Magazine, Hall, Barbara. "317th TAW Flies the Unfriendly Skies Over Rio Hato," March 1990.

Philadelphia Inquirer, Bowden, Mark, *"Black Hawk Down"* (Series), 16 November–14 December 1997.

Popular Mechanics, "Special Ops," pp. 50–53, January 1999.

The Ranger Link, United States Army Ranger Association.

Altieri, James. "William Orlando Darby," Winter 1994, pp. 20–21.

Ivers, Larry E. "The First Ranger in America," Summer 1994, p. 25.

Ivers, Larry E. "2nd Ranger Infantry Company (Airborne) 1950–1951," Winter 1994, pp. 25–26.

Ivers, Larry E. "3rd Ranger Infantry Company (Airborne)," p. 17.

"Our Heritage," Summer 1994, p. 19.

Soldiers Magazine.
Rogers, Jerry. "New Ship Honors Army Hero," September 1996, pp. 4–5.
Sheftick, Captain Alan. *"Shughart* Sails," March 1997, pp. 46–47.
U.S. News & World Report, Letters, August 1, 1994, p. 4.
Washington Post,
Richburg, Keith B. "Pakistani Says UN Bungled on Aidid," November 3, 1993.
Atkinson, Rick. "The Raid That Went Wrong," January 30, 1994.

CORRESPONDENCE/PHONE CONVERSATIONS

Bolger, Lieutenant Colonel (Promotable) Daniel P.
Black, Colonel (Ret) Robert
Medal of Honor Society, 40 Patriots Point Road, Mount Pleasant, South Carolina, 29464.
Gordon, Mrs. Carmen.
Hackworth, Colonel (Ret) David H.
JFK Special Forces War Museum
McKnight, Colonel Danny
Moore, Lieutenant General (Ret) Harold G.
Puckett, Colonel (Ret) Ralph
Sisk, Sergeant First Class
Stanton, Shelby L.

INTERNET BULLETIN BOARDS

Task Force Ranger – Black Hawk Down
http://www3.phillynews.com/packages/somalia/
United States Army Ranger Association
http://www.ranger.org/~ranger/history.htm
Special Operations Aviation Regiment (SOAR) Gothic Serpent Memorial
http://www.nightstalkers.com/tfranger/memorial/

Index

B

Kearney, Captain Francis 397
Kelly, Private First Class William 418–420
Kemmer, Ranger Bill 278
Kennedy, Captain Quinton 116, 121–122
Kennedy, Lieutenant Samuel 41
Kerchner, Lieutenant 240
Kernan, Colonel William F. 414, 426, 428, 430
Kerrey, Lieutenant (j.g.) J. Robert 522
Kesselring, Field Marshall Albert 234
Kester, Lieutenant Colonel John W. 189
Khanh Hoa Province, Vietnam 362
Khomeini, Ayatollah 387
Kien Hoa Province, Vietnam 312
Killer Rangers 353
Kim Son Valley, Vietnam 330
Kimble, Private David 44–45
King George III 129
King Philip 10–11
King Philip's War 10–11
King's American Regiment 152
King's Rangers 133–135
Kingston 144, 146
Kingstree 142–143, 146–148, 152, 156
Kit Carson Scouts 366
Knowles, General Richard T. 324
Knyphausen, General 132
Kontum Province, Vietnam 295, 300, 350, 361
Korean Conflict 271
Korean Conflict Ranger Units 513
Koster, General Samuel W. 327
Kowalewski, Private First Class Richard 462–463, 466
Kozach, Specialist 4 309
Kraft, Sergeant James W. 335
Krueger, General Walter 258–259
Kubinak, Ranger Sumner 279
Kudzu Rangers 313
Kuhn, Sergeant Jack 243
Kuwait 431
Kyle, Colonel 392–393
Kyoto, Japan 267

L

L'Ange Gardien 94
La Barbue Creek 35, 42, 44
La Barque Island 47
La Comandancia, Panama 423–424

La Conquet Peninsula, France 253
La Corne, Partisan 70, 85
La Force, Partisan 101–102
Lacy, Chaplain Joe 250
Laden, Terrorist Osama bin 494–495
Lake Champlain 16, 23–24, 26–27, 29–32, 35, 55, 70, 78, 81–82, 99–100, 104, 134–135
Lake George 16–17, 19–20, 23–24, 27–29, 32, 34, 40, 44–46, 55, 57, 59, 63–64, 66–69, 78–79, 82, 92, 134
Lake Oneida 90, 115
Lake Ontario 73, 115, 117
Laker, Specialist 4 Carl J. 337–338
Lam Don Province, Vietnam 362
LaMacta, North Africa 225
Lancaster, Specialist 4 Kenneth R. 309
Langlande, Partisan 94
Lannon, Specialist 4 Joseph 410
Latin, Private First Class Wilber J. 340
Law, Specialist 4 Robert D. 345–346, 522
Lawson Army Airfield, Georgia 424–425
Lear, Specialist Philip 429
Lechner, Lieutenant James 470
Lee, General Robert E. 154, 176–177, 183–184, 193, 199, 208–209, 216–217
Lee, Lieutenant Colonel Henry 'Light Horse Harry' 154, 160–163, 165–170
Lee's Legion 155
Leerburg, Specialist 336
Leesburg 188, 190–192, 195, 214
Legion of Honor 199
Lemon, Specialist 4 Peter C. 522
Lento, Sergeant Stanley J. 335
Leonard, Sergeant Paul 462
Lepre, Specialist Phil 479
Levis, General Francois-Gaston 94, 100, 102, 110–113, 115
Leyte Gulf, Philippines 259
Lima Rangers 365–366
Lincoln, President Abraham 182, 196
Lindman, Captain Allen A. 342–343
Linnell, General Frank H. 325
Little Peedee River 144
Little Peedee Swamp 142, 144
Littrell, Sergeant First Class Gary L. 295–297, 523
Live Free or Die 16
Loi-kang Ridge, Burma 269
Lomell, Sergeant Leonard 243
Long Binh Province, Vietnam 305, 339, 369

548   To Fight with Intrepidity...

N

About the Author

John Lock is a 1982 graduate and former assistant professor of the United States Military Academy at West Point. He enlisted in the Army in 1974 and served as a Non-Commissioned Officer until 1978. His commissioned assignments include the 1st Armored Division, Nuremberg, West Germany, the 82d Airborne Division at Fort Bragg, N.C., and Stabilization Forces (SFOR), Bosnia and Herzegovina.

His military and advanced civil education includes the Engineer Officer Basic Course, the Infantry Officer Advanced Course, the Combined Arms Services Staff School, the Command and General Staff College, and a Master of Science degree from Rensselaer Polytechnic Institute. His decorations include the Master Parachutists Wings and the Ranger Tab.

In 1998, the first edition of his first book, *To Fight with Intrepidity: The Complete History of the U.S. Army Rangers, 1622 to Present,* was published by Simon & Schuster/Pocket Books. His second work, *The Coveted Black and Gold: A Daily Journal Through the U.S. Army Ranger School Experience* was published in 2001.

Endorsements for
The Coveted Black and Gold

FOREWORD: John Lock's *The Coveted Black and Gold: A Daily Journey Through The US Army Ranger School Experience* will cause every Ranger graduate to say, "Yes, I remember that! That's the way it was!" As he reminisces, he'll also exclaim to himself, "I'm glad I did it but I'll never do it again!" Lock's attention-riveting account is based on the contraband daily log that he kept without being detected by the ever-present RI (Ranger Instructor). That Lock succeeded is a tribute to his perseverance and adroitness in avoiding detection. He has achieved in writing what may be acclaimed as the seminal work on the Ranger Training Program at the Infantry School. By so doing he has explained clearly that a Ranger is a soldier with a special attitude — self-assured, determined, demanding of himself and of those with whom he soldiers, a person for whom only the best is acceptable, a person who strives to be all that he can be.

Lock brings to the reader's attention the stark reality of the demands of Ranger training by indicating each day in his log the number of hours of sleep (the average is three each day) and the meals missed. Even recounting the meals missed does not indicate accurately the caloric deficiency because the "meal" received may have been only a modicum of food. But to a Ranger, any meal is a banquet!

As Lock expresses so well in "Final Thoughts," Ranger training provides a unique opportunity for a person to learn about himself. "The deprivations, adversity, exhaustion, and stress will quickly strip away any facade and reveal the true core of any man. In the process, it will assist your transformation into a warrior and leader of combat soldiers. It is an experience and accomplishment that no one can take from you."

Colonel Ralph Puckett, USA (Ret)
Honorary Colonel of the 75th Ranger Regiment

Lieutenant Colonel Lock has written a fascinating and informative work on the most elite of the Army's troops and tells us what it takes to earn the coveted Black and Gold Ranger Tab. A good read for any student of the warrior ethic.

General Colin L. Powell, USA (Ret)
Former Chairman of the Joint Chiefs of Staff

JD Lock captures the essence of the best course in the world to prepare a man to fight and win in sustained close combat. No other course I know of, including the SEAL's premier BUDS program, prepares a man psychologically for the rigors of infantry combat. I know that I personally must have faced greater gut checks in training and combat but nothing seems to match the seemingly endless challenges faced by my Ranger buddies and me during January patrols in the mountains of north Georgia or the freezing waters in February of the Florida swamps. I thank God I had this Ranger School benchmark early because it served me well during the following 34 years and even into retirement. Everything seems to pale in comparison to those stark, uncompromising Ranger school tasks we had to accomplish despite the difficulties. The Mission always came first and could never be compromised.

Rangers, do in fact, *Lead the Way*!

General Wayne A. Downing, USA (Ret)
Third Colonel of the Regiment
and Former CINC, US Special Operations Command

The U.S. Army Ranger School is a nine-week challenge to a man's self-confidence, physical fitness, and above all, his determination to prevail. A nine-week trip from hell designed to cull out the mentally and physically weak and to make the survivors far more capable leaders. A nine week witches brew of misery; rain, mud, slime, snakes, chiggers, heat, cold, humidity, numbing fatigue, life or death situations, very little sleep or food, 70 pound rucksacks and Ranger Instructors in omnipresent wolf packs yapping, snapping and hounding the students day and night to drive out the weak.

And drive them out they do, adding those who quit due to what Rangers call an "MWA" (massive wimp attack) to those who fail one of the technical portions of the course—Land Navigation; the Leadership challenges; knot tying tests; the Peer ratings and those who are recycled or fail due to injury or sickness. On average, only 25% of the men who begin with a class finish it with that class and earn the Ranger Tab.

This book takes the reader vicariously through Ranger School. I have never been to Ranger School but I have always respected greatly the accomplishment of those who have. Lieutenant Colonel (then U.S.M.A. Cadet) John Lock's diary gave me a comprehensive appreciation of what a Ranger graduate has accomplished. He spares none of the details. Carrying a hidden diary, he avoided being caught by the Instructors as he scrawled daily entries. Remarkably objective he captured it all; the hours of sleep each day (the average was 3); the meals missed; the rare humorous events; the sadness of seeing companions fail because of their own shortcomings or the inaction or incompetence of others in a patrol they were leading; the personal heroism of men in actual life-threatening situations. So far as I know Lock's diary is the only day-to-day student chronology of the great stress and pressure on an aspiring Ranger to perform 100% correctly while physically miserable, worn out and severely undernourished.

I highly recommend this book to those who would like to know more about Army Rangers. And to those who are about to go into Ranger School, it will provide an excellent "recon."

> Lieutenant General Harold G. Moore, USA (Ret)
> coauthor of the *New York Times* Best Seller
> *We Were Soldiers Once ... and Young*

A must read to understand the Ranger community and for those aspiring to become RANGER QUALIFIED — the right of passage for leaders who can be depended on when the going gets tough. The coveted BLACK and GOLD establishes a standard for setting the example, leading the way and to live by for the rest of your life.

> Brigadier General USA (Ret) Dave Grange
> 7th Colonel of the Regiment

For those getting ready to attend the United States Army Ranger School or those who want to get the "feel" for the rigors of Ranger training, John Lock's *The Coveted Black and Gold* is a must read. For those who have the Ranger tab, reading this superb day-to-day narrative will bring back memories long suppressed! While reading this book will not get you closer to earning the coveted "Ranger Tab" it could be a major step to mentally preparing yourself for the best small unit leadership training in the world.

HOOAH! RLTW!

> Colonel P.K. Keen
> Eleventh Colonel of the Regiment

Professional soldier and West Point graduate John Lock takes you into the heart of America's most intense military experience, United States Army Ranger School. Here is Ranger training up close and personal, so real that you feel the pain, taste the sweat, and learn just what it takes to wear *The Coveted Black and Gold*.

Colonel Daniel P. Bolger
Author of *Savage Peace*

In prose as spare and sharp as a soldier's bayonet, John Lock shows what young men of character can and will endure in pursuit of a dream to become the best.

Ed Ruggero
USMA & Ranger School graduate, author of *38 North Yankee*

The author is a wonderful writer who has captured the Ranger course experience like no other I have read. If published in its present form it would likely do well as preparatory reading for those who are about to go to Ranger school and for those who are its graduates an insightful narrative describing the challenges they faced.

Review Comments AUSA, 20 July 2000

CPSIA information can be obtained at www.ICGtesting.com
Printed in the USA
LVOW06*1358290514

387778LV00004B/23/P